The
Greenwood Encyclopedia
of
World Folklore
and Folklife

Volume 4
North and South America

The Greenwood Encyclopedia
of World Folklore and Folklife

VOLUME 1
Topics and Themes, Africa, Australia and Oceania

VOLUME 2
Southeast Asia and India, Central and East Asia, Middle East

VOLUME 3
Europe

VOLUME 4
North and South America

The Greenwood Encyclopedia of World Folklore and Folklife

VOLUME 4
North and South America

Edited by William M. Clements

Thomas A. Green, Advisory Editor

GREENWOOD PRESS
Westport, Connecticut • London

Library of Congress Cataloging-in-Publication Data

The Greenwood encyclopedia of world folklore and folklife / edited by William
    M. Clements.
      p. cm.
    Includes bibliographical references and index.
    ISBN 0–313–32847–1 (set : alk. paper)—ISBN 0–313–32848–X
    (v. 1 : alk. paper)—ISBN 0–313–32849–8 (v. 2 : alk. paper)—
    ISBN 0–313–32850–1 (v. 3 : alk. paper)—ISBN 0–313–32851–X (v. 4 : alk. paper)
    1. Folklore—Encyclopedias.   2. Manners and customs—Encyclopedias.
I. Clements, William M., 1945–   .
GR35.G75   2006
398'.03—dc22   2005019219

British Library Cataloguing in Publication Data is available.

Library of Congress Catalog Card Number: 2005019219
ISBN: 0–313–32847–1 (set)
       0–313–32848–X (vol. 1)
       0–313–32849–8 (vol. 2)
       0–313–32850–1 (vol. 3)
       0–313–32851–X (vol. 4)

First published in 2006

Greenwood Press, 88 Post Road West, Westport, CT 06881
An imprint of Greenwood Publishing Group, Inc.
www.greenwood.com

Printed in the United States of America

The paper used in this book complies with the
Permanent Paper Standard issued by the National
Information Standards Organization (Z39.48–1984).

10 9 8 7 6 5 4 3 2 1

Contents

Foreword

In many ways, *The Greenwood Encyclopedia of World Folklore and Folklife* represents the completion of a two-volume work published in 1997, *Folklore: An Encyclopedia of Beliefs, Customs, Tales, Music, and Art*. As editor of that encyclopedia, I endeavored to bring together a set of general entries on folklore forms, methods, and theories. Attempting to confine such diverse topics within a two-volume work often compelled those of us who took on the task to violate a guiding principle of folkloristics—the consideration of cultural contexts. To paraphrase a disclaimer included in the Preface to *Folklore*: the variety and wealth of the world's traditions demanded a severely abridged treatment of the subjects.

This concern returned to haunt me in the person of my former editor, Gary Kuris, who had changed presses and saw the opportunity to build on our earlier collaboration. Other obligations compelled me to pass along the editorial duties to William Clements, who had played a major role in the original project. Unable to resist involvement in such an ambitious and meaningful enterprise, I accepted the role of advisory editor. Thanks to Bill, this role has allowed me to be associated with what I believe will prove to be an extraordinary research tool, while requiring very little effort on my part.

Thus, almost a decade after the publication of *Folklore*, Greenwood Publishing Group, in this four-volume *Greenwood Encyclopedia of World Folklore and Folklife*, has provided a venue for redressing the omissions of that earlier project. These volumes flesh out the relatively economical treatments of concepts, forms, and theories with specific discussions of folklore in context; comparisons of art forms and lifeways within the various culture areas of the world; and consideration of topics that transcend cultural, social, and disciplinary borders. As such, the vision of folklore as a culturally situated phenomenon, arising from and contributing to the lives of its bearers, becomes fully apparent.

THOMAS A. GREEN
Texas A&M University

Preface

The term "folk-lore" entered the English language in 1846 when William J. Thoms, writing as Ambrose Merton, proposed it as a "good Saxon substitute" for the Latinate "popular antiquities," which British enthusiasts for the beliefs, behaviors, and objects of the "olden time" were using to denominate their interest. Thoms's contribution was a word (one that had been occasionally in use before his coinage); what it referred to already existed. And, in fact, other European languages had already found their own words for what Thoms was calling "folklore." (The hyphen disappeared in the twentieth century.) Germans were already studying *Volkskunde*, for example, by the time "folklore" appeared over the name Ambrose Merton.

The term may be English and of fairly recent coinage, but the kind of cultural material that it has come to encompass exists in every society, and many societies have been taking an interest in their folklore (by whatever name they refer to it) for quite some time. *The Greenwood Encyclopedia of World Folklore and Folklife* is an attempt to assess this cultural material on an international basis and also to provide some idea of what has been done in each of the represented groups by both group members and outsiders to document, analyze, preserve, and revitalize it.

Like language, religion, politics, and economics, folklore is a cultural universal found everywhere in the world. That fact—and the fact that the materials of folklore often show remarkable similarities in different places and at different times—makes a survey of folklore materials on a worldwide basis especially relevant. Moreover, although the foundations of folklore study—at least in Europe—lay in romantic nationalism, a tradition of internationalism also exists. One need only think of such compendiums as Frazer's *The Golden Bough* (1890 and many subsequent editions), which, although driven by a view of culture that few serious folklorists would endorse today, nevertheless brings together a vast amount of folklore material from all over the world. The first edition of Stith Thompson's monumental *Motif-Index of Folk-Literature* (1932–1937; 2nd edition, 1955–1958) catalogued narrative elements from a range of traditional genres from throughout the world. The *Funk and Wagnalls Standard Dictionary of Folklore, Mythology, and Legend* (1949)—famous among folklorists for its twenty-one different definitions of the term "folklore"—has unsystematic worldwide coverage. Beginning in the 1960s, the University of Chicago Press's Folktales of the World series also adopted the globe as its bailiwick. Each of the twenty or so volumes in that series focuses on the narrative traditions of a particular country (for example, Japan, China, Mexico, France, England, Israel, and India). In 1961, Richard M. Dorson edited *Folklore Research around the World*, a collection of essays that assessed the state of folklore scholarship in several different countries. When he inaugurated the *Journal of the Folklore Institute* (now *Journal of Folklore Research*) at Indiana University, he intended that its coverage be international. Of course, these few examples do not exhaust the attempts by folklorists to highlight what Dorson, in an essay entitled "The Techniques of the Folklorist," called "international relations" in folklore. They do, however, suggest the academic tradition out of which the current work emerges. As far as I know, a vision such as that of Thomas Green and the editors of Greenwood Publishing Group has not found expression in any previous work; the purpose of these four volumes is to survey the world's folklore heritages in a way that emphasizes the international nature of folklore in general and of specific folklore materials, while placing folklore within particular cultural milieus.

The aim of this encyclopedia is to examine folklore within the broad contexts of culture areas and the more narrow contexts of specific societies. To that end, the goal was to sample from every continent and subcontinent and to represent as many of the specific societies on those land masses as seemed feasible. The result is a series of substantial essays by specialists in the folklore of particular groups.

Given that both the specific nature of the folklore and the availability of resources on each topic vary from society to society, contributors had considerable latitude in what they felt to be important to represent the folklore of their societies and in how they decided to present it. However, they were given the following template—intended to be more suggestive than prescriptive—with ten areas that they might attend to in their essays:

1. *Geographical Setting.* The topography, climate, and other features of the physical and natural environment that help to shape the society's culture.
2. *Sociocultural Features.* Subsistence activities, political organization, social organization, and other aspects of the culture that will help readers understand how folklore works in the society.
3. *Ethnohistorical Information.* Migration patterns, political developments, watershed events, and interactions with other societies.
4. *Belief System.* Worldview and traditional religion (including medical practices).
5. *Verbal Art.* Myth, legend, folktale, and other oral forms, approached from an indigenous perspective.
6. *Musical Art.* Vocal and instrumental.
7. *Sports and Games.*
8. *Graphic and Plastic Arts.* Arts, crafts, architecture, clothing, and foodways.
9. *Effects of Modernization and Globalization.*
10. *References and Bibliographical Essay.* A brief history of the study of the society's folklore with a list of works from which the entry has drawn and recommendations for additional reading.

Contributors were encouraged to think not just in terms of folklore "texts" but of the processes of storytelling, singing, and performing folklore.

The four-volume *Greenwood Encyclopedia of World Folklore and Folklife* contains 205 entries written by more than 200 folklore scholars from around the world. To facilitate the comparison of geographically related countries and cultures, the volumes are broken down into the following regional subdivisions:

Volume 1: Topics and Themes, Africa, Australia and Oceania

Volume 2: Southeast Asia and India, Central and East Asia, Middle East

Volume 3: Europe

Volume 4: North and South America

Volume 1 opens with an alphabetically arranged collection of thirty-nine short essays on processes, research tools, social and intellectual movements, and concepts important for understanding folklore on an international, intercultural basis. These introductory entries should equip the reader to appreciate the dynamic nature of folklore through time and as it passes across cultural boundaries. Volume 1 then proceeds to a series of entries on the peoples and cultures of Africa, Australia, and Oceania, which, like all the entries in the other three volumes, are listed alphabetically within a series of regional subdivisions (e.g., Southern Africa, Western and Central Africa, Polynesia).

Most entries run between 3,000 and 5,000 words, although those for older and more complex cultures and societies (e.g., China, India) are often longer. Useful subheads (e.g., Geography and History; Myths, Legends, and Folktales; Music and Songs; Challenges of the Modern World) divide the entries into topical sections, allowing readers quickly to find the aspect or genre of a group's folklore that may be of most interest to them. Written in a clear, readable style, the entries are also based on the best and latest scholarship, offering detailed, current information on the folklore and folklife of particular peoples and cultures. The *Encyclopedia* can thus serve a variety of users, from students (both high school and undergraduate) requiring information for projects and papers in a wide variety of subjects and interdisciplinary classes, to general readers or travelers interested in knowing more about a particular culture or custom, to folklore specialists needing to stay current with the latest work on peoples and cultures beyond or related to their own areas of expertise. By promoting cultural diversity and stressing the interconnectedness of peoples and cultures around the globe, the *Encyclopedia* can also help any user who wishes better to understand his or her own cultural heritage and the influences neighboring and even more distant groups have had on its development. Most entries also help readers understand how the emerging global society and economy have and are affecting the customs and beliefs of peoples around the world.

The *Encyclopedia* also contains maps located at the start of the relevant geographical section and numerous photographs of the peoples and artifacts of a culture. Volume 4 contains a number of additional features, including a glossary that briefly defines some of the terms that recur throughout the entries. The purpose of the glossary is to give the reader a point of departure for understanding some of the language of folklore studies and anthropology used by the authors, and most of these terms merit the much more extended treatments they have received elsewhere, in such works as Thomas A. Green's *Folklore: An Encyclopedia of Beliefs, Customs, Tales,*

Music, and Art (1997). Volume 4 also includes a geographical guide of peoples and cultures to help readers put an unfamiliar culture in geographical context, and a highly selective general bibliography that identifies works offering intercultural perspectives on folklore.

Besides concluding with extensive bibliographies of important information resources, the entries are also cross-referenced, with entry names highlighted in **boldface** type when they are first mentioned in the entry or listed in a "See also" line at the end of the text. To make the cross-references useful across the set, each volume contains a listing of the entries found in the other volumes so that users can quickly identify where to find the entry for a highlighted reference. Each volume also contains a volume-specific table of contents and a complete subject index to the set.

Acknowledgments

Obviously, this work is a team effort. Most of the members of that team are named in the Editors and Contributors section in Volume 4 and appear with their contributions throughout the work. I want to call special attention here to individuals whose contributions might otherwise be unclear and underestimated: Thomas A. Green, who had the idea for this encyclopedia; Gary Kuris, vice president, Editorial, and George Butler, senior acquisitions editor, of Greenwood Publishing Group, who contacted me and helped to devise the formal proposal for the project; John Wagner, senior development editor at Greenwood Publishing Group, who has been the principal editor for this project, with whom I have been in almost daily contact for the last several years, and whose influence is felt in every aspect of the work; Charles R. Carr and Clyde A. Milner II, administrators at Arkansas State University, who arranged for me to have help from graduate assistants and other amenities; William Allen, Jennifer Majors, Cliff Stamp, and Diane Unger, who provided technical assistance; and Frances M. Malpezzi, who helped to keep the work focused during the three years that it has been the major professional aspect of my life. I would also like to thank Tom Brennan for preparation of the maps. The production staff at Westchester Book Group also deserves thanks: production editors Rebecca A. Homiski and Carla L. Talmadge; copyeditors Jamie Nan Thaman, Frank Saunders, Carol Lucas, and Krystyna Budd; and Enid Zafran, who prepared the index.

I also believe I was particularly fortunate in my formal folklore education in having instructors whose view of folklore was truly international. These include Richard M. Dorson, who, though an Americanist, never lost sight of the importance of thinking of folklore globally; Warren E. Roberts, whose work in historic-geographic folktale studies and in material folk culture had a strong international flavor; Linda Dégh, who brought a continental perspective to the Indiana University Folklore Institute in the late 1960s; and John C. Messenger, an anthropologist whose fieldwork has taken him to Nigeria and to the west of Ireland. They and others reminded us that folklore cannot be understood only by looking at it within the context of a single culture. I hope that this work will impress that point on its readers.

Comprehensive List of Entries

North America

American Indian

APACHE

GEOGRAPHY AND HISTORY

The North American Indian groups subsumed under the name Apache—Chiricahua, Jicarilla, Lipan, Mescalero, Western Apache, and Kiowa-Apache with the Navajo, who are now regarded as distinct enough from their fellow Southern Athapaskan speakers to constitute a separate society—apparently migrated to the American Southwest (Arizona, New Mexico, and Texas) and northern Mexico from the Mackenzie Basin in what is now Canada. That population movement began perhaps as early as the tenth century C.E. and continued for the next several hundred years. Before the eighteenth century, the Chiricahua were established in southeastern Arizona and northern Mexico, the Western Apache to the north and west beyond the Gila and Salt Rivers, the Jicarilla in north-central New Mexico, and the Mescalero in southeastern New Mexico and Texas. The Kiowa-Apache affiliated loosely with the Kiowa after the latter arrived on the southern Plains, and the Lipan lived in southwestern Texas.

Like other Athabaskan-speakers, the Apaches referred to themselves as "the people" (*Ndé* or *Diné* in variant forms depending on dialect). The outsiders' designation, Apache, was first used by the Spanish explorer Juan de Oñate in 1598. Most authorities believe it derives from the Zuni Pueblo word *ʔapaču*, used to refer to all the foraging groups, including the Navajo, who had recently become a nuisance for the settled Pueblo communities. Pre-contact Apaches lived primarily as foragers, though some groups—especially the Western Apache, Jicarilla, and Lipan, who established *rancherías*, where they raised maize, beans, pumpkins, and melons—did engage occasionally in horticulture. Kinship stressed matrilineal descent, and residence was matrilocal. Similar to other foragers, Apaches aggregated into small bands consisting of extended families, which might coalesce periodically during the course of the annual cycle for economic, religious, or other collective endeavors, especially a young woman's initiation ceremony. Except for the Jicarillas and Kiowa-Apaches, who lived in Plains tipis (and, in fact, adopted and adapted many aspects of Plains culture), the characteristic Apache dwelling was the easily assembled and dismantled wickiup, a cone-shaped structure with pole framework covered with brush, grass, reeds, and sometimes animal skins.

Apaches apparently made their first contact with Euro-Americans during Coronado's *entrada* of 1540, and before the Spanish *conquistador* had made his way back to New Spain he or his men had probably encountered several of the Apache groups. Sustained interaction with Europeans began with Oñate's expedition in the late

WESTERN INUIT
AND YUPIK

WESTERN INUIT
AND YUPIK

TLINGIT

TLINGIT

TLINGIT

HAIDA   TLINGIT

CANADA

OJIBWE

OJIBWE

NEZ PERCE

L A K O T A

LAKOTA

IROQUOIS

CHEYENNE

U N I T E D
S T A T E S

Pacific
Ocean

Atlantic
Ocean

CHEROKEE

Appalachia

HOPI
NAVAJO

KIOWA

Mississippi
Delta

APACHE

CHOCTAW

SEMINOLE

MEXICO

Gulf of
Mexico

N

0   600 km

0   600 mi

Regions and Native Peoples of North America.

sixteenth century. The Apaches responded to Spanish settlements as they did to the Pueblos who had preceded them into the Southwest by constantly posing the threat of raids. The pressure of Apache raiding was an enabling factor for the Pueblo Revolt of 1680, when the Spanish temporarily abandoned New Mexico. When they returned twelve years later, the Apaches were the most formidable force in the region. For the next century the Spanish worked at pacifying the Apaches and were generally successful in offering subsidies to individual bands if they would settle near missions. The resulting peace lasted until the Mexican Revolution, after which a return by the Apaches to an economy based partially on raiding occurred. The state of more or less constant tension increased following the Mexican War. When the United States took over Apacheria following the Treaty of Guadalupe Hidalgo in 1848, they attempted to subjugate the Apaches militarily. Several reservations were established for Apaches in New Mexico and Arizona, but the rigidity of American military control and foolish errors such as the false arrest of the Chiricahua leader Cochise in 1861 kept tensions high. The "Apache Wars" lasted for more than a generation, ending only with the surrender of Geronimo, a Chiricahua, in 1886. Instead of being restored to his homeland as he and his band had expected, Geronimo was shipped eastward first to Florida and then to Alabama before ultimately being settled at Fort Sill, Oklahoma. Though many of the descendants of Geronimo's followers were moved to the Mescalero reservation in New Mexico in 1913, others have remained in southwestern Oklahoma. The U.S. government also implemented their policy of assimilation by sending many Apache children to the Carlisle Training School in Pennsylvania, where they were supposed to learn the ways of Western civilization.

The history of contact between Europeans and the Lipan Apaches in Texas had a different trajectory. The Lipan were the dominant group on the southern Plains during the eighteenth century. Pressures from the Spanish to the south and from the Comanches to the north undermined their preeminence. By the mid-nineteenth century, Lipan presence in much of their ancestral territory had become negligible, and many individuals affiliated with other Apache groups, especially the Mescalero.

According to the 2000 federal census, 96,833 people identified themselves as Apache, making them the seventh largest American Indian group in the United States. Many live on three reservations: Fort Apache and San Carlos—both in Arizona—and Mescalero in New Mexico. Other Apaches remain in southwestern Oklahoma near Fort Sill.

MYTHS, LEGENDS, AND FOLKTALES

An important cosmogonic pattern in Apache mythology is that of the emergence, a scenario that resembles that found among the Pueblos. Emergence mythology, which frequently appears in matrilineal cultures and metaphorically defines the earth as a maternal force, usually begins with the cosmos already in place. The ancestors—often pre-human—of the mythtellers live in a paradisaical world within the present earth. Ultimately and often through their own missteps, the ancestors are forced to move into the next world—often through a hole in the sky. As they emerge from level to level, they become more and more human. Their final emergence (at least for the time being) brings them into the present world, for most Apaches the fourth in which they and their ancestors have lived. Several versions of the emergence have been recorded among the Jicarillas, and most posit the pre-existence of at least some of the features of the landscape before their ancestors emerged.

The Mescalero Apache creation myth describes a four-stage process, which occurs over as many days. Creator begins by separating sky from earth and producing light and water. Then plants and small animals take their place in the cosmos. They are followed by larger animals and then by humans. The implications of this creation myth continue in contemporary Apache life: the creation of humankind after what they must depend upon for survival has already appeared, a sense of egalitarian kinship with animals and plants, the interdependence of everything in the cosmos, and the significance of four as the pattern number that organizes much of what Apaches do and how they perceive their world. Myth provides a model for contemporary life; it is not simply a story set in the prehistoric past.

Traditional Apache storytellers distinguish narrative genres. Among the Western Apache, two important categories of stories are *nagodi'é* and *ŀe'gocho*. The former are regarded as true stories set in the past, similar to myths and legends. The style adopted for telling these stories may be relatively formal and reserved. *Nagodi'é* are especially suited for adult audiences. They are subdivided into *godiy¿hgo nagodi'é* (myth), *'ágodzaahí* (historical tale), *nŀt'éégo nagodi'é* (saga), and *ch'idii* (gossip). Raiding and warfare provided ample material for the historical tales, and anthropologists and historians have used them as source material not only for an Apache perspective on the events of the latter half of nineteenth century that captured the public imagination then and now but also for cultural data that are not otherwise accessible.

Ŀe'gocho are fictional stories traditionally told only at night during the winter months. A favorite topic is Ba'ts'oosee, the Western Apache trickster, among many native groups of the Southwest and southern Plains manifested as Coyote. Often told to children, **trickster** stories require a livelier performance style than legends and elicit spirited audience response, usually laughter at trickster's shenanigans. Like many other tricksters, Ba'ts'oosee is a wanderer whose adventures consist of episodes in which he lives up to his reputation by manipulating those whom he encounters and sometimes suffering (temporary) consequences as a result. Stories about Ba'ts'oosee also have a satirical purpose, sometimes even pointing out the foibles of the stereotypical "Whiteman."

Like many such inter-group stereotypes, depictions of Whiteman demonstrate what Apaches are not: hypocritical, shallow in their social relations, intrusive, bossy, rude, greedy, and ostentatious, among other characteristics. Trickster stories do not afford the only vehicle for portraying Whiteman. He may appear in other kinds of narrative—even *na'godi'é*—as well as in staged enactments in which an Apache assumes the role of Whiteman and behaves as he does (and as a Western Apache does not). Such portrayals serve an integrative purpose by clearly differentiating Apaches from people of another **ethnicity**. They also help to educate, since portrayals of Whiteman in both stories and enactments produce derisive laughter, which identifies behavior that is likely to evoke ridicule.

RITUALS AND CEREMONIES

The Girls' Puberty Ceremony has been of particular importance throughout Apacheria. Each year, perhaps on the Fourth of July to take advantage of the extended holiday period, people assemble to celebrate the transition to womanhood of those girls who have attained maturity during the past year. This rite of passage eases the young women's transition into their new status, and it also reinforces all Apaches' sense of identity. Typically a four-day affair whose agenda is scheduled according to the "star-clocks" by which the organizers measure the passage of the nighttime hours, the event provides plenty of chances for Apaches who live apart from their communities to return home, to forget for a time their roles in mainstream culture, and to share memories, conversation, and food.

The ceremony affords an opportunity for the young women at the beginning of their maturity to identify with White Painted Woman, a culture **hero** and transformer who helped to reshape the world into a place habitable for human beings. Her myth emphasizes important themes associated with the cycle of life. When she first appears to the *Ndé*, she is a young girl coming from the east. When she reaches adulthood, she becomes associated with the south. Old age takes her to the west, and finally she goes toward the north to die. But she is immediately reborn to begin the cycle again.

Among the Mescaleros the young girls who are participating in the puberty ceremony become reincarnations of White Painted Woman, and much of the symbolism recalls the fundamental elements of her myth. For example, the ceremonial lodge where much of the ceremony takes place is structured around four holy lodgepoles, called grandfathers. These recall both the cardinal directions and the stages of life through which White Painted Woman passes in mythic time. Many of the activities that the initiates must perform require fourfold repetition. Moreover, the ceremony strongly emphasizes circularity, reminding everyone of the cyclic nature of White Painted Woman's journey.

The Mountain Spirits, who dwell in the interiors of mountains, may dance at the Girls' Puberty Ceremony. Typically dance teams consist of four spirits accompanied sometimes by two clowns, figures who enact some of the escapades related in trickster narratives. The Mountain Spirit dancers wear elaborate garments: buckskin kilts, colorful waist sashes, arm streamers to which eagle feathers are attached, and—most strikingly—headdresses that may extend four feet above the dancers' heads. They emphasize the community-wide implications of the rite of passage, for their appearance at the ceremony helps to ensure the fortunes of everyone, not just the young women who are making the transition into adulthood.

Although the Girls' Puberty Ceremony is often the central event in the ceremonial calendar, Apache festive life has consisted of many other observations, connected with the seasonal and astronomical cycles. An example is the Jicarilla Relay Race—perhaps borrowed from neighboring Pueblo cultures—in which young men who had attained puberty but had not yet married were expected to participate at least once. Held each fall, the race divides the Jicarillas into two loosely defined moieties. One side represents the sun and animals; the other is associated with the moon and plants. The point of the race seems to have been to emphasize the necessary balance between what the two moieties represent if the cosmos is to continue to operate in the best interests of humankind.

Singing and instrumental music accompany Apache ceremonies and occur in non-ritual circumstances as well. Particularly important for the Apache has been the *tsii'edo'a'tl*, colloquially known as the Apache violin. Usually made from the dried flower stalk of the agave, which could be hollowed out easily, the violin was strung with horsehair and played with a bow made from any flexible wood. Violinists placed the instrument against their chests to perform ceremonial songs, love songs, or drinking songs. Some authorities believe that the Apache violin is an adaptation of a Spanish original, but Athabaskan-speaking groups in the Northwest, whence the Apaches migrated, may have had similar instruments.

ARTS AND CRAFTS

Basketry, traditionally the province of women, has been one of the preeminent art forms among Apaches, who have been particularly known for three-rod coiled baskets made principally from willow shoots. Peeled, the shoots are whitish in color but with time often take on a golden patina. Designs on baskets, usually geometric forms emphasizing fourfold structures, are produced by interweaving black and dark brown devilsclaw or occasionally yucca root, which is red. In the early twentieth century, a variety of baskets were being manufactured among the San Carlos Apache: conical carryalls, which might be decorated with buckskin fringes; the more elaborately decorated plaques, which were intended only for sale; and large baskets like ollas or jars. Some argue that the golden age of Apache basketry ended during the years of the Great Depression, when increased availability of Western mass-produced pots, pans, and other receptacles diminished indigenous need for baskets. Meanwhile, the slackening of tourist trade discouraged artists from producing traditionally structured baskets. Nevertheless, the market for Apache baskets revived after World War II, and many artists are now producing objects for galleries and for tourists.

Another important art object from Apache tradition is the cradleboard, which is constructed within a day or two of a birth. Using a willow frame, the artist attaches cross pieces made from soft wood. The hood of the cradle is made by bending several reeds and connecting them with sinew. A soft layer of cedar bark or grass provides comfort for the child. As the child grows, he or she graduates to larger cradleboards until the age of fifteen to eighteen months. The most apparent function of cradleboards is to provide security for children and to allow the mother free use of her hands. However, they are also objects of beauty. Apaches have frequently decorated them with strips of calico and other bright-colored cloth.

CHALLENGES OF THE MODERN WORLD

Despite the reduction of size in Apacheria to only several reservations and despite the changes that the twentieth and twenty-first centuries have brought, Apaches continue to preserve their identity by retaining forms of traditional culture and adapting them to new circumstances. The Girls' Puberty Ceremony is still an important occasion, for example, and as many as 15,000 people—most of them Western Apaches—speak the Apache language. Apaches meet threats to their cultural heritage forcefully, enlisting a range of methods for asserting their claims. For example, the telescope complex that a consortium of astronomers are building on Arizona's Mt. Graham has met with considerable resistance from Western Apaches, for whom the mountain, *Dzil Nchaa Si An*, is a sacred site. Although most of the American institutions involved in the project have withdrawn, the project still has support from the University of Arizona and from foreign sources, such as the Vatican, despite resolutions from the San Carlos Apache Tribal Council and objections from several Indian rights organizations.

Meanwhile, Apaches have found their places in the context of **globalization**. The Chiricahua sculptor and painter Allan Houser (1914–1994) has been recognized for blending elements of his heritage with elements of modernism. Economically, the Inn of the Mountain Gods on the Mescalero reservation in southern New Mexico has become one of the premiere resorts in the Southwest, and nearby Ski Apache provides an important venue for winter sports. The Jicarillas have also taken advantage of **tourism** both through developing a casino and by tapping into the crowds that flock to nearby Chama, New Mexico, each summer to ride a steam train through the Sangre de Christo Mountains.

STUDIES OF APACHE FOLKLORE

The earliest folklore "research" among Apaches was probably that of John Gregory Bourke (1887–1888), aide-de-camp for General George Crook during his pursuit of Geronimo in the 1880s. Other early figures of note in American anthropology also published material on Apache folklore during the late nineteenth and early twentieth century: for example, James Mooney (1898), Frank Russell (1898), Pliny Earle Goddard (1911), and Aleš Hrdlička (1905). Significant work on the subject was done in the 1930s by Grenville Goodwin (especially 1971 [1939]) and by Morris Edward Opler, who published several collections of oral narratives as Memoirs of the American Folklore Society (1938, 1940, 1942) as well as many other ethnographic books and articles, primarily on the Jicarillas. Keith Basso (1979) has been the principal student of Western Apache culture, including folklore, during the latter half of the twentieth century, and Claire Farrer has worked extensively with Mescalero folklore (1996).

BIBLIOGRAPHY

Basso, Keith. 1979. *Portraits of "the Whiteman": Linguistic Play and Cultural Symbols among the Western Apache*. Cambridge, MA: Cambridge University Press.

———. 1996. *Wisdom Sits in Places: Landscape and Language among the Western Apache*. Albuquerque: University of New Mexico Press.

Bourke, John Gregory. 1887–1888. The Medicine-Men of the Apache. *Annual Report of the Bureau of American Ethnology* 9: 443–603.

Evers, Larry. 1979. *Ba'ts'oosee*, an Apache Trickster Cycle. *Southwest Folklore* 3.4: 1–15.

Farrer, Claire R. 1991. *Living Life's Circle: Mescalero Apache Cosmovision*. Albuquerque: University of New Mexico Press.

————. 1996. *Thunder Rides a Black Horse: Mescalero Apaches and the Mythic Present.* 2nd edition. Prospect Heights, IL: Waveland Press.

Goddard, Pliny Earle. 1911. Jicarilla Apache Texts. *Anthropological Papers of the American Museum of Natural History* 8: 1–276.

Goodwin, Grenville. 1971. *Western Apache Raiding and Warfare*, edited by Keith H. Basso. Tucson: University of Arizona Press.

————. 1994 (1939). *Myths and Tales of the White Mountain Apache.* Tucson: University of Arizona Press.

Hrdlička, Aleš. 1905. Notes on the San Carlos Apache. *American Anthropologist* 7: 480–495.

Mooney, James. 1898. The Jicarilla Genesis. *American Anthropologist* 11: 197–209.

Opler, Morris Edward. 1938. *Myths and Tales of Jicarilla Apache Indians.* Memoirs of the American Folklore Society, No. 31.

————. 1940. *Myths and Tales of the Lipan Apache Indians.* Memoirs of the American Folklore Society, No. 36.

————. 1942. *Myths and Tales of the Chiricahua Apache Indians.* Memoirs of the American Folklore Society, No. 37.

Rhodes, Willard, ed. n.d. *Apache* (sound recording). Library of Congress AFS L 42.

Russell, Frank. 1898. Myths of the Jicarilla Apaches. *Journal of American Folklore* 11: 253–271.

Tanner, Clara Lee. 1982. *Apache Indian Baskets.* Tucson: University of Arizona Press.

William M. Clements and Frances M. Malpezzi

CHEROKEE

GEOGRAPHY

The Cherokees dominated the southern Appalachian region of North America for thousands of years. The Eastern Band of Cherokee Indians still lives there today, while most Cherokee people—the Cherokee Nation of Oklahoma and the United Keetoowah Band (UKB)—live throughout the United States as a result of the 1838 removal. Cherokee language, folklore, and values persist though the Cherokee people have adopted modern technology and participate in twenty-first-century life.

The Cherokees once dominated the whole southern highland region, their original territory encompassing approximately 140,000 square miles, parts of eight present-day states. This area of the United States includes the highest mountains east of the Mississippi River and is a temperate rainforest, with elevations ranging from near sea level to 6,684 feet. The extreme differences in elevations have produced tremendous biodiversity. More kinds of trees grow here than in all of Europe. Seventy-five percent of all the medicinal plants in the United States grow here. On the mountaintops, more than ninety inches of rain fall annually, and streams, creeks, rivers, springs, and waterfalls dominate the landscape.

The Cherokee people say that they have always been here in the mountains, placed here by the Creator, who gave them their language and traditions. Today the Cherokees consist of the three federally recognized tribes mentioned earlier. The Cherokee Nation of Oklahoma and the UKB live primarily in Oklahoma. According to the 2000 census, the Cherokees were the largest American Indian tribe in the United States.

HISTORY AND SOCIAL STRUCTURE

The primary concern of Cherokee culture is a sense of balance. The Cherokees believe that a person must balance spirit, mind, and body. Being in balance also means living in harmony with neighbors and the earth, taking only what is needed. Their social organization and customs reflect this pattern. For example, men's roles are balanced with women's roles; both are regarded as essential. The personal autonomy and freedom of the individual, which has always been considerable, is balanced with a concern for the good of the whole.

The Cherokees have been successful horticulturalists for more than 1,000 years. They developed their own varieties of corn, beans, and squash. Villages were surrounded by hundreds of acres of cornfields and orchards. Mostly women farmed while men hunted and fished in the highlands and streams near the village.

The Cherokee nation was a loose confederation of autonomous villages. Each village had a peace chief, a war chief, and a priest with different roles. The seven clans, based on women's lineages, also had leadership roles. The peace chief took care of issues within the village concerns, while the war chief dealt with trade and war. The priest mediated between this world and other worlds and was in charge of ceremonies.

Balancing these important roles filled by men, the clan system played an important part in maintaining social order and structure. The clan system was based on women's lineages: a child inherited its mother's clan. The clans were Wolf, Deer, Bird, Blue, Paint, Long Hair, and Wild Potato, and each had special knowledge or abilities. Long Hair clan people were often leaders, for example. Laws maintained through oral tradition were enforced by the clans, and one of the most important of these was the law of blood revenge, which was based on corporate responsibility. If someone from the Bird clan was killed by someone from the Wolf clan, then the Bird clan had the right to execute the killer. If the killer was not available, another member of the Wolf clan was executed. Balance was thus restored.

Cherokee society was matrilineal and matrilocal. Both the clan affiliation and property were passed through the mother's line, making the mother's brothers important relatives for children. Extended families based around several generations of women shared a household. This house and any farm or garden areas were passed down through the women.

The seven clans gave structure to many aspects of Cherokee life. In the council house and at the dance grounds, Cherokees sat in one of seven sections designated for their clan. When traveling, a Cherokee would find people of his of her clan, who were obliged to provide food and hospitality for any clan member as though the person were a member of their immediate family.

Cherokee society was democratic. All members of a village participated in discussion and decision making, including men, women, and children. They practiced democracy through consensus of the group as a whole, which led to well-developed traditions of persuasive rhetoric and oratory. Children were taught from an early age to balance considerations of their own personal freedom with the good of the tribe as a whole. As a result, Cherokee society combined a high degree of personal autonomy with responsibility to the larger family, clan, and village.

Cherokees believe they have always lived in the southern Appalachians, that the Creator placed them there and gave them their language and customs. Legends locate the first Cherokee man and woman at Shining Rock (now on the Blue Ridge Parkway) and the first Cherokee village at Kituhwa (near present-day Cherokee, North Carolina). Archeologists believe that people have been present in the southern Appalachians for more than 14,000 years. Village sites like Kituhwa show that people have lived there continuously for more than 10,000 years. With regard to Cherokee culture, archeologists trace sequences of material remains from present-day Cherokees back approximately 3,000 years. Linguistic scholars say that Cherokee language became a distinct language more than 3,500 years ago and that it is related to other Iroquoian languages such as Mohawk, Huron, and Oneida. Beginning about three thousand years ago, people in the southern Appalachians began settling in villages, growing some crops, and making distinctive pottery. These characteristics were widespread throughout the region that belonged to the Cherokees at the time of European contact.

Beginning about 600–900 C.E., people in the southeast began building mounds surmounted by council houses, temples, or residences. Throughout the southeast, they depended on maize agriculture, had extensive trade networks, and were organized socially in chiefdoms. They shared an iconography that appeared on gorgets and petroglyphs. This area included the tribes that came to be known as the Cherokee, Chickasaw, Choctaw, Creek, Caddo, and others.

Contact with Europeans for the Cherokees came in 1540 with Hernando De-Soto's expedition. Scholars speculate that European diseases decimated the Cherokees in the sixteenth century, reducing their population from 40,000 to less than 10,000. In the eighteenth century, epidemics swept through the Cherokee nation three times, each time reducing the population by 30 to 50 percent. During this time, the Cherokees engaged in trade with the British, exchanging deerskins for guns and ammunition, bells, cloth, steel knives, and other trade items. Cherokee women traded corn and baskets for stroud cloth, calico petticoats, ribbons, beads, bells, kettles, hoes, plows, and other items. During the eighteenth century 75 percent of the Cherokee lands were taken in treaties. Cherokee delegations visited the King of England in 1730 and 1762. The Cherokees sided with the British in the American Revolution and, as a result, had many of their villages destroyed in 1776 by colonial militia.

Beginning in 1789, the U.S. federal government encouraged the Cherokees to become "civilized." Within fifty years, the Cherokees developed their own system of writing, a bilingual newspaper, schools, churches, a capital city, a written constitution, a police force, courts, ferries, blacksmiths, toll roads, and other innovations. But the American belief in manifest destiny, greed for land on which to produce cotton with slave labor, and the removal of the French as a threat from the west resulted in the forced removal of all southeastern tribes to Indian Territory (now Oklahoma). The forced Cherokee removal became known as the Trail of Tears, and during this time from 4,000 to 8,000 Cherokees died—between 25 and 50 percent of the population. As a result of Removal, most Cherokee people today live in Oklahoma, though the Eastern Band lives on a small remnant of the Cherokees' original homeland in the mountains of western North Carolina and includes the descendants of people who owned land, those who hid in the mountains, and those who returned from Oklahoma.

RELIGIOUS BELIEFS

The Cherokees say that they have always believed in one creator, Unelvnvhi, whom they also address as Grandfather. They believe that all life is connected and that they are spiritually related to all of creation. In this creation, however, human beings have special responsibilities as caretakers of the earth. To live in balance, one must show respect to all one's relatives. This is exemplified in the traditions of plant gathering. When a medicinal plant is identified, the first specimen is not taken; one must find four or even seven plants before gathering one. In return, the gatherer must leave a token of thanks such as a pinch of tobacco.

The Cherokee belief system regards medicine, religion, spirituality, psychology, and ecology holistically. Spirituality permeates all aspects of life. The stickball game, for example, has associated religious rituals and ceremonial dances. Ceremonies are designed to help maintain balance. The Going-to-Water Ceremony, for instance, was performed every morning so that a person could begin the day cleansed both spiritually and physically.

Traditions of conjuring balance traditions of healing. Both use prayer formulas and ritualistic actions to accomplish certain effects, which might include healing from disease, safe childbirth, or gaining someone's affections. Healers are distinguished from conjurers in that they work for the good of others, whereas conjurers work for their own gain. The extensive Cherokee plantlore is orally transmitted from generation to generation and is guarded from outsiders.

The numbers four and seven are important throughout Cherokee folklore because they represent the four cardinal directions as well as the directions of above and below. The seventh direction is considered the spirit at the center of all things. Seven clans give structure to many aspects of Cherokee life.

Colors also are associated with directions and qualities, some positive and some negative. Red is associated with the east and with power and success. White is associated with the south and peace. Black represents the west and death: the direction of the darkening land, where the spirits of the dead travel. Blue represents the north and defeat or sometimes just thoughtfulness.

Today many Cherokee people are Christians. Some practice Christianity while maintaining traditional Cherokee religious beliefs as well. The Cherokee National Council invited the first Christian missionaries to teach Cherokee children to read and write English. Moravians came in 1800 and were rapidly followed by Presbyterians, Baptists, and Methodists. Rev. Samuel Worcester worked with Elias Boudinot (Buck Watie) to translate hymns, psalms, the gospels, and the New Testament into the Cherokee language and syllabary. By the time of Cherokee Removal in 1838, Cherokee people had hymnbooks and gospels printed in their own language and had written tracts and sermons. Cherokee ministers went on the Trail of Tears, and people today sing hymns in the Cherokee language that, according to oral tradition, their ancestors sang on the Trail of Tears. Gospel music has become a Cherokee tradition that preserves the language as well as shape-note musical traditions from the nineteenth century.

Myths, Legends, and Folktales

Verbal folklore among the Cherokees takes many forms. Myths, legends, folktales, jokes, proverbs, and healing formulas are all rich and varied. Origin stories, legends about places, animal tales, folktales, personal experience narratives, jokes, and proverbs have been passed down for generations. Stories about "little people" form an important part of the **repertoire**. Humor is part of many stories and informal verbal interactions as well.

These are not the categories observed by the Cherokee, however, who tend to call all myths, folktales, and other stories legends. Folklorists more narrowly describe legends as stories told as though true about a person or place. This folk taxonomy sheds some light on the Cherokee attitude toward folklore: people recognize that these stories are not literally true but that they illuminate aspects of truth.

Origin myths provide detailed accounts of how things came to be. In the story of the creation of the earth, for example, mud is brought up by *dayunishi*, the water beetle, and this mud grows into the earth. The great buzzard flies low and makes mountains and valleys with his wings. The first man and woman, Ganadi (the Cherokee word for "hunter") and Selu (the Cherokee word for "corn"), lived at Shining Rock, a location about thirty miles from present-day Cherokee, North Carolina. The first Cherokee village was Kituhwa, a location where a mound still exists on the Tuckaseegee River about ten miles from the town of Cherokee. This site is still so significant to the Cherokees that the Eastern Band bought it back in 1996. It had been owned by non-Cherokees since the time of Removal.

In the sacred origin stories several themes emerge. Often the person or animal who accomplishes a heroic deed is not the biggest and strongest, but instead a small creature like the water beetle, who brings mud for the earth, or the water spider, who brings fire to the people. The moral of these stories is that every creature has a purpose and that even the smallest member of the community can do something for the good of the whole. Another theme holds that good can come out of horrendous events. When Selu's sons kill her because they think she is a witch, she tells them to drag her body around the clearing; corn sprouts where her body passes. From this tragic matricide comes corn for the people. The theme of balance is apparent in the myth of the origin of disease and medicine. When the animals create diseases to punish man for not showing respect to them, the plants create a cure for every disease.

Other origin myths account for specific characteristics of plants and animals. These are based on close observations of nature and often involve a moral that reinforces the Cherokee system of beliefs and values. For example, the story of why the possum's tail is bare teaches that one should not brag. The story of the origin of strawberries teaches that one should be slow to anger. Both of these cultural values enable people to live in harmony with each other. Dozens of stories explain the appearances of animals: why the turtle's shell is cracked, why the chipmunk's back is striped, why the deer has antlers. In addition to transmitting cultural values, these stories teach children to look closely at the natural world around them. Cherokee people today often say that they were not physically punished as children but were corrected by being told stories.

Stories about the "little people" or *yvwi usdi* are told as though true, and people claim to have seen them, heard them, or witnessed the results of their actions. This race of small beings lives mostly unseen but alongside the Cherokees. They dress like Cherokees and have clans like the Cherokees. Their clans live in different settings, though: some live in laurel thickets, others in rock cliffs, by streams, near cemeteries, or elsewhere. The little people can be helpful, as in stories where they help lost children find their way home. But their help can be dangerous; adults are prohibited from telling about their encounters with little people on pain of death. Stories of little people also reinforce Cherokee values of respect and the idea of balance. Children are taught not to pick up or disturb things in the woods (for instance, a rock or feather) because those things might belong to the little people, and if you take something belonging to the little people, they will take something of yours in return. This tradition explains why things around one's house sometimes seem to disappear.

Still other stories tell of a race of immortals, or *nunnehi*, who live in a sort of parallel universe. Their world is accessed through whirlpools or waterfalls or mounds, and humans who venture there see strange sights and consider themselves lucky to return alive. In one story, the immortals issue forth from Nikwasi Mound in the form of warriors and help the Cherokees defend their village from attack. This same story appeared during the Civil War, when Nikwasi was no longer a Cherokee village but the Appalachian town of Franklin. In this local legend, the Union Army bypassed Nikwasi because their scouts saw armed men standing on every corner, even though all the able-bodied men of the town were away at war.

Monsters, giants, and mythical creatures also have a place in Cherokee folktales. Stonecoat and Spearfinger were fearful creatures who devoured one's liver, causing death. The giant Judaculla or Tsulkalu lived in the rugged Balsam Mountains. The horned serpent Uktena terrorized whole villages until it was defeated by a magician from another tribe.

Accounts of historical events have also entered Cherokee oral tradition. Many Cherokee families pass on stories of what happened to them during the Trail of Tears. Stories from the boarding school era, when children were taken from their families to be educated in the ways of Euro-American civilization, are also part of family folklore. Narratives about ghosts, spirits, big snakes, local characters, and humorous events have also become part of family and community folklore.

Until the twentieth century, all Cherokee folklore was in the Cherokee language. Because of federal policies of acculturation and the policies of boarding schools operated by the Bureau of Indian Affairs (1893–1948), Cherokee children were physically punished for speaking their language. This was particularly humiliating because in Cherokee culture, children were never struck by adults. Consequently, most parents did not teach their children to speak the language. The Cherokee dance songs continued to be passed on in the language, and Christian gospel songs were sung in both English and Cherokee. At the beginning of the twenty-first century, the Cherokees are trying to preserve and revitalize their language before it disappears.

Although myths and folktales are today told in English, their rhythm reflects the rhythms of the Cherokee language.

The creation of a form of writing by Sequoyah in 1821 was unprecedented. Sequoyah is the only individual in recorded history to have created a writing system without being literate. Within months of approval of Sequoyah's syllabary by the Cherokee National Council, 90 percent of the Cherokee people could read and write in their own language. They used the syllabary to write letters to relatives and in 1828 began printing a bilingual newspaper, the *Cherokee Phoenix*. People preserved medical formulas by writing them down and also kept records that enabled them to keep from being cheated.

MUSIC AND SONGS

Cherokee music includes instrumental and vocal traditions, and music is connected with dances, ceremonies, and stories as well as everyday life. Traditional instruments include flute, whistle, water drum, pottery drum, and rattles. The flute was made from a length of rivercane or from the legbone of a deer. It was played without accompaniment, and one of its traditional uses was the greeting of visitors. Whistles were made from the legbones of birds and were played by shamans to encourage the stickball teams or were blown by warriors in battle. The traditional vocal war cry for the Cherokees imitated the gobble of the male wild turkey. Percussion instruments were important for dance traditions. The water drum was made from a short length of hollow log, covered with skin drawn tight by a hoop placed over it and snugged down against the side of the drum. The level of water in the drum determined the tone. Pottery drums were made of ceramic vessels covered with a head of tightly stretched deerskin. The dance leader or shaman traditionally played the drum or used a small rattle. Men sang the dance songs while rhythmic accompaniment was provided by women wearing turtle shell rattles on their legs, tied just below the knee.

Song traditions include lullabies, dance songs, prayer formulas, and songs for ceremonies. Lullabies were sung mostly by women to children. Dance songs were sung mainly by men, balanced by women's rhythmic accompaniment. Songs for the prayer formulas would have been the specialized knowledge of medicine people.

Cherokee songs traditionally are in major more often than minor keys. They are very melodic. Often they consist of short sections that are repeated four or seven times. Dance songs may begin and end with a whoop.

By 1800, Cherokee people were playing fiddles and singing Christian songs introduced by missionaries. One of the first publications in Sequoyah's syllabary was a book of hymns in the Cherokee language. Both of these traditions carried on through the nineteenth and twentieth centuries. The hymn tradition includes shape-note songs, translated into Cherokee.

Oral history about the Trail of Tears maintains that the Cherokees sang specific hymns in the Cherokee language during the removal experience, and people still perform these. The hymns include "Amazing Grace" and "The Trail of Tears Song." The latter uses the words to "Guide Me Thou Oh Great Jehovah" sung to a tune in a minor key.

The Cherokee gospel singing tradition in the twentieth century and into the early twenty-first century has been very strong. Cherokee gospel groups sing in white churches, at festivals, at "singings" in the communities, and on tours as well as in their home churches. These groups are often quartets with soprano, alto, tenor, and bass. They may perform with just one guitar or with guitar, bass, and additional instruments. The harmonies evoke shape-note arrangements, with contrapuntal parts, and in some cases the groups use shape-note hymnals. Some songs are performed only in Cherokee; others are sung with some verses in English and some in Cherokee. When the Cherokee Nation and the Eastern Band met officially for the first time since the Trail of Tears in 1984 at Red Clay, Tennessee, gospel groups had already been traveling back and forth to sing in each other's churches.

The tradition of singing and drumming for powwow dancing became popular in the twentieth century as a pan-Indian tradition, and these events became even more widespread after World War II. Although some powwow dances come from particular tribes, the powwow is a celebration of Indian identity that crosses cultural lines. In the powwow tradition, singers (usually men) gather around one large drum, with each singer using a drumstick. They play together on the beat, creating a powerful sound.

FESTIVALS, CELEBRATIONS, AND DANCES

Cherokee festivals as described by eighteenth-century observers included traditions lost today, though the Green Corn Ceremony continues, as do Stomp Dances. Seven festivals were described, along with informal dramas that re-enacted stories about hunting and war. Pantomimes of war or hunting—sometimes serious, sometimes comedic—were enacted in the council houses as entertainment.

The Green Corn Ceremony, an annual ceremony of renewal, is celebrated when the first corn is ready to eat. Traditionally held sometime in late August or early September, this ritual includes purification ceremonies, dances, and feasting. This was a time to make amends and forgive others. Marriages often took place at this time.

Dances occurred before stickball games to prepare the players and at other times determined by the shamans. Within the larger Stomp Dance Ceremony, some dances were social in nature and others were more sacred. Some dances were considered a form of prayer. Some such the Bear Dance and Quail Dance honored animals. Another dance, called the Booger Dance, made fun of evil spirits or people who threatened the tribe. In historic times, some of the masks representing evil spirits came to resemble Europeans and African Americans. Stomp Dances still take place today as part of traditional Cherokee religion.

Distinct from these sacred traditions are the demonstration dances for the public at festivals and performances. These might include the Friendship Dance. Powwow dancing is more of a competition for the participants, based on dances from many tribes from throughout North America.

Festivals today include events for both the Cherokee and the general public. For the Eastern Band of Cherokee Indians, the Fall Fair held the first week of October annually since 1914 combines agricultural displays, arts and crafts, community booths, food, and performances. For the Cherokee Nation of Oklahoma, Labor Day weekend is their annual National Holiday.

Beginning in the 1930s, the Eastern Band of Cherokee Indians began performing a drama about the Trail of Tears and their origin as a distinct group. In the late 1940s, this became an outdoor drama, *Unto These Hills*, which is still performed and which has given rise to traditions of its own. The Cherokee Nation likewise tells its story in an outdoor drama held through the summer months.

SPORTS AND GAMES

Although Cherokee cultural values emphasize the importance of cooperation more than competition, in sports and games competition is sanctioned and enjoyed with the understanding that any grudges are left on the playing field. The stickball game was called The Little Brother of War, acknowledging that its skills prepared men for war. Cherokee cultural values also emphasize that players should not get angry even in the heat of a game. To lose one's temper is considered childish and bad form. The stickball game brings together many aspects of Cherokee folklore: dances, medicine, songs, and an important origin story. "The Ball Game of the Birds and Animals" tells of a mouse rejected by the team of animals but accepted by the birds, who gave him wings. He won the game for the birds, and we know him today as the bat. The story ends with moral instructions to include everyone on your team or in your community even if they look different.

In the stickball game, two teams (often representing communities) with equal numbers of players oppose each other on a large playing field. The object is to get the small leather ball between two goal posts at the opposite end of the field. Each player has two ballsticks. These are made of hickory with a small net of sinew at one end. These must be used to pick the ball up from the ground. Players can touch the ball with their hands only if it is above the waist. The only other rule is that a player cannot hold his stick with one hand and hit another player with it; he must use both hands. This rough sport involves running, tackling, and wrestling. "Drivers" with switches serve as informal referees and can break up fights. The object is to score twelve points. All-night dances and ceremonies for the ball players conducted by a shaman preceded stickball games. Betting was heavy. The Going-to-Water Ceremony following the game was intended to wash away any lingering bad feelings and restore the players to everyday life.

Other contests such as shooting a blowgun or bow and arrow were held to highlight individual skills. Wrestling matches and footraces also determined the strongest and fastest members of the community, and stories are still told about legendary strong men.

The marble game was originally played with stone spheres about 1.5 inches in diameter on a field with several holes. Teams played against each other. This game survives in Appalachian folklore on the Cumberland Plateau as "Roley Holey." Cherokee people in Oklahoma still play this game, often using billiard balls as marbles.

The chunkey game was played mostly in the past, and its stone disks continue to be found in fields throughout the southern Appalachians. This game was played between individuals, usually male, on a flat playing ground. One person rolls the chunkey stone and attempts to either hit it with his spear or throw the spear where the stone will come to rest.

The butterbean game, or dice game, was played by teams as a social pastime. Large beans, black on one side, or carved dice are tossed in a flat, shallow basket. The number of light and dark sides showing on each toss gives a score. Scores are tallied with corn kernels, and the first team or person to reach twenty-five wins.

ARTS AND CRAFTS

Cherokee folk art traditions include such activities as basketry, pottery, doll-making, beadwork, clothing, weaving, weapon-making, and carving masks, figures, and canoes. These traditions are often passed down within families, where children learn by observation and trial and error. Gathering materials requires extensive knowledge of the natural world. These traditions were originally all functional within Cherokee society, where everything that was needed was gathered or made from natural materials from the southern Appalachians. In addition, for thousands of years trade brought materials from the Gulf of Mexico, the Great Lakes, and the Atlantic coast. Today some of these traditions have changed because of new materials and new technology; others have changed because artists are making items for tourists and art galleries rather than for their original functions. The number of skilled Cherokee folk artists dedicated to practicing these traditions remains significant.

Cherokee baskets have been important trade items for centuries if not millennia. Originally made from rivercane, these baskets were used for storing items, gathering, sifting flour, making hominy, and catching fish and in ceremonies. Rivercane was gathered from the extensive canebrakes surrounding each Cherokee village. Split into four or eight pieces, the cane was smoothed with a knife. Splits were dyed with bloodroot, walnut, butternut, and yellowroot. Finally, splits were woven into baskets with distinctive patterns. Some baskets were "doublewoven"—meaning that the basket was woven in one continuous piece with an inside and outside layer. A few Cherokee people still make this type of basket today. Other items woven from rivercane included flat mats. When much Cherokee land was lost and women no longer had access to cane beginning about 1800, they began making baskets from white oak. A century later, as oak became rare because of extensive timbering, they began using honeysuckle and finally maple for baskets.

Cherokee pottery traditions extend back 3,000 years in the southern Appalachians. The Eastern Band of Cherokee Indians has the longest continuing pottery tradition on their own land of any tribe in the United States. Their handmade, coiled pottery was stamped with wooden paddles while the clay was still wet, imprinting it with patterns of cords, cloth, or carved designs. Pottery was also incised with geometric designs. It was fired in an open fire and then smudged with burning corncobs to create a smooth interior surface. The functional pots were used for cooking, serving, and holding water. A typical cooking pot might hold about one gallon, though larger pots were used in the council houses. During the Mississippian period from 600 to 1600 C.E., pots were also painted with red and white clay slips and formed in the shapes of frogs, birds, and humans. Influenced by the tourist market in the twentieth century, most Cherokee pottery became decorative rather than functional while still retaining some of the earlier incised patterns and designs. Beginning in 2002, Cherokee potters in the Eastern Band revitalized their pottery tradition by again making stamped, waterproof functional pottery.

Weaving and manufacture of clothing date back millennia. Cordage was made from a variety of plants and used to make fishing nets. Cloth was originally woven from the inner bark of the mulberry and from Indian hemp. The tradition of finger weaving (without a loom) continues today. Feather capes were made from turkey feathers fastened on a net of twine. Deerskins were used for leggings, shirts, breech-clouts, and other clothing. Cherokee moccasins, typically of elk or bearskin, had a distinctive front center seam. Changes in clothing began in the eighteenth century with the availability of trade goods. Cherokee women later began growing, spinning, dyeing, and weaving cotton. Today Cherokee men and women wear ribbon shirts and tear dresses with fingerwoven sashes and corn beads to represent their traditional dress. Dolls have been made from clay, cornshucks, wood, and fabric, and this tradition has taken on some new forms today.

Beadwork as a folk tradition has undergone changes because of newly available materials. The oldest beads were of bone and shell, strung together or sewn on clothing. Wampum belts made of quahog shells from the north Atlantic coast denoted sacred obligations of war and peace between tribes. Shell gorgets made during the Mississippian period were carved with elaborate designs representing myths and legends on shells from the Gulf of Mexico. With the introduction of trade beads and the organic corn beads or Job's tears, beadwork has changed. Today people use tiny glass beads from the Czech and Slovak Republics or Japan to create elaborate designs on bolos, barrettes, belt buckles, sneakers, and ball caps in modern beadworking traditions that still embody Cherokee esthetics. Some people are reproducing shell art as well.

Weapons were originally made by hand, and the earliest Cherokee weapons included spears, atlatls, bows and arrows, and blowguns. Spear and arrow points were knapped from flint. Atlatls were made from wood with a weight carved from stone. Bows were carved from locust, and arrow shafts made from rivercane tipped with turkey feathers. The blowgun is made by straightening and hollowing a length of rivercane. Its darts are made from a small shaft of honey locust tipped with thistledown wrapped in sinew.

Carving has been a technique resulting in many functional as well as beautiful items made from different kinds of wood and stone. Cherokee people have carved bowls, spoons, bows, and canoes as well as stone effigy figures, rock art, pipes, masks, and animal figures. Fish sinkers, chunkey stones, ball sticks, and weapons all require carving in their manufacture.

ARCHITECTURE

Cherokee architecture was traditionally wattle-and-daub, replaced by log cabins about 1800 and modern housing in the twentieth century. The traditional extended family dwellings included a winter house, a summer house, food storage house, and *asi* or hot house. The winter house measured about sixteen by twenty feet with a central hearth and raised platforms for sleeping. Locust posts were set in the ground several feet apart, maple or willow saplings woven between them, and the wall plastered inside and out with clay mud. A central structure of four posts surmounted by a conical construction supported slabs of bark for the roof with a smoke hole at the top. The summer house was a roof supported by four poles, where the family worked, ate, and slept in the summer. The hot house or *asi* had a low roof covered with earth and served as a warm place for older family member to sleep in the winter as well as a site for ceremonies.

Cherokee public architecture included mounds, constructed as the center of towns along rivers throughout the southern Appalachians. The mounds were built in ceremonies that are still carried on. Rising as much as forty feet above the surrounding floodplain, mounds were the center of village life. The townhouse or council house was constructed on top of the mound and was built large enough to hold the entire village so that everyone could participate in discussions, hear news, and reach decisions by consensus.

At the beginning of the nineteenth century, a few Cherokee families built plantation houses of brick and wood. The Vann house in Chatsworth, Georgia, was designed by James Vann and constructed by Moravian carpenters, Cherokee workers, and African American slaves. Its colors and designs reflect a combination of federal and Cherokee style. Another good example of Cherokee plantation architecture can be found at Rome, Georgia.

As lands were taken and Cherokees moved away from the southern Appalachians, the log house became a common solution to housing problems. Households still often included summer houses and *asis* as well as the cabin of hewed or rounded logs, and these persisted into the twentieth century in western North Carolina.

FOOD

Cherokee traditional foodways involve hunting, fishing, gathering wild foods, farming, and gardening. For more than a thousand years the Cherokees have been expert farmers, relying on maize, beans, squash, pumpkins, sunflowers, and other crops. They used a system of crop rotation that allowed wild strawberries, blackberries, and other fruits to grow up in old fields near villages. Over the centuries they developed their own genetically unique corn, which they still grow today, as well as many varieties of beans and squash for which they save seeds every year. Foods are preserved through drying, canning, pickling, and more recently freezing.

Gathering wild foods is still an important activity for Cherokee families at different times of year, especially for the Eastern Band, who live in the mountains of western North Carolina. Early in the spring people go to their family's traditional gathering places in the woods to gather ramps, a wild onion. The whole community celebrates a Ramp Festival with a meal of fish, potatoes, greens, and wild ramps. Another early green is *souchan*, which is steamed. Through the seasons, different greens are gathered. Families also go on journeys to pick huckleberries and blackberries when they ripen.

Cherokee women make "bean bread," a kind of dumpling. It is molded from cornmeal and beans, wrapped in corn husks or hickory leaves, and boiled. It is served with grease for seasoning.

CHALLENGES OF THE MODERN WORLD

Modernization, globalization, and the policies of the U.S. government have affected the Cherokees. Nevertheless, the Cherokees have managed to retain the essence of their culture while adapting and surviving both physically and culturally. Early in the eighteenth century diplomatic relations with the American colonies were based on recognition of Cherokee national sovereignty, but these relations rapidly became policies of conquest. After the American Revolution, the government recommended that the Cherokees become "civilized" and live together with the Americans. Within fifty years, they had developed their own system of writing, schools, churches, a written constitution, toll roads, and ferries and were living as prosperously as their white neighbors. The federal government then pursued a policy of Removal that split the Cherokee nation, killed at least one fourth of its members, and set back its economy for generations. In the late nineteenth century, the government began an aggressive policy of acculturation in order to try to eradicate all Native American cultures and to educate children in boarding schools. After World War II the federal government tried to eradicate American Indian cultures by relocating individuals to cities to work. Despite all these programs and policies, Cherokee people have survived with a unique culture and the determination to preserve and carry it into the future.

STUDIES OF CHEROKEE FOLKLORE

The Cherokees have been the subject of descriptions and study for more than three centuries. Eighteenth-century accounts by James Adair (Williams 1930), Henry Timberlake (Williams 1927), William Bartram (1996), and John Norton (1970) provide detailed descriptions of Cherokee life and culture. In the early nineteenth century, the Cherokees began producing their own written documents. At the time of Removal in the 1830s, they were documented in census materials, maps, spoliation claims, letters, and other materials. The Payne Manuscript from the 1830s describes many traditions and ceremonies. From 1880 till 1920, James Mooney visited the Cherokees and recorded stories, formulas, and other ethnographic information for the Bureau of American Ethnology. Frans Olbrechts followed his lead in the 1920s. John Witthoft from the University of Pennsylvania studied the Cherokees in the mid-twentieth century. Studies of the Cherokee language by William Cook, Duane King, Durbin Feeling, and others began in the late twentieth century.

Archeological studies began to shed light on Cherokee culture beginning with the Valentine family excavations in the 1880s, the collections of Gustav Heye, and the Works Progress Administration activities of the 1930s. Post-war archeology used radiocarbon dating to examine Cherokee origins. Teams of archeologists from the University of Tennessee and the University of North Carolina worked from the 1950s through the 1970s. Salvage archeology in the late 1970s in response to Tennessee Valley Authority projects in east Tennessee yielded additional information. Today the Cherokees are directing archeological excavations and studies through tribal archeologists and historic preservation officers. They are using non-invasive research techniques to reveal information about sacred sites such as Kituhwa. The

Museum of the Cherokee Indian in Cherokee, North Carolina, has been publishing the *Journal of Cherokee Studies* since 1976.

BIBLIOGRAPHY

Bartram, William. 1996. *Travels and Other Writings*. New York: Library of America.

Calhoun, Walker. 1989. *Where the Ravens Roost* (sound recording). Cullowhee, NC: Mountain Heritage Center.

Cook, William. 1979. A Grammar of North Carolina Cherokee. Diss., Yale University.

Duncan, Barbara R., col. and ed. 1998. *Living Stories of the Cherokee*. Chapel Hill: University of North Carolina Press.

———, ed. 2001. *Where It All Began: Cherokee Creation Stories in Art*. Cherokee, NC: Museum of the Cherokee Indian.

Duncan, Barbara R., and Brett H. Riggs. 2003. *Cherokee Heritage Trails Guidebook*. Chapel Hill: University of North Carolina Press.

Feeling, Durbin. 1975. *Cherokee-English Dictionary*, edited by William Pulte and Agnes Cowen. Tahlequah: Cherokee Nation of Oklahoma.

Hill, Sarah H. 1999. *Weaving New Worlds: Southeastern Cherokee Women and Their Basketry*. Chapel Hill: University of North Carolina Press.

King, Duane. 1975. A Grammar and Dictionary of the Cherokee Language. Diss., University of Georgia.

———. 1979. *Cherokee Nation: A Troubled History*. Knoxville: University of Tennessee Press.

Mooney, James. 1992 (1900). *History, Myths, and Sacred Formulas of the Cherokee*. Asheville, NC: Bright Mountain Books.

Norton, John. 1970. *The Journal of Major John Norton*, edited by Carl F. Klinck and James J. Talman. Toronto: Champlain Society.

Olbrechts, Frans M. 1931. Two Cherokee Texts. *International Journal of American Linguistics* 6: 179–184.

Payne, John Howard. 1962. *Indian Justice: A Cherokee Murder Trial in Tahlequah in 1840*, edited by Grant Foreman. Muskogee, OK: Star.

Perdue, Theda. 1997. *Cherokee Women, 1700–1835*. Lincoln: University of Nebraska Press.

Speck, Frank G., Leonard Broom, and Will West Long. 1951. *Cherokee Dance and Drama*. Norman: University of Oklahoma Press.

Williams, Samuel Cole, ed. 1927. *Lieut. Henry Timberlake's Memoirs, 1756–1765*. Johnson City, TN: Watauga Press.

———, ed. 1930. *Adair's History of the American Indians*. Johnson City, TN: Watauga Press.

Witthoft, John. 1946. The Cherokee Green Corn Medicine and the Green Corn Festival. *Journal of the Washington Academy of Sciences* 36: 213–219.

Barbara R. Duncan

CHEYENNE

GEOGRAPHY AND HISTORY

Not only has Cheyenne oral, customary, and material folklore been among the most documented in Native America, but the Cheyenne, the westernmost Algonkian language group, also represent the quintessential Plains Indian tribe in American popular culture. At present, some 5,000 Northern Cheyennes are enrolled at their southeast Montana reservation, while some 5,700 Southern Cheyennes are more widely scattered from their former reservation in and around Colony and Corn, Oklahoma. They are exogamous and matrilineal: they traditionally married outside their bands, which numbered ten, to join the band of the bride's mother. Archeology and tribal tradition agree that the people who called themselves the Tsistsistas originally inhabited the woodlands north of Lake Superior, migrating south into northwestern Minnesota at the end of the 1600s under pressure from the northeast by Assiniboines and Crees armed by the English and from the east by French-supported Chippewas. Later violence from the Chippewas led them to settle among the upper Missouri River tribes in present-day central South Dakota. They adopted these tribes' lodges made of sod or branches packed with clay and covered with woven rush mats. They grew corn, squash, and beans, made clay pottery, and took hunting trips onto the forbidding plains with travois, the dog-sled used by Indians and white trappers alike before horses gradually reached the region from Mexico. "Cheyenne" probably derives from the Sioux term *Sha hi' e la*, "red paint people," or "red [that is, foreign] talkers." Their name *Tsistsistas* means either "the people" or "the gashed people" in reference to their traditional manner of identifying themselves in sign language.

Sometime in the mid-eighteenth century the Tsistsistas and Suh'tai, who spoke an Algonkian dialect very close to Cheyenne, met west of the Missouri River. They moved west together to escape new threats from Assiniboines, Ojibwa, and Sioux, the last of whom were not yet the Cheyennes' close allies. The Suh'tai merged into the tribe fully by the 1830s, though distinctive Suhtai ancestry is still remembered by some Cheyennes. This is also the time when the tribe found Nowa'wus, their sacred mountain—nowadays called Bear Butte, South Dakota. Stories about the Cheyenne and Suh'tai culture heroes Sweet Medicine and Erect Horn sometimes include both of them entering the Sacred Mountain to learn Cheyenne tribal law and government.

Historically, circa 1800 is the dawn of the high period of Cheyenne culture on the Plains, when young men rode the newfound horses into what John Stands in Timber calls "the Blue Vision," the far horizon of the Great Plains. Nomadic buffalo hunting, ritual warfare centering on warrior societies, vision quests, and material culture that Cheyennes broadly shared with Arapahoes, Sioux, Kiowas, and other Plains tribes followed. Ironically, this period lasted only from about 1800 to 1876. It is important to remember that though American popular culture defines Cheyennes through imagery from this period, the reservation period has lasted longer, as have earlier periods of Cheyenne history.

Around 1830 they further divided into Northern and Southern Cheyennes, partly because of the lure of trading posts on the southern Plains. This division was solidified when wagon train trails split the buffalo into northern and southern herds. The tribe's long and bitter resistance against the U.S. Army on the southern Plains from 1864 to 1875 and on the northern Plains until 1877 is well documented. The two most tragic moments of this resistance were the Sand Creek massacre of Southern Cheyennes in 1864 and the bloody exodus northward of Northern Cheyennes from the Southerners' Oklahoma reservation in 1878 and 1879.

Cheyennes since the late eighteenth century were governed by a Council of Forty-Four chiefs: four principal chiefs and four from each of the ten bands. Though this Council of Forty-Four became inactive around 1900, it was revived in 1940 and 1960 and continues today. The chiefs' ideal was simple, as Stands in Timber says Sweet Medicine prescribed:

> You chiefs are peacemakers. Though your son might be killed in front of your tepee, you should take a peace pipe and smoke. Then you would be called an honest chief. You chiefs own the land and the people. If your men, your soldier societies, should be scared and retreat, you are not to step back but take a stand to protect your land and your people. Get out and talk to the people. If strangers come, you are the ones to give presents to them and invitations. When you meet someone, or he comes to your tepee asking for anything, give it to him. Never refuse. Go outside your tepee and sing your chief's song, so all the people will know you have done something good.

Throughout the classic **fieldwork** period from 1890 to 1935, ethnographers noted the stability of Cheyenne culture under the Council of Forty-Four, but more recently anthropologist John H. Moore has criticized this concept as "simplistic" and suggests a dynamic of constant tension between the chiefs' society and the warrior societies. Cooperating and often conflicting with the chiefs, these warrior societies numbered six. The first four, Kit Foxes, Red Shields, Elks, and Dogs, were founded by the culture **hero** Sweet Medicine. The Bowstrings were founded by Owl friend, an early-nineteenth-century warrior. The Crazy Dogs were the newest, founded in the mid-nineteenth century. By the mid-twentieth century Kit Foxes, Elks, Dogs, and Bowstrings survived in Oklahoma, while Kit Foxes, Elks, and Crazy Dogs were active in Montana. In recent decades the societies have attracted Cheyenne Vietnam and Gulf War veterans. In 1993 various society members were witnessed guarding the remains, repatriated from the Smithsonian Museum, of Cheyennes killed in the 1879 Fort Robinson, Nebraska, massacre. Another group, Contraries, were men who for fear of Thunder had vowed to do everything backward. Only a few men of each generation could afford the psychic stamina to live like this.

RELIGIOUS BELIEFS AND RITUALS

When a Cheyenne smoker offers the sacred pipe, he offers it above to Maheo (the All Father), to Esceheman (Grandmother Earth), and to the four cardinal spirits called the *maheyuno*. The lesser deities, including cosmological and animal spirits, are called *maiyun*. Cheyenne religious narratives, especially the stories of men fasting for visions in pre-reservation and reservation times, are deeply concerned with the negotiation of power and harmony with these various spirits. The story Edward Curtis collected around 1911 from legendary medicine man White Bull or Ice about his own vision quest, for example, is densely symbolic and layered with exchanges of knowledge and power.

Cheyenne religion centers on two major ceremonial objects: the Sacred Arrows (*Mahuts*) and the Sacred Buffalo Hat (*Esevone*). Both require regular renewal as well as special circumstantial renewal, as when the Arrows were captured by Pawnees in 1830 or when the Hat Keeper's wife mutilated it in 1874. (The Hat was renewed shortly before Cheyennes and Sioux defeated Custer's Seventh Cavalry in 1876.)

More recent examples of their ceremonial role have occurred in the twentieth century. The Sacred Arrows Keeper normally is Southern Cheyenne, whereas the Hat Keeper is a Northerner. *Mahuts* are male. They give power over other men and animals. *Esevone* is female and represents the buffalo and cattle herds. The long and continuous line of Sacred Hat Keepers on the Northern Cheyenne reservation speaks to the enduring power of these objects.

The main Cheyenne religious ceremony is the Sun Dance, a ritual shared with other Plains tribes. Traditionally eight days long but in modern times four or five, the Sun Dance or Medicine Lodge was banned for ten years around 1897 on the Northern Cheyenne reservation and was restricted or discouraged by government officials on both reservations from 1875 to 1934. The Sun Dance is traditionally pledged by a man who seeks to avert misfortune or fulfill an earlier vow. Its most dramatic aspects are the swinging of pledgers from the Sun Dance pole and their dragging buffalo skulls by means of skewers through their pectoral muscles. Another controversial element, which caused missionaries and government officials to attempt its suppression, has been ritual copulation between the wife of the pledger and his instructor. Though torture and the Sacred Woman get the most attention from outsiders, the Cheyenne Sun Dance is a meticulous, slow-moving affair that includes elaborate pre-arrangements among pledger, instructor, Medicine Lodge maker, and the warrior society or societies assigned to supervise the ceremonies: creation of a *tsih moh' no iv* or "gathering lodge" and then a *nukeyum* or "lone medicine lodge" for the actual priests involved; and instruction, painting, dancing, lodge- and body-painting, and feasting.

During the past 130 years, other religions have gained followings in Cheyenne country. The Native American Church, an intertribal rite that uses peyote in all-night ceremonies, was established on both southern and northern reservations by the early twentieth century. Even before then, in the 1880s, Ursuline nuns established a mission on the northern reservation. Its successor is the present-day St. Labre School, a strong Catholic presence on the reservation. The most enduring Protestant presence is Mennonite, thanks largely to a half-century's work by Rev. Rodolphe Petter, a legendary reservation figure who helped save Cheyenne language while suppressing traditional Cheyenne religion.

Many Cheyennes, no matter what their formal religious persuasion, perform daily religious rituals just as their ancestors did. In the morning, mothers burn cedar to bless their families. In the evenings, men chop and burn wood for backyard sweatlodges. In these, prayer turns are taken as the host pours water over glowing lava rocks. Then he burns some cedar as participants slap their arms with sage bundles. Nowadays many women join their husbands or other male relatives in the sweatlodge, which used to be rigidly segregated by gender. Later that evening, after the traditional post-sweatlodge meal of dried deer meat soup and frybread, men might start drumming and singing.

Another folk custom with quasi-religious overtones that has endured throughout reservation life is the giveaway, in which families give away traditional crafts or more contemporary objects in celebration or as an expression of thanks, such as when a prayer or wish is answered.

Fourth of July on the Northern Cheyenne reservation is typically powwow week-end. Families camp for the weekend on the powwow grounds south of Busby to watch and participate in competitive dances and songs that include the sometimes racy "49er songs," reservation-era intertribal folksongs. Distinguished members of the tribe are honored during powwow. Indian and white teenagers, the latter from off-reservation towns, parade and flirt along the circular track of the grounds, stopping at frybread, *menudo* (tripe soup), and Indian taco stands.

In summer, some Cheyenne families travel the approximately 200 miles to Nowa'wus or Bear Butte State Park, the sacred mountain where tribal members have special camping privileges. The butte's slopes are dotted with ribbons in the trees, left by praying and fasting Cheyennes. Bear Butte is central to the tribe's most important myth, that of the culture hero Mut'siev, Sweet Medicine or Sweet Root Standing. The myth's ending prophecy of the coming of whites and cultural loss is often anthologized. In about two dozen collected versions of the Sweet Medicine myth from 1890 to the present, a structural pattern persists. Sweet Medicine, an apparent orphan, appears at a poor old woman's tipi and is adopted by her and sometimes her aged husband. He miraculously provides for them, often in four instances. In other versions, he is simply the natural child of a married couple, extremely precocious first in speech and then in his decision to enter a spiritual dance, where he miraculously decapitates and heals himself. Then he kills or injures an elder over a buffalo hide. Magically escaping through the tipi smoke hole when men come for him, he appears to his pursuers four times on four different ridgetops in the insignias of the warrior societies he will later form. During this exile or sometimes in a later visit after reconciling with the tribe, he enters Nowa'wus and receives from the *maiyun* the Sacred Arrows, the buffalo, names of the other tribes that will be their friends and enemies, and tribal law. Returning to feed the starving Cheyennes in some versions, he instructs them in sacred ways and lives a long life—sometimes four lives—before prophesying the coming of white (and sometimes black) men, their hunger for gold and their technology, the end of the buffalo and the coming of cattle, and worse. He predicts Cheyennes will forget their old ways, lose their children to the new ways, join in tearing up the earth, and finally forget this very prophecy. To this day Cheyennes remind themselves of Sweet Medicine's prophecy so as *not* to fulfill it.

MYTHS, LEGENDS, AND FOLKTALES

Cheyennes tell other culture hero and tribal origin myths, perhaps older than Sweet Medicine's. The Suhtai culture hero Erect Horns and his wife received the Sacred Buffalo Hat, *Esevone*, and instruction on the Sun Dance from Maheo and Thunder inside a different sacred mountain. The myth of the origin of the Chiefs' Council of Forty-Four may be earlier than Sweet Medicine's story too. In a story collected by E. Adamson Hoebel, the society was founded by Mukije, a young woman who is wrongly accused with her brother of killing her mother, tied to a stake, and abandoned. However, she is taught by a stranger how to prepare buffalo meat, which she teaches to the tribe along with the chiefs' ways. At the end she predicts the arrival of Sweet Medicine.

Cheyennes share some tale types with other Plains tribes. They tell of Maheo, the creator, blowing life into humans after making them from earth. In the former Massaum or Animal Dance are elements of The Great Race, in which humans and buffalo compete to see who will eat whom. They share the story of the seven brothers who became the Seven Stars with other Plains tribes. Other myths concern the **trickster** *wihio* (spider), who has been conflated with *veho* (white man). Both get caught in their own elaborate webs. In a story reported by John Stands in Timber, for example, *veho* bargains with an Indian medicine man for an ill-fitting pair of eyes.

Cheyenne legend concerns warriors and their exploits, especially against traditional enemies like Assiniboines, Crows, Shoshones, Kiowas, and Pawnees. Though some legends of the fighting with the U.S. Cavalry exist—one enduring story tells how the dead Custer's ears were pierced by Cheyenne women so he would hear better in the next world—whites were not regarded as traditional enemies. Cheyenne men's vision quest narratives, like the war narratives to which they sometimes attach, are often structured in four-part segments, exploring the tension among pre-enactment, enactment, and ritual reenactment of visions. Even today Cheyenne men tell autobiographical narratives in this framework of vision and reenactment.

Two young Cheyenne men, in ceremonial paint, prepare for the Sun Dance (1910). (Courtesy Library of Congress)

In the past eighty years, Cheyenne women's life stories, collected by fieldworkers from several disciplines, have emerged as a post-reservation oral history tradition. Iron Teeth Woman (born 1834) told interviewer Thomas B. Marquis how she started life as a girl traveling with her band north of the Platte River in present-day Nebraska and ends her account by describing how at age ninety-two she lives on handouts alone in a tarpaper shack. Mostly reticent about fighting with the soldiers, she concludes nonetheless with the heroic memory of her son at the Fort Robinson massacre, fighting off surrounding troopers until he was killed while saving his little sister. More recently Belle Highwalking, born in 1892, recalled early reservation games, courtship and visits to the neighboring Crow reservation, Christmas and Memorial Day giveaways and other customs of the decades between the world wars, and reservation life in the 1960s—including a complaint that Cheyenne girls have abandoned their once legendary modesty and are now "boy-crazy."

SONGS AND DANCE

Cheyenne songs were and are numerous. Traditionally, as Stands in Timber recalls, men learned songs in dreams or visions, from animals, or during other supernatural occasions: thus the Elk Society mourning song came from the ghostly song of a young man heard the day after his death. Warrior songs continue to the present. One from World War II urged young men: "When you arrive there, growl like a bear! / If the airplane falls, growl like a bear! / If the big boat sinks, growl like a bear!" Sacred songs abound, too, for example, Sun Dance songs learned from instructors as well as contemporary peyote songs. Many such songs consist of one to four lines, with varied repetitions and drum accompaniment. More secular songs, like the powwow songs (one has the singer "riding with my honey in my one-eyed reservation Ford," sung in English *or* Cheyenne) as well as women's guild songs and giveaway songs, have also flourished. While many songs are accompanied by drum, the flute was traditionally used in courtship. Grover Wolf Voice, who died in the mid-twentieth century, was perhaps the last traditional Northern Cheyenne flutemaker.

The importance of sacred dance to Cheyennes is highlighted by a story Belle Highwalking told in the early 1970s about a Sun Dance pledged by her father, which was to be followed by a Contrary Dance:

Before this ceremony, a dog was killed and cooked. When the ceremony started, someone pounded on a drum and the dancers scattered around and acted scared. They hid way off, some of them under small sage brushes with no shade. After the drum stopped, the dancers came back and lay in the shade with their feet up on the tipi and their heads on the ground. . . . The dancers danced around the pot in which the dog was cooking, and then they lifted the arms of the person putting on the ceremony. They did this four times, after which they stirred the boiling dog soup with their bare arms.

Animal dance performed by the Cheyenne Buffalo Society (1927). (Courtesy Library of Congress)

This particular Contrary Dance lost attendance thanks to a simultaneous Massaum or Buffalo Dance, also called the Crazy Dance, associated with the buffalo priests who got their power from *Esevone*. In this dance men painted as animals—yellow deer, red buffalo, black magpies—followed the dance's pledger and behaved as their respective animals while Contraries tried to disrupt events (the Contraries did double duty away from their own dance). Powwow dancing is nowadays the main form of traditional social dancing, taking place over the July Fourth weekend on the Northern Cheyenne reservation and on weekends through the summer on reservations across the western United States for Cheyennes who travel the powwow circuit. There are competitive gender and age groups of "fancy" intertribal dancers as well as social dances open to all. Cheyenne boys trained for the warrior life from early on with frequent competitive shooting, stick throwing, wrestling, and the "kicking game." These persisted among men till middle age, George Bird Grinnell reports. Boys mimicked hunting and war-partying while girls mimicked women's camp duties. Games shared by both genders included *Ne e' wat se' um* (Carrying Head Downward) and *Ma mau' is kan it'* (Jumping from Side to Side). Girls' games included *Nit an i tai sin un*, an ice game resembling bowling, and *O assi oph* (Football), in which girls competed kicking and balancing a ball on their insteps and on which women wagered beads, earrings, and bracelets.

SPORTS AND GAMES

The best-known games are the Wheel Game and the Hand Game. The former, one of many versions found across North America, involves *hohktsim*, wheels made from meshed rawhide and willow hoops. After "capturing" these wheels with sticks, boys send the wheels flying at one another. There was also a men's version of playing with the *hohktsim* in which sticks were thrown into the wheel's mesh as it rolled by. On this game men wagered horses, blankets, robes, arrows, and other items. The Hand Game involves two parties who bet against each other on which hand a member of the opposing team is using to hide a marked bone. This latter man moves his hands in time to singing and drumming from the players in an effort to confuse the guessers.

ARTS AND CRAFTS

Cheyenne art is among the most highly regarded of traditional Plains Indian art. Realistic war scenes were painted on chiefs' and warrior society lodges and, starting in the 1860s, in white ledgers and sketchbooks. Southern Cheyenne warriors Cohoe and Howling Wolf, imprisoned in Florida after surrendering to the army in 1875, produced pictorial renditions of the old buffalo days in ledger books; Northern Cheyenne High Bull did likewise on a roster captured from the Seventh Cavalry at the Little Bighorn in 1876. Cheyenne women's art was considered sacred and was produced by guilds of women. Quillwork, robe painting, and more recently beadwork have been the province of these guilds. Nowadays Cheyenne beadworkers produce work for sale at powwows and at cultural centers such as the Little Bighorn Battlefield museum near the Northern Cheyenne reservation.

CHALLENGES OF THE MODERN WORLD

Cheyennes fought harder for and lost more of their culture than most Indian tribes. By the time the Northerners got a reservation in 1884, the tribe was decimated and disheartened. Nomadism and ritual warfare with other tribes were forbidden, the buffalo were gone, the most important religious ceremonies outlawed, and children forcibly removed from their homes to learn white culture and language. The effect of this suppression was devastating, leaving many Cheyennes today no longer fluent in their language or conversant with their tribe's history, folklore, and religion. However, even during the worst years of repression, Cheyennes continued to hold secret ceremonies in the northern reservation's remote backcountry. In some ways, the twentieth century enriched Cheyenne folklife. Powwow, evolving from the pre-contact tradition of summertime intertribal visits, has spread together with frybread and *menudo*, dance styles, and clothing such as ribbon shirts and feathered bustles. Certainly Cheyenne traditions have changed, but from the long view of the early twenty-first century, it is clear that new folkways have evolved.

STUDIES OF CHEYENNE FOLKLORE

The wealth of Cheyenne material collected since 1890 by anthroplogists, oral historians, and even legal and religious scholars is also unusual, making for its own fascinating history of the **ethnography** of an individual tribe. George Bird Grinnell, who had encountered Cheyennes when he rode with cavalry and cowboys in the 1870s and 1880s, came to the Northern Cheyenne reservation as a scholar in 1890 and continued his fieldwork on summer visits to both reservations over the next thirty-six years. He relied on interpreters. He was followed by some of the era's leading ethnographers: George A. Dorsey, James Mooney, Edward Curtis, Truman Michelson, A. L. Kroeber, and E. Adamson Hoebel did fieldwork among either or both Cheyenne divisions. Kroeber, first to follow Grinnell, collected tales in English probably from young adults who had already been through the white school system or from Christian southern families. Between 1901 and 1903, Dorsey interviewed various Southern Cheyenne Medicine Lodge priests and recorded a Sun Dance in 1903. Curtis visited the Northern reservation around 1910 to record the ceremonies and narratives. On the fiftieth anniversary of the Battle of the Little Bighorn in 1926 and subsequently, Thomas B. Marquis, a reservation doctor, recorded the life stories of several Northern Cheyennes by means of sign language; his most famous publication was *Wooden Leg: A Warrior Who Fought Custer* (1962 [1931]). Marquis was also the first ethnographer to record Cheyenne women's narratives, including that of Iron Teeth. This autobiographical tradition continued through the twentieth century. John Stands in Timber's *Cheyenne Memories* (1972 [1967]), recorded by Margot Liberty in the late 1950s and early 1960s, comprises warrior legends, myths, reservation anecdotes, and ceremonial descriptions. So does *Dance around the Sun* (1977), written by Alice Marriott and Carol K. Rachlin from the memoirs of Southern Cheyenne beadworker Mary Little Bear Inkanish. Katherine Weist collected and published Belle Highwalking's narrative in 1979. Late in life Stands in Timber befriended and adopted Father Peter J. Powell, who over the past forty years has become the main documentarian of Cheyenne religion and the major collector of Cheyenne narrative.

BIBLIOGRAPHY

Cohoe. 1964. *A Cheyenne Sketchbook by Cohoe*, edited by E. Adamson Hoebel and Karen D. Petersen. Norman: University of Oklahoma Press, 1964.

Curtis, Edward Sheriff. 1970 (1911). *The Cheyenne*. Vol. 6 in *The North American Indians: Being a Series of Volumes Picturing and Describing the Indians of the United States and Alaska*, edited by Fredrick W. Hodge. New York: Johnson.

Dorsey, George A. 1971 (1905). *The Cheyenne*. Glorieta, NM: Rio Grande Press.

Giarelli, Andrew. 1984. The Temporal Structure of Cheyenne Narrative. Ph.D. diss., State University of New York at Buffalo.

Giglio, Virginia. 1994. *Southern Cheyenne Women's Songs*. Norman: University of Oklahoma Press.

Grinnell, George Bird. 1972 (1915). *The Fighting Cheyennes*. Norman: University of Oklahoma Press.

———. 1972 (1923). *The Cheyenne Indians: Their History and Ways of Life*. 2 volumes. Lincoln: University of Nebraska Press.

Highwalking, Belle. 1979. *Belle Highwalking: The Narrative of a Northern Cheyenne Woman*, edited by Katherine M. Wiest. Billings, MT: Montana Council for Indian Education.

Hoebel, E. Adamson. 1978. *The Cheyennes: Indians of the Great Plains*. 2nd edition. New York: Holt, Rinehart and Winston.

Hoebel, E. Adamson, and Karl Llewellyn. 1941. *The Cheyenne Way: Conflict and Case Law in Primitive Jurisprudence*. Norman: University of Oklahoma Press.

Marquis, Thomas B. 1962 (1931). *Wooden Leg: A Warrior Who Fought Custer*. 2nd edition. Lincoln: University of Nebraska Press.

———. 1973. *Cheyenne and Sioux: the Reminiscences of Four Indians and a White Soldier*, edited by Ronald H. Limbaugh. Stockton, CA: Pacific Center for Western Historical Studies.

Marriott, Alice, and Carol K. Rachlin. 1977. *Dance around the Sun: The Life of Mary Little Bear Inkanish, Cheyenne*. New York: Crowel.

Michelson, Truman. 1932. The Narrative of a Southern Cheyenne Woman. *Smithsonian Miscellaneous Collections* 87.5: 1–13.

Mooney, James. 1964 (1907). The Cheyenne Indians. *Memoirs of the American Anthropological Association*, Vol. 1, No. 6. Millwood, NY: Kraus. 357–442.

Moore, John H. 1999. *The Cheyenne*. Oxford: Blackwell.

Powell, Peter J. 1980a (1969). *Sweet Medicine: The Continuing Role of the Sacred Arrows, the Sun Dance and the Sacred Buffalo Hat in Northern Cheyenne History*. 2 volumes. Norman: University of Oklahoma Press.

———. 1980b. *People of the Sacred Mountain: A History of the Northern Cheyenne Chiefs and Warrior Societies, 1830–79. With an Epilogue, 1969–74*. 2 volumes. New York: Harper and Row.

Stands in Timber, John, and Margot Liberty. 1972 (1967). *Cheyenne Memories*. 2nd edition. Lincoln: University of Nebraska Press.

Andrew L. Giarelli

CHOCTAW

GEOGRAPHY AND HISTORY

Two sacred myths explain how the Mississippi Band of Choctaw Indians came to call central Mississippi home. The first is an emergence myth in which the Creator made the southeastern Indian tribes from the earth at the sacred Nanih Waiya mound in Kemper County, Mississippi. The Seminole, Cherokee, Creek, and Chickasaw were created in turn and then sent off in different directions to find their homes. The Choctaw were created last and were chosen to live at their birthplace. In the other myth, the Choctaw initially lived out west. When game became scarce and the land infertile, the prophets relayed a message from the Creator that they were to move east, following a sacred pole that would point the way. When they reached the Nanih Waiya

Sacred Nanih Waiya mound located in present-day Kemper County, Mississippi. (Photograph by Tom Mould)

mound, the pole stood straight up, indicating their journey was over, their home found. Archeological, historical, and linguistic records corroborate elements of these myths, both literally and figuratively, identifying probable migration patterns from the west as well as subsequent banding together in the Nanih Waiya area as a tribal unit.

The Choctaw then and now have been a dynamic community quick to adapt the technology and customs of their neighbors when they found them useful. This philosophy of openness led to regular alliances with European settlers during the eighteenth and the nineteenth centuries. During this time, the Choctaw adapted missionary women's dress, men's hats, and the military drum into their culture and today use these items as symbols of their ethnic heritage. Further, many also adopted Christianity, and today the majority of tribal members are Christian.

The Choctaw have not always found the social and political life of Mississippi welcoming. Alliances with Europeans inevitably meant involvement in war. With the military arena in constant flux, the Choctaw increasingly found themselves employed as pawns in a battle for land rights that ironically excluded them. Such manipulation climaxed in President Andrew Jackson's policy of removal, an attempt to clear the Indians from the American southeast to make room for the fledgling nation's white settlers. The Choctaw were the first to be removed after signing the Treaty of Dancing Rabbit Creek in 1830. Throughout the rest of the century and into the first decade of the next, the government succeeded in removing as much as 75 percent of the tribe to lands in Oklahoma, where a thriving community lives today as the Choctaw Nation.

The Choctaw who remained in Mississippi were driven into inhospitable swamps to eke out a living as farmers. Eventually, they became sharecroppers on land once theirs. In a biracial South of black and white, the Choctaw did not fit any neat category. Not granted the rights of whites and unwilling to accept the discrimination afforded blacks, the Choctaw retreated socially as well as geographically and lived in virtual isolation. This has been changing slowly, a result of the tribe's increasingly visible and powerful role in the Mississippi economy. Beginning in 1979 with an industrial park, the tribe began creating jobs for themselves. Led by Chief Phillip Martin, the tribe continued to develop industry and factory jobs. In 1994 they built their first casino, adding to an already thriving tribal business. Today, the tribe is one of the largest employers in Mississippi.

There are approximately 8,900 tribal members, the majority of whom live in one of eight established areas in central and south-central Mississippi in communities that roughly mirror tribal settlements of the eighteenth century. Modern transportation has led to far more interaction between these communities, but differences remain particularly in dialect and perceived levels of traditionality. Bogue Chitto, for example, is widely recognized as one of the most traditional communities, where the language remains spoken by virtually all, Christianity is still met with resistance, and people conduct their daily lives "the old way," which often means cooking outside, wearing Choctaw shirts and dresses, and relying more heavily on farming, hunting, and cottage industries such as basketweaving than on nine-to-five jobs.

THE CHOCTAW FAIR

As with the labeling of Bogue Chitto, there has been a growing impulse to label elements of Choctaw culture as traditional. One result is that the utility of Choctaw material arts has been pushed more heavily toward the decorative, as woven cane baskets move from cupboards to walls. The availability of cheaper and more easily attained substitutes for hand-woven baskets and hand-stitched quilts has clearly contributed to this trend as well. Another result is that the private social spheres of folklore performance of the past have moved into the public arena of formal performance. House dances, for example, once held regularly on weekend nights at friends' homes are now performed almost exclusively at the annual Choctaw Fair and at elementary school festivals as symbolic enactments of cultural heritage. However, rather than codifying their culture, these more formal performances continue to be arenas for negotiation and change. The pinnacle for such public performance today is the annual Choctaw Fair.

The fair is a synthesis of Choctaw and mainstream American cultures. The brightly colored beads strung into sashes and jewelry reflect the flashing lights of the midway rides. The smell of cotton candy, elephant ears, and corn dogs mingles with that of slow bubbling hominy. The fairgoer can wander in and out of these activities, but for as much as the Choctaw have synthesized a unique ethnic culture with a more modern, mainstream one, divisions are clearly marked. Hominy is sold on one side of the road, corn dogs on the other. The amusement park rides rattle and whirr on the ballfield while the dancing is held in an arbor across the road. One can win a stuffed pink elephant on the sunny midway, but must move to the shade down the road to find a carefully stitched star quilt. The division is not just Indian versus non-Indian. One can buy a Choctaw quilt, basket, or beaded sash in the Choctaw artists' pavilion, but must move inside to a separate building to buy a Navajo silver ring or Plains-style dreamcatcher.

Young social dancers from the Red Water community performing at the annual Choctaw Fair. (Photograph by Tom Mould)

Choctaw is Choctaw. There is a closer affinity to other American Indians than to non-Indians, but tribal distinctions are maintained to avoid tribal confusion among tourists. The Choctaw have prided themselves on maintaining their tribal identity. While the Choctaw Fair is a chance to synthesize the elements of their daily lives as Choctaw, as Indians, and as Mississippians, it functions more powerfully as a means of distinguishing themselves by publicly performing their identity.

Stickball players fight for control of the ball during the World Stickball Championship at the annual Choctaw Fair. (Photograph by Tom Mould)

This declaration of identity is perhaps most vividly and aggressively proclaimed with the stickball tournament. While the carnival rides are thrilling and country music performances appealing, the focal point of the Choctaw Fair for most tribal members is stickball, as it has been at similar community gatherings for over a century. Today's fair emerged loosely from the inter-community ballgames that have been played since at least the eighteenth century when Europeans travelers described them. Elders in the community today remember gathering a few times a year with other communities to play stickball, dance, eat, and tell stories. The games were intense, play was controlled but rough, and families often wagered their most prized material possessions on the outcome. Success was important, and teams employed what resources they had to ensure victory, including aid from the supernatural. Choctaw doctors, rain witches, or ballplay witches stood on the sidelines and evoked the supernatural to sway the game's outcome. While the medicine men and ballplay witches are not evident on the sidelines today, drummers accompany each team to set the pace of the game, intimidate the other team, and garner support for their side. Further, the question of supernatural involvement in stickball as well as other sports is often raised, particularly when an unusual spate of bad luck or amazing skill is displayed.

DANCE

Integral to these extended weekend gatherings of the past was dancing. While some of the dancing was done by doctors to aid their team in winning, most of it was performed by all members of the tribe. These social dances—both honorary and social—continue to be performed today. A number of the dances are named for the animals they honor such as the duck dance, quail dance, raccoon dance, turtle dance, and snake dance. Such dances often mirror the movements of the animal while acknowledging the importance of the animal for the Choctaw. Chanters guide the dancers with their voices—chanting rhythms with repeated vocables (non-lexical syllables)—and with sticks that they strike together to pound out a beat. Sometimes a drummer will serve instead, employing similar percussive rhythms. The dances are generally slow, except for the playful raccoon dance, and performed together by old and young, male and female.

With strict interdictions against marrying within one's family or clan, social dancing among different communities was integral for courtship. Some dances functioned quite explicitly in this regard, such as the friendship dance and the stealing partners dance, which not only permits, but mandates, social engagement among peers known or unknown, initiated by both men and women. Dance for courtship and entertainment was carried into house dances during the twentieth century. Choctaw musicians left their sticks and drums at home, adopted guitars and fiddles, and adapted square dance music and steps to fit Choctaw dance esthetics, slowing down the pace and limiting physical contact during the dances. Today, most house and social dancing occurs in formal, public performance by community-organized dance groups, negating the possibility for courtship since the dancers are all from the same community and are often related.

ARTS AND CRAFTS

While stickball teams and dance groups are generally organized by community, community lines are less clearly drawn for material artists. Booths of different arts from different communities are scattered around the open-air pavilion. Here, tribal members move the private work of the back porch and living-room into the shared space of the fairgrounds. Artistic performance is altered only slightly by the change in venue. Artists happily answer tourists' questions but rarely seek the sale. Most sit in chairs behind their tables, working intently or laughing with family members working alongside them, just as they do at home where family remains the primary source for social interaction.

Most of the material arts—basketweaving, quilting, beading, dressmaking, dollmaking—are exclusive to women. Men, however, dominate woodworking. Today that means primarily stickball sticks, though not long ago it would also have included split oak baskets, rabbit sticks, and drums. Stickball stick makers begin by hunting hickory trees in the surrounding woods, felling and splitting the logs, carefully shaving the wood into sticks with a thin, malleable end, soaking the wood in water, and heating it over an open flame to shape the cups. The work is hard and time-consuming. The women's work is often no less physical and also demands patience and skill achieved only after many years. Basketweaving in particular demands much the same process as stickball stick making: hunting the increasingly difficult-to-find cane in nearby swamps, chopping it down and splitting the cane into thin strips, boiling the dyes over an open fire, and dyeing the cane. The task of weaving demands fingers tough enough to avoid cuts from the sharp cane, but nimble enough to weave the strips into tight, geometrically designed baskets.

For both artists, the primary goal has been function. A stickball stick that is warped, misshapen, too long or short, with cups that do not fit together is of

Estelline Tubby dressed in a formal Choctaw dress that she hand-stitched. Her star quilt covers the sofa. (Photograph by Allyson Whyte)

little use to the player. The basket with cracked cane, sharp edges, and gaps in the weave was equally useless, though this has been changing as baskets move from practical to decorative use. For both, artistry exceeds function. Craftsmanship in the stickball stick is evidenced in the smooth handle, the balance in the stick from end to end, and the tight leather straps that form the cup basket. The art is in the form. It is generally left to the player to customize the sticks further, painting designs or nicknames on them.

The basketweaver is responsible for the artistry of form as well as of design. Virtually all Choctaw baskets are designed geometrically with the diamond dominating both in baskets and throughout Choctaw art. The diamond echoes the eastern diamondback rattlesnake, a **motif** present in Choctaw dances and stories as well. Both revered and feared, the snake frequently signals the world of the supernatural, particularly at the margins where humans may encounter this world. In one legend, for example, a man learns a recipe to become a snake. Doubting its effectiveness, he prepares it and turns into a snake. His wife is horrified but tries to protect him, feeding him at his hole in the backyard where he has chosen to live. Feared by his neighbors, the snake-man is eventually attacked and killed. The fear that drives the neighbors to kill the snake comes partly from the fear he will eat their children, but it derives also from the cultural belief that people able to shape-shift are often witches, bad doctors intending to harm people. In legend, that form is often a snake or an owl; in contemporary life, the range of woodland animals in Mississippi is possible. A widespread legend in the Conehatta community tells of a huge snake that lives in a local pond. When one pond dried up, it slithered to another, creating the ditch visible today. There is also a prophecy that one day, snakes big enough to eat men will exist in Mississippi. Some wonder whether the snake of Conehatta legend fulfills this prophecy. Snakes also appear in the humorous folktales or *shukha anumpa*—literally "hog talk." In one story, two hunters are out hunting when one mistakes his toe for a snake. Frightened, he shoots at it, severing his toe. In daily life, the snake has been appreciated for its role in ridding the fields of mice, weevils, and other small animals that damage crops. This is the honor referenced in the snake dance. The Choctaw view of the snake is emblematic of a more general relationship with the natural and supernatural worlds, one of healthy fear and proper respect.

MYTHS, LEGENDS, AND FOLKTALES

As with all communities that until recently depended on spoken rather than written word, the oral traditions of the Choctaw continue to serve an important role in constructing tribal history, tribal identity, and the more pervasive worldview that is reflected throughout Choctaw culture. Arguably, the stories can be divided along two axes,

Luke Frazer using a hatchet to whittle a piece of hickory before shaving and shaping it into a stickball stick. (Photograph by Tom Mould)

A collection of hand-woven swamp cane baskets housed in the tribal archives. (Photograph by Tom Mould)

time—passed down versus contemporary—and tone—serious (where truth is important) versus humorous (where truth is negotiable). Divisions blend, however, and while audiences recognize the dominant role and function of each story, the oral traditions of the Choctaw are rife with sacred stories that make audiences laugh and funny stories that make audiences think. The humorous stories are *shukha anumpa*. Some use the term to indicate animal stories, accounts of how possum lost the hair on his tail and how turtle's shell got broken and reglued into the mosaic pattern seen today. These include trickster tales where rabbit fills the alternately clever and foolish role. Others use the term *shukha anumpa* for the joking and teasing stories they tell on each other, where "hogwash" becomes a more accurate translation than "hog talk." In both, the characters are foolish and silly; and in both, deeper lessons can be learned and underlying value systems expressed and negotiated.

The serious stories, the important stories, are those passed down and constructed by older generations and comprise what many understand as myths, legends, historical narratives, prophecies, and memorates or accounts of encounters with the supernatural. Though they may have humorous elements, the stories are presented as true and important to maintain and tell. By far the most frequently recounted subject of these stories is the encounter with the supernatural. Virtually all adult tribal members either have a story of their own encounter with a supernatural being or recount one of a close relative. In many ways, these stories serve as a sign of cultural heritage, particularly since most of these supernatural beings cannot be seen by or do not show themselves to non-Choctaw people. The panoply of supernatural beings is vast, and distinctions between one being and the next are often difficult to draw. Choctaw doctors were—and still are, though doctors are becoming more rare—often consulted after an encounter to help determine what the person saw and what meaning should be drawn from the experience. An encounter with *bohpoli* or the little people, for example, often indicates the potential for that person to become a Choctaw doctor, particularly when the encounter comes early in life. *Bohpoli* are fairly easy to recognize: they stand about three feet high and have the wrinkled, wizened features of old men. Other beings are more ambiguous. A ball of light could be *hashok okwa hui'ga*—translated loosely as "dew drop" and suggestive of a will-o-the-wisp—or a witch. A hog could be *na losa chitto*—literally "big black thing" and one of the most dangerous of the supernatural beings—or a shapeshifting doctor or witch. Or both could be simply lights or hogs. Most storytellers discuss the confusion of what the being was and what it might mean, opening the stories for negotiation rather than cementing them as declarative fact.

SUPERNATURAL LORE

The supernatural world remains dominant in the Choctaw **worldview**. In the past, men and women who were chosen and skilled to interact with the supernatural had clear roles. Prophets conveyed messages for how to live and how to prepare for the future. Doctors learned the art of healing from the supernatural beings in the woods and often consulted them for diagnoses. Ballplay witches appealed to the supernatural for success in stickball games. Bad doctors or witches depended on the supernatural for their power to harm others. Today, most of these roles are disappearing or are being transformed. People are generally uncomfortable talking about witches, fearing that such talk might attract the attention of one and make them the target of an attack. But people sense that there are fewer witches today, just as there are fewer doctors. Many people lament the fact that they must travel over an hour to find a Choctaw doctor and even then are wary about going, since they may not know the doctor well enough to trust. With the spread of Christianity, the prophets have become priests and ministers, though again many in the community lament that they are not filling the role fully, contenting themselves with interpreting the past and present but not the future.

Despite some criticism of ministers and priests within the tribe, the synthesis of tribal customs and Christianity has been fairly smooth. Generally, people have searched for parallels and common ground rather than areas of difference and conflict. Recounting the important stories of their community, people often narrate the prophecies of the Bible along with the prophecies of tribal oral tradition, sometimes combining the two in search of coherent meaning.

CHALLENGES OF THE MODERN WORLD

This acceptance of outside cultural influences is most visible in the performed arts. Like many North American Indian tribes, the powwow, once confined to the Plains, has recently gained popularity among the Choctaw. The sweat lodge has also become more popular, particularly as people find resonance with their own traditions of sweating for purification. Design motifs and arts from Plains and Pueblo tribes are also popular as inspiration to artists and as home decoration. Beadworkers in particular have borrowed and adapted a number of Southwest designs such as the thunderbird, adding them to the more abstract, geometrical designs seen in beadwork pictured in the oldest photographs of the Choctaw. The easily recognizable silhouette of the dejected Indian on horseback, head down, spear lowered, appears on cloth and wood canvases. It is almost as common to see dreamcatchers hanging from automobiles' rearview mirrors as it is to see small wooden stickball sticks.

Yet the Choctaw retain a sense of individual ethnic identity. The adaptation of outside traditions is overshadowed by the constant internal impulse to challenge, test, and create. Inspiration is both internal and external. Thanks to globalization, the external arena is growing every day as the Choctaw engage in ever-wider interactions socially, politically, and economically. This external influence is balanced, however, by a determined sense of shared identity that tribal members use to construct dynamic folk traditions.

STUDIES OF CHOCTAW FOLKLORE

Arguably the most useful book on the Choctaw remains Swanton (1933), which gathers all the major historical accounts of the Choctaw beginning in the eighteenth century through when he published the book and presents a view of Choctaw life before, during, and after European contact. The picture is generally monolithic, but the resources compiled are incomparable. The majority of books dealing with the Mississippi Choctaw are historical, few moving beyond the removal era: Galloway

(1995), Kidwell (1995), DeRossier (1970), and Debo (1966 [1940]). Of the books dealing with the Choctaws since removal, most continue to examine Choctaw political and economic life with scant attention to folklore traditions. Wells and Tubby (1986) contains a few articles that attempt a more socioanthropological study of Choctaw culture, as do many of the articles by Peterson (1972, 1979) and not least of all McKee and Schlenker (1980). For books more specific to the study of folklore, Howard and Levine (1990), Blanchard (1981), and Mould (2003, 2004) are useful not only for their specific folklore focus, but also for their inclusion of broader cultural contexts.

BIBLIOGRAPHY

Blanchard, Kendall. 1981. *The Mississippi Choctaws at Play: The Serious Side of Leisure*. Urbana: University of Illinois Press.

Debo, Angie. 1966 (1940). *And Still the Waters Run*. New York: Gordian Press.

DeRossier, Arthur H., Jr. 1970. *The Removal of the Choctaw Indians*. Knoxville: University of Tennessee Press.

Galloway, Patricia. 1995. *Choctaw Genesis, 1500–1700*. Lincoln: University of Nebraska Press.

Howard, James, and Victoria Lindsay Levine. 1990. *Choctaw Music and Dance*. Norman: University of Oklahoma Press.

Kidwell, Clara Sue. 1995. *Choctaws and Missionaries in Mississippi, 1818–1918*. Norman: University of Oklahoma Press.

McKee, Jesse O., and Jon A. Schlenker. 1980. *The Choctaws: Cultural Evolution of a Native American Tribe*. Jackson: University Press of Mississippi.

Mould, Tom. 2003. *Choctaw Prophecy: A Legacy of the Future*. Tuscaloosa: University of Alabama Press.

———. 2004. *Choctaw Tales*. Jackson: University Press of Mississippi.

Peterson, John H., Jr. 1972. Assimilation, Separation, and Out-Migration in an American Indian Group. *American Anthropologist* 74: 1286–1295.

———. 1979. Three Efforts at Development among the Choctaws of Mississippi. In *Southeastern Indians since the Removal Era*, edited by Walter L. Williams. Athens: University of Georgia Press. 142–153.

Swanton, John R. 1933. *Source Material for the Social and Ceremonial Life of the Choctaw Indians*. Bureau of American Ethnology Bulletin, No. 103.

Wells, Samuel J., and Roseanna Tubby, eds. 1986. *After Removal: The Choctaws in Mississippi*. Jackson: State University Press of Mississippi.

Tom Mould

HAIDA

Geography and History

Haidas live on Haida Gwaii—which literally means "the islands of the Haidas"—a northwesterly Canadian archipelago of over 100 islands in the Pacific Ocean. Haida history dates back to "mythtime" preserved in the oral tradition of creation stories, songs, ceremonies, history, and mythology of the tribe. The curator of the National Museum of Canada suggests that the Haida presence on Haida Gwaii spans 9,000 years. However, the last 400 years have seen an exodus of some Haidas into Alaska. Only recently have the islands secured the traditional name, Haida Gwaii, for their homeland, though most maps still designate these islands as the Queen Charlotte Islands.

The location of these islands significantly influences Haida culture and identity. The splendor of the oceans and diversity of geography exert a strong bind that is difficult for Haidas to separate from their essence. The vast forests are some of the most spectacular in Canada—and even the rest of the world—with trees more than 2,000 years old. Logging currently endangers these forests, and Haidas are committed to halting the full-scale destruction of the forests. These trees have contributed to Haida skill in architecture, woodcarving (particularly their great totem poles), and canoe design. The pervasive unique flora and fauna on these islands also earned them the nickname the Canadian Galapagos. The climate is rather mild with winters dipping into the mid-thirties Fahrenheit and summers averaging 68 degrees. The ocean provides wealth in many ways: an abundance of food including salmon, herring, shrimp, crab, halibut, and kelp; clothing and blankets from seals, sea otters, and sea lions; tools from the bones of mammals; and mythology. While much of the Western tradition sees blessings descending from the heavens, Haidas see the blessings ascending from the ocean. Since the mainland is approximately eighty miles to the east, Haida Gwaii remained largely unaffected by the tribal interaction common to mainland coastal communities. The distance also served as protection, since few other tribes dared to attack the Haida homeland when occasional conflicts occurred.

Historically, Haidas had two dwellings, one inland for the winter months and another near the shores used from late spring till late fall. The late spring, summer, and early fall seasons were full of activity, mainly centered on securing sustenance for the winter and materials for making clothes, blankets, baskets, and hats. Salmon, caught and dried during the fall and summer, served as the staple during the winter months. In the summer, daylight lasts from 4:00 A.M. until just after 11:00 P.M. In contrast, winter days have less than eight hours of daylight. Thus, the seasonal cycle determined that most outdoor activity would occur when the weather was best. When the winter winds began to blow, the winter cycle of retreat inland with all the gathered supplies and food began. Winter weather usually hindered long-term food and material gathering—such as berries to dry and spruce roots for weaving—as well as hunting and fishing, though this was occasionally necessary.

SOCIAL STRUCTURE

Largely matrilocal and exogamous, Haidas typically married outside of their clans. Haida society consists of two moieties, Ravens and Eagles. If a Haida man from the Eagle clan wanted to marry, his choices were limited to women from the Raven clan.

A Haida village. Haida houses were large wooden structures with an entrance in front surrounded by the totems of the family. (Picture Collection, The Branch Libraries, The New York Public Library, Astor, Lenox and Tilden Foundations)

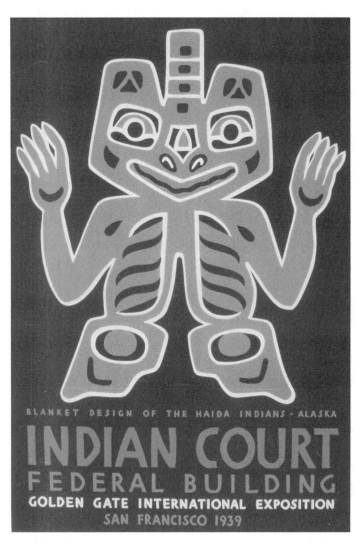

Blanket design of the Haida Indians used for the Indian Court poster at the Golden Gate International Exposition in San Francisco, 1939. (Courtesy Library of Congress)

When a couple did marry, they usually lived in the same village as the wife's mother, sometimes in the same house. Houses were especially large wooden structures with an entrance in front surrounded by the totems of the family. These houses are important, since families within each clan identify and refer to themselves with regard to a house. Their family name is also traced back to a single house. Matrilineal kinship determined which families lived in the same house. A fireplace, usually in the middle of the house, heated the structure and served as the cooking place. Over the fireplace was what Haidas call *ginaa*, the smoke hole in the roof which provided the necessary ventilation. This smoke hole played an important role in practical daily living and had a particular role in one very important story.

MYTHS, LEGENDS, AND FOLKTALES

Like many other cultures in North America and the rest of the world, the Haida are an oral society. One common feature of oral societies concerns their creation mythology. Haidas have many different stories that account for their presence in the world today along with their islands and the rest of the cosmos. With Haidas, the creator Yehl, a white raven, is a trickster character. Raven's transformation from white to black is a theme common in stories among Native Americans in Alaska and First Nations communities in Canada. A Haida version reveals not only how the sun, moon, and stars came to be but also how and why Yehl created them. The following account comes from Henry Geddes, a Haida elder, and tells how the eulachon, a small fish in the Northwest Canadian waters that is prized for its oil, serves as the impetus for Yehl:

It was always dark. There was no daylight. Raven could see some boys getting lots of eulachons, and he wanted some.

"Hey," he said, "how about some eulachons?"

"Go on, go away! You're always telling lies. You better go away."

So then Raven found out where they kept the light—big and round. The wealthy ones had it. They had a big huge house, and they had a daughter. So Raven figured the only way he could get in there was to be born. So that's how he did it, the young girl had a baby, and it was Raven. And he grew rapidly. And as he got a little bigger he used to roll the light around. He used to play with it.

Then he would sit and cry, yell and cry, "*Ginaa. Ginaa Ginaa.*" *Ginaa* means— you know those big Indian houses built long and in the middle they had something come up? That's where the smoke came out—they call that *Ginaa.*

So Raven, it was all closed in, and he cried all the time and he'd say "*Ginaa*" all the time. So his mother said, "He wants that hole a little wider."

He kept on crying and crying. One day he started practicing flying with the light under his wing. He kept on practicing until finally he knew he could get out. So he flew out. So he went back up the river and he tell them people, he hollered at them, he said, "Now if you people give me eulachons, I'll give you day light."

"Go on, go away! You're always lying!"

"No," he says, "it's true. No." So he says, "I'm going to show you—I'm going to give you just a little bit of daylight." And he showed a little bit, and the whole place was light. And he put it away, and it was dark again.

So everybody brought in—oh—loads after loads of eulachons. He couldn't ever eat all that up. So he flew down to where there were some rocks, sharp ones. So he gets this big disk, and he starts hammering away at it. And he broke it in half. And breaks it in half, and he said, "Well,"—he throws it, and he said, "This will be the sun. And this one," when he threw it, he said, "this one will be the moon."

So after he gathered up all the crumbs, he threw that up there, and he said, "[These] will be the stars."

Thus, we have here the beginning of light. What this account reveals is that hunger drives Yehl to steal the light in exchange for the eulachons he craves so much. Missing from this account is how Yehl turns black because of squeezing out of the smoke hole and rubbing himself in the soot as he tries to escape. What is also evident in this story is the nature of Yehl. The boys refer to him as a constant liar. In fact, they do not want to have anything to do with Yehl. But he proves them wrong as he bargains for the eulachons with the promise of letting them see the light. The end of the story reveals Yehl receiving so many eulachons that he could not ever eat them all, but he would try. As Geddes brings the story to a conclusion, he mentions that this is merely a part of the Raven cycle of stories that could easily last a week if all the stories were told.

The cyclical nature of the stories such as this one also affords important insight into the Haida worldview, since they believed in human reincarnation. Haidas held that every new baby born into the community was someone in the family who had recently died. Thus, often whenever people would make the comment, "Gee, she looks just like her auntie!" or "Gee, he sure looks like his uncle!" it was usually a reference to the idea that the child was a reincarnation of that person. As in Geddes's account of how light came to this world, the birth of a baby is part of the cycle of reincarnation.

This portion of the Raven cycle reveals two typical aspects of Haida oratory as well. The first aspect concerns the purpose of the oral literature, which is to provide knowledge of history from the Haida **worldview**. The advent of light to the world is one of the most important aspects of all creation accounts. The Haida version addresses both how and why the light began, since we learn Yehl longed for the eulachons and then devised a scheme to obtain what he wanted. Implicit in sharing this knowledge is the warning not to be like Yehl. While never stated explicitly, such stories are often used to socialize Haida children into correct behavior. The second aspect is a very misunderstood one and concerns the supernatural dimension of Yehl's creative nature. When early accounts first appeared in English, the misunderstanding concerned the clash of Western and Haida creation accounts. The Western tradition ascribes creation to God or a number of different gods, but with a much different perspective on the nature of deity. The Western worldview reveres and worships the creator or creators for their ability and power, but the Haida did neither. This is most evident in the boys' calling Yehl a liar whenever he speaks to them. However, when mainstream North Americans encountered stories of Yehl, they assumed that since Yehl was the creator, he must be the Haida's god. Thus with this false assumption which still exists, they concluded that Haidas worship a raven god.

This oral literature also reveals Haida social structure. The boys' willingness to give their eulachons for the light represents not only a sacrifice on their part but also an opportunity. They would enjoy elevated status in the society for achieving or obtaining visible wealth—in this case, light. Social standing was and remains very important in Haida culture. The abundance of the natural resources in, on, and around Haida Gwaii enabled Haidas to pursue not mere subsistence living but wealth and prestige as well. But the most interesting aspect of wealth in Haida society was not how much one could personally accumulate and show off; it was how much one could give away. The potlatch, a ceremony common among Alaskan natives and First Nations communities, became the standard for measuring the wealth of a person or family. Potlatches were held for different reasons, including becoming a chief, moving into a new home, honoring another person, or raising a personal or village totem pole. Within each community, individuals could host their own potlatch, or the community could combine efforts to host a large one and invite other communities and even other tribes to attend.

POTLATCH

Largely misunderstood by the Canadian government, potlatches were banned from the mid-1880s until 1954. Outsiders misconstrued the cultural significance of the event, the giving of presents to the potlatch guests. To give away as much as possible was essential to the gathering. The measure of wealth was not how much the potlatch host had at the end of the event, but how much he had given away to his guests during the potlatch. Blankets, pelts, copper, argillite (a black stone indigenous to Haida Gwaii), baskets, hats, carved paddles, spoons, bowls, boxes, and walking sticks were among the early gifts, with silver and gold later becoming prominent gifts as well. Many of the gifts were often made by the host or the host's family and then presented to the guests. A family could spend a year carving argillite and wooden gifts, making blankets, and weaving hats and baskets just to have enough to give away at a potlatch. Haida carvings were unmatched for skill and design, and their weaving skills could produce baskets that were watertight.

The reciprocal function of the potlatch was very important. Potlatches were celebrations of songs, stories, dancing, feasting, and gifts often lasting more than three days. The food would include all sorts of salmon, smoked and fresh, halibut, cod, shrimp, crab, seaweed, and eulachon grease. The food was also part of the measure of wealth, and it was important to have all the best staples to offer guests. The event would culminate in the host achieving a higher status in the village because of having held the potlatch.

For the Haida, dancing and singing are two of the greatest expressions of cultural identity. Events like a potlatch serve as a perfect venue for elaborate presentations of stories with songs and dances. The singers, using only a drum made from an animal skin, would sing songs from their history, family, and community to entertain guests or as part of the winter cycle of stories, songs, and dances. Often the dances were elaborate recreations of the myths accompanying the songs. Dancers wore ornate masks and costumes as they performed particular dances. Raven, killer whale, wolf, bear, and eagle masks were common, as was that of Gagiht (or Gagid), the crazy half-man, half-beast. One of the most popular topics for the celebrations was Yehl.

While many the potlatch activities are currently extant, potlatches are a rare event now. The increased visibility of Haida culture has led to new developments in artistry, especially silkscreen prints and paintings. Carving silver and gold bracelets, earrings, and necklaces has also become prominent. Carving totem poles, masks, paddles, and canoes (though this has only recently been revived) has always been relatively popular. Dancing and singing are currently not as actively pursued as carving or painting, but there are some youngsters learning the dances and songs. While they do learn the songs in Haida, the young singers most likely do not understand what they are singing, since Haida is not their first language and they have had little experience in speaking it. Thus, though able to sing the songs, they may not have enough proficiency to analyze the specific features of the songs except to talk generally about what the songs mean. This is common among many First Nations communities and Native American tribes that have assimilated English as their first language. Despite integration into mainstream society, Haidas still maintain their connection to Haida Gwaii as part of their identity and pursue the arts to express that bond to the world.

STUDIES OF HAIDA FOLKLORE

Interest in Haida folklore, other than from Haidas themselves, has occurred only in the last 125 years, with the most interest occurring in the last 25 years. Finding a single source that addresses Haida culture and folklore is not possible, but from these selected references, an adequate overview is possible. The first two references offer cultural background. Blackman (1982) offers cultural information from a Haida woman's perspective. Her book is important, since so much of the early information that ethnologists and linguists gathered was largely from male sources. Swanton (1909) reveals the typical androcentric approach to culture.

While the study of Haida folklore has been popular only since the last quarter of the twentieth century, much of the literature has its basis in linguistics. The study of the Haida language has motivated and resulted in much of the folkloric research. Two examples are Bringhurst (2002) and Enrico (1995). Both authors offer contemporary translations of stories gathered by John Swanton and his work with the Haida language at the end of the nineteenth century and the beginning of the twentieth century. Since there are so few native speakers of Haida alive, the opportunity to research the language and oral traditions with live consultants is slowly ending. Soon any future research concerning both the language and folklore will have to rely on consulting books or other data and not living persons.

BIBLIOGRAPHY

Blackman, Margaret. 1982. *During My Time: Florence Edenshaw Davidson—A Haida Woman.* Seattle: University of Washington Press.

Bringhurst, Robert. 2002. *Masterworks of the Classical Haida Mythtellers.* Vancouver: Douglas & McIntyre.

Enrico, John. 1995. *Skidegate Haida Myths and Stories.* Skidegate: Queen Charlotte Islands Museum.

Swanton, John. 1909. *Contributions to the Ethnology of the Haida.* American Museum of Natural History Memoirs, No. 8.

Frederick White

HOPI

GEOGRAPHY AND HISTORY

The country of the Hopi people is starkly beautiful, a land of subtle color and muted wildlife, which is the essence of the Hopi way of life. Situated on the Colorado Plateau of northern Arizona, the Hopi Indian Reservation today encompasses 1.6 million acres, although the Hopi *tutskwa*, the people's ancient traditional land base, covers more than 18 million acres. This geography is tremendously diverse, from rugged desert canyons to expansive grasslands and mountains blanketed in evergreens. It is also a delicate landscape, as most areas receive less than ten inches of rainfall per year. The land fosters the Hopi virtue of balance, for it is the earth that provides the means for all living things to thrive and endure.

Modern Hopi communities are concentrated on three high mesas, ordered from east to west, with three villages on each. On First Mesa are Wàlpi, Sitsomovi, and Tewa; on Second Mesa are Songòoqavi, Musangnuvi, and Supawlavi; on Third Mesa are Orayvi, Hotvela, and Paaqavi. Other towns include Kiqötsmovi and Moencopi, and many Hopi families live in field houses and farmsteads throughout the reservation. Although Hopis tend to be sedentary, traditionally focused on farming, the broader region has long been used for ranching, gathering, hunting, and offering prayers at dispersed sacred sites.

The Western world first met the Hopi people in 1540, when Pedro de Tovar of the Francisco Vàzquez de Coronado expedition sought a route to the Pacific Ocean. This contact led to a long history of colonialism that involved the exchange of radical new materials (tools and foodstuffs), ideas (Christianity and capitalism), biology (diseases and genes), and identities ("Indians" and "Others"). Hopis habitually sought peace, but they did fight against the oppressive policies and practices of the Euroamerican invaders, most famously in the Pueblo Revolt of 1680. In part because of their geographic isolation, Hopis successfully resisted Spanish authorities into the late 1700s. However, life was not altogether easy as new diseases impacted

Hopi communities. An outbreak in 1780 and 1781 led to more than 5,025 Pueblo Indian deaths, with heavy losses at Hopi. When the Americans arrived in 1848, Hopis were primarily concerned with stopping **Apache** and **Navajo** raiding and protecting lands from settlers. In the late 1800s, many Hopis opposed the American government's policies of land distribution and the forced placement of children in schools. In 1935, the Hopi Tribal Council was established and ushered in a new era of government action, even as some community members challenged the authority of this new form of political administration. In the twentieth century, Hopi community members became gradually more engaged with outsiders as they increasingly depended on the emerging cash economy and battled for land and water rights.

The Colorado Plateau has archeological remains that are more than 12,000 years old. The first Indian groups lived by hunting and gathering, though agriculture was incorporated when corn was introduced from Mexico 5,000 years ago. Around 1,000 years ago, native peoples in the American Southwest began living in distinctive above-ground masonry compounds with contiguous rooms—some growing to be more than 1,000 rooms—and large, open plazas. In this period, distinct traditions of material culture emerged, such as multicolored pottery and ornate paraphernalia associated with unique religious societies. Many of these ancient places are now ruins around the Hopi mesas, though some, such as Orayvi founded 900 years ago, are still occupied.

HOPI ORIGINS AND ANCESTORS

Hopi traditional knowledge says that long, long ago the ancient Hopi ancestors, the *Hisatsinom* (Persons of Ancient Times) emerged from below and came onto this, the Fourth World. After the ancestors surfaced, they soon met the spirit being Màasaw, who told them that the land was theirs and that they should begin their search for the center of the universe, the Hopi mesas. The people agreed, and Màasaw gave them a planting stick and a bag of seeds. They were to be humble farmers. As Màasaw directed the *Hisatsinom* on their journey to the Hopi mesas, groups formed, each becoming a clan. Dozens of clans materialized and were named for the natural or meteorological phenomena they encountered. They traveled to many places, pausing to rest at one village and then moving on to make another. Generation followed generation. At last the clans began to coalesce along the Hopi mesas, each bringing its own stories, rituals, and knowledge. Today, the Hopi people are unified through an array of histories, each encased in clan traditions that relate to their ancestors' migrations throughout the land.

While many scholars suggest the *Sípàapuni* in the Grand Canyon was the place of Hopi emergence, many clans associate the beginning place with *Yayniwpu* (The Beginning), located perhaps in Central Mexico. Wherever the Hopi ancestors began, the migration stories recount that they traveled throughout and beyond the Greater Southwest. These movements of migration were not linear and unidirectional but circuitous. Ancestral villages such as *Qa'ötaqtipu* (Burnt Corn), *Sikyatki* (Divided Valley), and *Awat'ovi* (Bow-High-Place) are still recalled, whereas the precise location of other villages has been lost to time. Many traditions refer to *Palatkwapi* (Red-Walled City), said to have been a stopping point for more than thirty clans. Various stories are told about *Palatkwapi*, but most relate a narrative about how the residents there lived in a fertile land and thrived for some time. However, the people soon turned careless and fell into moral and spiritual corruption. Solicited by inculpable priests, the *Paalölöquangw* (Great Horned Water Serpent) caused an immense flood that destroyed *Palatkwapi*. Some say the flood was only stopped when two children were sent into the fissure from which water poured forth. The survivors, cleansed and humbled, migrated northward to meet their destiny on the Hopi mesas.

Many Hopis believe that ancient artifacts and ruins survive into our modern age not by chance but through the designs of their ancestors. Along their migration routes, Màasaw instructed the clans to leave *Kuktota*, their "footprints" on the earth, by setting down ritual springs, trails, shrines, and petroglyphs. *Ang Kuktota* (along there, make footprints) is thus a central tenet of the covenant with Màasaw. Some Hopi even explain that the *Hisatsinom* would deliberately break pottery and peck out petroglyphs just before they moved to a new village. The surviving ruins and sacred spots are monuments that give proof of the ancestral migrations and Hopi commitment to land stewardship.

SOCIAL STRUCTURE, LANGUAGE, AND AGRICULTURE

The social organization of the Hopi is incredibly complex, based on each individual's cross-cutting social memberships and affiliations with village residence, clans, and religious societies. Each person traces his or her ancestry primarily through the mother's side of the family. Hopi society has matrilineal exogamous clans, matrilocal households, and a matrilineal kinship system. The father's side is generally supportive and secondary. The household is the smallest distinct social unit, and it is not uncommon to find several biological families living in one residence. Contemporary community leadership involves both the Tribal Council and traditional offices held by village and ceremonial leaders. Clans and societies not only organize social relations but also perform sacred rites and ceremonies that keep the world in balance. Although communities often work together amicably, they sometimes have split and separated because of political disagreements, increasing population, and physical conflicts.

The Hopi language is classified as Uto-Aztecan and appears related to the Great Basin Numic languages; however, different dialects are spoken on each mesa. The Tewa community on First Mesa is Tanoan-speaking, closely related to the Kiowa of the Great Plains. Hopis, though remarkably diverse, remain united by their shared land, language, history, economy, identity, beliefs, and values.

Hopi subsistence has long depended on agriculture, primarily the cultivation of corn, beans, squash, and cotton. With dry weather, little permanent surface water, and robust winds, farming is a precarious endeavor on the Colorado Plateau. Through the millennia Hopi farmers have perfected agricultural methods such as floodwater farming (planting crops near streams that overflow when flooding) and irrigation farming (using terraces and alignments to guide and control water flow). Land for farming has traditionally been controlled by the clans within each village, with the clans who arrived in the village first receiving precedence. Agriculture expanded with colonialism, as the Spanish introduced peaches, apricots, onions, chili, watermelons, and wheat as well as horses, mules, burros, sheep, and cattle. Anglos later introduced safflower, sorghum, turban squashes, peanuts, turnips, cabbage, carrots, tomatoes, peas, apples, pears, and cherries. The first plantings of corn are usually in spring so that the crops mature by mid-July in time for the *Niman* (Home Dance) ceremony. Historically, corn is mainly baked and then stored for use throughout the year. Hopis also make extensive use of wild plants, such as yucca for washing hair—a practical and ceremonial act—and using the leaves for making baskets. Hunting has primarily focused on deer, antelope, and rabbit. Since the days of the Spanish, Hopis have raised cattle and sheep, and these activities remain important today. Importantly, all these production activities have traditionally been tied to religious beliefs, and in fact they are often the same thing. Planting is a form of prayer—as prayer is a form of planting.

CEREMONY AND RITUAL—THE *KATSINA* SEASON

The order of the world is maintained through prayers and sacred rituals, Hopis believe, carried out by religious societies and clans, performed throughout the year in public and secrecy. Nearly every ceremony focuses on rain, which when combined with earth, constitutes the essence of all life. Unlike Western thought, Hopi worldview concentrates on continuity, relationships, and transformation. Death, for example, is not seen as the end of life but, rather, as birth into a new kind of being. The spirits of the dead return to the living as *katsinas* (kachinas) in the form of clouds and thus rain, snow, springs, streams, and lakes. The relationship between the spirit beings and Hopis is one of reciprocity, a cooperative exchange. The kachinas are symbolically fed with prayers and offerings, and the kachinas in turn feed the Hopis with the water that replenishes the earth. In this way, ritual acts help maintain the spirit world, and the spirit world maintains human life. In this view, all things are imbued with life force, and so all thoughts, actions, and beings are interrelated. There is no clear separation among places, animals, food, rocks, and water. The universe, however, is not without order. One fundamental structure is the directions, which are synchronized with color and the passing of time marked by the sun's movement across the horizon: *kwiningyaqw* (the northwest is yellow, the summer-solstice sunset), *taavangqw* (the southwest is blue, the winter-solstice sunset), *tatkyaqw* (the southeast is red, the winter-solstice sunrise), *hoopaqw* (the northeast is white, the summer-solstice sunrise), *oomiqw* (above is black), and *atkyaqw* (below is speckled, all the colors). This organizing system connects time and space and forms the basis of the Hopis' intricate system of ritual.

In many ways one might say that ceremony lies at the heart of Hopi traditional life, the ideal of equilibrium achieved through music and performance. Although Hopis have certainly been influenced by Western society for close to 500 years, Hopi ceremony today shows little sign of genuine syncretism. Ceremonies are enacted by different groups, including the kachina cult, men's societies, and women's societies. One clan, and sometimes several clans, control and organize each major ceremony. The ceremonial calendar, defined by the movements of the sun and moon, is divided into two key parts, the *katsina* season and the society ceremonies. In October or November, the *Wuwtsim* ceremony, a ritual involving four societies, the

Kwaakwant (Agave Society), *Wuwtsim* (Ancients Society), *Aa'alt* (Horn Society), and *Taatawkyam* (Singers Society), begins the year. This ceremony in part initiates Hopi men, re-enacting Hopi emergence and preparing men for their life and eventual transformation to the spirit world. The Winter Solstice Ceremony, a highly esoteric service that reverses the sun from its winter path, follows in December.

The *katsina* season then opens with *Soyalagnw*, and masked dancers appear until *Niman* (Home Dance) in July when the *katsinas* return to their abode in the San Francisco Peaks near present-day Flagstaff, Arizona. The society dances begin again, this time with the Snake-Antelope Dance and the Flute Society dances. The Women's Society dances of the *Mamrawt*, *Lalkont*, and *O'waaqöl* follow in early fall. The *Mamrawt* rites relate to war and fertility, among other facets of life, whereas the *Lalkont* and *O'waaqöl* mainly concern fertility.

Dances often entail elaborate and colorful costumes with headgear, body paint, and distinctive clothes. The masks of the *katsinas* are thought to be the manifestation of ancestors who live half the year with the Hopi. Singing and chanting are done by the dancers who also move in a synchronized fashion. Gourd rattles are often used, and sometimes tortoiseshell rattles are attached to the legs of dancers. The preparations of the dancers are rigorous—physically and spiritually intense. It is also a major commitment of time and energy. Dancers must refrain from salt, meat, and sexual intercourse before, during, and shortly after each ceremony. Many ceremonies last eight full days, divided into two parts, in addition to a day of preparation. However, other ceremonies vary in length, perhaps four or sixteen days. When the ceremonies are finished, dancers resume their everyday life. Knowledge of these ceremonies, outlined only briefly here, is considered extremely potent and potentially dangerous. Mishandling the ceremonies can result in terrible sickness and even chaos.

The first part of ceremonies usually begins secretly in kivas, underground or partially underground ceremonial chambers; the second part is performed in public plazas with people watching from rooftops and in front of their homes. Ceremonies are connected to individual kivas. Among the Hopi, kivas are square and are entered by a ladder through the roof. The ladder is set over a fireplace in the center of the room. Kivas symbolically replicate Hopi cosmology on three levels: a platform, the floor, and a *sipapu*, a hole in the ground representing the place of emergence. Inside kivas, participants engage in praying, singing, erecting altars, weaving, storytelling, and smoking. Altars are panels painted with icons and symbols representing water, animals, and cult heroes with sacred objects such as effigies, medicine, and fetishes placed in front.

While prayers are formalized in public and secret ceremonies, more mundane aspects of Hopi life are often still connected to ceremony. For example, some ceremonies end with a foot race that begins at a sacred shrine and then leads the clouds gathered in the sanctuary back to the Hopi villages. Other games such as Shinny, which is played with a wooden stick and buckskin ball, and guessing games are played between ceremonies in moments of spare time. Pottery making, too, involving the mixture of water and earth, is often perceived as a kind of prayer making.

ARTS AND CRAFTS

Today, Hopi pottery is among the most celebrated Pueblo art forms. In the Colorado Plateau region, ceramic bowls and jars appeared more than 1,500 years ago and were based on basketry, a much older technology. Pueblo ceramics are crafted with a coil-and-scrape method, so called because long coils of clay are laid upon each other and then wiped to a smooth surface. Pottery was first decorated by incising the clay when it was wet or leaving the coils exposed, but soon black, red, and white paint was added to create designs of animals, geometric shapes, humans, and supernatural forms. Hopi ceramics took an especially distinctive turn when potters began firing their clay with coal collected near the Hopi mesas. The resulting yellow color uniquely identifies this pottery. Hopi pottery making declined somewhat in the colonial age, first with the arrival of the Spanish and then the arrival of the railroad in Arizona in the 1880s. For centuries, Hopi pottery was not primarily an esthetic object but, rather, a tool with utilitarian and ritual functions. In 1875, Thomas Varker Keam was licensed to trade with Hopis, and the trader exchanged Western goods for pottery. While this exchange maintained the Hopi craft, it was not until several decades later that the Hopi ceramics renaissance began. In the 1890s, anthropologist Jesse Walter Fewkes began excavating at a site called *Sikyatki*, and a young woman from Tewa Village named Nampeyo saw the old pottery styles there. Inspired, she began imitating and expanding on these ancient ceramics. Soon her pottery was sold across the country. Building on Nampeyo's legacy, subsequent generations have taken Hopi pottery to even higher artistic levels and have become celebrated throughout the world.

Although Hopi pottery is now widely collected, other arts are key to Hopi social practice, identity, and economy. For at least 900 years, Hopis have painted the walls of the ceremonial kivas. These designs are reminiscent of ceramic iconography but tend to be much more visually elaborate and steeped in ritual. Walls are painted in earthy hues in conjunction with a ritual, and when the ritual is finished, the painting is plastered over. At one uninhabited village, *Awat'ovi*, archeologists found a single kiva wall with 100 layers of plaster, more than 30 of them painted. Around 1912, Hopi artists began painting on easels with oils and acrylics and sold the paintings to collectors in Santa Fe. Although it is generally women who make ceramics, men paint the kiva murals and also do much of the weaving. Weaving is done from vertical and backstrap looms to make blankets, sashes, kilts, wedding robes, belts, garters, and the women's distinctive woolen black dress. Women do most of the basketry, making plaques, trays, and baskets using both wicker techniques and coiled techniques in which a bundle of grasses is sewn with strips of yucca leaves. In the early 1890s, silversmithing was introduced to Hopis. However, it was not until the 1940s that Hopi artisans launched the distinctive style celebrated today, a silver overlay technique. Kachina dolls were originally made by *katsinas* and distributed to children at dances. Long ago, they were primarily educational and so focused on the individual personalities of particular spirit beings. By the 1930s, with more Hopis receiving formal training in schools, the dolls became increasingly sculptural. The dolls are not actual supernatural beings but, rather, mimic humans adorned in kachina costumes.

Since the early twentieth century, the different mesas have tended to focus on particular crafts: on First Mesa are potters, on Second Mesa are basketmakers, on Third Mesa are weavers. These various crafts and arts play an essential role in Hopi life today. They allow Hopis to participate in the modern economy and honor their history by making traditional objects that are also infused with contemporary techniques, economics, and values.

STUDIES OF HOPI FOLKLORE

A good starting point to learn more is the Hopi Tribe's Internet site (www.hopi .nsn.us). Several important books can be found about Hopi ancient history, archeology, and oral tradition (Bernardini 2005; Lyons 2003; Malotki 1993). There are some good volumes about traditional knowledge, myths, legends, and recent history (Courlander 1982; Nequatewa 1967; Whiteley 1988). Ethnographies are an important source of information (Clemmer 1995; Geertz 1994; Whiteley 1998). Other general references are also helpful (Hopi Dictionary Project 1998; Ortiz 1979).

BIBLIOGRAPHY

Bernardini, Wesley. 2005. *Hopi Oral Tradition and the Archaeology of Identity*. Tucson: University of Arizona Press.

Clemmer, Richard O. 1995. *Roads in the Sky: The Hopi Indians in a Century of Change*. Boulder, CO: Westview Press.

Courlander, Harold. 1982. *Hopi Voices: Recollections, Traditions, and Narratives of the Hopi Indians*. Albuquerque: University of New Mexico Press.

Geertz, Armin W. 1994. *The Invention of Prophecy: Continuity and Meaning in Hopi Indian Religion*. Berkeley: University of California Press.

Hopi Dictionary Project. 1998. *Hopìikwa Lavàytutuveni: A Hopi-English Dictionary of the Third Mesa Dialect*. Tucson: University of Arizona Press.

Lyons, Patrick D. 2003. *Ancestral Hopi Migrations*. Anthropological Papers of the University of Arizona, No. 68. Tucson: University of Arizona Press.

Malotki, Ekkehart, ed. 1993. *Hopi Ruin Legends: Kiqötutuwutsi*. Lincoln: University of Nebraska Press.

Nequatewa, Edmund. 1967 (1936). *Truth of a Hopi*. Flagstaff, AZ: Northland Press.

Ortiz, Alfonso, ed. 1979. *Handbook of North American Indians*. Vol. 9, *Southwest*. Washington, DC: Smithsonian Institution Press.

Whiteley, Peter M. 1988. *Deliberate Acts: Changing Hopi Culture through the Oraibi Split*. Tucson: University of Arizona Press.

———. 1998. *Rethinking Hopi Ethnography*. Washington, DC: Smithsonian Institution Press.

Chip Colwell-Chanthaphonh

IROQUOIS

GEOGRAPHY

Generally acknowledged to have developed society and culture over many centuries in what is now central New York State and contiguous areas reaching from the St. Lawrence River on the east to the Great Lakes on the west, the Iroquoian-speaking peoples extended in pockets as far south as present-day Virginia. The area's location within the northern maize-cultivation belt is a major ecological factor impinging on Iroquoian culture. The terrain includes lakes and rivers, mountains, and agricultural flatlands. Their situation within the greater Eastern Woodland culture area and dependence on the forest have also unified the Iroquois.

SOCIAL STRUCTURE

The importance of agriculture to the Iroquois cannot be overstated. Besides the "three sisters" of corn, beans, and squash, garden crops—most important, the sunflower—are in evidence. Communal gardens could be im-

Iroquois Indians. (Picture Collection, The Branch Libraries, The New York Public Library, Astor, Lenox and Tilden Foundations)

mense with attached fruit orchards sometimes extending for miles. Traditionally, matrilineal sibs living in bark-covered longhouses forming sometimes large, fortified villages tend the gardens. Thus the female line provides the basis for social organization and even property ownership. The mother's brother is an important figure, whose role is often stressed in folktales. Clan membership is derived from the mother. Society is divided into several exogamous clans, with the clans making up moieties, or two halves of the community. Members of the same clan are considered relatives and not proper marriage partners. In the older practice, the ideal marriage was between members of opposite moieties, and a tendency to avoid marriage within the clan persists. The perception of dualities runs through society and politics as well as beliefs and folklore. Artificial or culturally determined pairings are the major theme throughout Iroquoian culture.

Perception of the political importance of pairings may have given formal impetus to the development of paired political alliances, the major feature of Iroquois history. The most famous and long-lasting of these is the Iroquois League, consisting of the present-day nations, east to west, of Mohawk, Oneida, Onondaga, Cayuga, and Seneca with the late-eighteenth-century addition of the Tuscarora. But other alliances have been historically important, including the Huron or Wendat, the Conestoga or Susquehannock, and perhaps political movements at the eastern end of Lake Erie. Probably because of a lack of intensive contact caused by the larger groupings, unaligned or only temporarily aligned Iroquoian peoples, especially groups along the upper Ohio River, have, however, sometimes been important transmitters of folklore.

CULTURAL HISTORY AND EUROPEAN CONTACT

Despite inevitable local diversity, Iroquoian folklore seems, for the most part, to be fairly similar. This view is affected, though, by focus on the Hurons and Senecas in the earliest and most extensive sources. These descriptions formed the bases for generalizations throughout Iroquoian culture. Iroquoian culture can best be seen as a consistent subset of Eastern Woodland culture, however, shaped for many centuries by interaction with nearby non-Iroquoian peoples, mostly Algonquian- and Siouan-speaking.

The manufacture of the utensils and paraphernalia of Iroquois life at the time of European contact involved little specialization, even in items needed in quantity such as stone tools. Plate-pressure making of flint arrowheads is still found among some scattered individuals who practice traditional hunting, but for the most part such practices no longer occur. Iroquoian ceramics are even less well preserved in memory. Metal utensils consigned ceramics to oblivion early on, and no folk tradition has preserved or revived them. Other Native Americans have preserved the ceramic craft as a hallmark of identity, but the Iroquois have not, perhaps because the tradition disappeared long before the idea of folklore as a vehicle of ethnic identity.

Early European contact fostered some aspects of folk craft, however. Steel tools certainly changed the technique and appearance of wooden and bark objects, but at the same time they gave diversity and facility, thus creating a resurgence of Iroquoian craft in mortars and pestles, ladles, paddles, dishes, chests, bows, clubs, and ritual paraphernalia. Hickory wood, being tough and standing up to wear, was the favorite for carved utensils. Basswood was the favorite for decorative artifacts such as masks. Paddles, dishes, and storage chests for such things as tree sugar were made mostly from elm bark. Canoes were also traditionally made from elm bark, and canoe paddles from hickory. It is not known if the practice of carving spoon handles in hickory with effigy patterns arose with the advent of steel or was practiced in precontact times. Iroquoian wooden spoons and ladles are still made, sometimes with effigy patterns similar to those in stone or ceramics dated many centuries ago. Sinew and woven fiber crafts have disappeared so that early clothing such as burden straps no longer exist, while bone and leatherwork have been rejuvenated with modern beadwork in association with the making of ceremonial costumes. Interestingly, bone is used today in a more pan-Indian style of jewelry rather than in the old Iroquoian style of decorated combs.

The period of most significant transition in culture occurred for most surviving Iroquoian groups with the disruption caused by the opening of the "Old Northwest," the inevitable conflicts, and finally the period of accommodation to pioneer life on reservations or in isolated communities up to 1840. Previously, the Iroquois influenced and received influences from colonial culture and folklore. During and after the Great Transition, the process became more unilateral, with the Iroquois adapting to pioneer ways, incorporating new lifeways, and changing the functions of many of the old ways that were retained. This process of acculturation has produced varying types of communities and identities among the descendants of the ancient Iroquois. During the period of change from pioneer to urban culture, the Iroquois went through stages of forestry, railroad, steel mill, and construction work in addition to farming. A more diversified and often urban pattern appeared after the mid-twentieth century.

The stages of development are reflected in changes in architecture. During the pre-colonial and colonial periods, the Iroquois were famous for the longhouse, which was ideally set with entrances east and west off a corridor of fireplaces dividing the house into apartments set on each side of the fire. The houses were framed in saplings and covered with bark sheets, generally elm. The beginning of the reservation period saw the introduction of the

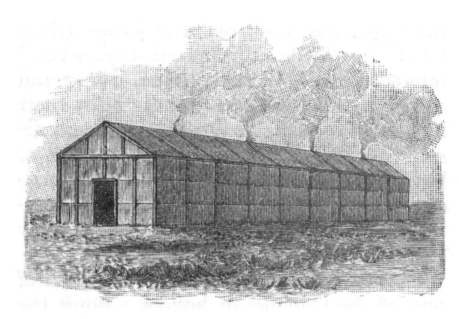

Hodenosote, or longhouse of the Iroquois. (Picture Collection, The Branch Libraries, The New York Public Library, Astor, Lenox and Tilden Foundations)

log cabin, which was used well into the twentieth century. The mid-twentieth century saw ranch-style houses on most Iroquoian reservations. Many Iroquoian people today are still familiar enough with the techniques to be able to produce the longhouse. Furthermore, the bark-covered hunting lodge, similar to the dwellings of the Algonquian-speaking neighbors of the Iroquois, is sometimes made for use even today. Architecture expresses the condition of Iroquois folklore as it has changed, borrowed, and preserved traditions.

The concept of official and popular culture, important to some definitions of folklore, is difficult to apply to Iroquoian tradition because of the highly institutionalized character of Iroquoian culture. Two examples especially illustrate this situation. While no large body of folksongs has been collected among the Iroquois, extensive collections of songs relating to large, public rituals as well as smaller, secretive society functions are available. The function of a truly folk tradition of songs has perhaps been assumed by personal songs. Similarly, there are no collections of Iroquoian riddles. Yet riddles have been institutionalized and form the basis of an important community ritual in the Mid-Winter cycle, the ritual of dream guessing. Riddles, which are usually part of folklore, are almost always part of what must be seen as official religion among the Iroquois. This characteristic of Iroquoian culture has resulted in the study of that culture being undertaken more often by archeologists, historians, anthropologists, ethnologists, sociologists, and even more exotic professionals than by folklorists.

Although few purely folkloristic studies of the Iroquois are available, our knowledge of early Iroquoian folkways is vast. The craft of basketry, for example, is well documented. Iroquoian baskets come in traditional styles reflecting local diversity and made for many purposes. Black ash is one of the most common materials used at least during the last century and a half. It is soaked, pounded, and cut into strips. Most of the basket-types are used for harvesting and preserving foods. Berry-picking baskets typically have belts to be attached to the waist, leaving both hands free for picking. A fairly unusual form of basket, no longer made, is the water basket, whose tight weave and resin lining made it useful for drawing, transporting, and storing drinking water. Contemporary communities continue the practice of traditional storytelling during basketmaking sessions. Another continuing tradition associated with basketmaking is corn husk crafts. White corn husks are used because they retain their color well. The most prevalent corn husk crafts are dolls and corn husk masks, both in miniature and in life size.

MYTHS, LEGENDS, AND FOLKTALES

With the transition to single household dwellings and individual farming by males, the communal taletelling sessions once associated with harvest ceased. However, the practice of taking in winter boarders became widespread, and boarders often paid for their keep by reciting folk traditions on long winter evenings. After a break in the tradition, this practice saw a renewal during the hard years of "Reaganomics" of the 1980s, as some Iroquois call them.

Most of the folktales found among the Iroquois have parallels in European folklore, especially accounts of the uncanny, the supernatural, and most particularly ghosts. The uncanny and supernatural among the Iroquois tend to focus on three specific areas: surprising events while hunting that suggest supernatural powers of animals; the reporting of cases of *kahaih* or shape-changing involving beings in animal shape who sometimes take human form and bring either misfortune or good luck to those who encounter them; and cases of witchcraft such as old people being able to move long distances in a short time. Almost all Iroquois folk narratives can be placed in one of these categories. Today such stories can sometimes be heard in fast-food restaurants and bowling alleys—wherever people may meet.

The grand, official myths, legends, and mythological stories are rarely told today, nor is there evidence that they formed a part of the public ritual. Some relate to the origin songs of the secret medicine societies. Others are variants of the creation story. Finally, there is the well-known origin story of the Iroquois League, the Deganawida myth. Collections of Iroquoian folk narratives contain other traditional material as well. While such collections apparently attempted to record a classical storytelling tradition, modern perceptions suggest that no such classical tradition existed. The stories in these collections actually represent the prevalent interests of the time. The transition from colonial culture to reservation culture was associated with a change in **worldview**. The old religion emphasizes a cyclical concept of time, whereas the post-1800 tradition focuses on the end of the world, a product not only of Christianity but of the decimation of Native society. The tension between these two perceptions determined the character of the "classical" tales collected in the nineteenth and early twentieth centuries.

Nevertheless, it is certain that gatherings from harvest to spring among the Iroquois must have included storytelling, which featured traditional figures such as the Stone Coats, the Flying Head or whirlwind and other wind creatures, Sharp-legs, the

Horned Serpent and other serpent figures, the Buffalo Man with his single rib, the Great Leech, and an assortment of fabulous animals and wizards often in magical combat, in chase and flight, and even in cannibalism and resurrections. These elements, both figures and motifs, must have formed a constant pool of resources for the folk narrator for many centuries.

One brief tale, collected on the Allegany Reservation in 1974, can illustrate the salient features of the tale tradition: "Long ago when the earth was new, the old people and my grandpa used to tell that the Indians living together in a village used to dance. They would keep dancing all night. That way the children were always left alone. Now once they heard the children shouting as the children started dancing too. Suddenly they started going up in the air where they were dancing. A round piece of ground went up in the air and the children just kept on dancing. Up into the sky it went, and they couldn't do anything to stop them. Now that is what is called the Pleiades. And now it shows us when they are dancing in the middle of the sky that they should have the Mid-Winter Festival."

This story is undoubtedly ancient and is the most frequently told story today as well. It embodies the typical structure of an implied prohibition, the breaking of the prohibition, and the results. It relates to the typical Iroquoian vision quest, which is generally reported as a sky journey. The story also supports the official ceremonial cycle, showing the way in which folk narrative and official religion are intertwined and difficult to separate conceptually.

Mask Making

Just as harvest events no longer provide a context for the transmission of such stories today, storytelling is missing from other traditional activities such as crafts. Iroquois carved wooden spoons seem to form a tradition going back at least to colonial times when steel tools became available. A tradition of making wooden masks goes back in more or less its present form to the same period. This is related to the official spirituality of the False Face Society. In former days this was exclusively official, but since the 1960s it has become a folk art not necessarily related to ritual. The same can be said for the cottage industry of Iroquois rattles. Only turtle rattles continue to be made for official ritual purposes alone. Other types are now made as crafts quite separate from the society rituals in which they have their origins. These include horn rattles (originally made of bison horns, but made today from cattle horns), bark rattles (originally made from elm bark, but now occasionally found in other bark), and gourd rattles still painted with traditional patterns.

Horn rattles and masks depended for several centuries on steel hand-tools. Masks were traditionally carved into living trees and painted red if they were made during the morning hours or black if they were made during the afternoon. This reflects the constant awareness among the Iroquois of the two-part division of the day. For several decades power tools have been used for making both masks and horn rattles. Meanwhile, masks are now made from cut trees rather than living ones. Both crafts are produced for decorative reasons as well as for the official and traditional society functions, and this is a departure from tradition. Craftwork for its own sake rather than ritual purposes can be identified by the failure to attach small bundles of tobacco. A lucrative business in making such artifacts has in recent years been suppressed as a desecration.

Masking relates to myths and legends that give body to the masking societies. The mask is particularly associated with the creation twins. Flint's failure to beat Sapling in the creation contest of moving mountains is sometimes taken as the origin of masking—the masks representing Flint or beings subjected to him. Flint now has the duty of helping people in illness, especially ailments of the head, neck, throat, and nose. It is difficult to separate folk and official beliefs among the Iroquois, and although official ritual is clear-cut and consists of the diplomatic and political protocol as well as public and society rites, the belief system does not break down into official and folk. Thus the same beliefs underlie unofficial use of masks or other society paraphernalia.

RITUALS AND CELEBRATIONS

Official and public ritual is based both upon the revitalization movement beginning around 1800 and the continuing older medicine societies. Although there is a definite break with older beliefs in contemporary Longhouse religion, the influence of the medicine societies has introduced conservative beliefs and practices. These are associated with old tale types, although tales are not told in public ritual, and they have specific non-narrative forms generally in the secret society ritual. Nevertheless, their continuing practice is associated with a knowledge of old tale types despite the fact that narrative situations have become atrophied. Both ritual and paraphernalia such as masks preserve a knowledge of such mythical figures as the creation twins.

Ritual events also function to some extent in the preservation of cooking lore. Traditional recipes exist for specific rituals, and these should be seen as quite official. However, two recipes merge ritual preparations with everyday cooking. The first is corn soup, which is made from hominy soaked in ashes, washed, hulled, and boiled with red beans. It is seasoned with mint, meat, often sugar or syrup instead of the traditional maple, and oils other than the traditional sunflower oil. Traditional meat seasoning is generally replaced with pork, reflecting changes in lifeways from the reservation period. The old pioneer cooking in an iron kettle over an open fire still occurs for ritual occasions. Traditional cornbread, a thick porridge cut cold and fried in slices, is very popular. Finally, the pan-Indian frybread is called frybread only in the Iroquoian languages. In reservation English, the Iroquois invariably call it ghostbread because of its role in some medicine society functions. Such traditional foods as corn soup and fried cornbread preserve the old Iroquoian taste for sweets. Most traditional recipes, even meat dishes, are sweet rather than salty.

ARTS AND CRAFTS

Traditional porcupine quill crafting is practically non-existent, but there has been a renaissance of beadwork since the late 1960s, though this had fallen into disuse among most of the Iroquois. Iroquois silver, once a well-known craft, has long disappeared.

The folk craft of beadworking reflects the pan-Indian identity that became prominent in the 1960s. Beading classes are found on reservations and in urban centers. Pan-Indian designs are common, but particular Iroquoian themes also occur. Among these are clan symbols, birds, or animals that are incorporated into beaded jewelry, but these have no connection to the trade-bead configuration of the sixteenth to eighteenth centuries. Since the origin of the craft is in recent pan-Indian identity, it displays two particular features. First, it lacks the diversity and skill of older Native American bead traditions. Fine, large pieces of tiny seed-beads are not as typical of the Iroquois as they are of some of the more westerly peoples. Second, motifs are limited to those that are consistent with the pan-Indian philosophy. Thus such images as footballs, baseball bats, and U.S. flags are not found among them. Some Iroquoian motifs such as the fir tree pattern seen in some wampum belts are also reviving.

SPORTS AND GAMES

Two traditional games still provide an outlet for folk craftsmen. The snowsnake is still made in reservation areas, and the lacrosse stick is even more widely known and crafted. Both games were originally part of the official healing ritual. Official healing is still determined by what in reservation English is called a fortune-teller. This specialist diagnoses the illness in terms of what is needed to treat it: the intervention of a particular medicine society with its songs and rites, specific herbs, and in some cases watching or participating in traditional games. The two sides in a ballgame, or in a bowl game at Mid-Winter, seem to represent the two major categories of forces called Oki and Otkon—the former a male and sky-oriented force and the latter female and earth-oriented. The balanced interplay of these is seen as conducive to healing.

Many games among the Iroquois are a part of official ceremonials. The most important of these is the bowl game performed at the Mid-Winter Festival in public ritual. This is a game of chance using five fruit pits, each charred on one side. The game pits the moieties of the community, representing the interplay of Oki and Otkon, against each other.

Like Native American games in general, most Iroquois games fit into the two categories of chance and prowess and rarely depend on cunning and wit. Chance as an expression of Oki and Otkon and skill as the dominant human means of meeting it are central values and express themselves in games. Traditional games such as snowsnake and lacrosse outside the context of the official ceremonial have entirely disappeared.

Among games of chance, the Iroquois almost exclusively used dice. The stick game is documented only for the Huron. Moccasin or hidden-ball games are fairly widely known, having been recorded among the Onondaga, Seneca, and Wendat. Among games of dexterity and skill, archery games were unknown, and ring-and-pin games were limited to the Huron. Hoop and pole and, of course, the snowsnake were once known. Ballgames were almost exclusively limited to racket games, although Shinny is recorded for the Tuscarora and football for the Wendat. Tipcat, otherwise known only among the Zuni and Teton Sioux, is recorded for the Mohawk.

DRAMA

Traditional dramatic arts are almost completely limited to medicine society ceremonials. These include the official secret rituals, generally conducted twice a year in the spring and autumn, the times when the year is divided in two. But the drama becomes public at the Mid-Winter Festival, which may last for up to ten days with sacred speeches and rites in the morning and society participation in afternoon and evening. The societies entertain the evening audiences with masking and semi-sacred clowning. Boisterous clowning, feats of prowess and dexterity, walking barefoot on ice, and carrying live coals in the bare hands occur at the Mid-Winter Festival. Dream-guessing ritual as well as the bowl game also have a dramatic character. The blind mask, which lacks eyeholes, also provides an element of dramatic entertainment reminiscent of magic acts.

HERBALISM AND SUPERNATURAL LORE

Herbalism is very important among the Iroquois. The concepts of Oki and Otkon are foundational to this, but on the surface Iroquoian herbalism may differ little from folk remedies in the Midwest and Appalachians in general. An enormous Iroquoian folk pharmacopoeia has been documented. Both simple and rather complex mixtures are known for practically every ailment. Two aspects of modern practice are clearly ancient, though most plants have been used by the Iroquois for some purpose over the centuries. Some herbals are documented in the earliest sources. One ancient traditional aspect of herbalism is gathering material with respect for the natural direction of flow or growth. This is associated with the older practice of burning tobacco and making an invocation before gathering herbs. Another clearly ancient practice is personal purification, the use of a traditional emetic in spring and autumn. This relates to the perception of things in pairs. The year is divided into two halves, and purification is needed at the transition between them. In the same way the day is divided into two parts, not day and night, but the time from dawn till noon as distinguished from the rest of the twenty-four-hour period.

Herbal concoctions as well as simple herbs are administered as poultices, teas, and infusions. They were also sprayed from the mouth, a practice that appears to have disappeared. Iroquoian herbalism and European folk remedies very much influenced one another. A number of plants such as the plantain used as a poultice for sores and bruises that were originally introduced from Europe have become ingredients in Iroquoian medicines.

A little studied but immensely rich area of folk medicine among the Iroquois is an entire herbarium of recipes for various female disorders. Especially among the southern Iroquois many of these are related to spells and other non-medicinal practices, but in the northern areas they are richly herbalist in character and require a specialized pharmacopoeia. Recipes are known for the onset of menstruation, maintenance of regularity, various forms of irregularity, premenstrual depression, menstrual pain, and menopause.

Folk beliefs are today an amalgamation of contributions from ancient Iroquoian beliefs, beliefs borrowed from other Native Americans, and beliefs borrowed from

Europeans. The belief in ghosts and the telling of ghost stories predominates. Sometimes these take a native twist, particularly when they refer to funeral traditions or the belief in the ancestors coming to dance with the living. More often they are indistinguishable from mainstream ghost stories. The hooting of owls and birds flying against windows are omens. The Iroquois would put a key on the back of the neck to reduce fever just as their European neighbors might do.

MUSIC

In the public sphere, as is typical of everything Iroquoian, music is divided into sacred dance (performed in the morning) and social dance (performed in the afternoon and night). The latter overlaps to some extent with the enormous body of society song and dance. Although much of this music is traditional, some of it today is also composed—especially social songs and dances forming the traditional repertoire of professional and semi-professional dance groups. The tradition of courting flute playing was apparently subject to individual improvisation and spontaneous composition. Unfortunately this area of folk tradition was never well documented. Although the tradition has disappeared, there is a pan-Indian resurgence of Indian flute-playing. Quite a number of Iroquoian musicians compose and perform today in traditional ways, though these do not have roots in the original local practice.

Official ceremonial has contributed to the development and preservation of the crafting of musical instruments. An Iroquoian specialty is the water-drum, required for certain ceremonies. The drum is a keg whose bottom is pitched with beeswax. The other end is covered with a skin, which is soaked with water from the inside before playing. The pitch can be changed by adjusting the amount of water in the drum. The drumstick is carved from hickory and often decorated with effigy figures.

The snapping turtle rattle is prepared by having the turtle bite a steel wire, hanging the creature aloft, and cutting off tail and limbs. The shell is cleaned by ants and filled with grains of corn or cherry pits. The tail and legholes are sewn up. A stick in the neck and head hole provides a handle, which, held in both hands, allows the side of the rattle to be beaten against a bench.

Christian hymns began to appear in the early 1800s. The first were translations of English texts, but soon Native hymns were added to these. Many resemble earlier Iroquoian personal invocations used for hunting and healing. Examples are found in practically all the Iroquois hymnals. Similarly, Christians began producing Native hymns, often with the name of a hymnwriter being known, but in some cases in the form of a folk hymn. Some of these folk hymns are popular in Iroquoian Christian congregations, but after enjoying 100 years of brilliant use, they began to decline in most communities around the 1960s.

STUDIES OF IROQUOIS FOLKLORE

The earliest sources of knowledge about Iroquoian folklore are the Jesuit *Relations* and other early travelers' journals. Later captivity journals also provide material. Reports of later missionaries and officials are generally meager sources. The body of Iroquoian sources is enormous and uneven, but few peoples have enjoyed so much attention from scholars as have the Iroquois. Morgan (1962 [1851]) remains the primary source for nearly every area of knowledge. Beauchamp (1922) gathered early material from a folkloristic perspective. Kurath (1961) is a fundamental source on music and dance traditions. Converse (1908) and Smith (1883) are two generalized sources among many excellent studies of folk narratives in particular communities. Fenton (1968) and Waugh (1916) are the major early sources on Iroquoian food lore.

BIBLIOGRAPHY

Beauchamp, William M. 1922. *Iroquois Folk Lore Gathered from the Six Nations of New York*. Syracuse: Dehler Press.

Converse, Harriet, 1908. *Myths and Legends of the New York State Iroquois*. New York State Museum Bulletins, No. 125.

Fenton, William N., ed. 1968. *Parker on the Iroquois: Iroquois Uses of Maize and Other Food Plants; the Code of Handsome Lake, the Seneca Prophet; the Constitution of the Five Nations*. Syracuse: Syracuse University Press.

Kurath, Gertrude P. 1961. *Effects of Environment on Cherokee-Iroquois Ceremonialism, Music, and Dance*. Bureau of American Ethnology Bulletins, No. 180.

Morgan, Lewis Henry. 1962 (1851). *The League of the Iroquois*. Chicago: University of Chicago Press.

Smith, Erminnie A. 1883. *Myths of the Iroquois at the Six Nations' Reserve*. Yale University Publications in Anthropology, No. 65.

Waugh, F. W. 1916. *Iroquois Foods and Food Preparations*. Canadian Geological Survey Memoirs, No. 86.

Thomas S. McIlwain

KIOWA

GEOGRAPHY AND HISTORY

Originally a Plains Indian people, Kiowas today reside mostly in rural southwestern Oklahoma and number about 10,000 to 12,000 persons. Officially, they are collectively known as the Kiowa Tribe of Oklahoma, a political entity that governs the economic workings of the tribe as a whole. Socially and culturally, however, Kiowas are enormously diverse: outside their everyday lives as typical Americans (who must find work and pay the bills), families, organizations, and localized communities approach Kiowa tradition from as many different perspectives as there are families, organizations, and localized communities. The Kiowa language is often spoken with significant variation from one community to the next; visions of heritage and tradition differ between and among the dozens of Kiowa organizations that host dances, powwows, hand games, and other so-called Indian doings; and storytelling varies greatly from family to family. This is not to suggest that Kiowas do not agree on "that which is Kiowa." On the contrary, Kiowas are a proud people with a rich, common heritage. But because their culture is vibrant and dynamic, there are varied interpretations of that culture.

Appreciating the varied and diverse roots of modern Kiowa traditions also resides with understanding their distinctive past. In the nineteenth century, Kiowas lived the vast majority of their lives in bands, traveling in small groups, gathering uncultivated plants and hunting wild game for food. Like other Plains peoples their lives revolved around hunting bison, which were once plentiful throughout the Great Plains. Through much of the year, small bands followed these buffalo as the animals migrated through the southern Plains—the territory that the Kiowas eventually settled after being driven from the northern Plains by the Lakota and other groups.

Like many other Plains peoples, Kiowas were master horsemen, collectively owning herds that numbered into the thousands. These horses were critical for both hunting and travel, but they also signified the status of their owners (that is, the more

Group portrait of Kiowa family, 1908. (Courtesy Library of Congress)

horses you owned, the more wealthy and powerful you were). Trading and raiding for horses was thus a major part of Kiowa life as was the warrior lifestyle that came to define the Plains way of life.

These small, mobile bands were often led by men who were both skilled leaders and tenacious warriors. Language, song, and narrative traditions developed within these individual bands in ways that made each band distinctive, but not so different that a member of one band could not get along in another band (indeed, people often moved fluidly from one band to another).

Each year in midsummer, these small bands came together to form even larger bands, who, in turn, camped together to hunt buffalo. During these gatherings, Kiowas held their annual *K'aw-tow*, "Gathering," generally known among Plains Indians as the Sun Dance. The Kiowas camped in a large camp circle, with each larger band, or "sub-tribe" (there were six, including the Plains Apache or "Kiowa-Apache," who are linguistically unrelated to the Kiowas), camped along the circumference. In the middle of this arrangement, the Kiowas built their Medicine Lodge, where the actual Sun Dance—an elaborate ceremony celebrating the buffalo hunt—was held. During and after the actual Sun Dance, various Kiowa organizations—often transcending band organization—came together to hold feasts, perform dances, and sing songs. The majority of these were men's military or warrior organizations, each of which performed their own dances and songs.

By the time of Euro-American contact in the early nineteenth century, the Kiowas, along with their allies the Comanches, dominated much of the southern Plains and warred against other powerful nations such as the Cheyenne and Arapaho. The Kiowas and Comanches presented a formidable threat to American settlement and expansion, especially to the railroad, which cut right through their territory. After several unsuccessful attempts to subdue the Kiowas, the U.S. government petitioned for peace in the Medicine Lodge Treaty of 1867, in which the Kiowas agreed to cease their hostilities and resettle (along with the Apaches and Comanches) on a reservation in southwestern Oklahoma in return for several annuities promised by the government. Among the promises were to prevent white settlement and hunting on the reservation, provide schools, and supply resources for learning how to farm. In the intervening years, these promises were only partially fulfilled—even when the Kiowas complained regularly and often of white encroachment on their lands and unfulfilled expectations of schools and other promised resources. These concerns repeatedly fell on deaf ears, especially because the prevailing attitude of the U.S. government was most often one of apathy and indifference for the plight of Indian peoples. This began to change, however, when Christian reformers convinced President Ulysses S. Grant to initiate the so-called Peace Policy, which would place the Indians' assimilation in the hands of Christian churches. Christians had a moral responsibility, the argument went, to lift their fallen brethren from their state of savagery. Although this attitude may repulse us today, it directly challenged the contemporary attitude that "the only good Indian was a dead Indian." Indians were people, argued church leaders, who were perfectly capable of American civilization if given the chance.

RELIGIOUS BELIEFS AND PRACTICES

Like the promises of the U.S. government, many "official" church policies ultimately failed because, as historian Francis Paul Prucha has argued, they were based on white rather than Indian goals. Paradoxically, however, the church activities on the Kiowa-Comanche-Apache (KCA) reservation had both devastating and beneficial consequences for Kiowa people. In general, the Kiowas practiced an open cosmology—that is, they added and subtracted religious beliefs and practices as their needs changed. For example, they had learned and adopted the Sun Dance from other Plains tribes in the pre-reservation era. Replacing one belief system for another wholesale—which the missionaries demanded—was not fully and willingly embraced by most Kiowas, although some most certainly did. While missionaries often strongly discouraged traditional Kiowa practices, the Kiowas—to the chagrin of many missionaries (but with the encouragement of some)—integrated Christian beliefs with their older beliefs, which would lead to a unique blending of the old and new in a syncretism that lasts to the present.

One particularly powerful way this blending emerged was through song, in which Kiowa people would combine the general sound and structure of old Kiowa songs with Christian themes. In some cases, Kiowa singers replaced English with Kiowa words in popular Christian hymns such as "Amazing Grace." But the vast majority of these Kiowas hymns were original compositions in the Kiowa language. Like the rest of Kiowa song, they were received by the godly through inspiration, prayer, or meditation. The Kiowa word for song, *daw-gyah*, literally means to "receive," "gather," or "catch" power. Over the years, Kiowa singers would receive hundreds of these songs, many of which still exist and are sung throughout Kiowa country in various community churches.

Each of these community churches has always approached the singing and interpretation of these Kiowa hymns in varying ways. But this is not surprising given that when the Kiowas settled on the KCA reservation, they generally settled in small communities that reflected their original, relatively independent "sub-tribes" or bands. The Kiowas were probably most attracted to the Baptist and Methodist faiths—the dominant religious denominations then and now—because of the relative community independence that these church organizations stressed at the time.

The Kiowas' approach to Christianity paralleled their approach to other emergent religious traditions such as the Ghost Dance and the Native American Church (NAC). The Ghost Dance was a messianic movement that spread throughout the Plains in the later nineteenth century—a tradition that the Kiowas practiced, after a short respite near the turn of the century, until the 1920s. Many Kiowas say that some of its tenets, including parts of its song practice, were integrated into Pentecostalism, which has grown in influence since the decline of the Ghost Dance. The NAC, or the "Peyote Road," brought together traditional beliefs and practices (and eventually, Christian beliefs and practices as well) with Peyotism, a movement that began with the Comanches and eventually spread throughout Indian country. Today many Kiowa families hold Peyote meetings, which feature an all-night service held outside in a tipi and include singing Peyote songs and taking the Peyote sacrament, a morning breakfast, a lunch, and lots of visiting that usually lasts well into the afternoon. And in true Kiowa style, each family—who may also be Methodist or Baptist or Pentecostal—approaches their Peyote meetings through the lens of their own family background.

DANCE

In addition to their religious traditions, the Kiowas also have a vibrant dance culture. Soon after the turn of the century, the Dawes Act of 1887, a plan to break up reservation land, was applied on the KCA reservation. Individual families were forced to accept 160-acre plots of land, and the rest of the reservation was opened for white settlement. To be sure, the Plains life that the Kiowas had known just a few decades before had rapidly disappeared. The Sun Dance, for example, had lost its significance; so too had warrior organizations, their dances, and their songs. But this began to change during World Wars I and II, when a common American and Kiowa experience with and focus on warfare coincided. The Kiowas' old warrior dances and songs found renewed significance as individual families began to hold dances such as the War Expedition Dance for their sons (and recently daughters) who were going off to fight or serve overseas. And when their sons and daughters returned, they held dances for their newest Kiowa warriors, dances such as the Scalp Dance and Victory Dance, which are performed by women. Kiowa families continue to host these dances for their sons and daughters who are in the military.

This revival of old dances was perhaps most pronounced during and after World War II and the Korean War. One warrior's organization, Tonkonga, or "Black Legs," was revived in 1958 as the Kiowa Veterans Association. Membership was restricted to male veterans of war, and twice a year the organization continues to host a weekend dance, which features the original dances and songs of the organization, the public recitation of battle stories, and lots of eating and visiting.

Several years before the Tonkonga was revived, however, a new women's organization, called the Kiowa War Mothers, was started. The organization originated in 1944 as a local chapter of the American War Mothers, a national organization for mothers of war veterans. But unlike the national organization, the Kiowa War Mothers would come to have their own dance and song tradition. Kiowa singers put new Kiowa words into the songs of the Round Dance (a social dance) and created a new song genre, Kiowa War Mothers songs. Importantly, these songs reflected a new experience of being both American and Kiowa. One song, for example, says, "Our warriors went to fight the Germans overseas; they returned to us safe." Dozens of songs like this were made during and after the war years; and once a year the Kiowa War Mothers still host a dance, which, of course, features the singing of War Mothers songs, perhaps the most anticipated part of the event.

Although the celebrations of the Kiowa Black Legs and the Kiowa War Mothers are extremely important to Kiowa culture and identity, not all Kiowa dances have evolved directly from the warrior tradition. The story of the Kiowa's O-ho-mah Lodge is a case in point. During the reservation era, native peoples were in increased contact with one another. The railroad, for example, made travel easy and accessible. And popular movements like the Ghost Dance and the Native American Church spread rapidly. Another popular movement that spread throughout Plains Indian communities was the so-called War Dance, although it had little to do with war. On the northern Plains it was also known as the Grass Dance; on the southern Plains it was also known as the Omaha Dance, among other names. Many different Plains tribes tell stories about its origin, but the story the Kiowas tell originates the dance with the Omaha (another Plains Indian tribe), who passed the dance and its songs to the Cheyenne, who in turn passed it to the Kiowas in the 1880s: hence why Kiowas call the dance *O-ho-mah* (a derivative of "Omaha"). The Kiowas would organize their own version of the dance, calling it the O-ho-mah Lodge.

THE O-HO-MAH LODGE

Since the 1880s, the O-ho-mah Lodge has never ceased in its practice. Each year during the summer months, the organization holds its yearly celebration, which features the organization's official dances and songs, giveaways, and lots of visiting and eating. An anticipated part of the event is the recitation of stories about the dance's songs: families regularly announce their ownership of individual songs, often publicly giving away to singers and others in honor of the song's performance. The formal dance is for men and boys only. The O-ho-mah Lodge is a men's organization, but since O-ho-mah is also a social dance, women and children join in the dancing in the evening when the "official" afternoon dances are complete.

The social component of O-ho-mah quickly spread throughout the Kiowa community during the war years, often supplementing other dances like the War Expedition Dance. The same was true in other Plains Indian communities. In fact, the popular manifestation of the dance would eventually incorporate men's and women's styles of dress and dance, and by the 1960s and 1970s the "powwow," as it came to be known, dominated the public life of Indian dances throughout the Plains. While today the powwow has spread all over Indian country, the popular style of the War Dance evolved in very different trajectories from the original Omaha or Grass Dance. Nevertheless, the O-ho-mah Lodge as well as the many organizations like it in other Plains communities still practices the original ceremony.

The O-ho-mah or War Dance is important to consider because it helped to popularize and disseminate another dance—perhaps the Kiowas' most popular dance. Like that of the War Dance, its English name has little to do with its actual practice. Its pre-reservation history is very different from O-ho-mah, but it took a similar route in its popularity and incorporation into the powwow. The Gourd Dance was originally the dance of another warrior organization, the *Taimpego* (which has a number of different translations, including "Skunkberry Peoples," "Crazy Horses," or "Unafraid of Death"). In the original dance, members of the Taimpego stood in place shaking to the rhythm of song rattles made of buffalo hide. When the dance was revived in the 1950s, these rattles were generally made of tin. The Kiowa men who revived the dance called their new organization the Kiowa Gourd Clan and opened its practice not just to veterans, as was the custom of the Kiowa Black Legs, but to all men. But like the War Dance, the Gourd Dance became extremely popular as it was integrating into the powwow tradition. It would, by the 1970s and 1980s, replace the popularity of the War Dance. Today dozens of organizations host Gourd Dances, often under the heading of powwow, throughout the year. Although it is "officially" known as a men's dance, in its popular form, women, men, and children all participate in contemporary Gourd Dances, though only men shake rattles.

GAMES, ARTS, AND CRAFTS

Although the Kiowas are perhaps best known for their dance and song traditions (and many more remain unmentioned here), they have other less visible, albeit still public, traditions as well. One such practice is the Handgame, an old gambling game. Teams made up of both women and men sit directly across from one another. Singing lively songs and using complex hand signals, each team guesses the whereabouts of small sticks, which the opposing team hides in their hands. It seems simple enough, but Handgamers are extremely talented in tricking their opponents: the game's real challenge is to follow the sticks through tricky and fast hand movements while the opposing team is distracting you with their jokes, taunts, and songs. Its practice is popular throughout the Plains, and Kiowas from Kiowa communities regularly compete against each other and with teams from other tribes—especially the Crows, with whom the Kiowas have a long, enduring relationship.

These relatively public traditions such as the Handgame, the Gourd Dance, or Kiowa hymns also go hand in hand with more individualized traditions and practices. These include the more traditional arts—for example, beadwork and tipi making—as well as modern art, with which the Kiowas also has longstanding affiliation. In the 1920s and 1930s, a group of Kiowa artists (known as the Kiowa Five) became famous for their skill in building on older drawing traditions such as ledger art and the famous "Kiowa calendars" to create a new form of popular art. Since then, dozens of Kiowa artists have also built on this popular art tradition. But importantly, traditional and modern arts now coincide in everything from the making of dance clothing to painting on canvas. And through their individual and differing approaches to these arts, well-known Kiowa artists such as Vanessa Paukeigope Jennings and Robert Redbird actively continue to maintain a vibrant, dynamic, and evolving tradition.

STORYTELLING

This recalls an earlier point: from popular art to dance and song, Kiowas have always approached their traditions in various and differing ways. In no tradition is this more evident than in storytelling. It is, as anthropologist and Kiowa tribal member Gus Palmer Jr. argues, perhaps the most important of all Kiowa traditions. While story maintains the significance and meaning of song, dance, or art, it also maintains connections between Kiowa people, powerfully elaborating their relationships to one another. Distinctive versions of stories circulate through the Kiowa community, and when Kiowa people gather—even in today's world where television has come to replace storytelling traditions—narrative still takes a central role in defining the dynamism of Kiowa culture. Indeed, everyday life is imbued with story; and when it comes to maintaining "our Kiowa ways," narrative gives life and continuity to every other tradition.

STUDIES OF KIOWA FOLKLORE

A good place to begin learning about this narrative tradition and its importance to Kiowa life is Palmer (2003) (see also Parsons [1929]). For a much larger survey of Kiowa folklore, see Boyd (1981, 1983). For general discussions of Kiowa history and culture, see Ellis (1996), Marriot (1945), Mooney (1898), and Momaday (1969). On dance, song and art traditions, see Ewers and Mooney (1978), Hail (2000), Lassiter (1998), and Meadows (1999). On Kiowa religion, see Kracht (1989) and Lassister, Ellis, and Kotay (2002). A plethora of materials are available on Kiowa song, sold mostly by commercial dealers, including Canyon Records (Phoenix, Arizona), Indian House Records (Taos, New Mexico), and the Smithsonian Institution. Two Kiowa song recordings, produced by Billy Evans Horse and Luke Eric Lassiter, are available in most major university research libraries: "Billy Evans Horse Sings Kiowas Gourd Dance Songs" and "Kiowa Powwow Songs." Finally, a sample of Kiowa songs (to accompany Lassiter 1998) can be heard at www.uapress.arizona .edu/extras/kiowa/kiowasng.htm.

BIBLIOGRAPHY

Boyd, Maurice. 1981, 1983. *Kiowa Voices*. 2 volumes. Fort Worth: Texas Christian University Press.

Ellis, Clyde. 1996. *To Change Them Forever: Indian Education at the Rainy Mountain Boarding School, 1893–1920*. Norman: University of Oklahoma Press.

Ewers, John C., and James Mooney. 1978. *Murals in the Round: Painted Tipis of the Kiowa and Kiowa-Apache Indians*. Washington, DC: Smithsonian Institution Press.

Hail, Barbara A. 2000. *Gifts of Pride and Love: Kiowa and Comanche Cradles*. Bristol, RI: Haffenreffer Museum of Anthropology.

Kracht, Benjamin. 1989. Kiowa Religion. Ph.D. diss., Southern Methodist University.

Lassiter, Luke E. 1998. *The Power of Kiowa Song: A Collaborative Ethnography*. Tucson: University of Arizona Press, 1998.

Lassiter, Luke Eric, Clyde Ellis, and Ralph Kotay. 2002. *The Jesus Road: Kiowas, Christianity, and Indian Hymns*. Lincoln: University of Nebraska Press.

Marriot, Alice. 1945. *The Ten Grandmothers*. Norman: University of Oklahoma Press, 1945.

Meadow, William C. 1999. *Kiowa, Apache, and Comanche Military Societies: Enduring Veterans, 1800 to the Present*. Austin: University of Texas Press.

Momaday, N. Scott. 1969. *The Way to Rainy Mountain*. Albuquerque: University of New Mexico Press.

Mooney, James. 1898. Calendar History of the Kiowa Indians. *Annual Report of the Bureau of American Ethnology* 17: 129–445.

Palmer, Gus, Jr. 2003. *Telling Stories the Kiowa Way*. Tucson: University of Arizona Press.

Parsons, Elsie Clews. 1929. *Kiowa Tales*. Memoirs of the American Folklore Society, No. 22.

Luke Eric Lassiter

LAKOTA

GEOGRAPHY AND HISTORY

Best known by the nineteenth-century term *Sioux* (a French corruption of the Algonkian word for "vipers"), the Lakota are part of the Seven Council Fires, a confederation of eastern, central, and western peoples speaking mutually intelligible dialects and sharing a set of common customs and beliefs. These dialects are part of a larger language family, Siouan, that includes Crow, Hidatsa, Mandan, Omaha-Ponca, Iowa, Otoe, Missouri, Assiniboine, and Quapah. The easternmost group, the Santee, account for four of the fires: Mdewakanton (Spirit Lake Village), Wahpeton (Leaf Village), Wahpekute (Leaf Shooters), and Sisseton (sometimes translated as Fish Scale Village). The centrally located Yankton make up two council fires: the Yankton (End Village) and Yanktonai (Little End Village). The Teton are the westernmost council fire. The eastern groups refer to themselves

Four Lakota women standing, three holding infants in cradleboards, and a Lakota man on horseback, in front of a tipi, probably on or near Pine Ridge Reservation (1891). (Courtesy Library of Congress)

in their own language as the Dakota, whereas the Tetons call themselves Lakota. This word means "friend" or "ally." The Tetons are themselves divided into seven groups: Sicangu (also Brule, Burnt Thighs), Hunkpapa (End of the Camp Circle), Miniconjou (Planters by the Water), Oglala (They Scatter Their Own), Oohenonpa (Two Kettles), Itazipco (also Sans Arcs, Without Bows), and Sihasapa (Blackfeet). Social scientists today use these specific terms as well as the collective *Sioux* to refer to the people of the original Seven Councils.

Seven Council Fires territory spans three ecological zones: woodlands, tall-grass and short-grass prairies. There are also isolated mountain ranges in the west. Groups followed a seasonal pattern—breaking into smaller units and camping in the bottomlands during the harsh winters, reassembling into larger groups in the spring and summer for communal hunts and rituals. Summers are hot and dry with spectacular lightning and hailstorms. Winters can be severe, and people sought protection from the weather by camping in the river and stream valleys and insulating their tipis with brush windbreaks. Long dark winter evenings were one of the traditional times for telling stories. These tales often reflected and even explained the surrounding landscape and were told both to entertain and to put children to sleep. Adults also were interested in hearing these stories, particularly if narrated by an expert teller.

The Lakota and Dakota believe in the kinship of all creation, symbolized by the closing of Lakota prayers with the phrase "for all my relatives." Without set doctrine or central authority, religion balances innovative personal experience with tradition governed by spiritual leaders familiar with beliefs and rituals handed down through time. One seeks a vision on one's own, but it is authenticated and validated by the larger community and by spiritual leaders who act as ritual specialists, healers, seers, and guides. Religion still permeates the Lakota and Dakota worldview. Events are begun with prayer, and the contemporary revival of Lakota and Dakota culture is seen primarily as a spiritual revival. These people were organized into bands based on kinship and social alliance. Leaders where chosen for their abilities in warfare and their generosity. Storytelling was an important way to validate individuals' qualifications for leadership.

Two Lakota men, Stands and Looks Back and Kills the Buzzard, in canoe on river (1902). (Courtesy Library of Congress)

During times when the U.S. government and European church groups actively suppressed Lakota rituals, Native practices went underground, while Christian rites were more openly adapted to fit Lakota beliefs. Traditional Lakota leaders assert that everyone prays to the same God, and today widespread tolerance for different religious expression exists on the reservation. Active Christians, often catechists or lay readers, also continued to practice traditional religion. But some tension occurs over who may engage in traditional Lakota religious rituals. Some hold that because the Lakota recognize and include in religious rituals the four colors, red, white, black, and yellow, the religion is open to all believers. Others hold that Lakota ritual was given to the Lakota and should not be exploited by outsiders or sold by Lakota to a willing audience of those seeking authentic religious experience. The respect that Lakota pay to individual choice has worked against a consistent policy on non-natives engaging in Lakota rituals, but all would agree that these sacred ways must always be treated respectfully.

Historians hold that the Lakota gradually moved west under the pressure of expanding populations of Europeans who where extirpating native peoples from their homelands. These people also moved to utilize the resources of the prairies, using new technologies of the horse, firearms, and later the fur trade. Some Lakotas, however, cite ethnoarcheology and traditional oral narratives to substantiate their claims that they were always located in the Black Hills area. They contend that stories of Indians coming to North America by a land bridge and Lakota only recently occupying the Black Hills (that is, during the 1770s) are ways to disfranchise the Lakota and not honor treaty obligations, particularly the illegal taking of the sacred Black Hills.

The United States made a series of treaties with the Dakota and Lakota. In 1851 the Eastern Dakota signed the treaties of Mendota and Traverse des Sioux. A diminishing land base and pressure from white settlers fomented the Minnesota Conflict of 1862. As a result the Santee fled west and into Canada. Those remaining were exiled, eventually to Nebraska. The Yankton signed the Treaty of Prairie de Chien in 1830. This and subsequent treaties diminished the Yankton land base and consolidated the bands onto reservations. The Yankton generally maintained peaceful relations with the United States. The most important in a series of treaties signed with the Yankton and Tetons were the Fort Laramie Treaties of 1851 and 1868. Conflicts with the United States arose as more and more Americans moved through the Lakota territories first as part of the gold rush and then as settlers. When the government ordered all bands to return to the reservations, some Lakota and Cheyenne refused, resulting in the Battle of the Little Big Horn. Difficult conditions on the reservations, diminishing resources, and the hope of reviving the old ways encouraged Lakota acceptance of the Ghost Dance, a ritual designed to resurrect the ancestors and restore the buffalo. In December 1890, the Indian agent on Pine Ridge Reservation brought in soldiers to curb this ritual. During an altercation at Wounded Knee the soldiers began firing on a whole encampment of Indians, resulting in a horrifying massacre.

While their land base was further diminished by the General Allotment Act of 1887, which assigned set amounts of reservation land to individual men and women and then sold off the "surplus," the Lakota and Dakota struggled both to adapt to the world around them and to maintain their own traditions and identity. The government and churches followed an assimilationist program through boarding and day schools and the teaching of English.

The Indian Reorganization Act of 1934 allowed the Lakota greater self-governance, though the structure of government, the tribal council, remains a point of contention on many Lakota reservations. In the 1960s and 1970s a series of public protests by Native American people such as the occupation of Alcatraz Island and the takeover of the Bureau of Indian Affairs office in Washington, D.C., demonstrated dissatisfaction with government treatment of Indians. The most prominent of these protests occurred in 1973 at Wounded Knee. Although Lakota people have mixed opinions on the appropriateness of these actions, most agree that they helped restore pride in being Lakota and in following Indian traditions. The Supreme Court recognized the illegality of the alienation of the Black Hills, and while the federal government has offered a monetary settlement to compensate for the loss of these lands, which the Lakota hold sacred, the struggle for their physical return continues.

MYTHS, LEGENDS, AND FOLKTALES

Because Lakota and Dakota once lived in nomadic bands, some traditions are unique to specific individuals, small groups, or groups of religious leaders. Trade and social interaction with surrounding groups brought in stories from and about neighboring tribes. The way in which the people themselves group their rich tradition of stories falls into two categories: those that are fanciful (not true in a literal sense) and those that are true (stories of a historical nature). Content, actors, and rhetorical devices mark the differences. Historical narratives were told during the day, and fanciful tales were told at night. Some say if you tell the stories at the wrong times, you will grow hair all over your body.

Some stories are familiar to all. Others are less widely known, often the product of a creative mind engaged in the ongoing tradition. Elements from one story can be incorporated into another, and skilled storytellers have considerable creative latitude. Stories tend to be brief and episodic, focusing on what the characters do and how they behave. They often address social or political situations, but the moral of the story is situated in the context of the telling as much as in the content of the tale. Thus, the hearer can draw conclusions about his or her own undesirable behavior when compared to that in the story without being shamed publicly.

A variety of actors appears in these stories: human, animal, and supernatural. Both genders are represented, generally within their cultural and social roles but sometimes violating these roles. The most sacred person in Lakota stories is the White Buffalo Calf Woman. This supernatural figure appears to two hunters, one of whom has evil designs on her and is destroyed. The other lives to tell the people to prepare for her coming. When she arrives at the camp, she gives the people the sacred pipe and teaches them how to live properly. When she departs, she transforms herself into a series of differently colored buffalo.

Heroes such as Iron Hawk, White Plume Boy, Falling Star, and Stone Boy have mystical origins and superhuman powers. They go on adventures, defeat powerful enemies, and rescue people. The Stone Boy story is a good example. Four brothers and a sister once lived together. One day each of the brothers goes hunting, and none returns. Their saddened sister swallows a stone and miraculously gives birth to Stone Boy, who quickly grows up and leaves to find his uncles. He discovers their bundled bones in an old woman's tent. He cleverly destroys the old woman, builds a fire, and sets up a sweat lodge, where his uncles' bones are restored to life. Stone Boy has many other adventures, often triumphing through use of mystical power.

The trickster Iktomi (in the east: Unktomi) is a human with spider-like characteristics who is rarely helpful, often causing other people trouble, which usually backfires upon him. In one story, Iktomi hears music and discovers mice having a big dance inside a buffalo skull. He decides to push his head into the skull, and the mice run away. Iktomi has not only ruined the dance, but now he has the skull stuck on his head. In one version of the story, he smashes the skull on a rock and hurts his own head. In another, he decides to soak the skull in water and drowns himself. In yet another, he sets the skull on fire and burns his own head.

Fearsome figures abound. Thunder Beings are imagined as large birds whose eyes flash and voices cry out. Giants from the north bring cold. Old women have mystical powers; serpents live in lakes, rivers, and streams; cannibals eat everything and everyone in sight; and horrible creatures have two faces. A Double Face story can serve as an example. Once a young lady refused to marry anyone in her tribe but agreed to elope with a handsome suitor from far away. She and her pet beaver sneak off with him one night, but soon she realizes it is the wicked Double Face, not her handsome suitor. Double Face makes her pull lice from his hair to put him to sleep. When he is soundly asleep, she ties lengths of his hair to each of the tipi poles like a spider web. She runs away, but Double Face gets loose and pursues her to a riverbank. There her pet beaver quickly constructs a bridge for her, just strong enough for her to escape, but just weak enough to plunge Double Face into the torrent, where he drowns. The girl returns home and marries the handsome suitor, and all honor the beaver.

Animals in Lakota stories have human qualities: they speak, hunt, go off on quests, have social institutions, and interact with human beings and other animal species. Humans who respect animals are rewarded, as are animals who care for humans. Often all but one of a group of animals abuse a hero. When the tables are turned, all the animals are punished or destroyed except for the one kind animal. Animals have their own political and social organization, but no sharp divide exists between animals and humans, and each can transform themselves from one form to the other.

Transformation in general is an important theme in Lakota stories. Orphan boys turn into handsome young men. Ugly men turn into beautiful young women. Old women are sometime dangerous monsters in disguise. Even the landscape can transform. The following story uses transformation to explain the shape of the landmark Devil's Tower, known to Lakota as Bear Lodge. A bear was chasing two children, a brother and sister. They prayed for divine intervention as they ran, and suddenly the ground rose to form a very high butte. The frustrated bear repeatedly jumped up to grab the children, scratching long lines into the side of the butte that can be seen even today. The brother and sister lived their lives atop the butte, and their spirits can be seen as two small clouds visible from time to time.

Love is also an important theme. Men achieve war honors or accumulate horses to gain brides. Parents sometimes spurn and other times encourage the suitors of their daughters. People fall in love with stars or with animals disguised as humans. They are tricked into loving someone who looks beautiful but is really horrible or spurn someone who looks horrible but is secretly beautiful. One story tells of a Lakota man married to an Arikara woman. When he decides to take a second wife, his first wife becomes angry, refusing to strike camp when the rest of the group moves. She remains alone in her tipi. Later, the husband sends his brother back to see if she has relented. When the brother enters the tipi, he discovers that she has changed to stone. The name of the Standing Rock reservation derives from this story. In another version the daughter of a chief was scolded for telling a lie and turned into this rock.

Kinship is essential to Lakota stories. Older brothers rescue younger ones. Tricksters call someone "brother" to deceive him. Younger brothers or nephews rescue older brothers and uncles. The Lakota believe in a relatedness of all creation. Being a relative implies social and moral responsibilities among the people, and enlarging families through adoption is common. Orphans, widows, strangers, and beloved children seek their place in the social world and succeed insofar as they fulfill their kinship obligations.

Dakota and Lakota creation stories are concerned less with the beginnings of physical reality than with how people come to the earth or how society begins. One important creation account chronicles the life of the Lakota when they lived with the Buffalo people in the underworld until some of them were tricked into emerging through a cave. Another tells of a great flood that destroyed many peoples (their blood is found today as pipestone in Minnesota quarries). One maiden retreated to a high hill to avoid the flood and was taken up into the sky by an eagle. The woman had twins whose father was the eagle himself. They began a new tribe, the Dakota.

Most Lakota stories have humorous elements while others are completely farcical. The humor often revolves around someone being deceived. One tale combines the traditional ghost story with the humor of tricking people. Four warriors go out to raid horses from the Pawnee. Unsuccessful, they start home, but because they forgot to bring extra pairs of moccasins on the raid, the ones they have soon wear out. They spot a tipi in which a dead man is laid out. Three of them decide to pay their respects to the man and then take his shirt to repair their moccasins. The fourth warns of vengeance from the man's ghost and leaves. Out of sight, he quickly covers himself with mud and an animal skin. He sneaks back to the tipi and scares his three companions so badly they faint from sheer terror. The deceiver then cleans up, rejoins his companions, and listens straight-faced while they tell him what happened. When they return to their people, the deceiver tells everyone what he did, so the whole community can laugh at the other three.

Vision Talks, War Stories, "As-Told-To" Stories

Not all Lakota and Dakota storytelling treats the fanciful. To become a spiritual leader, men and women must have engaged in a variety of religious rituals and had visionary experiences. A vision talk is the equivalent of presenting credentials or a resume when applying for a job. Given before a ritual begins, the talk is never meant as an opportunity to show off and often features self-deprecating humor, statements of the speaker's unworthiness to lead rituals despite his or her accomplishments, and advance apologies in case the ritual is not carried out perfectly. While religious experience is intensely personal, receivers of a vision can explain the experience to spiritual leaders, who help interpret and validate the vision. Vision talks are considered sacred and are not discussed in everyday conversation.

War stories are a very important part of Lakota and Dakota life, allowing an individual to demonstrate his bravery and leadership abilities by telling of his accomplishments in battle at large communal gatherings, particularly the Sun Dance. Normally witnesses verify the speaker's story. Today war veterans are held in high esteem and have important roles at social events such as powwows and funerals.

Before literacy came to the Dakota and Lakota with the missionaries, they relied on memory and artistic representations to record history. The winter count chronicled the single most important event for each year in a group's history, which was represented by a simple drawing that served as a mnemonic device. With literacy, a phrase associated with that event was added to summarize and start the story for the keeper of the count.

Individuals painted images of their war deeds on hides, on tipi covers, and inside liners. With the coming of Europeans, paper became available, often bound into ledger books. Amos Bad Heart Bull was one of the most important ledger book historians, expanding war deed drawings to include explanations of Lakota ritual while documenting important interactions with the government and chronicling early life on the reservation. He added written Lakota text to many drawings, thus shifting the genre from pure representational art to a mixture of text and image, and he wrote down his narrative instead of reciting it. While ledger drawings and winter counts were intended to serve as historical narratives, they have become a form of commercial art, copied for sale to outsiders.

With the coming of missionaries both Dakota and Lakota learned how to read and write their own language as well as English and adapted their oral traditions to the written word. There is a long tradition of autobiography. The Dakota physician Charles Eastman not only recorded folklore but also wrote his autobiography and general works about Indian life. This is also true for Luther Standing Bear, Susan Bordeaux Bettelyoun, Josephine Waggoner, and most recently Delphine Red Shirt. Ella Deloria wrote cultural descriptions as well as a novel, edited and posthumously published as *Waterlily*, about Lakota life at the time of European contact.

A form of autobiography is the "as-told-to" story in which Dakota or Lakota narrate their experiences to an outsider (sometimes an anthropologist but often scholars from other disciplines or simply interested individuals). The most prominent of these narratives is *Black Elk Speaks*, recorded and reshaped by poet-scholar John Neihardt. This work includes folk stories along with Black Elk's vision talk and kill talk.

Although the Lakota and Dakota did not have theater in the Western sense, they did develop an important tradition of acting out visions. (One noted instance of this was Black Elk's acting out his horse vision with the help of his community.) This sacred performance is more like a medieval mystery play than a stage show. In the late 1800s, Lakota and Dakota adapted dancing, horsemanship, and prowess in battle through staged conflicts, helping to create the popular Wild West show. This tradition continued with cultural performances of dance and religious ritual. They were and continue to be important ways for Lakota and Dakota to travel, enjoy different experiences, and create friendships and alliances with a vast network of people. The Lakota have also been involved in movie performances for a considerable period of time.

MUSIC AND SONGS

The Lakota have a variety of musical forms and instruments, and contemporary Lakota music spans the gamut from traditional to highly innovative. In addition to voice, drum, flute, and rattle were the traditional instruments. Art and regalia can also have a musical dimension: bells, dewclaws, and tin cones play as people move about, especially in dances. Lakota songs can roughly be divided between ceremonial and social, one used for religious rituals and honors and the other used at powwows (which many consider sacred events) and other community gatherings. Some Lakota songs are considered public so that any group can sing. Other songs belong to individuals and are received through dreams and visions. Sacred songs include those sung at major rituals such as the Sun Dance, in sweat lodge ceremonies, during curing and healing rituals, and at adoption rituals, namings, wakes and burials, and death anniversary memorials. During the Ghost Dance era, many people received songs that referred to the coming world renewal anticipated by this belief. A large number of Christian hymns in Dakota and Lakota are sung at church services, funerals, and memorials. Native American Church (peyote) meetings also have a distinctive set of songs accompanied by rattle and water drum. Flute music was traditionally used for courting. Today it is an important performance piece with many accomplished players using both traditional and newly composed melodies. Finally, Lakotas and Dakotas have also adapted the genres of country-and-western, classical, rock, rap, and even jazz.

SPORTS AND GAMES

The Lakota have a wide variety of traditional games. Some of these such as the Hoop Game have mythic roots. This particular game was taught by a young man with a vision who rolled a hoop, whose wake revealed buffalo hoofprints. He taught the game to four respected men. Men played the game to ensure an abundance of buffalo and a successful hunt. It entailed throwing poles at a hoop with four scoring points on it. The Elk Game was also played by men before elk huts to ensure success. It involved tossing a hoop into the air and catching it or taking it from one's opponent on a special wand. Another skill game for men was the Webbed Hoop, in which spears were thrown into hoops with webbing with hope of striking the hoop in the center. The Moccasin Game also has mythic associations, one story saying that the trickster Iktomi invented the game and that it was first played among the spirits. Like the Hand Game the Moccasin Game entails guessing where an object is placed.

Women played a Peach Pit Game. Six pits were decorated on one side and left plain on the other. The pits were tossed, and different images earned different points. Sticks were used to keep the score and determine the winner. Another woman's skill game involved catching deer bones on a skewer. Although everyone might play this game, only women did so formally in competition. Many children's games and entertainments often taught social and economic roles. Boys played with miniature bows and arrows and had various games in which they shot at targets and played at hunting or warfare. Girls played with dolls and toy domestic items such as miniature travois, tipis, and baggage.

ARTS AND CRAFTS

Lakota art is integrated into Lakota life. Common implements such as bowls and pounding mallets were carefully decorated and colored. Tipi covers were painted with designs and graphic representations of great deeds, stone pipes used in religious rituals were artistically carved and decorated, and hide containers and buffalo robes were decorated with bright geometrical shapes. With the incursion of European art, the Lakota adapted new media such as glass beads, fabric, and paper to their own work. Today a strong artistic tradition of beadwork, quillwork, quilting, silver work, dollmaking, and carving flourishes. Lakota also engage in graphic arts such as painting, drawing, ceramics, and sculpture. Oscar Howe utilized both traditional drawing as well as the artistic styles of his day to create beautiful drawings, illustrations, and paintings. Other Lakota artists include Arthur Amiotte, Martin Red Bear, and Don Montilleaux.

CHALLENGES OF THE MODERN WORLD

When considering the folklore of the Lakota and Dakota, it is important to note that these people have themselves become part of the folklore of the American West and indeed part of world folklore. Elements of history and fantasy intertwine, making the Lakota into the iconic Plains Indian (or even the iconic Indian) in the minds of many. That tends to freeze these people in a partly mythic past and lead many to assume that contemporary Sioux are simply poor imitations of these mythic heroes. Many historians end the story of the Dakota with the Minnesota Uprising and the Lakota with the tragedy of Wounded Knee.

Despite deliberate attempts to suppress their culture in the 1800s and despite the global changes that all cultures experienced in the 1900s, Lakota and Dakota cultural life remains vibrant at the beginning of the twenty-first century. Efforts are being made today to preserve the Lakota and Dakota languages and to increase the number of speakers through language programs embedded in the educational system. Culture learned in the homes is now reinforced in grade school and high school and at tribal and non-tribal colleges and universities. Religious rituals flourish, and the people continue to tell their stories, historical and fanciful, in the day and in the evening, "for all our relatives."

According to the U.S. Bureau of the Census, in 1990 there were a total of 103,255 Sioux living on sixteen reservations in Minnesota, Montana, Nebraska, North Dakota, and South Dakota. Sioux live on eight Canadian reserves in Manitoba and Saskatchewan and number 5,420, according to the Canadian Department of Indian Affairs and Northern Development. Sioux also live in urban areas such as Rapid City, Sioux Falls, Chicago, and Minneapolis and—particularly as a result of their high enlistment rate in military service—on and near installations throughout the world. Many migrate frequently between the reservation and urban areas for work and to maintain kinship ties.

These people thrive today. The children play basketball and computer games while learning to honor their spiritual traditions and their relationships to one another. Adults not only retell and recreate the stories of their ancestors, but they also create new stories and retell history in newspapers, on the radio, and in popular and scholarly journals and books, contemporary music, and films.

STUDIES OF LAKOTA FOLKLORE

The most useful reference work on the Lakota is Volume 13 of the *Handbook of North American Indians*. This work has articles on each of the three subdivisions of the Dakota as well as two historical articles (DeMallie 2001a, 2001b, 2001c; Christaffererson 2001; Albers 2001). Significant cultural accounts from the nineteenth and early twentieth century include, for the Dakota, the writings of Pond (1986) and, for the Lakota, the works of Walker (1980, 1982, 1983). Contemporary historical works include those by Anderson (1984, 1986), Anderson and Woolworth (1988), Landes (1968), and Meyer (1993) for the Dakota and Gibbon (2003), Utley (1963, 1993), and Price (1996) for the Lakota and Dakota. Authors writing on Lakota religion and culture include anthropologists William Powers (1975, 1982, 1986, 1987), Marla Powers (1986), Grobsmith (1981), DeMallie and Parks (1987), and Bucko (1998).

Lakota and Dakota stories readily accessible in print include those recorded by Marie McLaughlin, who was part Santee (1974). Santee doctor Charles Eastman was a prolific writer, devoting many of his works to stories (Eastman 1904, Eastman and Eastman 1990 [1909], Eastman 1991 [1918]). Zitkala-Ša, a Yankton whose American name was Gertrude Bonnin, wrote stories for popular journals, which have been collected in two books: one specifically on oral narratives (1985a), the other containing creative stories of a more autobiographical nature (1985b). Anthropologist Ella Deloria collected an important series of stories (1974 [1932]). Lakota Luther Standing Bear also published a collection of stories (1988). Lakota storyteller Rosebud Yellow Robe also wrote a book of Lakota stories for children told to her by her father (1979). Virginia Driving Hawk Sneve has published a considerable amount on Lakota and European, two stories that intertwine in her own life (1972a, 1972b, 1974a, 1974b, 1993, 1995, 1997, Sneve and Himler 1993).

Two volumes of Santee stories were collected as part of the Depression-era Federal Writers' Project in Nebraska in 1939 (1939a, 1939b). These stories were culled from a Santee missionary newspaper called *The Word Carrier* published between 1883 and 1887. The Nebraska Curriculum Development Center also produced an anthology of Santee stories, some from published sources and some told by contemporary Santee (Frerichs and Olson 1979). A collection of Lakota stories was made at the same time (Workers of the South Dakota Writers' Project 1987). The work was illustrated by noted Lakota artist Oscar Howe. Another collection of stories was made on the Rosebud reservation in the summer of 1973 (Theisz 1975). A group of stories collected by German Jesuit Fr. Buechel, S.J., were reproduced and translated by Fr. Paul Manhardt, S.J. (1998). Authors of children's books have frequently drawn upon Lakota stories. Many Iktomi stories have been collected and published by English-American writer and illustrator Paul Goble (1988, 1989, 1990, 1991, 1994, 1998, 1999).

Helen Blish published and commented on Amos Bad Heart Bull's ledger (1967), Janet Berlo on Black Hawk's ledger (2000), and James Howard and Raymond Bucko on one of White Bull's ledgers (1998). Garrick Mallery was an early commentator on Winter Counts and picture "writing" in general (1972 [1888–1889]).

Individuals who have narrated their biographies, often including a wide variety of stories, to outsiders, include Bishop Harold Jones (Cochran 2000), John Lame Deer (Erdoes and Lame Deer 1972), his son Archie Fire Lame Deer (Erdoes and Lame Deer 1992), Mary Brave Bird (Erdoes and Brave Bird 1993), Severt Young Bear (Young Bear and Theisz 1994), Leonard Crow Dog (Erdoes and Crow Dog 1995), the Dull Knife family (Starita 1995), Pete Catches (Catches and Catches 1999), and Joseph Eagle Elk (Mohatt and Eagle Elk 2000).

Works on Lakota and Dakota music include those by Densmore (1918), Paige (1970), Theiz (1996), Powers (1968, 1980a, 1980b, 1988, 1990a, 1990b), and White Hat with John Around Him (Around Him and White Hat 1983). Recordings of Lakota music are readily available on compact discs from a variety of publishers.

The University of South Dakota houses a rich collection of Lakota oral narrative performances, which may be sampled at www.usd.edu/iais/oralhist/. Several recordings of Lakota oral performances are available. Frank Fools Crow tells the story of the White Buffalo Calf Woman in Lakota (Fools Crow and others 1977). The other side of the record is narrated in English. Episcopal priest and cultural expert Vine Deloria Sr. recorded a series of stories and songs (1976). Ben Black Elk, son of Holy Man Nicholas Black Elk, recorded a series of stories and reminiscences, which were later put on compact disc accompanied by Lakota songs performed by Warfield Moose Jr. (Black Elk and Moose Jr. 2002). A recent television special dramatized four Lakota stories in the context of a story of a Lakota boy journeying to a powwow with his grandfather (Barron 2003).

Although a remarkable number of Lakota and Dakota people either wrote their own versions in their native languages as well as in English or narrated stories to non-Native transcribers, the tellers have provided little commentary on these stories. The majority of commentary on Lakota folktales has been done by two scholars, Elaine Jahner and Julian Rice. Jahner has written about Lakota stories in general in her introduction to *Lakota Mythology* and has also produced analytical essays on Blood Clot Boy (1982), Stone Boy (1983), and White Plume Boy (1992). Rice has discussed the role of Lakota storytelling and storytellers in general as well as analyzed specific stories (1989, 1991, 1992, 1993, 1994).

The Buechel Memorial Lakota Museum has a virtual exhibition of traditional games at www.sfmission.org/museum/exhibits/games/woskate.shtml and of Winter Counts at www.sfmission.org/museum/exhibits/wintercounts/. For more extensive references, see Bucko's bibliography of Dakota and Lakota sources on-line at puffin.creighton.edu/lakota/biblio.html.

BIBLIOGRAPHY

Albers, Patricia. 2001. Santee. In *Handbook of North American Indians*, Vol. 13, Part 2, edited by R. J. DeMallie. Washington, DC: Smithsonian Institution. 761–776.

Anderson, Gary C. 1984. *Kinsmen of Another Kind: Dakota-White Relations in the Upper Mississippi Valley, 1650–1862*. Lincoln: University of Nebraska Press.

———. 1986. *Little Crow: Spokesman for the Sioux*. St. Paul: Minnesota Historical Society Press.

Anderson, Gary C., and Alan R. Woolworth, eds. 1988. *Through Dakota Eyes: Narrative Accounts of the Minnesota Indian War of 1862*. St. Paul: Minnesota Historical Society Press.

Around Him, John, and Albert White Hat. 1983. *Lakota Ceremonial Songs*. Rosebud, SD: Sinte Gleska College.

Barron, Steve. 2003. *Dreamkeeper* (film). Hallmark Entertainment.

Berlo, Janet Catherine. 2000. *Spirit Beings and Sun Dancers: Black Hawk's Vision of the Lakota World*. New York: George Braziller.

Black Elk, Benjamin, and Warfield Moose Jr. 2002. *Ben Black Elk Speaks* (sound recording). Yellow Spider. ASIN B00007802P.

Blish, Helen, ed. 1967. *A Pictographic History of the Oglala Sioux*. Lincoln: University of Nebraska Press.

Bucko, Raymond A., S.J. 1998. *The Lakota Ritual of the Sweat Lodge: History and Contemporary Practice*. Lincoln: University of Nebraska Press.

———. 2004. Lakota Woskate–Lakota Games. In *Lakota Material Culture Collection and Associated Notes*, edited by R. A. Bucko, M. Marshall, and F. Sapienza. Saint Francis, SD: Rosebud Educational Society.

Buechel, Eugene, S.J. 1998. *Lakota Tales and Texts in Translation*, translated by Paul Manhardt, S.J. 2 volumes. Chamberlain, SD: Tipi Press.

Catches, Pete S., Sr., and Peter V. Catches Jr. 1999. *Sacred Fireplace: Life and Teachings of a Lakota Medicine Man*. Santa Fe, NM: Clear Light Publishers.

Christaffererson, Dennis M. 2001. Sioux, 1930–2000. In *Handbook of North American Indians*, Vol. 13, Part 2, edited by R. J. DeMallie. Washington, DC: Smithsonian Institution.

Cochran, Mary E. 2000. *Dakota Cross-Bearer: The Life and World of a Native American Bishop*. Lincoln: University of Nebraska Press.

Deloria, Ella C. 1974 (1932). *Dakota Texts*. New York: AMS Press.

Deloria, Philip. 1989. *Eyanopapi—the Heart of the Sioux* (film).

Deloria, Vine, Sr. 1976. *Stories of the Lakota* (sound recording). Canyon Records C-6151.

DeMallie, Raymond J. 2001a. Sioux until 1850. In *Handbook of North American Indians*, Vol. 13, Part 2, edited by R. J. DeMallie. Washington, DC: Smithsonian Institution.

———. 2001b. Teton. In *Handbook of North American Indians*, Vol. 13, Part 2, edited by R. J. DeMallie. Washington, DC: Smithsonian Institution.

———. 2001c. Yankton and Yanktonai. In *Handbook of North American Indians*, Vol. 13, Part 2, edited by R. J. DeMallie. Washington, DC: Smithsonian Institution.

DeMallie, Raymond J., Jr., and Douglas R. Parks, eds. 1987. *Sioux Indian Religion: Tradition and Innovation*. Norman: University of Oklahoma Press.

Densmore, Frances. 1918. *Teton Sioux Music.* Bureau of American Ethnology Bulletins, No. 61.

Eastman, Charles. 1904. *Red Hunters and the Animal People.* New York: Harper.

———. 1991 (1918). *Indian Heroes and Great Chieftains.* Lincoln: University of Nebraska Press.

Eastman, Charles, and Elaine Goodale Eastman. 1990 (1909). *Wigwam Evenings: Sioux Folk Tales Retold.* Lincoln: University of Nebraska Press.

Erdoes, Richard, and Archie Fire Lame Deer. 1992. *Gift of Power: The Life and Teachings of a Lakota Medicine Man.* Santa Fe, NM: Bear.

Erdoes, Richard, and John Lame Deer. 1972. *Lame Deer—Seeker of Visions.* New York: Simon and Schuster.

Erdoes, Richard, and Leonard Crow Dog. 1995. *Crow Dog: Four Generations of Sioux Medicine Men.* New York: HarperCollins.

Erdoes, Richard, and Mary Brave Bird. 1993. *Ohitika Woman.* New York: Grove Press.

Erdoes, Richard, and Mary Crow Dog. 1990. *Lakota Woman.* New York: Grove Weidenfeld.

Federal Writers' Project. 1939a. *Nebraska Folklore Pamphlets: Santee-Sioux Indian Legends.* Vol. 21. Lincoln: Federal Writers' Project.

———. 1939b. *Nebraska Folklore Pamphlets: More Santee-Sioux Indian Legends.* Vol. 23. Lincoln: Federal Writers' Project.

Fools Crow, Frank, Man Noble Red, Noah Kills Enemy at Night, and Steve Red Bow. 1977. *Fools Crow* (sound recording). Tatanka Records. TLP 100.

Frerichs, Robert, and Paul Olson, eds. 1979. *A Few Great Stories of the Santee People Told by Many Nineteenth Century Santee and by Edna Peniska and Paul Robertson of the Modern Santee.* Lincoln: Nebraska Curriculum Development Center.

Gibbon, Guy E. 2003. *The Sioux: The Dakota and Lakota Nations.* Malden, MA: Blackwell.

Goble, Paul. 1988. *Iktomi and the Boulder: A Plains Indian Story.* New York: Orchard Books.

———. 1989. *Iktomi and the Berries: A Plains Indian Story.* New York: Orchard Books.

———. 1990. *Iktomi and the Ducks: A Plains Indian Story.* New York: Orchard Books.

———. 1991. *Iktomi and the Buffalo Skull: A Plains Indian Story.* New York: Orchard Books.

———. 1994. *Iktomi and the Buzzard: A Plains Indian Story.* New York: Orchard Books.

———. 1998. *Iktomi and the Coyote: A Plains Indian Story.* New York: Orchard Books.

———. 1999. *Iktomi Loses His Eyes: A Plains Indian Story.* New York: Orchard Books.

Grobsmith, Elizabeth S. 1981. *Lakota of the Rosebud: A Contemporary Ethnography.* New York: Holt, Rinehart and Winston.

Howard, James H., ed. 1998. *Lakota Warrior: Joseph White Bull.* Introduction by Raymond Bucko. Lincoln: University of Nebraska Press.

Jahner, Elaine. 1982. Cognitive Style in Oral Literature. *Language and Style* 15: 32–51.

———. 1983. Stone Boy: Persistent Hero. In *Smoothing the Ground: Essays on Native American Oral Literature*, edited by B. Swann. Berkeley: University of California Press. 171–186.

———. 1992. The Moment of Dilemma. The Lakota Story of White Plume Boy. *Parabola* 17.4: 58–62.

Landes, Ruth. 1968. *The Mystic Lake Sioux: Sociology of the Mdewakantonwan Santee.* Madison: University of Wisconsin Press.

Mallery, Garrick. 1972 (1888–1889). *Picture-Writing of the American Indians.* New York: Dover Publications.

McLaughlin, Marie L. 1974. *Myths and Legends of the Sioux.* Bismarck, ND: Tumbleweed Press.

Meyer, Roy W. 1993. *History of the Santee Sioux: United States Indian Policy on Trial.* Revised edition. Lincoln: University of Nebraska Press.

Mohatt, Gerald Vincent, and Joseph Eagle Elk. 2000. *The Price of a Gift: A Lakota Healer's Story.* Lincoln: University of Nebraska Press.

Nauman, Charles. 1978. *The Grass That Never Breaks* (film). Nauman Films.

Paige, Harry W. 1970. *Songs of the Teton Sioux*. Los Angeles: Westernlore Press.

Pond, Samuel. 1986. *The Dakotas or Sioux in Minnesota as They Were in 1834*. St. Paul: Minnesota Historical Society Press.

Powers, Marla N. 1986. *Oglala Women*. Chicago: University of Chicago Press.

Powers, William K. 1968. Contemporary Oglala Music and Dance: Pan Indianism versus Pan-Tetonism. *Ethnomusicology* 12.3: 352–372.

———. 1975. *Oglala Religion*. Lincoln: University of Nebraska Press.

———. 1980a. Oglala Song Terminology. In *Selected Reports in Ethnomusicology*, Vol. 3, edited by C. Heth. 23–41.

———. 1980b. Plains Indian Music and Dance. In *Anthropology of the Great Plains*, edited by M. Liberty and W. R. Wood. Lincoln: University of Nebraska Press. 212–229.

———. 1982. *Yuwipi: Vision and Experience in Oglala Ritual*. Lincoln: University of Nebraska Press.

———. 1986. *Sacred Language: The Nature of Supernatural Discourse in Lakota*. Norman: University of Oklahoma Press.

———. 1987. *Beyond the Vision: Essays on American Indian Culture*. Norman: University of Oklahoma Press.

———. 1988. Foolish Words: Text and Context in Lakota Love Songs. *European Review of Native American Studies* 2.2: 29–34.

———. 1990a. *Voices from the Spirit World*. Kendall Park, NJ: Lakota Books.

———. 1990b. *War Dance: Plains Indian Musical Performance*. Tucson: University of Arizona Press.

Price, Catherine. 1996. *The Oglala People, 1841–1879: A Political History*. Lincoln: University of Nebraska Press.

Rice, Julian. 1989. *Lakota Storytelling: Black Elk, Ella Deloria, and Frank Fools Crow*. New York: Peter Lang.

———. 1991. *Black Elk's Story: Distinguishing Its Lakota Purpose*. Albuquerque: University of New Mexico Press.

———. 1992. *Deer Women and Elk Men: The Lakota Narratives of Ella Deloria*. Albuquerque: University of New Mexico Press.

———. 1993. *Ella Deloria's Iron Hawk*, translated by J. Rice. Albuquerque: University of New Mexico Press.

———. 1994. *Ella Deloria's The Buffalo People*, translated by J. Rice. Albuquerque: University of New Mexico Press.

Sneve, Virginia Driving Hawk. 1972a. *High Elk's Treasure*. New York: Holiday House.

———. 1972b. *Jimmy Yellow Hawk*. New York: Holiday House.

———. 1974a. *Betrayed*. New York: Holiday House.

———. 1974b. *When Thunders Spoke*. Lincoln: University of Nebraska Press.

———. 1993. *The Chichi HooHoo Bogeyman*. Lincoln: University of Nebraska Press.

———. 1995. *Completing the Circle*. Lincoln: University of Nebraska Press.

———. 1997. *The Trickster and the Troll*. Lincoln: University of Nebraska Press.

Sneve, Virginia Driving Hawk, and Ronald Himler. 1993. *The Sioux*. New York: Holiday House.

South Dakota Oral History Project. 2003. *Index of South Dakota Oral History Project Resources*. South Dakota Oral History Project.

Standing Bear, Luther. 1988. *Stories of the Sioux*. Lincoln: University of Nebraska Press.

Starita, Joe. 1995. *The Dull Knifes of Pine Ridge: A Lakota Odyssey*. New York: Putnam.

Theisz, Ron D. 1996. *Sending Their Voices: Essays on Lakota Musicology*. Kendall Park, NJ: Lakota Books.

————, ed. 1975. *Buckskin Tokens: Contemporary Oral Narratives of the Lakota*. Rosebud, SD: Sinte Gleska College.

Utley, Robert. 1963. *The Last Days of the Sioux Nation*. New Haven: Yale University Press.

————. 1993. *The Lance and the Shield: The Life and Times of Sitting Bull*. New York: Henry Holt.

Walker, James. 1980. *Lakota Belief and Ritual*, edited by R. DeMallie and E. Jahner. Lincoln: University of Nebraska Press.

————. 1982. *Lakota Society*, edited by R. DeMallie. Lincoln: University of Nebraska Press.

————. 1983. *Lakota Myth*, edited by E. Jahner. Lincoln: University of Nebraska Press.

Workers of the South Dakota Writers' Project. 1987. *Legends of the Mighty Sioux*. Rapid City, SD: Albert Whitman.

Yellow Robe, Rosebud. 1979. *Tonweya and the Eagles and Other Lakota Indian Tales*. New York: Dial Press.

Young Bear, Severt, and Ron D. Theisz. 1994. *Standing in the Light: A Lakota Way of Seeing*. Lincoln: University of Nebraska Press.

Zitkala-Ša. 1985a. *American Indian Stories*. Lincoln: University of Nebraska Press.

————. 1985b. *Old Indian Legends*. Lincoln: University of Nebraska Press.

Raymond A. Bucko, S. J.

NAVAJO

GEOGRAPHY AND HISTORY

Navajo folklore exists in a plurality of perspectives. Recently, the name Navajo itself has been a point of discussion, given that many prefer the indigenous *Diné* (The People) as the Navajo call themselves in their own language. Diné College—the first college established by Native Americans for Native Americans in 1968—was formerly Navajo Community College. In contrast, the tribal government and newspaper have retained the names the Navajo Nation and the *Navajo Times* respectively. Such diversity among community members about so fundamental a part of their identity offers a window into understanding the current cultural reality of there being many different interpretations of what it means to be truly Navajo.

Folklore is integral to every aspect Navajo life. Songs and prayers accompany such daily activities as herding sheep, planting crops, and weaving. The front door of a *hooghan* (the traditional dome-shaped Navajo dwelling crafted from earth and wood) faces east toward the rising sun, inviting inhabitants to greet the new day. Coyote tales, told exclusively during the winter months, provide instructions for thinking and acting correctly. Because of its association with mythological and historical events, the Navajo Reservation or *Diné Bikéyah* (literally "under Navajo feet") is itself alive with significance. Folklore is the glue that integrates the people, the natural world around them, their homes and livestock, their beliefs and relationships. It is often said that in Navajo, as in other Native American languages, there is no word for "art." The same could be said of "folklore"; it permeates all of Navajo life.

The practice of cultural traditions is a balance of many variables, reflecting individual interpretation, innovation, and choice against the backdrop of a larger cultural frame. This cultural frame is itself in a state of continual transformation, as environmental and historical change impacts people's lives. Here, "Navajo" will refer to the larger cultural frame. Yet it is important to remember that culture is lived by individuals inhabiting particular communities, living in particular moments in time. The Navajo philosophy *aashi bi'bohlii*, "it's up to you," expresses culturally sanctioned independence of thought and action but is balanced by accountability to one's community.

In the larger Native North American cultural landscape, the Navajo are Athabaskan, tracing their geographic, cultural, and linguistic descent from western Canada, migrating south to their present home in the American Southwest by approximately 1300 C.E. The Southwest has long been home to diverse cultures—the Pueblo peoples, the Utes, Paiutes, Mexicans, and later Spanish and Anglo-European settlers. Interaction between the Navajo and their neighbors has been peaceful in the case of trading, friendship, and intermarriage; but warfare, conflict, and tension have also pervaded intercultural relationships. Following the Pueblo Revolt of 1680 and the subsequent Spanish Reconquest, many Pueblos took refuge in Navajo communities, introducing traditional practices that, blended with Athabaskan roots, have contributed to Navajo culture as it is known today.

Euro-American westward expansion and colonization in the latter half of the nineteenth century fueled intercultural tension that culminated in the Long Walk or *Hweeldí*, an event that had a pivotal impact upon Navajo life and culture. In 1863, the United States recruited retired colonel Kit Carson to lead a scorched-earth campaign that forced approximately 9,000 Navajo people to walk across 300 miles from their homeland to the Bosque Redondo at Ft. Sumner in eastern New Mexico, where they lived for five years under harsh conditions. The intent of the Long Walk was the permanent removal of the Navajo from their land. However, negotiations between Navajo leaders and the U.S. government—and according to some a ceremony held by Navajo prisoners—ultimately paved the way homeward. The 1868 treaty, signed by Navajo headmen and U.S. government officials, restored the Navajo to their home (henceforth the Navajo Reservation), banned hostility between the Navajo and their neighbors, and required that Navajo children attend school.

Today the Navajo Nation is the largest Native American cultural community in the United States, with a population of approximately 290,000. The Navajo Reservation covers a varied landscape of alpine meadows and mountains, sage-covered grasslands, expansive desert, piñon-juniper-covered hills and plateaus, and crimson red rock country. It spans 25,000 square miles of northeastern Arizona, northwestern New Mexico, and southeastern Utah, with elevations ranging from 4,300 to

Tsegi Canyon, Arizona. (Photograph by Laura Marcus)

11,300 feet. The natural landscape is interwoven with the traditional economy. Along the San Juan River sumac and willow, the plants from which baskets are made, are plentiful, making the northern part of the reservation a good area in which to buy or trade for baskets. Each region has its own specialty based on its natural resources, a biodiversity that has long fed the barter economy.

One universal phenomenon across Navajo country is the presence of livestock—cows, horses, and most importantly sheep or *dibé*. The Spanish introduced sheep to the American Southwest in the late fifteenth century, and over time they have become a mainstay of Navajo culture, well-being, and economy. Traditionally, a family's wealth is measured by the size of its flocks. Mutton stew is a staple of the Navajo diet. Wool has long been an invaluable resource as a commodity to be traded for other goods and to be spun and woven into blankets and rugs. The Navajo seasonal cycle is shaped by caring for sheep. Spring is the time for shearing, an event that brings families and communities together to work side by side. Fall is the lambing season.

Upon their liberation from the Bosque Redondo, Navajo families were issued commodities with which to return home, including the sheep that became the foundation for rebuilding their flocks. The five years spent at Bosque Redondo introduced the Navajo to unfamiliar goods such as coffee and flour, which became staples of the Navajo diet, and manufactured items such as enamel cookware and factory-made cloth, which ultimately replaced Navajo pottery and handwoven clothing in everyday use. These items were available at the trading posts that began appearing on the newly formed Navajo Reservation. At the trading post, Navajo customers exchanged their own goods—wool, livestock, piñon, and traditional arts such as woven blankets and jewelry—for food staples, cookware, rope, velveteen and calico, and even ready-to-assemble buckboard wagons. Ultimately in the mid-twentieth century, a cash economy replaced the indigenous barter system. Wool, livestock, piñon, and artwork enjoy continued prominence, but most Navajo people also participate in the mainstream cash economy as wage-earners and consumers.

THE NAVAJO LANGUAGE AND RESERVATION

In contrast to many native communities now struggling to revitalize their languages, a majority of Navajo people are native speakers. Language is of central concern for parents who wish their children to retain their culture, even as they participate in American mainstream society. Often, English is spoken at school and work, while Navajo is the language of home and community events. Because of its complexity, the Navajo language was developed into a code that successfully eluded the Japanese during World War II. The code arranged Navajo words into a list that, when translated into English, became an alphabet. Additionally, coded words were developed for military terms, such as *beshlo* or "iron fish" for submarine. The Code Talkers and their role in defeating the Japanese in World War II remain a source of pride, and this group of veterans is held in high esteem and honored at public events.

In pre-reservation times, the Navajo were a politically decentralized people, living in family and community-based clusters. Prominent headmen, *naat'áani*, were decision-makers and arbiters of justice, providing governance at the local level. Following the establishment of the reservation, the twelve Navajo headmen who had signed the 1868 Treaty were entrusted with the supervision of their followers, acting as the liaison between their people and the federally appointed superintendent. This system was successful for a time, but ultimately the U.S. government took matters into its own hands and by 1909 established six regional sub-agencies, each with its own supervising agent. The elected twelve-member Navajo Tribal Council was established at Window Rock in 1923, largely in order to negotiate the leasing of oil and timber on the reservation, but also to centralize Navajo internal governance. In 1927 the chapter house became a localized organizational unit based loosely on kinship networks and centered at trading posts. Today the Navajo Nation provides self-governance through its own political and judicial system and a police force, along with departments overseeing education and economic affairs, among others. Local civic activities remain the jurisdiction of the 110 chapters across the reservation.

Navajo communities stretch out expansively and are focused on cooperative activities such as sponsoring ceremonials, farming, and sheep grazing. A typical camp consists of various structures, including Western-style houses, trailers, satellite dishes, and corrals in addition to *hooghans* and shade houses—three-sided lean-to-like structures crafted from cottonwood branches, often used as summer kitchens or a reprieve from the season's heat. As architectural styles blend, it is not uncommon to see a Western-style house in the shape of a *hooghan* with the door facing east, an adaptation that extends to the design of public buildings on the reservation. The traditional Navajo *hooghan* is often the site for a family's ceremonial occasions as well as the dwelling where family elders tend to live. Navajo people trace their descent through clans—extensive networks that establish familial relationships of caring and help. Because Navajo culture is matrilineal, a person is born *for* his or her mother's clan and *to* his or her father's clan, the mother's clan being the primary affiliation. Rooted in the Emergence and the interaction between the Navajo and other cultures, the clan system ensures that wherever one travels in Navajo country, one will find family and community.

The Navajo Reservation is the longstanding home of The People. On a map, the shifting political boundaries of the Navajo Nation have been drawn by a series of treaties. Yet it is the Four Sacred Mountains that form the spiritual borders of the Navajo homeland. These are *Sis Najiní*, Blanca Peak, to the east, near Alamosa, Colorado; *Tsoodził*, Mt. Taylor, to the south, in northwestern New Mexico; *Dook'o'oosłííd*, San Francisco Peak, to the west, near Flagstaff, Arizona; and to the north in southwestern Colorado, *Dibé Nitsa*, Hesperus Peak. Not only do the Four Sacred Mountains frame the spiritual parameters of Navajo country, but they are each associated with specific Holy People or *Diyin Dine'é*, the cardinal directions, a time of day, a color, a precious stone. The number four pervades Navajo traditional life: there is morning, day, dusk, and night time; we are infants, young people, adults, and elders; the seasons cycle through spring, summer, autumn, and winter. Four is the number of power in Navajo belief, giving a sense of completeness.

NAVAJO COSMOLOGY AND THE CONCEPT OF BALANCE

The story of the Navajo Emergence to the present world is the foundation of Navajo cosmology. It describes the journey through which the Navajo arrived in their present home, explaining how and why things are the way they are, providing the etiology of Navajo geography, and prescribing the details of ceremonial and daily life. Before arriving in the Fourth or Glittering World as the Earth Surface People they are today, the Navajo ascended through the First or Black World, the Second or Blue World, and the Third or Yellow World. Navajo belief establishes the Emergence as the true history of the Navajo people and their homeland. Traditional accounts and archeological research agree and diverge in places; for instance, the question of the time and route of the Navajo arrival in the Southwest has long been the subject of debate. Regardless of which explanation one embraces, the inseparability of folklore and lived experience cannot be denied.

The Holy People are the Navajo pantheon, participating directly in the Emergence and returning as invited guests at ceremonials that invoke their presence. They are the figures whose stories are told in the Emergence, and whose experiences gave rise to the need for the original, foundational ceremonials that have come down through time and continue to serve people today. After the Emergence to the present world, First Man and Talking God found a baby girl, Changing Woman, *Asdzáá Nádleehí*, on Gobernador Knob in present-day northwestern New Mexico. First Man and First Woman raised Changing Woman, who grew up in four days (in some versions, four years) and was the patient for the first *kinaaldá*, the Girls' Puberty Ceremony which continues to mark the passage into womanhood. Changing Woman is considered to be the mother of all Navajo people and the ideal for Navajo women. An encounter between Changing Woman and the Sun resulted in the birth of the Navajo Hero Twins, Monster Slayer and Born for Water, who ultimately delivered the Navajo people from the monsters who were inhabiting the earth and making it a dangerous place to live.

Central to Navajo culture is the concept of *hózhǫ'*, a state of beauty, balance, and order resulting from living in harmony with one's human, supernatural, and natural surroundings. In contrast to the duality between good and evil characteristic of many religions, the Navajo worldview recognizes that life inevitably presents situations that can disrupt a person's sense of *hózhǫ'*. When a person becomes ill, she or he is considered to be out of balance. Ritual provides the means through which one can be restored to *hózhǫ'*. Someone who is sick might consult a hand trembler or a stargazer—a diagnostician who determines the cause of an illness and prescribes the proper ceremonial treatment to restore the patient to good health. A person's symptoms might be of a physical or emotional nature. The mind/body dichotomy is not present in Navajo belief, which considers the physical and emotional realms inextricably connected. An illness could be caused by the patient's spiritual transgression or by external forces beyond the patient's control. Some ceremonies are quiet, private family occasions, whereas others are large community events in which many people participate by attending and providing various kinds of help.

CEREMONIES, MEDICINE, AND RELIGION

The Blessingway ceremony, *Hózhóójí*, is the most widely practiced of all Navajo ceremonials. It is held throughout the year and is invoked as circumstances require. The Blessingway may be held for anyone for diverse reasons as either a preventative ceremony or a restorative ceremony. Specific occasions for which a Blessingway might be performed include the blessing of ceremonial items, medicine men, livestock, political officials upon inauguration, pregnant women, departing and returning travelers, and houses. Other ceremonials such as the *Ye'iibichei* or Nightway and the Mountainway or *Dziłk'ijí* may only be held during the winter season, and the *'Anaa'jí* or Enemyway takes place exclusively during the summer months.

The ceremonial knowledge that upholds Navajo ritual practice lives in the minds of medicine men or *hataałii* (literally, "singers"), who represent the combined equivalent of doctors and clergymen. Medicine men acquire their knowledge through long-term apprenticeships that are as rigorous as medical school. Like medical doctors, medicine men specialize in particular ceremonials. For each ceremonial, a medicine man must learn all the relevant songs and prayers as well as the proper preparation and use of sandpaintings and medicine bundles. Sandpaintings are literally illustrations from the *nakéé nááhane'* or stories from the past. With the performance of the correct songs and prayers and gestures, sandpaintings become *alive*, inviting the presence of the Holy People who are associated with a particular ceremony. In the course of a ritual, the patient is often seated on the sandpainting and, through the power of association with the Holy People depicted in the sandpainting, acquires the ceremonial means to overcome illness. Despite precise attention to detail, inevitably there is individual variation among medicine men. Ritual exemplifies the interrelatedness of Navajo folklore genres. It is the constellation of myth, ceremonial objects, prayer, dance, song, and family and community support that renders a ritual a powerful conduit between the realm of the Holy People and the Navajo, with the capacity to effect healing.

From the time when hospitals and doctors first appeared on the Navajo Reservation, there has been tension between Navajo and Western philosophies regarding medical treatment. Some have integrated these practices harmoniously, combining visits to the medicine man and the doctor to maintain health; others struggle to find the balance, especially when the medicine men and doctors detract from each other's treatment modalities. More recently, there is growing

A Navajo shaman gives medicine to a participant as two others look on (1905). (Courtesy Library of Congress)

recognition of the need to integrate both healing systems. Today it is not uncommon for hospitals on the reservation to make arrangements for Navajo and Western medicine to work in tandem.

The first missionaries to establish a presence on the Navajo Reservation were the Mormons, who came to Moencopie in northeastern Arizona in 1871. More intensive missionary activity began during the 1890s, when the U.S. government bestowed land grants to various religious organizations. However, these early efforts had little impact on Navajo spiritual practices. From the 1950s and continuing into the 1960s and 1970s, the number of missions and missionaries proliferated, bringing practitioners of the Mormon, Catholic, Baptist, Pentecostal, and Assembly of God faiths to the reservation and attracting many more Navajo parishioners and clergy. Another outside spiritual influence on the Navajo Reservation has been the Native American Church, or Peyote religion, which began attracting adherents in the 1930s and has continued to grow, not without conflict with Navajo non-practitioners, the Navajo tribal council, and various governmental agencies. Although some people still oppose its practice on the Navajo Reservation, the Native American Church has become a permanent presence in Navajo culture and is practiced by many. Encompassing a blend of Christian symbolism and nativistic beliefs and practices, the Peyote ceremony is known as the Medicine Way or 'Azee'jí. A Peyote ceremony is conducted for a range of occasions, including to mark a birthday or holiday, to cure a patient of an illness or problem, to attract good fortune, to send a person safely on a journey, or to give thanks for a successful return. Whereas some adhere exclusively to one spiritual practice, others engage in any combination of traditional Navajo religion, Christianity, and the Native American Church.

MUSIC AND SONG

Regardless of the spiritual tradition(s) a person practices, the importance of music is a common denominator among all religions found on the Navajo Reservation. Navajo medicine men are *hataałii* or "singers," and the patient in a ritual is "the one sung over," attesting to the prominence of music in ritual. In the context of ritual, songs are sung or chanted by medicine men either a cappella or accompanied by a pottery-and-buckskin water drum played with a wooden beater or rhythms played on a rattle. Depending on the occasion, a rattle might be made from a gourd filled with various objects, rawhide or deer hooves or dew claws. Each Navajo ritual has its own particular cluster of songs performed at specific moments during the ceremonials. Because of their association with myth, these ritual songs often contain narratives. There are literally thousands of such songs. In addition to the ceremonial songs, there are songs that have ritual power during such activities as farming or hunting, providing protection and prosperity for the singer. In pre-reservation times, when trading parties left Navajo country to barter with other tribes, they sang songs at various moments in the journey to assure them a safe passage, friendly treatment by the hosts, and a return with a cache of trade goods. In the days of the historic trading post, traders recall hearing such songs as customers approached on horseback. Following are the first and the final verses of a trading song referring to horses and other trade goods as recorded by W. W. Hill in 1948:

The beautiful thing is starting toward me
I being the son of the sun
The white shell bead horse is starting toward me
From the center of the sun's home, it is starting toward me
It eats out of the white shell basket
The dark clouds' dew streams from it as it starts toward me
The pollen from the beautiful flowers streams from its mouth
    As it starts toward me
With its beautiful neigh it calls as it starts toward me
Soft goods of all sorts are attached to it as it starts toward me
Hard goods of all sorts are attached to it as it starts toward me
It shall continue to increase without fail as it starts toward me
It shall be beautiful in front of it as it starts toward me
It shall be beautiful behind it as it starts toward me
Good and everlasting one am I as it starts toward me.

They eat
I being the son of the moon
The turquoise bead horses they eat
From the center of the moon's home they eat
They eat out of the turquoise basket they eat
The dew of the dark fog streams from them as they eat
The pollen from the beautiful flowers streams from their mouths
    As they eat
With their beautiful neighs they call us to eat
Soft goods of all sorts are attached to them as they eat
Hard goods of all sorts are attached to them as they eat
They shall continue to increase without fail as they eat
Behind them shall be beautiful as they eat
In front of them shall be beautiful as they eat
Good and everlasting one am I as they eat.

Additionally in the realm of sacred music, Christian hymns or gospel songs as well as Peyote songs associated with the Native American Church are prevalent musical traditions on the Navajo Reservation. Among secular music genres are traditional songs, *diné biyiin*, such as lullabies and occupational songs (for silversmithing, weaving, planting corn, and other occupations) as well as personal songs, which are composed by individuals for their own enjoyment. Traditionally, some songs are owned and must therefore be bought with money or something of equal value to obtain the right to perform them.

DANCE

Dance is a central feature of some of the winter ceremonials, such as the Nightway, which includes masked *Ye'ibichei* dancing, and the Mountainway or Dark Circle of Branches, which features the Fire Dance. Navajo rituals are held to effect healing, but they also serve to bring far-flung neighbors together for socializing. Held during

the summer months, the Enemyway includes a social dance consisting of pairs
dancing a two-step in a circle to the accompaniment of a singing group and drum. An
offshoot of this social dance is the Traditional Song and Dance, which has become
an exclusively social event taking place during the warmer months of the year. The
songs that accompany Traditional Song and
Dance are secular and are sometimes humorous, occasionally containing English words
or phrases. Recordings of these songs can be
heard on the Navajo radio station, KTNN
AM ("The Voice of the Navajo Nation"),
and are available for sale at trading posts
across the reservation. The Navajo musical
repertoire expands to include various forms
of popular music such as folk, rock and roll,
and disco. Navajo bands and performers
play and record music in every style imaginable, often expressing Navajo experiences
and ideas through popular musical forms.

Characters from Navajo mythology appear in a *Ye'ibichei* dance (1906). (Courtesy Library of Congress)

Traditional Song and Dance events are most commonly advertised through word
of mouth and homemade signs that appear at chapter houses, trading posts, and
other public venues. Joining these signs in growing numbers across the reservation
are announcements for country-and-western dances. The Navajo Two-Step once referred exclusively to the Traditional Song and Dance, but it has also become a reference to the distinctively Navajo style of country-and-western dancing. Another
secular context for music and dance is the powwow, an intertribal gathering where
participants specialize and compete in various pan-tribal dance traditions. Navajo
dancers and singing groups travel the powwow circuit throughout the western
United States and, in some cases, nationally. Navajo ceremonial and secular dances
are also performed at various public events like the Shiprock Fair, Eastern Navajo
Fair, Navajo Nation Fair, or the Gallup Intertribal Ceremonial. The Shiprock Fair,
the first of these fairs, was introduced by Indian agents and superintendents in 1909
and modeled after the county fair or harvest festival. The fairs also became an occasion for Navajo events such as horse racing and rodeo, traditional performing arts,
and the display of visual art forms. Now under tribal and local supervision, these
events continue to be high points on the Navajo calendar.

SPORTS AND GAMES

During the winter months, families and communities enjoy *késhjéé*, the Shoe Game or
Moccasin Game, in which one team hides a yucca root ball in a shoe and the other
tries to find it. The teams keep score with yucca branches. The first Shoe Game took
place during the Emergence, when nocturnal and diurnal animals competed to determine whether it would always be day or night. Because there was a tie, day and night

both have their place in our lives. Among other popular forms of Navajo entertainment is rodeo—a natural, given the prevalence of livestock on the reservation. During the summer months, the All Indian Professional Rodeo Cowboys Association (AIPRCA) sponsors many rodeos across the Navajo Reservation. Additionally, some families build their own arenas, where they host family and community rodeos. Basketball is also extremely popular both in the context of schools and official championships and on the home courts that are a common sight throughout the reservation.

ARTS AND CRAFTS

Navajo culture is probably best known to the world beyond the reservation for its material culture traditions: weaving, silversmithing, basketry, sandpaintings, and, more recently, pottery and figurative art. All these art forms originated in traditional indigenous use but have become part of the trade to outsiders. The spiritual roots of Navajo weaving recount that Spider Woman taught First Woman to weave, giving her a means of artistic expression and meditative well-being as well as a way to provide for her family. The earliest textiles were wearing blankets, worn over the shoulders for warmth and beauty. In the days of pre-reservation intertribal barter, such blankets were highly coveted for their fine weaving and designs. The yarn was spun from wool sheared from Navajo flocks and then dyed—in the early days with indigo, cochineal (an insect that gives a red color), and other natural materials. Following the Long Walk, Navajo textiles remained a valuable commodity in the barter system, but weavers soon realized that the better economy was to weave for trade and wear manufactured clothing. Trading posts stocked manufactured yarns and dyes, which Navajo weavers continue to use today in addition to their own homespun, vegetally dyed yarns. When the wool market failed in the 1890s, traders recognized that Navajo weavers would see a better return on their wool if it was woven into floor rugs that could compete in the market for Oriental carpets, which were popular at that time. The establishment of regional rug designs associated with particular trading posts began then and continues today. Whereas most rugs are woven for sale to outsiders, saddle blankets and cinches, sash belts and *bííl* (the traditional two-piece dress) are still made for Navajo use.

Other art forms also illustrate traditional patterns of use as well as Navajo relationships with the outside world. The Navajo learned the art forms of blacksmithing and silversmithing around the middle of the nineteenth century from Mexi-

Navajo Indian blanket and belt weavers. Photograph taken by James Mooney, 1892–1893. (Courtesy Library of Congress)

can and Spanish metalsmiths living in the Rio Grande valley and near the south-eastern edge of the present-day Navajo Reservation. Beginning with relatively simple pieces with unadorned surfaces, Navajo silversmiths developed stamped designs and in the 1870s began creating jewelry set with turquoise, a tradition that has become a hallmark of Navajo culture. In addition to its beauty, Navajo jewelry was early on a visible form of wealth—bracelets, rings, earrings, pins, necklaces, collar decorations, bolos, belt buckles, buttons, and more—which could be pawned or traded when livestock and agriculture were a less certain means of income. Toward the end of the nineteenth century, the Fred Harvey Company commissioned lighter pieces for the tourist trade that grew steadily following the advent of the railroad to the Southwest. Whereas Navajo silversmiths made relatively substantial pieces for their own use, they created daintier work for the outside market, a differential esthetic that continues today. The surge in interest in all things Indian in the 1960s and 1970s contributed to a boom in Navajo jewelry. With the impact of non-Navajo esthetics and the availability of new materials, Navajo silversmithing encompasses diverse techniques from the more traditional sandcasting to inlay and the incorporation of semi-precious stones imported from around the world in addition to locally mined stones.

Baskets continue to play an important role in Navajo life but are also woven for sale to outsiders. Baskets are an essential feature of most Navajo ceremonials either to contain medicine or, when inverted, to serve as drums. They are also a form of payment to medicine men in exchange for ceremonial services. Until fairly recently, baskets were woven with the traditional red, black, and white stepped "wedding basket" design, associated with clouds, mountains, spiritual well-being, and the Navajo wedding ceremony. In the 1960s, pottery and basketry were revived in the context of classes offered at Navajo Community College and the Rough Rock Demonstration School. These classes not only revitalized cultural traditions that had become increasingly rare but also inspired the exploration of pictorial basketry and pottery designs. At this time, Navajo basket weavers began creating representational pieces depicting figures such as animals, birds, flowers, and scenes from Navajo mythology and history. Pictorial baskets are made mostly for sale to tourists and collectors. Ceremonial use still calls for the old-style wedding baskets.

Early Navajo pottery was made exclusively for cooking, storage, and ceremonial use. As manufactured cookware replaced Navajo pottery for everyday use, this art form became scarce except for ceremonial contexts. In the early stages of the Navajo pottery revival, artists began by re-creating traditional utilitarian ware, which was distinctively Navajo in its thick walls, "fire clouds" (created in the firing process), and undecorated surfaces—except for the "necklace," a broken band of etched design around the pot's rim. Over time, Navajo potters began experimenting with designs by adding geometric patterns and pictorial scenes of traditional Navajo life to pottery surfaces, refining the thickness of the walls or creating a fine burnished surface. A departure from the earlier replicas of the authentic utilitarian vessels, these pieces are clearly created as works of art.

Another art form that has undergone a transformation in recent years is the carving of representational figures. Traditionally, medicine men carved fetishes for ceremonial use and children crafted toys from mud for their own entertainment. In the

1980s, however, there began a movement to make representational figures from sandstone, wood, ceramics, or cardboard. This work depicts traditional scenes of Navajo life such as herding sheep, but it also presents social commentaries on such current issues as gaming or alcoholism. Building on the tradition of Navajo rock art, which is found on sandstone walls across the reservation, Navajo easel painting began in the early years of the twentieth century. Painting continues to be a medium through which artists represent traditional life and contemporary themes.

Since they are esthetically pleasing and suggest cultural authenticity, ceremonial designs have long provided inspiration for commercial sandpaintings, rugs, wood carvings, pottery, paintings, and jewelry. Yet, because of their powerful and sacred nature, the reproduction of sandpaintings as permanent art works for sale is controversial. To avoid the risk of harm resulting from invoking the Holy People in a casual way, artists who use sacred designs might alter the symbolism in a piece so that it lacks ceremonial power or they might undergo ceremonies as a preventive measure. In all the Navajo material culture genres, imagination and innovation have taken traditional artists in many new directions, dramatically expanding the repertoire of Navajo visual arts.

CHALLENGES OF THE MODERN WORLD

The Southwest has long been shared by diverse cultural communities. In pre-reservation times and the early reservation years, it was predominantly men who traveled away from Navajo country to conduct trade and warfare, representing the interests of those who stayed at home. As wage work, military service, and boarding schools increasingly took Navajo people off the reservation, and as the railroad, paved roads, and pickup trucks facilitated travel to reservation border towns, contact with the world beyond the Navajo Reservation inevitably increased. Additionally, the reservation era ushered in higher numbers of outsiders: traders, government agents, schoolteachers, missionaries, and tourists, who gradually became part of the cultural landscape. Yet, even as mainstream society has encroached upon their world, the Navajo have claimed the very forces of **modernization** that have threatened their way of life and adapted them to support traditional culture. When Navajo children first began attending boarding schools, their teachers were Euro-American instructors whose mission was to "educate" and assimilate Navajo children by eradicating indigenous culture. Cruel punishments awaited Navajo students who outwardly displayed their native culture. This policy's devastating effects are widely known, and personal experience narratives about running away are a prevalent genre among those who attended boarding schools. Today most students attend schools in their home communities, and a growing number of teachers in reservation schools are Navajo. Bilingual programs incorporate Navajo culture into the curriculum, providing encouragement for students to learn about their cultural heritage and for families to take an active role in school-based activities.

Despite their changing relationship with the world around them, the Navajo have held as tenaciously to their cultural identity as they have to their land. If folklore is integral to all of Navajo life, it also lives at the interface between Navajo culture and the outside world, a porous boundary through which knowledge, skills, and ideas flow.

Navajo culture has always incorporated new esthetic forms, techniques, and ideas while maintaining basic core beliefs and values. It is the resilience of the Navajo people and their culture that has allowed for their survival through intercultural conflict and colonization, through massive transformations in their economy and lifestyle, and through the impact of the fast-paced, high-tech industrial culture of mainstream America. A new tradition, the decoration of satellite dishes with the traditional wedding basket design, attests to this adaptability and to the constant communication between traditional Navajo life and the world beyond the reservation.

STUDIES OF NAVAJO FOLKLORE

Since the first Spanish explorers arrived in the Southwest, written accounts of interaction with the Navajo have provided abundant documentation of their folklore and culture. Additionally, military personnel, ethnographers, missionaries, traders, medical professionals, and teachers among others have contributed to the wealth of literature on Navajo folklore. Because of its relevance to all areas of life, Navajo folklore is best understood in the broader context of culture and history. Several resources—Kluckhohn and Leighton (1946), Link (1968), Ortiz (1983), Bailey and Glenn (1986), and Iverson (2002)—present overviews that incorporate Navajo folklore and provide extensive bibliographies of both primary and secondary sources for further reading. Military surgeon Washington Matthews was among the first to publish accounts of Navajo folklore, including oral literature and ritual (1994 [1897]), weaving (1884), and silversmithing (1883). His documentation of Navajo folklore at the turn of the twentieth century provides a historical barometer during an era of vast cultural change. Matthews's contribution to the literature on Navajo culture and several of his previously unpublished pieces are presented in an edited volume of essays (Halpern and McGreevy 1997). *An Ethnologic Dictionary of the Navaho Language*, compiled by the Franciscan Fathers of St. Michael's Mission in Arizona (1910), provides one of the earliest orthographies of Navajo language; it is also rich with folkloric detail. Because of its sheer poetic and visual beauty and the fear that the forces of modernization would eradicate Navajo religion, several twentieth-century ethnographers undertook the recording of Navajo ceremonials, including Haile (1938), Haile and others (1957), Wheelwright (1946), Wyman (1970), and Luckert (1977). Reichard (1944, 1950), Spencer (1957), Witherspoon (1977), Aberle (1982), Frisbie (1987, 1993), and Faris (1990) provide in-depth analyses of Navajo ritual. Because of its historical longitude, Toelken's series of interpretations of Navajo folklore, most notably Coyote tales, offers an evolving perspective based on decades of fieldwork, but just as importantly presents the author's insights into fieldwork ethics. To learn about Navajo music, see McAllester (1954), McAllester and McAllester (1980), and McCullough-Brabson and Help (2001).

Navajo folklore has been carried forward in time, generation to generation, by the people themselves, who have kept their own culture alive without assistance from the written word, though ethnographic resources occasionally provide helpful documentation for cultural practitioners. Increasingly, Navajo authors and artists are documenting and presenting their own culture and history through scholarly writing, literature, visual arts, and music. For Navajo perspectives that include folklore, see Yazzie (1971), Roessel (1980), Benally (1982), and the Rock Point Community School (1982). Based in oral history, Dyk (1938), Roessel (1973), Mitchell (1978), Bighorse (1990), and Benedek (1995) chronicle Navajo culture and experience through vivid personal accounts by community members. Two contemporary Navajo authors, poet Luci Tapahonso (1993) and novelist Irwin Morris (1997), present Navajo folklore through literature. The official Web sites for the Navajo Nation (www.navajo.org) and the *Navajo Times* (www.navajotimes.com) provide updated information about Navajo life and culture. To learn about current Navajo education and scholarly work on a variety of topics, including folklore and culture, see the Diné College Web site (www.dinecollege.org) as well as the Web site for the annual Navajo Studies Conference (www.navajostudies.org). The Navajo Studies Conference is a unique event convening Navajo and non-Navajo scholars and cultural practitioners to discuss a range of contemporary issues (see Piper, Roberts, and Smith 1993; Piper 1999). The film *Seasons of a Navajo* presents a year in the life of a Navajo family and includes folklore in context. In the documentary *A Weave of Time*, anthropologist John Adair revisits the Pine Springs community in Arizona, where he conducted fieldwork fifty years earlier; the film illustrates the tension between Navajo tradition and contemporary American life.

Several authors who have written about Navajo weaving have learned the craft as a means of understanding it from an insider's perspective. Reichard (1934) and Bennett (1974) are narrative ethnographies that provide detailed information about the weaving process as well as beliefs, practices, and personal experiences that surround the art form. Hedlund (1992) and Bonar (1996) offer profiles of weavers as individual artists and contemporary weavers' insights into their tradition. The film *Woven by the Grandmothers: 19th Century Navajo Textiles* (based on the same exhibit as Bonar [1996]) presents weaving in historical and contemporary context. For information about the history and technique of Navajo silversmithing, see Woodward (1938) and Adair (1944). Edison (1996) and Simpson (2003) give an overview of Navajo basketry while presenting commentary from individual artists and others involved in the art. Hartman and Musial (1989) trace the revival of Navajo pottery from its historic roots. Through her work with medicine man Hosteen Klah, Newcomb (1964) explores sandpainting as a ceremonial art; Parezo (1983) examines the evolution of this tradition as a commercial art form. Bernstein and McGreevy (1988) and Rosenak and Rosenak (1994) present more recent innovations in Navajo traditional art, and Kluckhohn, Hill, and Kluckhohn (1971), and Ortiz (1983) provide overviews of Navajo material culture. The literature on Navajo folklore is enormous; the resources listed here are a good starting point for further exploration.

BIBLIOGRAPHY

Aberle, David F. 1982. *Peyote Religion among the Navaho*. 2nd edition. Chicago: University of Chicago Press.

Adair, John. 1944. *The Navajo and Pueblo Silversmiths*. Norman: University of Oklahoma Press.

Alvord, Lori Arviso, with Elizabeth Cohen Van Pelt. 1999. *The Scalpel and the Silver Bear: The First Navajo Woman Surgeon Combines Western Medicine with Traditional Healing*. New York: Bantam.

Bailey, Garrick, and Roberta Glenn. 1986. *A History of the Navajos: The Reservation Years*. Santa Fe: School of American Research Press.

Benally, Clyde. 1982. *Dinéjí Nákéé' Nááhane': A Utah Navajo History*. Monticello, UT: San Juan School District.

Benedek, Emily. 1995. *Beyond the Four Corners of the World: A Navajo Woman's Journey*. New York: Alfred A. Knopf.

Bennett, Noël. 1974. *The Weaver's Pathway: A Clarification of the "Spirit Trail" in Navajo Weaving*. Flagstaff, AZ: Northland Press.

———. 1987. *Halo of the Sun*. Flagstaff, AZ: Northland Press.

Bernstein, Bruce D., and Susan Brown McGreevy, eds. 1988. *Anii Ánáádaalyaa'ígíí: Continuity and Innovation in Recent Navajo Art*. Santa Fe: Wheelwright Museum of the American Indian.

Bighorse, Tiana. 1990. *Bighorse the Warrior*. Tucson: University of Arizona Press.

Bonar, Eulalie H., ed. 1996. *Woven by the Grandmothers: Nineteenth-century Navajo Textiles from the National Museum of the American Indian*. Washington, DC: Smithsonian Institution Press.

Borden, John, producer. 1984. *Seasons of the Navajo* (film). Tempe: Peace River Films, KAET.

Brady, Margaret. 1984. *"Some Kind of Power": Navajo Children's Skinwalker Narratives*. Salt Lake City: University of Utah Press.

Dyk, Walter. 1938. *Son of Old Man Hat: A Navaho Autobiography*. Lincoln: University of Nebraska Press.

Edison, Carol A., ed. 1996. *Willow Stories: Utah Navajo Baskets*. Salt Lake City: Utah Arts Council.

Fanshel, Susan, Deborah Gordon, and John Adair, producers. 1987. *A Weave of Time: The Story of a Navajo Family, 1938–1986* (film). Los Angeles: Direct Cinema Limited.

Faris, James C. 1990. *The Nightway: A History and a History of Documentation of a Navajo Ceremonial*. Albuquerque: University of New Mexico Press.

Franciscan Fathers. 1910. *An Ethnologic Dictionary of the Navaho Language*. Saint Michaels, AZ: Navajo Indian Mission.

Frisbie, Charlotte J. 1987. *Navajo Medicine Bundles or Jish: Acquisition, Transmission, and Disposition in the Past and Present*. Albuquerque: University of New Mexico Press.

———. 1993. *Kinaaldá: A Study of the Navaho Girl's Puberty Ceremony*. Salt Lake City: University of Utah Press.

Haile, Father Berard. 1938. *Origin Legend of the Navaho Enemy Way*. New Haven: Yale University Press.

———. 1984. *Navajo Coyote Tales: The Curly Tó Aheedlíinii Version*. Lincoln: University of Nebraska Press.

Haile, Father Berard, Maude Oakes, and Leland C. Wyman. 1957. *Beautyway: A Navaho Ceremonial*. New York: Pantheon Books.

Halpern, Katherine Spencer, and Susan Brown McGreevy, eds. 1997. *Washington Matthews: Studies of Navajo Culture, 1880–1894*. Albuquerque: University of New Mexico Press.

Hartman, Russell P., and Jan Musial. 1989. *Navajo Pottery: Traditions and Innovations*. Flagstaff, AZ: Northland Publishing.

Hedlund, Ann Lane. 1992. *Reflections of the Weaver's World*. Denver: Denver Art Museum.

Hill, W. W. 1948. Navaho Trading and Trading Ritual: A Study of Cultural Dynamics. *Southwest Journal of Anthropology* 4: 371–396.

Iverson, Peter. 2002. *Diné: A History of the Navajos*. Albuquerque: University of New Mexico Press.

Kelley, Klara Bonsack, and Francis Harris. 1994. *Navajo Sacred Places*. Bloomington: Indiana University Press.

Kluckhohn, Clyde, W. W. Hill, and Lucy Wales Kluckhohn. 1971. *Navaho Material Culture*. Cambridge, MA: Harvard University Press.

Kluckhohn, Clyde, and Dorothea Leighton. 1946. *The Navaho*. Cambridge, MA: Harvard University Press.

Lewett, Linda, producer and director. 1998. *Woven by the Grandmothers: 19th Century Navajo Textiles* (film). Washington, DC: WETA.

Link, Martin A., ed. 1968. *Navajo: A Century of Progress, 1868–1968*. Window Rock, AZ: The Navajo Tribe and K. C. Publications.

Luckert, Karl W. 1977. *Navaho Mountain and Rainbow Bridge Religion*. Flagstaff: Museum of Northern Arizona Press.

———. 1978. *A Navajo Bringing-Home Ceremony: The Claus Chee Sonny Version of Deerway Aijilee*. Flagstaff: Museum of Northern Arizona Press.

Matthews, Washington. 1883. Navajo Silversmiths. *Second Annual Report of the Bureau of Ethnology, 1880–81*. Washington, DC: GPO.

———. 1884. Navajo Weavers. *Bureau of American Ethnology Annual Report, 1881–1882*. Washington, DC: GPO. 371–391.

———. 1994 (1897). *Navaho Legends*. Salt Lake City: University of Utah Press.

McAllester, David P. 1954. Enemy Way Music: A Study of Social and Esthetic Values as Seen in Navajo Music. *Papers of the Peabody Museum of American Archaeology and Ethnology, Harvard University* 41.3: 1–96.

McAllester, David P., and Susan W. McAllester. 1980. *Hogans: Navajo Houses and House Songs*. Middletown, CT: Wesleyan University Press.

McCarthy, Tom, director. 1986. *Navajo Code Talkers* (film). New Mexico Film and Video.

McCullough-Brabson, Ellen, and Marilyn Help. 2001. *We'll Be in Your Mountains, We'll Be in Your Songs: A Navajo Woman Sings*. Albuquerque: University of New Mexico Press.

Mitchell, Frank. 1978. *Navajo Blessingway Singer: The Autobiography of Frank Mitchell, 1881–1967*, edited by Charlotte J. Frisbie and David McAllester. Tucson: University of Arizona Press.

Morris, Irwin. 1997. *From the Glittering World: A Navajo Story*. Norman: University of Oklahoma Press.

Newcomb, Franc Johnson. 1964. *Hosteen Klah: Navaho Medicine Man and Sand Painter*. Norman: University of Oklahoma Press.

Ortiz, Alfonso, ed. 1983. *Handbook of North American Indians*, Vol. 10. Washington, DC: Smithsonian Institution.

Parezo, Nancy. 1983. *Navajo Sandpainting: From Religious Act to Commercial Art*. Tucson: University of Arizona Press.

Piper, June-el, ed. 1999. *Diné Baa Hane Bi Naaltsoos: Collected Papers from the Seventh Through Tenth Navajo Studies Conferences*. Window Rock, AZ: Navajo Nation Historic Preservation Department.

Piper, June-el, Alexandra Roberts, and Jenevieve Smith, eds. 1993. *Papers from the Third, Fourth, and Sixth Navajo Studies Conferences*. Window Rock, AZ: Navajo National Historic Preservation Department.

Reichard, Gladys A. 1934. *Spider Woman: A Story of Navajo Weavers and Chanters*. Glorieta, NM: Rio Grande Press.

———. 1944. *Prayer: The Compulsive Word*. Seattle: University of Washington Press.

———. 1950. *Navaho Religion: A Study of Symbolism*. New York: Princeton University Press.

Rock Point Community School. 1982. *Between Sacred Mountains: Navajo Stories and Lessons from the Land*. Chinle, AZ: Rock Point Community School.

Roessel, Robert A. 1980. *Pictorial History of the Navajo from 1860 to 1910*. Rough Rock, AZ: Navajo Curriculum Center, Rough Rock Demonstration School.

Roessel, Ruth, ed. 1973. *Navajo Stories of the Long Walk Period*. Tsaile, AZ: Navajo Community College Press.

Rosenak, Chuck, and Jan Rosenak. 1994. *The People Speak: Navajo Folk Art*. Flagstaff, AZ: Northland Publishing.

Simpson, Georgiana. 2003. *Navajo Ceremonial Baskets: Sacred Symbols, Sacred Space*. Summertown, TN: Native Voices.

Spencer, Katherine. 1957. *Mythology and Values: An Analysis of Navaho Chantway Myths.* Philadelphia: American Folklore Society.

Tapahonso, Luci. 1993. *Sáanii Dahataal/The Women Are Singing.* Tucson: University of Arizona Press.

Toelken, Barre. 1976. The "Pretty Languages" of Yellowman: Genre, Mode, and Texture in Navaho Coyote Narratives. In *Folklore Genres*, edited by Dan Ben-Amos. Austin: University of Texas Press. 145–170.

———. 1981. Poetic Retranslation and the "Pretty Languages" of Yellowman. In *Traditional Literatures of the American Indian: Texts and Interpretations*, edited by Karl Kroeber. Lincoln: University of Nebraska Press. 65–116.

———. 1987. Life and Death in the Navajo Coyote Tales. In *Recovering the Word: Essays on Native American Literature*, edited by Arnold Krupat and Brian Swann. Berkeley: University of California Press. 388–401.

———. 1996. *The Dynamics of Folklore.* 2nd edition. Logan, UT: Utah State University Press.

———. 1998. The Yellowman Tapes. *Journal of American Folklore* 111: 381–391.

———. 2004. Beauty Behind Me; Beauty Before. *Journal of American Folklore* 117: 441–445.

Wheat, Joe Ben. 2002. *Blanket Weavers of the Southwest*, edited by Ann Lane Hedlund. Tucson: University of Arizona Press.

Wheelwright, Mary Cabot. 1946. *Hail Chant and Water Chant.* Santa Fe: Museum of Navajo Ceremonial Art.

Witherspoon, Gary. 1977. *Language and Art in the Navajo Universe.* Ann Arbor: University of Michigan Press.

Woodward, Arthur. 1971 (1938). *Navajo Silver: A Brief History of Navajo Silversmithing.* Flagstaff, AZ: Northland Publishing.

Wyman, Leland C. 1970. *Blessingway.* Tucson: University of Arizona Press.

———. 1983. *Southwest Indian Drypainting.* Albuquerque: University of New Mexico Press.

Yazzie, Ethelou, ed. 1971. *Navaho History.* Chinle, AZ: Navajo Curriculum Center, Rough Rock Demonstration School.

Zolbrod, Paul G. 1984. *Diné bahane': The Navajo Creation Story.* Albuquerque: University of New Mexico Press.

Laura R. Marcus

NEZ PERCE

GEOGRAPHY AND HISTORY

The activities of the characters, the imparted values, and the physical culture described in Nez Perce myths allude mainly to the culture of aboriginal times when the Nez Perce occupied roughly 13 million acres in what is now north-central Idaho, southeastern Washington, and northeastern Oregon in the United States. Nez Perce territory included the Clearwater and portions of the Salmon River and Snake River drainages. This area has many mountains, rivers, and deep canyons that provided a wide variety of food resources, protection from invaders, and shelter from the extreme cold in winter. The Nez Perce migrated throughout their territory on a seasonal basis. They made expeditions into what is now southern Idaho and eastern Oregon and Washington, down the Columbia River, and even into the northern Great Plains for buffalo and became more mobile after they adopted the horse.

The early Nez Perce lived primarily in small settlements of from 30 to 200 people. These villages were politically unified into bands that were in turn organized into composite bands. This pattern of political organization resulted largely from the location of the villages along streams and tributary systems. Villages were identified with the small streams, bands with the larger tributaries, and composite bands with rivers. A typical village consisted of several related extended families, usually led by one headman (generally the eldest able man, occasionally a shaman) whose powers were sharply limited by the village elders who elected him. The headman's duties were to demonstrate good behavior, be a spokesperson for the village, resolve disputes, and attend to the people's general welfare. Women did not speak in most council proceedings but normally influenced their male relatives to achieve their goals. The elected band leader was usually the leader of the largest village in the group and was often assisted by prominent warriors. Composite band councils were composed of band leaders but tended to be led by prominent warriors who elected a temporary leader. This type of organization made large operations such as buffalo hunting in the Great Plains easier. The head chief system in which the entire tribe was represented by a permanent leader was a product of later treaties and the reservation system that emerged after 1840.

Childhood betrothals were common. Families decided if the couple were compatible in terms of personality, relative wealth, and social prestige. Marriage between known relatives, even distant cousins, was forbidden. Marriage of more than one son into a family was common as was sororal polygyny, the practice of a man marrying two or more sisters. The levirate and sororate (the option to marry the eldest brother of the groom or a sister of the bride in the event of their deaths) were also observed. Couples lived with the parents from whom they could expect to gain the most, usually those of the groom.

MYTHS, LEGENDS, AND FOLKTALES

The Nez Perce believed that humans and natural objects had souls, without which they ceased to exist. Mythical characters share much in common with the teaching spirits that Nez Perce individuals traditionally acquired during vision quests. Teaching spirits differ from souls in that they are acquired during life and are rarely lost. At adolescence, children of both sexes were sent out to seek tutelary spirits in vision quests. Teaching spirits could give special powers and abilities to those who followed the proper rituals and taboos, or they could cause misfortune and death to those who violated taboos. The Nez Perce believe that although the animals became mute after humans arrived, they can still reveal their full power to humans in visions and dreams. Heaven and hell were concepts brought by Christian missionaries, but conceptions of an afterlife predated Christianity. Shamans were people who demonstrated particularly strong supernatural powers during medicine dances and in healing and who performed various ceremonial services in the community.

A legend for the Nez Perce was more than entertainment. Important lessons about local geography and natural resources were found in heroes' and villians' trials. Probably the most important lessons taught the morals and behaviors expected of a Nez Perce man or woman.

The stories implied that to be happy and successful, one should or should not do certain things. Along with each story's special points, several general lessons can be found in the myth cycle as a whole: no matter how hard you try to gain by cheating and deception, everything will go wrong and you will be left with nothing in the end; if a child is mean to others or disobedient to his parents, his friends will leave him all alone in the world, making him an unwanted and lonely child; if a person is greedy for more than his share, he is apt to lose everything, thus stressing the importance of sharing with others; jealousy of a friend's good fortune can lead to a bad end; people should give encouragement instead of ridicule; even the strongest can be defeated by weaker but more intelligent beings; one should not judge a potential marriage partner especially based upon looks alone without realizing what is in that person's heart; the strong should learn to protect the freedom of the weak; people will help you if they believe you are sincere and have good intentions.

Nez Perce culture has undergone rapid transformation since first contact with Euro-Americans, but Nez Perce myths are quite conservative and reveal few new materials. For example,

Four Nez Perce Indians dressed for a dance on Colville Indian Reservation. (Courtesy Library of Congress)

although horses played a large role in shaping Nez Perce life after about 1700 C.E., horses do not appear as characters in the narratives, are rarely mentioned, and appear only as minor details. The values associated with the behavior and activities of mythical characters in particular contexts as well as the physical culture described in the narratives almost always allude to traditional Nez Perce culture before the horse. Nez Perce myths do not directly or systematically reflect traditional Nez Perce culture in a typical structural-functional manner. Instead, the myths form a semi-independent sector of Nez Perce culture and depict a distinct reality whose construction is based on its own rules. Myths are mechanisms for educating children, for stimulating social interaction and cohesion, and for amusement. Nez Perce myths were traditionally recounted by elders during winter. They are inhabited by a cast of characters that includes animals, plants, rocks, rivers, celestial bodies, and other figures who behave like humans yet exist in an era before humans were created. The myth cycle has survived largely unchanged despite massive changes in other sections of Nez Perce culture.

Narratives that include Coyote make up more than half of Nez Perce myths. (© Tom Brakefield/The Image Works)

Coyote Tales

Narratives that include Coyote make up more than half of Nez Perce myths. Because Coyote created them, the Nez Perce consider themselves to be the children of Coyote: *Iceye.yenm mamayac*. Many other mythical characters inhabit the world where Coyote's adventures take place, but he is the most complex figure in Nez Perce mythology. Few other characters manifest a survival capacity equal to his. He represents and expresses many of the most basic human drives: lust for power, hunger for food, and unrestrained sexual desire. His methods for satisfying these drives often include deception, evasion, trickery, and disguise. His actions may disrupt the lives of his mythical associates, yet he seems to be aware that his activities can benefit the human beings whom he is soon to create.

It is also worthwhile to note several other things about Nez Perce Coyote. He is not a god in the Western sense; he is not a hero in the sense used by Joseph Campbell; he is not a creator in the sense of the figure from the book of Genesis; and he is not merely a picaresque figure. The term **trickster**-*transformer*, often applied to Coyote, also omits several important aspects of his character because he is not only the perpetrator of tricks but also the victim of tricks perpetrated on him by others. His role as a transformer has been exaggerated, especially in view of his motives, which are self-centered.

Like myths from other cultures, Nez Perce myths impart basic values and beliefs and provide moral instruction. They help explain the creation of the world and its inhabitants, the origins of rituals and customs, and the meaning of birth, death, and other natural occurrences such as origins of animals, environmental features, and customs. This type of story helps answer questions about why certain things in nature came to be the way they are now: how the seasons started or why there is a frog in the moon, for instance. Many of the tales are humorous, as when Eel loses his bones in a gambling game, but important information is found in all of them. Some stories deal with the seasons and the sun and moon. Many other stories teach about the markings and habits of different animals or which plants are edible or useful. A few tales such as "How the Salmon Found They Shouldn't Go up Potlatch Creek" and "Coyote Builds a Dam" teach about landmarks still visible in Nez Perce territory today or how various rivers were not suitable for spawning because of a lack of spawning beds and gravel. The story of the salmon as related by Alan Slickpoo (1979) illustrates this design:

Once, Coyote was sitting on top of a hill when he saw that the salmon were starting to swim upstream. They were heading toward the place where the falls at Wasco, on the Columbia River, were broken. Coyote saw the salmon pass as he went up the first branch of the great Snake River. It goes up that way from the Columbia River, and its water is clear. Coyote saw then that the salmon were on their way up the Clearwater River to spawn, and were heading on upstream to Potlatch Creek.

Suddenly, he remembered that there was no gravel at the headwaters of that creek where the Chinook salmon could spawn. So he hollered after them, "You are going up where there are only split rocks. If you want to go to a good place to spawn, go on up the big clear river."

And so they did. Some of them went up to *Tamso-ypa*, one mile up from the mouth of Potlatch Creek. From there they jumped on over to the Clearwater River, over the saddle. Some of the other salmon were up near the mouth of the stream. They heard the other fish say, "We are going up this stream [the Clearwater River]. It is better."

So they jumped over to Eagle Point, where the saddle is. From then on, the Chinook salmon never went up Potlatch Creek, for its headwaters are only split rocks. The Chinook salmon and steelhead salmon migrate on up the Clearwater River and the upper branches to spawn.

Disobedience Tales

Tales of disobedience teach the same lesson: that children should not disobey their relatives. Most older relatives took part in training children. Nez Perce children developed close ties with grandparents, who typically cared for them after weaning. In contrast to a more formal relationship maintained with their parents, children could joke with and tease grandparents, whom they tended to regard as equals. Grandfather would usually direct a boy's first attempts at hunting, fishing, sweatbathing, and riding, while Grandmother would usually direct a girl's first root-digging or berry-picking. Grandparents also spent many hours telling myths, which were a primary means of education. Siblings and cousins were viewed as brothers and sisters, and aunts and uncles were called by the same terms used for father and mother. By the age of six, boys and girls were already contributing substantially to the family's well-being.

In the story of the "Disobedient Boy," a boy finds that the entire tribe abandons him because he misbehaves. In "*Kiw-kiw-lu-ye*'s Grandchildren," both parents leave their children alone after they disobey their mother. The children must then face many dangers all alone. Both stories show, however, that if one is truly sorry, his relatives will return and care for him again.

The behavior of characters in myths instructed children in proper behavior and taught them practical lessons such as the habits of game animals, the location of food and other resources, how to use implements and tools, and the geography of their territory. Some emphasize the positive or negative outcomes of various types of behavior, reinforcing the prized values of honesty, justice, bravery, generosity, self-discipline, and self-reliance. In vengeance tales, someone seeks revenge for a wrong that has been done to him. The reader or listener decides whether the character is right or wrong in taking revenge. One character, for example, kills his wife because she told a lie. In another tale, Coyote comes back to life several times in these stories to kill a few "Old Time Killers" who have killed him before. The lesson of vengeance tales is, "Beware those who feel wronged by you, for they may be plotting revenge."

Coyote and the other mythical actors are pre-human combinations of animal, human, and superhuman qualities. Their behaviors are not entirely human, and we should not assume that these actors reflect traditional Nez Perce culture. Coyote acts largely on his immediate urges and impulses and is only marginally social in the human sense, which helps to explain the amoral actions that conflict sharply with traditional Nez Perce behavior.

Shrewdness Tales

In shrewdness tales the characters have to think up very clever ways to get what they want, be it a wife, revenge, or supper. Coyote is in good form as the "trickster" as he disguises himself as a baby ("Coyote Breaks the Fish Dam at Celilo"), pretends to die and be buried ("Coyote Marries His Daughter"), and plays several other tricks throughout the stories. Sometimes, though, Coyote plays tricks to help people, as when he breaks the Celilo dam so that those upstream could have some salmon too. Other characters such as "Bed-wetting Boy" and "Bluejay" also show much cleverness in these enjoyable tales. For example, Alan Slickpoo (1972) related the story "How Coyote Roasted Salmon":

> Coyote was on his way upriver one day when he became very hungry. He was swimming up the Columbia River, but instead of following the mainstream, he decided to go up the *Tu-sa* (Touchet River in Washington). There he saw some salmon going by. Coyote asked them as he sat down, "Why is it that not even one of you swim out to the shore? Come out of the water this way. Once I saved your life by breaking the dam at Celilo."
>
> The salmon said to each other, "He is right about that. He has given us these good streams to swim up. You go out to him." So one Chinook salmon swam out to the shore. Suddenly Coyote grabbed him with a blanket, but the Chinook salmon tore up the blanket and got away. So Coyote went upstream farther, still hungry.
>
> A little while later, he broke the leg of Meadowlark as he was walking. Coyote said, "Aunt, tell me what I can do to hold the salmon, and I will make you a new leg."
>
> Meadowlark said, "You'll never succeed by wrapping the salmon in a blanket. Next time, tell them to swim out to you, and when they are near the shore, have a stick ready. When you see a salmon, hit it." Then Coyote made the Meadowlark a new leg.
>
> That day, Coyote said to the salmon, "Swim out to shore. I saved you once, remember?" Just as one came to shore, Coyote hit it with a club. He then cut the sides of the salmon off and roasted each side on a stick. Then he went to sleep.
>
> Fox, Raccoon and Skunk came along and saw the delicious salmon roasting and the Coyote fast asleep. The Fox said, "Let's eat the salmon while he is asleep."
>
> They ate up all the salmon that Coyote was roasting over the fire. Then they cut off a piece of his rump and placed it on the roasting sticks and set it before the fire to roast, and they departed.
>
> Coyote woke up saying, "Urn, I am hungry and the salmon looks as if it is cooked." So he grabbed a piece that was roasting and tasted it, "Yum, Yum, it tastes good." In the meantime an ant began to crawl up his leg and reached his cut-off rump. It itched and he began to scratch. He suddenly discovered that a part of him was gone, and learned that he had been eating his own flesh that was roasting in the fire.

He looked around and saw that on the hill Fox, Raccoon, and Skunk were rolling around laughing at him. "Hmmm," he said. "I shall get even with them."

So he waited until they too went to sleep, tired from laughing. Seeing this, he found some eggs. He sneaked up to the three and began "painting" them. He used the yellow of the egg and painted the Fox up all yellow. He then took the dark coals from the fire and made circles around the Raccoon's eyes and tail. He also took the white ashes and painted the stripes on the back of the Skunk.

When the trio woke up they looked at each other and began laughing, because they looked so funny. Soon they learned that someone had played a trick on them. They saw Coyote laughing, rolling around on the ground. He had got even with them for playing such a trick on him.

That is why the place is now named *Tu-sa*, which means to roast something.

Tales of Food and Bravery

Plants traditionally used by the Nez Perce for food include camas bulbs, wild carrot, wild onion, many kinds of berries, seeds, pine nuts, mosses, and bark. Game animals include salmon and other fish, elk, deer, moose, mountain goats and sheep, bear, small game, and birds, many of which show up in Nez Perce myths.

In several of these tales, the greed is for food. "Racoon-Boy," for example, takes all the food from his hungry grandmother and is finally eaten by her when she turns into Grizzly Bear. The "Glutton" does not let his wife have any meat and is finally deserted by her. Other forms of greed are also found in these stories. In "Coyote, His Friend Fox, and Woodtick," Coyote is greedy for another man's teepee, skins, and other possessions. But, as always, he finds out that those who are too greedy lose everything in the end.

Tales of bravery are full of adventure as the different characters win battles, fight terrible monsters, and go to strange places. Like most of the other tales in the Nez Perce repertoire, other information is presented during the telling of the adventures. "Coyote and the Monster of Kamiah," for example, takes place just as the *La-te-tel-wit* (Human Beings) come. This story also describes some of the looks and traits of certain Indian peoples, such as the Flathead, Cayuse, and Nez Perce.

BIBLIOGRAPHY

Slickpoo, Alan P., Sr., Leroy L. Seth, and Deward E. Walker Jr. 1972. *Nu Mee Poom Tit Wah Tit (Nez Perce Legends)*. Lapwai, ID: Nez Perce Tribe of Idaho.

Walker, Deward E., Jr., and Daniel N. Matthews. 1998. *Blood of the Monster: The Nez Perce Coyote Cycle*. Norman: University of Oklahoma Press.

Deward E. Walker Jr.

OJIBWE

GEOGRAPHY AND HISTORY

The term *Ojibwe* (also *Ojibwa*, *Ojibway*, and *Chippewa*) is used variously to refer to overlapping but non-congruent linguistic, ethnic, and political groups. Perhaps the most common usage is to identify a group of indigenous people whose forebears lived in the vicinity of the Great Lakes, especially on the northern shores of Lakes Huron

Ojibwe mending a canoe with tipis in the background (1913). Despite centuries of disruption and change, the Ojibwes have clung tenaciously to their identity. (Courtesy Library of Congress)

and Superior, at the time of contact with Europeans approximately 400 years ago. As such a geographically delimited population, the Ojibwe are often distinguished from other groups such as the Ottawa and Algonquins. From a linguistic point of view, however, defined in terms of chains of mutual intelligibility, all these groups speak interlocking dialects of the same language, customarily self-designated as *Anishinaabemowin* (also *Nishnaabemwin*, *Anishiniiniimowin*, and *Nakawemowin*). Over the course of four centuries, these different peoples interacted with Europeans and other indigenous groups in various ways, giving rise to political, cultural, and linguistic amalgamations and diasporas that have transformed pre-contact relations.

The most important changes derive from the effects of European military and economic interests, including the fur trade and struggles by the French, British, and Americans for control of the geographic areas that constitute the traditional homelands of Great Lakes indigenous peoples. The various Ojibwe-speaking groups initially interacted with the French through the Hurons, who were located just to the east of Lake Huron. The material advantages that attended the exchange of furs for European trade goods, especially weaponry, created a crisis in the region that led to a devastating attack by Iroquoians on the Hurons in 1649, precipitating a westward flight by Algonquian peoples that extended their range west across the Great Lakes and adjoining regions as far as Minnesota and thus into territory formerly held by other Algonquian people such as the Fox as well as Siouan peoples. Ojibwe people also moved west with the Great Lakes fur trade, extending their range across the boundary waters area of Minnesota and Ontario to Lake Winnipeg in contemporary Manitoba and ultimately west to the eastern slopes of the Rocky Mountains.

At the same time that the French were actively trading furs in the Great Lakes region, the British were establishing trade relations with Algonquian peoples living in the Hudson Bay drainage. Many of the inland groups with whom the British interacted were also speakers of languages identifiable as belonging to the Ojibwe-language complex. With the defeat of the French on the Plains of Abraham in 1759, the fur trade came under British control from its initial base on Hudson Bay, which had devastating repercussions for the Ojibwe, since it effectively resulted in a monopoly that undermined the bargaining power of indigenous people involved in the trade. At the time of American independence at the end of the eighteenth century, the fur trade was in steady decline, and European interest in the Great Lakes region as well as elsewhere shifted from the relatively less intrusive extraction of fur to wholesale agricultural settlement and mining, resulting in a vast influx of European immigrants who dealt with the "Indian problem" initially through removals and later with the establishment of reservations. Faced with economic ruin from mounting debts incurred from the fur trade and exacerbated by the depletion of game upon which they had relied for their subsistence, the Ojibwe were induced to enter into a long series of treaties in which they ceded their lands to the American and Canadian governments. Such cessions ultimately produced the contemporary situation, in which the descendants of original Algonquian populations find themselves located either on small, widely separated reservations existing within a sea of European settlement or as part of a contemporary urban diaspora.

In the latter half of the nineteenth century, the American and Canadian governments pursued aggressive assimilation programs, the most notorious component of which was the removal of Indian children from their families to distant residential schools, where they were not allowed to speak their indigenous languages and where they were taught farming methods, related vocational skills such as blacksmithing, and the Christian religion. In the twentieth century, the adoption of European technology has resulted in further transformations of Ojibwe domestic life. Yet despite centuries of disruption and change, the Ojibwe people have clung tenaciously to their identity, and their contemporary social and cultural life shows identifiable reflexes of the many periods of their pre-contact and post-contact history. Today Ojibwe life consists of a richly articulated cultural mosaic that is at once hybridized with European culture while simultaneously retaining core Ojibwe elements.

MYTHS, LEGENDS, AND FOLKTALES

Ojibwe oral tradition represents the first indigenous verbal lore to be documented in depth by Europeans, having received the attention of Henry Rowe Schoolcraft, who served as Indian Agent in what is now northern Michigan from 1822 to 1841. Taking his initial impulse from an ethnographic questionnaire developed by Lewis Cass, Schoolcraft sought to document local Ojibwe language and culture, a task that was facilitated by his marriage in 1823 to Jane Johnston, whose father was a prominent fur trader and whose mother was Ojibwe. The Johnston family were fluent speakers of Ojibwe. Schoolcraft was amazed to discover the existence of such a rich oral tradition among the Ojibwe and ultimately published a substantial number of stories in translation, though his bowderlizations and stylistic changes often obliterated the form and force of the originals. Schoolcraft's stories also served as the basis for one of the most famous poems in American literary history, Longfellow's *The Song of Hiawatha*, which fueled romantic nationalist interests by casting sanitized heroic Ojibwe oral tradition, a distinctly "American" legacy, in the meter of the epic Finnish poem, the *Kalevala*. Longfellow confused Iroquoian and Algonquian tradition, naming the poem for an Iroquoian hero but featuring the central figure of Ojibwe traditional cosmology, the culture-hero and **trickster** Nenabozho (also Nanabush, Wenebozho, and Wiizakejaak). Nenabozho was conceived when his mother was impregnated by the wind or, according to some accounts, by the sun.

Hiawatha of the Iroquois Indians. Longfellow confused Iroquoian and Algonquian tradition, naming the poem for an Iroquoian hero but featuring the central figure of Ojibwe traditional cosmology, the culture-hero/trickster Nenabozho. (© Topham/The Image Works)

The Nenabozho myth cycle traditionally served as a cosmogonic account of such important events as how fire was obtained, the origin of death, protocols for engaging enemies in battle, the emergence of hunting as a primary cultural practice, and the formation of the present world. In contemporary usage, the character of Nenabozho is central to a host of oral and literary forms, running the gamut from casual adaptations of English language jokes to professionally produced plays such as Tomson Highway's *Dry Lips Oughta Move to Kapuskasing* (Highway is Cree, but his plays are set in Ojibwe communities) and important novels such as Gerald Vizenor's *Griever: An American Monkey King in China* and Louise Erdrich's *Tracks*. This continuing centrality of Nenabozho to verbal art and written literature underscores the centrality of imagination, humor, irony, and humility to Ojibwe cultural life. In recent years, too, a popular text for programs in Ojibwe culture taught by Ojibwes has been Edward Benton-Banai's *The Mishomis Book: The Voice of the Ojibway*, which uses the traditional Nenabozho cycle to respond to the moral idealism and arrogance of European Christianity by casting Nenabozho in almost hagiographic terms. Another consummately skillful popularizer of Ojibwe oral tradition is Basil Johnston, whose work includes *Ojibway Heritage* (1976), *Moose Meat and Wild Rice* (1978), *Ojibway Ceremonies* (1982), and *Bear-Walker and Other Stories* (1995), among many others.

Ojibwe oral tradition is by no means limited to stories of Nenabozho, since stories traditionally had a central role in education, critical thinking, and entertainment. Other thematic types include precautionary tales of marriage to animals, vision-quest stories, bungling host stories, animal tales, wendigo stories, and journey tales. Traditional motifs are sometimes used as a template for casting historical experiences—for example, the common story in Wisconsin explaining contact with Europeans in terms of a distinguished elder first dreaming of Europeans and then setting out eastward in a canoe eventually to find them on the St. Lawrence River.

Many traditional European stories have been adapted and adopted into the Ojibwe canon from both French and English sources. Such stories often include references to princesses and kings, gold coins, and European domestic animals, but they also feature traditional Ojibwe characters such as wendigoes and a heroic orphan boy living with and protecting his grandmother. There are, for example, stories of Taazhaanh or Zhiizhaan (an adaptation of French Petit Jean, which was shortened to Ti-Jean in North America). Such stories abound, and representatives can be found in the vast collection of stories compiled by William Jones in the early twentieth century, which includes the Ojibwe texts alongside careful English translations, and Victor Barnouw's collection of Wisconsin Ojibwe myths and tales, which unfortunately provides only heavily edited English and rhetorically flawed translations with disconcerting analyses based on Freudian sexual fixations.

PUNNING AND ORAL HISTORIES

Another popular hybridized form of humor is that of cross-language punning. Punning is a verbal form central to Ojibwe humor. In one widely found story in Minnesota, an Ojibwe and a white man go hunting for ducks. They take along a lunch, which the bossy white man puts in the care of the Indian. When a duck flies over, the ever imperious white man shouts to the Indian, "Get down! Get down!" But his companion hears instead the Ojibwe *"Gidaan! Gidaan!"* meaning "Eat it up! Eat it up!" The Indian obliges by eating the lunch. Later, when the white man desires to eat, he asks the Indian for the food only to discover that it has been eaten as instructed, at which point he shouts, "You damn Injun!" This the Ojibwe interprets to be *"Gide-miijin,"* meaning "You've eaten to your fill," at which point he replies, *"Enh, inde-miijin!"* (Yes, I've eaten to my fill). Word play of this sort is extremely popular and is particularly manifest in the artful creation of new words. Because Ojibwe is a polysynthetic language, a single word can be equivalent to a whole sentence of English. Much stock is put in the apt and concise coinage of a new term. For example, when northern Ojibwe elders first observed young people gyrating to the rhythms of a rock dance, they promptly coined the word *wewebidiyeshimo,* which has the components *weweb-,* "throw repeatedly," *-diy-e,* "one's backside," and *-shimo,* "do dancing"—literally, "she or he dances in such a way as to repeatedly throw his or her backside about." The precision of such coinages has been compared to the esthetic economy of expression found in Japanese haiku. Perhaps the most impressive form of this sort of compounding wordplay is the Ottawa-Odawa single-word tongue-twister *Gga-gchi-niisaakye-zaagji-ziinkiigmaane-bskiigdigwe-bmiboojgesahin,* which translates as "I'm going to throw you down the hill so hard the snot will come out of your nose and your knees will buckle."

Another creative aspect of Ojibwe oral tradition is that of oral history. In the early 1800s William Warren, half-Ojibwe and a fluent speaker of the language, traveled about his native region of Wisconsin and Minnesota and recorded Ojibwe elders' accounts of their history, which he compiled into his *History of the Ojibway People,* published in 1885, thirty-two years after his death. Many of Warren's accounts relate to military engagements, particularly with the Sioux. In the east, similar accounts describe encounters with the Iroquois or Ojibwe participation in European conflicts. A particularly striking example is the late Sam Osawamick's account of the deeds of the military leader Niibaakhom, who assisted the British in the War of 1812. At a critical point in the narrative, Niibaakhom sends two scouts in the form of bats to reconnoiter the number of troops in an American camp, and with this intelligence his warriors are able to prevail over their opponents, thus preventing Canada from falling to the Americans. Such accounts rather obviously encode a **worldview** cast in Ojibwe cultural terms and grade by degrees into more formulaic traditional verbal forms such as Andrew Medler's story of a young man who receives the protection of a mirror-being during his vision-fast and is later able single-handedly to overcome a host of the enemy with the aid of his tutelary. As the battle ensues, the young man is rendered invisible by the mirror-being, which further aids him by flashing blinding light to confound the enemy. Such stories highlight a traditional epistemology that grounds itself in an articulated relationship between dreaming, personal relationship with other-than-human tutelaries, and singular heroism in the service of community. Almost all such stories have protagonists who react decisively to foreign aggression rather than initiating it. Such service is at the core of Ojibwe values, as testified in the twentieth century by the inordinate response of Ojibwe men to the call to service in time of war. A striking account of such sacrifice can be found in the oral history provided by Joe Chosa of Lac du Flambeau, Wisconsin, who served thirty-seven months in Europe and North Africa in World War II.

MUSIC AND SONGS

Music is also a prominent component of Ojibwe creative expression. Traditionally, musical forms and functions were of many varieties, including, for example, those used by specialists in their medical procedures, courtship and love songs, songs of war, game songs, and various songs for children. Traditional narratives also sometimes contained song components. Traditional instruments were various kinds of drums, rattles, and flutes. Many contemporary Ojibwe musicians have created popular hybridized styles incorporating both traditional Ojibwe and contemporary Western musical styles. One such artist is Keith Secola, originally from the Iron Range district of northern Minnesota, whose signature song is "NDN Kars," in which the hapless Indian owner of a broken-down car with expired license plates drives precariously from one powwow to the next, constantly being stopped by local police officers because of the dilapidated state of his transportation. With characteristic Ojibwe punning, Secola has dubbed his musical style as Alter-Native, playing on the popular contemporary rock genre alternative.

ARTS AND CRAFTS

Traditional crafts included various kinds of basketry, grass-work, birch-bark incisions, decorative beading, and dyed porcupine quilling. Many of these crafts are still practiced, primarily to produce goods for sale, many of which are consummately artful. The dreamcatcher, originally used as a charm and toy to be hung from a child's cradleboard, continues to be a popular handicraft. It is typically made with a twig or piece of metal formed into a ring to enclose and support a system of strings resembling a spider's web. Many traditional crafts such as quilting and appliqué work have been professionalized to a very high degree and are of such quality as to command thousands of dollars for a single work.

Graphic art is also very popular, and Ojibwe artists who have achieved national and international fame most notably include Norval Morrisseau, Leland Bell, Carl Ray, Arthur Schilling, and Daphne Odjig. Morrisseau, a native of the Lake Nipigon area of northwestern Ontario, provided a mural for the Canadian Indian Pavilion at the 1967 Canadian Exposition in Montreal, winning instant acclaim. Morrisseau's art is characterized by vividly colored figures that take their inspiration from traditional Ojibwe mythology and the pictography of rock paintings and birch-bark scrolls. Often figures are represented in a black outline "X-ray" style that reveals compartmentalized interiors in saturated colors, and traditional "spirit-lines" sometimes make explicit connections between the people, animals, and flora represented in the paintings. For Morrisseau, the bright blocks of color in his paintings provide a means by which the Ojibwe people (and others) can begin to heal themselves from the profound alienation and loss that they have experienced over the centuries of contact with Europeans. His style has been dubbed (New) Woodlands or, sometimes, Legend painting and has inspired generations of Ojibwe and Cree painters. Daphne Odjig, often classified as a Woodlands painter, is also nationally recognized. While Odjig's work shows clear connections with the Woodlands tradition, she distinguishes herself from it by her central concern with womanhood and family, as opposed to the more explicitly spiritual, questing, nature of typical Woodlands-style art. Both Odjig and Morrisseau are recipients of the Order of Canada, the country's highest award for personal social achievement.

FESTIVALS AND CELEBRATIONS

The most important social event for many Ojibwe people is the powwow. While drawing from traditional themes such as ceremonial dance and drumming, the modern powwow simultaneously blends the social and spiritual in a celebration of community. The powwow is also an affirmation of traditional Ojibwe culture and heritage. As with other tribal groups, the powwow is structured in terms of a series of social and honor dances performed to the accompaniment of drum groups. The honoring of war veterans figures prominently in powwow ceremony.

Other traditional activities of significance to many Ojibwe people include wild rice harvesting and maple-sugaring, each with attendant ceremonies of gratitude, community, and respect. In northern Ontario, where Christianity was introduced to the Ojibwe people by Cree missionaries, the Anglican Church in particular has been heavily indigenized and provides a rich source of spirituality and community for many people. In many such communities, Cree, written with a syllabary, remains the liturgical language of choice.

While their total population equals that of a modest American or Canadian city, the achievements of the Ojibwe people in all forms of creative expression testify to the place of imagination and art in Ojibwe society and the consummate skill of its practitioners. The best way to experience Ojibwe folklife is of course firsthand, which can readily be done through attendance at powwows and other cultural events hosted by Ojibwe people and communities. Many universities and colleges in the Great Lakes region offer courses in Ojibwe language and culture, and various heritage programs open to the public are also common in Ojibwe communities. Many communities have museums and heritage centers that display and explain local traditions and history. Casinos and bingo halls continue the long tradition of gaming in Ojibwe society, and many feature cultural exhibits and themes. Many communities have Web sites as well that provide an abundance of cultural and historical materials, which can be readily accessed through a simple Web search.

BIBLIOGRAPHY

Barnouw, Victor. 1977. *Wisconsin Chippewa Myths and Tales, and Their Relation to Chippewa Life*. Madison: University of Wisconsin Press.

Benton-Banai, Edward. 1979. *The Mishomis Book: the Voice of the Ojibway*. St. Paul: Indian Country Press.

Berbaum, Sylvie. 2000. *Ojibwa Powwow World*, edited and translated by Michael M. Pomedi. Thunder Bay, Ontario: Lakehead University Centre for Northern Studies.

Densmore, Frances. 1913. *Chippewa Music—II*. Bureau of American Ethnology Bulletins, No. 53. Washington, DC: GPO.

———. 1929. *Chippewa Customs*. Bureau of American Ethnology Bulletins, No. 86. Washington, DC: GPO.

Dunning, Robert. 1959. *Social and Economic Change among the Northern Ojibwa*. Toronto: University of Toronto Press.

Hallowell, A. Irving. 1992. *The Ojibwe of Berens River, Manitoba: Ethnography into History*, edited by Jennifer S. H. Brown. Montreal: Harcourt Brace Jovanovich.

Hilger, M. Inez. 1951. *Chippewa Child Life and Its Cultural Background*. Bureau of American Ethnology Bulletins, No. 146. Washington, DC: GPO.

Johnston, Basil H. 1976. *Ojibway Heritage*. Toronto: McClelland and Stewart.

———. 1978. *Moose Meat and Wild Rice*. Toronto: McClelland and Stewart.

———. 1982. *Ojibway Ceremonies*. Toronto: McClelland and Stewart.

———. 1988. *Indian School Days*. Toronto: McClelland and Stewart.

———. 1995. *Bear-Walker and Other Stories*. Toronto: Royal Ontario Museum.

Jones, William. 1974 (1917, 1919). *Ojibwa Texts*, edited by Truman Michelson. 2 volumes. New York: AMS Press.

Kegg, Maude. 1983. *Nookomis gaa-inaajimotawid: What My Grandmother Told Me*, edited by John D. Nichols. St. Paul: Minnesota Archaeological Society.

———. 1991. *Portage Lake: Memories of an Ojibwe Childhood*, edited by John D. Nichols. Edmonton: University of Alberta Press.

Lindquist, Mark A., and Martin Zanger, eds. 1993, 1994. *Buried Roots and Indestructible Seeds: The Survival of American Indian Life in Story, History and Spirit*. Madison: University of Wisconsin Press.

Morrisseau, Norval. 1997. *Norval Morrisseau*. Toronto: Key Porter Books.

Nichols, John. 1988. *An Ojibwe Text Anthology*. Text+ Series, No. 2. Studies in the Interpretation of Canadian Native Languages and Cultures. London, Ontario: Centre for Research and Teaching of Canadian Native Languages, University of Western Ontario.

Odjig, Daphne. 1992. *A Paintbrush in My Hand*. Toronto: Natural Heritage/Natural History.

Rogers, Edward. 1962. *The Round Lake Ojibwa*. Toronto: Ontario Department of Lands and Forests for the Royal Ontario Museum.

Tornes, Elizabeth M., ed. 2004. *Memories of Lac du Flambeau Elders. With a Brief History of Waaswaagoning Ojibweg*, by Leon Valliere Jr. Madison: University of Wisconsin Press.

Valentine, J. Randolph. 1998. *Weshki-Bmaadzijig ji-noondmowaad: That the Young Might Hear: The Stories of Andrew Medler as Recorded by Leonard Bloomfield*. London, Ontario: Centre for Research and Teaching of Canadian Native Languages, University of Western Ontario.

Valentine, Lisa P. 1995. *Making It Their Own: Seven Ojibwe Communicative Practices*. Toronto: University of Toronto Press.

Vennum, Thomas. 1988. *Wild Rice and the Ojibway People*. St. Paul: Minnesota Historical Society Press.

———. 2000. Review of *Ojibwa Powwow World* by Silvie Berbaum. *Minnesota History* 57.5: 212–214.

Warren, William. 1957 (1885). *History of the Ojibway People*. Minneapolis: Ross and Haines.

Williams, Angeline. 1991. *The Dog's Children: Anishinaabe Texts Told by Angeline Williams*, edited and translated by Leonard Bloomfield; edited by John D. Nichols. Publications of the Algonquian Text Society. Winnipeg: University of Manitoba Press.

Rand Valentine

SEMINOLE

GEOGRAPHY AND HISTORY

A late-forming group of Native Americans, the Seminoles organized in Florida in the early eighteenth century from many tribes in the southeastern colonies of North America in consequence of government attempts to relocate them. They came from the states that are now Georgia, Alabama, North Carolina, South Carolina, Tennessee, and Mississippi. The core indigenous group was the Creeks or Muskogee, joined by runaways from the Oconee, Hitchiti, Sawokli, Tamathli, Apalachicola, and the Chiaha, who later became the Mikasuki. Other people from the ravaged Yuchi, Apalachee, Yamasee, Timucua, and Calusa tribes were also absorbed. During the 1770s, these Florida Indians collectively became known as the Seminole.

Etymologically, *Simano-li* is the Muskogee word believed to derive from the Spanish *cimarron*, meaning "wild" or "runaway." Black slaves were sold at first to Seminole chiefs and over a period of twenty years integrated into the society in a non-subservient relationship. These slaves were valuable members of the community and not held in the traditional owner-slave relationship. They demonstrated skills in harvesting and caring for livestock and lived in a reciprocal setting. Since they had lived among whites, they became interpreters for the Seminoles because they both understood European languages and rapidly learned the Muskogean dialect of their captors (who were actually more like patrons). The Seminole group attracted more and more slaves from Georgia and South Carolina because, unlike the white owners, Seminoles encouraged autonomy as the slaves developed social relationships within the group. Soon the white settlers wanted their slaves back as well as more Indian land. But the Seminoles steadfastly refused to return these now-integrated people to their former owners.

The United States waged three wars against the Seminoles. The first, in 1817, was led by Andrew Jackson, who invaded Florida and destroyed the homes of the Seminoles because they were allegedly harboring slaves. The second was in response to the Indian Removal Act of 1830, through which the United States attempted to send the Indians to Oklahoma. The tribe, led by Osceola, won that war, but unfortunately he was tricked

Osceola of Florida. Drawn on stone by Geo. Catlin, from his original portrait. (Courtesy Library of Congress)

into surrendering seven years later when the U.S. troops pretended that they wanted to hold a truce. Osceola was imprisoned at Fort Marion in St. Augustine, Florida—now Castillo de San Marcos—in a special cell apart from the twenty other Seminoles captured with him. One story tells that they ate special herbs and grasses to make them shrink small enough to escape. They actually did get away, but Osceola remained, too ill with malaria to leave. The third Seminole war, in 1858, ended the conflicts. More than 3,000 people had been banished to Indian Territory west of the Mississippi River. At the end of the second Seminole war, there were approximately 500 living Seminoles. After the third, far less survived, and those who did remain in Florida hid in the swamplands of the Everglades.

Miraculously, they avoided detection while building their families and homes and retaining their traditions and what they could of their culture. Perhaps the most enduring faculty of this group has been their ability to change their lives to meet the demands of the modern world without giving up what is distinctly Seminole. In their Everglades environments, they tended gardens, processed cornmeal, and raised hogs.

The U.S. government continued to infringe upon their rights by relocating the Seminoles and transporting them under the harshest conditions to live on reservations in what is now Oklahoma. This tragic journey is known as the Trail of Tears. Those who were relocated to Oklahoma became known as the Seminole Nation, one of the five civilized tribes. Heartbreaking stories tell of children removed from their families and spirited across the country to be "re-educated" and "retrained" in the ways of the whites. This "Christianizing" consisted of forcing the children to abandon their language, cut their hair and style it in the fashion of whites, dress in Euro-American clothing, and be subjected to a severely cold climate without adequate protection from the elements. Many children died on the trains while being transported to such schools as that at Carlisle, Pennsylvania. However, enough Seminole were stubborn and brave enough to escape and return to Florida to re-establish their culture, and for that reason they are regarded as the only Native American group able to resist total expatriation.

Since the Seminole culture derived from North American eastern tribal culture, they originally shared many characteristics known throughout the culture area such as clothing, food production, tools, shelter, religion, and sociopolitical organization. But adaptation to the heat and humidity of Florida in all aspects of their lifeways was necessary to survive in this challenging environment.

CLOTHING

Traditional southeastern Native American clothing included fitted skins, dresses, skirts, aprons, shirts, breechcloths (for men), leggings, deerskin robes, and coats. In warm weather, men wore a leather loincloth held in place with a leather thong or belt made from plant material. When it became cooler, or when going through forested areas, they wore leggings held in place with garters and rabbit, marten, or bear fur robes. Women dressed in leather aprons that extended to the knee and added longer skirts, leggings, and fur robes in the winter. The cloth was woven from natural fibers found in the inner bark of the mulberry tree or a combination of animal hair with plant fibers. Children were naked except for foot protection. Shoes were moccasins made from deer or bearskin. Feathers in general indicated social status: the more ornate, the higher on the social scale. Eagle feathers epitomized rank and were followed by turkey. Both men and women wore head coverings decorated possibly with feathers appropriate to their standing in society. As trade developed between Europeans and the Seminoles, cotton fabric replaced fur and skin, and by the late 1800s, children were clothed, men wore shirts that extended to midthigh, and women wore long skirts, blouses, and a shawl that looked like an additional skirt worn around the neck. One of the most ornate and impressive accoutrements of dress was the bandolier bag or beaded pouch, which looked like a shoulder bag but was elaborately decorated with beads and embroidery. When the Seminoles found trade needles too large to fit through the small holes in their beads, the style of beading changed: stringed lengths of beads rather than individual beads were sewn onto the bag. During the industrial revolution of the 1880s, the hand-cranked sewing machine was enthusiastically acquired by women who began to experiment with contrasting bands of colorful strips of cloth to replace the lengths of calico. Seminole clothing evolved to patchwork, a highly colorful and ornate tradition of making fabric for dresses, skirts, shirts, and jackets. The patchwork that formed the patterns was made from strips of cloth cut and then combined to make larger pieces. These had names for patterns such as spools, flash, Xs, checkers,

By the late 1800s, Seminole children were clothed and women wore long skirts, blouses, and a shawl that looked like an additional skirt worn around the neck. (Courtesy Library of Congress)

rattler, and other themes in nature. Women sewed a distinctively styled shoulder shawl that appears to be a skirt without sleeves and extends to the wrist. Later, these shawls were shortened to mid-arm length. In the early twentieth century rick-rack trim was incorporated and can be used as an indicator of the time period when the particular garment was manufactured.

Food

Corn, beans, and squash are the traditional Native American staples supplemented by occasional protein from deer and small game, as well as from fish, turtle, and shellfish if a group lived near the water. Berries, nuts, and seeds were gathered from surrounding ecosystems. In Florida, alligator were hunted and later became the focus of a highly controversial tourist attraction on Seminole reservations known as alligator wrestling. Tobacco, an ancient crop brought across the Siberian Peninsula with the first migrations of people from the Eastern Hemisphere, was also grown by the Seminoles. It was smoked for ceremonial and religious purposes, a ritual that was incorporated and played an important part in medical treatment and healing of the sick.

When the remaining Seminole in southern Florida settled, they developed three foods as distinctively theirs: *sofki*, frybread, and swamp cabbage. *Sofki* is made from corn that is mashed, pounded, and then boiled in water. It is a high-calorie, high-nutrition energy drink, similar to that used by the Maya before embarking on a long journey. It has symbolic meaning to the Seminoles, a way of guaranteeing good health in much the same way that Euro-Americans perceive milk. Frybread is made from wheat flour, baking powder, salt, and lard. It is shaped into a round patty and then fried. It too is heavy in caloric value, but because of its fat content and way of preparation it has been partially blamed for the unusually high degree of diabetes mellitus among the Seminoles. Swamp cabbage is derived from the sabal palmetto. The Seminoles must first fell the tree and then go inside the trunk to get to the bud. Known as hearts of palm to non-native Americans and sold as a delicacy, Seminoles eat it raw, boiled, or lightly fried.

ARTS, CRAFTS, AND HOUSING

Predictably, the tools used by cultural groups correspond to their natural resources and the crafts that they produce. Typically, eastern tribes used the bow and arrow for hunting and warfare with arrowheads made from chert until the rifle was introduced and adopted. Wicker armor and bark shields to use for body protection are documented in ethnographies. For fishing, they used hooks carved from deer antler, bone, or shell. Fishing line was made from the inner bark of trees or plant fibers. Fish poisons were compounded to temporarily stun the fish so that fishermen could remove them from the water by catching them with their hands. Traps or weirs were fabricated from branches, and reeds or dams were constructed from stacked stones. The inner bark of trees was used to make fishing line and nets. Lures were made from small sharp pieces of bone or wood tied to a line. Early Seminoles used shell scrapers to remove flesh from the deerskin they used for clothing.

The housing unit of the Seminoles was the *chickee*, of which there were four types: one for sleeping, one for dining, one for relaxing, and one for childbirth. The number four is significant in Seminole folklore because it symbolizes the world. The four directions of the world—east, south, north, and west—have particular significance, spirits, and meanings. The *chickee* has a thatched roof made from cabbage palm and is supported by poles hewn from cypress or palmetto wood. Most of the dwellings had platforms raised about thirty inches to provide protection from snakes and high water when it rained. During a hurricane, the roof could be removed from the poles and used as protection as the people crouched under the fronds.

Built with four posts, a birthing *chickee* was a separate hut used only for women. This *chickee* was kept at a distance from the other habitations. The pregnant woman was assisted by two or three other women, and after the child was born, both mother and child stayed in the hut for four days. Unlike Western cultures where mother and baby are protected from other members of society, some tribal people felt the need to be protected from blood and other discharges from the new mother. Like many Native American cultures, the Seminoles believed that during times of menstruation and after childbirth, women had to remain isolated because their blood was dangerous and polluting. They remained in isolation for four days.

SOCIAL STRUCTURE, RELIGIOUS BELIEFS, AND ORAL TRADITIONS

Sadly, none of the pristine creation myths of the Seminole have survived. Those that are available reveal the effects of syncretism with the Judeo-Christian story of creation. According to John Swanton, general cosmological beliefs held that the world was flat and the sun, moon, and stars were attached to the sky, which was like an overarching vault. The constellations were perceived in terms of Seminole flora, fauna, and technology. For example, the Big Dipper was described as a canoe. When an eclipse occurred, it was described as a frog swallowing the moon. The rainbow was thought to be a large snake, a cutter of the rain. The importance of the Native American concept of the number four survived in Seminole folklore. There are four cardinal directions, each with its significant spirits. The construction of a *chickee* required four poles. In drumming and music, the time signature is 4/4, and four days of confinement follow childbirth.

When a person died in camp, the site was abandoned, and the group moved to establish a new location. The rationale behind relocating was because a ghost of the recently deceased might want to take the soul of a close relative to keep him company. As recently as 1980, a ritual was held after the death of a significant member of the Seminole community during which men shot guns into the air to make enough noise to prevent the soul or ghost of the deceased from returning to capture the soul of a living relative. The shaman then entered and made medicine, boiled roots, and gave the liquid to all who were related so they could either bathe in it or drink it.

As land became more populated by non-Seminoles, the Seminoles again adapted their folkways and, instead of moving the entire camp away from the sick or dying person, erected a *chickee* far enough away from the camp so that the sick person could go there and not endanger the rest of the village. A medicine man, or shaman, was the specialist who had the power to mix a substance with the drugs used in healing to prevent the diseased person's soul from seeking company with the healthy and the living.

Native American belief systems usually do not separate religion from healing or art. It is integrated into every aspect of life so that even when hunting, people feel a connection to their creator and ask forgiveness for taking the life of another creation. Albino animals were believed to be especially sacred.

The Green Corn Dance (*busk, puskita, buskita*) ceremony introduced the New Year in many Native American cultures of the Southeast. It lasted eight days. When crops ripened, the event commenced when a religious specialist lit a new fire. Broken pottery was thrown away, and women took pieces of wood, lit them from this original fire, and brought them to their homes. A drink called the Black Drink was imbibed. Then the first corn of the season was collected from the fields, cooked, and shared. A series of dances began with women who danced for three hours during the middle of the day when it was the hottest. That same evening they danced again and were joined by the men, who formed an outer circle around the women and wove in and out, avoiding physical contact with each other. On the third day, young men and warriors began a long dance led by two falsetto singers. They danced until dark and then grew silent. For the next five days, tribes socialized, feasted, danced, and held conference-type ceremonies during which they forgave their friends and neighbors their prior trespasses and started the New Year afresh. A peace pipe was lit and passed around. Seminole tradition modified this ceremony. It still is held in early June and includes all the clans. There are ball games similar to rugby, and the ceremonial fire is lit. A tribal medicine bag is passed around from the eldest to the youngest and then used to light the fire. Important discussions, ususally political in nature, are held. The Green Corn Ceremony is the unifying event of religious, social, and tribal life.

Originally the Seminoles were matrilineal, meaning that the goods passed from generation to generation through the women or mothers. A husband's first responsibility was to his sister's children, not his own. Because discipline was harsh and administered by the maternal uncle, the child could maintain a friendlier relationship with his or her father, who did not administer punitive behaviors.

Today the Seminoles consist of two tribes: the Seminole Tribe of Florida, which has approximately 2,000 people, and the smaller Miccosukee, numbering only 500. Most Seminole live on reservations in Big Cypress, Brighton, Immokalee, Ft. Pierce, and Hollywood. The Miccosukee live in their own reservation and along the Tamiami Trail in south Florida. The Seminole language derives from the original integration of the upper and lower Creek Indians who spoke similar but distinct languages, the Muskogee and the Mikasuki. Since the Creeks were the dominant culture, the other tribes learned to speak either one or the other. Artistic traditions now center on crafts that appeal to tourists: little dolls, patchwork clothing, and small models of alligators and Indians made from woven fibers and cloth. The fabrication of *chickees* as a way for Seminoles to earn money has been encouraged and protected in the State of Florida.

STUDIES OF SEMINOLE FOLKLORE

Some good general sources about the history of the Seminoles and their culture include Garbarino (1972, 1989). For information about the slaves who joined the tribe, see Porter, Amos, and Senter (1996). On current Seminole folkways see West (1999). An oral history written by Betty Mae Tiger Jumper and Patsy West (2001) is an excellent firsthand narrative with interspersed text.

BIBLIOGRAPHY

Garbarino, Merwyn. 1972. *Big Cypress: A Changing Seminole Community*. New York: Holt, Rinehart, and Winston.

———. 1989. *The Seminole*. Langhorne, PA: Chelsea House.

Jumper, Betty Mae Tiger, and Patsy West. 2001. *A Seminole Legend: The Life of Betty Mae Tiger Jumper*. Gainesville: University Press of Florida.

Porter, Kenneth Wiggins, Alcione M. Amos, and Thomas P. Senter. 1996. *The Black Seminoles: History of a Freedom-Seeking People*. Gainesville: University Press of Florida.

Swanton, John R. 1929. *Myths and Tales of the Southeastern Indians*. Bureau of American Ethnology Bulletins, No. 88. Washington, DC: GPO.

———. 1946. *The Indians of the Southeastern United States*. Bureau of American Ethnology Bulletins, No. 137. Washington, DC: GPO.

West, Patsy. 1999. *The Enduring Seminoles: From Alligator Wrestling to Ecotourism*. Gainesville: University Press of Florida.

Lana Thompson

SIOUX. *See* Lakota

TLINGIT

GEOGRAPHY AND HISTORY

The Tlingit Indians live predominantly on the southeast Alaskan coast from Yakutat to Dixon Entrance as well as along the Chilkat and Stikine Rivers and in Southwest Yukon and Northwest British Columbia. This part of Alaska is an archipelago roughly the same size and shape as Florida with few communities connected by road, so contact occurs primarily by ferry or air. Native people live in scattered villages of several hundred people and in larger cities such as Juneau, Ketchikan, and Sitka.

Coastal Tlingits live in and on the edge of a rainforest—the most extensive temperate rainforest in the world, reaching from Puget Sound to Kodiak Island—and this environment has shaped their lifestyle and material culture. Known as the Northwest Coast, the culture area extends roughly from southeast Alaska to Puget Sound and the mouth of the Columbia River. After California, the Northwest Coast is the second most diverse linguistic area of aboriginal North America. Although the groups are linguistically distinct, the cultures are strikingly similar. With their immediate neighbors to the south, the Haida and Tsimshian, the Tlingit comprise a northern subgroup of Northwest Coast culture. Native American culture of the Northwest Coast has captured the imagination of explorers since first contact. These are the people of totem poles, elaborately carved wooden bowls and bentwood boxes, plank houses, ocean-going canoes, Chilkat robes, button blankets, and other well-known cultural features, especially the ceremony known in English as potlatch.

Tlingit society is divided into two moieties, or halves, generally called Raven and Eagle, but in some places Crow and Wolf. The society is matrilineal, meaning that a person is born into his or her mother's moiety and clan. The moieties are exogamous, so that traditionally one married a person of the opposite moiety. Each moiety also includes many clans. The clan was the major traditional unit of political, economic, and social power, determining ceremonial identity and ritual interaction, but this system has weakened in the last 100 years. Each clan had its leader, developed an autonomous "foreign policy," and owned a variety of real and intellectual property. Stories, songs, dances, and graphic art designs are included in the concept of property, as are a range of spirits. Often the spirits are depicted in visual art or referenced in song, dance, and oratory. Stories remember the history of acquisition of certain spirits by clan ancestors. Song, dance, and oratory are vehicles for recalling the spirits to the present time and place in a ceremonial context. These concepts of ownership and prerogative are common to most of the Northwest Coast. The Tlingit term for this, *at.óow*, means "a purchased object." Purchase was frequently through the death of an ancestor. Because of this overarching concept of ownership, any genre approach to Tlingit folklore must at all times be matched by a dynamic (contextual, functional) approach: the totem design is one thing, but who owns it, and who was commissioned to carve it? The song is one thing, but who has the "right" to sing it, and to whom and under what circumstances? Kinship terms are central images in the texts of songs and oratory. Knowledge of these songs, histories, and designs was and is not secret or esoteric. In fact, to be competent in ceremonial interaction one must know the names, songs, stories, and images of other clans, but the right to wear certain designs or perform certain songs or stories is restricted by clan identity.

The Tlingit language belongs to the Na-Dene family and is grammatically related to the Athabaskan languages (such as Navajo and Apache) and Eyak. Tlingit oral tradition and a variety of scientific data suggest that the people migrated from the interior to the coast in prehistoric times and gradually expanded from the southern end of their present territory to the north. The most significant impact on Tlingit history and culture is contact first with Russians (1794–1867) and then with Euro-Americans (following the sale of Alaska by the Russians to the United States in 1867).

RELIGIOUS BELIEFS

Traditional, pre-contact Tlingit religion was shamanism of a classical circumpolar or Siberian type. All nineteenth-century observers stressed the centrality of the shaman to the entire Tlingit sociocultural order. John Swanton considered that among all the Northwest Coast people only among the Tlingit did shamanism reach its climax. The source of the shaman's power was his control over powerful spirits, called *yéik*, who served as his helpers. Each *yéik* has a personal name, a special song, and associated ceremonial objects such as bone amulets, rattles, and masks. The spirits had the capacity to choose the person whose helpers they wished to become, and it was extremely dangerous to refuse such a call.

As in other shamanic religions, candidates were not ordained into a pre-existing religion as much as they became recipients of personal spirits who revealed themselves to the individual. Where Tlingit shamanism seems distinctive or significantly different is that the spirits are "owned" not by the entire community but, rather, by the clan of the shaman. Individual revelation of shaman spirits is common, but for spirits to be perceived as clan property is unusual. Shamanism is typically individualistic and unstructured, and sedentary cultures with complex social structures tend to have more codified religious systems. Tlingit traditional religion is characterized by an unusual combination of shamanism and complex social structure, from which it is inseparable.

None of the early European observers found any evidence of collective worship of any spirit or deity, including Raven (Yéil). Nor was there a hierarchical and centralized pantheon of spirits. Instead, much of the traditional religion focused on acquiring and maintaining spirit power for and by the individual. A complex system of taboos and concern with good and bad luck was part of traditional religion.

In Tlingit tradition, shamanism was ideally positive, benevolent, and focused on healing. Since the spirits were potentially dangerous, though, extreme caution was exercised in dealing with them. Reciprocity with a clan of the opposite moiety is part of this traditional protocol. The popular Tlingit concept is balance. The spirits of clans of the opposite moieties balance each other out and keep the supplicants from harm.

In contrast to shamanism, witchcraft was negative and malevolent. Like shamanism, beliefs about the witch, called *nakws'aatí* (master of medicine), *nukws'aatí*, or *neekws'aatí* (master of sickness or master of pain), were central to the pre-Christian Tlingit **worldview**, and vestiges survive today. The terms for witches refer to the belief that they cause sickness and death by casting spells on other persons. Part of the job of the shaman was to combat witchcraft. These are, of course, ideal categories. As in all religion we can assume the occasional presence of personally corrupt "professional" clergy. Historical evidence suggests that many accusations of witchcraft, as in other cultures, targeted weak or marginal persons or were linked to personal rivalries in the community.

It is safe to say that today there is no purely traditional Tlingit religion in any organized sense. Most Tlingits are members of some Christian denomination, and among the more traditionally minded there is much syncretism of the traditional belief system with newer religions to the extent that the belief systems are compatible. Thus many communities still continue potlatching and other traditional practices, whereas some communities and individuals do not. Many traditional practices were syncretized into the "pan-Protestant" funeral services of the Alaska Native Brotherhood and Sisterhood, governed by *Robert's Rules of Order*. The older Christian churches are the Russian Orthodox, Presbyterian, Salvation Army, and Roman Catholic. Since World War II a variety of fundamentalist churches as well as the Mormons and the Baha'i have taken root.

POTLATCH

Because each clan has its own spirits and no single clan owns the total or collected spirits of the community, the concept of reciprocity becomes very important. The best example of this is the Tlingit memorial for the departed, commonly called pot-

latch in English, to which each moiety brings half of the spirits or provides access to half of the spirits needed for the removal of grief. From the point of view of folklore, the potlatch is the single most important event in Tlingit folklife because it combines so many genres of verbal and visual folklore, foodways, and other components operating in the context and dynamics of social structure and spiritual worldview. Typically songs and speeches are exchanged across moiety lines as part of the ceremonial exchange of goods and services. They are generally held in the fall because this allows maximum time for harvest of traditional food such as salmon, seal, deer, and berries.

The memorial is hosted by the clan of the departed, with direct support from other clans of the same moiety and indirect support from the in-laws of the opposite moiety. They invite guests of clans of the opposite moiety. The Tlingit term for "potlatch," ḵoo.éex', means "to invite." Food and gifts are distributed to guests of the opposite moiety. Traditional belief holds that by sharing food and gifts such as blankets with the living, we can also share them with the spirits of the departed. In fact, only by sharing with the living can we share with the departed. Traditional regalia is displayed, and traditional

Tlingit woman in full potlatch dancing costume, 1906. (Courtesy Library of Congress)

songs and dances are performed in turn by hosts and guests. Thus the potlatch represents several levels of mediation: between the living members of a community; between the living and the spirits of the human departed; and between humans and the disembodied shaman spirits of the spirit world. Thus, while much of pre-contact Tlingit religious life was individual-oriented with no collective worship of powerful spirits or deities, extremely elaborate death-related ritual activities such as the ḵoo.éex' formed the traditional core of the entire sociocultural order and continue to do so, though to a lesser degree and in changing ways.

The important feature of post-funeral cycle is the Forty Day Party, which is similar to the memorial potlatch but less complicated and without gift-giving and elaborate display of regalia with accompanying dirges and oratory. It is essentially a dinner given forty days after a person's death and is more light-hearted in tone. This custom was certainly reinforced by, if not derived from, the Russian Orthodox practice of prayer and dinner forty days after death, modeled on the Ascension of Christ.

Myths, Legends, and Folktales

Verbal art is one of the richest genres in Tlingit folklore, and many genres (naming, for example) must remain beyond the space limits of this article. Personal names follow complicated systems of clan ownership, genealogy, kinship, and remembrance of the deceased. Indigenous place names are extremely important for a number of reasons, and, as in the folklore of other cultures, the naming of dogs, cats, boats, and other objects is also interesting.

We use the conventional Western folklore definitions: *myth* is that which is sacred and true, usually in the remote past, with divinities, superhumans, or non-humans as characters; *legend* is that which is historical and true, with human characters; *memorate* is a remembrance of limited distribution, usually personal or family; *folktale* is fiction. Folktales and deliberate fiction are conspicuously absent in traditional Tlingit oral literature. To date, we have found only one Tlingit folktale, and that is a borrowing from Russian. But since a narrative may change categories over time, it is safe to say that a story considered true in the past may not be considered true by contemporary Tlingits.

The Tlingit terms for narratives are *tlaagóo*, specifying a narrative of ancient origin or time, and *shkalneek*, referring to any story or narrative in general. Another type of narrative is called *át kookeidí*, which translates roughly as parable, or extended metaphor or simile, and frequently appears in ceremonial oratory. As a final distinction in terminology, we are treating myth here as narrative form in contrast to a discussion of Tlingit religion in general.

Myth is the single event in the past that establishes the covenant. Ritual is the ongoing imitation, remembrance, or representation such as the Jewish Seder, Christian Communion, or Tlingit ḵoo.éex'. In many shamanic traditions the right to hunt and engage in other subsistence activity is typically established in ancient covenants (myth). Continuing luck or success is confirmed through ritual observances and correct personal thought and behavior in remembering these covenants. Many of the stories from what we call legendary time record how clan ancestors or progenitors acquired particular spirits.

Narratives in Tlingit oral literature may be grouped into four broad categories based on style, content, and the internal relationship of the narratives: (1) early myth time; (2) Raven myth time (Raven as culture **hero** and Raven as **trickster**); (3) legendary time; and (4) historical time. Other than historical time, all are types of Tlingit mythology. These categories are descriptive and not prescriptive. While not arbitrary, neither are the boundaries rigid. Tlingit oral literature as we know it today seems to have involved flow among the categories over time. For example, history may become legend. Thus a personal or family memorate of recent origin might attain the status of a community or national legend. Likewise, recent historical, non-mythic events may be understood or reshaped according to the mythic and mythologizing patterns of the culture. Over even longer periods of time, legend may blend with myth.

The concept of early myth time provides a convenient way to group what now seem like the odds and ends of Tlingit mythology: creation accounts involving cosmic phenomena (sun, moon, thunder, earthquakes, wind, and the Milky Way, for instance) and stories of various monsters and marvelous creatures such as the sea monster or "Lucky Lady." Stories in this group are the most

Tlingit totem pole. Animals, places, and spirits are figures that are commonly depicted on totem poles and other visual art. (Courtesy Library of Congress)

enigmatic in Tlingit mythology. They are outside the Raven cycle or describe events prior in time to the Raven cycle. The cosmic phenomena described were created before Raven entered the scene. Also, most of these stories seem un-Tlingit in their absence of the personal names and clan affiliations so characteristic of the narratives from legendary time. The motifs are not unique to Tlingit (for example, Sun and Moon being brother and sister who committed incest), and it is unclear if these myths are very ancient or borrowings from other Native American groups.

The most popular character in Tlingit mythology is certainly Raven, and the most significant feature of Tlingit Raven is his dual or multiple personality. In many societies, the roles of culture hero and trickster are filled by two different figures. In Tlingit, they combine in Raven. This has intrigued and confused observers from the earliest Western accounts to the present day. Raven stories can be divided into two categories: "culture hero" and "trickster." The culture hero is a character in mythology who gives the world its present shape. Raven is popularly called a creator, but we disagree with this. He actually creates little or nothing. He is certainly not god-like, much less a god. Raven is the great rearranger, a mythic handyman and jack-of-all-trades. Anthropologist Claude Lévi-Strauss described him with the French term *bricoleur*. Typically, Raven redistributes things, making the already created world more user-friendly for people and animals. Thus, the world as we know it today was largely shaped by Raven out of the elements that already existed but were inaccessible. Fresh water, fire, low tide, the salmon run, the sun, moon, and stars all existed but were hoarded by one individual who refused to share them with the rest of creation. Through trickery Raven steals and redistributes these. In the process, other features of the world such as rivers, the hydrogen cycle, and various animals and their characteristics are created. An etiological aspect often appears in Raven stories.

It is important to notice that Raven's motives are not altruistic. He is driven by lust, gluttony, ego, and greed. Benefits to the rest of creation are entirely accidental, coincidental, or created from leftovers as an afterthought. Raven cheats and manipulates his fellow creatures, whence the term *trickster*. He is incapable of having a "meaningful relationship" with others. In the Tlingit language, the stem for *Raven* and *liar* is the same. The best one can hope for in a partnership with Raven is to emerge alive and simply hungrier and with damaged pride from having been robbed or cheated out of something. Raven tricks the small birds out of their share of the King Salmon, and he redesigns their plumage as a consolation prize. Many are not so lucky: Cormorant loses his tongue; Deer becomes Raven's dinner when he slips off the high log Raven dares and tricks him into crossing; Brown Bear dies a painful death after Raven tricks him into cutting off his genitals for fishing bait; Brown Bear's Wife dies a horrible death when Raven tricks her into swallowing hot rocks whole (telling her it is his special fish recipe). Raven, of course, eats them. Many Raven stories would today be considered X- and R-rated.

A large and important category of Tlingit myth deals with the acquisition of clan spirits and the crests visually representing them by human ancestors in what might be called legendary time. Technically these narratives are legends by definition because the events happened to the human ancestors and progenitors of today's clans, but they overlap with myth in their concern with the acquisition of spirits. Through their human element, the stories are owned by the various clans, and protocols concerning the rights to claim, use, and display the crest art related to the stories remain central in Tlingit culture today. These animals, places, and spirits are the figures commonly depicted on totem poles and other visual art. Songs and dances usually accompany the story and visual art. In this genre of Tlingit myth, humans are the main characters, and their actions and encounters with the animal, natural, and spiritual worlds have established the covenants by which humans interact with animals and the environment.

The general pattern of these stories has a human offending some animal or force of nature and being taken by that form of life to live among them, learn to understand and appreciate them, and gain their power as a spiritual guide. Sometimes the humans die, as do the Woman in the Ice in the "Glacier Bay History" and the Woman Who Married the Bear. Sometimes the human returns from this "out-of-body" experience and becomes a spiritual mediator or a shaman, as does Aak'wtaatseen, the boy who is taken by the Salmon People. In all cases, the clan of the ancestor involved gains exclusive access to the particular spirits involved. Typically the mythic event remembered in the story is ritually re-enacted through behavior in daily life or in special ceremonial events.

We can assume that in oral tradition as in written literary history, the appeal of certain genres may wax and wane over time while certain classics endure. Swanton's storyteller Katishan explains at the end of his Raven cycle that since the time of the Raven stories, "everything is about spirits." We understand this to mean that the spirit acquisition legends had been gaining in popularity over time. It also implies a concept of time-depth, with the spirit and crest acquisition stories being more recent than the Raven stories and increasingly capturing the popular imagination.

When we enter historical time, in which events can be recorded orally and also be confirmed with other ethnohistorical documentation, we leave the categories of myth (at least in their generic form). One clear example are historical narratives dealing with the Battles of Sitka of 1802 and 1804 between the Kiks.ádi clan of Sitka and the Russians. There is remarkable agreement between Tlingit oral traditions tape-recorded within the last 50 years and Russian eyewitness accounts written down about 200 years ago. These will differ in opinion, point of view, and frame of reference (for example, the navy log will record date and time, whereas the oral account will not), though the same events are addressed. This shows that oral history can be accurate and reliable when canonically received and carefully transmitted over many generations. Conversely, not all written accounts are intrinsically or equally accurate as a result of literacy alone.

ORATORY

If legends record the acquisition of a particular spirit power or clan crest, in the genre of oratory the images and spirits operate in real time. Oratory differs from narrative in performance, style, and content. Whereas a story can be told into a tape recorder, oratory is delivered in real time to a live audience, typically in a ceremonial setting across moiety lines. At a potlatch, a Raven guest will deliver a speech to the Eagle hosts designed to remove their grief. In Tlingit narratives, simile is extremely rare and metaphor virtually non-existent (although on a larger scale, the whole story may be a metaphor). In contrast, simile and metaphor are the mainstays of Tlingit oratory. These are typically extended, as in Homeric simile or the extended metaphors of English Elizabethan and metaphysical poetry. The content usually begins with establishing the social context of the speech event by connecting the orator to others present often through genealogy. Once this is done, simile and metaphor come into play, based on the visual art present in the form of hats, blankets, and other regalia. The regalia and spirits and persons they recall and represent are used for the removal of grief. The speeches are not memorized in the form of a liturgical text but are improvised according to conventional patterns, but with the specific details determined by the circumstances.

MUSIC AND SONGS

Songs are very important in Tlingit folklife. There is no flute tradition, but as with most other Native American groups, drums and rattles are the main instruments. Songs usually begin with vocables or "burden syllables" that establish the melody. There is nothing comparable to the Euro-American folksong or ballad. As with other genres, songs are clan owned, and performance rights are restricted. Most were traditionally performed in ceremonial contexts, so there are few if any "secular" songs in Tlingit.

The most common genres are love songs, lamentations, and Raven songs. These differ in structure and seriousness. Imagined in Western, literate terms, the typical structure of a Tlingit song might be described as having four lines: an opening image or statement, a genealogical or kinship reference, and two lines of further development, comparison, or resolution. Love songs are directed across moiety lines, and the second line usually addresses the opposite moiety as a "child" or "children" of the composer's (father's) clan. These images are difficult for outsiders to follow, and they demonstrate that an understanding of Tlingit social structure underlies all Tlingit folklore and folklife. These are popularly called love songs because members of the opposite moiety are eligible marriage partners, and the songs and teasing are acceptable strategies of flirting and courtship, mock or serious.

In lamentations, the kinship reference is within the clan and moiety, usually to a maternal uncle or grandparent, and the content typically deals with separation, loss, or death. Raven songs extend the comic nature of the Raven stories and sometimes overlap in form and function with love songs.

With the coming of Euro-American influence, several musical genres emerged in the early twentieth century, especially village brass bands, dance bands, and Hawaiian steel guitar. Orthodox choral music as well as Salvation Army and other Protestant hymns developed in the Tlingit language. Gospel music remains popular.

DANCE

The most important genre in the area of Tlingit dramatic art today is dance. For earlier periods, and especially for cultures lower on the Northwest Coast, there is documentation of theater-like performances in the context of potlatch, but this no longer exists in Tlingit, though in recent years there has been a revival of theater and storytelling blending Northwest Coast traditions with Western theater. The older practice often included magic acts and optical illusion. One particularly joyful contemporary example of potlatch dramatics in one community has the men of one clan stamp their feet rapidly, imitating glaciers calving, while the women of the opposite moiety imitate kittywakes startled from their rookery. This is a good example of the congruence of "spiritual geography," natural science, social structure, and folklore. Kittywakes do nest and feed around glaciers. These are emblems of clans of opposite moieties who interact as marriage partners and in ceremonial and ritual exchange. The rookeries and glaciers are important as sacred places. These appear in visual art, in crest-acquisition legends, and as images (simile and metaphor) in oratory.

Perhaps the most important extinct genre of dramatic art is the riddle, for which the clues were not verbal, but behavioral. From what elders told us over thirty years ago, people often acted out certain things in the potlatch, and others had to guess what they were. When Nora Dauenhauer asked about the genre, one elder was amazed, told her she was too young to know about it, and explained that he had not seen or heard of it since he was a child. Vestiges of non-verbal riddle may survive in the dramatics mentioned above, and verbal riddling may be subsumed in the simile and metaphor of oratory, but nothing in Tlingit today compares to the riddle traditions in Alaskan Athabaskan languages, which may also function as a kind of catechism for learning to use metaphor in oratory and storytelling.

Several sub-types of Tlingit dance are defined primarily by the motions, accompanying songs, and clothing worn. The most common type of dance is the "regular" dance, which requires no special gestures or wardrobe and is performed especially when one is named by the opposite moiety in the love songs. One stands and dances during that verse of the song. Two other common styles are the entrance and exit songs and dances that are performed as a group enters or leaves the performance area, traditionally the clan house, today generally the stage.

Several special kinds of dances are performed during the potlatch, each with a distinctive feature. The motion or yarn dance is one of the joyous styles. It is done by women and is sometimes called the sway dance, after the motion of the bundles of yarn attached to a headband and hanging in front of each ear as the women sway in place, dancing to spirit songs. Another distinctive dance, the *yéik utee* or "Imitating the Spirit" dance, is performed by one or more dancers, usually men, each wearing an ermine headdress with a carved wooden frontlet (*shakee.át*) and dancing behind a blanket so that only the bobbing of the headdress shows. They dance to spirit songs that are serious and generally imitate animals. A third kind of dance, also performed by men, is the "Haida Style" dance. The origin of the name is unclear. The dancer wears a headdress and a Chilkat robe or button blanket and dances to love songs.

ARTS AND CRAFTS

Tlingit graphic and visual art are world famous, and little needs to be said about them here because of the wealth of material in print. Of note, however, is that many of these studies deal only with form and technique, whereas context, clan ownership, and function are essential in Tlingit folklife and worldview. Major genres are woodcarving, silver carving, beadwork, and weaving. Silver work is mostly bracelets, earrings, and pendants. Beadwork is applied on a variety of items of clothing ranging from bracelets, watchbands, belt buckles, and pendants to bibs, vests, and felt blankets (usually also decorated with buttons). Weaving includes a variety of media: spruce root, cedar bark, and fabric weaving using a combination of mountain goat wool and cedar bark. Bark and root objects include hats, baskets, mats, and capes. Woven objects include blankets, tunics, shirts, dance aprons, and leggings. The earliest forms seem to have been geometric or "raven's tail," and this style was revived in recent years. In the nineteenth and twentieth centuries the major style was "form line," in which animals and clan crests were depicted, often in abstract form with three-dimensional figures projected onto two planes, combining side and front views.

Woodcarving includes hats, masks, wall plaques, dance paddles, bentwood boxes, and, of course, totem poles, for which this region is famous. Some missionaries mistakenly equated totem poles with "graven images," but they were never worshipped or prayed to. They were and are essentially heraldic and refer to the genealogy of the person or group that commissioned the pole to be carved and erected. The images do not "tell" as story as much as allude to stories already known, much as the Christian cross does not "tell the Easter story" but alludes to a story familiar from other sources. As an art object, it is simply a geometric design. Totem poles are one of the many forms of Tlingit visual art that allude to narratives from Tlingit myth and legend.

Canoe carving is now enjoying a revival. In the early to mid-twentieth century many Tlingit men were involved in designing and building skiffs and commercial fishing boats. The region is also known for its traditional plank housing, replaced in the early twentieth century by Western frame housing.

CHALLENGES OF THE MODERN WORLD

The ethnohistorical experiences described above blend steadily into experiences of **modernization** and **globalization**. The Russian period resulted in relatively little disruption of Tlingit language, lifestyle, spirituality, and social order. In contrast, the American period brought many changes accompanied by a far greater and longer lasting influx of newcomers, lured by the gold rush, timber, and fishing. Presbyterian missionaries brought compulsory education conducted in the English language only and increasingly at boarding schools. Tlingit language, culture, and lifestyle were actively suppressed. Conservative Tlingits tended to remain Orthodox; modernists tended to become Presbyterian.

Assimilation was also a Tlingit strategy and social agenda as they organized politically to fight for civil rights on several fronts, including citizenship, voting rights, and integration of schools, restaurants, and public facilities. Important landmarks are the forming of the Alaska Native Brotherhood in 1912 and the Central Council of Tlingit and Haida Indians of Alaska in 1941, the latter in order to bring suit against the U.S. government, resulting in the Alaska Native Claims Settlement Act of 1971. This act reorganized Alaska Native people into profit-making corporations. By 1981 the Tlingit corporation, called Sealaska Corporation, was one of the Fortune 1000 companies.

These obvious legal and political changes have been accompanied by more subtle changes in and conflicts within tradition. For example, a corporation board is required to make a profit for its shareholders, but corporate practice may be in conflict with the traditional land ethic and ecological values regarding the environment. Most significantly, Tlingit sociopolitical organization over the last 100 years has slowly changed from a clan-based structure to a Western community and nation-based structure. Corporate structure requires a leader for all the Tlingit people, whereas traditionally each clan was autonomous; a "Tlingit national anthem" has become extremely popular; and a modern, corporate-sponsored folk festival called Celebration has become extremely popular. From the folklore point of view, the text or content of the songs and dances performed at Celebration remains traditional, but the context is new and different with active dancers performing for a passive, secular audience in contrast to the reciprocal dynamics of a traditional ceremonial performance situation such as potlatch. In narratives, we now experience a much higher level of editorializing in contrast to performances of thirty or forty years ago, which were more laconic and where much more freedom was given to the listener to make sense of the story with little or no imposition from the storyteller. All this is influenced by the patterns of discourse in the broader American culture.

BIBLIOGRAPHY

Dauenhauer, Nora Marks. 1986. Context and Display in Northwest Coast Art. In *Voices of the First America: Text and Context in the New World*. Special Issue of *New Scholar* 10: 419–32.

———. 1995. Tlingit *At.óow*: Tradition and Concepts. In *The Spirit Within: Northwest Coast Native Art from the John H. Hauberg Collection*, edited by Helen Abbott and others. Seattle: Rizzoli and Seattle Art Museum. 20–29.

———. 1998. Five Slices of Salmon. In *First Fish, First People: Salmon Tales of the North Pacific Rim*, edited by Judith Roche and Meg McHutchinson. Seattle: University of Washington Press. 100–121.

———. 2000. *Life Woven with Song: Poetry, Prose, and Plays*. Tucson: University of Arizona Press.

———. 2002. Have Patience—Some Things Cannot Be Rushed. In *Alaska Native Ways: What the Elders Have Taught Us*, edited by Roy Corral. Portland, OR: Graphic Arts Center Publishing. 60–71.

Dauenhauer, Nora Marks, and Richard Dauenhauer, eds. 1987. *Haa Shuká, Our Ancestors: Tlingit Oral Narratives*. Seattle: University of Washington Press.

———. 1990. *Haa Tuwunáagu Yís, for Healing Our Spirit: Tlingit Oratory*. Seattle: University of Washington Press.

———. 1994a. *Haa Kusteeyí, Our Culture: Tlingit Life Stories*. Seattle: University of Washington Press.

———. 1994b. "Glacier Bay History" by Amy Marvin and "Speech for the Removal of Grief" by Jessie Dalton: Essay and Translations. In *Coming to Light: Contemporary Translations of the Native Literatures of North America*, edited by Brian Swann. New York: Random House.

———. 1995. Oral Literature Embodied and Disembodied. In *Aspects of Oral Communication*, edited by U. Quasthoff. Berlin: De Gruyter. 91–111.

———. 1998. "Tlingit Origin Stories" and "Raven Makes the Aleutian Islands and the Alaska Peninsula" (told by Suzie James). In *Stars Above, Earth Below: American Indians and Nature*, edited by Marsha C. Bol. Niwot, CO: Roberts Rinehart Publishers. 29–46, 57–61.

———. 1999. The Paradox of Talking on the Page: Some Aspects of the Tlingit and Haida Experience. In *Talking on the Page: Editing Aboriginal Texts*, edited by Laura J. Murray and Keren Rice. Toronto: University of Toronto Press. 3–41.

———. 2000. Raven and the Tide: A Tlingit Narrative by Emma Marks. *Worldviews and the American West: The Life of the Place Itself*, edited by Polly Stewart and others. Logan: Utah State University Press.

————. 2001. Tracking Yuwaan Gageets: A Russian Fairy Tale in Tlingit Oral Tradition. In *Native American Oral Traditions: Collaboration and Interpretation*, edited by Barre Toelken and Larry Evers. Logan: Utah State University Press. 58–91.

————. 2003a. Tlingit Speeches for the Removal of Grief. *Arctic Anthropology* 40: 30–39.

————. 2003b. Louis Shotridge and Indigenous Tlingit Ethnography: Then and Now. In *Constructing Cultures Then and Now: Celebrating Franz Boas and the Jesup North Pacific Expedition*, edited by Laurel Kendall and Igor Krupnik. Washington, DC: Arctic Studies Center, National Museum of Natural History, Smithsonian Institution. 165–183.

————. 2004a. Three Tlingit Raven Stories. In *Voices from Four Directions*, edited by Brian Swann. Lincoln: University of Nebraska Press. 25–41.

————. 2004b. Evolving Concepts of Tlingit Identity and Clan. In *Coming to Shore: Northwest Coast Ethnology Past and Present*, edited by Marie Mauzé, Michael Harkin, and Sergei Kan. Lincoln: University of Nebraska Press. 253–278.

Dauenhauer, Richard. 1981. Notes on Swanton Numbers 80 and 81. *Journal of American Folklore* 94: 358–364.

————. 2000. Synchretism, Revival, and Reinvention: Tlingit Religion, Pre- and Postcontact. In *Native Religions and Cultures of North America*, edited by Lawrence E. Sullivan. New York: Continuum. 160–180.

Richard Dauenhauer and Nora Marks Dauenhauer

WESTERN INUIT AND YUPIK

GEOGRAPHY AND HISTORY

Long ago, when the earth was thin, people and animals could converse with each other. Like humans, each animal species lived in its own village and spoke its own language. In those days, the first people often traveled to the animals' homes, where they were shown the universe from their hosts' perspectives. They learned to be aware of how a seal feels when it is taken for food but its meat is left to rot along the coast. They were shown that certain types of snares were especially painful to some animals. They aided and were in turn assisted by the animals, establishing long-lasting reciprocal relationships. From these experiences, the people developed an ethic of respect for the natural world around them. They were assured that as long as they showed respect through personal behavior and community ceremonies, the animals would return to give themselves up for food again and again.

These experiences are recounted in stories, called *unikkaatuat* in Canada, that have guided the Arctic and Subarctic people for centuries. In Alaska, they form a genre of stories from the distant past called—in various languages—*qulirat*, *unigkuwat*, or *unipkaat*. They are part of the verbal folklore of the people commonly called Eskimos by outsiders, but whose names for themselves are Inuit, Yupiit, Sugpiat, or Inupiat, depending on their language and homeland.

The verbal folklore of many hunting and gathering societies concerns relationships between people and the plants and animals that comprise their diet. In this, the Yupik (one form of the singular for Yupiit) and Inuit people are not unique. What is most distinctive are their performing and visual folk arts. Dramatic musical performances open with an individual or row of synchronized dancers gently bobbing to a tentative-sounding drumbeat. When the song leader is satisfied that musicians and dancers are ready, he increases the volume and beat. The dancers leap or sway—as the story-dance demands—to the drumbeat and male and female voices. The tone can be joyful, comical, pensive, competitive, or angry. Audience reaction is sought, and participation is expected. The second characteristic form of this northern folklore, the visual arts, consisted traditionally of utilitarian objects fashioned with unparalleled care, enhanced with distinctive designs, and made of materials basic to survival in the far north. Today this legacy continues in the re-creation and reconceptualization of traditional forms for the modern art market.

Despite similarities regional variations in Arctic and Subarctic folklore derive in part from differences in languages, history, and geography. The region is home to speakers of four closely related languages in the Esk-Aleut language family. Derived from a common parent language between 1,000 and 2,700 years ago, these four languages have similar grammars, sound systems, and alphabets and share a fair amount of vocabulary.

Since the sixteenth century, Europeans have used the designation "Eskimo" to refer to these people, but its use is controversial. It is now accepted by some Alaskan Yupiit and Inupiat but repudiated by others, most vehemently Canadian Inuit. Unfortunately, there is no term that satisfactorily encompasses all the groups despite a move to extend the Canadian designation "Inuit" into Alaska. In the United States, the name fits only the Inupiat, who speak the same language as their Canadian neighbors. It is inaccurate to refer to the three Yupik groups (Siberian or St. Lawrence Island Yupik, Central Yup'ik, and Sugpiaq) as Inuit. Most Yupiit of southwestern Alaska call themselves Yup'ik or Yup'ik Eskimos. To further confuse matters, the Sugpiaq-speakers further south have called themselves Alutiiq (when speaking their own language) or Aleut (when speaking Russian or English) since the earliest days of the Russian fur trade in the eighteenth century. A designation imported by the Russians to Alaska when it was a Russian colony, "Aleut" vies with the original Sugpiaq as the term of choice. Ethnographic and linguistic literature often refers to the Sugpiaq as Pacific Eskimos, but the people themselves are adamant that they are neither Yupik nor Eskimo.

The Yupik, Sugpiaq, and Inuit people and their ancestors have inhabited the coastal areas of Greenland, northern Canada, and Alaska south to and including Prince William Sound for at least 4,000 years. Their way of life has been hugely affected, if not completely determined, by geography, climate, and available resources. The people have adapted to extremely cold weather conditions with a complex technology of unexcelled beauty and ingenuity. Most of the territory is treeless, so people have used sod, rocks, packed snow, ice, skins, whale bones, and driftwood to fashion shelters. Depending on the reliability of supplies of fish and game, people have followed a nomadic life or settled in villages, some quite large. Even village-dwellers have customarily moved seasonally to fish camps, returning to their central settlement in the fall, then breaking winter up with short hunting or trapping trips to outlying areas. This pattern is still followed today to the extent that school schedules and the few available office jobs allow.

In addition to the coastal dwellers, two groups have deep roots inland. These include the Inuit-speaking caribou-hunters of northern Canada and Alaska and the Central Yup'ik river-dwellers of southwest Alaska, who rely on Pacific salmon for much of their food. These interior groups have maintained close trade and marriage relationships with coast-dwellers, ensuring a rich supply of oil from sea mammals while they have provided furs and fish from the interior.

The food quest for all Eskimo peoples is both thorough and opportunistic. Whatever is available is closely studied and then hunted, trapped, or snared. The people are most known for their heavy reliance upon sea mammals (seals, whales, walrus, sea lions) and fish (Arctic char, salmon, pike, sheefish, tomcod, herring, halibut). Caribou form an important source of protein as well. People add migratory birds, especially swans, ducks, and geese, to year-round available ptarmigan and grouse to vary their diets. Snowshoe and Arctic hare are considered starvation foods, not highly nutritious but often the only game available before seasonal migrations of larger mammals arrive. These creatures are the subjects of many of the oldest stories.

The technological genius of the Inuit and Yupiit is evident in the immense array of tools and weapons used until recently to survive in the Arctic. Specialized arrows, spears, fishing implements, knives, fleshers, nets, snares, harpoons, and traps abounded. The skin boat, or *qayaq* (commonly spelled "kayak"), was used throughout the region to hunt on the open sea or along rivers. Dog sled technology was perfected by 1600 C.E., with variations in the harness type and sled length, depending on local terrain. The hooded skin parka was both an instrument of survival and a thing of beauty. A different parka design is distinctive to each Canadian and Alaskan community and, in some cases, to each family. Intricate implements were fashioned out of ivory, bone, baleen, driftwood (which was carved, bent and sewn, and painted), grass (for socks and baskets), furs and skins, horn, antler, stone, feathers, and, when available, metal. Decoration was achieved by etching, drawing, sewing, piecing, grass-weaving, inlaying, carving, and painting.

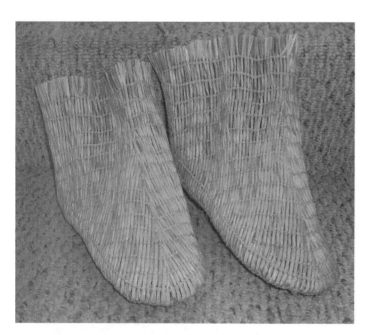

Grass socks (*alliqsak*), made by Yupik elder Lena Atti of Kwigillingok, 2001. (Photograph by Patricia H. Partnow)

The Eskimo people inhabit three modern states: Greenland, Canada, and the United States. Their experiences with European colonizers have been diverse but have followed a similar trajectory toward larger and more permanent settlements and the adoption of English (in Canada and the United States) as the common language. The ultimate results of colonization have been a decreasing role played by storytelling as the use of indigenous languages was discouraged or forbidden and the supplanting of traditional education by a Western model. Despite these trends, oral transmission of ancient and contemporary stories in English remains a favorite pastime. In addition, the performing arts are enjoying a renaissance as **tourism** provides a paying audience, while the visual arts, supported by schools dedicated to indigenous arts, have benefited from a burgeoning market for work by native and First Nations artists.

The remote location of Canada's far north, its weather, and the absence of desired minerals allowed the Inuit people centuries of freedom from economic and social exploitation. The Arctic region was fully mapped only in the mid-nineteenth century, slightly in advance of the heyday of commercial whaling. With this new industry came the end of isolation as Euro-American visitors arrived, bringing new technology and trade along with disease and alcohol. Subsistence rounds were disrupted when people moved to whaling stations where work and desirable Western goods were available. Traders followed whalers as the fur trade expanded into the farthest reaches of Canada. Even more than the whaling stations, trading posts disrupted the traditional food quest, notably the winter seal hunt, as men sought fur-bearers rather than the multipurpose seal. Through the years, dependence on the traders increased. Settlements became permanent and were located not where hunting was good but where transportation was convenient. Traders were accompanied or quickly followed by missionaries, who provided what education and health services were available until the government assumed these functions after World War II. Of all the Canadian Inuit groups, the Copper Inuit of the Central Canadian Arctic were the last to come face to face with white men when they encountered Stefansson and his expedition in 1908–1912. Major changes followed the opening of the first government school at Tuktoyaktuk in 1947. By 1982 there were more than thirty schools in the Canadian Arctic, one in each settlement of any size. In the 1980s reliable air service came to all settlements, bringing them into regular and relatively easy communication and contact with the rest of the world.

Alaska's Inupiat and Siberian Yupiit also suffered from the impact of commercial whaling during the mid-nineteenth century, but this was not the first time Europeans had had an effect on the lives of Alaska Eskimos. Sugpiaq territory was among the earliest to be affected by the fur trade. Russian traders established the first permanent post in the region in 1784, following it with a dozen others, mostly small two-man posts throughout southern and western Alaska. As in Canada, one effect of the posts was the relocation of previously mobile people to permanent settlements and the concomitant reliance on trade goods in preference to hunted or gathered materials. The effect on the folklore of the Sugpiaq people was enormous. While storytellers continued to recount the ancient tales, the ceremonial round was completely altered. People abandoned some ancient traditions and melded others into a new Alutiiq version of Christianity. Thus traditional songs are sung in Church Slavonic, people celebrate namedays to commemorate the Russian Orthodox saints they are named after, and Christmas celebrations combine ancient Sugpiaq elements with biblical stories.

Meanwhile, whalers from the United States and Europe had begun plying the waters of the Bering and Chukchi seas, bringing trade goods, disease, alcohol, and, in time, shortages of large sea mammals to the northern and westernmost peoples. Large whaling communities grew around the whaling stations, some such as Barrow on the coast of the Arctic Ocean taking hold and transforming themselves into modern social service and industrial hubs.

The late nineteenth century saw the arrival of U.S. government–sponsored but church-run schools and missionaries who doubled as teachers. Depending on the denomination that dominated a particular region, language and local traditions were either encouraged, permitted, or, most often, forbidden. Because church schools, widespread from the 1920s to the 1960s, often discouraged use of Native languages, the folklore of Alaska's Eskimo people suffered too. Three of Alaska's Eskimo languages, excepting only Central Yup'ik, are today endangered if not moribund.

Two final blows undermined the isolation of the Inupiaq and Yupik people of Alaska: first, a series of gold rushes from 1896 to the early twentieth century that brought hordes of temporary gold-seekers to a few Inupiaq areas but, more lastingly, resulted in transportation and communication corridors that made future immigration possible; and second, World War II. The latter produced a modernized infrastructure that allowed the location and supply of schools in previously isolated villages, which in turn became inhabited year-round rather than seasonally. Under the impact of these influxes of outsiders, Native people have gradually adopted more and more of the trappings of Western life and culture.

SOCIAL STRUCTURE

The social structure of the Inuit and Yupik groups in Canada and Alaska varies with location, but among all groups the building block is kinship. First the nuclear family, then the extended family (everywhere but among the Copper Inuit in Canada), reckoned along both mother's and father's line, are the primary economic and social units. This fact is reflected in many stories, ancient and contemporary, that stress the need for solidarity within a family or the dire consequences of living in isolation without family.

In pre-contact days, named groups formed communities, bands, or, in Alaska, "nations" consisting of several families who harvested resources in specific areas, cooperated in large communal hunts (of caribou or whales, for instance), traded as a group, engaged in warfare together, and returned to the central settlement during deepest winter.

The Suqpiaq, particularly those who lived on Kodiak Island, differed in social structure from other Inuit and Yupik peoples. Theirs was a complex society with elements from their Northwest Coast neighbors (particularly Tlingits), with whom they were in contact. Their houses were large, matrilineality was favored, and they arranged themselves into social classes. Even so, leadership was marked not by heredity but by ability, charisma, and intelligence and was limited to the family group as in other Eskimo societies.

Many Inuit and Yupik communities were physically dominated by one or more buildings called the *qasgiq* (Central Yup'ik), *qargi* (Inupiaq), or *qaggiq* (Inuktitut), either a men's house where the men slept and worked (the first) or a community hall where men worked together during the day and the entire community gathered for ceremonies, parties, or conferences (the latter two). The whaling communities of northern Alaska from Wales north and east along Alaska's Arctic coast were divided into whaling crews, each presided over by an *umialik* (owner of the large skin boat, or *umiak*, that took hunters to sea) and crewed by family and in-laws.

The Arctic can be a dangerous place. Besides the perils of starvation and freezing, inter-group wars and raids were common in the days before contact with Europeans. At the same time, Inuit and Yupik people developed ingenious strategies to turn non-kin into kin, strangers into allies. These include formal and informal adoption (an adopted person retains his or her original family and gains a new one as well), recognition of namesakes as relatives of a sort, co-spouse arrangements (sometimes called wife-swapping), recognizing "kin-of-kin" as one's own kin, and establishing lifelong trade and hunting partnerships. These strategies overlay the practice of sharing food among relatives and neighbors, a basic and persistent norm among all Eskimo peoples, and allowed distant people to avoid conflict or war while establishing contacts with each other that could ensure future trade or intermarriage. The formation of such relationships was often marked by a dance and public celebration.

Relationships within a family were close but subject to rules. Mother-in-law and sister-in-law avoidance by men was common. In some groups, the husband was required to work for the father-in-law for a year before the marriage was officially sanctioned. Among one group of Suqpiaq, preferred marriages were contracted between cross-cousins, whereas in other Eskimo societies, this "teasing cousins" relationship was considered incestuous. Joking, particularly poking fun at one's own or one's cross-cousin's quirks or mistakes, was enjoyed. This form of verbal play continues in casual conversation, the recounting of anecdotes and memorates, and as the content of songs or dances composed for public performance.

Grandparents are revered and cared for. Except in times of extreme starvation, heroic measures were taken to tend to the needs of the elderly who were past the age of productive hunting or sewing, but whose wisdom contributed to group survival. Elders are still offered the best parts of meat recently hunted and are particularly honored with a gift of food when a youngster makes his first kill of a particular species. They then help host a dance in the boy's honor. Similar celebrations occur when a girl gathers her first berries. In both cases, the child dances with older relatives for the first time at the celebration.

Children are highly valued and welcomed. They are understood to be reincarnations of deceased relatives or ancestors and are respected both for themselves and for their identities as incarnations of past elders. In fact, respect for the individual is a paramount value in Yupik and Inuit societies. Perhaps because people historically lived in small houses and settlements where everyone's business was common knowledge, social norms forbid people to assault an individual through loud noises, prying eyes, or demands for responses or answers. This has repercussions in child-rearing, since it is considered more appropriate and effective to point out positive examples and praise success rather than to scold. Criticism is often conveyed indirectly to an individual—for instance, from an elder relative through a cross-cousin or trusted relative. Corporal punishment is discouraged. A "readiness" philosophy of education was traditionally followed—that is, a child learned what was needed when it was needed and when he or she was ready to learn it with prompting from adults. The most common methods of instruction were teaching by example, repeating aphorisms, prescriptions, or injunctions (still a common practice)—particularly to boys while they worked with their elder male relatives in the *qasgit*—and conveying lessons and information through story. A common motif in Eskimo tales concerns the coming of age of a boy or girl who moves from self-indulgence to understanding of his or her proper role in society. This entails learning physical skills as well as acknowledging the priority of the group's well-being over individual desires or impulses.

RELIGIOUS BELIEFS AND RITUALS

Similarly, an important theme in Eskimo folklore is the complementarity of men and women, rich and poor, old and young. Many stories begin with a marked imbalance of ownership, power, and ability, resolved during the story by a redistribution so that everyone in the community has enough and is satisfied with the situation. For instance, one type of story involves a young girl of marriageable age who refuses all suitors—an intolerable situation in Inuit society, for every man needed a wife, every woman a husband. A person could not survive alone, and families could not afford to support unmarried adults. The situation is intrinsically dramatic and demands a resolution.

The world of the Inuit and Yupiit is inhabited by people of different nations and ethnicities, but it is also the realm of animals and geographic features (such as streams, mountains, and rocks) that, like humans, have a life force or spirit (the *yua*, *sua*, or *inua*) and are sentient. Many ancient stories recount the beginnings of a social and spiritual relationship between people and these other beings. In ancient days, all humans could communicate with spirits of animals or features, but certain spiritual advisors or practitioners were more gifted than others. These shamans (the different kinds of practitioners had different titles) presided over ceremonies with a goal of affecting weather or travel conditions, migrations of game, and general hunting luck. The people saw an immediate connection between hunting success and adherence to rules of behavior and respect shown to previous animals killed. If the rules were broken, a shaman could determine how to repair the severed rapport between human and animal.

The Inuit and Yupik religion was more involved with daily survival than concerns about life after death. Still, a recognized cosmology included a universe populated by forces that affected the lives of humans. Central Yupiit and Sugpiat recognized a supreme being, *ellam yua/lam sua*, which roughly translates as "personification of the universe." This being is the sky, the world, and awareness itself, the being that makes possible all cognizance. Canadian Netsilik Inuit recognized three extremely strong spirits, which some ethnographers call deities: Nuliajuk, the sea goddess (known as Sedna and Arnapkapfaaluk in other parts of the Arctic); Narssuk, the god of the sea and bad weather; and Tatqiq, the moon spirit. Other deities or powerful spirits were recognized in other parts of the Arctic. In addition, the creator-**trickster** Raven—recognized as the creator of the land out of a vast sea and the bringer of light to a dark world—figures prominently in the cosmology of Alaskan groups. Canadian Inuit have a cycle of stories about the Tunrit, a race of giants who preceded the Inuit on the land.

Illness was a physical and spiritual affliction, often requiring the intervention of both physician and shaman—who could be the same individual. A vast body of knowledge related to massage, medicinal plants, heat treatments, and other methods served the people for generations and is now being recorded and studied from a Western scientific approach.

Ceremonialism reached a high level in Central Yup'ik and Sugpiaq areas of the far north. An annual round called on the animals at the beginning of the season to request a good year, thanked and honored them at the end of the season, and brought people together to share their bounty in the middle. Games, songs, and dances, marked by costumes and regalia, specialized apparatus, and masks, were elaborate and extensive. In Alaska and Canada alike, a shaman might demonstrate his ability to travel to the moon or to transform himself with the help of a spirit helper during a community gathering.

MYTHS, LEGENDS, AND FOLKTALES

Not only is the oral tradition of the Inuit and Yupik people rich, but much has been recorded in both the indigenous languages and English. In Alaska, the Eskimo people generally divide stories into two large categories, the first roughly analogous to myths (ancient stories that recount origins or deal with universal issues of being human in the world). The second is a very broad category consisting of more recent stories. The former are called, variously, *unigkuwat*, *qulirat*, or *unipkaat* and are set in the distant time when the boundaries between human and animal, life and death, day and night were permeable and unstable. This was when dry land was fashioned from a flooded landscape, when the darkness was relieved by the placement of the sun, moon, and stars in the skies, when the first killer whales were formed from an abandoned wife and her baby son. The Inuit cognate for the Inupiaq *unipkaat*, *unikkaatuat* is not restricted to the most ancient stories, but is used as a general gloss for "story."

A few notable themes and motifs appear in the ancient tales. In Alaska, Raven is greedy trickster and creator. One *unipikaaq* cycle about the Inupiaq culture hero Qayaqtuagingñaqtuaq takes a month to tell. The Canadian Inuit culture hero Kiviuq engages in many adventures similar to this Alaskan counterpart. The story about an unwanted woman named Sedna, Nuliajuk, or Arnapkapfaaluk who is shoved into the sea by her father and brothers, later to become mistress of all sea creatures, is common from northern Alaska to Greenland. Orphan stories, in which a fatherless boy must find his way in the world often with the help of a spiritually powerful grandmother, abound throughout the region. A story told in all parts of the region involves a mistreated blind boy whose sight is restored with a loon's help. Another common tale chronicles the marriage of a man and a bear. The husband is foolishly unfaithful, resulting in his brutal demise. "How-so" stories also fit within this genre. They are told primarily by women to children. Imbedded in many ancient tales are songs.

The second category of verbal art is not a genre but, rather, a grouping of stories that happened within living memory and can be attributed to specific individuals within the past several generations. This group includes extemporaneous expressions as well as accounts of historic and legendary exploits. The Yupik warrior Apanuugpak of the early nineteenth century is characterized as a "killing machine" who has narrow escapes and makes life miserable for his enemies throughout much of the lower Yukon and Kuskokwim deltas. These stories also narrate the exploits of legendary shamans. When the subject is personal experience, men most commonly talk about hunting in Alaska, while they are taking a steambath. They detail each step of the hunt, and the audience attends the recitation with intense interest. Most exciting are close calls, often involving large predators such as brown bears or polar bears or extreme weather conditions. The raconteur invariably learned a valuable lesson from the experience, which he readily passes on to his listeners.

A relatively new kind of story is the *gussuk* or *tannik* (Whiteman) tale. These often feature whites as hapless ignoramuses who can easily be duped by their Eskimo hosts. Women's memorates often relate to experiences of their youth or biographical sketches of people important in their lives or villages. Both men and women tell of their strange or scary experiences, often with a supernatural bent. These include encounters with "little people" (*ircinrat*) on the tundra, the spirits (*sua*) of streams or other geographic features, or "Outside men" (*a'ularaat*), Bigfoot-like creatures who abscond with unwary travelers. People of all ages also love to recount funny stories about themselves or someone else.

String stories—similar to cat's cradle—are still learned and retold throughout the Arctic and Subarctic, though they have survived as a viable form of lore only in pockets. A string story performance consists of a tale about particular animals, geographic features, or adventures, told while the performer is twisting and knotting a long loop of string into a picture that illustrates the story's punch line. In Inuit areas, string stories may be told only in the winter, a restriction that does not apply in southern regions.

Another genre combining verbal and visual art that was popular among Central Yup'ik girls until some twenty years ago was storyknifing. Girls' fathers would fashion graceful arching forms from ivory that look like flattened shoehorns. They carved and etched designs along the top edge and left the bottom edge smooth. More recently girls used stainless steel butter knives. Three or four girls went outside and squatted in the snow or over a patch of wet mud. They smoothed out the snow or mud with their knives, then drew squares, rectangles, and lines to represent a house and its inhabitants. Each girl told a story about the family that lived in the house, illustrating the action with deft knife strokes.

DANCE, SONGS, AND MUSIC

Performance and dance styles vary throughout the Inuit-Yupik region, but humor was always appreciated and generally a part of each evening's program. Equally prominent might be ridicule or competitive songs, particularly in the Canadian Arctic. A Central Yup'ik tradition holds that dance originated at the end of a long period of warfare. The elders from different villages agreed that fighting was depleting human and animal resources. They decided to institute dancing as an alternative.

The primary musical instruments are a round tambourine-like drum, beaten with a long thin stick, and the human voice. Rattles and whistles are sometimes used as well, though not in all parts of the region nor

The Miracle Dancers of Anchorage, Alaska, perform at a local cultural center, January 2002. (Photograph by Patricia H. Partnow)

with all songs. In some parts of the Arctic, the men drum and sing while the women dance in a row before them. Elsewhere men kneel in front of the women, dancing with their upper bodies only, while the women stand behind them dancing. Drummers are seated to one side or behind the women. In still other areas, the men are the main performers with women as backdrop singers. Dancing styles vary, but in general dance accompanies a strong drumbeat and consists of motions that tell the story that is being sung. Men usually dance with energy and force, women with smoothness and grace.

Songs are composed for the occasion, and today may depict an airplane ride, a hunting incident, or a mishap on the ice. People also perform older songs learned from parents or grandparents. A brief story about the author and how he or she came to compose it introduces each song. The number of verses varies, with Central Yup'ik performances showing the most elaboration. After many verses, the song leader shouts, "Pamyua!" meaning "its tail end!" This signals to the dancers that the drumming and singing will become loud and fast, and the dancers are expected to move with similar enthusiasm. If the audience approves the performance, anyone can shout, "Pamyua!" Singers and dancers must repeat the verse with greater verve if possible. This can continue until the audience tires of the song.

Today a resurgence of interest in performance arts that originated in the winter ceremonials but then went underground during years of repression by various Christian churches is evident. Regalia, long unused in many communities, is now fashioned out of skins, feathers, beads, bones, ivory, wood, puffin beaks, and cloth. In Alaska, dance groups make matching qaspeqs, cotton indoor parkas, and practice many hours before performances. Regional and statewide gatherings allow the groups to perform in school gymnasiums and museums, dancing long into the night for several days at a time. But the legacy of the missionaries remains in villages where devout church members consider dancing immoral. Another ancient tradition, now limited to the eastern part of the Arctic, is the enactment of

Ivory grouping, Inupiaq and St. Lawrence Island Yupik. The grouping of four ivory seals was carved by St. Lawrence Island artists. (Photograph by Patricia H. Partnow)

Inuit owl stone carving by Shorty Killiktee of Lake Harbour. (Photograph by Patricia H. Partnow)

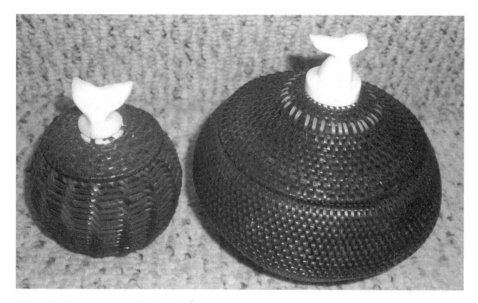

Baleen baskets with ivory knobs in the shape of whales' tails. Left, James Omnik; right, Carl E. Hank, both of Point Hope. (Photograph by Patricia H. Partnow)

stories through interactive throat singing, in which air bursts past the vocal cords.

FESTIVALS AND GAMES

Throughout the Arctic and Subarctic, trade fairs or other opportunities for gatherings of groups occasioned games, contests, and dances. Merging fierce competition with a playful spirit, men and women played games of strength, speed, and agility. These continue in Alaska and Canada in the formalized annual World Eskimo Indian Olympics. Contests include one- and two-foot high kicks, ear pull, leg wrestling, seal hop (one of the most painful races imaginable with contestants hopping on toes and knuckles until all but one drops out with bloodied and swollen joints), and others that relate directly to survival in the past. Today the games are characterized by competition just as fierce as in the past, yet competitors regularly coach and assist each other. Universal euphoria occurs when a record is broken, no matter who accomplishes the feat.

ARTS AND CRAFTS

While personal use items had previously been made beautiful and distinctive, today the visual arts are put to the service of commerce as well. In Canada, carving from soapstone, serpentine, and other stones often into characters from ancient stories is a vital industry. Similarly, stone cuts, etchings, stencils, and lithographic prints, an innovation of the 1950s as a way of providing income for an activity that allowed people to engage in culturally meaningful work, have become collectors' items in galleries and living rooms throughout the world. Pieced wall hangings using wool and yarn originally imported by the Hudson's Bay Company are another important art form produced by Canadian Inuit women. Jewelry representing traditional subjects in ivory, beads, and fine metals is popular. In Alaska, the baleen baskets of the Point Hope Inupiat command high prices, as do exquisite walrus and mammoth ivory carvings of animals and people made by St. Lawrence Islanders and Inupiat. Coiled grass baskets by Central Yup'ik women regularly sell out in bazaars throughout Alaska. Masks, particularly those from Nunivak Island in Alaska, have a ready market, while Sugpiaq areas specialize in fine twined grass basketry and bentwood hunting visors that are delicately painted in swooping lines and festooned with sea lion whiskers. Dolls from all regions of the far north depicting traditional activities in exquisite detail have captured the attention of collectors. In Alaska, the ancient practice of etching figures and

All baskets—with the exception of the open-weave basket in the front row—were made by Yupik women from coiled beach grass, both dyed and natural. The basket on the far right is decorated with dyed seal gut. These baskets were made between 1972 and 2002. The open-weave basket in the front left is in the twined Sugpiaq/Alutiiq style. (Photograph by Patricia H. Partnow)

designs on personal belongings and tools finds expression in pen, pencil, and ink drawings on seal skin and paper. Each art form derives from a traditional object used in everyday life in the past or in the ceremonial round, but today most are made for sale. Museum catalogs provide excellent information about Inuit visual arts, both traditional and contemporary.

CHALLENGES OF THE MODERN WORLD

Many children's games are in danger of being forgotten under the onslaught of television and video games, but the baby boom generation remembers playing jack-like games, ballgames where the ball is bounced from hand to hand and person to person, keep-away, pin-and-ball games, and a group game that can incorporate as many people as are available, today called Eskimo baseball.

A system of apprenticeship wherein young boys were tutored to become storytellers ensured the persistence of oral tradition. They were required to learn not only episodes and plots but also exact phrasing and intonation, particularly when depicting

Yupik mask by Peter Smith of Nunivak Island, 1980. The rings with attached appendages and the red ocher and chalk-textured off-white pigments are characteristic of Nunivak woodworking. (Photograph by Patricia H. Partnow)

Inuit "packing doll," Kalluk ("Thunder"), and her brother "Lightning." Made in 1988 by "Maudie" of Spence Bay. (Photograph by Patricia H. Partnow)

different characters. The most talented young men practiced telling the stories among themselves and in front of their mentors before they went public. Women too learned stories and songs from their mothers, grandmothers, and aunts, but in the home rather than in a formal or public setting. Stories are not owned and can therefore be told by anyone, but non-specialists customarily defer to acknowledged storytellers. Today that role is assumed by traditionally trained elders or by young people interested in a career in drama and performance.

Today many Yupiit and Inuit bemoan the loss of the oral traditions, noting that their children and grandchildren spend more time in front of the television than with their elders. They have devised three antidotes: annual regional Elders' Conferences that provide a venue and audience for the recounting of oral traditions; recording and subsequent archiving of stories told in indigenous language and English on audio- and videotape; and publication of books of stories. All lack important parts of oral performance: the first suffers from lack of cultural context, the second from lack of authentic audience, and the third from the loss of live performance style. Still, they ensure the preservation of the content, if not always the dynamics, of folklore.

STUDIES OF INUIT AND YUPIK FOLKLORE

There are many print sources for information about Yupik and Inuit verbal folklore. The most readily available, but unfortunately least reliable, sources can be found in children's sections of bookstores. Most Arctic **ethnographies** and explorers' journals written over the past century and a half contain a section on folklore and folkways of the indigenous people—for example, Balikci (1970), Birket-Smith (1953), Burch (1998), Condon (1996), Hawkes (1970 [1916]), and Nelson (1971 [1899]). Readily available are publications by the Alaska Native Language Center at the University of Alaska Fairbanks. This center, whose mission is the study, recording, and preservation of Alaska's indigenous languages, has an extensive collection of audio-recordings, many transcribed and published in limited edition. School districts throughout Alaska and Canada have been active since the 1970s in recording and printing information from student oral history projects. They have also produced instructional materials based on ancient traditions. Unfortunately these materials can be difficult to locate and obtain, since they are generally printed in small numbers and have no distribution network outside their locales. Cultural centers and Native organizations, particularly in Alaska, have published the transcripts of Elders' Conferences. More readily available are overviews of oral literature (Morrow 1994, Nungak and Arima 1969, and Senungetuk and Tiulana 1987). The University of Alaska at Anchorage has produced a special edition of its journal *Alaska Quarterly Review* called *Alaska Native Writers, Storytellers & Orators* (Spatz, Breinig, and Partnow 1999) devoted entirely to Alaska Native literature, both oral and written. Some Canadian collections—including, for instance, Petrone (1988)—contain selections that span a broad geographic and historic range.

A few dramatic and media productions have been based on Yupik and Inuit folklore in both Alaska and Canada. The most successful are produced by the National Film Board of Canada. In 2001, an award-winning feature film based on an oral tradition, *Atanarjuat: The Fast Runner*, enjoyed wide distribution throughout North America. This film offers hope for Yupik and Inuit oral tradition. It is a model of excellent film-making and storytelling that was written, directed, produced, and acted by an Inuit crew. This is the sort of endeavor that many see as insurance that Eskimo folk tradition has a future as well as a long and rich past.

Yupik dolls made of cloth and seal skin. (Photograph by Patricia H. Partnow)

BIBLIOGRAPHY

Balikci, Asen. 1970. *The Netsilik Eskimo*. Garden City, NY: Natural History Press.

Birket-Smith, Kaj. 1953. *The Chugach Eskimo*. Etnografisk Raekke 6. Kobnhavn: Nationalmuseets.

Burch, Ernest S., Jr. 1998. *The Inupiaq Eskimo Nations of Northwest Alaska*. Fairbanks: University of Alaska Press.

Condon, Richard G. 1996. *The Northern Copper Inuit: A History*. Norman: University of Oklahoma Press.

Hawkes, E. W. 1970 (1916). *The Labrador Eskimo*. New York: Johnson Reprint.

Morrow, Phyllis. 1994. Oral Literature of the Alaskan Arctic. In *Dictionary of Native North American Literature*, edited by Andrew Wiget. New York: Garland. 19–26.

Nelson, Edward William. 1971 (1899). *The Eskimo about Bering Strait*. New York: Johnson Reprint.

Nungak, Zebedee, and Eugene Arima. 1969. *Eskimo Stories—Unikkaatuat*. Ottawa: National Museums of Canada.

Petrone, Penny. 1988. *Northern Voices: Inuit Writing in English*. Toronto: University of Toronto Press.

Senungetuk, Vivian, and Paul Tiulana. 1987. *A Place for Winter: Paul Tiulana's Story*. Anchorage: The CIRI Foundation.

Spatz, Ronald, Jeane Breinig, and Patricia H. Partnow, eds. 1999. *Alaska Native Writers, Storytellers & Orators: The Expanded Edition. Alaska Quarterly Review.* Special Issue.

Zacharias, Kunuk. *Atanarjuat: The Fast Runner.* 2001. Igloolik, Canada: Igloolik Isuma Productions.

Patricia H. Partnow

YUPIK. *See* Western Inuit and Yupik

African American and Regional Non-Native Cultures

AFRICAN AMERICAN

ROOTS OF AFRICAN AMERICAN FOLKLORE

Many strands of oral and material traditions from Africa have blended with European and other cultures to form the basis from which most recognizable African American folklore genres have emerged: spirituals, **trickster** tales, toasts, the dozens, proverbs, legends, the blues, and rap. These genres, all noted for their verbal artistry, serve as vehicles through which views toward the sacred and the secular and ideas about the community versus the individual, cleverness overcoming the powerful, greed, sex, violence, alcohol and drug abuse, male-female relationships, dominance and subordination, identity and race, and other such themes are transmitted from generation to generation. Along with material folk culture, they represent some of the most important cultural resources that comprise the African American experience.

Because of the importance of the spoken word among African groups from which slaves were captured, many of the most ubiquitous folklore forms are cast in Black English dialect. A subject that has received considerable interest among sociolinguists and folklorists, Black English dialect varies from Standard English in at least three ways: grammar (for example, dropping the /s/ in nouns to indicate plurality and lack of verb tense, such as "He got five dollar"), pronunciation (for instance, substituting *d* for *th* in "the"), and vocabulary (such as "gumbo," "jazz," and "okra").

Zora Neale Hurston offers an excellent example of dialect in *Mules and Men* (1935), in which she records a number of folk narratives she collected in Florida during the 1930s. Her collection of stories and jokes contrasts with Joel Chandler Harris's earlier publication *Nights with Uncle Remus* (1883), a collection of tales that Harris (who was white) heard from blacks while growing up in the South. Uncle Remus, a fictional black servant who tells the plantation owner's son the stories Harris edited, employs phonetic dialect (often called eye dialect) as a literary device to underscore the quaintness of black southern characters. That and later publications by Harris offered to white readers the richness of folk wisdom but also sparked a scholarly debate about the origins of these so-called dialect tales. Conversely, Hurston's collection was based on ethnographic research she conducted among fellow blacks in and around her hometown of Eatonville, Florida, and comes closer to capturing the spoken word in print.

Did the tales from these and other collections originate

Zora Neale Hurston offers an excellent example of dialect in *Mules and Men* (1935), in which she records a number of folk narratives she collected in Florida during the 1930s. (Courtesy Library of Congress)

from Europe or from Africa? Folklorist Richard Dorson, who employed research tools which indexed folk narrative motifs and folktale types, favored a predominantly European origin. After reviewing the work of black and white collectors of African American folklore who preceded him, Dorson concluded that his collection of tales was non-African in origin. For example, he claimed that "Coon in the Box," among the best-known Old Marster stories, derives from a **motif** (K1956, "Sham wise man"), which appears in "Doctor-Know-All" (AT 1641), collected and published by the Grimm brothers.

"The Coon in the Box" is a story of black servant Jack who endangers himself when his boss wagers that Jack is a "know-it-all" who can guess the contents of a box. What the boss does not realize is that Jack always investigates the facts ahead of time so that he appears to have an uncanny ability to know things in advance. But this time, Jack did not know the contents of the box, in which the boss had placed a raccoon. Jack gives up and proclaims, "You got that old coon at last," thereby correctly "guessing" the contents and guaranteeing his boss considerable financial gain. William Bascom effectively countered Dorson's claims of European origins by drawing from a considerable number of collections in both the Eastern and Western Hemispheres, and his comparative analysis makes the strong connection between African and African American folktales unquestionable.

Later scholars furthered the debate by revisiting "The Coon in the Box" in Dorson's earlier collection. According to John Minton and David Evans (2001), "The Coon in the Box" as a version of "Doctor Know-All" represents an African American adaptation of a universal trickster tale. What is important is the culturally specific understandings of the tale and its concern with the connections African Americans probably drew between the tale and their circumstances in which they were unable to escape from a system that linked race and class. Jack (aka John) helps his boss (Marster) win the bet, but the protagonist merely escapes with his life. Rarely is he the beneficiary of any material gain. In short, "The Coon in the Box" demonstrates that as blacks assimilated European culture, they nevertheless expressed African modes of thought, recasting these as distinctly African American traditions. The reinterpretation of European expressive forms that have also drawn from African sources and in many cases have distinctly African roots, which Bascom argued, renders the argument of origins of African American tales meaningless if scholars ignore the context in which such forms emerge.

Lawrence Levine's *Black Culture and Black Consciousness* (1977) offers a fine example of how blacks in the Americas incorporate folklore into their everyday lives. Employing ex-slave narratives and other primary sources, Levine gives a compelling argument that there is no doubt that since European colonization of the Americas, Africans figured prominently in shaping its history and culture, transporting their traditions and customs with them as they were forced from their homelands and onto plantations. Yet some early scholars claimed black slaves suffered from cultural amnesia, given the traumatic experience of the trans-Atlantic crossing. Other theories that Melville Herskovits in his *Myth of the Negro Past* (1941) challenged included the notion that because blacks were thought biologically inferior to white Europeans, they were incapable of possessing any kind of artistic or creative abilities of their own and certainly had no way of forming a unifying body of folklore, particularly given the diverse linguistic stocks from which they came. However, changes in ways of speaking eventually evolved from the pidgin languages to a creolized form that simplified verb tense and other linguistic forms. Children learned this creole, which moved toward the dominant language form that became known as Black English dialect. Moreover, there are a number of similarities among the trickster and animal tales in Africa that resulted in a distinctly African American corpus of folklore, much of which Hurston's *Mules and Men* captures in print. That African slaves were childlike savages, a *tabula rasa* upon which Europeans could force their own values and **worldviews**, was a racist idea roundly debunked by Herskovits.

SLAVERY AND SPIRITUALS

Entering North America along the eastern seaboard and the coast of the Gulf of Mexico, slaves who survived the trans-Atlantic crossing affected plantation culture in all aspects of life. Out of the slave experience grew a rich body of expressive culture reflecting a distinct set of values and attitudes. The oral traditions that emerged were vehicles by which they expressed their joys and sorrows and their beliefs, giving them a means of coping with this oppressive system.

To encourage black slaves to work under harsh conditions while draining, clearing, and cultivating huge areas along river systems, white overseers and plantation owners felt it would be beneficial for their investment in human property to teach them about God and the dire consequences that would be visited upon those who rejected God's commandments not to steal or lie and to work hard for the white man. However, slaves found aspects of the Old Testament particularly relevant to their own captivity. It was easy to identify with the story of Moses, who freed the Hebrews from the Egyptian pharaoh. Belief in a better world gave slaves hope that the day would come when they would also be free. Such images of escape, even if it meant in the afterlife, helped them cope with their secular world of hard work. However, indentured servants also brought with them their own distinct religious system replete with a variety of deities and means of protection from the forces of evil. The religion of vodou is a magico-religious system whose leaders (priests) played important roles in inspiring rebellious slaves to resist brutal plantation life. A central figure was Legba, a god of West Africa and vodou, a cunning, intelligent trickster who holds the key to the gate that separates the human's world from the world of the gods. European Christian beliefs did not destroy many of the beliefs that slaves brought with them to the Americas.

Spirituals invoking images from the Bible did not all necessarily imply an acceptance of the slave's lot on earth. Some early spirituals had subversive messages:

> I don't want to ride in no golden chariot,
> I don't want to wear no golden crown,
> I want to stay down here and be
> Just as I am without one plea.

Spirituals were also masked messages about freedom and escape in this world: for example, "Go down Moses, way down in Egypt land / Tell Ole Pharaoh to let my people go" and "Swing low, sweet chariot, comin' for to carry me home." "Follow the Drink' Gourd" may have been a celestial map, a guide to the underground railroad for blacks seeking to escape slavery. Nevertheless, as most folklorists have observed, spirituals—which W.E.B. DuBois dubbed "sorrow songs"—also express the hardships slaves endured and the hope for freedom that would come to God's chosen people, espousing their confidence of getting into heaven while assuring them that sinful whites would not. In short, spirituals could appeal either to the secular world of enslaved people or to the sacred one that offered hope for freedom.

This chapter in the emergence of a distinctly African American expressive form is a recurring one as American blacks find cause to remember their cultural legacy in the form of folk festivals, or what have been called freedom celebrations. Freedom celebrations remind celebrants of their legacy, the saga of which passes from one generation to another through colorful pageants. William H. Wiggins Jr. (1987) describes the saga as having four epochs. The first deals with the African past with scenes that depict the glories of Egypt, Ethiopia, and other ancient civilizations. The second period is slavery, which include episodes such as forms of physical and psychological torture, slave revolts, the underground railroad, and the emergence of slave spirituals. Emancipation follows slavery, with scenes of Lincoln issuing the Emancipation Proclamation, the Civil War, the role of black soldiers, slaves who felt morally obligated to run the plantation while their masters were away at war, and their subsequent experiences of freedom. The final epoch describes the continual struggle for freedom that began with Emancipation, underscoring that forms of slavery still exist, and this part of the saga also includes the disfranchisement of blacks during Reconstruction, mass migrations from the South to the North, participation of black soldiers in American wars, the civil rights movements, the rise of black nationalism, race riots, and the emergence of blues, jazz, gospel, and other musical contributions blacks have made to American culture and history. These annual events give celebrants opportunities to pass along to younger generations their histories, songs, and stories, thereby reminding them of their roots and their continuing struggle for first-class citizenship in the New World.

The plantation culture that depended upon slavery represented the second epoch in these freedom celebrations. Such a context gave rise to spirituals as a worldview emerged that linked the slave's world with that of the Hebrews under Moses and also included aspects of a belief system with African antecedents. In this worldview, certain gifted individuals such as conjure doctors could manipulate supernatural forces to achieve their own ends. Practitioners of these beliefs were sometimes at odds with Christian converts, though in some respects the two systems influenced each other. Moses, like the fictional John de Conqueror popular in plantation oral traditions, was a mystical figure possessing the power to help others. However, conjurers were also capable of countering a bad spell, or *juju*, and believers seeking to control supernatural forces as well as faith healers combined both natural remedies for the sick and injured with magic. For those who worked close to the soil, knowledge of plants with medicinal properties played an important role in combating the numerous maladies slaves regularly faced. Many overseers and slaveowners relied on the skills of black healers and midwives familiar with such herbs and plants. These folk healers were indispensable on plantations, particularly those lacking access to trained physicians. However, if natural cures or everyday methods for solving problems were ineffective or unavailable, then a patient might find it necessary to consult a specialist who could manipulate unseen forces to thwart an enemy, avenge a wrong toward oneself or loved one, or create a love potion. The belief system therefore incorporated both religion and magic, though practitioners of vodou, derived from the Caribbean Vodun religion, were often held in awe and often feared by both blacks and whites. Stories abound on plantations of hoodoo doctors capable of transforming themselves to evade capture, while folk healers such as midwives were depended upon by whites on plantations where white doctors were not always available. The efficacy of such healers was sometimes even preferred at times. When white physicians were unsuccessful in delivering the mistress's baby, she often sent for a black plantation midwife. According to one account, two white doctors attempted to discredit a particular midwife's claims in a successful delivery and ridiculed her, warning, "Get back darkie, we mean business an' don' won't any witch doctors or hoodoo stuff." Nevertheless, the white woman insisted she stay and perform her work. Such healers were more inclined to place their faith in their knowledge of plants and herbs than in controlling supernatural forces characteristic of hoodoo doctors.

However, many who believed that supernatural forces could be controlled through magic and ritual received reinforcement in those beliefs whenever misfortune befell their white captors, such as when the dreaded boll weevil destroyed cotton crops or when floods threatened to ruin a white landowner's investment. These were acts of an angry God who sought revenge against evil whites who mistreated slaves. These conditions also fostered the development of a rich body of trickster tales, stories that often depicted the subservient black slave outwitting his master such as the cycle of Marster-John tales that was pervasive throughout plantation communities in the southern United States.

Typically in these tales, John would invert the power relations between him and his white master. In a version of "Old Master Eats Crow" recorded by Richard Dorson, John was caught hunting on Master's place and was warned not to do so anymore, but John did anyway and shot a crow. Marster told John to give him his gun, and he then aimed it at him and demanded John to pick the feathers off the crow, saying, "Now start at his head, John, and eat the crow up to where you stopped picking the feathers at." After John finished eating, Marster returned his gun, but when John started walking away, he turned toward Marster, pointed the gun at him, and said, "Lookee here, Old Marster," and threw the rest of the crow at him. "I want you to start at his ass and eat all the way, and don't let a feather fly from your mouth."

Stories also circulated that would teach young listeners about what happens to careless slaves who fail to adhere to an informal code of conduct such as not telling others everything you know or cooperating with white authority figures. "Talking Turtle" is about a turtle who scolded John: "Black man, you talk too much," whereupon John ran to get Old Marster to come with him to the bayou to see the talking turtle. But Old Marster did not want to go see a talking turtle because he did not believe John. He warned him he would give John a good beating if he was lying. When they arrived at the bayou, the turtle said nothing as his head receded into his shell, so John received a beating. A bewildered John returned to the bayou, and the turtle said, "Black man, didn't I tell you you talked too much?"

TRICKSTER TALES

The trickster figure played a prominent role in folktales heard on southern slave plantations, but the animal tricksters bore the closest resemblance to their African counterparts. Tricksters such as Hare or Rabbit (found throughout East Africa) and Spider (a transformation of Anansi common in much of West Africa and the Caribbean) were relatively small and weak creatures and therefore reached their goals through wit and guile rather than through physical power. What they craved—food, sex, and other prizes—were much the same as the desires of the slaves who told of their exploits. Storyteller and listeners identified with them, and such animal tales explained how the alligator got his mouth, why the rabbit has a short tail, and how a protagonist outwits his stronger foe (for example, "Tar Baby"). Most important, the victories of Brer Rabbit became the victories of the slave. Narrators also told supernatural and religious tales as well as other kinds of explanatory tales: how the church evolved, why the black man's hair is nappy, and why African Americans are black. But after slavery, these tales gave way to a different kind of protagonist, one who figured in a type of narrative that came to be known as toasts and who was also often incorporated into other expressive forms.

In the animal tale "Tar Baby," which Harris popularized in his early Uncle Remus collection, the trickster Rabbit "signifies" on his antagonist Fox, imploring him not to throw him into the briar patch, which is of course the rabbit's natural habitat and thus ridiculing his adversary's ignorance. The rabbit's signifying is one of the most striking features in black oral traditions and most often implies indirect insult. The toast "The Signifying Monkey" tells how Monkey tells Lion that Elephant has been saying bad things about him and that it is Elephant who is king of the jungle. This causes Lion to seek Elephant in a duel, much to the delight of Monkey, whose satisfaction comes from his ability to create chaos through his verbal skills. When Lion discovers Monkey's deception, he returns to the tree where Monkey is laughing hysterically. Monkey further incurs the wrath of Lion, again signifying on him by hurling insults at Lion and ridiculing his gullibility while sitting safely high on a tree limb. But while jumping up and down in laughter, the monkey slips and falls and finds himself at the mercy of Lion. He again quickly fools Lion into forgiving him, scurries back up the tree, and continues ranting and berating the Lion's gullibility. This toast illustrates some of the most important features of signifying, and the situational context in which the word applies narrows its meaning.

TOASTS

Toasts, sometimes known as jokes, are long narratives often in rhymed couplets that frequently employ signifying as one of their most significant features. They are often heard in prisons, on street corners, and at barbershops, restaurants, meeting halls, or wherever men gather to tell stories. Besides the well-known "Signifying Monkey," there are other toasts that include a trickster-badman figure. Unlike trickster John in the John-Marster tale cycle specific to southern slave plantations, the protagonist in black toasts takes on much different characteristics. For instance, the character Shine appears in one of the best-known toasts in black oral tradition, "The Titanic."

After the superliner *Titanic* sank in 1912, the toast appeared in a variety of versions in both song and prose narrative among blacks and whites, but the toast most popular in black oral tradition depicted the character Shine, a lowly boiler-room worker, rebelling against the ultimate white authority figure aboard ship, the captain. Perhaps because the *Titanic* refused passage to African Americans (except those who worked in subservient positions like Shine), including black heavyweight boxing champion Jack Johnson, the toast must have had a particular appeal among those it circulated. Essentially, Shine, a trickster-type character who possesses badman qualities, responds to the captain's demands for him to return below and continue shoveling coal, despite Shine's warning that the ship is sinking, by ultimately refusing the order. The following excerpt comes from a collection of toasts that Bruce Jackson recorded from a black convict at a southeast Texas prison farm:

> Up popped Shine from the deck below,
> says, "Captain, captain," says, "you don't know."
> Says, "There's about forty feet of water on the boiler-room floor."
> He said, "Never mind, Shine, you go on back and keep stackin' them sacks,
> I got forty-eight pumps to keep the water back."
> Shine said, "Well, that seems damned funny, it may be damned fine,
> but I'm gonna try to save this black ass of mine."
> So Shine jumped overboard and begin to swim,
> and all the people were standin' on deck watchin' him.
> Captain's daughter jumped on the deck with her dress above her head and her
>   teddies below her knees.
> and said, "Shine, Shine," say, "won't you save poor me?"
> Say, "I'll make you rich as any Shine can be."
> Shine said, "Miss, I know you is pretty and that is true,
> but there's women on the shore can make a ass out a you."
> Captain said, "Shine, Shine, you save poor me,
> I make you as rich as any Shine can be."
> Shine say, "There's fish in the ocean, whales in the sea,
> captain, get your ass in the water and swim like me."

The toast underscores institutionalized racism and plays on stereotyped images of sexually promiscuous blacks who prey on white women. The laughter that comes from listening to a gifted raconteur depict white people drowning as the outrageous Shine swims to safety gives this particular toast special prominence in black oral tradition. The style of delivery also affects audience response, and a good speaker includes such paralinguistic devices of communication as facial and hand gestures and voice inflections. Other toasts have transformed the heroic qualities of the trickster slave into a character who not only boasts of his physical abilities but associates himself with some of the most dangerous elements in society: prostitutes, pimps, and gamblers. One of the best badman toasts that illustrates this type of character is Stagolee, who kills Billy Lyons over a Stetson hat in a bar called the Bucket of Blood (a generic term for juke joints).

THE DOZENS

The dozens, a form of verbal dueling, is often associated with toasts. The dozens is embedded in the "The Signifying Monkey" as Monkey exchanges insults with Lion, but the dozens primarily involves black adolescents who engage in ritual insults until somebody "loses."

"Playing the dozens" also goes by names that vary regionally, such as "signifying" or "sigging" (Chicago), "joning" (Washington, D.C.), "woofing" (Philadelphia), and "capping" (West Coast). Played by and performed among an audience that most often involves black adolescent males, the object is to hurl creative insults or "snaps" against one's opponents (often targeting a close relative such as one's mother), whereupon the recipient of the snap responds accordingly. "Sounding" also refers to the ritualized insult, and for somebody to "sound on" somebody else refers to a ritualized attribute of that person: for example, "If ugliness were bricks, your mother would be a housing project." A clever response would build on this insult, receiving either praise or groans from listeners. It is a verbal activity that can take on a wide range of meanings. According to the civil rights leader H. Rap Brown, "The real aim of the Dozens was to get a dude so mad he'd cry or get mad enough to fight." Moreover, Brown pointed out, "Some of the best Dozens players were girls." Therefore, the game is not necessarily gender-specific, although the content of the insults differ according to a performer's gender.

Major themes of the dozens include poverty ("Your family is so poor, they go to Kentucky Fried Chicken to lick other people's fingers"), ugliness ("Your mother is so ugly, when she walks in the bank they turn off the cameras"), stupidity ("Your sister is so stupid, she went to the baker for a yeast infection"), and sexual promiscuity ("Your mother's like a bag of chips, she's free-to-lay").

Other interpretations of the dozens include the notion that this form of activity is a reflection of tensions black males face in an environment where one must prove masculinity and reject femininity. Roger D. Abrahams (1970) suggests that the dozens enables a boy to attack some other person's mother and consequently diminish his own mother's influence. Another explanation, proposed by Onwuchekwa Jemie (2003), holds that the disrespect shown the mother in the dozens is the means by which a boy eventually disengages himself from the comfort of his mother's intimacy—an issue more important for African American males than their African counterparts, given the abuse black males have suffered in the New World and their frequent difficulties in protecting family members. Playing the dozens includes considerable signifying, as is evident in "The Signifying Monkey."

PROVERBS AND RUMOR STORIES

Verbal artistry may also be seen in African American proverbs, a form that can be most easily understood within the context in which it is heard. Sw. Anand Prahlad cites an example, "Different strokes for different folks," that has been used in a variety of circumstances, and "You reap what you sow," a proverb often found in slave narratives. These succinct forms contrast with the longer narrative forms that have more recently appeared in collections such as the various urban legends recorded and analyzed by Patricia Turner (1994).

Turner's best-known work is her analysis of the rumors that suggested FBI culpability in its lack of enthusiasm in investigating the Atlanta child murders that were committed from 1979 until 1981. Other conspiracy rumors appeared after the arrest of a suspect whom many thought was innocent and suggested a plot by the Ku Klux Klan (KKK) to destroy young blacks. Additional stories have circulated about the KKK's efforts in this and other plots, such as its purported involvement in contaminating chicken in a fast-food chain to make young black men sterile.

FIELD HOLLERS AND WORKSONGS

While spirituals influenced the development of gospel music, which focused more on themes from the New Testament than from its predecessor, contemporary African American folk music forms such as blues and later rap and hip-hop also draw heavily upon a rich body of earlier traditions.

Oral traditions associated with plantation culture include field hollers and worksongs. These forms are rooted in black American culture going back at least three centuries. They sometimes contain words but as often as not wordless sounds to call others from the field or communicate with neighboring fieldworkers. Worksongs, by definition, accompanied labor on plantations and could still be heard in southern prisons well into the twentieth century. They not only helped pass the time but often helped to prevent slow workers from attracting the attention of a brutal overseer or prison guard. While they helped to regulate and coordinate work of all kinds (including hoeing, chopping cotton, cutting down trees, and aligning railroad ties), they also were an acceptable means by which singers expressed their discontent with harsh and unfair working conditions, their longing to be home, or concern over who might be home sleeping with a worker's girlfriend or wife. Military analogues to these worksongs include marching chants such as "Jody songs" popular among black soldiers, who disseminated them throughout the ranks while they were away from home. Jody was the character thought to be sleeping with one's wife.

Field hollers and worksongs dealt with themes that also appeared in the blues such as a rule-breaking aggressive protagonist who challenges white authority and the status quo (for example, "John Hardy" and "Railroad Bill"). Such ideas in song suggest a certain amount of thematic continuity in black oral tradition that manifested itself in the blues. The blues often emphasizes an emotional intensity registering concerns

Worksongs accompanied labor on plantations and could still be heard in southern prisons well into the twentieth century. Pictured here are African American convicts working with axes and singing in a woodyard, Reed Camp, South Carolina (1934). (Courtesy Library of Congress)

common to black listeners. Audience members had opportunities to participate in blues performances, given the nature of the genre's call-and-response pattern, in such contexts as juke joints.

BLUES, RAP, AND HIP-HOP

Blues most often conforms to or varies somewhat from a basic twelve-bar, AAB pattern. Lyrics frequently contain several stanzas, each one twelve measures of 4/4 time in length. The first line (A) is repeated by the second, and the stanza's third line (B) usually rhymes with the first two. However, each of the three lines may take only a few measures to sing, allowing two measures for an instrumental "response" to the vocal line. The most common blues sequence in these musical phrases is tonic, subdominant, and dominant chords (for example, A major, D major, and E major). However, the scale of most blues is based on so-called blue notes that fall somewhere between the cracks of the piano keys and are thus slightly lower or flatter than they normally would be in a Western musical scale. Such notes include both major and minor thirds, major and minor sevenths, and perfect and flatted fifths. The music of the blues is very similar to that of its precursors, and the line between sacred and secular music is not always clear.

The religious experience, particularly chanted speech, affected the blues. Indeed, the preaching tradition and the blues tradition involve verbal skills their practitioners acquire by supernatural means. For example, songster Robert Johnson is reputed to have "bought" blues skills by selling his soul at the "crossroads." Both black preachers and bluesmen employ a pattern of call and response. Phrases that are formulaic in preaching are also typical among blues performers. Other parallels are evident during performances, such as audience-congregation participation.

Early hymnody, spirituals, and gospels helped shaped the blues. "Dr. Watts" hymns, named after the late-eighteenth-century composer Isaac Watts, were performed among non-literate black congregations by "lining-out," a style wherein a song leader recites a line that congregants repeat in a slow rhythmic tempo. Although spirituals had their settings in the Old Testament, they contained livelier melodies than Dr. Watts hymns, with patterned stanzas, a chorus easily learned and sung and that was infinitely expandable. Spirituals stressed other-worldliness and the rewards of the life to come, themes with potential for a good deal of emotion. Gospel music took shape during the last quarter of the nineteenth century with the advent of the gospel quartet, and it is more upbeat than spirituals with lyrics concerned with this world rather than the afterlife, focusing on more positive images of proper behavior in the here and now. It remains one of the most popular kinds of religious music in black oral tradition. It is not unusual to see blues performers beginning their careers singing hymns, gospels, and spirituals while growing up with a church and later turning to blues and other types of secular music.

Having emerged at least by the 1890s, the blues draws from traditional motifs, images, and stanzas. A performer was flexible in his composition particularly in non-thematic, country, and folk blues (and more so than in city, urban, popular, and thematic blues). The songs' themes deal with problems in the everyday secular world, especially male-female relationships. This topic is common because of the uncertainty of relationships, but also because of the festive contexts in which bluesmen often performed such as juke joints, known for gambling, sexual promiscuity, and sometimes even lethal fights over women. Other subjects a bluesman might raise include unemployment, ill health, crime and prison, and other kinds of tragedy that formed part of the everyday experience of black audiences. Lyrics employ culturally specific images and metaphors, such as comparing the object of one's desire to a horse or to a "handyman." A distinctive blues vocabulary—such as "rider" referring to "woman" and "diddy-wah-diddy" as an ideal community or place—emerged in the tradition.

Scholars have classified blues in terms of regional styles and the musical instruments frequently accompanying their performances: "country," "classic," and "urban." Country blues includes the eastern seaboard blues of Peg Leg Howell, Brownie McGhee, and Sonny Terry; Delta blues exhibits "heavy" texture, shouting, and frenetic vocal style typical of songsters Robert Johnson (dubbed "King of the Delta Blues") and his predecessor Charley Patton; Texas blues commonly has a single-string guitar, relaxed vocal qualities, and "light" texture, as heard in recordings by Blind Lemon Jefferson, Mance Lipscomb, and Lightnin' Hopkins; and jug bands use jugs, washboards, and kazoos as exemplified in the music of ensembles from Memphis, Tennessee, such as that of Gus Cannon and Will Shade. "Classic" blues, sometimes referred to as city blues, is typically associated with early recording artists Bessie Smith and Ma Rainey and featured string bass, electric guitar, drums, and sometimes a piano as accompanying instruments. These singers were popular blues artists whose recordings appeared on "race" records that targeted black customers and that often inspired the careers of other blues performers who heard them. Urban blues include bands with drums and electric instruments—for example, groups fronted by B. B. King, Jimmy Reed, Muddy Waters, and Howlin' Wolf.

Growing out of these earlier forms is the rap music of modern hip-hop culture. Unlike its predecessors, rap music relies on the manipulation of technology as it explores poverty, urban blight, and violence. Rap is a form of music employing rhyme, rhythmic speech, chanting, and street speech—all performed over a musical soundtrack. Economic development that has changed areas of cities such as the Bronx in New York generated an outcry among adolescents who have reacted by employing expressive forms that resulted in rap music. The word *rap* is very similar to terms that have been used to refer to the dozens (for example, *joning*, *capping*, and *sounding*) and therefore has considerable affinity with earlier black oral traditions.

ARTS, CRAFTS, AND ARCHITECTURE

The most visible evidence of the contributions of African American folklore to the shaping of American culture and history is in material culture. John Michael Vlach (1978) gives a compelling argument connecting the shotgun house to West Africa, a "signpost to African-derived culture," suggesting that the name shotgun may even stem from the **Yoruba** *to-gun*, a word that means "place of assembly." The Yoruba house comes from slaves of Angola-Zaire origin, and Vlach has demonstrated that the most common slave house in Haiti was a rectangular gable-roofed house comprised of wattle-and-daub walls and a high thatch roof, like those among the Yoruba.

Evidence suggests that a prototype of the shotgun house resulted from the interaction of African slaves, French colonials, and Arawak Indians in Haiti. Scattered throughout the lower Mississippi River Delta and the South in general, it derives its name from the ability to view the structure's back exit from the front door, enabling one to fire a shotgun through the entire length of the house. A typical shotgun house has three or more small rooms connected directly to one another. Like its West African and Caribbean counterparts, the shotgun house matched perfectly the warm southern climate in which African slaves found themselves, but it also reveals a worldview that values close interactions among its occupants.

There is a distinct tradition of highly ornamental ironwork in African American blacksmithing, though ironworking has also taken on a more utilitarian dimension as well—as seen in the work of African American blacksmiths in East Texas and elsewhere who are continuing a tradition in which the blacksmith is the pivotal craftsman of his community. His importance in the New World is tied to an African legacy in which he was master of the four elements—air, earth, fire, and water—and capable of transforming himself at will into various animals and plants. He is an ambivalent figure in West African folklore, an intermediary between the living and the dead. In Central Africa blacksmith-kings appear in legend as founders of their state, and in the Congo the blacksmith's authority ranks him with chiefs, priests, and sorcerers. Although such mythical powers did not manifest themselves in the Western Hemisphere, the African American blacksmith's social status in southern rural communities today reveals parallels to the status enjoyed by his African forebears. Intense involvement in their communities allows black ironworkers in East Texas and elsewhere to enjoy a status similar to the role of a blacksmith in the pre–Civil War South. Writers have noted that some blacksmiths were particularly capable of subversive activities such as making weapons for uprisings. Because so much depends upon the work of a skilled ironworker, slaveowners recognized their value. The interrelationship of a blacksmith with his community and an accounting of the role blacksmiths have played in southern communities is revealed in many of the ex-slave narratives collected by federal workers during the Great Depression.

Another aspect of the plantation experience that continues today is the quilt, also a subject embedded in ex-slave narratives. African American appliqué and strip quilts often juxtapose contrasting colors and designs, a distinct African American characteristic. An appliqué quilt of Harriet Powers of Georgia, for example, included two pictorial quilts, and her 1896 Bible quilt contrasts eleven panels arranged in three horizontal bands, rendering scenes from the Bible in an overall arrangement that appears random despite following a linear sequence. Asymmetrical and unpredictable designs or "offbeat" patterns are esthetic options in West and Central African fabrics, which folklorists have recently recognized in other expressive forms among African Americans in the southern United States. Among West Africans, colors are also extremely important in cloth. African American women in Suriname value strong colors in their pieced textiles so much that colors should "shine" or "burn." The color of one piece should "lift up" the one next to it—that is, it should provide strong contrast.

The esthetic at work in this kind of material culture manifests itself in similar ways in African American folk art, such as that of Nathaniel Barrow of Helena, Arkansas. Barrow has been painting telephones; carving airplanes, boats, and trucks; crafting whirligigs; and fashioning wall hangings from wood since 1977. The content in his artworks include color schemes and asymmetry similar to what appear in the quilts. Some paintings by Barrow include drawings of snakes, an important motif in African American folklore that also figures into voodoo rituals.

The African American experience cannot be understood unless traditional expressive forms, whose contents and forms have changed over the centuries, are considered. Folk music and song, trickster tales, toasts, the dozens, proverbs, legends, and folk arts and crafts are a small sampling of many more cultural resources that comprise much of the black diaspora and give meaning to a diverse ethnic group that continues to shape American culture and history.

BIBLIOGRAPHY

Abernethy, Francis E., Patrick B. Mullen, and Alan B. Govenar, eds. 1996. *Juneteenth Texas: Essays in African-American Folklore*. Denton: University of North Texas Press.

Abrahams, Roger D. 1970. *Positively Black*. Englewood Cliffs, NJ: Prentice-Hall.

———. 1985. *Afro-American Folktales: Stories from Black Traditions in the New World*. New York: Pantheon Books.

———. 1990 (1963). Playing the Dozens. In *Mother Wit from the Laughing Barrel: Readings in the Interpretation of Afro-American Folklore*, edited by Alan Dundes. Jackson: University Press of Mississippi. 295–309.

———. 1992. *Singing the Master: The Emergence of African-American Culture in the Plantation South*. New York: Penguin Books.

———. 1994 (1962). *Deep Down in the Jungle . . . Negro Narrative Folklore from the Streets of Philadelphia*. Chicago: Aldine Publishing.

Bascom, William. 1992. *African Folktales in the New World*. Bloomington: Indiana University Press.

Burns, Richard Allen. 1996. African-American Blacksmithing in East Texas. In *Juneteenth Texas: Essays in African-American Folklore*, edited by Francis E. Abernethy, Patrick B. Mullen, and Alan B. Govenar. Denton: University of North Texas Press. 166–193.

———. 2002. The Shotgun Houses of Trumann, Arkansas. *Arkansas Review* 33: 44–51.

Christian, Marcus. 2002. *Negro Ironworkers of Louisiana, 1718–1900*. Gretna, LA: Pelican Press.

Cooke, Benjamin G. 1972. Nonverbal Communication among African Americans: An Initial Classification. In *Rappin' and Stylin' Out*, edited by Thomas Kochman. Urbana: University of Illinois Press. 32–64.

Dance, Daryl Cumber, ed. 2002. *From My People: 400 Years of African American Folklore*. New York: Norton.

Dillard, J. L. 1972. *Black English: Its History and Usage in the United States*. New York: Vintage Books.

Dorson, Richard M. 1970 (1956). *American Negro Folktales*. New York: Fawcett World Library.

Dundes, Alan, ed. 1990 (1973). *Mother Wit from the Laughing Barrel: Readings from the Interpretation of Afro-American Folklore*. Jackson: University Press of Mississippi.

Holloway, Joseph E. 1990. *Africanisms in American Culture*. Bloomington: Indiana University Press.

Hurston, Zora Neale. 1990 (1935). *Mules and Men*. New York: Harper Perennial.

Jackson, Bruce. 1999 (1972). *Wake up Dead Man: Hard Labor and Southern Blues*. Athens: University of Georgia Press.

————. 2004 (1974). *Get Your Ass in the Water and Swim like Me: African-American Narrative Poetry from the Oral Tradition* (with sound recording). New York: Routledge.

Jemie, Onwuchekwa, ed. 2003. *Yo' Mama! New Raps, Toasts, Dozens, Jokes, and Children's Rhymes from Urban Black America*. Philadelphia: Temple University Press.

Keyes, Cheryl L. 2002. *Rap Music and Street Consciousness*. Urbana: University of Illinois Press.

Kochman, Thomas, ed. 1972. *Rappin' and Stylin' Out*. Urbana: University of Illinois Press.

Labov, William. 1972. Rules for Ritual Insult. In *Rappin' and Stylin' Out: Communication in Urban Black America*, edited by Thomas Kochman. Chicago: University of Illinois Press. 265–314.

Levine, Lawrence. 1977. *Black Culture and Black Consciousness: Afro-American Folk Thought from Slavery to Freedom*. New York: Oxford University Press.

Lomax, Alan. 1993. *The Land Where the Blues Began*. New York: Pantheon Books.

Minton, John, and David Evans. 2001. *"The Coon in the Box": A Global Folktale in African-American Tradition*. Helsinki: Academia Scientiarum Fennica.

Mulira, Jessie Gaston. 1990. The Case of Voodoo in New Orleans. In *Africanisms in American Culture*, edited by Joseph E. Holloway. Bloomington: Indiana University Press. 34–68.

Oliver, Paul. 1990 (1960). *Blues Fell This Morning: Meaning in the Blues*. London: Cambridge University Press.

Palmer, Robert. 1981. *Deep Blues*. New York: Penguin Books.

Perkelay, James, Monteria Ivey, and Stephen Dweck. 1994. *Snaps*. New York: William Morrow.

————. 1995. *Double Snaps*. New York: William Morrow.

Prahlad, Sw. Anand. 1996. *African-American Proverbs in Context*. Jackson: University Press of Mississippi.

Puckett, Newbell Niles. 1969 (1926). *The Magic and Folk Beliefs of the Southern Negro*. New York: Dover.

Rawick, George P., and others, eds. 2000 (1972). *The American Slave: A Composite Autobiography*. Westport, CT: Greenwood.

Turner, Patricia A. 1994. *I Heard It through the Grapevine: Rumor in African-American Culture*. Berkeley: University of California Press.

Vlach, John Michael. 1978. *The Afro-American Tradition in Decorative Arts*. Cleveland: Cleveland Museum of Art.

————. 1991. *By the Works of Their Hands: Studies in Afro-American Folklife*. Charlottesville: University Press of Virginia.

Wahlman, Maude Southwell. 1993. *Signs and Symbols: African Images in African-American Quilts*. New York: Studio Books in Association with Museum of American Folk Art.

Wiggins, William H., Jr. 1987. *O Freedom! Afro-American Emancipation Celebrations*. Knoxville: University of Tennessee Press.

Richard Allen Burns

APPALACHIA

GEOGRAPHY AND HISTORY

Appalachian folklore constitutes a distinctive set of traditions that emerged historically through the intermingling of several cultures in an often-misunderstood region of the United States. Living among the mountains, Appalachia's people have usually resided in valleys or hollows and so have been accustomed to feelings of entrapment and isolation as well as the security of familiar and seemingly unchanging surroundings. While scholars have debated its specific boundaries, this particular region—in recent years most often called Appalachia, though formerly referred to by such names as the southern Appalachians or, simply, the southern mountains—certainly encompasses northeastern Alabama, northern Georgia, the northernmost tip of South Carolina, western North Carolina, eastern Tennessee, eastern Kentucky, western Virginia, and all of West Virginia. Other definitions of the region incorporate southeastern Ohio, western Maryland, and western Pennsylvania, whereas the Appalachian Regional Commission, a federal agency established in the 1960s to serve the region's economic needs, includes northeastern Mississippi and southwestern New York in its definition of Appalachia.

Whatever its outer boundaries, the Appalachian region inarguably consists of at least five distinct sub-regions. These are, from east to west, the Blue Ridge Province (extending from south-central Pennsylvania to northern Georgia and encompassing the Blue Ridge crest and parallel mountain ranges on the North Carolina–Tennessee border, including the Great Smokies and the Unakas as well as in-between ranges, most notably the Black Mountains); the Valley and Ridge Province (incorporating the Great Valley of the Appalachians and featuring a network of rivers and ridges); the Alleghenies (located primarily in West Virginia, western Maryland, and western Pennsylvania); the Cumberland Mountains (a range on the Virginia–Kentucky border known for its coal deposits); and the plateau (collectively referred to as the Appalachian Plateaus, including the coal-rich Cumberland Plateau of eastern Kentucky and eastern Tennessee).

Because its mountains block eastward-drifting air carrying moisture from the Gulf of Mexico, the Appalachian region generally receives more rainfall than do the lower elevation areas to its west or east. Frequent rain, the region's temperate climate, and its wide range of elevations have encouraged considerable diversity of plants and animals. The first human inhabitants of Appalachia were aboriginal people who lived in the region during the Paleo-Indian period, approximately 10,000 years ago. During the sixteenth and seventeenth centuries C.E., Europeans in Appalachia—first, Spanish and, later, French and English explorers—encountered two Native American tribes: the **Cherokee** and the Shawnee. European groups who settled on the Appalachian frontier during the eighteenth century—Scots-Irish, English, German, French Huguenot, Swiss, and Welsh—engaged in warfare with Native Americans before the American Revolution, then co-existed peaceably in southern Appalachia for several decades through the late 1830s, when the Cherokee were forced to march to Indian Territory by the federal government during the notorious Trail of Tears. Historically, Appalachia's distance from population centers, combined with the region's mountainous terrain and extensive forestland, necessitated that settlers from Europe learn survival techniques from indigenous peoples as well as from settlers of other ethnicities. For instance, Scots-Irish settlers, when arriving in Appalachia, had little prior experience living in wilderness, having previously dwelled in deforested, densely populated Ulster. Hence, they needed to learn hunting-gathering and woodcraft techniques from members of other ethnic groups—specifically, Cherokees and Germans—already in Appalachia. Each of the aforementioned ethnicities contributed to the repository of folkways used and shared in Appalachia.

The primary migration route for the European settlement of Appalachia—from central Pennsylvania southwestward into Virginia, then through the Great Valley of the Appalachians into North Carolina—created the historical circumstances that led to the mixing of cultural influences. In the early eighteenth century, Germans from eastern Pennsylvania established many of the first farmsteads along Virginia's Shenandoah River. During this same era, economically marginal people of English descent ventured westward from the Virginia Tidewater over the Blue Ridge into the fertile Shenandoah Valley. By the mid-eighteenth century, Scots-Irish immigrants, also journeying from eastern Pennsylvania, bypassed that already occupied valley for available properties on the slopes of the Virginia and North Carolina Blue Ridge.

From the early eighteenth century through the late nineteenth century, most people of European ancestry residing in rural Appalachia maintained a largely self-sufficient way of life combining various food-producing folkways (foraging, hunting, stock-raising, and crop-farming) with such traditional trades as blacksmithing, gunsmithing, and woodworking. Before the twentieth century, most products—whether wagon axles, tools, quilts, musical instruments, or moonshine—were hand-made within home communities or were obtained through bartering.

RELIGIOUS BELIEFS

Belief systems within Appalachia were based on Protestant Christianity (even the region's Native American groups such as the Cherokee had embraced European faiths), and yet many Appalachian people observed traditional beliefs structured around non-standardized interpretations of Christian doctrine. Folk religions emerged and proliferated in Appalachia because of the region's longstanding geographical remoteness from population centers. Beginning in the mid-eighteenth century, members of several European Protestant denominations—including German Dunkards, Mennonites, and Amish—intentionally settled in Appalachia to preserve their anti-establishment belief systems in relative distance from mainstream society. As a general rule, rural Appalachian communities relied on formally untrained, sometimes illiterate preachers whose interpretations of scripture were inherently esoteric. Embracing the teachings of such preachers, sects prospered with little or no obeisance to mainline churches. Most such sects were fundamentalist, reflecting strictly literal readings of the Bible. Several Baptist sects in Appalachia, for instance, practiced such traditional Christian rituals as full-immersion baptisms

"Shall we gather at the river." Mountain people have an inherent interest in what follows after their stay on Earth has ended. (Photograph by Earl Palmer. Courtesy of Jean Haskell)

in rivers and creeks (metaphorical re-creations of Christ's baptism in the River Jordan) and footwashing (based on John 13:14–15). Serpent handling, another Appalachian ritual from a biblical source, allegedly emerged in the early twentieth century after east Tennessean George Went Hensley was directed by God in a vision to take literally lines of scripture from the Book of Mark (16:17–20), which urged believers to "take up serpents" and to observe other "signs" in order to prove their faith. A small number of Pentecostal and Holiness congregations in Appalachia and the wider South subsequently incorporated the handling of snakes into special worship services, during which time congregations also engaged in displaying other ritual "signs" of faith, including poison-drinking (most often strychnine) and fire-touching (for example, hot coals or a lit torch).

Some facets of the Appalachian belief system evolved from non-Christian influences, reflecting traditional secular ideas about causal relationships between two phenomena or two actions. Most so-called superstitions involved notions brought to Appalachia by European settlers, though over time Appalachian people rejected many superstitions as scientifically unsupportable or as untenable because unauthorized by scripture. One folk belief in Appalachia, "planting by the signs," involved farmers making decisions about planting and harvesting crops based upon astrological charts printed in commercial mail-order almanacs. These charts, assigning a few days per month to each of the twelve zodiac signs, asserted that every day of a given month was controlled by a sign and therefore possessed some of that sign's characteristics. For example, a day designated as belonging to one of the zodiac's "water signs" (Cancer, Scorpio, Pisces) was deemed to be the best time of the month for planting crops. "Planting by the signs" fell out of use as Appalachian people increasingly relied upon daily or weekly weather reports from professional meteorologists.

MYTHS, LEGENDS, AND FOLKTALES

Verbal traditions in Appalachia include local **repertoires** of proverbs, riddles, rhymes, sayings, legends, folktales, and folksongs. The region's people have historically employed proverbs in everyday situations to communicate moral perspectives and to encourage socially appropriate behavior. While most regional proverbs were of British origin, some were introduced into Appalachia by Germans and African Americans. Riddles, never as common as proverbs in Appalachia, were either allusive rhymes or one-sentence questions used by a person to test another's wit or knowledge base. Some rhymes were verbal components of traditional games for children. In many parts of the region, folk sayings have historically been painted on handmade signs to make public pronouncements of religious conviction.

The first myths told in Appalachia were Native American creation stories, some of which were documented by white ethnologists (most notably James Mooney, who collected, transcribed, and published Cherokee myths). Virtually all the myths held sacred by whites in Appalachia were from Judeo-Christian sources. Many white settlers in Appalachia told local legends that communicated the significance of places (for instance, the mysterious lights seen near Brown Mountain in the North Carolina Blue Ridge), events (such as the railroading disaster commemorated in the song "The Wreck of the Old '97"), or people (such as Daniel Boone).

Historically, folktales abounded in Appalachia. Most of these oral narratives either related seemingly supernatural occurrences or endeavored to explore human morality (overtly through stories about human characters or covertly through anthropomorphic, fable-like "animal" stories). The best-known cycle of folktales associated with the region, the Jack tales, originated in the British Isles. Absorbing certain American traits, including mountain settings, Jack tales also retained European elements, including such traditional characters as giants, devils, and kings. The protagonist of these tales was a poor Appalachian boy named Jack, a **trickster** figure who outsmarted all who would oppress him. Several tales from this cycle, especially "Jack and the Bean Tree," became widely popular in the twentieth century after members of the Hicks, Harmon, and Ward families—whose ancestors first told Jack tales in western North Carolina during the eighteenth century—shared their versions with folklorists and writers (most crucially, Richard Chase), who disseminated the Appalachian Jack tale repertoire to the American public.

SONGS, BALLADS, AND MUSIC

Appalachia is equally renowned for its ballad and folksong traditions. The oldest non–Native American musical genre in the region, Appalachian balladry evolved from British ballad tradition. Eighteenth-century settlers from England, Scotland, and Ireland continued to sing in Appalachia at least 100 of the approximately 300 different British ballads categorized in the nineteenth century by scholar Francis James Child. Appalachian people sang variant texts of British ballads, and those often-truncated narratives, incorporating a blend of European and American characters and settings, were set to simplified (often minor-keyed and pentatonic) melodies. Women were the main practitioners of ballad singing in Appalachia, and they tended to sing ballads a cappella and to employ asymmetrical rhythm and unemotional delivery when performing them.

An indigenous ballad tradition, known collectively as Native American balladry, was emerging among Appalachian people of European ancestry by the early nineteenth century. A number of these ballads, including "Omie Wise," "Tom Dula," and "John Henry," chronicled actual historical events that occurred in Appalachia. Two other song traditions in Appalachia were lyric songs—that is, non-religious songs that were less narrative and more overtly emotional than ballads—and sacred songs (including hymns). Both traditions influenced the rise of commercial country music and commercial southern gospel music.

Native Americans during sacred ceremonies performed the first instrumental music heard in Appalachia. Cherokee musicians, for instance, played drums and cane flutes to accompany ceremonial dancing and singing. The most common instrument among eighteenth-century European settlers was the fiddle. Another European instrument, the Highland bagpipe, was never widely played in Appalachia until being revived across the region during the late twentieth century. Appalachian fiddlers played a diverse repertoire of tunes—many of which were based on British folk melodies—for dances and for other social gatherings. The banjo, derived from an African American instrument, was transported into Appalachia by black tradesmen traveling on riverboats during the early nineteenth century. White performers soon embraced the banjo, playing it in minstrel shows that visited Appalachian communities. By the late nineteenth century, fiddle-banjo duos were common in the region, and by the early twentieth century newly introduced instruments—guitar, mandolin, and Hawaiian-style steel guitar—were combined with fiddles and banjos. This string-band music was increasingly fast-paced, with more accomplished groups of musicians playing a remarkably complex music that incorporated jazz-influenced syncopation and improvisation. Numerous Appalachian string bands made commercial recordings during the 1920s, and some such as the Skillet Lickers from north Georgia became nationally popular. By the mid-1940s, string band music had evolved into bluegrass music, a commercial music initially shaped by Bill Monroe, a musician from western Kentucky, and by several musicians from Appalachia, including Earl Scruggs and Lester Flatt. During the urban folk music revival of the 1950s and 1960s, both native and non-native musicians began to play Appalachian music on instruments formerly unheard or uncommon in Appalachia, including harmonica, autoharp, fretted dulcimer, and hammered dulcimer.

FESTIVALS AND CELEBRATIONS

People in Appalachia have commemorated their cultural heritage by establishing and maintaining a variety of festivals. Regional festivals have promoted local agriculture (such as the Shenandoah Apple Blossom Festival in Winchester, Virginia); represented the range of folklife traditions in Appalachia (for instance, the Blue Ridge Folklife Festival in Ferrum, Virginia); showcased a specific regional tradition (the National Storytelling Festival in Jonesborough, Tennessee); acknowledged the heritage of an ethnic group (notably, the Grandfather Mountain Highland Games and Gathering of Scottish Clans in Linville, North Carolina); celebrated a historic event (for example, Gold Rush Days in Dahlonega, Georgia); or honored a prominent individual associated with the region (the John Henry Days Festival in Talcott, West Virginia). Today Appalachia not only hosts the longest running annual folk music festival in the United States (the Mountain Dance and Folk Festival, held in Asheville, North Carolina, since 1928), but also the nation's largest music festival (Merlefest in Wilkesboro, North Carolina).

DANCE AND DRAMA

Despite the fact that dancing was often officially viewed in Appalachia as a forbidden activity, the people of the region created some distinctive dance traditions. Appalachian people danced at Saturday night get-togethers and at such celebratory events as harvest gatherings. Buckdancing—a solo dance from the region combining elements of Cherokee ritual dancing, Irish jigs, and **African American** flatfoot—encouraged improvisation and individualism. Many regional dances were integral parts of social activities, including the play-party, a socially condoned courtship dance for younger people. Participants in this dance acted out through the use of gestures the lyrics of traditional play-party songs, most of which reflected everyday routines of rural life. Other social dances from the region were intended for adults and incorporated elements from English reels, French quadrilles, and Scottish country dances. Most Appalachian social dances were led by a caller who would guide

A home in the wilderness in Clay County, Kentucky. This log cabin fenced in by palings of native-grown chestnut provides mute testimony to the durability of things built by our forebears. (Photograph by Earl Palmer. Courtesy of Jean Haskell)

Sam "Thumpkeg" Dehart peels some strips of slippery elm from an elm tree growing on his place on Shooting Creek in Franklin County, Kentucky. Among the many herbaceous plants and trees possessing therapeutic powers, the inner bark of the American Sweet Elm tree ranks high in use by many mountain folks. (Photograph by Earl Palmer. Courtesy of Jean Haskell)

dancers—whether organized in squares, circles, or lines—through a sequence of maneuvers to the accompaniment of live music. Each dance routine constituted a specific sequence of dance moves that callers would request from dancers by such descriptive names as Dive and Shoot the Owl. Clogging, a traditional regional social dance, spawned a modern team dance known as precision clogging, which attracted widespread attention because of its intricate choreography and colorful costumes.

Appalachia has not produced a true folk drama. Several "outdoor dramas" are regularly staged in Appalachia, yet these are the antithesis of folk drama, since they are commercial events intended for mainstream audiences. Presented in open-air theaters during the summer tourism season, "outdoor dramas" are scripted and choreographed to portray stories from Appalachian history. One well-known example, *Unto These Hills*, is staged each summer in Cherokee, North Carolina, and takes a romanticized, even sentimentalized approach to telling the story of the Trail of Tears.

SPORTS AND GAMES

Traditional Appalachian games, which usually contained verbal, customary, and material components, included indoor games for two to several people and outdoor games for both small and large groups. All regional games were intended to help people pass the time constructively. The indoor game Fox and Geese, for example, bore rules that resembled checkers but utilized corn kernels and a homemade board. Some traditional indoor games from Appalachia (including Old Granny Wiggins Is Dead) provided groups with opportunities to solve imaginary problems through teamwork. Outdoor chase games were popular not only because they required minimal equipment, but also because they encouraged mingling among males and females. Other outdoor games formerly or presently popular in Appalachia involved specialized equipment including horseshoes, marbles, mumblety-peg (a knife game), and various rope and stick games. Several ballgames were once popular in the region, including catball, fieldball, and townball. (The latter two, both team sports, were forerunners of baseball.)

ARTS, CRAFTS, AND ARCHITECTURE

Appalachia's folk architecture emerged out of the confluence of several ethnic traditions in the region. The Appalachian log cabin, for instance, combined German woodworking and Slavic mortaring techniques with British design features. Log cabins were either square, reflecting an English design brought into Appalachia from the Virginia piedmont, or rectangular, a modification of either an Irish or a Scandinavian design transported into Appalachia by settlers from Pennsylvania. Other traditional architectural structures in Appalachia, including barns, outbuildings, and mills, were all likely based on designs brought by German settlers from Pennsylvania. Historically, one of the more distinctive barn designs built in Appalachia was the cantilever barn, today still visible in a few eastern Tennessee and southwestern Virginia counties. This design, accommodating Appalachia's topography, allowed farmers to carry crops grown up the slope directly onto the barn's second floor for storage and also

Rufus Duncan says making chairs is an in-born art. Here he starts the weaving of a bottom for a tall kitchen chair he made in his wayside shop by the banks of Indian Creek. (Photograph by Earl Palmer. Courtesy of Jean Haskell)

An ox yoke is honed to smoothness with a drawing knife. This particular ox yoke is made of cucumber tree wood. (Photograph by Earl Palmer. Courtesy of Jean Haskell)

permitted the easy loading of crops onto wagons parked on the barn's first floor. To protect crops and control animals, people in Appalachia built fences—generally out of wood, since that was more accessible than stone. Two general types of wooden fences were dominant in Appalachia—picket and split-rail, the latter of which was probably a variation of a Scandinavian prototype.

Given the abundance of trees in the region, Appalachian craftspeople created an array of furniture—tables, chairs, stools, benches, and beds—for their own use according to localized traditional designs. Furniture makers in Appalachia utilized only basic tools—axes, saws, knives, braces, and bits—and often worked without nails, screws, and glue, yet they built furniture of lasting quality using a system of tightly fitted, interlocking wooden parts. Also made from wood were containers (including baskets, bowls, and boxes); decorative figurines; toys (stilts, tops, limberjacks, and whimmy diddles); and musical instruments (fiddles, banjos, dulcimers, and whistles).

Some common toys in Appalachia—such as dolls and cornstalk constructions—were built from materials other than wood. Additional regional crafts included shoes (generally incorporating leather produced at home), clothes (woven on the loom from local wool), and quilts featuring a range of designs from the highly structured Log Cabin design to the essentially random Crazy Quilt.

FOOD

Appalachian foodways combined European food traditions with those borrowed from Native Americans. The earliest European settlers in Appalachia survived by hunting wild game (primarily deer and bear), fishing, gathering wild plants (including berries, nuts, roots, leaves, stems, and edible mushrooms and fungi), and growing cultivated vegetables (corn, beans, pumpkins, and squash) obtained from Native Americans. As the availability of wild animals decreased as a result of over-hunting, Appalachian people began to depend upon the meat of domesticated animals, primarily pigs, cows, and chickens. In addition to the aforementioned foodstuffs, people in the region ate orchard fruits (especially apples and cherries), enjoyed sweeteners (primarily honey and molasses), and drank various beverages (ranging from milk, tea, and cider to various liquors—whiskey being the most popular—brewed in local stills). Historically, cooking was done either in outdoor fire pits or indoor fireplaces, and cooking paraphernalia (racks, hooks, pokers, shovels, pots, and pans) were made from iron obtained outside the community but crafted by local blacksmiths.

A man pours a bushel of hickory grain corn into the hopper of his gristmill on Stone Mountain Creek. (Photograph by Earl Palmer. Courtesy of Jean Haskell)

CHALLENGES OF THE MODERN WORLD

By the twentieth century, industrialization—whether coal mining, logging, or other extractive industries within the region or factory jobs outside the region—forced countless Appalachian people to leave farms and abandon agricultural ways of life, which led to the steady decline of many regionally specific, rural traditions. However, since Appalachia's population continued to be comprised primarily of people with ancestral ties to the region, some older Appalachian folkways have persisted into the twenty-first century, while other regional traditions have been consciously revived during the past several decades by younger generations of both natives and non-natives—groups that today recognize Appalachia as having produced one of the more distinctive regional cultures in the United States.

STUDIES OF APPALACHIAN FOLKLORE

Holistic studies of Appalachian folklore and folklife include several volumes in the University Press of Mississippi's Folklife in the South Series, each of which concerns the traditional culture of a specific Appalachian sub-region: Montell (1993); Williams (1995); Olson (1998); and Suter (1999). The semi-

Children are always ready to lick the pot after another kettleful of apple butter has been boiled down. (Photograph by Earl Palmer. Courtesy of Jean Haskell)

nal collection of Cherokee folklore is Mooney (1992 [1900]). The various *Foxfire* books (twelve volumes: 1972–2004—for example, Wigginton 1972) offer general interest articles on numerous genres of traditional culture from Appalachia. *The Frank C. Brown Collection of North Carolina Folklore* (seven volumes: 1952–1964), while covering only one state within Appalachia, documents a broad cross-section of the genres of folklore found across the region. There are many respected studies investigating specific genres of Appalachian folklore, including, for ballads, Sharp and Karpeles (1932); for regional occupational folksong associated with coal mining, Green (1972); for instrumental music, Conway (1995); for Appalachian dialectical speech, Montgomery and Hall (2004); for customary folklife, Crissman (1994) and Cavender (2003); for folk architecture, Glassie (1968); and for foodways, Dabney (1998). Two comprehensive historical studies of the region are Drake (2001) and Williams (2002). Important academic studies exploring issues in Appalachian cultural history include Shapiro (1978); Eller (1982); Whisnant (1983); McNeil (1995); Dunaway (1996); and Billings and Blee (2000).

BIBLIOGRAPHY

Billings, Dwight B., and Kathleen M. Blee. 2000. *The Road to Poverty: The Making of Wealth and Hardship in Appalachia*. Cambridge: Cambridge University Press.

Cavender, Anthony. 2003. *Folk Medicine in Southern Appalachia*. Chapel Hill: University of North Carolina Press.

Conway, Cecilia. 1995. *African Banjo Echoes in Appalachia: A Study of Folk Traditions*. Knoxville: University of Tennessee Press.

Crissman, James K. 1994. *Death and Dying in Central Appalachia: Changing Attitudes and Practices*. Urbana: University of Illinois Press.

Dabney, Joseph Earl. 1998. *Smokehouse Ham, Spoon Bread, & Scuppernong Wine: The Folklore and Art of Southern Appalachian Cooking*. Nashville: Cumberland House.

Drake, Richard B. 2001. *A History of Appalachia*. Lexington: University Press of Kentucky.

Dunaway, Wilma A. 1996. *The First American Frontier: Transition to Capitalism in Southern Appalachia, 1700–1860*. Chapel Hill: University of North Carolina Press.

Eller, Richard D. 1982. *Miners, Millhands, and Mountaineers: Industrialization of the Appalachian South, 1880–1930*. Knoxville: University of Tennessee Press.

The Frank C. Brown Collection of North Carolina Folklore. 1952–1964. 7 volumes. Durham: Duke University Press.

Glassie, Henry. 1968. *Pattern in the Material Folk Culture of the Eastern United States*. Philadelphia: University of Pennsylvania Press.

Green, Archie. 1972. *Only a Miner: Studies in Recorded Coal-Mining Songs*. Urbana: University of Illinois Press.

McNeil, W. K., ed. 1995. *Appalachian Images in Folk and Popular Culture*. 2nd edition. Knoxville: University of Tennessee Press.

Montell, William Lynwood. 1993. *Upper Cumberland Country*. Jackson: University Press of Mississippi.

Montgomery, Michael, and Joseph S. Hall. 2004. *Dictionary of Smoky Mountain English*. Knoxville: University of Tennessee Press.

Mooney, James. 1992 (1900). *History, Myths, and Sacred Formulas of the Cherokees*. Asheville, NC: Bright Mountain Books.

Olson, Ted. 1998. *Blue Ridge Folklife*. Jackson: University Press of Mississippi.

Shapiro, Henry D. 1978. *Appalachia on Our Mind: The Southern Mountains and Mountaineers in the American Consciousness, 1870–1920*. Chapel Hill: University of North Carolina Press.

Sharp, Cecil J., and Maud Karpeles, eds. 1932. *English Folk Songs from the Southern Appalachians*. Oxford: Oxford University Press.

Suter, Scott Hamilton. 1999. *Shenandoah Valley Folklife*. Jackson: University Press of Mississippi.

Whisnant, David E. 1983. *All That Is Native and Fine: The Politics of Culture in an American Region*. Chapel Hill: University of North Carolina Press.

Wigginton, Eliot, ed. 1972. *The Foxfire Book*. Garden City, NY: Anchor.

Williams, John Alexander. 2002. *Appalachia: A History*. Chapel Hill: University of North Carolina Press.

Williams, Michael Ann. 1995. *Great Smoky Mountains Folklife*. Jackson: University Press of Mississippi.

Ted Olson

MISSISSIPPI DELTA

GEOGRAPHY AND HISTORY

The essence of Mississippi Delta folklore may be found in an area between Memphis, Tennessee, and Vicksburg, Mississippi, in the southern United States. It is here that African American verbal art has flourished and where black folksong forms part of the soundscape that persists into the twenty-first century. What historian-journalist David Cohn called "the most southern place on earth" is the land where the blues began. It is where blacks and whites wrestled a living from a vast alluvial floodplain that stretches from southeastern Illinois to the Gulf of Mexico. The river has been a blessing for a few and a curse for many: the Delta's climate; unsanitary living conditions that promoted malaria and dysentery, especially among poor inhabitants with no access to medical facilities; the boll weevil's ability to destroy cotton-

Typical shotgun house. (Courtesy Library of Congress)

fields; economic disparities between the rich and the poor; an obsession with race; and efforts to control blacks are all themes reflected in the region's folklore.

Plantation culture included the "big house" (often a European-styled mansion where the landowner lived), slave cabins, and numerous outbuildings. Like the sharecroppers' shacks that replaced them, slave cabins were cramped and crowded, often unsanitary. A simple cabin typically had a dirt floor, an area for cooking, and an area for sleeping. Although slave cabins and sharecropper shacks are fast disappearing, shotgun houses, structures that have a distinct African legacy, still dot the landscape. These

houses are usually three rooms deep with no hallways and with doorways opening from one room to the next so that if you opened the front entrance and fire a shotgun straight into the house, the shot would exit the back door. Blending African ideas of living space with European and Native American concepts, many black workers responded to the Delta's hot, humid climate by building these inexpensive structures, and a few refurbished houses are even available for tourists to rent at the Hopson Plantation near Clarksdale, Mississippi. Such buildings reflect the bare necessities of their occupants.

A crew of 200 laborers, many of them former tenant farmers, were brought to Aldridge Plantation near Leland, Mississippi, to hoe cotton for one dollar per day. (Photograph by Dorothea Lange. Library of Congress Prints and Photographs Division)

FIELD HOLLERS AND WORKSONGS

The soundscape of the Delta includes more ephemeral folklore forms such as field hollers, worksongs, spirituals, and the blues. To some extent, these forms overlap, and some scholars suggest hollers and worksongs were pre-blues forms. Unaccompanied by musical instrumentation, field hollers consisted of a melodic phrase with various vocal techniques such as falsetto and vocables. Sung in the fields and in levee camps, hollers communicated shared emotions and attitudes with fellow workers and helped make hard work more tolerable. Worksongs, also lacking musical accompaniment, were common among fieldhands as well. Until the 1960s, hollers and worksongs could still be heard twenty-five miles south of Clarksdale on the eastern fringes of the Delta at Parchman Penitentiary. In 1947, Alan Lomax recorded "Levee Camp Holler," loosely structured in its jumps from one image to another:

> Ohhhh, Lord, I woke up this mornin',
> Man, I was feelin' bad.
> Woah, baby, I'm ["feelin'"] bad, man.
> Well, I was thinkin' about the good times, Lord,
> I once have had.
>
> Well, Lord, Oh mmmmmmmm!
>
> Oh well, ohh, boy,
> If you want to go to Mr. Charley's,
> Go down the mornin' when the boys work,
> You'll be all right. . . .
>
> Lord, Lord, Lord, Lord, Lord.
> Boy, I got a woman looking for me, Lord, Lord, man.
> Boy, she lookin' for me;
> She lookin' for me, Lord. . . .

Unlike field hollers, worksongs among black prisoners at Parchman were more timed in relation to the work convicts performed. Worksongs served as vehicles for protest against a harsh guard, for dreams of freedom, for concerns over faithful and faithless women, or for rebellion against whites. Lomax captures the essence of worksongs in "Rosie":

> LEADER: Be my woman, gal I [chop]
> GROUP: Be yo man [chop]
> LEADER: Be my woman, gal I [chop]
> GROUP: Be yo man [chop]

Worksongs put control of the work, as indicated by the bracketed "chop" in the above transcription, into the hands of a work leader who sets the pace of work and often prevents a slow worker from being singled out by a guard. In contrast to the field holler, "Rosie" is a much more structured performance and provides workers with a distinct rhythm in a call-and-response form so crucial in completing tasks that require strict adherence to chopping or a timed ax swing. Worksongs were more often avenues for social protest than one generally finds in other folksong types, such as the blues, but there are still many similarities between worksongs and blues that suggest a strong link between them. Sometimes such a song could voice criticism and ridicule of the slavemaster or overseer. Worksongs also drew from and shaped the development of African American spirituals.

Plantation overseer near Clarksdale, Mississippi. (Photograph by Dorothea Lange. Library of Congress Prints and Photographs Division)

SPIRITUALS AND BLUES

Spirituals reflected the Old Testament ethos of "an eye for an eye" and freedom for God's people, themes particularly relevant and appealing to a black congregation expecting God to punish those whites who brought misery to them. Scholars have noted that African Americans exercised control over their churches, though these institutions were the product of the belief by early-nineteenth-century planters that Christianity helped to make slaves more docile.

Many blues performers recognized that their singing could be likened to preaching in style and in audience impact. Many early bluesmen such as Charley Patton heard sermons that beckoned for sinners to seek salvation through Jesus, and toward the end of a chanted sermon both preacher and congregation were using rhythm to exert emotional appeal. Some have compared a call-and-response between a preacher and his congregation to the call-and-response feature of the blues. A chanted sermon might be punctuated with an "Amen!"

The heart of bluesland is where the "Southern cross the Dawg," referring to a place in Moorhead, Mississippi, where the east-west Southern Line Railroad (now the C & G) crosses the north-south Yazoo and Mississippi Valley Lines, affectionately called the Yellow Dawg. In 1903, blues popularizer W. C. Handy heard one of his first blues songs in the Tutwiler, Mississippi, train station from an unknown singer using the back of a knife for a slide as he sang about going "where the Southern cross[es] the Dawg." This was one of the first documentations of the blues, and the form continues as a vital part of Delta musical traditions into the twenty-first century.

During Reconstruction and into the twentieth century, railroads and highways took black Deltans away from the brutalities of life in the fields. Consequently, the theme of escape has shaped much of the Delta's folklore. The Great Migration of freemen northward in the early twentieth century was a response to the cycle of intimidation and debt that accompanied agrarian life and kept black people on the lower economic rung in the Delta. Bluesmen Sam Chatmon, Charley Patton, and Robert Johnson drew from these and other themes prevalent in early Delta blues.

Patton, often referred to as the "Father of the Delta Blues," was the son of a preacher. He ignored his father's attempts to discourage him from playing the "devil's music" and became enthralled with the area's musicians, especially Sam Chatmon, and eventually developed a guitar style specific to the Delta, one that others emulated. A few years later, Robert Johnson, the "King of the Blues," recorded "Terraplane Blues," a song about an automobile that presumably traveled the well-known U.S. Highway 61 that runs north and south through the center of the region. Though an automobile might afford a bluesman a means to travel, Johnson sang about a sexy automobile: "I'm gonna get down in this connection, keep on tanglin' with these wires / And when I mash down on your starter, then your spark plug will give me fire." The double entendres and sexual innuendos are characteristic of many blues songs, which allowed an appreciative audience to identify with the singer's life experiences both on and off the road.

Many African traditions were rooted in a belief system that included several gods, such as the trickster god Eshu, who could empower others. In the Western Hemisphere, the bluesman makes a pact with this figure (identified with the Devil) to achieve his maturity as an accomplished musician. Delta bluesman Tommy Johnson tells a story repeated in other narratives concerning the mysterious manner in which he suddenly acquired his musical talents:

> If you want to learn how to play anything you want to play and learn how to make songs yourself, you take your guitar and go to where a road crosses that way, where the crossroad is. . . . A big black man will walk up there and take your guitar and he'll tune it. And then he'll play a piece and hand it back to you. That's the way I learned how to play everything I want.

Black plantation workers suffered and sang not only of their forced servitude but also of the region's frequent floods. For example, in a 1929 recording, Charley Patton sang of the floods of 1927 that left many homeless. This excerpt from Patton's song depicts the singer's personal experiences as he identifies whole towns, known well by his audience, within the Mississippi Delta that were inundated from this tremendous flood:

> Now looka here Leland, river was risin' high,
> Looka here boys round Leland tell me the river is risin' high,
> I'm goin' to move over to Greenville, fore I say "Goodbye"
>
> Looka here the water now, Lordy, done broke out, rolled most
>   everywhere,

The water at Greenville and Lula it done rose everywhere,
I would go down to Rosedale but they tell me there's water there

Now the water now Mama, done struck Charley's town,
Now the water now Mama, done struck Charley's town,
Well I'm goin' to Vicksburg for the higher mound.

FOLK MEDICINE

Because whites have done little to ensure the health of the Delta's black population, many African Americans have relied on traditional folk remedies. Plantations had midwives who often had knowledge of roots and herbal remedies. Conjurers drew their power from both natural and supernatural sources and are most often associated with voodoo. Sources in Arkansas and Mississippi reported three kinds of individuals possessing special gifts of the supernatural: the hoodoo doctor who diagnoses and treats diseases caused by hoodoo evil, the fortuneteller who prophesies the future, and the healer who cures natural ailments that baffle doctors through his secret arts.

Numerous beliefs associated with plants and animals manifested themselves in the customary behavior of those whose interpretations of events dictated their responses. Driving a stake into a crossroads kept enemies away, roots chewed and spat on courthouse steps assured acquittal in a criminal trial, and charms hidden in tree limbs restored sexual potency. These practices offered blacks a sense of protection from the harsh realities of daily life in the Delta, particularly for those lacking an education and the various forms of health care afforded by whites.

FOLKTALES

Many of the oral traditions among the Delta's black inhabitants included stories of the weak outwitting the strong and of folk **heroes** who sometimes successfully challenged the white authority structure. Examples include the John and Old Marster stories ubiquitous in southern folklore in the United States. Folktales depicting the **trickster** John outwitting (or sometimes punished by) his master during slavery gave rise to a new kind of folk hero who challenged white authority figures, the "bad" man in black oral tradition. "Stackerlee," the subject of blues songs and of black toasts, was dubbed by Alan Lomax "the badman hero of the Delta." After recording prison worksongs and field hollers outdoors at Parchman Penitentiary in 1947, Lomax moved indoors and recorded eight stanzas of "Stackerlee":

Now Stackerlee, he was a bad man,
He wanted the whole round world to know,
He toted a .32–20
And a smokeless .44.

Now Stackerlee told Billy Lyon,
"Billy, I'm sho gon take your life,
You have winned my money
And I found a fow-ul dice."

Now Billy Lyon, he told Stackerlee,
He said, "Stack, please don take my life,
I've got two little chillun
And my po lil weasley wife."

"Now one of them is a boy, Stack,
And the other one is a girl."
"But if you love your children, Billy Lyon,
You will have to meet them in the other world."

In some versions, Stackerlee goes before a white judge who sentences the badman to death. Nevertheless, he continues to wreak havoc even in death as he takes over hell from Satan.

Songs and stories about Stackerlee (or "Stagolee") were common and sung at least as early as 1895 in Coahoma, Mississippi, and it is tempting to view Satan as a thinly veiled white authority figure whose powers the black man now possesses. Perhaps the character's appeal among blacks stems from his emergence from the trickster and conjure figures prominent in oral traditions on slave plantations throughout the Delta. His rebellion against white law and white values are some of the heroic qualities narrators celebrate. Parchman Penitentiary was a typical setting in which such a figure might flourish in the Mississippi Delta's black oral traditions, a context similar to a nineteenth-century slave plantation.

Residents of the Mississippi Delta interject a strong sense of place and knowledge of natural resources in their folklore. Although work on plantations required the skills of various craftsmen, levee building included the making of wheelbarrows to haul sand and soil, and railroad building relied upon tie-hackers, folklorists have tended to focus on more readily identifiable crafts, especially those that are available at folk festivals such as folk instruments, canemaking, and other such woodworking.

Jitterbugging, Clarksdale, Mississippi. (Photograph by Dorothea Lange. Library of Congress Prints and Photographs Division)

MUSICAL INSTRUMENTS

African American one-string guitar maker Louis Dotson of Lorman, Mississippi (near Vicksburg), learned to play guitar from his father and learned to make a "diddley bow," formed from a piece of broom wire stretched vertically over the outside of a house, which serves as a resonator. A precursor to slide guitar, the string is struck with the right index finger while sliding a bottle in the left hand up and down the string's surface. This instrument may be found in West Africa and throughout the Mississippi Delta.

Like Dotson, bluesman Othar Turner continued a tradition he learned growing up. Born in 1908, he could make a cane fife by age thirteen and later played the blues before pursuing the fife-and-drum tradition, a type of African American hymnody that emerged in the northern Mississippi hill country before spreading to the Delta. He made and mastered the fife, which is a hollow, flute-like instrument made from bamboo cane.

Cane maker Victor "Hickory Stick Vic" Bob of Vicksburg also drew from the Delta's environment, especially hickory trees, from which he made walking sticks. Born in 1892, he explained to folklorist William Ferris the steps in crafting a walking stick, claiming that the best tree comes from the poorest soil: "It's got to be very poor ground so that the tree will grow slow."

Non–African American Folklore

A survey of folk groups that have contributed to the region's folklore would not be complete without including Chinese, Italians, Mexicans, and Jews. Chinese immigrants who worked as farm laborers as early as 1870 and on construction gangs on the railroad eventually opened small stores and became merchants. Burdened with an ambiguous racial identity as perceived by blacks and whites, members of this group have also shared in the Delta's history of race relations. Some rose in status as they aligned themselves with whites; others remained lower in the social hierarchy as they intermarried with blacks. In Bolivar County, Mississippi, wealthy citizens bought lots or talked to property owners to make it nearly impossible for a Chinese family to buy or build a home within the city limits. Conversely, Chinese merchants have had little difficulty in getting along with other ethnic groups. Race relations in the Delta manifest themselves in the customary behaviors that residents display toward one another, whether in the form of overt ethnic slurs or institutionalized racism such as segregated schools.

In an effort to reduce the region's dependence on black labor as blacks started leaving the Delta during the Great Migration, a few planters recruited Italian immigrants. Originally from the agricultural provinces of northern Italy, they brought with them values, attitudes, and outlooks rooted in an Italian heritage. Family experiences of some of these immigrants in Mississippi include a story that recounts a family's leave-taking from the Delta as family members left for Arkansas: "We were amazed to see nearly all the families by the roadsides to bid us farewell. One of the women took mother's broom from among the furniture in the trailer. 'Taking a broom with you when you move brings bad luck,' she yelled as we moved on." Foodways such as making *sfoglia*, a flour and egg pasta, constitute an important cultural expression Italians used to maintain cultural identity. Nevertheless, Italians were afforded only slightly better treatment than other ethnic minority groups, as exemplified by one condescending Mississippi planter who found Italians to be "industrious, peaceable and thrifty" as well as "healthy, hearty and virtuous." He had never had an Italian woman give birth to an illegitimate child on his plantation. But Italian workers took exception to the attitudes and values of a system that considered planting and cultivation of cotton something that even many blacks were resisting. In some instances, Italians were even barred from attending white-only schools because they were considered racially inferior to whites.

Delta Jews feared becoming targets of discrimination because of their identity and empathy with black Deltans during the civil rights movement in the 1950s and 1960s. The White Citizens' Councils that emerged as a result of civil rights activities pressured Jews to join them in their movement to prevent blacks from gaining access to educational and other public services, but those Delta Jews who acquiesced to such demands also struggled to maintain their own heritage through customs and practices passed on through generations before them. While temples and synagogues provide places of worship as well as arenas where language, custom, and foodways continue, Delta Jews have also identified themselves as southerners who live in the Mississippi Delta.

Mexicans have also been an important source of labor on many of the farms that needed day labor, and Dorothea Lange's photographs during the 1930s capture many of these laborers at work in the field or in transit between plantations. Because they are one of the fastest-growing ethnic minority groups in this part of the United States, it is reasonable to assume that Mexican American folklore will become increasingly prominent in the Mississippi Delta, particularly with respect to foodways, one of the region's most visible expressive forms.

By considering the Mississippi River Delta folklore in terms of the material and oral traditions specific to folk groups comprising the region, it becomes evident that each group reveals specific values and attitudes toward one another, toward friend and foe, toward the sacred and the profane. In their responses to this "most southern place on earth," Deltans' sense of place unsurprisingly incorporates worldviews often in conflict with one another as all groups struggle to survive in a climate where cultural differences collide and where economic disparity between the rich and the poor continues into the twenty-first century. Despite population decreases throughout the Delta as residents find economic advantages elsewhere, the land still holds an attraction for those interested in one of the most distinctive sources of American folklore.

STUDIES OF MISSISSIPPI DELTA FOLKLORE

In addition to the print, sound, and film sources listed in the bibliography, the folklore of the Mississippi Delta can be explored at several Web sites. The American Folklife Center at the Library of Congress maintains a guide to its collections from the region at www.loc.gov/folklife/guides/Mississippi.html. An expanding site developed by students at Starkville (Mississippi) High School focuses on Mississippi musicians, writers, and actors (www.shs.starkville.k12.ms.us/mswm/MSWriters AndMusicians). The Mudcat Café (www.mudcat.org) is an on-line magazine focusing on blues and folk music, and the National Park Service maintains "Welcome to Nile of the New World: Lower Mississippi Delta Region" at www.cr.nps.gov/delta/home.htm.

BIBLIOGRAPHY

Cobb, James C. 1992. *The Most Southern Place on Earth: The Mississippi Delta and the Roots of Regional Identity*. New York: Oxford University Press.

DeWitt, Mike. 1999. *Delta Jews: Jews in the Land of the Blues* (film). New York: Filmmaker's Library.

Dorson, Richard M. 1970 (1956). *American Negro Folktales*. Greenwich, CT: Fawcett.

Evans, David. 1982. *Big Road Blues: Tradition and Creativity in the Folk Blues*. Berkeley: University of California Press.

Ferris, William. 1982. *Local Color: A Sense of Place in Folk Art*. New York: McGraw-Hill.

LaPin, Deirdre. 1982. *Hogs in the Bottom: Family Folklore in Arkansas*. Little Rock, AR: August House.

Levine, Lawrence. 1977. *Black Culture and Black Consciousness*. New York: Oxford University Press.

Loewen, James W. 1988 (1971). *The Mississippi Chinese: Between Black and White*. Prospect Heights, IL: Waveland Press.

Lomax, Alan. 1985. *The Land Where the Blues Began*. New York: Pantheon.

———. 2001. *Blues in the Mississippi Night Featuring Big Bill Broonzy, Memphis Slim, Sonny Boy Williamson* (sound recording). Rounder Records ROUN 1860.

Oliver, Paul. 1990 (1960). *Blues Fell This Morning: Meaning in the Blues*. Cambridge: Cambridge University Press.

Palmer, Robert. 1981. *Deep Blues*. New York: Penguin.

Titon, Jeff Todd. 1994 (1977). *Downhome Blues: A Musical and Cultural Analysis*. Chapel Hill: University of North Carolina Press.

Wilson, Charles Reagan, and William Ferris, eds. 1989. *Encyclopedia of Southern Culture*. Chapel Hill: University of North Carolina Press.

Richard Allen Burns

South and Central America and the Caribbean

South America

CAIPIRA (BRAZIL)

GEOGRAPHY AND HISTORY

Covering a large geographical area of southeastern Brazil and shaped by the expanding influence of people from São Paulo, who first entered the Brazilian interior in search of gold and slaves, the Caipira culture area encompasses the states of São Paulo, Paraná, and Minas Gerais. This culture reflects the blending of the lifeways of indigenous Tupi-Guarani–speaking people with those of *paulistas* from São Paulo, who began to settle there in the nineteenth century.

Caipira comes from the Tupi language and means "woods inhabitant"—a modification of its previous meaning, "jungle inhabitant." It has been used to refer to any inhabitant of interior Brazil and usually has negative connotations. The Caipira tradition developed in rural areas among *posseiros*—people living in places where the property rights were not clearly defined—and laborers attached to large plantations. These were closed, self-supporting societies characterized by isolation, communal labor, rustic living conditions, disregard for the future, simple foodways with clear Indian influences, romantic and nostalgic music, and religious and healing practices that fused indigenous and medieval Christian elements.

Two ethnic components contribute to Caipira culture: the *paulista-meztizo* mixed-bloods and the indigenous Tupi-Guarani. The former, also called *bandeirante*, specialized in slave trading and prospecting for gold. Many of the indigenous people were connected with Christian missions or lived in Portuguese villages. Since the Villa de São Paulo is far from the coast, where all commercial, cultural, and ethnic interchange with Europe occurred, *paulistas* drew as much from indigenous culture as from that which had been imported from abroad. In addition to the use of native language, their way of life resembled that of the Tupi-Guarani: going barefoot, using bows and arrows for hunting, sleeping in hammocks, living in rustic houses, and relying on hunting and local vegetation for food.

Indigenous contributions to the cultural mix of Caipira have come from two peoples: the now-extinct Tupinikim and the Guarani. Like all Tupis, the Tupikinim were nomadic hunters. They frequently visited related groups and were involved in almost constant warfare. Consequently, bravery and vengeance figured significantly in their value system. Since they were also extremely religious, the most prestigious person in a Tupinikim community was the *pajé*, or shaman. They believed in a god who created the world and in culture **heroes** such as Mairá and Sumé. Among the most feared deities were Tupan—owner of rain and thunder—and Anhangá, lord of

Regions and Peoples of South America.

evil. Deities—most often evil ones—ruled the world of the living, who protected themselves through propitiatory rituals and offerings. The souls of the dead were also feared, and therefore funerals had to follow strict rules. Otherwise the living would be visited by a variety of misfortunes. After death, warriors and brave women would go to a realm of happiness, The Land Without Evil. Cowards, effeminate men, and mean people would be transformed into animals. Although they had a similar culture, the Guarani were more peace-loving and conciliatory.

RELIGIOUS BELIEFS AND RITUALS

Among the current religious practices in the Caipira region, one finds the cult of the souls. Souls can help the living in several ways, provided that certain rituals are observed scrupulously. For instance, in order to locate a lost object, one lights a candle from the cooking fire. To deliver someone from a curse, a candle must be lit at a crossroads. Successful business transactions will follow if one ties a knot in a piece of cloth and keeps it until the business has been completed. To guarantee a successful journey, the traveler should light a candle at the foot of a cross. Souls are believed to be located at particular places such as the foot of a cross, the door of a church, a kitchen door, termites' nests, and the openings in an armadillo shell. Every Monday is a day of ritual, but the most important date for religious practices is 2 November, the Day of the Dead.

Traditional remedies and cures include the following: to stop a nosebleed, a cross made from cornhusks is placed over the victim's head; to cure dermatitis, one draws four crosses in blue ink around the affected one for three consecutive days; and to thwart an earthworm (*gusano*) infestation, the sufferer should wear a collar of garlic or one made from seeds known as eyes of a goat. Another way to cure worm infestation requires the person to drink milk boiled with garlic and salt for three months when the moon is waning. Traditional medical specialists are the *rezador*, who prays for cures and remedies, and the *curandeira*. The *curandeira* often has a principal role in treating maladies that do not respond to home remedies.

Spirits—many evil, but some benevolent—populate Caipira culture. Among them is the *Saci-Perere*, who is a playful black child with only one leg and is always ready to effect some sort of mischief on both humans and animals. He lives at the edges of farmlands and at crossroads. In order to protect one's horses, the *Saci-Perere*'s preferred targets, one should put garlic in the beasts' snouts. The *Caipora* is a hairy, heavyset individual with a small head and flat nose. He usually appears riding a wild boar (*jabali*) and driving a herd of wild pigs. He often chases people who dare to go hunting on Fridays. He is responsible for protecting wild animals. Offering him tobacco, though, will usually appease him. The *Yara*, or water monster, lives in rivers and lakes and drags people who believe her words to the bottom of the waters. A female spirit, she usually appears late in the afternoon. Therefore, one is advised not to bathe at this time or to urinate into bodies of water.

GAMES AND FOOD

The most common game of native origin is the *peteca* (from a Tupi word meaning "to beat one's palms against each other"). The play involves a straw toy that has a core of feathers or straw and feathers at one end. Players form a circle, and the person who allows the toy to fall loses the game.

Caipira food reflects many influences from the indigenous culture. For example, *tutu* is a dish consisting of beans on a thick paste made from cornmeal. Bean *tropero* is a typical dish for groups of travelers on the move. It is prepared with cornmeal or manioc flour with fried eggs or pork sausage. Manioc flour, boiled or roasted, is very commonly found on Caipira tables along with native produce such as pumpkin, *inhame*, and *cará*. Manioc flour is also used in the preparation of *pirao*, in which it is mixed with fish or beef broth. In addition, manioc flour is used to prepare a bread eaten with cheese and a cake called *biscocho de polvilho*. *Frango con urucu* is chicken fried in pork lard and steamed with *urucu* seeds, which give it a reddish color, and *pazoca de carne* is dried beef ground with a mortar and mixed with manioc flour or cornmeal. *Farofa de izá* is fried parts of the winged ant mixed with manioc flour. Cornmeal is a staple, eaten almost everyday with rice, beans, and beef. Desserts include *bolo de fubá*, or corncake; *pomonha*, a soft corn pastry wrapped and steamed in a corn leaf; *curau*, cream with grated soft corn; and *canjica*, a creamy soup of shelled dried corn cooked with milk.

Music and Festivals

Important Caipira music forms include *cateretê*, or *catira*, and *moda de viola*. *Cateretê*, which means "dancer" in Guarani, is a dance in which the participants form two rows, one of men and the other of women. They stand in front of each other and move to the rhythm of clapping hands and stamping feet while following the music of a guitar. In some parts of Caipira country, this dance is reserved for men. *Cururu*, or "dance of the frog," is a male-only dance. It originated in the religious dances of the Christian missions among the natives. Specific sub-types of this dance form are the Saint Gonzalo dance and the Holy Cross dance. Other Portuguese-derived dances have also been incorporated under this rubric. The *cururu* dances have three parts: a greeting to the audience, praise to the saint, and challenge among the participants. *Moda de viola* are love songs. They are either nostalgic, tragic, or satiric and are usually performed as a duet.

Caipira festivities are those derived from Portuguese tradition. Among them are Santos Reyes (Three Wise Men), which occurs on 6 January; the Santa Cruz (Holy Cross) festival on 3 May; Divino Espíritu Santo (Pentecost), fifty days after Easter; and saints' days celebrated in the month of June: Saint Anthony, Saint John the Baptist, and Saint Peter.

Arts, Crafts, and Architecture

The homes in the Caipira region reflect indigenous influences. Most of them are supported by walls of intertwined branches covered with mud and clay, and the roof is made from the plant *sapé*. Furnishings are minimal. Beds consist of wooden planks or strips of leather, which support mattresses filled with corn husks. Benches or doorsteps provide the only seating.

Caipira handicrafts include woodworking to produce pots and containers, spoons, and mortars for grinding grains. Bowls are made of the shells of a gourd called *cuia*. Some parts of the Caipira region produce ceramics using native designs and decorations. Straw and cane are used to make baskets, fans, hats, and traps designed to catch fish and small animals.

BIBLIOGRAPHY

Araujo, Alceu Maynard. 1973. *Cultura popular brasileira*. São Paulo: Melhoramentos/Instituto Nacional do Livro-MEC.

Cândido, Antônio. 1964. *Os parceiros do rio Bonito*. Rio de Janeiro: Livr. José Olympio.

Cascudo, Luís da Câmara. 1988 (1954). *Dicionário do Folclore Brasileiro*. 6th edition. Belo Horizonte: Itatiaia.

Pires, Cornélio. 1987 (1921). *Conversas ao pé do fogo*. São Paulo: Imprensa Oficial do Estado.

Xidieh, Oswaldo Elias. 1972. *Semana Santa Cabocla*. São Paulo: Instituto de Estudos Brasileiros da Universidade de São Paulo.

Benedito Prezia (Translated from the Spanish by Ernesto Lombeida)

CANDOSHI

GEOGRAPHY AND HISTORY

An Amerindian group numbering around 3,000, the Candoshi live along the tributaries of the Pastaza and Morona rivers to the north of the Peruvian Amazon in South America. The ecosystem is the tropical rainforest, rich in biodiversity, though many parts are uninhabitable marshland. Much of the region is covered by an extensive network of lakes and rivers, including Lake Musa Karusha, one of the largest in the Western Amazon. In this environment, the generally male activities of hunting and fishing yield abundance. Women dedicate their time to the cultivation of bananas and manioc. Other foodstuffs and virtually all materials necessary for houses, canoes, weapons, and tools are gathered from the forest. The Candoshi are economically self-sufficient despite trading forest products for manufactured items such as ammunition, batteries, or clothes.

Daily life is organized around the single-family, and often polygynous, household. The Candoshi family household is normally isolated. Indeed, Candoshi households may be separated by several kilometers, forming units that are almost politically independent. Two or three households might be grouped together, and today one can find a few small villages that have been set up by missionaries. However, such settlements are of recent origin and very unstable. In some instances, the extreme isolation of the Candoshi household is offset by supra-domestic structures, formed by a dozen residences located within a relatively circumscribed space. These groupings (there are around twenty) are based on alliances between two groups of brothers and sisters who intermarry in order to create a network of solidarity. A warrior-chief of recognized authority, who shares his power with another warrior-chief, leads the group. The relationship between these local groups

Candoshi daily life focuses on single-family households, which are often isolated from one another by several kilometers. (Photograph by Alexandre Surrallés)

181

is one of relative hostility, which can turn into open aggressiveness. Shamanism is regulated by the same logic of aggression. The social philosophy is therefore founded on the conviction that the self is constructed at the expense of the identity of enemies, which finds its symbolic representation in the former practice of head-shrinking.

The Candoshi are closely related to the Shapra, which can be considered a subgroup. They also share considerable cultural affinity with the members of the Jivaro language family (consisting of the Achuar, Aguaruna, and Shuar) located to the north and west. The Candoshi and Shapra languages are mutually intelligible, but differences between Candoshi and the Jivaro languages are much more pronounced to the point that speakers of these languages cannot understand each other. Nevertheless, many expressions and a significant portion of vocabulary are common to all these languages.

Any consideration of Candoshi history must confront the lack of rigorous archeological research and the scarcity of archival information on both the geographic area and its inhabitants. It is possible, however, to affirm that the region was impacted early on by the colonial era. As early as the sixteenth century, Spanish expeditions pushed their way through Candoshi territory. At that time, the area was home to three main ethnic groups: the Mayna, Andoa, and Roamainia. Assuming no large-scale migration occurred (of which there is no record), these ethnic groups can be considered the ancestors of the modern Candoshi, even though they occupied a much larger area than the Candoshi do today.

The history of relations between the Candoshi and colonial society is one of love and hate. Periods of trade and negotiation gave way to turbulent times marked by indigenous rebellion and subsequent armed repression. The first such uprising was the notable Mayna rebellion against the Spanish, which took place in February 1653. The various extractive industries that have passed through the region since then invariably provoked further revolt and uprisings. As happened during the colonial era with gold prospectors in the Marañon River, during the rubber boom, and during the arrival of the timber, fishing, and hydrocarbon industries in the 1960s, brief periods of collaboration and attempted negotiation soon erupt into irrevocable hostilities.

The most recent significant impact on the Candoshi was the arrival of missionaries from the Summer Institute of Linguistics (SIL) starting in the 1950s. SIL representatives began living with the Shapra and later with the Candoshi to learn their languages to translate the Bible and convert them to Christianity. The missionaries' presence entailed a damaging demonization of many aspects of Candoshi culture. Nevertheless, some Candoshi learned to write their own language in the course of working with the missionaries. And despite pressure from the missionaries, many aspects of Candoshi culture, such as polygyny, the use of hallucinogens, isolated settlements, shamanic practices, and war, remain largely unchanged to this day. To defend their cultural and territorial rights, the Candoshi organized an indigenous federation in the early 1990s.

RELIGIOUS BELIEFS, RITUALS, AND CELEBRATIONS
According to the Candoshi all entities possess a form of subjectivity. General "animism" results from this perspective. Stars, vegetation, and animals perceive the

world as subjects with their own relative perspectives. However, even if every entity has its own subjectivity, communication between humans and non-humans is not always possible. It depends on the connections and the incompatibilities between the respective faculties of perception that the entities are believed to possess such as language, will, and vision. A hierarchy is thus created based on the type of interaction made possible by these connections. Entities that have a particularly strong presence called *vani* (translated as "soul" by the missionaries) are at the top of the hierarchy. Such entities include toothed animals, in particular large predators, various humanoid forms, and, of course, human beings.

One characteristic these entities share is a heart (*magish*), considered one's center because it is the point from which the world is perceived. In ritual practices involving the use of hallucinogens to search for a favorable premonition of future activities, called *magómaama*, the practitioner makes contact with these entities to adopt the traits they possess in order to increase his heart's perceptive potential. The most important of these ritual practices is the search for *arutam*, the spirit of a warrior with the *vani* of a jaguar. This community of "people" (*tpoots*) forms the social space beyond humanity. However, among all the entities that shape this heterogeneous society, there are those who are known as *kadoazi*. Who are they from the native's point of view?

The Candoshi usually refer to themselves as *kadoazi*, the term from which the name of the ethnic group is derived. It is also a common name, and it is possible that this name has its origin in the title of a great warrior of the past just as local groups today take the name of their chief. If *kadoazi* is employed as a synonym of "human being," then other ethnic groups are not necessarily included. Because they lack a notion of universal humankind, the Candoshi represent the human condition through their own particular experience of humanity. As a consequence, *kadoazi* refers primarily to the Candoshi themselves. Thus the most accurate translation of the term would be "we and the people like us." In fact, *kadoazi*, when understood as "human being," can take on many meanings that vary according to the speech context and the position of the speaker. For example, the meaning of *kadoazi* in a conversation among Candoshi is different from what it would mean in a dialogue between a Candoshi and an Achuar. Thus the meaning of *kadoazi* can range from "we" as the local group along with the wide circle of relatives living on the same stretch of river to "we" as indigenous people who share the same values and ways of life as opposed to the Spanish-speaking river-dwellers found south of the territory. Between these two extremes, *kadoazi* refers to the ethnic group, also a rather vague concept, but which could be defined as the community with which a feeling of belonging is shared—forged by the historical memory of interethnic confrontations which have been perpetuated until today among other factors. The antonym of *kadoazi* is *tonari*. Depending on the context, *tonari* can refer to a non-relative, a non-indigenous person, an unknown person, and even an enemy. In fact, *tonari* connotes potential enmity.

The character of the system of collective denomination suggests that the Candoshi do not perceive their surroundings as a space of peace and quiet. In their view, with the endemic hostility between local groups, isolation of the settlements, difficult conditions of transport within tropical forest marshlands, and low population density (0.16 per square kilometer), meetings by two people in the Candoshi social landscape are by no means coincidental. In such circumstances visits are rare, and a household may spend long periods of time without any social contact outside the local group. To break this isolation the Candoshi, like many other Amazonian societies, have developed formal visits between household settlements of different local groups. These visits are inaugurated by long welcoming ceremonies called *tasànomaama*, which literally means "to be face to face" and comes from words like *tasàsasàvo*, meaning "in front," or *tashi*, meaning "face."

Essentially, the *tasànomaama* ceremony consists of a dialogue involving only adult males, held between the residents of a household, on the one hand, and very occasional visitors from distant locations, on the other. The latter may belong to local groups located farther away than the neighboring local groups or those living on the same riverbank. Among the residents, the head of the family, his grown-up sons, and sons-in-law who may live there (because of uxorilocal postmarital residence) or are only passing through take part in the dialogue. The visiting group of adult males who will take part in the dialogue may consist of a father and a few of his sons or sons-in-law, two or three brothers, or two brothers-in-law traveling together. Hosts and visitors may be relatives, but very distant relatives.

Visitors announce their arrival by blowing a horn or by blowing down the barrel of a shotgun. If they come by canoe, the visitors remain in the canoe in the river in front of the house, pretending to row backwards, waiting for a sign of invitation. When the sign is given, the male visitors enter first, but only into the part of the house reserved for them. They enter in single file and in order of rank (essentially based on a combination of personal reputation and age), surrounded by the striking formality present throughout the ceremony. On entering the house, the highest-ranking male visitor, wearing facial paint and a crown of feathers and armed with a loaded gun, offers the first words of greeting. The head of the receiving household, himself armed with a gun, replies to the greeting and signals where the visitor should be seated. The visiting women and children as well as the host women and children remain outside, sometimes hidden. Once the male visitors are seated in the designated place, the master of the household requests his wife, sister, or daughter to offer a bowl of manioc beer to the guests. In the meantime, the host, still armed, finishes his own facial painting while sitting on a high stool between the male and the female sections of the house. The tense silence is finally broken when, after all eye contact had been carefully avoided, the master of the house suddenly looks at the leader of the visitors and begins to speak.

The ceremony begins with a few preliminary sentences concerning good manners and tradition. The master of the house then improvises variations on stereotyped formulas in a vigorous manner. After his intervention, the host asks the chief of the visitors to respond in similar fashion. The master of the household asks each of the male visitors to speak with him. He chooses the speakers in order of rank and delivers his own speech at the end of every intervention. If other male adults are present within the household, they also carry out a series of ceremonial dialogues with the visitors. The ceremony can last for several hours.

After the formal welcoming ceremony, the real celebration begins when manioc beer especially prepared for such occasions is served. The celebration continues until two or three jars containing thirty liters of fermented manioc have been consumed. During the day, participants drink to the point of inebriation; during the night they sleep. Early before dawn the next day, the men convene around the fire (normally in the female part of the house) to drink tea made from the *vayoosa* (*Ilex sp.*) plant, which has emetic effects. With no face paint or other adornments nor the rest of the paraphernalia common to visits, the men begin an intimate conversation that touches on the real topics of interest for the visit: the establishment of marital or military alliances, the exchange of goods or services, and the relay of information related to conflicts, for example. The meeting ends when the congregants disperse to the river to bathe and vomit the tea they drank earlier. After decorating themselves once more, they take their seats again on the men's side of the house to begin another day of drinking manioc beer. This can continue for several days until the beer runs out.

SONGS AND MUSIC

One of the celebration's culminating moments comes when the participants, euphoric from the effects of the beer, begin to sing and play musical instruments. Sometimes celebrants will dance, forming a male line that moves into a circle around a woman who dances spontaneously for several minutes before another takes her place. The most popular type of music at these festivities is songs dedicated to the singer's brother, spouse, or sometimes a special visitor usually performed by women while offering the honoree manioc beer from a jar. These songs are called *yashina*, a term derived from *yashisi* (which means "manioc") and from the verbal form *yashimaama* (which means both "to offer manioc beer" and "to sing" in the context of these celebrations). These songs are sung during the end of the celebration, when the pleasure of having visitors begins to turn into a sense of despair at the impending farewell. The songs use similar poetic images such as fraternal or conjugal love, death that will separate us, the manioc beer we are sharing, and our good fortune for having been able to visit. A humorous note is frequently interjected in these female songs, and often the humor serves as a way for the singer to gently mock herself before her visitors.

In the following translation we can appreciate one of these songs dedicated to the singer's brother, sung by an elderly woman, Tsirta of the Upper Nucuray, at one of the first celebrations in which Alexandre Surrallés had the opportunity to participate in 1993. The singer had been traveling with her husband, and she and Surrallés coincided at her brother's house, where he had been staying for a few days. It was nighttime, and her singing was accompanied by flute music:

> Brother, my brother, drink this manioc beer although it is not very strong.
> Brother, my brother, we do not know the moment we will die;

> When you die, I will remember how I offered you a drink, my brother,
> And so I will remember you when you are dead.
> Man always dies too soon, you are my only brother; when you die I will
> remember this moment when I served you manioc beer, face to face.
> Brother, my brother, if we did not know each other, I would not invite you
> to drink, but since you are my only brother, I do it in this way.
> I have come from far away, and when I go, I will say that I have kept my
> word by offering you a drink.
> I have come from far away, and when I go, I will say that I have kept my
> word by offering you a drink.
> Brother, my brother, this is how our ancestors did it.
> Brother, my brother, drink my beer even though my arm looks like that of
> a spider monkey (*Ateles belzebuth*).

These celebratory songs form part of the varied registry of Candoshi secular music. Secular songs are performed publicly and are partially improvised, though they always follow the canon of the musical genre. Both men and women can perform the songs individually or in a group. Sometimes the singer is accompanied by a pentatonic two-holed flute, a hand-crafted violin, or a drum. Candoshi secular music is richly varied, beautiful, and meaningful. The songs evoke lyric emotions often expressed through allegories of animal life or other aspects of the natural world. The fullness of youth, the forms and colors of life, love, friendship, the passing of time, and the pain of saying goodbye are some of the classic themes. Multiple themes often appear together in one song, as is the case in this brief song performed by Isigoro, the owner of the house where Alexandre Surrallés lived during his stay in Western Candoshi territory in 1992. Isigoro had just learned that a woman he loved had contracted marriage with someone else:

> I am like a leaf hanging from a tree branch;
> A strong wind will come and take me away, leaving me who knows where;
> Perhaps there I will be happy.

In addition to secular music, Candoshi folklore encompasses another category of songs that we could term magical or incantational. This type of music is extremely diverse, but all songs communicate a desire to influence others (human beings or otherwise) in order to improve some aspect of reality. These songs are performed *sotto vocce* in ritualistic settings for various ends: to resolve a problem or conflict, improve an interpersonal relationship, increase agricultural production or the spoils from a hunt, or assist in shamanic interventions, for example.

In addition to these types of music and other forms of expression common among Amerindian societies such as mythic narratives, the Candoshi possess other means of artistic expression such as the decoration of ceramics and intricately made feather costumes. The relative isolation that the Candoshi strive to maintain has meant that the external influences of a still weak but ever-growing colonizing front have had little impact on their rich and varied folklore, in contrast to the vast majority of indigenous communities in the upper Amazon.

STUDIES OF CANDOSHI FOLKLORE

Published works on the Candoshi are not extensive. Notable works include the Candoshi-Spanish dictionary by John Tuggy (1966), articles by Massimo Amadio and Lucia D'Emilio on Candoshi history and sociology (1983, 1985), and the most recent works of Alexandre Surrallés (1992, 2000a, 2000b, 2003b, 2004), including the only monograph to date on the Candoshi (2003a).

BIBLIOGRAPHY

Amadio, Massimo. 1985. Los murato: Una síntesis histórica. *Amazonía peruana* 6.12: 117–131.

Amadio, Massimo, and Lucia D'Emilio. 1983. La alianza entre los candoshi murato del Alto Amazonas. *Amazonía peruana* 5.9: 23–36.

Surrallés, Alexandre. 1992. A propos de l'ethnographie des Candoshi et des Shapra. *Journal de la Société des Américanistes* 78.2: 47–58.

———. 2000a. Passion, mort et maladie dans une culture amazonienne. In *En substances. Systèmes, pratiques et symboliques. Textes pour Françoise Héritier*, edited by J.-L. Jamard, E. Terray, and M. Xanthakou. Paris: Fayard. 387–396.

———. 2000b. La passion génératrice. Prédation, échange et redoublement du mariage candoshi. *L'Homme* 154–155: 123–144.

———. 2003a. *Au coeur du sens. Perception, affectivité, action chez les Candoshi*. Paris: Centre national de la recherche scientifique et Maison des sciences de l'homme. Collection Chemins de l'ethnologie.

———. 2003b. Face to face: Meaning, Feeling, and Perception in Amazonian Welcoming Ceremonies. *Journal of the Royal Anthropological Institute* (N.S.) 9: 775–791.

———. 2004. Horizontes de intimidad: Persona, percepción y espacio en los candoshi. In *Tierra adentro: Territorio y percepción indígena del entorno*, edited by A. Surrallés and P. García Hierro. Copenhagen: IWGIA. 137–162.

Tuggy, John. 1966. *Vocabulario candoshi de Loreto*. Yarinacocha, Peru: Instituto Lingüístico de Verano.

Alexandre Surrallés

ECUADOR

ROOTS OF ECUADORIAN FOLKLORE

The study of Ecuadorian folklore follows a historical tradition based on the various manifestations of folkloric expression throughout Ecuador's unique chronological trajectory toward nationhood as well as the fact that two completely different cultures have contributed to Ecuadorian identity: a European culture from the Iberian Peninsula and the native Amerindian culture of the Andean region of South America. Both currents have influenced each other to produce a rich and varied folklore that includes popular and oral poetry, traditional narratives, folk speech and linguistic innovations, magical beliefs and practices, popular theater, holidays, funeral practices, folk costume, games, music and dance, traditional musical instruments, cattle herding, food and meals, and popular arts and crafts.

These have been studied and recorded since the sixteenth century with the arrival of Spanish missionaries such as Fray Bernabé Cobo, who in his 1653 *Historia del Nuevo Mundo* included among other topics a report on the elaboration and use of a native alcoholic drink called *chicha*. The historical and chronological study of Ecuadorian folklore finds its best expression in the moumental work of Paulo de Carvalho-Neto, *Antología del Folklore Ecuatoriano, 1653–1969* (1994)—the first edition of the first and second volumes of which appeared in 1964 and 1970, respectively. In this anthology Carvalho-Neto gathers sixty-nine texts by forty-four different authors. He organizes the material into four chapters that offer a convenient overview of Ecuadorian folklore. The study of Ecuadorian folklore begins with travelers and explorers from the seventeenth through the nineteenth centuries. Their work, mainly descriptive, was followed by the beginnings of analytical study in the mid-nineteenth century. The "Modern Period" of Ecuadorian folklore study began in 1920 and gave way to the Contemporary Period in the early 1960s.

POETRY

Popular poetry appeared very early in the documentation of Ecuadorian folklore. The earliest compositions revealed the cultural encounter that gave particular color to the meter and language that the poets used. Early compositions have survived the passage of time and, in the small towns of the highlands, are still sung in their original form. They were originally composed in the style of the Spanish romance in lines of eight syllables that can easily be recited or sung. But the most interesting characteristic of this poetry is the mixture of Spanish and Quechua, a native language, in alternating lines. The following example uses Quechua in the first and third lines and Spanish in the second and fourth:

Ashku apanay, mapa runa	Let that dog away, useless man!
Quién dizqué te ha de querer	Who is going to love you?
Tukuy moza warmikuna	All the young women never
Nunca te han podido ver.	Have been able to look at you!

Some of this poetry was originally composed in Quechua only, but a translation in Spanish was made for those who did not understand the Amerindian language. The translation resulted in a version that appealed to the educated Spanish-speaking elite. The best and more extensive collection of this type of popular poetry is that of Juan León Mera. An example from his *Cantares del pueblo ecuatoriano* (1898) follows:

Llullu shunguta charini	Spanish: *Tengo tierno el corazón*
Kantami warmi kuyani	*Por eso te amo mujer*
Kanmanta ñuka llukini	*Más tú causas mi aflicción*
Kanmanta ñuka wakani.	*Y me haces llanto verte*

A closer translation of the original would produce a much simpler composition, as does this English rendering:

I have a tender heart.
I love you, woman,
Because of you I'm sad,
Because of you I cry.

Poetic compositions also express people's feelings toward current events, as in the case of a man given the death penalty for killing his wife in a moment of jealousy and rage:

Dizqué van a fusilarlo	He will face the firing squad
Porque a su esposa mató	Because he killed his wife.
Ella lo mató primero	She killed him first
Pues por otro lo dejó	By leaving him for another [man].

Compositions of this type are printed and sung by professional singers who perform in the plazas and markets and then sell them as *cancioneros* (song pamphlets).

SONGS AND NARRATIVE GAMES

Popular songs, poems, and narratives carry a cultural content corresponding to the different geographic zones and regions of the country. Those discussed in the preceding section are found in the Highland Region. But the example that follows below is a song-dance-game combination from the tropical-coastal region:

EL SOMBRERITO	THE LITTLE HAT
El juego del sombrerito	The hat game
Se juega de esta manera	Is played like this:
Dando la media vuelta	Turning around,
Dando la vuelta entera	making a whole circle,
Y dando la media vuelta	Turning around,
Diciendo el verso primero	Telling a verse first.

At this point a man may jump to the middle of the circle and sing:

Las estrellas en el cielo	The stars in the sky
Salen de dos en dos	come out in pairs.
Quiéreme zambita Linda	Love me, beautiful Zamba,
Como yo te quiero a vos	As I love you.

Then a woman will come to the middle of the circle and sing:

Los jovencitos de hoy día	Today's young men
Son como papaya madura	are like a ripe papaya.
Cuando les piden un medio	When asked for a penny,
Les dan frío de calentura	they get the chills.

Then the leader of this dance and game will come to the middle of the circle and sing:

Sombrerito, sombrerito	Little hat, little hat
Que estás caído en el suelo	that had fallen to the ground,
Yo vengo a levantarte	I come to pick you up
Por ser prenda de tu dueño	because you belong to me.

This game continues with more songs and dancing.

Songs and verses that show a deep African influence appear in the subtropical region. In fact these types of folksongs were heard only on the coastal plantations among the descendants of African slaves. The sample that follows is incomprehensible to an outsider:

Arriple bellá bombola
Y abajilbe macucano
Me la propia zamuquita
Mi melé bellá parrando.

It tells that while there is much fun upstairs, downstairs one finds only the old man, father of the *chicha*, with his girlfriend talking to him.

Of course, the variety of folksongs and narratives is representative of geographic locale as well as religious beliefs. Some of the most common are the *Mashalla*, a wedding song to offer advice to the newlyweds; the *Coplas del carnaval*, which are sung during the pre-Lenten festivities; and the *villancicos*, carols sung during processions that take place before and after mass in honor of the child Jesus. The processions are called *El pase del niño*. These *villancicos* can be heard in Quechua, Spanish, or both languages, depending upon the place. This author once had the opportunity to attend a comic presentation based on the *Mashalla*, now appropriated by the town's elite and sung in Spanish in front of a character representing the Justice of the Peace—the *Intendente*. First a lady sang, "*Señor Intendente, justicia le pido / Que mi marido no duerme conmigo*" (Your Honor, I demand justice / That my husband doesn't sleep with me). Then a man appears and sings:

Señor Intendente, justicia le pido	Your Honor, I demand justice.
Esta chola miente	This woman is lying.
Yo duermo con ella	I sleep with her,
Pero no me siente!	But she ignores me.

Then after each exchange between the woman and her husband, the chorus sings: "*Mashalla, mashalla / Kashulla, kashulla*" (Dear little son-in-law / Dear little daughter-in-law).

Traditional Ecuadorian narratives include legends such as those concerning the presence of the Apostle Saint Thomas among the natives long before the arrival of the Europeans. Folktales are numerous and combine native and European elements.

MEDICINE AND MAGIC

Medicine and magic seem to go hand in hand, as do the practitioners and the types of medicinal elements. First, every village seems to have a *curandero* or *curandera*, a healer who operates outside of regular medical practice. Then there is the *brujo* or *bruja*, a "witch doctor" most commonly found in small and isolated villages as well as in the tropical rainforests. Then there is *el adivino* or *la adivina*, a fortune-teller common to several levels of society. Although this character has displaced the "gypsy," people still have a preference for an exotic fortune-teller, one who comes from outside the village, city, or country. Finally we find the *fregador*, who is called to fix broken bones and sprains, and the *limpiadora*, usually a woman who uses a handful of fresh herbs and flowers that she rubs lightly over a patient suffering from the evil eye or *espanto* (fright).

In 1912 there appeared *Enumeración botánica*, a very interesting work by Luis Cordero that listed medicinal plants and herbs and the ailments they cure. Many of these plant cures are still in use today.

FESTIVALS AND CELEBRATIONS

The celebration of traditional holidays and festivities follows the Roman Catholic religious calendar, but with a striking emphasis on those holidays that take place on the same date or time of the year as indigenous Amerindian holidays celebrated before the arrival of the Europeans. Thus we have the *San Pedro*, a week-long celebration to honor Saint Peter, which falls on 29 November. This is the time when corn is ripe to be cooked—usually as corn on the cob. At the time of the Inca Empire, corn was regarded as a gift from the sun god, *Inti*, and the celebration of *Inti Raymi* took place to honor this event.

Another holiday that follows a similar pattern is *El día de finados*, which honors the dead. It is in reality a three-day holiday when special foods are prepared and a table is served during the evening before All Saints' Day (1 November) as an offering to the souls of departed relatives. *Carnaval* is another of the important holidays that blends traditional pre-Lenten celebrations brought from Europe. In some towns and cities these celebrations last for a whole week with much feasting, dancing, serenading, and parades called *comparsas*. Throwing water balloons, now outlawed, was very common until recently. Another important and characteristic cyclic ceremony in Ecuadorian tradition is *Los Inocentes*, or more a properly *La temporada de inocentes* (the season of the innocents). This takes place during the Christmas season and consists in people of

Festival at a small village near Ambato, Ecuador. (© Topham/The Image Works)

all ages dressing in costumes or disguises to mock or ridicule authorities, neighbors, friends, and others. The most common disguises are those of *payasos y monos*, clowns and monkeys. *Payasos* carry a *chorizo*, a sausage made of rags and cotton that they use to hit bystanders, and *monos* carry a whip that is sometimes used on children who should be in school or at home instead of lingering in the streets. *Los Inocentes* occurs at the same time the Catholic Church observes the feast day commemorating the massacre of the innocents recorded in the New Testament accounts of the life of the infant Jesus.

Popular *corridas de toros* (bullfights) and *peleas de gallos* (cockfights) are also among celebrations that have taken root in Ecuadorian folklore. Popular bullfights differ from those that take place in the capital city Quito around 6 December or in the city of Riobamba around 21 April. These are as formal, elegant, and expensive as those of Spain. Cockfights are regulated to ensure that the damage inflicted on the animals is minimal. However, in virtually any town where cockfights take place one may observe that during this event in the confines of the enclosure of a *gallera* (the cockfight arena) the mayor of the town, the governor of the province, and other local authorities receive the same treatment as the street vendor, the tradesman, the farmer, and minor bureaucrats. These traditional games thus operate as a social leveling mechanism.

ARTS AND CRAFTS

Ecuador has maintained a significant tradition in handicrafts that are well known for their quality and design. Quito has been the center of that tradition thanks to what was called *La Escuela Quiteña* in colonial times. Among the members of this school are painters and sculptors, and right behind them in reputation are a group of woodcarvers and weavers. At present woodcarvers have concentrated in San Antonio de Ibarra. Weavers have settled in the same province of Imbabura but in the city of Otavalo, north of Quito. Other centers of handicraft production and creation are located in the provinces of Chimborazo and Tungurahua in the center of the Highland Region and in the province of Azuay to the south, particularly in the city of Cuenca, which is also well known for the quality and design of pottery pieces of considerable variety.

The well-known Panama hats are handcrafted in Ecuador, mainly in the coastal province of Manabí and in Azuay. In addition to these hats, manufacturers also produce a variety of straw hats of different quality, shapes, and colors.

The Ecuadorian tradition of love for poetry finds expression nowadays in a recent urban art form found in such cities as Quito, Cuenca, Loja, and others. Graffiti consists of perhaps one or two poetic lines, usually scrawled on the walls of public buildings.

BIBLIOGRAPHY

Carvalho-Neto, Paulo de. 1994. *Antología del folklore ecuatoriano, 1653–1969.* 2nd edition. Quito: Abya-Yala.

Cobo, Fray Bernabé. 1983 (1653). *History of the Inca Empire,* edited and translated by Roland Hamilton. Austin: University of Texas Press.

Cordero, Luis. 1911. *Enumeración botánica de las principales plantas, así útiles como nocivas, indigenas ó aclimatadas, que se dan en las provincias del Azuay y de Cañar de la república del Ecuador.* Cuenca: Imp. de la Universidad.

Mera, Juan León. 1898. *Cantares del pueblo ecuatoriano.* Quito: Museo del Banco Central del Ecuador.

Ernesto Lombeida

KAINGANG

GEOGRAPHY AND HISTORY

The Kaingangs are among the five largest indigenous groups of Brazil with an approximate population of 28 million. Their language belongs to the Jê language group of the Macro-Jê linguistic family. The name Kaingang appears in the literature at the end of the nineteenth century. Before this time, the Kaingangs were called *Coraodos* (Crowned) because of the shape of their haircuts. In the ethnographic literature of Brazil, some confusion between the Kaingangs and the Xoklengs o Laklano exists because of Jules Henry, who first studied the latter, now numbering around 1,000. The Xoklengs are linguistically and culturally similar to the Kaingangs, and he erroneously referred to them as Kaingangs too.

The Kaingangs live in more than twenty Indian areas over four different states within Brazil from São Paulo to Rio Grande do Sul. This territorial dispersion corresponds to the distribution of the local pine woods (*Araucaria angustifolia*), which provided an important component of their diet.

The Kaingangs and Xoklengs are related to some of the oldest settlers of southern Brazil, dating to 8600 B.C.E. Researchers have found underground housing units and round mounds encircled by trenches characteristic of the Southern Jê. These cultural groups underwent very significant changes at the beginning of the first century C.E., primarily as a result of the introduction of ceramics and agriculture.

In the past the Kaingang economy was based on hunting, fishing, gathering, and agriculture. Hunting was limited to the rainforest mammals such as the *tapir*, *caititu*, and *coati* and many varieties of fowl (for example, *yacutinga* and *macuco*). Trapping was done with a rope stretched to catch parrots and *baitacas* (a species of macaw), and the *émbitkô* technique was used to catch a sort of water mouse. The most popular hunting tool was the bow and arrow, the tips of arrows being wooden or bone.

FOOD

Gathering activities centered upon the collection of pine seeds in the extensive araucaria forests. These seeds were consumed roasted, and the Kaingangs made a flour out of them. Another way to conserve the seeds was to store them in baskets, whose lids were secured with vines and then lowered into a deep spot in the rivers—hence, the name *fágfy õkór*. They also used the seeds to make a fermented drink called *kyfe*. The Kaingangs gathered honey (*guaraipo*, *jeteí*, and *irapuá*), often used to prepare a fermented drink for the *kiki* ritual; wild fruits such as the *yaboticaba*, *pitanga*, and *ariticum*; *palmito*, used after it has been milled into flour; insect larvae (*corós*), which are found in the palm, *tacuaras*, pine, and *yaracatiá* trees (the Kaingangs

Baskets for sale at an urban market. (Photograph by Wilmar da Rocha D'Angelis)

would fell an occasional pine tree and leave it on the ground to decompose in order to harvest the larvae that would appear); vegetables such as the *fuá* or *erva moura* as well as the *kumi* (mendioca leaves), *cambuquira* and *pyrfé* (burning weed leaves); and *yerba mate* (*Ilex paraguayryensis*), which is still in use for the preparation of tea or *mate* (*kógwuin*) and once was used in divination rituals. In addition to food items, the Kaingangs also gathered medicinal plants such as the *ortiga Brava*, used in weaving a type of shirt, and shawls called *kurus*.

They also gathered the *tacuara* species of bamboo, which is employed in the manufacture of baskets, currently sold as handicrafts.

Fish also constituted an important component of the Kaingang diet. *Paris* was a fishing trap made with *tacuaras* or rods. In addition, fish were caught by use of poisons extracted from plants such as the *timbó* and from barks from other trees.

Kaingang farming includes the production of corn, beans, and pumpkins. Kaingangs adopted the cultivation of other products thanks to cultural contacts that have taken place. Currently, farming and farm labor are basic elements of Kaingang economy.

SYMMETRY IN MYTHS AND FOLKTALES

For the Kaingangs the world is perfectly symmetrical, made of antithetical but complementary pairs. This basic world principle is personified in the mythical heroes Kamê and Kairu, the founders of society. The exogamic divisions of society stem from these culture heroes and their respective sons: Kamê is subdivided into Kamê and Wónhétky; Kairu is divided into Kairu and Votor. Affiliation with any of these subgroups is determined by patrilineal descent, and each is referred to by a **repertoire** of names that constitute personal Kaingang identity. Any Kaingang name once belonged to an ancestor and comes with a number of prerogatives and duties. During the festivities of *Kikikoi* (festivities for the dead) the Kaingangs take for themselves the names of the deceased, thus legitimizing the usage of former names.

The Kamês are related to the sun as well as lower places and long objects. They confront risks coming from the world of the dead. They are characterized by persistence, permanence, and strength. The Kairus are related to the moon, the dew, and humidity. They are also associated with higher places and short or round compact objects. They confront the threats coming from the world of the living and are characterized by their mobility and agility. For the Kaingangs, unity is the sum of these opposing principles.

Kaingang aversion to the union of identical parts stems from the sterility attributed to such unions, which are therefore considered a negation of social life. In their daily lives, they emphasize the relationship of opposites as ideal and harmonious; any relationship to members of the same "half" is considered conflictive. On everything they insist on the interchange of different parts. In medicine and healing, for instance, they must mix a Kamê plant with a Kairu one.

The relationships of exchange between the two halves are considered permanent: Kaingangs marry someone from the opposite half; the dead are buried by the other half; and when a person is going through a difficult situation, he or she is assisted by a member of the other half. A boy's first take from a hunt is offered to his maternal grandfather, for example, a member of the opposite half, a practice that assures good luck to the hunter. It is also expected that someone from the other half will tell a person the secrets of shamanism and become his or her *iangre* (special friend), a spiritual double of a *kuiâ* (*xama*).

Symmetry becomes a constant search for the ideal, and thus life is dependent on such dynamics and conflicts for existence. This becomes very clear in the myth concerning the origin of the moon:

> In the beginning there were two suns. They had a fight. One hit the other in the eye, and this became the moon, now half blind. And the moon says, "Now I am weaker, but I am going to favor water." Moon is the dew; it comes out in the evening to give dew. But the sun is to provide heat, to dry the soil and even the water. If the two suns had continued to exist, there would be no plants, people, or anything at all.

This confirms that for life to exist, differences are necessary. Therefore the two halves Kamê and Kairu are perceived as cosmological. Every living creature belongs to one of them. For example:

KAMÊ		KAIRU	
Rõ	sun	*Kyxõ*	moon
Fâg	pine tree	*Fwó*	cedar
Tõin	palm	*Tõinror*	palm
Kokamẽ	spotted cavy	*Xê*	coati
Kémbê	deer	*Fẽfẽn*	armadillo
Ngrud	leopard	*Ngro*	toucan
Krĩntkĩr	macaw	*Fókféi*	otter
Krengufãr	minnow	*Rig-mbâg*	catfish
Mangmbâg	bee	*Engpéi*	mosquito

The fundamental division observed by the Kaingangs in their cosmological vision and their social life—the division of the world and of society always in two halves—appears very clearly in the myth of their origin, which was documented for the first time in the nineteenth century. It appears as follows:

> At first there was a great flood which covered the land except the top of the *Crinjijimbé* mountain. The Kaingangs, Cayurucrés, and Camés swam toward the

mountain carrying a lighted torch (firewood) in their mouths. The Cayurucrés and the Camés became tired and drowned, and their souls went to live on the mountain. The Kaingangs and some of the Curutons reached, with great effort, the top of the mountain, and there they spent many days without food because the water was still high. They thought they were going to die, but then they heard the songs of the Saracuras (the slaty-breasted wood-rail), who were coming with baskets filled with dirt, which they threw on the water, making it recede slowly. With the help of the ducks the Saracuras were able to reach the top, building a sort of bridge that the Kaingangs and Curutons used to to get out of the water. Those who were saved on the branches of the trees became monkeys.

The Cayurucrés and Camés, whose souls have gone to the center of the Earth, opened a path inside it and came out by two paths. In the path opened by the Cuyurucrés a beautiful brook appeared. This path was flat and without stones, and for this reason they still have small feet. But the Camés opened their path over a stony ground that hurt their feet, which became swollen, and that is why the Camés still have large feet. On the path they opened there was no water, so they had to ask for it from the Cayurucrés, who allowed them to drink as much as they needed.

Once outside they asked the Curutons to bring the baskets and calabazas they had left below, but the Curutons were lazy and did not climb back and so still remain at the bottom of the mountain. For this reason they are considered as runaway slaves who are to be captured when found.

In the following nights, after they came out of the mountains the Cayurucrés and Camés made the animals out of ashes and charcoal. At the same time that the Cayurucrés were creating such animals as tigers, ants, and bees, the Camés were creating others to confront them such as mountain lions, wasps, and poisonous snakes. However, after they finished these tasks, they went to join the Kaingangs. When they arrived at a large field, all of them came together and decided to marry the young men and women: first the Cayurucrés married their sons to the Camé girls, and then the other way around. And since there were still some young men left, they were married to the daughters of the Kaingangs. Therefore, the Cayurucrés, Camés, and Kaingangs are relatives and friends.

Other historic moments in their mythic narrative appear in connection with the adoption of farming and in all probability with the male dominance in Kaingang society. What follows is the myth of Ñara:

According to these natives Ñara was the first to teach them how to clear the land and plant crops. Ñara was the chief of the Kaingang nation, and in a time of scarcity he gathered all the members of the nation and took them to a place in the jungle where he ordered each one to use their tools and fell the trees, then to burn the underbrush to clear the land.

When the cleared land was ready, Ñara ordered them to tie a big rope to his neck and drag him over the newly cleared land, where he was to be buried when dead. He further instructed them to return after three months to find the food they needed.

After this voluntary sacrifice of their chief the natives left very sad and went into the jungle hunting and gathering food for three months. After this time they returned to the previous place and found there plenty of corn, beans, and pumpkins.

Corn had grown from Ñara's penis, beans had grown from his testicles, and pumpkins from his head.

However, there are some variations of this myth. Some believe that white corn with a few black kernels come from Ñara's eyes, the small beans from his fingers, and the large beans from his toes.

RELIGIOUS BELIEFS AND RITUALS

The most common religious and shamanic rituals among the Kaingangs are related to death. They believe that the spirits of those recently deceased are very dangerous because of their nostalgia for the loved ones left behind. They thus linger in the places they frequented most when alive, often longing to encounter their spouses and children. The Kaingangs also believe that any contact with the dead brings all sorts of cosmic disorder, illness, and death.

As soon as a person dies, the spouse is taken from the house and carried to a shelter in the jungle by an individual from the other half (a *péin*), who then assumes the role of a *péin*. In the shelter the widow or widower is left alone to lie prone upon the ground, having to eat meats without any fat and roasted directly over the fire—meals served, of course, by the *péin*. This period of isolation lasts from seven to twenty days. The Kamês, though stronger, spend less time in isolation. During this time the widow or widower is purified to eliminate any vestiges of the deceased spouse so that he or she will not endanger the rest of the people. Mud

The widow purification ritual requires that the woman be doused with a bath of medicinal plants. (Photograph by Juracilda Veiga)

During *Kikikoi* (festivities for the dead) the Kaingangs assume the names of the deceased. (Photograph by Wilmar da Rocha D'Angelis)

and plant extracts are used to purify the eyes. It is also sometimes necessary to bathe the person with medicinal plants to purify the entire body. These baths also serve to repel the *wéinkupring* or spirit of the deceased person. At the end of this period of isolation, the children are painted with charcoal, and the widow or widower has hair and nails trimmed. Then follows a public ceremony of purification, during which the shaman (*kuiâ*) prepares a bath with medicinal plants for the widow or widower, the children, and close relatives. With a broom made of branches the *kuiâ* cleans the house, especially the spots most frequented by the deceased, who is commanded to leave his or her family alone. Nowadays, however, Kaingangs have added the Roman Catholic prayer of the rosary, which is performed at the cemetery on the seventh or thirtieth day after death.

Meanwhile a more elaborated ritual "guarantees" that the spirit of the deceased will remain in the place of death. The *Kikikoi* festival represents the essence of Kaingang cosmology. Several publications have already described this ritual. It seems, however, that in the last thirty years only the community of Xapecó (Santa Catarina) has performed it, doing so as late as the 1990s. *Kikikoi* is performed for the recently deceased and includes as ritual participants those villagers related by family ties. For this ritual to take place, the presence of prayers from the four subgroups, who happen to possess the powerful prayers and hymns that carry the souls to a desired destination, is absolutely crucial. Using their *xygxyg* (maracas made of gourds) and their songs, they show the path for the *wéinkupring* to follow toward the place of the dead.

During the festival the community seems to return to earlier times, so the Kamês and the Kairus are not together. During the evenings of the ritual each group gets together around a fire: the Kamês on the west side and the Kairus on the east side. This brings them to the mythical time when Cayurucré and Camé emerged from the ground in the mountains and, night after night, created all the animals. On the last evening all the guests come to the village, including those for the "village" of the dead, and during the following day, they perform the final rituals in the cemetery to send the *wéinkupring* to their village accompanied by the spirits of those who have died recently. At the conclusion of this ceremony the shamans close the gate between the two worlds, and the two groups (halves) come to the dancing field, where they drink and dance together, reestablishing their original alliance.

A third ritual is still performed every year in the village of Inhacorá in Rio Grande do Sul during the month of August. The *Festa do Kuiâ* (Feast of the Shaman) coincides with the Brazilian Catholic Feast of the Good Lord Jesus. For the Kaingangs, it consists of a communal meal and the raising of a mast under the blessings of the shaman.

During this festivity the *kuiâ* narrates the myth detailing the first action of *Topẽ* (The Creator). To raise a new mast, according to the *kuiâ*, is to repeat the first action undertaken by their creator god the day he discovered this land for the Kaingangs. In his "sermon" the *kuiâ* assumes the place of that god and says, "I am He here in this land. What He did on this land, I am doing it now." Then he calls on his people to follow him in his ceremonial actions around the mast. He repeats: "What I am doing now must be continued always by all our people. When something bad happens you must come to the mast, because this is the real 'Miguel'"—that is, the real *kuiâ*.

When the mast is taken out, the participants place some bean seeds at its base and a head of corn on its upper end. In southern Brazil this annual ritual corresponds to the time of clearing the land in preparation for new planting of corn and beans following winter. Therefore, these festivities can be considered as a ritual of cosmic renewal and an offering for a good harvest.

BIBLIOGRAPHY

Maniser, Henry H. 1928. Les Kaingangs de São Paulo. *23rd International Congress of Americanists*. New York: Science Press. 760–791.

Métraux, Alfred. 1946. The Kaingang. *Handbook of South American Indians*, edited by Julian Steward. Bureau of American Ethnology Bulletin, No. 143.1:445–475.

NIT/UFRGS and others. 2002. *Kanhgág jykre—Pensamento Kaingang* (sound recording). Porto Alegre: Museu Antropológico do RS, NIT-UFRGS, Selo Quartavia.

Tommasino, K., and J. F. Rezende. 2000. *Kikikoi. Ritual dos Kaingang na Área Indígena Xapecó/SC. Registro Áudio-Fotográfico do Ritual dos Mortos*. Londrina: Midiograf.

Veiga, Juracilda. 1994. Organização social e cosmovisão Kaingang: uma introdução ao parentesco, casamento e nominação em uma sociedade Jê Meridional. Dissertação de Mestrado, Campinas: IFCH-UNICAMP.

———. 2000. Cosmologia e práticas rituais Kaingang. Tese de Doutorado, Campinas: IFCH-UNICAMP.

Veiga, Juracilda, and Wilmar R. D'Angelis. 1996. *A festa do Kikikoi* (film). Campinas, SP: Author's edition.

Juracilda Veiga

PERU

Geography and History

Located in west-central South America, Peru is bordered on the north by Colombia and **Ecuador**, on the south by Chile, and on the west by the Pacific Ocean. Peru (including islands) covers 1,280,000 square kilometers. Lima is its capital. Peru's topography is divided into three areas: coast, sierra, and mountain. The coast is a long dry stretch of land that runs the length of the country. The coast is the economic center of Peru, where many of the nation's crops are grown. East of the coastal plain is the sierra area, including the Andes mountain ranges, plateaus, and valleys. The main mountain range is the Cordillera Occidental. The sierra covers approximately 30 percent of the country and runs southeast to northwest with an average height of approximately 3,600 meters. The highest peak in Peru is Husascaran at over 6,500 meters. The sierran slopes and a less elevated area are known as the Montaña region and encompass approximately 60 percent of Peru's land area. It is covered by forests in the west and tropical growth in the east. This area is the least developed and explored of the country.

The complex geography of Peru is reflected in the central native Andean concept of *huaca*, referring to anything imbued with supernatural power. Notable features of the landscape—from mountain crags to stones—are seen as having this power. This conception of sacred geography continues today, centuries after the introduction of Catholicism.

Exterior of Santo Domingo Catholic Church showing a Spanish colonial doorway and remnant of a wall of an Incan temple of the moon, Cuzco, Peru. Peru remains nearly 90 percent Roman Catholic. (Courtesy Library of Congress)

Approximately 6 percent of Peruvians work in the farming, fishing, or forestry industries. Along the coast the majority of the export crops are grown, whereas in the mountain region local crops are grown. Many Peruvian farms are small and function to produce subsistence crops. Chief crops include sugarcane, potatoes, rice, corn, seed cotton, coffee, and wheat. In addition, Peru grows more coca than any other country.

The division in Peru's political and economic structure can be seen in the stratification between social and ethnic classes, from the Spanish-speaking Europeans along the coast at the top to the **Quechua** and Aymara peoples living in the highlands and in the poor areas of major cities such as Lima. The mestizo class forms the middle, making a living in a variety of professions including business, government, and the military.

The military government that operated from 1968 to 1980 somewhat minimized the power of wealthy Peruvians and benefited those below them economically. This was accomplished through land redistribution, transforming plantations into cooperatives, and extending the government's role in the general economy. The upshot of these reforms, however, was rampant inflation and unemployment that ultimately left many Peruvians just as poor as before. The general standard of living in Peru remains low, particularly in rural areas.

In a country that remains approximately 90 percent Catholic, family life is characterized by participation in fiestas organized around the sacraments and rites of passage. In addition, a distinctive aspect of Peruvian society at the local level is the tradition of *compadrazgo*, or the relationship between parent and godparent. This form of ritual co-parenthood has important economic and social as well as religious components. In Peru the relationship between the parents and godparents (*compadres*, or co-parents) is also highlighted to extend the network of fictive kin that can be called upon for support.

Nearly one-half of Peru's inhabitants are indigenous, particularly Quechua- and Aymara-speaking people. The Quechua trace their lineage to the Inca, who rose to power in the centuries before the arrival of Francisco Pizarro in the sixteenth century. In addition, approximately 100 other indigenous groups populate the rainforests in the eastern part of the country. These groups remain virtually isolated from the rest of Peruvian society. Almost 40 percent of the country's inhabitants are *mestizos*, people of mixed Spanish and Native American heritage. In addition, approximately 15 percent of Peruvians are of Spanish or other Caucasian heritage; the remainder trace their heritage from the African diaspora, **Japan**, or **China**.

The Spanish, led by Pizarro, arrived in 1531. Members of Roman Catholic religious orders came shortly thereafter. These included Dominicans, Franciscans, and Mercederians by 1550, Augustinians in 1551, and Jesuits in 1568.

During the colonial era the *encomienda* system operated to spread Christianity to the native population. Adopted in 1503, this system obligated indigenous peoples to supply labor and tribute to *encomenderos* (colonists who were usually large landowners) in return for protection and education in Christianity. In practice, however, the *encomienda* system more closely resembled slavery and was not eliminated until the late eighteenth century. However, the *hacendado* (large landowner) system—similar in many ways—persisted in the northern coastal area until the 1970s.

After Pizarro and the Spanish arrived in the sixteenth century, Catholicism was imposed on the native population, and the religious rituals and artifacts of the indigenous groups were suppressed or destroyed. Although Peru remains nearly 90 percent Roman Catholic, clear pre-Christian, pan-Andean elements of a religious cosmology can be seen. Because the Spanish Catholic Church used syncretism to convert the indigenous peoples, Catholic saints came to substitute for local gods, and Catholic shrines were superimposed on native sacred places. For example, the Christian God came to be associated with the Incan solar deity, and the Virgin Mary came to represent Pachamama or the Earth Mother. Meanwhile, certain local topographical features such as rocks or lakes continue to be held sacred (referred to as *huacas*) as sites inhabited by *apus* (spirits of natural sites) and *naupa machus* (ancient ancestors).

Ultimately, the combination of forced conversion and lack of ongoing priestly and sacramental involvement with much of the Peruvian population, particularly in rural areas, has resulted in a localized version of Roman Catholicism. For example, a tree that naturally resembled a cross might be dressed in a priestly cloth and venerated as both a Christian and a native Andean sacred symbol. In the more Hispanicized coastal areas of Peru, people follow pan-Catholic practices more closely, with an emphasis on venerating patron saints and manifestations of Christ and the crucifix.

LIFE-CYCLE RITES AND FOLK MEDICINE

Rites of passage celebrated in Peru are often connected to the sacraments of Catholicism. Birth is marked by a *bautismo*, or baptism, initiation by a coming-of-age party or wedding, and death by a funeral. Particularly in the coastal areas of Peru, death customs are distinctive and include a wake, formal *luto* (or mourning), and a funeral procession often accompanied by music. Generally, the individual life-cycle is punctuated by fiestas, for which the preparation and expense can be significant. This may result in a delay in receiving a sacrament—as when a family needs to save for as long as two years before they can afford to throw a lavish party for (and therefore baptize) a child. Similarly, in a ritual complex most clearly seen in coastal areas, when a family member dies, it is the duty of the recently bereaved to hold an all-night vigil wake during which food and drink such as *chicha* (corn alcohol) or beer and tortillas or similar food is traditionally served to the community. This may continue for nine nights according to the custom of the novena or nine-night praying of the rosary for the repose of a soul.

In addition, *curanderismo* (folk healing) and *brujería* (witchcraft) are still prevalent in the coastal areas of Peru such as Piura, a department in the far north of the country. Catholic images and rituals such as saints, crucifixes, rosaries, novenas, and processions are incorporated with aspects of African-derived religious beliefs including witchcraft. For example, Saint Ciprian is considered the patron saint of *brujería* and is represented as an old bearded monk with his book of prayers for different "cures" and a skeleton as companion. This syncretism is especially clear in the case of *rezadores* or *santiguadores* (those who pray or use holy water) who cure by a combination of prayers and sprinkling of holy water and have a *mesa* (table) filled with images of Saint Ciprian and Saint Martin of Porres among others.

MYTHS, LEGENDS, AND FOLKTALES

Myths of ancient Inca Peru include creation stories about the god Viracocha—who created humans out of darkness after turning the first beings into stones—and the well-known "Coniraya [also known as Coniraya Viracocha] and Cahuillaca," a tale in which the god Coniraya pursues and fathers a child with Cahuillaca, only to have her reject him as a potential suitor. The tale ends with Coniraya taunting society from the upland villages. Among the myths still in oral circulation today is the tale of "The Condor Seeks a Wife," which tells a somewhat similar tale about loss of innocence and the separation of the genders. In this tale a woman is tricked into marrying a condor when he appears to her in human form and later convinces her to scratch his back—which precipitates his transformation into a condor. She is homesick and hungry, though the condor tries to be a kind husband. Eventually a parrot returns the woman to her mother and is punished by being torn to pieces: the origin of today's parrots. Also in circulation are modern fables and animal tales, including "Why the Fox Has a Huge Mouth" and "The Mouse Husband."

A post-Columbian myth cycle about the culture hero Inkarri circulates in the contemporary southern Andes. This tale prophesies the return of the Inca to overcome Spanish-*mestizo* domination and return rule of Peru to the Quechua as descendants of the Inca. In this myth cycle the ninth dynastic Inca Pachakuti clearly resembles the god Inkarri: both are the offspring of a sun-god father and a mortal woman, and both have supernatural powers.

Sculpted stele representing the god Viracocha, a creator deity originally worshipped by pre-Inca inhabitants of Peru. A god of rain, he was believed to have created the sun and the moon on Lake Titicaca. (Werner Forman/Art Resource, NY)

A host of local legends cover both supernatural and secular themes. For example, in the northern department of Piura, these stories tell about subjects ranging from the origin of patron saints to the exploits of famous military leaders. The tale of "La Virgen de las Mercedes de Paita" (The Virgin of Mercy of Paita) relates the miracle of the statue of the Virgen de las Mercedes—later the basis of veneration by townspeople: when pirates tried to raid the chapel and steal the statue of the Virgin, they were unable to decapitate it with their swords. "Castilla y Los Piuranos" tells about the nineteenth-century governor Ramon Castilla, who upon becoming a military leader, they say, retained his special preference for Piuranos when it came to deserters. Similarly, in the Cajamarca area the legend of "La Cruz Maldita" (The Cursed Cross) relates the tragic tale of two young lovers and an evil friar.

Contemporary Quechua folktales collected from San Martin incorporate tales in Quechua as well as Spanish, including well-known animal tales such as that about the turtle and the hare ("El conejo que compitió una carrera") and "Una señorita hija de un viudo" (A Young Woman, Daughter of a Widower) with parallels to Cinderella and containing the **motif** of impossible tasks.

The etic categories of myths, legends, and folktales are clearly found in Peruvian folklore. From an emic perspective, however, there is a tendency to categorize Quechua verbal art forms on the basis of spatial distinctions with attention to the setting of narrated events. Such stories break down into *kwintu* and *leyenda*. *Kwintus* are those whose action takes place in an area that remains undefined, whereas *leyendas* center upon a place identified by local toponyms.

PROVERBS AND RITUALIZED INSULTS

Proverbs are another form of Peruvian folklore. Popular themes include agriculture, cattle herding, agricultural labor, folk medicine, astronomy, and jurisprudence. Many of these proverbs might be characterized as fatalistic, but another way to view them would be as commonsensical or practical. For example: "*Cristal vasullam vidaqa, sas nispa urmaykun, chall nispa chayaspa, manana impayas kutimuq*" (Spanish: *La vida es como un vaso de crystal, se cae, se rompe y ya no vuelve*. English: Life is like a crystal vase; it falls, breaks, and doesn't return), or "*Junan noqapaq, pazarin qampaq*" (*Hoy para mí, mañana para ti*. Today for me; tomorrow for you). The latter might be compared to the English-language proverb, "But for the grace of God go I."

Ritualized insult and verbal dueling also figure in Peruvian folklore. The Quechua genre of *tratanacuy*, particularly popular in Ayacucho, consists of formularized insults exchanged between individuals—for example: "*Mojino Senqa Maqta*" (*Indio de cara sucia*. Indian with a dirty face). In Morropon, located in the northern department of Piura, the genre of the *cumanaña*, in which poetry is composed using a combination of conventional formulas and improvisation to comment upon current situations or offer a challenge to another person, is still practiced.

POETRY AND FOLKSONGS

Folk poetry, meanwhile, in agrarian communities has always had a communal quality and multiple functions. It played a vital role in agricultural tasks and the daily life of the community. Themes include love, agriculture, and departure. Andean music is characterized by a rhythmic irregularity and asymmetry, and most Quechua songs are composed in a pentatonic scale. Quechua folksongs are distinctive for their parallelism of metaphors and themes. Another trope found in some Quechua folk poetry is called *qenqo*, a rhetorical figure that involves circumlocution. Quechua folksongs and poetry are typically described as having a sad quality, though certainly joy and sarcasm are to be found as well, particularly in songs related to *carnaval* or *pukllay*. For example, the following song relates an attitude of contempt (the Spanish and English translations follow):

En el morro de Ahuaycha una botella vacia,	On the nose of Ahuaycha an empty bottle,
en el morro de Acraquia una botella vacia.	On the nose of Acraquia an empty bottle.
¿Con qué cosa tuya vamos a confrontarnos?	With what are you going to confront us?
¿Con qué cosa tuya vamos a preguntarnos?	With what are you going to question us?

Two particularly popular Quechua folksong genres are the *huayno* and the *yaravi*. *Huaynos* are distinctive in juxtaposing happy-sounding polyphonic tunes sung in 4/4 time with melancholy themes, though not all *huaynos* are sad in tone. An example of a typically plaintive-sounding *huayno* lyric would be "Ayacuchano Huérfano Pajarillo":

Ayacuchano	One from Ayacucho,
huérfano pajarillo	little orphan bird
a que has venido	that has come
a estos lugares	to these places,
alza tu vuelo	your flight takes off.
vamos a tu tierra	Let's go to your land
donde tus padres	where your parents
lloran tu ausencia.	weep for your absence.

The *yaravi* actually has the same music as the *huayno* but is played more slowly. It may also be characterized as having a more tragic tone than the *huayno*, though the lyrics may not necessarily correspond to the musical tone:

En mi pueblo de Santiago	In my home town of Santiago
al Apostol veneramos	We venerate the apostle
porque siempre nos defiende	Because he always takes care of us
y nos colma de milagros.	And heaps miracles upon us.

Certain folksong genres are associated with particular festivals or calendar customs, such as singing *villancicos* (Christmas carols) during Christmas or singing and dancing the *marinera* during the festival of the Virgen de la Puerta (Virgin of the Door) in the department of La Libertad. The *marinera*, a fast and lively song and dance style, originated in the coastal area of Peru and is related to the Chilean *cueca*. This song tends to be an expression of affection for a particular woman:

Cuando yo veo que miras	When I see you looking,
que miras a algún galán	Looking at some ladies' man,
siento que mi alma se parte	I feel that my heart is breaking,
se parte por la mitad.	Breaking in half.

A number of traditional handmade musical instruments are created in Peru. These include the *travesera*, a panpipe constructed from reeds commonly used to play *huayno* music. It is usually played with one hand while the other hand plays a drum made of a hollowed-out tree trunk covered in cowskin. Other traditional instruments include the *quena, antara, pinkullo, pututo, wacra pucu, clarin de Cajamarca, tinya, wankar, cajón, charango*, and indigenous harp. The *quena* also figures in a popular legend from Huamanga about a priest who fell in love with a girl and after her death made a *quena* of her bone and played it until he went mad.

FESTIVALS AND CELEBRATIONS

Peruvian festivals can be assigned to several different categories. The first and main type of festival in Peru is the religious festival (538 total), the majority of which have as their major theme saints the Virgin Mary, Christ and the Christ child, or crosses. For saints (51 saints and a total of 213 festivals), the most popular are Saint Isidore the Worker, patron of farmers (15 May), Saint John the Baptist, patron of cattle (24 June), Saint Peter, patron of fisherman (29 June), Saint James the Apostle, associated with the bearing of the cattle (end of June), Saint Rose of Lima, patron of Peru and the Americas (30 August), and Saint Martin of Porres, patron of social justice in Peru (3 November). Festivals for the Virgin Mary (39 different Virgins, celebrated in 185 festivals) include the Virgin of Candelaria (2 February), Virgin of Carmen (16 July), Virgin of the Snows (5 August), Virgin of the Assumption (15 August), Virgin of the Nativity and of Cocharcas (8 September), Virgin of the Mercies (24 September), and the Immaculate Conception (8 December). Those for Christ and the Christ child (86 festivals) include the Adoration of the Child in January and the Lord of the Miracles in October. Festivals dedicated to crosses (42 local festivals) take place particularly during May and September. In addition, there are ninety-nine so-called folkloric or customary festivals that focus on activities including artisan and farming fairs, Peruvian stepping-horse and regional dances, and other community celebrations such as Day of the Compadre. Finally, there are civil fiestas (25 total) to commemorate the founding of cities. The majority of these festivals are local and religious in character.

The following are highlights of the Peruvian festival calendar throughout the year. In January, New Year's celebrations take place throughout Peru, with variations according to specific locale. In the department of Huancavelica the Lost Child Feast is celebrated dramatizing the adoration of the infant Christ. From 9 until

16 February the Feast of the Virgin of Candelaria occurs in several areas of Peru, including Puno, characterized like other festivals by music, dancing, and traditional costumes. In mid-February Carnival in Cajamarca is celebrated. Characteristic of *carnaval* here is the raising of *unshas* (trees strewn with fruits and gifts) that are cut during dancing. In Ica during the last week of February the Black Summer Festival is celebrated, focusing on typical Afro-Peruvian dances such as the *lando, alcatraz,* and *festejo. Lando*—with origins in Angola (where it is called *londu*)—was brought by slaves to the coastal areas of Peru to form a dance with a combination of Spanish and African rhythms. *Alcatraz* is a couple's dance during which a woman holds a tissue between her legs while the man dances around her with a candle with which he tries to light the tissue. If it catches fire, according to tradition, the two belong together. *Festejo* involves a musical competition between men playing *cajones,* a musical box drum made from wood. In April, Holy Week is celebrated throughout Peru in areas including Arequipa, Ayacucho, Cusco, Junin, and Piura. Each locale has particular ways of celebrating the week. For example, in Morropon, located in the department of Piura, a Camino de la Cruz (Way of the Cross) procession takes place on Good Friday, when it is customary to eat a dish called *malarrabia,* made with mashed plantains and accompanied by cheese and olives. In southern Peru (including Cuzco, Ayacucho, and Huancavelica) the festival of the Virgin of Carmen is celebrated in mid-July. At the end of July in Apurimac the Yawar Feast or Feast of Blood is observed by trapping the condor and then having bullfights with it before it is released in a celebration marked by dancing. From mid to late October the Señor de los Milagros festival is celebrated in Lima among other places in Peru. The original image of the Lord of the Miracles was painted by a slave on a wall in 1650. The procession has the painting placed on a silver- and gold-covered platform. Finally, the Madonna of the Door from Otuzco is celebrated in La Libertad in the third week of December.

Generally speaking, each village, town, and city in Peru has its own church with its own patron saint or religious figure as the basis of an annual festival. The major festival in Peru is in honor of the Lord of the Miracles (October). Devotion to the Lord of the Miracles began in the colonial era with the religious and social discrimination against blacks and indigenous peoples. Slaves erected a chapel, on the wall of which an anonymous artist in 1651 painted an image of the crucified Christ that is said to have later survived a massive earthquake. This is the basis of the annual festival. In addition, native Andean conceptions of the sacredness of topographical features persist and have become intertwined with Christianity. This can be most clearly seen in the celebration of the Feast of Corpus Christi in Cuzco. Because the festival overlaps with the Inca June solstice called Inti Raymi as well as native Andean harvest festivals, the native and Christian traditions have become intertwined.

In addition, there are several distinctively Peruvian Catholic festivals which tend to relate to natural disasters such as earthquakes, resulting in the veneration of "disaster saints" in a manner combining Catholic with Andean spiritual concerns. One of these "disaster saints" is the Señor de los Temblores (Lord of the Earthquakes), who serves as patron of Cuzco and who commemorates a great earthquake in 1650. Similarly, in Huanchaco, near Trujillo on the northern coast, the Virgen del Perpetuo Socorro (Virgin of Perpetual Help) is celebrated in commemoration of an earthquake in 1619.

GAMES, ARTS, AND CRAFTS

Dice games that were customary in the ancient Inca Empire have survived among Quechua-speaking peoples in Peru. This game was typically played after a death to determine the distribution of the deceased's possessions, to protect survivors from the contagion or cause of death, and to honor the dead. The game known as *picha* or *taba* is played with a four- or five-sided die usually made of bone. The players arrange themselves on either side of the corpse and toss the dice over the corpse to players on the other side. The winner is the person who throws the die upright, and the prize is usually an animal. The game may also be used as a form of divination to determine, for example, the cause of an illness.

Among the many arts and crafts currently created in Peru today are masks. Masks are made for use in folk dances, particularly in the regions of Puno, Cuzco, and Junín. Masks made for ritual dances include *Los shapish* (made of cardboard-stone and with a terrified expression used in war dances), *Los condors* (condors—used in totemic dances), and *El huacón* (made of carved wood with a grotesque expression and having a moralizing function). Those made for humorous dances include *Los reilones* (a mask with a humorous expression), *Calistrada* (made of cloth), *Corcovado* (representing the Spanish), *Avelino* (made of chamois in simple designs with added pieces and having a commemorative function), and *Machu* (made of woven wool and wearing a normal expression). Those made for satirical purposes include *Chonguino* (constructed from a mesh of fine wire, representing the Spanish), *Pachahuara* (made of bandana), *Huatrila* (made from a mold with added pieces and wearing a satirical expression), and *Viejos* (made of plaster with simple molds).

Other folk arts include the well-known Torito de Pukara and the tradition of *retablos*. The Torito de Pukara (Bull of Pukara), made from clay and decorated with different colors, is considered a kind of good luck charm and is associated with the fecundity of cattle. The devotional art known as *retablos* is a also a popular form of folk art. These are three-dimensional representations of scenes, often religious, made from potato paste and painted bright colors.

CHALLENGES OF THE MODERN WORLD

Like the indigenous people of other countries, the Quechua- and Aymara-speaking people of Peru are adapting to the increase in recent decades of cultural **tourism** and its effects on their folk traditions. An example is Taquile Island, one of the few remaining areas in Peru where exquisitely woven textiles and traditional dress are still created during the course of daily life; its position as a prime tourist destination led to the commercialization of the cloth in the 1960s. One consequence of the popularity of the tourist market in the community has been that the demands on their time required by catering to tourists has left little time for weaving.

BIBLIOGRAPHY

Alva Plascencia, Juan Luis. 1968. *Leyendas y cuentos peruanos*. Lima: Ediciones El Quique.

Baquerizo, Manuel. 1998. La poesía quechua: De lo oral a lo escrito. In *Folklore: Sobre dioses, ritos y saberes andinos*, edited by Luís Millones and others. Huancayo, Peru: Sociedad Científica Andina de Folklore. 21–43.

Bierhorst, John. 1976. *Black Rainbow: Legends of the Incans and Myths of Ancient Peru.* New York: Farrar, Straus and Giroux.

Cuentas Ormachea, Enrique. 1995. *Presencia de Puno en la cultura popular.* Lima: Empresa Editora Nueva Facultad.

Dean, Carolyn. 1999. *Inka Bodies and the Body of Christ: Corpus Christi in Colonial Cuzco, Peru.* Durham: Duke University Press.

Dobyns, Henry, and Paul Doughty. 1976. *Peru: A Cultural History.* New York: Oxford University Press.

Engl, Lieselotte, and Theo Engl. 1969. *Twilight of Ancient Peru: The Glory and Decline of the Inca Empire,* translated by Alisa Jaffe. New York: McGraw-Hill.

Frisancho Pineda, David. 1986. *Curanderismo y brujería en la costa peruana.* Lima: Talleres Gráficos de Lytograf.

Helguero Seminario, Federico. 1974. *De la patria vieja: Antología de cuentos y leyendas piuranas.* Piura: Universidad de Piura.

Hijar Soto, Donato Amador. 1990. *Raices del folklore peruano.* Lima: Editorial Inkari E.I.R.L.

Howard-Malverde, Rosaleen. 1990. *The Speaking of History: "Willapaakushayki" or Quechua Ways of Telling the Past.* London: University of London Institute of Latin American Studies.

Hudson, Rex. 1992. *Peru: A Country Study.* Washington, DC: Federal Research Division, Library of Congress. September.

Instituto Lingüístico de Verano. 1981. *Aku Parlanakuypachi: Cuentos folklóricos de los quechua de San Martín.* Verano: Instituto Lingüístico de Verano.

Karsten, Rafael. 1930. *Ceremonial Games of the South American Indians.* Helsinki: University of Helsinki.

Leonardini, Nanda. 1996. *Calendario de fiestas en el Perú.* Lima: Alamar.

Martínez Parra, Reynaldo. 1985. *Paremiología quechua.* Lima: Máximo Ascarza Flores.

Orellana Valeriano, Simeon. 1998. Las mascaras en el valle de Jatun Mayu. In *Folklore: Sobre dioses, ritos y saberes andinos,* edited by Luis Millones and others. Huancayo: Sociedad Científica Andina de Folklore. 107–123.

Rodrigo, Luis, and Edwin Montoya Roja. 1997–1999. *La sangre de los cerros: Antologia de la poesía quechua se canta en Perú.* Lima: Universidad Nacional Federico Villareal.

Sallnow, Michael. 1987. *Pilgrims of the Andes: Regional Cults in Cusco.* Washington, DC: Smithsonian Institution Press.

Smith, Robert. 1975. *The Art of the Festival, As Exemplified by the Fiesta to the Patroness of Otuzco, La Virgen de la Puerta.* Lawrence: University of Kansas Publications in Anthropology.

Valencia Vargas, Faustino. 1961. *Algunos aspectos del folklore de la convención.* Cuzco: Editorial H. G. Rozas.

Vivanco, Alejandro. 1930. *Cantares de Ayacucho.* Ayacucho, Peru: Ediciones Folklore.

———. 1988. *Cien temas del folklore peruano.* Lima: Distribuidora BENDEZU E.I.R.

Zorn, Elayne. 2004. Ancient Andean Cloth in the 21st Century: Crafts, Tourism, or Both? Paper presented at the 2004 Florida Folklore Society Annual Meeting, Orlando, FL, 21 February.

Natalie Underberg

QUECHUA

GEOGRAPHY AND HISTORY

The Quechua (or Quichua) language is spoken by some 8.5 million people in the northern and central part of the Andes mountain range of South America. Quechua speakers comprise a wide spectrum of people from village farmers in fairly isolated rural districts to largely Hispanized but still Quechua-Spanish bilingual townspeople in provincial capitol towns, to proletarianized miners and other workers in urban centers. Quechua is spoken not only by rural native Andeans but also by urban *mestizos* (literally "mixed-bloods") whose cultural practices draw on a mix of Hispanic and indigenous cultures. Thus one cannot speak of a single Quechua people or culture. On the other hand, there are continuities in the folklore of Quechua speakers from **Ecuador** through **Peru** and Bolivia and into northern Argentina. Many of these cultural commonalities are also shared with speakers of other indigenous languages such as the Aymara of Bolivia and southern Peru, meaning that it may be better to think of the folklore, not of specific ethnic groups or language communities, but of multiethnic and multilingual regions within the Andean area.

One factor shaping the folklore of native Andeans, including Quechua speakers throughout the region, is the precipitous topography of the Andes themselves. Indigenous perceptions of the mountain environment with its variety of ecological zones and micro niches at different elevations have formed the basis for many beliefs and expressive practices. The organization of rural subsistence is based on understandings of how different crops and other resources are distributed over different ecological zones in the mountains and valleys with important implications for indigenous cosmology and esthetic expression.

The region today inhabited by Quechua speakers largely corresponds to the area covered by the former Inca Empire, a multiethnic and multilingual polity. The common Inca practice of relocating entire ethnic groups from one part of their territory to another (*mitimaes*) resulted in a patchwork of populations with similarities still found in place names, names of ethnic groups, and expressive practices in widely separated areas. Quechua was the *lingua franca* and administrative language of the empire, but the Incas generally followed a policy of allowing ethnic groups within their empire to keep their culture and language. This situation changed with the coming of the Spanish in 1532 and the beginning of the colonial period. The expansion of Quechua to the detriment of other languages did not actually begin in earnest until the colonial period, as the Spanish used Quechua as a vehicle for the Christianization of the population.

RELIGIOUS BELIEFS, LIFE-CYCLE RITUALS, AND FOLKTALES AND RIDDLES

Spanish Christian missionary activity resulted in a complex syncretism of sixteenth- and seventeenth-century Iberian devotional Catholicism with existing indigenous religious beliefs and practices, resulting in a religious system that intermingled the two sources. Catholic saints were identified with indigenous Andean deities and concepts of the supernatural such as the Iberian patron saint Santiago (the apostle St. James the Greater, whom Jesus called "son of thunder" because of his violent temper) becoming identified with the Andean god of thunder and lightning Illapa and the Virgin Mary with Pachamama, the Andean Earth Mother. Catholic celebrations of All Souls and All Saints Day became intertwined with already existing indigenous beliefs about and practices surrounding the dead to the extent that it is difficult to distinguish specifically "Spanish" and "indigenous" traits in current religious beliefs and practices.

This complex syncretism can also be seen in beliefs and practices about sickness and bodily health. The traditional healers of the Kallawaya people of northwestern

Bolivia understand the body as a hydraulic system in which different kinds of fluid circulate. Certain aspects of their body concept and theory of illness resemble European humoral theory, though researchers have yet to decide if they assimilated this theory from the Spanish or if it is an independent Andean invention. Herbs used by Kallawaya curers include both native Andean species and European plants introduced by the Spanish.

Life-cycle rituals play an important part in Quechua life, from a child's first haircut (*uma ruthukuy*) to elaborate mourning rites for the dead. In the rural areas of Cochabamba, Bolivia, *Todos Santos* (All Saints Day) is celebrated with festivities at the local cemetery. Graves of the recent dead are decorated with small bread figures of babies and doves, and villagers go from grave to grave chanting prayers for the dead. In the neighboring region of northern Potosí, people build elaborate altars over graves including decorated ladders to aid the soul's journey to heaven. Women also perform elaborate Quechua lamentation songs for the recent dead in Bolivia and Ecuador. Rituals for children who have died (*wawa velorio*) are particularly elaborate in highland Ecuador.

Supernatural characters do not play a large role in Quechua folktales (*willay*), which are dominated by animal stories. The fox (*atuq*) is especially prominent in these stories, in which he is a trickster who constantly gets himself in trouble because of his arrogance and short-sightedness. Other common characters include the condor and the rabbit. One particularly well-known story involves the fox challenging the condor's supremacy as ruler of the high altitudes. To settle the dispute, the two agree to spend the night at the top of a mountain. The fox cannot stand the cold and freezes to death.

Riddle games are common among children. Quechua riddles often involve animals and other objects from the natural environment, as in the following examples from southern Peru:

Day or night, it never walks on feet.—A snake.

A town with no streets.—A honeycomb.

You knock him down, roll up his sleeves, cook him, and eat him.—Corn on the cob.

SONGS AND MUSIC

Quechua verbal art is especially developed in song. Prominent here is the singing of short verses (*coplas*) in the form of song dueling (*takipayanaku*), which is common not only among rural peasants but also among urban *mestizos* in the valleys of Cochabamba, Bolivia. The fiesta of *Carnaval* (Carnival) especially is an occasion for performing song duels. Singers challenge each other to improvise humorous, earthy retorts to each other, as in the following two verses:

Challenge me with a verse, and I'll challenge you.
I'll marry you off to my old dog.

I'll sing and I'll dance.
Singing like this, I'll make you wet your pants.

The singing of the Quechua *qhashwa* performed by young people around Cuzco in southern Peru also may include such song dueling. Solo singing with instrumental accompaniment characterizes the *mestizo huayno* (also *huayño*), the characteristic couple's dance performed throughout Peru and Bolivia, and also known in Ecuador as the *sanjuanito*. *Huayno* texts may be in Quechua, Spanish, or a mixture of both and often treat themes of loss, sadness, and abandonment as in the following example from a Peruvian Quechua *huayno*:

> My mother gave birth to me
> In the ravine of silence
> Saying "Let her be eaten
> By condors and lions."
>
> The condor doesn't want me.
> The lion doesn't want me.
> They said to me,
> "You must pay for your faults."

Besides these songs sung for entertainment, different local traditions of ritualized worksongs associated with agricultural and pastoral tasks such as sowing, harvesting, cleaning irrigation channels, and animal branding or marking also exist. These songs are disappearing in many areas as traditional agricultural techniques change with the expansion of modern technology.

Fiestas such as Carnival are also a time for the performance of instrumental music. Especially common among Quechua speakers is performance on various kinds of flutes and panpipes. These instruments are played in large ensembles in which different sizes of a single type of instrument are played with or without drum accompaniment. Different kinds of flutes and string instruments are not mixed within a single ensemble. In southern Peru and Bolivia, panpipes are typically played using a hocket technique whereby the notes needed to play a melody are divided between two separate instruments played by different players. Each player fits his notes between those played by the other players in order to create a complete melody. In addition to these instrumental musical traditions, Quechua youth often use guitar-like string instruments called *charangos* to accompany song. Musical performance is strongly gendered, with men playing musical instruments and women singing.

A general principle throughout Quechua communities in Bolivia and southern Peru is the division of the year into musical seasons with different instruments

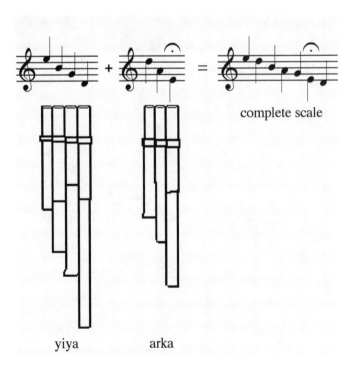

complete scale

yiya   arka

Distribution of pitches in the two halves of a *julajula* panpipe, northern Potosí, Bolivia. (Diagram by Thomas Solomon)

Julajula panpipe players, northern Potosí, Bolivia. (Photograph by Thomas Solomon)

and song types. An important fiesta in the religious calendar and agricultural cycle marks the beginning of each season, and the seasons are also punctuated by other festivals. The details of these musical calendars vary according to region or even from village to village within a single area. For example, in northern Potosí, Bolivia, the *paray timpu* (rainy season) from *Todos Santos* (1 November) until the movable fiesta of *Carnaval* (generally mid- to late February) is a time for performance on vertical duct flutes with whistle-type mouthpieces called *pinkillus* and on large string instruments known as *qhunqutas*, which accompany the song genre *wayñu*. The *kujicha timpu* (dry season, literally "harvest time") from *Paskwa* (Easter) until the end of October is a time for performance on various panpipes (*julajulas*, *sikus*, *sikuras*), vertical notched flutes (*lichiwayus*), and small stringed instruments known as *ch'ili charanku* and *ansaldo*, which accompany the song genre known as *takiy*. Traditionally in this region, no music is performed during *Kwarisma* (Lent).

Besides the *charango*, adapted from Iberian lute instruments, other instruments taken over by Quechua musicians from European sources include the harp and violin, often played together, and the brass band. All these instruments may be used in performing the Peruvian *mestizo huayno*.

The agricultural-religious festival is the primary context for musical performance, which is typically part of a larger ritual complex. Music and costumed dance are frequently associated with pilgrimage and other kinds of movement through space such as boundary-marking ceremonies. Communities in northern Potosí, Bolivia, make pilgrimages during dry season fiestas to *mestizo* towns that function as ceremonial centers. These fiestas are part of a regional cult of the cross, and each community brings its communal cross down to the church in town in order to have it blessed and recharged with spiritual power. During the pilgrimage from their home communities to the church in town, men continuously play panpipes called *julajulas*.

DRAMA AND THE *ENTRADA*

During the colonial period Spanish missionaries used drama as a way of teaching Catholic traditions. Presentations based on these religious dramas, depicting biblical stories or religious folktales such as the battle between Michael the Archangel and the Devil, continue to be offered today and include dialogue, music, and dance. Such dance-dramas often form part of larger fiesta celebrations.

In the urban areas of Bolivia, the fiesta often takes the form of the folkloric *entrada* (parade), such as the famous Carnival of Oruro or the fiesta of the Virgin of Urkupiña in Cochabamba. In these parades, large groups of costumed dancers perform stylized dance steps to the accompaniment of brass bands. The costumes of the individual groups may represent ethnic groups from various regions of Bolivia such as the Tarabuqueños from around Sucre, the Tobas from the southeastern Chaco region, or the Afro-Bolivian population of the lower Andean slopes of eastern La Paz Department, represented in the two dances called *morenada* and *saya*. The masks and costumes worn by dancers during such urban folkloric parades themselves constitute elaborate examples of material culture. In addition to costumes representing different indigenous groups from around Bolivia, animal characters including the bear and the condor are common as well as supernatural beings such as angels and devils. In the fiesta of the Virgen del Carmen in the town of Paucartambo in southern Peru, *mestizo* costumed dancers similarly impersonate indigenous groups from other regions of Peru or parody other social groups such as exploitative lawyers and government officials.

Diblada (devil dance), Llallagua, Potosí, Bolivia. The dancer with a cross is an angel, while the others are devils. (Photograph by Thomas Solomon)

SPORTS AND GAMES

In the valleys of Cochabamba in Bolivia, *Todos Santos* is the occasion for a unique swinging game involving *wayllunk'as*—large swings suspended from a high tree branch or tall wooden frame. The game involves swinging up very high and grabbing with one's feet baskets of flowers hung from high arches while singing traditional humorous verses about romance to the musical accompaniment of accordion or other instruments.

In northern Potosí, the dry-season pilgrimage festivals culminate in a ritual battle known as *tinku*. Fighters engage in a boxing match on the street in front of

Wayllunk'a swing game, Cochabamba, Bolivia. (Photograph by Thomas Solomon)

Tinku ritual battle, northern Potosí, Bolivia. (Photograph by Thomas Solomon)

the church. Opponents must come from two large opposing social groupings of ethnic groups roughly corresponding to high and low ecological zones with potatoes and corn as their respective identifying products. The fighters wear *monteras*, cowhide helmets resembling the metal helmets worn by Spanish *conquistadores*. Blood spilled during the fighting is said to fertilize the land for the upcoming growing season. Similar ritual battles take place in southern Peru and in the Otavalo region of Ecuador, where combatants trade strokes with whips aimed at each other's legs or hurl stones at each other with slings.

ARTS AND CRAFTS

Textile weaving is highly developed among the Quechua. Throughout the Andes one finds myriad local variations on the general principle of bilateral symmetry in textile design. According to this principle, the designs on the two halves of a textile, such as the figurative strips or broad colored bands of a blanket or carrying cloth, are mirror images of each other, arranged symmetrically around either side of a center line. Textiles such as woven belts (*chumpi*), scarves (*chupa*), and knitted caps (*ch'ulu*) may also incorporate complex geometric designs or animal motifs such as condors and llamas. Textiles may have ritual significance—for example, small woven bags (*ch'uspa*) used for carrying and ritually exchanging coca leaves.

CHALLENGES OF THE MODERN WORLD

As communities of Quechua speakers become more integrated into the larger state society, their expressive traditions become better known in the cities and are subject to incorporation into semi-official presentations of state "folklore." When performing in folkloric festivals or competitions sponsored and judged by non-Quechua city-dwellers, rural Quechua may adapt performance genres to the occasion by altering traditional texts, costumes, or performance practices. Folkloric ballet groups performing stylized versions of indigenous dances provide entertainment for the middle class in large cities.

New developments in Quechua folklore include the emergence since the 1960s of urban folkloric musical groups who perform stylized versions of rural indigenous music, including their own newly composed songs in Quechua. Representative of these groups is Los Kjarkas from Cochabamba, Bolivia, which was especially popular in the 1980s and 1990s. Departing from traditional rural practice, these groups typically mix different instruments such as notched flutes, panpipes, and *charangos* in a single ensemble, creating elaborate arrangements of traditional or newly composed tunes.

Globalization has also produced new contexts for Quechua folklore. Many Quechua musicians from Peru, Bolivia, and Ecuador travel to Europe and North America to perform and record albums as well as sell weavings and other handicrafts. A large Quechua-speaking community of migrants from southern Peru can be found in Washington, D.C. These migrants retain close ties to their home communities, returning home to Peru to take part in communal fiestas, even sponsoring fiestas with the new wealth they have earned overseas.

STUDIES OF QUECHUA FOLKLORE

The preeminent scholar in studies of Peruvian Quechua folklore was novelist and anthropologist José María Arguedas (1911–1969). In addition to his research, he also drew on his knowledge of Quechua folklore for his novels, several of which have been translated into English. In Bolivia pioneering folklorists include Manuel Rigoberto Paredes (1870–1950), Antonio Paredes-Candia (b. 1924), and Jesús Lara (1898–1980). Any of their many works are good starting points, though none has been translated into English. Stephan (1957) and Payne (2000) provide English translations of Quechua songs and stories. Contemporary anthropological studies such as those of Allen (2002), Bastien (1987), and Sallnow (1987) provide an understanding of Quechua folklore in context, focusing especially on ritual, religion, and cosmology. The Web site "Culture of the Andes" (www.andes.org) contains Quechua jokes, riddles, poetry, and songs with audio files and English and Spanish translations.

BIBLIOGRAPHY

Allen, Catherine J. 2002. *The Hold Life Has: Coca and Cultural Identity in an Andean Community.* 2nd edition. Washington, DC: Smithsonian Institution Press.

Arguedes, José María. 1970. *Mitos, leyendas y cuentos peruanos.* 2nd edition. Lima: Casa de la Cultura Perú.

———. 1985. *Yawar Fiesta*, translated by Frances Horning Barraclough. Austin: University of Texas Press.

Bastien, Joseph W. 1987. *Healers of the Andes: Kallawaya Herbalists and Their Medicinal Plants.* Salt Lake City: University of Utah Press.

Cohen, John. 1980. *Peruvian Weaving: A Continuous Warp—for 5,000 Years* (film). Berkeley: University of California Extension Center for Media and Independent Learning (25 minutes).

———. 1984. *Mountain Music of Peru* (film). Berkeley: University of California for Media and Independent Learning (60 minutes).

———. 1992. *Dancing with the Incas: Huayno Music of Peru* (film). Berkeley: University of California Center for Media and Independent Learning (58 minutes).

Lara, Jesus. 1985. *La literatura de los quechuas.* 4th edition. La Paz: Librería-Editorial Juventud.

López, Jaime, Willer Flores, and Catherine Letourneau. 1992. *Lliqllas Chayantakas.* La Paz: Programa de Autodesarrollo Campesino PAC–Potosí and Ruralter.

Meyerson, Julia. 1990. *'Tambo: Life in an Andean Village.* Austin: University of Texas Press.

Mountain Music of Peru. Vols. I–II (sound recording). 1991, 1994. Smithsonian Folkways CD 40020, 40406.

Paredes, Manuel Rigoberto. 1970. *El arte folklórico de Bolivia.* La Paz: Ediciones Camarlinghi.

Paredes-Candia, Antonio. 1976. *Fiestas populares de Bolivia.* 2 volumes. La Paz: Ediciones ISLA and Librería–Editorial Popular.

Payne, Johnny. 2000. *She-Calf and Other Quechua Folk Tales.* Albuquerque: University of New Mexico Press.

Sallnow, Michael J. 1987. *Pilgrims of the Andes: Regional Cults in Cuzco.* Washington, DC: Smithsonian Institution Press.

Stephan, Ruth. 1957. *The Singing Mountaineers: Songs and Tales of the Quechua People.* Collected by José María Arguedas. Austin: University of Texas Press.

Traditional Music of Peru. Vol. 1, *Festivals of Cusco* (sound recording). 1995. Smithsonian Folkways CD 40466.

Traditional Music of Peru. Vol. 3, *Cajamarca and the Colca Valley* (sound recording). 1997. Smithsonian Folkways CD 40468.

Traditional Music of Peru. Vol. 6, *The Ayacucho Region* (sound recording). 2001. Smithsonian Folkways CD 40449.

Thomas Solomon

SERTÃO (BRAZIL)

Geography and History

In the interior of northeast Brazil, three cultural traditions come into the contact: the Portuguese, the Tupi-Guarani, and the Kariri, one of the Jê-speaking people. The last is the most influential component of Sertanejo, the culture found in this vast region, which includes the Sertão (the southern and central sections of the state of Ceara and the western portions of Pernambuco and Paraiba), the *agreste* (central Pernambuco and Paraiba), the southern areas of Alagoas and Sergipe, and the north and central portions of Bahia.

The term *Sertanejo* comes from the Portuguese *sertão*, which designates a dry, un-inhabited area. It is used in this context to refer to semi-arid northeastern Brazil, whose climate has been a major factor in the lifeways of the inhabitants. Thanks to the native vegetation (especially *caatinga*—a Tupi-derived word that refers to plants that remain dry for most of the year), open fields, and mountains, Portuguese colonization introduced livestock, particularly sheep and goats, which required large grazing areas and little human supervision. This pastoral economy produced a population dispersed in centers throughout the culture area. Many of these population centers became cities; others remained small communities formed by extended family structures that emphasized endogamous marriages within clans.

The *vaqueiro* (or cowboy) appears here as the prototype figure who works at raising cattle for himself or for others. He learned to live a solitary and independent life. But the construction of dwellings or other large-scale projects brought *vaqueiros* together in a kind of communal labor, called *mutirão*, which followed indigenous patterns. Other occasions for gathering have included religious holidays and family events such as weddings, baptisms, and funerals.

Farming practices respond to climate. Horticulturalists grow beans, corn, manioc, and sweet potatoes in the valley and the foothills of the *serras*. Diet is therefore predictable and simple, utilizing a limited variety of vegetables, cereals, and manioc flour. To these staples some families add beef and the meat from hunting armadillo, guinea pig, *mocó* (a rock mouse), and other small game.

KARIRI CULTURE

The Kariri people have lost most of their indigenous culture, but it once had significant influence in the region. Positioned around a central yard, their houses were built of split bamboo and covered with a mud mixture called *sapé*. People slept in hammocks made from a local fiber called *caroá*. A newly born boy was immediately rubbed against a wild pig, considered a protector animal, and then bathed with *aluá*, a drink made of fermented corn. This was done to ensure that he would grow up to be a good hunter and a good drinker. His lip was perforated when he reached adolescence. During festivities, the Kariri drink *aluá* and *caium*, made from fermented yuca. But religious rituals called for *jurema*, a hallucinogenic drink prepared from the roots of a plant of the same name. They also smoke tobacco in pipes made from clay or cedar wood and also in hollow gourds (*calabazas*), which have been carved with mouth and eyes to allow the sacred tobacco smoke to emerge. A special flute made from the femur of the *caracará*, a bird considered a protector, was allowed to be seen by few men. Upon someone's death, his or her bones were burned, ground up, and then mixed with corn flour to be consumed later by relatives. The shaman, or *bisamu*, had a very important role not only as a healer but also as an intermediary with the divinity. It was he who could talk to Badzé, a god of the forest and of smoke, and to Badzé's two children, Podita and Warakidze, gods of rain and hunting. The supreme god is Nhinhó, a practically inaccessible deity. Periodically, the Kariri would retire to isolated places to perform purification rituals to expiate sins. These rituals would usually take place at the time of harvesting *ouricuri*, a type of coconut.

RELIGIOUS BELIEFS

Sertanejo religious practices mix Roman Catholic elements with indigenous traditions and especially emphasize penitence performed during religious processions and pilgrimages. The most common destinations for pilgrimage are places that recall the sufferings of Jesus Christ and the saints: Bom Jesús da Lapa and Monte Santo (in Bahia), Nossa Senhora das Dolores (in Juazeiro, Ceará), and São Francisco das Chagas (in Canindé, Ceará). Dressed in religious garments, pilgrims take long trips by bus or truck or perhaps on foot in search of some spiritual or material benefit. Most pilgrimages fulfill a promise made in exchange for God's positive response to a request. In some sanctuaries, pilgrims are attracted by a popular preacher whose word and testimonies draw large crowds. Examples include Antonio Consejero in Canudos, Bahia, during the nineteenth century, Father Cicero Batista in Juazeiro, Ceará, in the mid-twentieth century, and most recently Fraile Damião in Canindé, Ceará. In small cities and towns groups of penitents spend Lent praying the rosary and seeking forgiveness for the sins of the entire community.

Popular religious traditions directed against the evil eye or *quebranto*, negative spiritual energies that some people possess, are still practiced. To protect themselves from these forces, people may use a *figa*, a representation of a closed fist that signifies that the body is "closed" or protected. Children, who are considered to be particularly vulnerable, must wear the *figa* tied with a red ribbon to the right arm. If preventive measures fail, a person afflicted with the evil eye must consult a *curandeiro* (shaman), who will remove the curse using a cross made from the leaves of the *ruda* (*Ruta graveolens*).

To cure livestock of worms and flies, people collect a stone from near the tracks of the animal and pray a specific prayer that ends with the Lord's Prayer while holding the stone. Healing will occur within a few days.

FOLKTALES AND FOOD

Sertanejo folklore includes stories about indigenous and European-derived legendary creatures such as the Caipora and the Lobisomen (half-human and half-wolf). The Paid a Mata (Forest Father) is a half-human, half-animal man-eating creature of considerable size, especially its claws and ears. He cannot be killed by a firearm unless targeted directly in the navel. Meanwhile the Mãi da Mata (Forest Mother) protects the forests and the animals that live there. According to the Sertanejos in the state of Pernambuco, those who mistreat nature receive a beating from her and become lost in the forest.

Sertão meals are rich and varied, emphasizing such ingredients as beef, corn, manioc, and beans. Typical dishes include *buchada*, which is prepared from the entrails of a lamb or goat chopped and mixed with herbs and slow-cooked for five hours. *Sarapatel* is made from ox blood, kidneys, and liver, also cooked with herbs. *Cuscus* is steam-cooked cornmeal, and *saltet mugunzá* is made from soft white corn, beans, and beef. *Tapioca* is a thin mush made from manioc flour. Other important dishes in the regional culinary tradition are *pirão*, *pamonha*, and *canjica*, also called sweet *munguzá* and are similar to the *caipira* tradition.

MUSIC AND FESTIVALS

Important musical traditions of the Sertanejo culture are the *aboio*, a solitary song which *vaqueiros* sing while herding cattle, and the *forró*, a happy and vibrant dance. The latter is very popular and has dancing couples execute their rhythmic movements to the accompaniment of accordion, triangle, and percussion without ever lifting their feet from the ground. A flute quartet, the *pífano band*, derives from Kariri tradition. It performs both secular and sacred music. It contributes to the festivities at parties and on holidays. The musicians also perform in church, honoring a community's patron saint before the main altar.

Traditional Sertão festivities correspond primarily to those of the Roman Catholic liturgical calendar: especially Holy Week, the feast day of the community's patron saints, and the feasts of some of the more celebrated saints such as St. Joseph. The month of June provides the context for several important feast days: those of St. Anthony, St. John, and St. Peter. Celebrations of these feast days draw upon indigenous patterns, since they occur at much the same time in the annual cycle when Kariri cyclic festivals occurred. European-based traditions such as bonfires and dances assume a native character. The Festa do Milho, or corn fiesta, for example, focuses on consuming indigenous foods made from corn, especially pastries such as *canjica, mungunzá,* and *pamonha*. Also featured are *pipoca* (popcorn) and charcoal-broiled corn on the cob. The preferred drink is *quentão*, formerly made from fermented corn or manioc but nowadays made from *cachaca* and ginger. These holidays also provide the contexts for weddings and *compadrios* (baptisms), since priests may not be available at other times. These rituals may occur at the bonfire, and weddings often end with a satiric dance called the *quadrilla*.

The *Bumba-meu-boi* is a folk drama performed at Christmas. It comically recounts the story of an ox left by its master in the care of a *vaqueiro*. He kills the animal to satisfy his wife's craving for its liver. Several characters, human and animal, intervene until a *curandeiro* is able to restore the creature to life. This play occurs throughout the Sertão communities in several variants.

ARTS, CRAFTS, AND HOUSING

Traditional housing of the Sertão is made of rods intertwined and covered with a mud mixture called *taipa* or *pau-a-pique*. It is then covered with tiles. It is customary to build a veranda facing east, where people gather in the late afternoon for relaxation and conversation. The Sertanejo house is also a ritual site, where prayers, especially the rosary, are said.

Handicrafts—using such materials as cotton, clay, leather, bamboo fibers, and straw—reflect the indigenous Kariri tradition. Leather is used for hats, shoes, and the *gibão*, worn by *vaqueiros* for protection from the dry, thorny branches they encounter in the *caatinga*. Artisans use clay to manufacture items for domestic use as well as figurines representing daily activities. The best-known of these figurines come from Caruarú, Pernambuco. Bamboo fibers are used for a variety of items used domestically such as baskets and colanders. The blankets, hammocks, and other fabrics made from cotton are sold throughout Brazil.

BIBLIOGRAPHY

Azzi, Riolando. 1993. A paixão de Cristo na tradiçãp luso-brasileira. *Revista Eclesiástica Brasileira-REB* 53: 114–149.

Bruno, Ernani Silva, and Diaulus Riedel. 1960. *O sertão, o boi e a seca*. 2nd edition. São Paulo: Cultrix.

Cascudo, Luís da Câmara. 1988 (1954). *Dicionário do Folclore Brasileiro*. 6th edition. Belo Horizonte: Itatiaia.

Mota, Clarice Novaes. 1996. Sob as ordens da Jurema: o xamã Kariri-Xokó. In *Xamanismo no Brasil*, edited by Jean M. Langdon. Florinópolis: Ed. Universidade Federal de Santa Catarina.

Queiroz, Rachel de. 1978 (1930). *O quinze*. 24th edition. Rio de Janeiro: José Olympio Ed.

Siqueira, Baptista. 1978. *Os Cariris do Nordeste*. Rio de Janeiro: Ed. Cátedra.

Benedito Prezia and Francisco Josivan
(Translated from the Spanish by Ernesto Lombeida)

SHUAR

GEOGRAPHY AND HISTORY

The Shuar are a group of between 30,000 and 50,000 Indians, almost all of whom live in the eastern Ecuadorian province of Morona Santiago in a region known as *montaña*. This is the easternmost foothills of the Andes mountain range and the uppermost fringe of the Amazon rainforest. Traditionally, Shuar lived on the hills between streams and rivers and traveled primarily by land. Most Shuar today live in two parts of Morona Santiago: the Upano Valley (between the Eastern Cordillera of the Andes and the Cutucú Cordillera) and Trascutucú (east of the Cutucú, where its steep hillsides give way to gentle slopes). Shuar share the Upano Valley with Ecuadorian settlers and often travel on the dirt highway built by the government to support colonization.

Traditionally, Ecuadorians as well as anthropologists have drawn a sharp distinction between indigenous peoples of the highlands and of the lowlands. The former live in large, urban settlements based on agriculture; the latter live in small, semi-nomadic bands of horticulturalists. The two have been viewed as culturally antagonistic and politically and economically isolated. Recently archeologists and ethnohistorians have come to realize that prior to Spanish conquest and colonization in the 1500s, peoples of the highlands and lowlands understood their cultural differences as much in terms of complementarity as antagonism and enjoyed connections through complex economic and political relations. Although today it is relatively easy to identify and locate Shuar culture, the further one goes back in time, the more difficult this task becomes. The sparse extant evidence of the pre-colonial period reveals that people often migrated between the Andes and the Amazon. In the process, cultures diverged and merged.

From the 1200s on, imperial and colonial policies dominated this region. Indeed, Spanish colonization under the leadership of Francisco Pizarro only replaced prior colonial efforts by the Inca Empire. However, the Shuar were notoriously difficult to subjugate. The 1600s saw a number of attempts to conquer the Shuar (usually in response to their violent resistance to taxes) and establish permanent settlements in the area, but none was successful. Eventually the viceroy prohibited further attempts. From 1599 to 1870, Macas—small and isolated, populated by people who claimed descent from either the Spaniards or the Inca, but who had come to speak Shuar and follow many Shuar customs—was the only permanent white settlement in the region.

During the late nineteenth century, more Ecuadorians began to settle in the region. Shuar responded to this new wave of settlement, unsupported by the state, with characteristic spatial strategies. Some families retreated from the colonial frontier to search for more abundant game deeper in the forest; others settled hitherto unoccupied areas near Ecuadorian settlements in order to block further Ecuadorian expansion. Shuar otherwise welcomed the settlers as new opportunities for trade, exchanging forest products such as deer and salt for manufactured goods such as shotguns and machetes, which were useful for hunting and gardening.

Thus, when the Catholic Salesians (who were granted ecclesial jurisdiction over the region by the state in 1893) established a mission at Mendez in 1914, both settlers and Shuar welcomed them. In 1935 the state established a Shuar reserve under Salesian supervision and charged the Salesians with teaching Shuar Spanish and promoting commercial agriculture. The Mission Aviation Fellowship and the Gospel Missionary Union, evangelical Christian organizations from the United States, established missions in Sucúa and Macuma that were independent of the Salesians.

In 1931, the Ecuadorian government granted a subsidiary of Standard Oil a concession to explore for oil in the Amazonian lowlands. The region had strategic importance as well, since **Peru** contested the Amazonian claims of **Ecuador**. When the government revoked the original concession and awarded it to a subsidiary of Shell Oil, Standard Oil entered into an agreement with Peru. Peru declared war on Ecuador in 1941, and in a ceasefire brokered by the United States, Ecuador ceded 200,000 square kilometers of territory to Peru. The Shuar reserve was now situated on Ecuador's Peruvian border. The loyalty of the Shuar was now of strategic importance to the state, which renewed its agreement with the Salesians in 1944.

The dispersed settlement pattern of the Shuar, however, limited Salesian efforts to convert adults. In the late 1940s Alberto Gomezcoello, one of the missionaries at Sucúa, had some alumni of his school build a chapel near their parents' homes in the forest and invite other Shuar to move near the structure. The priest could then visit once a year and perform a mass for several Shuar families. Gomezcoello's successor, Juan Shutka, intensified this process in the 1950s, and by 1960 he had established eleven *centros* near Sucúa. The word *centro* refers specifically to a plaza of cleared forest, but also more generally to the chapel, schoolrooms, and houses built around the plaza. At first these *centros* functioned as mini-missions without priests, but under Shutka's guidance they developed into a new form of Shuar community, each with an elected headman (*síndico*, or trustee). In 1961 Shutka began meeting with the *síndicos* of the various *centros*, and in 1962 they united to form an association, the *Asociación de Sucúa*. These men encouraged graduates of other mission schools within the reserve to duplicate this process and form other associations. In 1964, leaders of seven associations met in Sucúa to form a federation, the *Federación de Centros Shuar*.

The federation quickly became an instrument of Shuar autonomy and response to a new wave of colonization. When the economy of the nearest highland city, Cuenca (the third largest city in the country), collapsed in the 1950s, government officials formed a regional agency to link the development of Cuenca with surrounding provinces by promoting the migration of poor people into the lowlands to raise cattle for the Cuenca market. The federation responded by promoting the formation of new *centros* and by securing collective title to land. Every two years all *síndicos* assemble in Sucúa to elect a president, vice-president, and directors who supervise programs in health, education, and economic development. In 1969 the state transferred control of the reserve from the Salesians to the federation. The next year the Evangelical Shuar formed their own federation, and various dissidents broke away to form a rival organization. Today there are over 200 *centros*.

SOCIAL STRUCTURE

Prior to the formation of the Shuar federation, the basic unit of Shuar social organization was the household. Shuar households were relatively autonomous and linked loosely by kinship, specifically polygyny (one husband with more than one wife) and matrilocality (married couples living with or near the wife's parents). The average household consisted of nine people: a man, his wives (typically two), married daughters and sons-in-law, and unmarried daughters and sons. After the birth of their first child, married daughters and their husbands would establish a new household not far from the daughter's natal household. Each household maintained a large garden or several smaller gardens (totaling up to 100,000 square feet). Houses were occupied for between five and nine years before a family relocated. Shuar recognized a family's rights to use a house and garden, but these use-rights traditionally did not translate into any notion of ownership or property. Shuar believed anyone had the right to occupy land that had been abandoned.

Although the rainforest itself is lush, its soil is thin and ill-suited for farming. Like many inhabitants of tropical forests, Shuar have relied on shifting, slash-and-burn horticulture. Shuar men traditionally cut down and burned patches of forests in order to liberate nutrients in plants and trees. Women then planted small gardens of root-crops such as manioc and potatoes as well as other plants like corn and plantains. The cultivation of such crops exhausted the soil after a few years, so men cleared new gardens and allowed the old ones to reforest. After repeating this process a few times, the family often abandoned their house and gardens, now overrun with weeds, to move to another location. Men supplemented garden production by hunting small game. The result of this subsistence strategy was dispersed settlement.

Preferential polygyny was in part a product of the disproportionate ratio of women to men owing to warfare. A major consequence of polygyny was to increase household food production: women produced over 65 percent of the calories for domestic consumption. Women also made manioc beer, which was essential for successful social functions that brought together people of different households. Combined with matrilocality, marriage also created bonds between a man and his father-in-law. Since young men left their homes upon marriage, they never entered into direct competition with their fathers over political power. Although in the early years of marriage matrilocality gave a father some control over his son-in-law, later sons-in-law formed their own autonomous households, often allied with that of the father-in-law. The result was a strong egalitarian social structure and ethos in which adult men valued independence from one another.

POWER AND RITUAL

Shuar value and aspire to power (*kakárma*), which they regard as an attribute of a person connected with certain spiritual components of the human being. Traditionally, the most important of these were the *arútam* that were acquired by men and women during various vision quests. A person who has thus acquired *arútam* is called *wáimiaku* (one who has seen). The incorporation of *arútam* by that person becomes manifest as individual proprieties and abilities that are a precondition for success in various fields of action. There are approximately forty different figures of *arútam* that can appear to a person in a vision. They represent certain types of power and skills that are related to various dimensions of life: some have been connected to violence and warfare, but the majority represent facets of everyday life and skills of conviviality and well-being (*pénker pujústin*). They provide the male or female vision-seeker with a special force to attain health, a long life, joy and happiness, material well-being, success, and skills in various gendered domains of work. In the masculine sphere, the accumulation of *arútam* was and often still is regarded as the precondition to become a powerful man (*kakáram*), famous for his abilities as a political leader with strong speech, an invincible warrior, or a shaman.

A vision quest could take place in various ritual contexts, and it was often integrated into special ceremonies, many of which centered on gender-specific spheres of life. A girl's vision quest was frequently combined with the female initiation ceremonies (*nua tsankram*). Fathers would often take boys of about eight years on a journey to a nearby waterfall (*tuna*), where they would be given *maikiúa* (an infusion from the plant *Datura arborea*, Solanaceae) in the hope they would then see momentary visions (often in the shape of an animal). If a boy were brave enough, he would approach and touch the vision, which would then explode and disappear. The boy was not to talk about this with anyone but was supposed to go to sleep. The *arútam* would then return in the form of an old man and would reveal himself to be the boy's ancestor. When the old man disappeared, the *arútam wakaní* entered the boy's body and thus augmented his *kakárma*, or power.

As long as the *arútam* remained attached to a person's body, he or she expressed confidence and intelligence and resisted disease, sorcery, and physical violence. If a man acquired special power for becoming a great warrior, he was invincible. Just as an *arútam* could be acquired, it could also be lost. This occurred if a young man talked about his visions with others. Shuar also believed that after inhabiting the same body for several years, an *arútam* began wandering at night as the person slept. During these nocturnal walks someone else could acquire the *arútam*. Shuar thus depended on a power that circulated but could never be controlled absolutely or permanently.

Tsantsas, or shrunken heads, were casualties of war. (Courtesy Library of Congress)

The ultimate sign of power for Shuar men was the possession of the *tsantsas* or shrunken heads of casualties of war. In fact, Shuar men went to war to acquire these heads (from non-Shuar) as signs of power. A successful returning party dispatched a message to an older warrior who subsequently sponsored a two- or three-day feast. The warriors returned to their homes and eventually hosted one or two additional feasts up to three years after the initial feast. These feasts lasted five or six days and were attended by up to 150 people who danced, ate, and drank huge quantities of manioc beer. One of the primary functions of these events was to initiate young men and women into the tasks connected with warfare, often through vision quests. Another was to promote and express inter-household solidarity. The *tsantsa* feasts were among the few times when significant numbers of Shuar came together.

The last reported *tsantsa* feast was in the 1930s, and today Shuar seldom take their children to the sacred waterfalls. Since the formation of the Shuar federation the *centro* has replaced the household as the fundamental unit of Shuar social organization, and the federation has provided a unifying political structure. As more and more Shuar enter the labor market, class inequality has begun to develop. However, Shuar do continue to see *tsantsas* and *maikiúa* as symbols of their identity and still value equality and autonomy as ideals, even when they are difficult to put into practice.

RELIGIOUS BELIEFS AND SHAMANISM

The contemporary Shuar belief system comprises various types of syncretism and parallelism that integrate traditional **worldview** and ritual with Christian beliefs and practices. Catholic and evangelical missionaries have made an intensive effort to promote Christianity during the past fifty years and continue to do so. Though priests, nuns, and other functionaries of Christian churches remain mainly non-Shuar (European and North American), the majority of the Shuar have been baptized and consider themselves Christians. In recent years the Native American Church has exercised some influence as well, particularly among shamans. Traditional beliefs are still relevant for many people, though a large number of Shuar rituals have been transferred from the public to the private sphere and have lost much of their social significance (for example, the *nua tsankram* or female initiation ceremony). Thus, there is no homogeneous belief system among the Shuar today. One has to think, rather, of a variety of elements of beliefs and practices that are combined and used by different people in many different ways.

According to the Shuar worldview, humans, plants, and animals share a spiritual element, *wakán*, and are classified as *aents*—conscious creatures or persons. *Wakán* provides all creatures with a subjectivity of their own, enabling them to communicate and maintain social relations with one another. In the case of humans, additional spiritual elements are acquired and incorporated into individuals during their lifetimes and may get lost again in the course of certain events. The Shuar notion of the person does not refer to a continuously stable and bounded entity but represents a process of transformations. The most important spiritual component of a human person is *arútam*.

After death, the diverse spiritual components of a person could then take various forms: the *arútam* could be transferred from one generation to the next in the vision quest; a *wakán* could be transformed into a deer, bird, butterfly, or ape-like monster; or it could act as a *wakán iwianch*, a malevolent spiritual being that endangers the living. Beliefs and narratives about *iwianch* vary considerably: *nekas* (real) *iwianch* are monstrous giants or spirits in the form of Spanish soldiers that live in the wilderness, whereas *wakán iwianch* are manifestations of the dead, especially the frightening *wakán* of fierce warriors.

Myths and individual narratives relate strange and dangerous encounters between Shuar and *iwianch*. Many people today can recall some type of confrontation with such a creature. The abduction of persons—very often children—by *iwianch* to their wild world is a widespread topic. It is common for adult Shuar to frighten their children with the threat that an *iwianch* will steal them away. The *iwianch* represents in many ways the opposite of a fulfilling life; it is an ugly spirit consumed by perpetual hunger and loneliness. Indeed, Shuar seem to fear the kind of existence that *iwianch* represent more than the *iwianch* themselves.

Shamans (*uwishin*) possess special spiritual power that allows them to exercise influence upon other persons' bodies, thoughts, and emotions, thus causing and healing disease and misfortune. Shuar conceptualize shamanic power elements mainly as magical darts (*tsentsak*)—little arrows of light in various shapes and colors—and as spirit helpers (*pasuk*) in the form of animals and mythical figures. Shamanism continues to constitute an important feature of Shuar social, political, and spiritual life.

Interregional and international migration and globalization have created new arenas for shamanic activities in recent years. Many Shuar shamans nowadays live in semi-urban environments, act as folk-healers (*curanderos*) in new social settings, and attend patients and clients from a variety of cultural and social backgrounds. The increasing differentiation of their social, cultural, and symbolic surroundings has presented new cultural flows reflected in the spiritual power of an *uwishin*. Many shamans today appropriate elements from a large number of spiritual traditions. The ability to coordinate, appropriate, and manipulate a multitude of spiritual fragments from various parts of Ecuador and the world is regarded an important quality of a Shuar shaman.

FOLKTALES AND NARRATIVES

Verbal art among the Shuar comprises a variety of genres that can be roughly divided into two categories: prose narratives and ritual dialogues. One generation transmits the corpus of tales (*jaunchu aujmátsamu*) orally to the next, mainly within the family or household. These tales are open to a fairly large degree of variation.

The Shuar consider *jaunchu aujmátsamu* to be moral tales that teach children values and instruct them in conviviality and "well-being" (*penker pujustín*). The tales are frequently told in informal settings. Narrators (men and women) will often choose a story with a connection to an event in everyday life. *Jaunchu aujmátsamu* relate a variety of events that comprise a series of transformations of the natural and social world from an undifferentiated past to a more differentiated present. Culture **heroes**, **tricksters**, man-eating monsters, animals, and the ancestors of humans (Shuar) interact in many ways and shape the contemporary world by their actions. Many stories are very entertaining and funny, enjoyed by both children and adults. Some mythical figures are endowed with more power and agency than others and are sometimes referred to as *arútam*. Thus, the concept of personhood and (spiritual) power—as expressed in the vision quest and other rituals—is also an important element of myth.

SONGS, SPELLS, AND CHANTS

The second genre of verbal art consists of songs and spells. Drinking songs (*nampet*) are performed during social events. They are often used to communicate emotions and are sometimes directed at a special person. *Nampet* are performed at various types of parties (*nampér*—from *nampék*: to be intoxicated, to sing) that take place after community work (*takát iniámpramu*) or at notable occasions such as national and Catholic holidays, the end of the school year, and sports events that involve several communities (*centros*).

Spells (*anent*) are recited or sung to exercise influence on people, events, and nature. They can be part of rituals closely linked to everyday life, celebrated privately, and performed by every adult. Men and women recite *anent* in the context of many activities such as gardening, hunting, love, childcare, and social relations. They are transmitted from one person to another or can be learned in dreams or visions. Everybody knows a few basic spells, but some people are famous for their profound and extensive knowledge.

The term *anent* also refers to the chants at public rituals such as the *tsantsa* (shrunken head) ceremonies or *úunt nampér* (great feast) dedicated to warfare, shrunken heads, the initiation of warriors, and the ritual production of power; *natemamu* (vision-quest ceremony for men and women); celebration of *uwi* (to enhance fertility and well-being); and the *napi* ceremony (celebrated after recovering from a snake bite). It also refers to chants at several initiation ceremonies for young men and women: *nua trankram* (the initiation of young women), *kusúm* (the initiation of young men to blowgun hunting), and *tuna* (the vision quest for young men at the waterfalls). These rituals were performed on a regular basis until the 1960s, when they were both prohibited by the Salesian Mission and the Ecuadorian state and abandoned by Shuar who were adopting the Ecuadorian settler lifestyle (especially commercial agriculture and sending their children to school). The oral transmission of the complex knowledge of verbal art and performance has thus been interrupted and lost to a large degree. Some *anent* are being preserved by the activities of shamans and of young Shuar scholars from the Instituto Intercultural Bilingüe in Bomboiza, Ecuador. Shamanic songs (*uwishín cantu*), also called *anent*, continue to form an important part of healing rituals.

Chanting was an important part of all the fiestas (*namper*), practiced by men and women according to their roles in the rituals. Musical instruments are almost exclusively played (and manufactured) by men to accompany either *anent* or *nampet*. Flutes (*peem, pinkiui, tiripish, yakuch*) and a type of violin, adapted from European music (*kitiar*), can be used to play a simple tune or a spell (*anent*), as the musician recites the words often to himself. A hollow log drum can be played to summon guests for a fiesta or spirits in a vision-quest ceremony (*natemamu*) or to communicate messages. Smaller drums (*tambur*) are mainly played at the secular part of feasts (*namper*) as rhythm instruments for dance (together with the rattle of shells on belts worn by dancing women).

MUSIC, DRAMA, AND DANCE

Some elements of Shuar secular musical art are performed today at various new types of fiestas, associated with schools, the Shuar federation, Catholic holidays, or Ecuadorian holidays. Singing and drumming at fiestas are limited to special occasions and have been largely replaced by radio and cassette players used to play Latin American music for dancing. "Radio Shuar," directed by the Shuar federation, regularly broadcasts programs dedicated to traditional music. Music also forms part of cultural performances that represent Shuar folklore at national and international events. Today Shuar public ritual music is practiced almost exclusively in healing ceremonies by shamans, who chant and occasionally play the jew's harp (*tumank*), using a bundle of leaves (*shushínk*) for rhythm and for the spiritual cleansing of the patient.

Most forms of dramatic art and dance have been part of public rituals but have not been practiced since the 1970s. Certain types of dance and dramatic performance were connected to war rituals, particularly to the *tsantsa* ceremonies. Other forms of dance and dramatic performance have been components of a series of different fiestas and rituals (*nampér*). Shuar dance style is mainly based on the movement of lines of men or women through the house in circles. Rhythm is provided by dance belts worn by women and by men beating drums. Whereas some dance sequences had specific ritual meaning, others (performed at the same occasion) were primarily meant for entertainment. Today social dances have been largely replaced by Latin American dance styles performed to recorded music, but some elements of traditional Shuar dance are staged at folkloric events.

A similar process applies to the elaborate ceremonial greeting and dialogue (*ushiar*), a combination of verbal and dramatic art, and was of considerable social and political significance in Shuar society when households were widely dispersed throughout the forest. Men performed it when visiting one another as part of the construction of alliances and conviviality between independent households. It is rarely practiced today except in staged cultural performances. This change is a reflection of the rise of the *centro*, which has both altered the political organization and dramatically increased the number and frequency of chance encounters between members of different households.

Arts, Crafts, and Trade

The production of certain objects and the respective skills (concerning pottery or canoe building, for example) are an important mythological theme. Many tales describe the process of learning a skill or art from a cultural hero and refer to the rituals and the moral standards connected with the application of this knowledge. Thus, the practice of crafts has been frequently associated with a set of rituals, especially with the use of spells (*anent*).

Evidence indicates that Shuar have been involved in trade networks linking the Andes to the Amazon since at least the time of contact. Moreover, Shuar have traded for manufactured goods such as machetes and shotguns since the Spanish colonial period. Nevertheless, until the flow of industrially produced commodities in the region intensified in the twentieth century, the Shuar manufactured a large number of items for daily use (including pottery, garments, baskets, hammocks, bags, canoes, and wooden objects). Some traditional objects that required special resources or expertise (for example, blowguns and feather headdresses) were often purchased from neighboring groups, however, particularly from the Achuar, who enjoy a reputation as especially skilled artisans. Today many traditional items have been replaced by industrial goods for daily use, though some objects are produced on a larger scale for *artesanía* in the national and international market (for example, necklaces, feather items, bags, dancing belts, and pottery). Especially prestigious items such as feather headdresses are still worn by some men at festive occasions and are used in a political context as an ethnic marker for the representation of Shuar culture and identity.

BIBLIOGRAPHY

Bianchi, Cesar. 1982. *Actividades y técnicas.* Quito: Mundo Shuar.

Harner, Michael. 1972. *The Jivaro: People of the Sacred Waterfalls.* London: Robert Hale.

———. 1973. The Sound of Rushing Water. In *Hallucinogens and Shamanism,* edited by Michael Harner. New York: Oxford University Press. 15–27.

Hendricks, Janet W. 1988. Power and Knowledge: Discourse and Ideological Transformation among the Shuar. *American Ethnologist* 15.2: 216–238.

———. 1993. *To Drink of Death.* Tucson: University of Arizona Press.

Karsten, Raphael. 1935. *Headhunters of Western Amazonas: The Life and Culture of the Jivaro Indians of Eastern Ecuador.* Commentationes Humanorum i Herorum, Vol. 7, No. 1. Helsingfors: Societas Scietiorum Finnica.

Lévi-Strauss, Claude. 1988. *The Jealous Potter.* Chicago: University of Chicago Press.

Mader, Elke. 1999. *Metamorfosis del poder: Persona, mito y visión en la sociedad shuar y achuar (Ecuador/Perú).* Quito: Abya Yala.

NACLA. 1975. Ecuador: Oil Up for Grabs. *Latin America and Empire Report* 9.8 (special issue).

Napolitano, Emanuela. 1988. *Shuar y anent: El canto sagrado en la historia de un pueblo.* Quito: Abya-Yala.

Pellizzaro, Siro. 1977. Cantos de amor de la esposa achuar. *Mundo Shuar,* Serie G, Nr. 2. Quito: Abya-Yala.

———. 1978a. *Mitología Shuar.* 12 volumes. *Mundo Shuar,* Serie F. Quito: Abya-Yala.

———. 1978b. *La celebración de Uwi.* Quito: Publicación de los Museos del Banco Central del Ecuador.

———. 1980. *Tsantsa: Celebración de la Cabeza Cortada. Mundo Shuar,* Serie F, Nr. 9. Quito: Abya-Yala.

———. 1990. *Arútam: Mitología shuar.* Quito: Abya-Yala.

Rostoker, Arthur G. 2003. The Formative Period Radiocarbon Chronology for Eastern Ecuador. In *Archaeology of Formative Ecuador,* edited by J. S. Raymond and R. L. Burger. Washington, DC: Dumbarton Oaks. 539–545.

Rubenstein, Steve. 2001. Colonialism, the Shuar Federation, and the Ecuadorian State. In *Environment and Planning D: Society and Space* 19.3: 263–293.

———. 2002. *Alejandro Tsakimp: A Shuar Healer in the Margins of History.* Lincoln: University of Nebraska Press.

Rueda, Marco V., and Ricardo Tankamash'. 1983. *Setenta mitos shuar.* Quito: Mundo Shuar.

Stirling, Matthew. 1938. *Historical and Ethnographical Material on the Jivaro Indians.* Smithonian Institution Bulletins, No. 117. Washington, DC: GPO.

Taylor, Anne Christine. 1996a. The Soul's Body and Its States: An Amazonian Perspective on the Nature of Being Human. *Journal of the Royal Anthropological Institute* (N.S.) 2: 201–215.

———. 1996b. The Western Margins of Amazonia from the Early Sixteenth Century to the Early Nineteenth Century. In *The Cambridge History of the Native Peoples of the Americas,* edited by Frank Salomon and Stuart B. Schwartz. Cambridge: Cambridge University Press. 2: 188–256.

Steven Rubenstein and Elke Mader

SIBUNDOY

GEOGRAPHY AND HISTORY

Nestled high in the Andes Mountains of southern Colombia at the eastern edge of the cordillera and just over a degree north of the equator lies the verdant oval known as the Sibundoy Valley. Measuring approximately 9 miles by 4.5 miles and poised some 7,500 feet above sea level, this flat expanse surrounded by steep mountains on all flanks is the home of two indigenous communities, the Inga and Kamsá. The remarkable feature of this cultural heritage is its merging of prominent South American prototypes with echoes of both Andean and tropical forest elements. The Sibundoy Valley is positioned at the northern fringe of Incan influence and just south of the large Chibchan states to the north. At the same time, it offers convenient passage between the Andes and the adjacent Amazonian basin. Inhabiting a veritable crossroads of native South America, the indigenous communities of the Sibundoy Valley have evolved traditional practices and beliefs blending these diverse influences as well as the impact of Spanish and later Colombian culture into a distinctive ethos.

The indigenous peoples of the Sibundoy Valley have retained their native languages, Inga, the northernmost dialect of the large Quechuan family of languages, and Kamsá, the last living dialect of the Quillasinga group of languages. Their isolation from the centers of administrative power in Colombia and Ecuador has allowed them to conserve and develop their native culture well into the modern period. During the last few decades, however, the national culture has made increasing inroads, placing the traditional culture under considerable stress.

The early history of the region is somewhat shrouded in mystery, pending further archeological and ethnohistorical research. The Sibundoy Valley is mentioned in early documents as a distant outpost known for its placer gold deposits, abundant agricultural output, and the prowess of its native doctors. It appears that the Ingas and Kamsás have resided in the valley since before the arrival of the Spaniards in the first decades of the sixteenth century. The Kamsá are an eastern projection of the pre-Columbian Quillasinga federation, a loose association of small states located in the Valle de Atris, where the modern city of Pasto is found, and in adjacent areas to the east and north of Pasto. The Ingas in the Sibundoy Valley are apparently derived from two different stocks: one branch, the Santiago Ingas, traces its lineage back to the Incas and claims to be a transported people moved from the interior of the empire to occupy this buffer zone on the northern fringe; the other, the San Andrés Ingas, most likely ascended from the adjacent lowlands in the colonial period.

These two peoples have shared residency in the Sibundoy Valley for several centuries now and have developed over the years a somewhat uniform indigenous culture with common subsistence patterns, means of governance, and traditional forms of thought and expression. This convergence derives in no small part from the manipulations of political and religious authorities who asserted control over the indigenous population of the valley. From the early times of the Spanish colony, the indigenous people of the valley were subjected to the *encomienda* system, which gave prominent Spanish settlers rights to the labor and goods of the native peoples, and to the evangelical efforts of one Catholic order after another, which proved successful in converting them to the Catholic faith. Well into the twentieth century, Sibundoy natives were essentially vassals within a feudal system controlled by a landholding elite and the dour Capuchin missionaries.

Today there are roughly 30,000 inhabitants of the valley, perhaps some 10,000 Ingas, 8,000 Kamsás, and the remainder descendants of Colombian *mestizos* (known as *blancos*, or whites, to the Indians) who settled in the valley during the last century or so. Some intermarriage between Indians and whites has recently taken place, though for the most part these communities remain separate from one another apart from commercial relations. Many members of the indigenous groups, especially the Inga, travel outside of the valley seeking a living in the cities of Colombia and neighboring Venezuela, returning primarily to help celebrate Carnival. Those who stay in the valley live a life with close links to the past. The native societies are historically based on the cultivation of maize, squash, beans, a number of edible roots, and a variety of local vegetables and fruits. Previously hunting and fishing contributed to the diet, but these natural resources have become scarce in recent decades. Poultry, pigs, and cuyes, the Andean guinea pig, are kept for their meat, and dairy cows are kept for milk that is shipped to nearby cities to generate cash income. Until quite recently, Sibundoy natives participated only to a limited degree in the commercial sector, and the indigenous families are still remarkably self-sufficient on their plots of cultivated land.

There are two units of community life that are important to understand: the *cabildo*, the community council, and the *vereda*, the hamlet or cluster of associated dwellings. There are several *cabildos* in the indigenous communities, each administering a segment of the population linked by geography and history. These councils are the center of community self-governance, with jurisdiction over most local matters. The *gobernador*, governor, elected each year by a popular vote, and his assistants run them. The *gobernador*'s most challenging task, apart from managing the day-to-day affairs of the community, is organizing a successful Carnival, the high point of the Sibundoy year. If the *cabildos* draw members of the indigenous communities into larger assemblies, the *veredas* are a more local expression of indigenous identity. These are groups of houses in a finite area, usually peopled by families who are related to one another. Many of the day-to-day activities of Sibundoy natives revolve around the *veredas*, and both Ingas and Kamsás tend to invoke their *veredas* as the first order of their social identity.

MYTHS, LEGENDS, AND FOLKTALES

The repertoire of Kamsá and Inga storytellers includes a corpus of tales that they trace back to a formative period when their ancestors essentially made the Sibundoy Valley and its environs safe for civilization. These tales are distinguished from other kinds of stories such as sacred history from the Bible or tales of international **tricksters** like Pedro Urdemalas, which are also performed by indigenous storytellers. This local corpus of tales is referred to by the Ingas as *antiwa parlo*, ancient tales, and by the Kamsás as *antewanos*, tales of the ancestors. Although the common root of these terms is the

Spanish word *antigua*, meaning "old" or "ancient," the content within the category is thought to be essentially native, depicting the actions of the "first people," mostly unnamed ancestors who endowed the Sibundoy native peoples with the knowledge that could sustain society in the valley.

Overall, the drift of Sibundoy mythic narratives is toward a gradual restricting of spiritual fluidity so that the stable institutions of civilized life might flourish. During the earliest phase of the ancestral period, according to this mythology, the sun and moon were personages who interacted with the first people, animals could take human form and speak like human beings,

Mariano Chicunque relates a humorous mythical episode. (Photograph by John Holmes McDowell)

and people lived without the benefit of many customs and practices that govern human society today. We glimpse a time before the first rising of the sun when there was neither sunshine nor fire nor food. At a later but still early phase, we hear about the *auca* (Ingas) or *yembe* (Kamsás), heathen savages who feasted on human flesh.

Much of Sibundoy mythic narrative tells how these heathens were vanquished, how fire and corn were introduced, and how the culture hero taught the early ancestors proper modes of subsistence and reproduction. In one episode after another, the rampant spiritual potency of these early phases is contained and moved to the perimeters of the valley, leaving a core friendly to the establishment of social and political institutions. There remains on the periphery a charged zone of spiritual power and danger that is the special domain of the native doctors and can be accessed by others through "sayings of the ancestors," proverb-like formulas for decoding the meaning of dreams and wakeful omens.

The Kamsás' Wangetsmuna cycle, with numerous parallels throughout the Andes, tells of the founding of Sibundoy civilization. It features the powerful thunder deity, who wields a sling to hurl thunder and lightning upon his rivals, and a culture hero, who wanders the world teaching people how to live properly, giving the animals their habits and voices, and dispensing justice. At one critical moment, Wangetsmuna sounds a horn, and from then on the boundaries between animals and people are permanently fixed. This Sibundoy mythic cycle evidently taps into an ancient bedrock of Andean cosmology.

A second strand of Sibundoy mythology points in an entirely different direction, toward the botanical science and visionary healing techniques of tropical forest shamans in the Amazonian basin just to the east of the Sibundoy Valley, who interact on a regular basis with Sibundoy native doctors. These mythic narratives are

231

Native doctor with curing branches and *huayra huahua* (spirit medium) in his hand. (Photograph by John Holmes McDowell)

focused on the spiritual resources of the native doctors, especially the mind-altering medicines *yagé* or *ayahuasca* and *borrachera* used in curing sessions to gain access to the spirit realm. Typically these stories tell of encounters with the masters or owners of these medicines, who instruct their human protégés in the preparation and proper uses of these substances. In one of these tales a respected elder and his daughter find an unusual egg in the forest. They care for it, and after a time a boy hatches from it. This child turns out to be the son of *indi waska*, the sun vine, a powerful form of *yagé* used to protect crops and control the weather. This boy quickly becomes a young man and joins the elders in their vision sessions, showing them how to cure effectively with the sun vine. At last he departs to rejoin his father, promising to return to the people in their visions as long as they do not misuse the sun vine.

A third strand of Sibundoy mythology depicts a series of animal suitors who attempt to marry into human families but are at last dismissed by the families of their intended spouses. This segment of the corpus expresses a dilemma, for the animal suitors often bring significant powers that might have alleviated life's hardships if the unions had been allowed. A bird woman, for example, could produce a barrel of *chicha*, the maize beer that serves as an elixir of life in the valley, from just a few grains of corn. The owl man could clear, plant, and harvest a patch of forest just by issuing a series of shouts. But the animal suitors never quite blend into their human environments. They remain unkempt, incommunicative, and ungainly even as they succeed in winning the affection of their intended mates. The message appears to be that these tantalizing improvements in the human condition must be reluctantly shunned to preserve a stable zone for the maintenance of social practices and institutions.

These mythic narratives may be performed in private settings within the family—as when a mother shares them with her children—or aired in more public settings, perhaps among members of a work crew when they gather in the late afternoon to drink *chicha* and socialize with one another. Typically, the older generation shares this knowledge with the younger people around them, having a strong didactic purpose in telling these tales so that people will be inspired by the example of the ancestors in order for things to go well in the present. Performances of mythic narratives can be very engaging, as narrators draw their audiences into the stories, mixing straightforward narration with dramatic re-enactments featuring the voices and gestures of story protagonists.

CEREMONIAL SPEAKING

Reverence for the ancestors is also a prominent theme in the ceremonial speaking known as the ritual language, which is used to transact community business in the *cabildo* as well as in rites of passage in the *veredas*. This special way of speaking has the acoustic and spiritual resonance of Catholic prayer. It is employed to confer a blessing on business at hand, whether in the *gobernador*'s greeting to the community at the commencement of the annual Carnival or during a baptism, wedding, or funeral celebrated in someone's home. Minor touches of this ritualized speech style can occur even in ordinary conversation to ask for favors or special consideration. Comparable forms of ceremonial speech are found among many peoples in lowland South America and in the foothills of the Andes.

The presence of ceremonial speaking cannot be missed because of its distinctive tonalities. Those who are masters of this speech genre are able to produce a rapid flow of specialized words voiced in chanted phrases, and their principal addressees respond in kind even as the speech continues, creating a remarkable interweaving of vocal production. In Inga or Kamsá, ponderous words are formed from a small set of weighty verbal roots, many of them derived from Spanish, by adding on an unusually large number of affixes. The content of these artful locutions is overtly religious in character, calling upon God, the Virgin Mary, and their ancestors to protect the health and well-being of all present. The underlying theme is that the present activity should replicate the models established by these forbearers and that the present is but a repetition of this hallowed past. One of the formulas common to most of these speeches is the affirmation that "we are following in the footsteps of our ancestors."

Ceremonial speaking ability grows with exposure to the civil institutions of Sibundoy society. Young adults begin to use it when they marry and become parents, for they will be expected to recruit *compadres* (ritual sponsors) for the celebrations that accompany these events, employing ceremonial speech in their transactions. The best speakers have entered into public service in the *cabildos*, where ceremonial speaking is prevalent. Venerable elders who have worked their way up the ladder to become *gobernador* are the ones who can really put on a show, exhibiting impressive skills in this stylized manner of speaking. These speeches are contrived through a practice of oral-formulaic composition, wherein the speaker improvises on the basis of a set of familiar formulas, mixing in content appropriate to the current occasion.

FESTIVALS AND CELEBRATIONS

The entire spectrum of Sibundoy tradition comes alive in the annual pre-Lenten Carnival, the cherished interval that Sibundoy natives identify as the high point of the year. Carnival draws heavily on the synthetic Andean folk religion practiced in the Sibundoy Valley, merging Roman Catholicism into the embracing traditional belief system. As Ash Wednesday approaches, people begin to gather in the *veredas*, going about from house to house sharing *chicha*, music, and dance. Carnival is the one time of the year when every house is stocked with *chicha*, and every door open to visitors. These visitations in the *vereda* are interrupted by a journey into town for a gathering of the entire community. On the Monday before Ash Wednesday,

Tapping the *chicha* barrel. (Photograph by John Holmes McDowell)

the Kamsás gather in the town of Sibundoy; on Shrove Tuesday, the Ingas do the same in the town of Santiago. These large-scale public events begin with a mass in the church of each town, where the *gobernador* asks for the blessing of the priest, offering him the *camarico*, a generous sampling of the harvest. After that the *gobernador* addresses the assembled community in the ceremonial speech form of their native tongue to release them to enjoy the Carnival. People then drift out into the main plaza, where they participate in a series of games and rituals, finally making their way to the *cabildo*, where they assist the *gobernador* in emptying whatever barrels of *chicha* (maize beer) he might have on hand for the occasion.

The material arts are well represented in the donning of Carnival outfits. Children and adults alike emerge from their houses and their *veredas* decked out in their finest woven ponchos and belts, attesting to the skills of the women, the exclusive masters of this craft among Sibundoy natives. Men of stature in the community—for instance, former *gobernadores*, accomplished native doctors—place on their heads the festive *coronas* or crowns, decked with strands of blue and green feathers from the macaw parrot and colorful woven belts. The masked dancers, *matachines* and *saraguayes*, place hand-carved wooden masks over their faces as they go about their dances in the plazas and along the main streets of the towns. The carnival mood is stoked by the ceaseless sound of Carnival music, played by musician-dancers on handmade reed flutes and wooden drums.

We have already taken note of the *gobernador*'s address to the community as mass comes to a close. Another Carnival speech genre is the ritual pardon, delivered in the ceremonial speaking style. This ritual begins as a junior member of the community approaches an elder, drops to his or her knees, and beseeches the Carnival blessing. The elder pronounces a blessing, whereupon the recipient arises, removes the elder's crown or hat, and spreads white petals of the Carnival flower over his or her head. Carnival is thought to be a time for uniting the community and reconciling personal differences, and these speech events play an important role in this process.

Although many people experience Carnival as essentially an interlude of social connection and license, on reflection it can be seen as a significant rite of renewal.

The preliminary ceremonies in the Catholic Church solidify the connection between the community and the Christian faith. Subsequent events in the plaza, along the main streets of town, and in the *cabildo* invoke the ancestral spirits and allude to mother earth, the sun and moon, the rainbow, and the thunder deity. The ritual slaughter of a rooster and spilling its blood, for example, are thought to replenish the earth. The rainbow plays a prominent role in mythic narratives about the founding of Sibundoy Carnival, and some Sibundoy natives perceive the entire Carnival celebration as honoring this figure. Under the influence of large quantities of *chicha*, the maize beer, and the insistent beat of the Carnival rhythm, people may enter an altered state of consciousness and experience a virtual return of the ancestors, reliving the conquest of the *aucas* and the acquisition of knowledge and power as these are portrayed in the mythic narratives.

CHALLENGES OF THE MODERN WORLD

The forces of **modernization** and the tide of civil war have radically altered circumstances in the Sibundoy Valley. Roads, electricity, and potable water have reached all but its most remote corners, and more and more young people have come under the influence of the national culture. Meanwhile, the brutal hostilities that have paralyzed Colombia over the last few decades have taken a toll on the native communities of the valley, who are too often caught in the middle of a war that is not theirs and does not much concern them. These developments have wrought major changes in the lifeways of the valley and placed the traditional practices and beliefs—and of course, the people themselves—in a vulnerable situation.

But there is reason to hope that the Sibundoy peoples will persist through these times of trouble and change. For one thing, children are still growing up speaking their native language, be it Inga or Kamsá, so the verbal environment for the persistence of culture remains strong. A second reason for hope is the flourishing trade of Sibundoy native doctors, who continue to cure within the community (and beyond it) using the traditional remedies and techniques. This medical practice, so deeply embedded in the traditional cosmology, ensures a continuing interest in mythic narratives, dream and omen proverbs, and other routes for apprehending the teachings of the ancestors.

A final component in this shifting scenario is the emergence of a campaign within the indigenous communities to recuperate and repossess the traditions of their elders. A good many younger Ingas and Kamsás are completing high school and enrolling in college these days. Most of those who obtain high school and university degrees are determined to give something back to the community. This cadre of indigenous activists and intellectuals has tended to value the forms of native folklore. They have established organizations and mounted aggressive campaigns to discover and recover the wealth of Sibundoy native traditions. *See also* **Quechua.**

BIBLIOGRAPHY

Bonilla, Victor Daniel. 1972. *Servants of God or Masters of Men: The Story of a Capuchin Mission in Amazonia.* London: Penguin.

Calero, Luis. 1997. *Chiefdoms under Siege: Spain's Rule and Native Adaptation in the Southern Colombian Andes.* Albuquerque: University of New Mexico Press.

Cobo, Bernabé. 1990. *Inca Religion and Customs*. Austin: University of Texas Press.

Demarest, Arthur. 1981. *Viracocha: The Nature and Antiquity of the Andean High God*. Monographs of the Peabody Museum, No. 6. Cambridge: Peabody Museum Press.

Dover, Robert. 1995. *Nucanchi Gente Pura*: The Ideology of Recuperation in the Inga Communities of Colombia's Sibundoy Valley. Diss., Indiana University.

Marzal, Manuel. 1996. *The Indian Face of God in Latin America*, translated by Penelope Hall. Maryknoll, NY: Orbis Books.

McDowell, John. 1981. Towards a Semiotics of Nicknaming. *Journal of American Folklore* 94: 1–18.

———. 1983. The Semiotic Constitution of Kamsá Ritual Language. *Language in Society* 12: 23–46.

———. 1987. The Kamsá Musical System. In *Andean Musics*, edited by R. Dover and J. McDowell. Andean Studies Occasional Papers, Vol. 3. Indiana University. 21–36.

———. 1989. *Sayings of the Ancestors: The Spiritual Life of the Sibundoy Indians*. Lexington: University Press of Kentucky.

———. 1990. The Community-Building Mission of Kamsá Ritual Language. *Journal of Folklore Research* 27: 67–84.

———. 1994. *"So Wise Were Our Elders": Mythic Narratives of the Kamsá*. Lexington: University Press of Kentucky.

McDowell, John, and Francisco Tandioy. In press. Recovering Inga Carnival: An Exercise in Ethnic Politics.

Schultes, Richard Evans, and Albert Hoffman. 1979. *Plants of the Gods: Origins of Hallucinogenic Use*. New York: McGraw-Hill.

Stoeltje, Beverly. 1992. Festival. In *Folklore, Cultural Performances, and Popular Entertainments: A Communications-Centered Handbook*, edited by Richard Bauman. Oxford: Oxford University Press. 261–271.

Tandioy, Francisco. 1987. *Muscuycuna y tapiacuna: Sueños ye agüeros en inga y castellano*. Pasto, Colombia: Comité de Educación Inga de Musu Runakuna.

Urban, Greg. 1986. Ceremonial Dialogues in South America. *American Anthropologist* 88: 371–386.

John Holmes McDowell

SURINAME MAROON

GEOGRAPHY AND HISTORY

Wherever slavery occurred throughout the Americas, there were also Maroons—men and women who fled their captivity, regrouped beyond the reach of the slave masters, and fought for their independence. Their communities ranged from tiny bands that survived for less than a year to powerful states encompassing thousands of members and surviving for generations or even centuries. Today their descendants in **Jamaica**, French Guiana, Colombia, Brazil, and elsewhere remain fiercely proud of their Maroon origins and, in some cases, continue to carry forward cultural traditions that were forged during the earliest days of African American history.

The Maroons of Suriname (formerly known also as Bush Negroes) have long been the hemisphere's largest Maroon population. Between the mid-seventeenth and late-eighteenth centuries, their ancestors escaped, in many cases soon after their arrival from Africa, from the coastal plantations of this Dutch colony in northeastern South America and fled into the tropical rainforest, where they regrouped into small bands. Their hardships in forging an existence in a new and inhospitable environment were compounded by the persistent and massive efforts of the colonial government to eliminate the threat they posed to the plantation colony.

The colonists reserved special punishments for recaptured slaves—hamstringing, amputation of limbs, and a variety of deaths by torture. The organized pursuit of Maroons and expeditions to destroy their settlements date at least from the 1670s, but these rarely met with success, for the Maroons had established and protected their settlements with considerable ingenuity and had become expert at all aspects of guerrilla warfare. By the middle of the eighteenth century when, in the words of a prominent planter, "the colony had become the theater of a perpetual war," the colonial government finally decided to sue the Maroons for peace. In separate treaties with the major groups, it agreed to guarantee Maroons their freedom and territory (even though slavery persisted for another 100 years on the coast) in return for promises that the Maroons would no longer raid plantations or harbor newly escaped slaves.

Today there are nearly 120,000 Maroons in Suriname and its neighbor to the east, French Guiana. The Ndyuka and Saramaka each have a population of about 50,000, the Matawai 4,000, the Aluku (Boni) and Paramaka each closer to 6,000, and the Kwinti only about 600. Though they still inhabit their traditional territories, many Maroons also live outside of these areas: in the capital city of Suriname, the coastal towns of French Guiana, or the Netherlands. Although the six societies were formed under similar historical and ecological conditions, they vary in everything from language, diet, and dress to patterns of marriage, residence, and migratory wage labor. From a cultural (and linguistic) point of view, the greatest differences are between the Maroons of central Suriname (Saramaka, Matawai, and Kwinti) and those to the east (Ndyuka, Aluku, and Paramaka).

Until the 1960s all six groups were referred to by anthropologists as tribes and as states within a state. Running their own political and judicial affairs under the authority of paramount chiefs and village captains and organizing their social life in terms of a matrilineal kinship system (in which the most important groupings for purposes of residence, ritual obligations, and marriage rules were those composed of people related through the female line), the Suriname Maroons were known to outsiders for such exotic practices as polygyny, oracular divination, spirit possession, body scarification, and ancestor worship, as well as distinctive styles of music, dance, and plastic arts and countless other aspects of daily life that reflected their uncompromised heritage of independence and their radical difference from the other populations of Suriname and French Guiana. Their dealings with the outside world were largely limited to the men's wage-labor trips, which provided the cash needed to supplement their subsistence base of slash-and-burn agriculture, hunting, and fishing with other necessities such as soap, salt, tools, cloth, kerosene, and kitchenware. Maroons felt tremendous pride in the accomplishments of their heroic ancestors and, on the whole, remained masters of their forest realm.

ROOTS OF MAROON CULTURE AND FOLKLORE
The Maroons, whose ancestors came from a wide variety of West and Central African societies, created new, vibrant African American cultures in the rainforest,

"March thro' a swamp or Marsh in terra firma." (Engraving by William Blake [1794] for John Gabriel Stedman, *Narrative of a Five Years' Expedition, against the Revolted Negroes of Surinam* [London, 1796])

drawing primarily on their diverse African backgrounds but with lesser contributions as well from American Indians (primarily subsistence techniques) and Europeans. Their enormously rich religious systems, their unique creole languages, and their vibrant artistic and performance achievements are strongly African in feeling, but at the same time they are unlike those of any particular culture or society in Africa. And their way of life, forged in an inhospitable rainforest by people under constant threat of annihilation, stands as enduring testimony to African American resilience and creativity and to the exuberance of a dynamic cultural imagination working itself out within the rich, broad framework of African cultural ideas.

Over the past three or four decades, the world of these peoples has undergone dramatic transformations. In the 1960s, the widespread use of outboard motors and the development of air service to the interior encouraged increased traffic of people and goods between Maroon villages and the coast. At the same time, the construction of a giant hydroelectric project by Alcoa and the Suriname government brought a dramatic migration toward the coast, with some 6,000 people forced to abandon their homes as the artificial lake gradually flooded almost half of Saramaka territory. Meanwhile in French Guiana, beginning in the 1970s, the Aluku Maroons were subjected to intense pressures for "*francisation*," which caused wrenching economic, cultural, and political transformations. Suriname's independence in 1975 brought little change in the life of most Maroons, but a civil war (1986–1992) between the national army of Suriname and Maroon "Jungle Commandos" (largely made up of Ndyukas but with a significant number of Saramakas as well) had devastating consequences. Whole villages along the Cottica River were annihilated, and some 10,000 Maroons were sent fleeing across the border into French Guiana. Today continuing battles over the control of the valuable mining and timber rights in the interior affect every aspect of contemporary Maroon life in Suriname, and many outside observers fear that the government has embarked on a policy of ethnocide toward the Maroons through its attempts to claim state ownership of their territories for the extraction of timber, gold, and other minerals.

RELIGIOUS BELIEFS AND RITUALS

The Suriname Maroons have always enjoyed an extremely elaborate ritual life. Such decisions as where to clear a garden or build a house, whether to make a trip, or how to deal with problems like theft or adultery are made in consultation with ancestors, spirits, gods embodied in snakes and other animals, and a variety of ritual powers that communicate with humans through such means as spirit possession, oracle sessions, and dreams. Both men and women participate in spirit possession, though mediums for some kinds of spirits (for example, *vodu* snake gods) tend to be women and those for others, such as *komanti* warrior gods, are almost always men. Gods and spirits, which are a constant presence in daily life, are also honored through frequent prayers, libations, feasts, and dances. Human misfortune is directly linked to other people's antisocial acts through complex chains of causation involving witchcraft or sorcery, gods, spirits, or ancestors. Any illness of other misfortune requires immediate divination and ritual action in collaboration with these spirits and others, such as warrior gods. Pregnancy—the key to continuity within the matrilineage—brings a period of heightened ritual danger and is managed in consultation with various spiritual powers. Birth, death, and other life crises are handled through extensive ritual, and much the same could be said of more mundane activities such as hunting a tapir or planting a rice field. Formal political life is also permeated with ritual. Village officials rule and adjudicate with the help of diverse oracles and shrines. For brief periods in Maroon history, particularly among the Ndyuka, authoritarian power has been exercised through religious means, as witch-finding cults or messianic movements have taken root for a time and then faded away.

Maroon religions incorporate a plethora of expressive forms, from esoteric ritual languages to formal prayer and oratory. Special drum languages, known for the most part only by ritual specialists, mark particular rites. And libations to ancestors and gods, with proverbial speech forming the core of invocations, are an everyday occurrence in every village. Particular matrilineal clans enjoy ownership of specialized cults (some dating back to the eighteenth-century wars of liberation), from those that conduct the rites for the birth of twins or find a person lost in the forest to others that set broken bones or cure gunshot wounds.

But Maroon culture emerges in its greatest intensity at funerals. Carried on over a period of many months and involving hundreds or even thousands of people, funerals unite the world of the living with that of the dead through a range of ritual practices and performance genres. The spirit of the deceased is interrogated regarding the cause of death, with two men carrying the coffin on their heads as a ritual specialist poses questions and the coffin moves its bearers back and forth or side to side in response. And specialized songs, drum rhythms, dances, festive foods, and riddling and folktale traditions join with the prayers, libations, proverbs (communicated by both speech and the *apinti*, "talking drum"), and spirit possession to effect the passage of the deceased person into the realm of the ancestors.

Amidst the hectic weeks of drumming, dancing, singing, feasting, and complex rituals that contribute to these festivities, the telling of folktales—which takes place during the night after the actual burial (as well as for some deaths on subsequent nights)—constitutes a special moment for people of all ages. The setting is more intimate than other funeral-related gatherings, typically involving some thirty to forty kinsfolk and neighbors, sitting on stools before the deceased's doorstep. Together, they in effect agree to transport themselves into a separate reality that they collectively create and maintain: "folktale-land," an earlier time as well as a distant place, where animals speak, where the social order is often inverted, where Maroon customs have been only partially worked out, and where the weak and clever tend to triumph over the strong and arrogant. Folktales are seen as entertainment and as fictions with deep moral lessons for the present—not as history or cosmological myths. Sitting by torchlight or the light of the moon, the participants at a tale-telling wake come face to face with age-old metaphysical problems and conundrums. By turns frightened by the antics of a villainous monster, doubled over with laughter at a lascivious song, or touched by a character's sentimental farewell, they experience an intellectually and emotionally rich evening of multimedia entertainment.

FOLKTALES

In the folktales of the Saramaka Maroons, the stock characters number in the scores and have a wide range of historical proveniences. Some, like the "scrawny little kid" (usually the youngest sibling who saves his sister from disaster), appear in some manifestation throughout African America. Others, like the giant, oafish "devils," have at least partial Christian and European roots. Still others, like Anansi the Spider or, more remarkably, Elephant (an animal whose memory is preserved by Saramakas at a remove of three centuries), are African to the core.

An evening of tale-telling among Saramakas begins with riddling, a long string of witty prompts and responses performed by two people at rapid-fire pace, ideally without pause, prefaced by the conventional exchange, *"Hílíti"* / *"Dáíti."* Then, after a few minutes, someone calls out *"Mató!"* the opening formula for tales. Another responds vigorously, *"Tòngôni!"* and everyone present steps over the invisible barrier into folktale-land. By calling out *"Mató!"* the first person takes center stage as the narrator of the first tale. And the person who replied by calling out *"Tòngôni!"* becomes the "responder" or "whatsayer," responsible for punctuating the narration at frequent intervals either with a conventional utterance, *"íya,"* or with interjections translatable as "That's true," "Really!" or "Right." Everyone present informally monitors the conscientiousness of this responder, whose performance is essential to the proper telling of the tale, complaining when the responses are too widely spaced or weakly delivered and collectively insisting that the telling maintain a clear call-and-response pattern. The teller and responder are often close friends or relatives and play out their interaction with joking, teasing, and collegial criticism that heighten the pleasure of the session.

Once underway, a tale should be punctuated at frequent intervals by short interruptions, each of which briefly evokes a longer tale, often simply through a song that plays a pivotal role in the fuller version. When the tale ends, some mix of compliments on its telling, animated discussion of its content and style, and extraneous conversation usually follow, but more or less quickly someone in the gathering calls out *"Mató!"* a second person responds with *"Tòngôni!"* and the next tale is already underway.

MUSIC

Musical forms are also at their most intense in the course of funerals. Special genres of drumming are brought into play and secular songs (which are also enjoyed on a daily basis in any number of formal and informal settings) are performed for the large crowds of participants, accompanied by handclapping and solo dances by men or women dressed in fashionable clothes, carefully done hairdos, and special accessories such as crocheted calfbands and multistranded beaded jewelry—some for beauty and others for protection against making a false step in the intricate footwork. Both songs and dances reflect concrete aspects of the performers' lives: lyrics evoke everything from local scandals and romantic dreams to coastal experiences and political rivalries, and dances imitate hummingbirds, urban factories, logging activities, and more.

ARTS AND CRAFTS

Perhaps the best-known aspect of the culture of the Suriname Maroons is their graphic arts, especially woodcarving. Men are the artists in this medium, producing exquisitely carved canoes, paddles, household furniture (stools and cabinets), architectural decorations (door lintels and even whole house façades), trays, kitchen implements, and combs. Eastern Maroons integrate vibrantly colorful painted designs in their carvings, whereas the Maroons of central Suriname limit their art to bas-relief, decorative tacks, and inlays of different tropical woods. The widely held notion that Maroon carvings are composed of symbolic **motifs** that can be "read" as messages of love is a fantasy of the Western imagination, but each decorated object does serve as a way for the artist to express his love for the woman to whom it is presented as a gift.

Women reciprocate with artistry of their own—often decorative sewing that reflects the latest styles of embroidery, patchwork, or appliqué. Women also carve beautiful organic designs, very different from the men's geometric carving style, on the inner surfaces of bowls made of calabashes, which grow on trees in the villages. These are used for elegant meal service to the men, who eat communally in small groups, separately from the women.

CHALLENGES OF THE MODERN WORLD

Maroons, sometimes imagined to be static holdovers from original African traditions, are in fact staunch enthusiasts for things new and innovative, especially in the verbal and visual arts. Young men are known for inventing play languages that are quickly superseded by the next generation's replacement. Newly introduced models of coastal imports such as pots and pans, enamelware, hammocks, and especially patterns of trade cotton are routinely celebrated with creative names that refer to current social events, whether marital gossip, political intrigues, or personal foibles. And artistic innovations such as a new woodcarving design or a

Saramaka woman dancing, 1968. (Photograph by Richard and Sally Price)

Aluku calabash (decorated gourd), collected in 1990. (From the collection of Richard and Sally Price)

241

Saramaka embroidered textile, sewn during the first half of the twentieth century. (From the collection of Richard and Sally Price)

novel sewing technique are the source of animated discussion. Despite an unmistakable underpinning that owes much to a generalized West and Central African heritage, all Maroon art and folklore is in its specific forms constantly on the move, producing what Amiri Baraka (writing about African American music in the United States) called "the changing same."

STUDIES OF MAROON FOLKLORE

Professional studies of Maroon folklore began in the 1920s, when Melville and Frances Herskovits conducted research for their *Suriname Folk-lore* (1936), which centers on the capital city of Paramaribo but includes a number of texts and observations on Maroons as well. For an analysis of the Herskovitses' pioneering **fieldwork** in Suriname, see R. and S. Price (2003.) Since that time, the major studies of verbal and graphic arts have been R. Price (2002), devoted to oral history; S. Price (1996), focusing on women's graphic and verbal arts; R. and S. Price (1991), a performance-based analysis and presentation of tale-telling and folktales; R. and S. Price (1994), which describes the participation of a troop of Saramaka, Ndyuka, and Aluku Maroons in the 1992 Festival of American Folklife; and R. and S. Price (1999), a heavily illustrated history and survey of the graphic, verbal, and musical arts of the different Maroon peoples of Suriname and French Guiana. For an account of religious movements among the Ndyuka Maroons, see Thoden van Velzen and van Wetering (1988). A recording of Maroon music, with extensive notes by R. and S. Price (*Music from Saramaka: A Dynamic Afro-American Tradition*) is available on cassette from Smithsonian Folkways.

BIBLIOGRAPHY

Herskovits, Melville, and Frances Herskovits. 1936. *Suriname Folk-lore*. Columbia Publications in Anthropology, No. 27. New York: Columbia University Press.

Price, Richard. 2002. *First-Time: The Historical Vision of an Afro-American People*. 2nd edition. Chicago: University of Chicago Press.

Price, Richard, and Sally Price. 1977. *Music from Saramaka: A Dynamic Afro-American Tradition* (sound recording). Smithsonian Folkways FW04225.

———. 1991. *Two Evenings in Saramaka*. Chicago: University of Chicago Press.

———. 1994. *On the Mall*. Bloomington: Indiana University Press.

———. 1999. *Maroon Arts: Cultural Vitality in the African Diaspora*. Boston: Beacon Press.

———. 2003. *The Root of Roots: Or, How Afro-American Anthropology Got Its Start*. Chicago: Prickly Paradigm Press/University of Chicago Press.

Price, Sally. 1996. *Co-wives and Calabashes*. 2nd edition. Ann Arbor: University of Michigan Press.

Thoden van Velzen, H.U.E., and W. van Wetering. 1988. *The Great Father and the Danger*. Dordrecht: Foris.

Richard Price and Sally Price

XAVANTE

GEOGRAPHY AND HISTORY

According to narratives told by Xavante (pronounced "Shah-vahn-te") elders, those who best know the tales of the beginning, Xavante people came from "the east"—from the place where the sun rises. Corroborating these narratives, documents from Brazil's colonial period locate the group on the eastern side of the Araguaia River in what is now the Brazilian state of Tocantins. Fleeing from slavers, settlers, mineral prospectors, and missionaries who intruded into their territory, during the late seventeenth and early eighteenth century Xavante peoples migrated west across the great river Araguaia and into the territory they now inhabit. Today approximately 11,000 Xavante live on six reserves in the state of Mato Grosso, Brazil. They are one of the largest indigenous groups in the Brazilian Amazon.

The move westward across the Araguaia separated the Xavante from their closest relatives, the Xerente, who remained on the eastern side of the great river. Scholars believe that historically the Xavante and Xerente constituted a single group. In narratives that recount their separation from the Xerente, contemporary Xavante elders tell of a huge freshwater dolphin rising up in the middle of the Araguaia, making the great river impassable. The dolphin terrified the people who had not yet traversed the river, and those who remained on the eastern shore, the Xerente, were left behind. This is how the Xavante divided from the Xerente, the elders say.

SOCIAL STRUCTURE AND RITUALS

Together the Xavante and Xerente make up the central branch of the Gê language family, one of the major families of the Amazon Basin. Like all Gê societies, Xavante social organization consists of cross-cutting binary groupings, or "moieties." One of these binary groupings, whose membership is determined through patrilineal descent, organizes individuals into two marriage categories called *poriza'õno* and *öwawê*. These groupings dictate that an individual marry someone from the other group, or "half." The other binary grouping consists of eight age sets, with four age sets in each grouping, or agamous moiety. Age sets bring together individuals from the two marriage halves so that individuals of both marriage groups, *poriza'õno* and *öwawê*, together form a single age-based group. A Xavante age set is somewhat analogous to a high school "class" that joins students from two rival middle or junior high schools into a single unified group. Xavante youth belong to the age set or class throughout their entire lives. Also like many middle-class North Americans, time and the increasing demands of family and professional activities diminish the importance

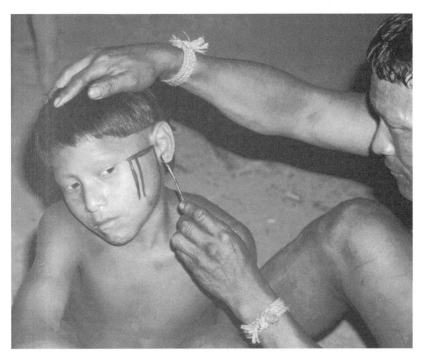

Father applying the *öwawē* patrilineal exogamous moiety marking to his son before the *ói'ó* club fight in 1986. (© by Laura R. Graham)

of one's age set (or high school class) affiliation as people grow older.

Numerous ceremonial activities create as well as publicly display these groupings that are the basis of much Xavante social life. The first public ceremony at which little boys engage is the *ói'ó* club fight. Boys participate from the time they can pick up a club and independently toddle into the fighting ring until they are ready to be inducted into the bachelors' hut, sometime between age seven and ten. This club fight highlights the opposition between the patrilineal exogamous moieties (marriage halves). *Ói'ó* also cultivate and display boys' fighting spirit and ability to withstand physical challenges, characteristics that are important to males in this traditionally hunting-gathering society.

On the eve of an *ói'ó*, fathers wash their sons with herb infusions that enhance these admirable male qualities. Fathers then lead their sons to the central plaza, where in the presence of the adult male community they paint their temples with the appropriate exogamous moiety insignia using a semi-permanent black dye extracted from the seeds of the genipapo plant. Before dawn on the day of the fight, fathers complete their sons' ornamentation by painting their bodies red with urucum, outfitting them with a white fiber waist-chord, and tying the signature-Xavante white cotton neck-tie under their chins. Once their ceremonial attire is com-

Boys battling in the *ói'ó* club fight in 1986. (© by Laura R. Graham)

plete, the boys are led to the central plaza, where each is given a mean-looking club fashioned from the stalk of a tuberous plant. One at a time, each boy is pitted against a boy of similar size from the opposite exogamous moiety. The little combatants attempt to hit each other as hard as they can until one of them throws down his club in defeat or, in the case of tiny tots, runs back to his father in tears. Strictly enforced guidelines limit hitting to relatively resistant areas of the back and shoulder and prevent anyone from getting seriously hurt. Xavante boys take great pride in their endurance and aggressive displays.

Two other ceremonial sporting competitions that Xavante enjoy are *Wa'i* wrestling matches and *buriti* log relay races called *uiwede*. These inspire and exhibit playful, competitive rivalries that exist between opposing agamous moieties. *Wa'i* wrestling matches publicly emphasize both exogamous and agamous divisions; log relay races emphasize agamous divisions by pitting age sets from opposing agamous moieties against each other. *Wa'i* wrestling matches take place prior to boys' induction into the bachelors' hut when they become members of an official age set. Young boys as well as girls who are the same age respond to taunts and challenges from a senior man and engage in lively standing wrestling matches that end when one (usually the senior male) successfully causes his opponent to fall. These are lighthearted challenges in which children wrestle with men (from the opposite marriage half who will become their age-set mentors once the age set is formed) who have a considerable size advantage over their opponents. When girls are called into the ring, several often join together to charge a single man whom they pursue in an amusing struggle that delights the onlookers, who laugh and cheer from the side.

Men apply body paint before ritual activity. (© by Laura R. Graham, 1987)

In *buriti* log relay races, runners sprint with an enormous and very heavy log (approximately eighty kilograms for men's races and sixty kilograms for women's races) before passing it onto the shoulder of a waiting member of the same age set or agamous moiety "team." Runners carry these tremendously heavy logs approximately six to eight kilometers from the race's starting point into the community center. Races always pit same sex agamous moiety teams against each other, and only adults are allowed to carry the logs. All able-bodied members of the community, however, join the race, making log-racing events exceptionally animated and fun. Log racing is, without a doubt, a favorite sporting activity.

After each log race, members of the principal participating age sets engage in collective song and dance performances, known as *da-ño're*. Performers sing and dance on the patios of designated houses on a performance tour that takes them from one end of the semicircular ring of houses to the other. The agamous moiety "teams" start their performance tours at opposite ends of the ring of houses and proceed in

The *uiwede* log race pits members of opposing agamous moieties against each other. (© by Laura R. Graham, 1987)

'Ritai'wa novitiates performing *da-ño're* in 1987. (© by Laura R. Graham)

opposite directions around the horseshoe-shaped ring of houses. The two groups' singing and dancing acoustically and visually highlight the opposition and rivalry between age sets from opposing agamous moieties, particularly when the groups sing and dance at adjacent houses near the apex of the semicircle of homes. Yet, within each group, individual participants, who are decorated with the same body paint designs and bodily ornaments, move identically while uttering the same vocables and short phrases over and over. The intersection of multiple expressive modalities formally displays the absorption of individual expression into collective expression and signals the merging of individual experience into collective experience.

SONGS AND DANCE

Da-ño're, collectively performed song and dance, is a quintessentially male form of expressive behavior, though women also perform on certain occasions. *Da-ño're* constitutes the single-most important public activity that pre-initiate bachelors' hut residents (known as *wapté*) and notiviates (known as *'ritai'wa*, adolescents) engage in as age-set groups. These performances, which the pre-initiate *wapté* present with the members of their sponsor or mentor group (consisting of an age set of initiated men from the same agamous moiety), engender extraordinarily strong emotional bonds between participants. Within the male life cycle, solidarity among members of a cohort varies in proportion to the frequency of *da-ño're* performance. Age-set bonds are strongest during the pre-initiate and novitiate phases when males regularly engage in frequent *da-ño're* performance.

Da-ño're express as well as engender social cohesion between other groups as well. For example, whenever senior men—who individually belong to several distinct age sets that no longer regularly sing and dance together as a group—wish to emphasize the collective solidarity of their group, they perform *da-ño're*. Senior men occasionally summon an entire community, including women and girls, to perform *da-ño're*. This occurs, for instance, following the resolution of an extremely divisive factional dispute. In such cases, *da-ño're* performance promotes as well as expresses cohesion among the disputing parties and among members of the community as a whole.

Da-ño're are compositions that initiated men "receive" from the ancestors in dreams. At the ear-piercing ceremony, a highlight of the male initiation complex, a new initiate obtains his first set of earplugs. These are little sticks crafted from woods considered to possess powerful dream-inducing capabilities. With the earplugs a boy acquires the means to "receive" songs from the ancestors through dreams. Today young men make the analogy between earplugs and antennae: earplugs give men the ability to "tune in" to the ancestors in their dreams. Earplugs point to a young man's ability to represent his dreams as songs, which constitute an important criterion for a man's social status as an adult. When women and girls perform *da-ño're*, they sing and dance together with men. In one ceremony that is part of the male initiation complex, however, a women's age set performs *da-ño're* without men. Since women do not possess earplugs, they are generally considered incapable of dreaming *da-ño're*.

Performing *da-ño're* with their age-set sponsors is the first activity that *wapté* pre-initiates do together as an official age set. In this performance the new pre-initiates display their membership in the age set, and the performance effectively establishes the existence of the new age set as a cohort. Subsequently during their residence in the bachelors' hut and throughout adolescence after initiation, pre-initiate boys and novitiate adolescents continually present *da-ño're* with the members of their age-set cohort. Repeated performances with the mentors teach pre-initiates the formal characteristics of different *da-ño're* types and proper performance practice as well as the entire *da-ño're* **repertoire** of the mentor age set. These performances expressively promote continuity between age sets of the same agamous moiety and create a cohesive soundscape within the village over time.

When Xavante speak of *da-ño're*, they refer to a unified performance complex, not just the acoustic features produced by voices. Participants sing and move together forming a circle with clasped hands. Xavante classify three distinct performance types under the generic term *da-ño're*. *Da-praba*, *da-dzarõno*, and *da-hipópó* are differentiated on the basis of the accompanying physical movements of the dance steps and the time of day suitable for their performance. *Da-praba* are performed in the late morning and throughout the day when the sun is full and strong. Male dancers mark time by stepping one foot to the side on one beat and bringing the other to join it on the next stressed beat. Women keep their feet together, as they do when dancing all types of *da-ño're*, and hop sideways. In this fashion the entire circle rotates in one direction. At transitional breaks in the song, the movements are reversed and the circle doubles back in the opposite direction. The physical movements that accompany *da-praba* are the most vigorous of all the *da-ño're* dances; *da-praba* are also perfomed at the quickest tempo. By engaging in this fast-paced and energetic dance form under the hot sun, performers display their physical stamina and endurance.

Xavante call *da-ño're* performed in the late afternoon and early evening *da-dzarõno*. Male dancers remain in a fixed spot while forcefully stepping one foot slightly forward and to the side. The third type of *da-ño're* is *da-hipópó*, "leg shaking" or "leg-bouncing" songs. *Da-hipópó* are performed in the evening, throughout the night, and into the early morning. Standing performers bend their knees outward in time with the metric pulse of the music. The knee bends cause performers' feet to shuffle back and forth, creating a brushing percussive sound. *Da-hipópó* that are performed from sundown until about midnight are simply called *da-hipópó*. Those that are performed between 1:00 A.M. and approximately 4:00 A.M. are called *marawa'wa* (middle morning), and *da-hipópó* performed between the time just before until just after sunrise are called *a'wê'u* (sunrise). Distinct types of *da-ño're* are thus considered appropriate for specific segments of a twenty-four-hour cycle or social soundscape.

CEREMONIAL WAILING AND HYMNS

Da-wawa, or ceremonial wailing, is another expressive vocal behavior that Xavante consider appropriate for specific slots within the twenty-four-hour soundscape. *Da-wawa* are highly melodic, stylized expressions of intense emotion that elders perform, typically at dawn or dusk. Both men and women use *da-wawa* laments to express powerful individual emotions associated with grief and loss, especially death, as well as extreme joy, particularly at reunions of close kin or friends after periods of prolonged absence. Specific events such as hearing a song that invokes powerful memories of nostalgia may also prompt an elder to keen at other times. In contrast to *da-ño're* singing and dancing, age rather than gender determines who can use this expressive form. Like *da-ño're*, however, *da-wawa* are dreamed compositions. An individual receives *da-wawa* through dreams only after she or he is considered to be an elder, usually after having many children.

The formal characteristics of *da-wawa* vocalizations emphasize intimacy and the experience of individual emotions. Individuals perform *da-wawa* in the most intimate of social spaces, from the sleeping mat or bed, far from the village center and the epitome of social space. In situations where wailing takes place in the presence of others, when a body is laid out or at interment, it is not a coordinated group expression. Individuals retain their separate forms and seemingly lose themselves, as if entranced, in their individual expressions of grief.

Although *da-wawa* are highly melodic and sound like "singing" to Western ears, Xavante do not consider *da-wawa* to be singing in any way. They classify *da-wawa* as a distinct expressive type. In contrast to their melodic complexity *da-wawa* are minimally linguistic. Their texts consist of a limited number of vowel sounds: [a], [e], and [i], which combine with a consonantal onset, either a glottal stop ['] or [h]. Consequently, *da-wawa* texts do not transmit propositions. Stripped of any referential content, the texts foreground the lament's message of affect. This affect is enhanced by creaking voice, wavering vocalic utterances, high-pitched falsettos, and audible gasps for breath that recall "natural" or spontaneous expressions of grief.

Hedza, "hymns"or "prayers," are a type of collectively performed dream-song predominantly performed by women but received through dreams by a few exceptional men, usually elders. Men also summon women to sing; this usually occurs when senior male leaders wish to promote harmony within the community. Men typically call the women to perform *hedza* in the early morning or in the evening before the men gather for their regular evening men's council in the central plaza.

MEN'S COUNCILS AND ORATORY

Initiated men gather in the central plaza twice daily, at dawn and in the evening, for the men's council or *warã*. Like the adolescents who gather in the central plaza in the middle of the night before singing around the village, men summon their cohort with short, high-pitched calls or shouts of "Kai, kai, kaaaaaaai." Morning reunions are typically less structured than evening meetings, which often commence as the bachelors' hut residents are singing around the village with their mentor group. As men lie on their backs gazing up at the stars or sit in the darkness, they listen to the intermingling of many voices, for when speaking in groups, Xavante frequently make simultaneous utterances producing an acoustically fascinating discursive pattern in which individual speakers interweave their discourse with the utterances of others.

Elders adopt a unique form of speech known as "*ĩhi*" (nasalized i) *mrémé*, "elders' speech." *Ĩhi mrémé* is the vocal hallmark of old age and prestige among the elderly and is considered eloquent and enjoyable to listen to. Characterized by extensive repetition and parallelism, a unique voice quality, and a special intonation patter, this speech style has a distinctive acoustic shape. Phrases uttered in *ĩhi mrémé* tend to be short and formally bounded. They are characterized by descending pitch and end with a slight rise instead of a decline, as in everyday conversational speech. Phrases are also spoken with greater pharyngeal constriction than is common in everyday speech, and speakers mark the end of phrases with explosive glottal stops and releases. Although it is impossible to identify acoustic pitch in this form of rhetorical speech, a "music-like" quality results from the repetition of phrases and clauses with parallel intonation contours that are framed by regular, staccato rhythmical patterns.

Very elderly men and some elderly women achieve eloquence as speakers of *ĩhi mrémé*. Adept speakers employ this speech style in other situations, when they wish to stress their age, wisdom, and the importance of their speech, especially when giving instructions to youth, making ceremonial greetings, and telling traditional tales, for example. When elders speak of the origin of the world—the savannah, a complex eco-zone consisting of upland grasslands with tropical forest galleries along the rivers—and the origin of foods, fire, and many other things that these traditionally semi-nomadic hunter-gatherers use when harvesting the natural resources of their land while on trek, they speak using *ĩhi mrémé*. Elders dramatize their narratives, quoting the speech of protagonists and assuming the identities of stories' characters to make the tales come alive for listeners.

The Jaguar tale that explains the origin of fire recounts how a young boy steals a burning ember from the fire of cunning old Jaguar, who wanted to eat him. Others relate the ways that various foods that form the basis of the traditional diet came into being. Star Woman brings produce down from the sky. Other "tasty things" are introduced through the transformations of two pre-initiate boys, the Parinai'a, who also metamorphose into animals such as dogs, which are essential for survival in a society of hunters. The Parinai'a invoked their superhuman powers after sneaking away from their trekking group and working when no one could see them. This excerpt illustrates how skilled narrators such as the elder Warodi assume protagonists' voices and how narrators embellish their stories with fascinating sounds that simulate listeners' imaginations. These techniques, combined with the unique features of *ĩhi mrémé* elders' speech, engage listeners and facilitate the transmission of Xavante traditions across generations.

> Now they are on trek.
> Next, they stay inside the little shelter and the two remained behind . . .
> "Hey, my friend, what will we be now?"
> "What will we be for real"?
> "Let's be dogs!" [whispered voice]
> "Yes! That's it! Let's be dogs for real!" [whispered voice]
> "Hau, hau, hau" [breathy voice, dogs barking]
> They are playing like dogs . . .
> Now they are following behind the trekkers.
> The elders are in single file.
> The two [dogs] nudge up against their legs.
> "Get away! They [dogs] always run too close!" [tense voice, elders' speech] . . .
> I don't know how they named their idea [dog] so quickly.

CHALLENGES OF THE MODERN WORLD

Contemporary Xavante are attempting to adapt to life within the limited, bounded territorial spaces of the six indigenous reserves they inhabit. They are adjusting their traditional semi-nomadic lifestyle to a necessarily more sedentary lifestyle and attempting to cope with the inability of their traditional subsistence patterns to meet their current needs. Their reserves are surrounded (sometimes invaded) by large ranches devoted primarily to cattle ranching or to monocrop soy or upland rice agribusiness. In some areas relations between Xavante and neighboring ranchers are extremely tense as heated disputes over land persist. Despite the challenges they confront, Xavante continue to practice the many expressive traditions they consider essential to their identity.

BIBLIOGRAPHY

Aytai, Desidério. 1985. *O Mundo Sonoro Xavante*. Coleção Museu Paulista, Etnologia, Vol. 5. São Paulo: Universidade de São Paulo.

Graham, Laura R. 1995. *Performing Dreams: Discourses of Immortality among the Xavante of Central Brazil*. Austin: University of Texas Press.

———. 1996. Three Modes of Shavante Vocal Expression: Wailing, Collective Singing, and Political Oratory. In *Native South American Discourse*, edited by Joel Sherzer and Greg Urban. Berlin: Mouton de Gruyter. 83–118.

———. 2000. "The One Who Created the Sea": Tellings, Meanings, and Intertextuality in the Translation of Xavante Narrative. In *Translating Native Latin American Verbal Art: Ethnopoetics and Ethnography of Speaking*, edited by K. Sammons and J. Sherzer. Washington, DC: Smithsonian Institution Press. 252–271.

Laura R. Graham

YANOMAMI

GEOGRAPHY AND HISTORY

The Yanomami, a Native American people numbering about 23,000, live in the Amazon Basin of southern Venezuela and northern Brazil. They are basically horticulturalists, who also hunt and gather. They have also engaged in trading with Europeans and European-descended peoples for centuries, adapting well to their environment. They have, however, come to the attention of most people through Napoleon Chagnon's description of them as fierce people in the many editions of his *Yanomamo: The Fierce People* (1968).

A number of good **ethnographies** of the Yanomami present a more rounded view of them and their periodic warfare (for example, Salamone 1997, Colchester 1984, and Lizot 1985). Some of these overlap Chagnon's **fieldwork**, especially Lizot (1985), Ramos (1995), and Saffirio and Scaglion (1984). These studies present a view of Yanomami family life, trade, naming practices, and adaptation to modern life. Familiarity with these aspects of life as well as with religion aid in understanding Yanomami folklore. The ethnographers agree that the Yanomami are far more complicated than Chagnon's portrait of them suggests. They have been put on reservations where until recently they were hunted by people. They have not had room to expand in more traditional ways, creating artificial situations for conflict. The now infamous measles epidemic that occurred during Chagnon's initial fieldwork exacerbated conflict. Chagnon's work has been used to paint the Yanomami as comparable to chimpanzees. His unrelenting grim portrait of them has been used to exemplify people stuck at an earlier stage of evolutionary development. Citing Chagnon, scholars have dehumanized the Yanomami. For example, Ghiglier (1999) states that the Yanomami routinely rape women as part of their survival strategy. Deriving his views from Chagnon's

A Yanomami woman spins cotton from her hammock as her child looks on, in the village of Demini. (© John Maier Jr./The Image Works)

"fierce people" image, Ghiglier also revives the theory of pre-logical thinking. He claims that the Yanomami are a prime example of a people trapped on the "logical" treadmill of war. As proof he cites a number of their traditional beliefs, especially those that attribute the cause of deaths to sorcery.

MYTHS, LEGENDS, AND FOLKTALES

It is not surprising that the Yanomami view other people in derogatory terms, especially those who come from over the waters. An origin myth makes the point. The son of Omauwa (one of the first beings) became very thirsty. Omauwa and his brother dug a hole for water, but they dug so deep that water gushed forth and covered the jungle. Many drowned. Some of the first beings survived by cutting down trees and floating on them. They became foreigners and floated away. The Yanomami survived by climbing mountains. Raharariyoma painted red dots all over her body and plunged into the lake, causing it to recede. Omauwa then caused her to be changed into a rahara, a dangerous snake-like monster that lives in large rivers.

Yanomami consider themselves to be "real" humans, whereas foreigners are degenerate copies of real humans. In another myth, a great flood drowns many people. Some floated off on logs and returned back speaking "crooked" Yanomami. A spirit fished these ancestors of non-Yanomami from the water downstream, made them come to life again, and sent them back "home."

Another myth articulates the Yanomami belief in levels of reality. It relates how the Yanomami dwell on a level of reality, Her Ka Misi, which was formed by the falling of a piece of a higher level, *hedu*. Original humans were part spirit and part animal. When they fell, their spirits burst forth.

The Yanomami share a flood story with many other peoples. This creation myth also serves to distinguish them from others. The myth holds that the "normal people" ran from the flood, climbing to high ground. These normal people became Yanomami. Those people who did not run from the flood by climbing up to high ground were the crazy people. These people sought to escape the flood through building sea-going vessels. The crazy people became foreigners.

Religious beliefs figure into Yanomami stories. They believe in four levels of reality. Things fall from a higher level to a lower one. The highest level of reality is a pristine one. It is the tender level from which many things originated, but it plays little role in everyday life. The Yanomami regard each of the levels differently, including the lowest level in which people fall to cannibalism. Each level has its stories about spirits, demigods, and evil people.

There is, for example, the story about the son of Omauwa, who was one of the original beings. This son became so thirsty that Omauwa and his brother dug for water. However, they dug so far that the rainforest became flooded and many people drowned. Some people cut down trees and floated away on them, while the Yanomami climbed mountains to escape. Raharariyoma, another of the original people, painted red dots all over her body. Then she jumped into the water and caused it to recede. Omauwa changed her into a dangerous snake.

This story displays a bit of the battle of the sexes. The creation story explaining the origin of men and women addresses the issue more explicitly. Men came about when an ancestor shot Moon in the stomach. Moon's blood fell to earth and changed into men. These men were fierce. There were degrees of fierceness. Thicker blood led to greater ferocity, thinner blood to less ferocity. Women, however, sprang from a fruit called *wabu*. A man saw a fruit on a vine that had eyes. He tossed it aside, and it immediately turned into a woman with a large vagina. Eventually, the man noticed her large and hairy vagina and copulated with her, as did all the other men. They produced many daughters and then copulated with them as well.

The Yanomami draw on their environment for stories. Unsurprisingly, there is a large body of folktales about the relationship of the jaguar and the Yanomami. The jaguar can take on human form. In this guise, it kills and eats men. This is related to the Yanomami fear of cannibalism. Like the Yanomami, the jaguar is a hunter. It also hunts men as do the Yanomami in warfare.

The jaguar stories also distinguish between nature and culture. The jaguar in the wild is part of nature, a creature of the forest. However, once caught and brought into the village, it becomes part of culture, a creature of the village. The jaguar presents a problem to the Yanomami because of its ambiguity. Jaguar is a natural creature that somehow has a number of human capacities. However, as compensation for their jealousy of him, he is portrayed in their stories as a stupid brute who is always defeated by the superiority of the Yanomami. Nevertheless, the Yanomami fear the jaguar, especially its ability to take human form and hunt and consume humans. They believe that they themselves have an innate disposition to eat humans. They are both attracted and repelled by the idea and express great disgust at anyone who eats meat not thoroughly cooked.

The jaguar story that best demonstrates the ambiguous attitude that Yanomami have for the jaguar is that of *misi*, the tortoise. Obviously, the tortoise is vulnerable when on its back. The story tells that the Original Beings from the village of Manakae-teri want through the forest hunting and collecting food. They found a tortoise, which they made into a pet. Meanwhile, unknown to them, Jaguar was killing everyone, and they were marked to be his victims. The Yanomami fled the village and left their tortoise dangling from a vine, a practice the Yanomami still use for their valuable possessions. Jaguar came into the village and saw the dangling tortoise. After Jaguar circled the village and found no humans, he came to the hut where the tortoise was dangling. The tortoise bit Jaguar on his snout. The more Jaguar struggled, the more the tortoise held on. Finally, the tortoise and Jaguar fell to the ground, and the jaguar died. Tortoise packed for a camping trip. On the way he found his owners. They had made a bridge. He crossed it and caught up with them. They were overjoyed to see their pet and to learn than he had survived his fight with Jaguar. When the owners returned to the village, they exclaimed when they saw

The Yanomami draw on their environment for stories. There is a large body of folktales about the relationship between the jaguar and the Yanomami. (General Research Division, The New York Public Library, Astor, Lenox and Tilden Foundations)

Jaguar and remarked on how big he was. Tortoise died on hearing this. The Yanomami cremated him and ate his ancestors. They recited his great deeds. People in other villages requested gourds of his ashes so that they could honor him as well. The simple tortoise at its most helpless had defeated the jaguar.

The Yanomami have an explanation in their flood story for the creation of humans. They do not, however, have an explanation for the first beings. They assume that these creatures existed when the cosmos came into being. These *no badabö*, or first creatures, played very specific parts in the processes of creation that took place after their own existence. For example, they are responsible for the origin of animals and plants.

Lest the Yanomami sound humorless, it should be noted that many of their stories are quite funny. People enjoy observing men, often high on hallucinogens, acting out the stories, improvising as they perform. The basic facts of the story, that the Caiman Ancestor, *Iwarwa*, was tricked into making his fire available to all because an obscene act caused him to laugh, are known to all. However, performers are free to elaborate on this outline. They can add details, prance as they wish, and use gestures.

As seen in the myth of the creation of men and women, sex is rather important in the Yanomami view of things. Both the relationship between men and women and the biological characteristics of each are important in their stories. There are many words for sex and its related activities in the Yanomami language. The Yanomami have separate origin myths for men and women. However, at least some Yanomami dispute these accounts. They cite a different version, one in which women were created from the thinnest blood of the moon. These women then mated with men. Men also mated with their female offspring, adding a double-incest theme to the story.

Stories focus on themes that are significant in the culture of the people. The fear of cannibalism and the ambiguity that Yanomami feel toward Jaguar are obvious in the relationship they feel to jaguars. The Yanomami are endocannibals. They consume the ashes of their own people. They hunt and kill people. In some sense, they identify with Jaguar. The wish-fulfillment aspect of Jaguar stories is that Jaguar is always outsmarted and made to look stupid by weaker creatures, obviously the Yanomami themselves. The creation stories offer another glimpse into Yanomami life. The problem of incest is common to creation myths. Men and women are seen as variations on a common theme. According to French anthropologist Claude Lévi-Strauss, creation myths characteristically struggle with significant intellectual problems. In the Yanomami myths, either males and females are equal or they are not. If they are equal, then all humans have descended from siblings through an act of incest. If a separate creation occurred for men and women, then humans are not equal. The Yanomami creation stories demonstrate that ambiguity quite clearly.

The separation of Yanomami from other peoples through a deluge indicates their belief in the craziness of non-Yanomami. In common with most peoples of the earth, they view others as not really human and consequently capable of inexplicable folly.

STUDIES OF YANOMAMI FOLKLORE

In addition to the ethnographies cited earlier, other useful sources on the Yanomami and their folklore include Chagnon (1979), Good (1995), and Smoles (1976).

Worthwhile Internet sites include the University of Manitoba homepage (www.umanitoba.ca/faculties/arts/anthropology/tutor/case_studies/yanomamo), the Yanamamo homepage (www.wugb.edu/~galta/mrr/yano/yano.htm), the Ethnographics Gallery (lucy.ukc.ac.uk/EthnoAtlas/Hmar/Cult_dir/Culture.7884), and the Yanomamo Research Group homepage (www.sscf.ucsh.edu/~cejal).

BIBLIOGRAPHY

Chagnon, Napoleon A. 1968. *Yanamamo: The Fierce People*. New York: Holt, Rinehart, and Winston.

———. 1979. Life Histories, Blood Revenge, and Warfare in Tribal Population. *Science* 239: 985–992.

Colchester, M. 1984. Rethinking Stone Age Economics: Some Speculations concerning the Pre-Columbian Yanomama Economy. *Human Ecology* 12: 291–314.

Ghiglieri, Michael P. 1999. *The Dark Side of Man: Tracing the Origins of Male Violence*. Cambridge, MA: Perseus Book.

Good, Kenneth. 1995. The Yanomamo Keep on Trekking. *Natural History* 104: 56–65.

Lizot, Jacques. 1985. *Tales of the Yanomami: Daily Life in the Venezuelan Forest*. New York: Cambridge University Press.

Ramos, Alcida Rita. 1995. *Sanuma Memories: Yanomami Ethnography in Times of Crisis*. Madison: University of Wisconsin Press.

Saffirio, Giovanni, and Richard Scaglion. 1984. Hunting Efficiency among Acculturated and Unaccculturated Yanomama Villages. *Journal of Anthropological Research* 38: 315–327.

Salamone, Frank A. 1997. *The Yanomami and Their Interpreters*. Lanham, MD: University Press of America.

Smoles, William J. 1976. *The Yanomama Indians: A Cultural Geography*. Austin: University of Texas Press.

Frank Salamone

Mexico and Central America

MAYA

GEOGRAPHY AND HISTORY

Although scholars still use descriptions like "Mesoamerica" and "Maya culture," it is difficult, if not impossible, to find articles or books that discuss Maya folkways in their broad diversity or cover all the regions where speakers of one of the twenty-six Maya languages currently reside. Most studies focus on a particular Maya-speaking community and situate the study within the region, state, or nation where that community is located rather than the "culture area." Even a recent supplement to the *Handbook of Middle American Indians* (2000), which contains general ethnographic and demographic information, contains three separate articles: one on highland Chiapas, a second on Guatemala, and a third on Yucatán. Information on the Maya of Belize is incorporated into the article on Yucatán, and Honduras and El Salvador are scarcely mentioned. To a certain extent, of course, this division of labor is understandable. Academic work requires specialization, the Maya languages spoken in Guatemala and Chiapas are very different from that of Yucatán and Belize, and the geography, history, politics, and economy of the Maya highlands (encompassing parts of Chiapas and Guatemala) are markedly different from the Maya lowlands.

At present it is difficult to generalize about the fate of spoken Maya. Yucatec Maya, the only Maya language spoken on the peninsula, seems safe for now. Although the percentage of Maya speakers continues to decline, the absolute number—estimated at 704,000—seems to be increasing, and the concentration of Yucatec Maya speakers in certain regions of the Yucatan ensures its use in daily life.

Peoples of Mexico.

A 1995 estimate suggests that in Chiapas approximately 950,000 people speak one of six Maya languages (Tzeltal, Tzotzil, Tojolabal, Ch'ol, Lacandon, and Mocho). However, Tzotzil and Tzeltal account for roughly three-fourths of this number. A recent estimate indicates that fewer than 900 people speak Lacandon, and Mocho is spoken only by individuals older than sixty. Therefore, it will soon suffer the fate of Chiapenec, which recently disappeared. Similarly, while more than 3 million people speak one of twenty different Mayan languages in Guatemala, the distribution of Maya speakers tilts strongly toward K'iche' with roughly 1 million speakers. At the other extreme, Itzaj, Tiko, and Mopan are nearly extinct, and several others (Awakatik, Sakapultek, S'pakapense, and Uspantele) are spoken in only one administrative district.

However, census data, which are questionable at best, do not fully reflect the fate of the language. One needs to look at the language itself, since languages begin to decay long before the last speaker dies. For example, despite the relatively large number of Yucatec Maya speakers, many noun classifiers have disappeared from the lexicon, and Spanish terms are routinely substituted for Maya. Languages begin to disappear because the people who speak them live in ecological zones that are being devastated or because they experience serious economic or political dislocations. Mesoamerican populations have faced more than their share of problems in recent decades.

NOTIONS OF SPACE AND TIME

Intimately related to language are notions of time, space, cosmos, body, and soul. For example, while English speakers use two terms to situate themselves in relation to objects in their perceptual field, Yucatec Maya speakers use five, including a term to describe spatial relations (for example, intermittent space) that English speakers lack. Moreover, space is rarely empty or secular. Every space has a *yuumil* (lord owner). Similarly, despite the violence and disturbances of the 1980s, the 260-day divinatory calendar (*tzolkin*) retains an important place in ritual healing and daily life among the K'iche' Maya of highland Guatemala. "Mountain maize," according to Dennis Tedlock (1989), "is sown, as humans are conceived on a particular day name and number and plants or babies vegetate or gestate for nine months, ideally culminating on the same name and number of the 260 day calendar as they got their start." Ethnographers have also written eloquently about the complexity of the Maya soul (which according to some accounts contains thirteen parts), the division of the cosmos into nine or thirteen planes, and the persistence of civil-religious hierarchies through which office holders meet their obligation to the community and pay homage to their ancestors.

At the same time, however, ethnographers have noted an erosion in traditional forms of keeping time, marking space, and religious practice. Although the ancient Maya calendar—with its division into eighteen months of twenty days and one five-day month—was the only calendar used by elderly people as recently as 1970 in certain highland communities, the Western calendar and the clock are now ubiquitous in Maya homes. In all regions, a shift from subsistence agricultural and maize production—which is central to Maya religious practice—to commercial agriculture and various types of wage labor has occurred. In many cases this entails the migration of men, and increasingly women, from their community of origin to lowland plantations, cities, or makeshift communities on the outskirts of tourist centers such as Cancún. While the problem may be most acute in highland Chiapas, where land shortages are severe, such emigration is also common in Yucatán and Guatemala. In addition, aggressive recruitment campaigns by Catholic and Protestant missionaries have targeted Maya communities and, more specifically, traditional Maya practices that involve the consumption of alcohol or are thought to be "wasteful" or "pagan." One hopes, though, that Maya communities will continue adding newer things "to older things rather than replacing them," something the Maya have done for centuries.

ZAPATISTA REBELLION

Political repression and neo-liberal economic reforms have also affected Maya during the last few decades. Although selecting the introduction of the North American Free Trade Agreement (1 January 1994) to stage an uprising might be considered an interesting act of "guerilla theater," the neo-Zapatista or EZLN uprising in Chiapas was, in fact, a response to reforms initiated by former president Salinas-Gotari (1988–1994). In particular, the rebellion is linked to the debt crisis of the 1980s that led to cuts in social welfare programs and a shift in national agrarian policy that effectively ended land distribution after 1992 and led to privatization of the *ejido* (public lands). Although the occupation of San Cristóbal was short-lived, a counterinsurgency campaign by the Zedillo government (1994–2000) continued for several years, resulting in uncalculated death and destruction. However, thanks to the popularity of *Commandante* Marcos (the leader of the insurrection), it was not long before the Zapatista movement itself became the object of contemporary folklore. In addition to a wide array of handicrafts, visitors to the highland Chiapas town of Amatenango in the mid-1990s could purchase a *supkomitanto* Marcos, a 15.5-centimeter masked figurine, as well as images of neo-Zapatista soldiers. While the political violence in Guatemala—which resulted in thousands of deaths in the 1980s—spawned no new cottage industries as it did in Chiapas, it did produce a number of very macabre jokes attributing the disappearance of Maya villagers to OMNIs (unidentified military objects), a play on the term OVNI (Spanish for UFO).

FOLKTALES

Within Mayan folklore the folktale has received more attention than any other form. An early example is Daniel Brinton's *Folk-lore of Yucatán*, a study of Mayan folk literature published by the London Folk-lore Society in 1983. Although Brinton's study is by no means systematic and contains no complete texts, the author does identify several characters and **motifs** that appear in later collections and are discussed throughout the peninsula today. One such character is X-tabay, a young, seductive woman who lives in the trunk of a large *ceiba* tree and captures the attention of hunters by combing her long, beautiful hair with a large comb (*xache'*). As the hunter approaches, X-tabay turns her back and runs away, but slowly enough—and with an occasional glance over her shoulder—so the hunter knows to pursue her. Soon the unsuspecting hunter catches up with her and ardently embraces the beautiful X-tabay. However, just as he begins to wrap his arms around her, X-tabay turns into a thorny bush or cactus with huge talons. Heartbroken and bloody, the hunter returns home, develops a high fever, becomes delirious, or dies. Because Maya villages, particularly in northwest Yucatán, were despoiled by large, agro-industrial *henequén* plantations during the late nineteenth and early twentieth centuries—and *henequén* is a type of cactus (*agave fourcroydes*)—the popularity of this story possibly relates to Yucatán's early insertion into the global economy. Brinton, however, was content to compare X-tabay with legendary women of European tradition like the sirens of Greek mythology and saw little need to contextualize or historicize the story. Indeed, although one would expect *henequen* to figure prominently in regional folklore because of its impact on social life, little or nothing has been written about this plant. In contrast, untold volumes have been written on maize deities and other ancient Maya symbols.

A more systematic approach to Mayan folk literature can be found in Margaret Park Redfield's study of Dzitas, Yucatán (1937), which was part of a larger study of the transformation of "folk" society into "civilization" conducted by her husband Robert Redfield, Alfonso Villa Rojas, and others in the 1930s and 1940s. In *The Folk Literature of a Yucatecan Town*, Margaret Redfield divides oral literature into three categories: the *cuento*, a fanciful tale; the *ejemplo*, a true story with a moral; and the *historia*, a more-or-less true story without a moral. Whereas the *cuento*—which includes Maya animal stories as well as tales of European origin—was considered a stable, well-defined form, Redfield found the *historia* difficult to define, since it often tended toward anecdote or fantasy. Like many ethnographers of her time, Redfield considered herself a "functionalist" and, therefore, was concerned less with the origin of a particular story than its contemporary use. For example, the following *ejemplos* from her collection might be used to teach children (or even adults!) not to spread rumors or say mean things about others:

> People said that I had twins because the children had two fathers. But God punished them for talking this way. It is not good to talk about other people, and so these same women had twins too.

> You should not make fun of people. Once there was a girl who used to go by a place where sat a hunchback. She would always make fun of him. Later when her child was born, it was a hunchback.

Moreover, many of the *cuentos* in Redfield's collection are of a religious character, inserting biblical figures like Jesus into distinctively Maya settings and narrating their ability to escape from devilish Jews who pursue them through forests and corn-fields. In this sense, Yucatec Maya tales are similar not only to tales collected in highland Chiapas by Robert M. Laughlin but also to dance-dramas in which certain performers are considered a composite of different demonic characters, including Jews, Moors, black men, monkeys, and occasionally priests. Although these dance-dramas were introduced by Spanish missionaries in the sixteenth century to teach the new religion, they are still performed, although under "new management," in several highland communities.

Unlike Redfield, Robert Laughlin *was* initially interested in the origin of particular tales as well as in discovering which themes are unique to Maya culture. Although he later abandoned this quest, it is interesting to read about the journey. In *The People of the Bat*, a collection of tales and dreams from highland Chiapas, Laughlin notes that a description of a woman's "pestiferous wound" was not only absent from other collections he had examined but seemed so typical of Zinacanteco thought that he assumed it must be their own addition to a common European tale. Only later did he discover an almost identical description in the work of Rabelais, the sixteenth-century French satirist. Similarly, Laughlin believed that a story describing how Christ punished a farmer by turning his field to stone was a Mesoamerican adaptation of Bible lore because he could find no version of the tale in Spain or other Latin American countries. Once again, however, the same tale was later discovered in a European text, in this case a thirteenth-century Latin manuscript. Ultimately, Laughlin concludes that the origin of maize (that is, how man obtained maize from a raven who stole it from a cave) is probably the only motif unique to the Maya highlands.

A more contemporary approach to oral literature appears in the work of Allan Burns. In *An Epoch of Miracles*, Burns not only broadens the scope of oral literature to include things not considered by Redfield but relates his typology to indigenous speech categories rather than the categories employed by previous scholars. For example, Burns notes that Maya speakers distinguish between playful speech (*baaxal tan*), which includes riddles, jokes, and songs and ancient conversations (*uchbin tzibalo'ob*), a stylized speech genre that includes creation tales or myths. Burns also draws attention to the contextual and performative aspects of storytelling. In addition to noting that Yucatec Maya like to tell riddles at wakes, he argues that Maya storytelling is best understood as dialogue or conversation. Whereas the Bible views creation as a monologue, the Quiché Mayan Popol Vuh views creation as the result of a conversation among the gods. Finally, Burns identifies poetic features of Yucatec Maya narrative such as parallelism, onomatopoeia, verbal reduplication, and other sound effects.

As Burns and others note, the Maya are neither prudish nor puritanical. The primary purpose of oral narrative is to entertain, and storytellers are not shy about discussing illicit sexual activities (though they prefer discussing sex in public rather than in private or in front of their wives). One of the more humorous stories in Burns's collection begins within an adulterous relationship. In "San Antonio," a woman and her lover have retired to her hammock when she hears her husband at the door. To avoid a violent confrontation, she ushers her consort into the tabernacle next door, where San Antonio is housed and instructs her lover to put on the saint's clothing. The adulterer does as he is told and remains standing in a saintly pose for many hours. Things go from bad to worse the next day when the husband sells his "image" of San Antonio, and the adulterer-saint is led away on a pedestal amidst an explosion of firecrackers. By the time he arrives in his new tabernacle, his eyes are burning, and he is about to collapse. Still he tries to maintain appearances as the new owners perform a novena on his behalf. As sweat drips from his brow, the parishioners discuss how wonderful and life-like the image is. Finally, San Antonio can endure no more and runs off, leaving many to believe a miracle has occurred while others shout insults.

DUMB PRIEST STORIES

Maya folk literature also contains many dumb priest stories, payback perhaps for abuses committed by nineteenth-century rural clerics. In *Of Wonder and Wise Men* (2001b), for example, Terry Rugeley not only points out that the priest and the hacienda owner were often one and the same, living fat off the labor of Maya workers, but includes some colorful complaints about priestly excess, including one alleging that Raymundo Pérez, the priest of Mascuspana, forced his parishioners to hunt alligators that were so ferocious "they will eat a Christian." While Rugeley views this complaint as an example of rhetoric rather than historical fact, it suggests a tradition of discussing *curas* (priests) in unflattering ways. Similarly, a humorous *cuento* in Allan Burns's collection features a clever Maya youth whose use of double entendre enables him to shock and insult a priest and then escape punishment. In a chance encounter, the priest meets Ahau and asks him about his family in broken Maya. In quick succession Ahau tells the priest to masturbate, that Ahau's mother is at home twisting her asshole, that the family ate out his sister the day before, and that his father "has gone to the rear of what he likes." Later, when the priest tries to have Ahau arrested, the youth explains to the police that he was simply offering the priest a cooked yam, that his mother has to sit on one end of the string while she twists *henequén* fiber into twine, that the family ate dough his sister made the day before, and that his father is happy when he stands behind his corn plants. The police have no choice but to let Ahau go.

DRAMA, RIDDLES, AND WORD PLAY

Irreverent humor can also be found in theatrical performances that follow more conventional celebrations held in honor of a village's patron saint. In his discussion of the San Bernardo *k'ub pol* (Yucatán), or Dance of the Pig's Head, for example, Loewe (2003a) details how the procession of the saints is transformed into satire through a series of substitutions: replacement of the saint by a corpulent pig, adornment of the beast with jewelry (for example, earrings) in emulation of Catholic saints who should be nicely dressed before they go outside, and incorporation of St. Pig into a raucous procession that ends at a thatched-roof "church." The most subversive element, however, is the recitation of vulgar Maya-Spanish quatrains or *bombas* during what is typically a solemn procession. The recitation not only mocks the procession of the saints but also ruptures the rhythmic, refined quality of the Spanish *cuarteta*.

The Maya also reveal their sense of humor through riddles and other forms of word play that can be traced back to Maya books of prophecy (the Chilam Balam) written in the early post-Conquest. The following, however, are of more recent vintage: "The bucket goes first, in the middle goes the drum, in back goes the brush—A horse"; "The point is drying out while the trunk is getting wet—A cigarette"; "It is being born, it is being baptized—Defecating and urinating at the same time."

CLOTHING

Much has also been written about Maya folk costume or *traje* (literally "clothing"), as it is referred to in Guatemala. In Yucatán the female folk costume has two main elements—a dress (*huipil*) and a scarf (*rebozo*). The *huipil* is a loosely fitting white cotton dress with embroidery around the hemline and neck in a broad, square pattern. Beyond this, *huipils* vary greatly in terms of color, quality, the complexity of the stitch, and the amount of thread used, so status differences are readily visible among *huipil* wearers. A more elegant version of the *huipil* called a *terno* (literally "three") contains a third layer of embroidery on a cloth inlay. The *rebozo* may also reveal something about the wearer's social status, since women can choose between nylon, cotton, or silk if they have the money. The male folk costume, rarely seen except during regional folk dances (*jaranas*), includes white trousers, a long-sleeved white shirt, a hat made of straw or a softer fiber, and a distinctive style of sandal (*alpargata*), which is open except for a narrow band of leather that crosses the toes. Like women, men distinguish themselves through the quality of the material used (linen versus rough-hewn cotton) and the type of buttons on the shirt (if buttons are even present). In the past, wealthy *mestizos* demonstrated their high social standing quite literally by adding layers of leather (*tiras*) to the soles of their sandals. Nowadays men may avoid the high-heeled sandal even on festive occasions to avoid being labeled homosexual.

In highland Guatemala, *traje* is made from heavier materials—the highlands being much cooler—and is considerably more complex than the folk costume of Yucatán. The complete female outfit can involve as many as twenty-two separate items and is worn differently. Here, multicolored *huipils* woven from a variety of different fabrics are tucked into ankle-length wool skirts (*cortes*). In addition, a broad apron (*delantal*) is tied around the waist. Like the *huipil* and the skirt, aprons are frequently embroidered in geometric patterns. While tourists quickly learn that certain designs or motifs are associated with particular communities, the Maya are not as parochial as many assume. A woman may select a *huipil* that is typical of her natal village, but she may opt for a design associated with the village of a close relative such as her husband or father or simply choose one that demonstrates good taste. Weather, respect for tradition, knowledge of other communities, and politics influence the decision about what to wear. Male attire, in contrast, is regional rather than community specific and, as in Yucatán, is seen far less often.

Nowadays the folk costume seems to be a more important marker of ethnic identity in the highland regions than in Yucatán. Nevertheless, describing trends or tendencies is somewhat hazardous, since ethnographers have been more inclined to count or estimate the number of people who speak a Maya language than the number of people who wear *traje*. Moreover, selecting an outfit depends on the situation. In Guatemala, women who normally wear Western dress (*ladinas*) may don *traje* during a pageant as an expression of national pride. Similarly, in Yucatán, women who would normally wear a plain cotton dress will put on an elegant *terno* to dance the *jarana*, a folk dance that is seen as a confluence of Spanish and Maya culture and thus a key symbol of regional identity. The definition of proper *traje* also changes with age, at least in Guatemala. For example, if an older woman does not adopt a particular *type* of skirt, she is no longer thought to wear *traje*, though her costume may appear quite Mayan to outsiders.

Tourism and the consumption of native handicrafts have also affected the way people dress. In the 1960s, middle-class Yucatecan women would not be caught dead wearing a *huipil*. It was too stigmatizing. However, following the establishment of Cancún in the 1970s, tourists from Europe and the United States descended upon Yucatán by the thousands, and many took home colorful *huipils* as souvenirs, suggesting that "modern," non-indigenous women could also wear such apparel. Shortly thereafter, the mini-*huipil* was born, a shorter, tapered, and thus more sexually appealing version of the original. In short, thanks to a few minor alterations, a symbol of subordination was quickly transformed into a symbol of regional pride. Ironically, perhaps, many low-income Maya women and their daughters stopped wearing *huipils* around this time because of the cost—in time and pesos—of producing them and the stigma associated with wearing them on something more than an occasional basis. Consequently it is more difficult to determine ethnic or status differences at a glance than it used to be.

Finally, although folk costume is often described as traditional, it is neither indigenous nor unchanging. What has come to be known as folk dress was introduced by Christian missionaries in the sixteenth century and continues to evolve, though the rate of change is somewhat slower than the non-indigenous fashion system.

MUSIC

No robust Mayan musical tradition exists in Yucatán. Now and again one may see a *tunkul*, a Maya drum made from a tree trunk, at political events, Maya congresses, or tourist venues, but its use in combination with electric guitars and other modern instruments makes it seem more like a historical anachronism than part of a living tradition. In the highlands, on the other hand, Maya musicians regularly perform during Carnival, at dance-dramas, and at other cultural events, and thanks to Smithsonian Folkway Records, the Instituto Nacional Indigenista, and the Instituto Chiapaneco de Cultura, there are a growing number of recordings. In 1992 Smithsonian Records produced *Music of the Maya-Quiché of Guatemala*, a sound cassette based principally on excerpts from dance-dramas recorded by Henrietta Yurchenco in 1945. In the 1970s and 1980s Glen Horspool recorded dozens of reels of Quiché Maya music performed in a variety of venues: processions, horse races, parties, parades, and church gatherings. Two sound cassettes produced by Jonatan López Rodríquez and the Instituto Chiapaneco de Cultura in 1993 contain Tzeltal music from Chiapas performed during Carnival and various religious processions, and a compact disc produced in 2000 by the Center for Indigenous Language, Arts and Literature includes Tzeltal dances recorded by two Chiapas radio stations in 1996 and 1997.

SPORTS AND GAMES

The recent literature on sports and games reveals little that seems distinctively Maya to contemporary observers. In rural Yucatán, children and young adults play baseball, soccer, and volleyball, much as in the United States, while older adults stand around and drink beer. During periodic celebrations held to honor a patron saint, one can also pay a small fee to watch amateur matadors chase scrawny bulls around a makeshift arena. However, unlike professional bullfights in which the matador impresses the audience with grace and unflinching courage, at the bullfights observed in Maxcanú, a transvestite toreador—known as *La Negra Tomasa*—entertained the audience with burlesque humor. Moreover, the decision to kill the underfed animal is more a business calculation (how much meat are the locals likely to buy?) than a response to audience's interest in seeing blood. In the 1940s, Santiago Pacheco Cruz observed other games such as *pa p'uul*, or Breaking the Pitcher. This later became known as *ts'oop sandia*, or Busting the Melon, when the pitcher was replaced by a watermelon. However, this game is now rarely played.

CHALLENGES OF THE MODERN WORLD

Commercialization of Maya culture has accompanied the growth of **tourism**. During **fieldwork** in Yucatán in the 1980s Ronald Loewe heard numerous stories about residents who survived the collapse of the *henequén* market by selling artifacts they collected from Mayan ruins or facsimiles they made on their own. The most popular story involved a clever Maxcanú artisan who purchased a number of plain ceramic vessels from a Mexico City vendor and "Mayanized" them by painting a faint, yet identifiably Maya design on the outside. He then gave them an aged, weathered appearance by chipping the edges and boiling them in a concoction of honey, *achiote* (a red spice), and mud. According to the story, the facsimiles were so authentic the artisan was able to sell them to prominent tourist establishments in Mérida for a hefty price. Not surprisingly, the federal police eventually noticed his handiwork, and one day just as the unsuspecting artisan opened up his shed, filled from top to bottom with forged artifacts, they arrested him. However, since it is illegal to sell *real* artifacts, not facsimiles, the wily entrepreneur was able to secure his release by showing the police the tools of the trade. While this story has all the features of a modern trickster tale—outsmarting or evading the *federales* is a common theme throughout Mexico—an archeologist from the National Institute of History and Anthropology who catalogs Maya artifacts, including those of recent vintage, acknowledged that some very good forgeries had come from the western part of the state in the late 1970s.

STUDIES OF MAYAN FOLKLORE

A large and rapidly growing sample of prayers, folktales, dreams, and oral histories has been published in one of the Maya languages and English or Spanish. Those interested in Chiapas can start by consulting Gossen's article on Tzotzil literature (1985). Köhler (2000) updates Gossen's article and includes references to texts that are published in other Maya languages of Chiapas. Oral histories of the Caste War of Yucatán as well as ethnic conflicts in highland Chiapas can be found in the appendices to Bricker (1981). Readers interested in folktales and dreams should also consult volumes published by Laughlin (1976, 1977). There is also a growing list of

Yucatec Maya folk texts, but only a few that are accessible to English readers. Two that are in English or include English translations are Burns (1983) and Redfield (1937). Rugeley (2001a) contains English translations of a number of interesting nineteenth-century texts, including a will that lists the possessions of a Maya worker, a letter sent from the governor's office to the mayor of a small village to dispel a rumor that a winged serpent had appeared in the village on 13 May 1842, and a variety of other documents. Those who read Spanish and are interested in oral literature should consult Ligorred Perramón (1990) and Boccara (1997)—which contains French, Spanish, and Maya—as well as bilingual Maya-Spanish works of Dzul Poot (1985). Those who read French should consult Boccara's fifteen-volume encyclopedia of Maya folklore (1997). Students of folklore may also find helpful information in Pacheco Cruz (1947), the works of renowned Maya linguist Alfredo Barrera Vásquez (1980), and Amaro Gamboa (1984). The latter's entertaining "encyclopedia" examines the unseemly underside of Yucatecan society through euphemism, insult, and innuendo and is popular among the regional intelligentsia for its candor. Those interested in political and economic aspects of Maya life in Guatemala should read Montejo (1987) and the autobiography of Nobel laureate Rigoberta Menchú (1984). Readers interested in Menchú may also want to look at Arias and Stoll (2001) and Nelson (1999). The latter argues that the proliferation of jokes about the Nobel laureate reflects concern about the instability of ethnic, **gender**, and class boundaries in contemporary Guatemala. A large selection of Maya tales from Guatemala (with English or Spanish translations) is available through Yax Te' Press: Maxwell (2001), Peñalosa (1995), and Montejo (1992). Yax Te' also distributes books on Mayan arts and crafts as well as novels about Maya life.

There are also a number of interesting and educational Web sites on Maya culture. The Mesoamerican Ballgame, www.ballgame.org, is an award-winning site that introduces children to the ancient Maya sport where losers were sacrificed to the gods. The interactive site takes one back to an ancient Mesoamerican city to watch a virtual ballgame. Visitors can even play the game themselves. Mayan Kids, www.mayankids.com, is a visually stimulating site that offers a good introduction to Maya culture, past and present, but is for a young audience. Mundo Maya, www.mayadiscovery.com/ing/default.htm, is a comprehensive site with links to such topics as archeology, nature, daily life, history, handicrafts, and legends. This site is a good reference to all things Mayan. Maya Family, www.sil.org/mexico/maya/familia-maya.htm, a bilingual (English-Spanish) site, gives a nice introduction to Maya language.

Although, for the time being, most Maya remain in Central America and Mexico, a growing number of Maya enclaves may be found in the United States. Ethnographic literature on the Maya of North America include Burns (1993), Fink (2003), Adler (2004), and Loucky and Moors (2000).

BIBLIOGRAPHY

Adler, Rachel. 2004. *Yucatecans in Dallas, Texas: Breaking the Border, Bridging the Distance.* Boston: Pearson Allyn and Bacon.

Amaro Gamboa, Jesús. 1984. *El uayismo en la cultura de Yucatán.* Mérida, México: Ediciones de la Universidad de Yucatán.

Arias, Arturo, and David Stoll. 2001. *The Rigoberta Menchú Controversy*. Minneapolis: University of Minnesota Press.

Barrera Vásquez, Alfredo. 1980. *Diccionario Maya Cordemex*. Mérida, Yucatán, México. Ediciones Cordemex.

Boccara, Michel. 1997. *Encyclopédie de la mythologie Maya Yucatèque: Les labyrinths sonores*. Paris: Editions Ductus.

Bricker, Victoria R. 1973. *Ritual Humor in Highland Chiapas*. Austin: University of Texas Press.

———. 1981. *The Indian Christ, the Indian King: The Historical Substrate of Maya Myth and Ritual*. Austin: University of Texas Press.

Brinton, Daniel. 1883. *The Folk-lore of Yucatán*. London: Folk-lore Society.

Burns, Allan. 1983. *An Epoch of Miracles: Oral Literature of the Yucatec Maya*. Austin: University of Texas Press.

———. 1993. *Maya in Exile: Guatemalans in Florida*. Baltimore: Temple University Press.

Centro Estatal de Lenguas, Arte y Literatura Indígenas. 2000. *Música Maya-Zoque de Chiapas* (sound recording).

Dzul Poot, Domingo. 1985. *Cuentos Mayas* (bilingual edition, Maya-Spanish). Mérida, México: Maldonado Editores.

Fink, Leon. 2003. *The Maya of Morgantown: Work and Community in the Nuevo New South*. Chapel Hill: University of North Carolina Press.

Gabbert, Wolfgang. 2004. *Becoming Maya: Ethnicity and Social Inequality in Yucatán since 1500*. Tempe: University of Arizona Press.

Gossen, Gary. 1985. Tzotzil Literature. In *Supplement to the Handbook of Middle American Indians*. Vol. 3, edited by Victoria R. Bricker and Munro S. Edmunson. Austin: University of Texas Press. 64–106.

Hanks, William F. 1990. *Referential Practice: Language and Lived Space among the Maya*. Chicago: University of Chicago Press.

Hansen, Asael T., and Juan R. Bastarrachea Manzano. 1984. *Mérida: Su transformación de capital colonial a naciente metrópoli en 1935*. México, D.F.: Instituto Nacional de Antropología e Historia.

Hendrickson, Carol. 1995. *Weaving Identities: Construction of Dress and Self in a Highland Guatemala Town*. Austin: University of Texas Press.

Hervik, Peter. 1999. *Mayan People within and beyond Boundaries: Social Categories and Lived Identity in Yucatán*. Amsterdam: Harwood Academic Publishers.

Horspool, Glen. 1982a. The Music of the Quiché Maya of Momostenango in Its Cultural Setting. Diss., University of California at Los Angeles.

———. 1982b. *Guatemala, Quiché Maya, 1977–1978*. Ms. deposited by at the UCLA Ethnomusicology Archive.

Köhler, Ulrich. 2000. The Maya of Chiapas since 1965. In *Supplement to the Handbook of Middle American Indians*. Vol. 6, edited by John Monaghan and Victoria Bricker. Austin: University of Texas Press. 179–206.

Laughlin, Robert M. 1976. *Of Wonders Wild and New: Dreams from Zinacantán*. Smithsonian Contributions to Anthropology, No. 22. Washington, DC: Smithsonian Institution Press.

———. 1977. *Of Cabbages and Kings: Tales from Zinacantán*. Smithsonian Contributions to Anthropology, No. 23. Washington, DC: Smithsonian Institution Press.

———. 1988. *The People of the Bat: Mayan Tales and Dreams from Zinacantán*. Washington, DC: Smithsonian Institution Press.

Ligorred Perramón, Francisco de Asís. 1990. *Consideraciones sobre la literatura oral de los mayas modernos*. México, D.F.: Instituto Nacional de Antropología e Historia.

Loewe, Ronald. 1995. Ambiguity and Order: a Study of Identity and Statecraft at the Mexican Periphery. Diss., University of Chicago.

———. 2003a. Yucatán's Dancing Pig's Head (*cuch*): Ion, Carnival, and Commodity. *Journal of American Folklore* 116: 420–443.

———. 2003b. Marching with San Miguel: Festivity, Obligation, and Hierarchy in a Mexican Town. *Journal of Anthropological Research* 59: 263–286.

López Rodríquez, Jonaton. 1993. *Voces indias de Chiapas: Música Tzeltal.* Tuxtla Gutiérrez, Chiapas: Instituto Chiapaneco de Cultura.

Loucky, James, and Marilyn M. Moors, eds. 2000. *The Maya Diaspora: Guatemalan Roots, New American Lives.* Philadelphia: Temple University Press.

Maxwell, Judith M. 2001. *Textos chujes de San Mateo Ixtatán.* Rancho Palos Verdes, CA: Fundación Yax Te' Press.

Menchú, Rigoberta. 1984. *I, Rigoberta Menchú: An Indian Woman in Guatemala*, edited by Elisabeth Burgos-Debray. London: Verso Press.

Montejo, Victor. 1987. *Testimony: Death of a Guatemalan Village.* Willimantic, CT: Curbstone Press.

———. 1992. *The Bird Who Cleans the World and Other Mayan Fables.* Willimantic, CT: Curbstone Press.

Nash, June. 1970. *In the Eyes of the Ancestors.* New Haven: Yale University Press.

———. 2001. *Maya Visions: The Quest for Autonomy in an Age of Globalization.* New York: Routledge.

Nelson, Diane. 1999. *A Finger in the Wound: Body Politics in Quincentennial Guatemala.* Berkeley: University of California Press.

Nettle, Daniel, and Suzanne Romaine. 2000. *Vanishing Voices: The Extinction of the World's Languages.* New York: Oxford University Press.

Pacheco Cruz, Santiago. 1947. *Usos, costumbres, religión y supersticiones de los mayas: Apuntes históricos con un estudio psicobiológico de la raza.* Mérida, México: By the author.

Peñalosa, Fernando. 1995. *Tales and Legends of the Q'anjob'al Maya.* Rancho Palos Verdes, CA: Yax Te' Press.

Pitarch Ramón, Pedro. 1993. Etnografía de las almas en Cancúc, Chiapas. Diss., State University of New York at Albany.

Redfield, Margaret Park. 1937. *The Folk Literature of a Yucatecan Town.* Carnegie Institute of Washington. Contributions to American Archaeology. 3.13: 1–50.

Redfield, Robert. 1941. *The Folk Culture of Yucatán.* Chicago: University of Chicago Press.

———. 1950. *A Village That Chose Progress: Chan Kom Revisited.* Chicago: University of Chicago Press.

Redfield, Robert, and Alfonso Villa Rojas. 1934. *Chan Kom, a Maya Village.* Pub. No. 448. Washington, DC: Carnegie Institution of Washington.

Rugeley, Terry, ed. 2001a. *Maya Wars: Ethnographic Accounts from Nineteenth-century Yucatán.* Norman: University of Oklahoma Press.

———. 2001b. *Of Wonders and Wise Men: Religion and Popular Cultures in Southeast Mexico, 1800–1876.* Austin: University of Texas Press.

Sullivan, Paul. 2000. The Yucatec Maya. In *Supplement to the Handbook of Middle American Indians.* Vol. 6, edited by John Monaghan and Victoria Bricker. Austin: University of Texas Press. 207–223.

Tedlock, Barbara. 1982. *Time and the Highland Maya.* Albuquerque: University of New Mexico Press.

Villa Rojas, Alfonso. 1978. *Los elegidos de dios: Etnografía de los mayas de Quintana Roo.* Mexico City: INI.

Vogt, Evan. 1978. *Bibliography of the Harvard Chiapas Project: The First Twenty Years, 1957–1977.* Cambridge: Peabody Museum of Archaeology and Ethnology, Harvard University.

Watanabe, John. 1992. *Maya Saints and Souls in a Changing World.* Austin: University of Texas Press.

————. 2000. Maya and Anthropologists in the Highlands of Guatemala since the 1960s. In *Supplement to the Handbook of Middle American Indians*. Vol. 6, edited by John Monaghan and Victoria Bricker. Austin: University of Texas Press. 224–247.

Yurchenco, Henrietta. 2002. *Music of the Maya-Quiché of Guatemala: The rabinal achi and baile de las canastas* (sound recording). Smithsonian Folkways Records F-4226.

Ron Loewe and Rebecca Read

MEXICO

GEOGRAPHY AND HISTORY

Mexico's official name is the United Mexican States, though most of the Mexican people and the rest of the world never use the official name. Its capital and most important city is Mexico City. The world's largest Spanish-speaking country, it acquired its name from the indigenous group that settled in central Mexico in the fourteenth century, the *Mexicas* (also known as *Aztecas*). Over sixty languages are spoken there, but Spanish is the only language recognized by the Mexican constitution. This situation has marginalized the indigenous populations throughout the years. While most Mexicans speak at least some Spanish, about 8 percent of the population speaks as their native tongue one of several Amerindian languages such as Náhuatl (the largest), Mayan, Zapotec, Otomí, and Mixtec. Mexican Spanish is very similar in syntax, grammar, and spelling to that of other Hispanic countries. The pronunciation and sound, however, differ, and Mexican Spanish is full of Náhuatl words that have been incorporated over the years.

Mexico has a population of 104,907,991. Most of the people are concentrated in Mexico City, Guadalajara, and Monterrey. Even though Mexico is geographically situated in North America, culturally it identifies with Central and South America. Mexico shares borders with the United States in the north and with Belize and Guatemala in the south. In the east and the west Mexico is bounded by the Gulf of Mexico and the Pacific Ocean respectively. The national territory of Mexico, which contains a diverse range of physical environments, is about 1,972,500 square kilometers. The *Sierra Madre Oriental* (Eastern Sierra Madre) and the *Sierra Madre Occidental* (Western Sierra Madre) go from north to south, meeting in central Mexico in a region that is called the *Cordillera Neovolcánica* (New Volcanic Mountains). Desert covers the states of Sonora and Chihuahua, and semi-tropical rainforest characterizes parts of the south and the Gulf Coast. The Yucatán Peninsula is the only flat area in the country and is located in the southeast. Mexico's narrowest point is at the Isthmus of Tehuantepec. Such variety of climates and geography has had a strong influence on Mexican folklore and folklife.

From a political perspective Mexico is a federal republic. The federal government is divided into three branches: executive, legislative, and judicial. In theory, the three branches have the same power, but in practice the presidency has controlled the legislative and the judicial powers over the years. The president serves for six years. No re-election is allowed at that level. The president is elected by popular vote. The legislative body is divided into two chambers: the Chamber of Deputies (500 members with three-year terms) and the Senate (128 members with six-year terms).

Mexico consists of thirty-one states and a Federal District (Mexico City). Each state has a governor who serves for six years. Even though Mexico is a federal republic, most of the power is concentrated in the president, who holds discretionary powers. Though a multiparty system, the political system is controlled by three parties: the PRI, the PAN, and the PRD. The Institutional Revolutionary Party (PRI), formed after the Mexican Revolution, ruled the country from 1929 till 2000. Throughout those years, the Mexican president was the head of this party. The PRI incorporated various socioeconomic sectors such as the peasantry, blue-collar workers, and the middle and upper classes. Ideologically the PRI is a center-left party. Because of its long period in power, however, it became the official party, a part of the establishment. The other significant parties are the National Action Party (PAN) and the Revolutionary Democratic Party (PRD). The PAN, which is identified as a conservative party, was created in the late 1940s and has become the loyal-opposition party without ever winning any election until the mid-1980s, when it won a governorship. Not until 2000 did the candidate of the PAN, Vicente Fox, win the federal presidency. This was the first time the PRI lost the federal election after more than seventy years. The PRD, created by former PRI members in 1987, is ideologically identified as a left-wing party. The PRD gained power in 1988, when it almost won the federal elections, and has held the governorship of Mexico City since 1997.

RELIGION

Today about 94 percent of Mexicans are Roman Catholic. Mexican Catholicism reflects a mix of Christian and pre-Hispanic rituals that have blended since colonial times. About 5 percent of the population is Protestant: Christian Evangelical, Baptist, Pentecostal, Mormon, Seventh-day Adventist, and Jehovah's Witness. Another 1 percent of the population is Jewish, atheist, or other religious persuasions. During the last twenty years, many American Protestant groups have financed Protestant churches in Mexico, particularly in the south. Two of the most successful religious groups in Mexico have been the Mormons and the Pentecostals. Mexico has had separation of church and state since 1857. As a consequence of this separation, the so-called *Guerra de Reforma* (Reform War) occurred between conservatives and liberals from 1858 till 1861. Benito Juárez, one of the most important figures during this time, wanted to decrease the control the Catholic Church had over Mexican life. Juárez and the liberals were able to accomplish the separation of church and state, giving the state ultimate power and control of most of the territory that the Catholic Church possessed since colonial times. After the war in 1861 Juárez—the first indigenous man to become president of Mexico—remained president until his death in 1872.

A second conflict between church and state happened after the promulgation of the Constitution of 1917 (the current constitution). Under this constitution the Catholic Church lost most of the privileges restored during the *Porfiriato* (1876–1911). The Constitution of 1917 established separation between church and state and lay education and removed special rights for clergy. Since 1917 small rebellions took place, but it was not until 1926 that an organized rebellion—the *Cristero* revolution or the *Cristiada* (1926–1929)—took place in central Mexico. As a consequence, the government closed many Catholic churches and imposed harsh laws against the clergy. In 1929, church and state reached an agreement that ended their conflict. Despite the separation of church and state, Mexicans are culturally Roman Catholic. Many of the customs, traditions, and festivities have a religious origin. The priests have a strong presence in small towns. Today the Roman Catholic Church has more power as a result of constitutional changes that former president Carlos Salinas de Gortari (1988–1994) proposed. Such changes gave judicial recognition to priests, ministers, and nuns. The good relationship between church and state was reinforced by current President Vicente Fox because his political party (PAN) has strong historical connections with the Catholic Church.

ETHNIC COMPOSITION

Mexico is a country with a rich ethnic tradition. Its Amerindian indigenous groups mixed with the European conquerors who arrived in 1519. The Spaniards conquered Mexico in 1521 after several years of struggle between them and some of the native groups. During the Spanish rule the natives were converted, and eventually European customs and folklore were added to native traditions. By the end of the eighteenth century, indigenous traditions, folklore, and customs had blended with European ones, creating new traditions that were no longer European or indigenous, but Mexican. Mexico exemplifies perfectly *mestizaje* or **hybridity** (the combination of European and Amerindian elements). The conquerors brought a new language and religion that gradually conquered the minds of the natives and mixed with their way of thinking. European thought has been predominant in Mexican intellectual life and has framed and influenced Mexican culture tremendously.

FOLK BELIEFS AND LIFE-CYCLE CELEBRATIONS

Mexican folk beliefs derive from pre-Hispanic and Hispanic practices. One of the most distinctive practices is herbal medicine, which was a very common practice among the pre-Hispanic indigenous groups and is still used today. The so-called *curanderos* (herbal healers) are bridges between the divine, spirits, and the people of this world. Mexicans believe that *curanderos* have the power to heal, to help them find a job or find love, to keep away bad spirits, and to protect them from evil such as the *mal de ojo* (the evil eye). The region of Los Tuxtlas, Veracruz, in southeastern Mexico is where many of the Mexican *curanderos* are concentrated. The town of Catemaco is nationally known as the home of *brujos* (sorcerers) and *curanderos* (healers). Catholic beliefs have played an important role in Mexican folk beliefs. All the magic rituals performed by

Patzcuaro, Mexico, woman painting skeleton decorations for Day of the Dead (*El Día de los Muertos*) celebration. (© Monique Salaber/The Image Works)

the *curanderos* or *brujos* involve Catholic prayers and Roman Catholic symbolism and iconography. Most Mexican holy days or fiestas are offered in honor of Catholic saints.

One of the best-known folk beliefs in Mexico is the legend of La Llorona (the Weeping Woman). The legend tells of a woman who falls in love with a nobleman and has his children out of wedlock. (The number of children varies as does their gender.) His family does not approve of the marriage because she is from a lower class and arranges for him to marry a richer woman. In different forms of the story, the man wants the children, does not want them, or does not even know about them. Either way, the children are drowned by their mother, and she dies from the remorse for what she has done. Other stories say that she drowns her children and then commits suicide. La Llorona grieves perpetually for her children and weeps near creeks, rivers, or lakes. She is described as a tall woman, dressed in white, who floats across these bodies of water. This legend has been known since colonial times.

Mexican people exhibit distinctive ideas regarding those who have passed from this world. Encounters with the dead evoke laughter and applause from Mexican people. As Octavio Paz points out, Mexicans are familiar with death. They joke about it, caress it, sleep with it, and celebrate it. Despite this apparent acceptance of death, Mexican society contains a strong element of sadness, and inventing their own celebrations in times of struggle is a valued attempt to heal their suffering.

In Mexico, festivities and religious events take place during all seasons of the year partially as a reaction to adverse economic circumstances. Through social events, Mexican people can forget their daily suffering and alleviate their worries often stemming from economic and social hardships. One of these celebrations is *El Día de los Muertos* (Day of the Dead), also known as All Souls' Day. The celebration is important for Mexicans, and the vast majority participate yearly. Even though All Saints' Day and All Souls' Day exist in most Catholic countries, it is celebrated very distinctively in Mexico. In other Catholic countries such as Spain, there are church services and people visit their dead relatives' graves. But Mexico has a unique interpretation of this traditional Catholic observance because of the fusion of its Spanish and indigenous cultural heritages. The syncretism between the Aztec concept of death in Mesoamerica and Spanish Catholicism gave birth to an exuberant *El Día de los Muertos* celebration. Such a *fiesta* takes place every year on 1 and 2 November to honor dead loved ones. On the Day of the Dead, the souls of the deceased are believed to come back to meet and share food, drinks, and time with their families.

The essence of the Day of the Dead, particularly in central and southern Mexico, consists of two spheres: public and private. The public sphere celebration takes place in the cemetery. People visit the cemetery, clean and decorate the graves, and eat with their relatives. The second element of the celebration is considered a private ritual and includes home altars with *ofrendas* or "offerings." Everybody, without exception, has a motive for rejoicing. One element that is extremely important for such an incredible celebration is the practice of placing *ofrendas* on these altars. *Ofrendas* are used yearly to welcome the souls of relatives who come from the other world. Since approximately 2000 B.C.E. *ofrendas* have been recognized in Mexico. The skull is a symbol that appears as a common ornament in most Mesoamerican cultures. Skulls were represented in the construction of the pyramids, relief sculptures, and freestanding sculptures. They were also depicted in murals, ceramics, and jewelry. These cultures considered death to be a promise for a new type of life filled with hope. The Aztecs believed all souls went to Mixtlan, the "paradise of the dead." They did not have the concept of a Hell that caused suffering and pain. For them, the transcendence of the dead did not depend on moral conduct. The Aztecs built *ofrendas* for the souls of their relatives so that their departed loved ones could enjoy the same things they had appreciated in the world of the living and to make their stay in the afterlife more comfortable. The objects put in the *ofrenda* represent the things given by the living to the dead so they can continue their existence in Mixtlan. It is important that those left behind feel that they are comforting their deceased family members in every way possible.

When the Spanish arrived in 1521, many of the existing ideas and customs were gradually blended into the calendar of the Catholic Church. As a result of the Spanish Conquest, the *ofrenda* became a mixture of indigenous and Spanish traditions. In contemporary Mexico, the *ofrendas* represent the maximum artistic and ideological expression of the people. They contain religious symbolism, beliefs, and ordinary customs. Many elements from both indigenous and European cultures are used in this celebration. It is extremely difficult to determine which elements came from Spain and which are indigenous to Mexico.

Mexicans celebrate the Day of the Dead in various ways. They set up altars to honor their loved ones. They decorate the graveyard with flowers, candles, and food. The *pan de muerto* (bread of the dead) is offered and consumed during this celebration. Altars are displayed at museums, schools, universities, public buildings, and churches. This celebration is particularly popular in central Mexico, the Purepechean towns (Michoacán), and in Oaxaca. People from different backgrounds come together to celebrate their deceased relatives. The different celebrations and fiestas give Mexicans an opportunity to show courage in their constructed view of reality. At the same time, these events represent their creative abilities toward the preservation of their traditional festivities and rituals.

Idealization of the indigenous past has promoted the idea that this celebration is full of native elements. However, it is clear that Spanish culture has influenced the ritual. On the other hand, native influence has also been pervasive in European folk practices brought to Mexico such as the *Semana Santa* (Easter, Holy Week) or the *Posadas* (Christmas celebration). *Semana Santa* (Easter) is one of the highest holy days for Mexicans. The holy week involves processions, prayer, masses, and other preparation for Resurrection Day. The *Posadas* are celebrations that take place from 16 to 23 December. They commemorate the journey of Mary and Joseph on their nightly search for a place to sleep in the town of Bethlehem. Family and friends reenact the biblical journey by visiting one another in their homes. They eat tamales, drink *atole* (chocolate drink), and sing *posada* carols.

As a consequence of modernization and globalization, celebrations of the Day of the Dead and the *Posadas* in some urban populations have lost their ritual tradition and meaning. In some towns, young people prefer to celebrate Halloween, or they observe the Day of the Dead with a celebration that is a hybrid between this celebration and Halloween. In the case of *Posadas* in the month of December, many parties called *posadas* do not differ from other parties except that they take place in December.

MUSIC AND SONGS

The rituals and celebrations are accompanied by a rich tradition of Mexican folk music. There are a number of forms of regional folk music in Mexico. One of the best examples of Mexican folk music is *mariachi* music. *Mariachi* is considered the Mexican folk music genre par excellence, not just because of its rhythms and instruments but also because of its place as a symbol of Mexican music and culture. A *mariachi* is an ensemble band of five or more musicians. These men or women wear the traditional Mexican costume of a *charro* (Mexican cowboy), a waist-length jacket, fitted pants and boots, and a large sombrero decorated with colorful metal ornaments. *Mariachi* music is a combination of sounds produced by trumpets, violins, and guitars with two traditional Mexican instruments, the *vihuela* and the *guitarrón*. The music accompanies romantic and humorous lyrics.

Another example of Mexican folk music is the *corrido*, a ballad that tells a story about people from the border and their adventures and interactions with others. It is the Mexican version of the Spanish romance. *Corridos* usually have a moral that instructs listeners in social mores. They narrate the adventures and lives of **heroes**, their women, and their battles. Men are the central characters of these Mexican ballads and at the same time comprise the usual audience. Although men assume cultural property of the *corridos*, female characters also play important roles such as the mother, the protective goddess, the lover, and the *adelita* (woman warrior). One of the best-known *corridos* scholars, Américo Paredes, indicates that *corridos* do not make reference to citizenship or blood but, rather, to the "Mexican" identity in a cultural sense. *Corridos* reflect the values and the way in which people conceive and interpret their own history. The *corrido* is a pivotal element that depicts Mexicans in their everyday lives.

Other popular Mexican musical forms are the *ranchera* (ranch song), the *norteña* (from northern Mexico), and the *banda* (band). *Ranchera* music developed during the Mexican Revolution. The music deals with rural life, unfaithful women, lost loves, and nostalgic and tragic themes. *Norteña* music is very popular in northern Mexico. Although this form of music has its origins in the *corridos*, it combines various musical forms such as the polka, the waltz, and American country-and-western music. The lyrics of *norteña* songs often deal with Mexican people living near the U.S.-Mexican border, undocumented immigrants, drug lords, and corruption.

MYTHS AND FOLKTALES: THE VIRGIN OF GUADALUPE

To understand Mexican folklore, one has to consider the way in which nationalism and identity developed in Mexico. During the colonial years and especially during the first years of Mexican independence, Mexicans used folk narratives to create a sense of identity and to discover the origins of their culture and history. The first category of folk narratives consists mainly of translations, chronicles, and summaries done by explorers or missionaries who created the first truly Mexican folkloric productions.

Among all the myths and symbols of Mexico, the one that is the most important is Our Lady of Guadalupe. The myth of Our Lady of Guadalupe helped to develop Catholicism in Mexico and also contributed to the development of Mexican nationalism. (Courtesy Library of Congress)

In pre-Hispanic Mexico, myth and prophecy were significant concepts. Myth helped indigenous peoples to remember their origins and their end. When the Spaniards arrived, Moctezuma thought that they were messengers from the culture hero Quetzalcoatl who came to inform them about the end of the Mexican empire. The Spanish conquistador Hernan Cortés interpreted these myths as a cession of sovereignty and sent a letter to the Spanish king telling him that the natives had recognized him as their king. Clearly the collapse of Tenochtitlán was partly caused by the Aztec prophecy of final catastrophe.

Among all the different myths and symbols of Mexico, the one that is undoubtedly the most important is Our Lady of Guadalupe. The myth of Our Lady of Guadalupe not only helped to develop Catholicism in Mexico but also contributed to the creation of a new identity and to the development of Mexican nationalism. The publication of the *Imagen de la Virgen María, Madre de Dios de Guadalupe, milagrosamente aparecida en la ciudad de México* in 1648 by Miguel Sánchez created a new era in the cultural history of Mexico. The image of the Virgin left in Juan Diego's *ayate* (or poncho) founded a considerable cult of devotion that grew even stronger when a basilica in honor of Our Lady of Guadalupe was completed in 1622 by the Archbishop Juan de la Serna.

In 1746, a ceremony took place announcing that the Virgin of Guadalupe was the universal patron of all the dioceses of New Spain. Years later, the Spanish crown and the papacy confirmed this status. This was a Virgin born in Mexico, one considered by the inhabitants of New Spain as a Virgin of their own. She was the protector of all the people born in Mexico. The Virgin of Guadalupe became a symbol that unified people from different races, social classes, **genders**, ages, and political ideas. The cult of the Virgin created a national and patriotic character. She remains the link between the *criollo* elite and the *mestizos* and Amerindians. The fact that she is the *Patrona de las Américas* was very important to the creation of a native American identity that had begun to break away from the shadow of its European origins.

On 12 December 1794 Fray Servando Teresa de Mier, a Dominican *criollo* priest, gave a speech at Tepeyac on the feast of Guadalupe. In the speech he made reference to Mary, the conqueror of America, suggesting that Guadalupe represented a new Ark of the Covenant between Mary and the Americas. This sermon is one of the ideological bases that inspired the independence movement. The image of the Virgin of Guadalupe that Hidalgo and the other founding fathers used later was the main symbol of the movement. With this symbol they identified themselves as Mexicans. The new nation developed myths that were becoming a part of its history. At the same time, these myths, particularly the myth of Our Lady, have lasted throughout the years and continue to be most influential. Every year on 12 December, millions of people make pilgrimages to the Basilica of Our Lady of Guadalupe in Mexico City. Outside Mexico, the Catholic community celebrates as well. Our Lady of Guadalupe has been named the patron saint of all the Americas by the Catholic Church.

FOLKLORE IN POST-CONQUEST AND COLONIAL MEXICO

Besides converting and conquering the natives, most of the visitors to the New World were eager to write about what they had seen. Christopher Columbus, Hernán Cortés, Bernal Díaz del Castillo, Bartolomé de las Casas, Bernardino de Sahagún, and many others wanted to use the pen as an instrument of persuasion, power, communication, and glory. The conqueror's pen invented America, created a new culture, a "New World" inspired by the idea of saving "lost souls." Such an atmosphere demanded the use of the pen as an instrument to express feelings about the natives, their presence, and their victories.

Bernal Díaz del Castillo collected documents and observed the people of Tenochtitlán and the rest of Mexico. His *Historia verdadera de la Conquista de la Nueva España* includes narratives with such cultural symbols as Doña Marina, or La Malinche. La Malinche was a native slave girl given to Cortés as a gift from Moctezuma. She became Cortés's interpreter and mistress. The fact that La Malinche helped Cortés has given her the reputation as a traitor to her race. In fact, the term *malinchista* means someone who prefers foreign things over Mexican things. La Malinche is one of the most important symbols of the *mestizaje* or the mix of Spanish and European traditions in Mexico because La Malinche, or Doña Marina, is depicted as the mother of the first Mexican.

Fray Bernardino de Sahagún's *Primeros Memoriales*, written in the mid-sixteenth century, resulted from the first close study of native cultures. He collected data systematically and wrote documents on the Nahua people's ancient rites, gods, religious beliefs, and medical, social, political, and moral practices. He used this collection to write his great work *Historia de las cosas de la Nueva España*, which has yielded some of the most important information we have of the Spanish understanding of early colonial and ancient Mexico.

The patriotic sentiment that started to grow in the Spanish population born in Mexico (the so-called *criollos*) increased with the control and power that the peninsular Spanish exerted over the rest of the population. The *criollo* group did not like the fact that all the power was in the hands of the peninsular Spaniards. The most important public manifestation of this dissatisfaction was the uprising in 1565 led by Martín Cortés, son of Hernán Cortés. Although this attempt was a failure and the uprising never took place, it was preceded by a dramatic manifestation of ritual language and of the *criollos'* vision of themselves and of the relationship they maintained with their place of birth. As members of a feudal aristocracy, the *criollos* of the sixteenth century based their cultural identity on an attachment to the land. Most of their claims were based on the fact that Cortés had received the Aztec Empire from the hands of its last legitimate ruler. By the middle of the seventeenth century the *criollos* had developed a clear sense of belonging to culture developed in New Spain and wanted to take for granted an ancient Amerindian past that would give them an independent historical identity.

Another group that also had an important role in the creation of the Mexican nation was the *mestizos* (people with Spanish and native blood). The *mestizo* writings of this time reflect a close relationship between folklore and history. Fernando de Alva Ixtlilxochitl and Diego Muñoz de Camargo were *mestizos* who argued that the true Mexican society was to be a *mestizo* one, a hybrid culture mixing Spanish laws and the Christian religion with native customs. In their historical writings, they used various literary genres such as myths, legends, and folktales. The authors share the same interest in rewriting their pre-Hispanic history. They use the same kinds of narrative and rhetorical strategies as the Spaniards. Ixtiloxochitl's *Sumaria relación* and Muñoz Camargo's *Historia de Tlaxcala* show that the chronicles written by the Spaniards reveal a lack of understanding of the language and culture of the natives. They pointed out that living and speaking the language was not enough to understand the culture. The fact that they are part of both cultures gives them some legitimacy. These authors wanted to demonstrate to the world the great mistakes that the Spanish conquerors made against their people. They assert the rights of the natives, of their elders, and of their tradition. However, the *mestizos* had only a small influence and power over society. The European elite did not give them space to make their voices heard.

Carlos de Sigüenza y Góngora was an influential Mexican scholar who contributed to the creation of Mexican nationalism. He regarded all myths as garbled versions of true historical events. Sigüenza y Góngora characterizes the mythical native and claims that the *criollo* descendants of the conquerors were the beneficiaries of "a Mexican ancient history." In *Teatro de virtudes políticas* Sigüenza y Góngora argues that Mexican history is part of the ancient world's history. This work argues for a link between the Mexica, the ancient Greeks, and the sons of Noah by means of an interpretation of the name Neptune. These myths presented the Spanish original conquerors as the natural rulers and the *criollo* descendants as the beneficiaries of the Mexican ancient history.

Another writer who contributed myths about origins was Francisco Clavijero. His *Storia antica del Messico*, which he wrote in his exile in Bologna, is the history of Mexico written by a Mexican. His contribution was pivotal in the discussion of Mexican folklore. He wrote the first cultural history of New Spain and emphasized the importance of accepting its ancient heritage as the only means by which Mexicans could come to terms with themselves and face the great changes in history. Clavijero wanted to re-establish the connection between the Amerindian past and the realities of the Amerindian present. Clavijero was in favor of a single cultural identity for *criollos*, *mestizos*, and Amerindians alike. He used the word *Mexicano* to describe the *criollo* and Mexican population. Clavijero's uses of adjectives of nationality were very successful in the development of a national culture of *criollos* and Amerindians. In order to be a Mexican it was necessary to have a share in both the European and the Amerindian worlds. The combination of myths and political ideas was of service to the creation of Mexican **nationalism**. The works of all the missionaries, conquerors, *criollos*, and *mestizos* slowly began to awaken a new consciousness in the people born in the Western Hemisphere.

MEXICAN INDEPENDENCE MOVEMENT

The *criollo* and *mestizo* cultural productions, the development of an emerging national identity, and the disagreements between the Spanish elite and the Mexican population were among the factors that came together to give birth to the Mexican independence movement from 1810 to 1821. Led by two priests as successive commanders-in-chief—Miguel Hidalgo and José María Morelos—with many of the lieutenants priests as well, the movement began on the night of 15 September 1810 in the town of Dolores Hidalgo, Guanajuato. Father Miguel Hidalgo rang the bell of the cathedral and cried, "Long Live Ferdinand VII! Long Live Our Lady of Guadalupe! Death to the *gachupines* [foreigners, particularly Spaniards, but since Napoleon invaded Spain during that time, he might also have been referring to the French]! Death to bad government!" Mexican official history records that the independence movement began at that moment. This independence movement was unique in that the principal leader raised the banner of the Virgin of Guadalupe to attract different segments of the society. The story of the beginning of the Mexican independence movement is very relevant in Mexican folklore today. In fact, Mexico celebrates its independence anniversary not the day it became independent from Spain, which was on 21 September 1821, but on the night of 15 September. Every year, a reenactment of this night takes place in every town or city in Mexico. Porfirio Díaz (dictator from 1876 till 1911) started the tradition on the centennial of Mexican Independence in 1910. Díaz reenacted the *Grito* or call for independence performed by Miguel Hidalgo 100 years before. Since then, the president of Mexico carries a Mexican flag from the balcony of the national palace and shouts the ceremonial *grito*: "*Viva la Independencia! Viva Hidalgo! . . . Viva México!*" to which the audience answers "*Viva!*" The president also rings a bell as Hidalgo did from Dolores. Throughout the country governors and mayors take on Hidalgo's role in their states and cities. This ritual is extremely important in Mexican folklore as a symbol of Mexican nationalism.

The war for independence in nineteenth-century Mexico gave place to new political, economic,

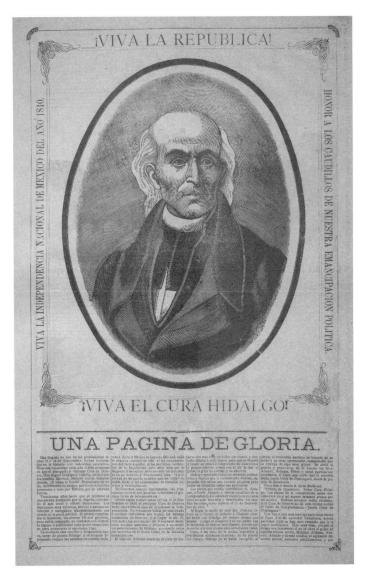

Broadside shows bust portrait of Father Miguel Hidalgo. (Courtesy Library of Congress)

cultural, and social problems. Mexicans had a stronger nationalistic consciousness, and in the area of literature and folklore a new movement, *costumbrismo*, evolved. This movement was based on different folk narratives that were descended from the works produced in colonial times but with a new twist. The new traditions were no longer identified as Amerindian or Spanish, but as Mexican. José Joaquín Fernández de Lizardi (1776–1827) was one of the most important representatives of *costumbrismo*. His *El Periquillo Sarniento* (1816) is a *costumbrista* novel that renewed interest in local folklore. All *costumbrista* publications describe and discuss the lifestyle of different groups of Mexicans, a portrait of social classes from the author's personal point of view.

NINETEENTH- AND TWENTIETH-CENTURY STUDIES OF MEXICAN FOLKLORE

In 1885 the word *folklore* appears in a speech entitled *Provincionalismos mexicanos* delivered by Joaquín García Icazbalceta at the meeting of the *Academia Mexicana de la Lengua* (Mexican Academy of Language). However, folklorist Vicente T. Mendoza insists that the first time that the term *folklore* was recorded in Mexico was in an article that appeared in the newspaper *El Nacional* on 7 February 1890. This article consists of an investigation of the familiar and vulgar terms of various towns in order to study human intellectual development.

Daniel D. Brinton's essay "The Folk-Lore of Yucatan," published in 1883 in *Folk-Lore Journal* in London, is considered by some scholars to be the first study of Mexican folklore. The article reappeared in Brinton's *Essays of an Americanist*, published in Philadelphia in 1890 and was then translated into Spanish by Enrique Leal as *El folklore de Yucatán*, published by the Archeological Museum of Yucatán in Mérida in October 1937.

The philologist and arguably Mexico's first folklorist Nicolás León (1859–1929) incorporated folklore into his class on ethnology at the National Museum in 1906. In 1906 León published his lecture number fifty-six with the title: *Foc-Lor mexicano* (published by the *Imprenta del Museo Nacional*). This was a comprehensive study of Mexican folklore that covered superstitions, proverbs, traditional narratives, and more.

During the Porfirio Díaz dictatorship, the Mexican population was upset with the injustices and foreign influence that Díaz promoted. The intellectuals were interested in popular manifestations

Mexicans aiming rifles from a mountain during the Mexican Revolution, which encouraged and created a strong Mexican nationalism. In turn, this helped the phenomenon of folklore as an intellectual subject. (Courtesy Library of Congress)

of a traditional character. Thus, the Mexican Revolution (1910–1917) encouraged and created a strong Mexican nationalism, and most artists oriented their works toward nationalism, which helped the phenomenon of folklore as an intellectual subject.

The Mexican Revolution affected the study of folklore in Mexico in two ways. The first consequence was the destruction of the scientific structure within the universities and research institutes in Mexico. This situation dissolved the scientific structure of folklore studies. However, this process had a positive consequence because it increased the interest of many people in the collection of folklore.

Manuel Gamio was one of the most important figures in anthropology, Amerindian studies, and folklore in Mexico. Gamio was the head of the *Dirección de Antropología* (Institute of Anthropology), a governmental agency created in 1917 with the goal of conducting anthropological research in the country. Gamio created the magazine *Ethnos* to promote the study of anthropology in Mexico and Central America. He published articles in this magazine as well as in other publications dealing specifically with indigenous folktales in Náhuatl.

Rubén M. Campos (1876–1945) was the pioneer folklorist of Gamio's generation. By the mid-1890s we hear of Campos as a government official and man of letters. In 1925 he held a position in folklore in the National Museum. Campos was the first person to occupy any academic position in the Mexican folkloric scene. During the time that Campos became a folklorist, the Ministry of Education created the so-called cultural missions, groups including social scientists and schoolteachers whose objective was to blend Mexican native subcultures into the Mexican nation. As the official folklorist, Gamio was in charge of this project, which intended to produce a book to serve as a guide for folklore scholars. The project resulted in three texts: *El folklore y la música mexicana* (1928), *El folklore literario de México* (1929), and *El folklore musical de las ciudades* (1930). These works contain a vast amount of folklore materials, including an excellent collection of urban lore, but unfortunately they are not rich in terms of theory and methodology.

During the 1920s Mexican folklore studies shifted from the occasional scholarship of men like León, Gamio, and González Casanova to the sustained but undisciplined enthusiasm of romantic nationalists, with a special interest in music. During this period Mexican folklore concentrated mostly on musical analysis. Folklorists developed an interest in the collection of folk music from small towns and have been credited with the introduction of the study of music into the discipline of folklore.

From 1914 to 1946 some eight folklore societies were created in Mexico. Six of them lasted for over a year; the other two had more longevity. In 1938 the American folklorist Ralph Steele Boggs promoted the creation of one of the two most influential Mexican folklore societies. Scholars in Mexico such as Vicente T. Mendoza and Virginia Rodríguez were very interested in the project. They decided to create a committee in folklore as part of the Mexican Society of Anthropology in 1938. Two years later this group became an independent entity but was still affiliated with its parent organization. The founder and first president of the *Sociedad Folklórica de México* was Vicente T. Mendoza, and the treasurer was Virginia Rodríguez. This society's purpose was to study folklore as an independent discipline. Other scholarly organizations in Mexico were interested in folklore, but only as a secondary concern. The *Sociedad Folklórica de México* organized research and conferences that promoted the development of folklore scholarship. Among its most important achievements was the publication of the *Anuario de la Sociedad Folklórica de México*. This journal first appeared in 1942, and twelve volumes followed, the last in 1955. A few issues of the *Anuario* appeared after that date, but the journal ceased publication in 1977, at the same time that the society stopped meeting. The *Anuario* primarily serves to give an overview of folklore studies in Mexico and folklore scholarship in the rest of the world.

In 1946 the *Academia Mexicana de Folklore* was created. This society got the support of the Ministry of Education. Until the 1970s the *Academia Mexicana de Folklore* met every Friday but never published any material. Folklore at this time was mostly viewed as based on the indigenous past—interpreted as a Mexican past. The heroes of the independence movement and the revolution were protagonists in the majority of the stories collected by the *Academia*.

By the end of the 1940s the scholarly bases of folklore in Mexico had been developed and promoted in the various institutions that had been created for folklore study. Vicente Téodulo Mendoza was a folklorist and composer who studied *corridos* and their origins and uses as expressions of national identity. Mendoza and his wife, Virginia Rodríguez, established the first Mexican School of Folkloric Studies in 1945. This project began by offering and organizing folklore courses. This decisive movement in folklore studies encouraged Mexican academia to take folklore seriously, and folklore scholarship in Mexico began to receive more support from the government and academic institutions.

Mendoza brought the field of Mexican folklore studies to an equivalent of any scientific endeavor and contributed significantly to the discovery of different historical roots of Mexican traditions. From 1936 until his death in 1964, Mendoza had his base of operations at the *Instituto de Investigaciones Estéticas de la Universidad Nacional Autónoma* (Institute of Esthetic Research of the National University). He produced an enormous number of works between 1920 and 1965, most of them dealing particularly with the roots of folklore. In 1939 he published *El romance español y el corrido mexicano*, a comparative study in which he proposes to uncover the detailed relationship between the Mexican *corrido* and the medieval Spanish epic poems or ballads. In 1954 he published *El corrido mexicano*. Among his most important publications are *La décima en México*, *La lírica infantil de México*, *La canción mexicana*, and *Panorama de la música tradicional de México*.

FOLKLORE STUDIES IN CONTEMPORARY MEXICO

Folklore scholarship in Mexico is currently conducted throughout other disciplines or by work done in other Latin American countries or in the United States. In April of 1940 the association Folklore of the Americas was created because many nations in the Western Hemisphere did not have well-formed and active national folklore societies. As such societies began to appear, they usually became members of Folklore of the Americas. The purpose of the association was to study and promote folklore scholarship in the Americas. This association published its first magazine,

Folklore Americas, in June 1941. Another association created to support the study of folklore in the Americas is the *Comité Interamericano de Folklore*. This association is affiliated with the *Instituto Panamericano de Geografía e Historia*, which is part of the Organization of American States. Most of the work related to folklore in Mexico produced during the 1980s and early 1990s was published in this Inter-American magazine, the last issue of which came out in 1992.

The study of folklore in Mexico has been limited during the last twenty years. Folklore in Mexico is generally considered as dependent on other disciplines such as anthropology, ethnology, history, literature, music, and linguistics. No universities offer a degree in folklore. Although some universities offer courses in folklore or have folklore researchers on their staffs, none even offers a folklore minor. Despite this lack of academic representation, some research in the field of folklore is being conducted.

Mexicans have always been obstinate about the idea of protecting the memory of the most important events that have marked their society, and this has colored the method that they picture their identity and destiny. From pre-Columbian times they have been engaged in a continuous battle to save their history and folklore from oblivion. Knowledge of the past was the foundation on which their priests and diviners based their astronomic calculations and their predictions of the future. Folklore has been one of the ways in which they have preserved their past. *See also* **Maya; Nahua; Otomí.**

BIBLIOGRAPHY

Anaya Monroy, Fernando. 1971. Dos investigadores ejemplares en el folklore: Vicente T. Mendoza and Virginia Rodríguez Rivera. In *25 estudios de folklore: Homenaje a Vicente T. Mendoza y Virginia Rodríguez Rivera*, México: Universidad Nacional Autónoma de México. 9–21.

Boggs, Ralph Steele. 1941. Genesis de Folklore Americas. *Folklore Americas* 1 (June): 1–4.

———. 1945. *Bibliography of Latin American Folklore*. New York: H. W. Wilson.

———. 1949. Mapa preliminar de las regiones folklóricas de México. *Folklore Americas* 9 (June–December): 1–12.

———. 1957. Prólogo del editor. *Folklore Americas* 17 (December): 1–3.

Brading, D. A. 1983. *Prophecy and Myth in Mexican History*. Cambridge: Center for Latin American Studies.

———. 1985. *The Origins of Mexican Nationalism*. Cambridge: Center for Latin American Studies.

———. 1991. *The First America: The Spanish Monarchy, Creole Patriots, and the Liberal State, 1492–1867*. Cambridge: Cambridge University Press.

Gamio, Manuel. 1925. The Utilitarian Aspect of Folklore. *Mexican Folkways* 1 (June–July): 7.

Gillmor, Frances. 1961. Organization of Folklore Study in Mexico. In *Folklore Research around the World: A North American Point of View*, edited by Richard M. Dorson. Bloomington: Indiana University Press. 97–104.

Gonzalez-Crussi, F. 1993. *The Day of the Dead and Other Mortal Reflections*. New York: Harcourt Brace.

Guzman López, Alfredo. 1943. Unas cuantas palabras con motivo de la Sesión de Clausura de esta Sociedad. *Anuario de la Sociedad Folklórica Mexicana 1942* 3: 183–187.

Ibarra, Alfredo. 1944. Vicente T. Mendoza. *Anuario de la Sociedad Folklórica Mexicana 1943* 4: 4–10.

Klor de Alva, Jorge. 1988. Sahagún and the Birth of Modern Ethnography: Representing, Confessing, and Inscribing the Native Other. *The Work of Bernardino de Sahagún: Pioneer Ethnographer of Sixteenth Century Aztec Mexico*, edited by Jorge Klor de Alva and others. Austin: University of Texas Press. 31–52.

León Portilla, Miguel. 1990. *The Broken Spears: The Aztec Account of the Conquest of Mexico*. Boston: Beacon Press.

Meierovich, Clara. 1995. *Vicente T. Mendoza artista y primer folclorólogo musical*. México: Universidad Nacional Autónoma de México.

Mendoza, Vicente T. 1948. Current State and Problems of Folklore in Mexico. *Journal of American Folklore* 61: 364–368.

———. 1953. Noticias de México. *Folklore Americano* 1 (November): 41–44.

———. 1957a. El papel de Manuel Toussaint en el folklore de México. *Anuario de la Sociedad Folklórica de México* 11: 39–49.

———. 1957b. Primera aparición y arraigo de la palabra "folklore" en Méjico. *Folklore Americas* 17 (December): 4.

Moedano Navarro, Gabriel. 1971. Bibliografía del Profesor Vicente T. Mendoza. *25 estudios de folklore en México: Homenaje a Vicente T. Mendoza y Virginia Rodríguez Rivera*. México: Universidad Nacional Autónoma de México. 1–5.

Nutini, G. Hugo. 1988a. Pre-Hispanic Component of the Syncretic Cult of the Dead in Mesoamerica. *Ethnology* 27: 57–78.

———. 1988b. *Todos Santos in Rural Tlaxcala*. Princeton: Princeton University Press.

Pagden, Anthony. 1987. Identity Formation in Spanish America. In *Colonial Identity in the Atlantic World, 1500–1800*, edited by Nicholas Canny and A. Pagden. Princeton: Princeton University Press.

Paredes, Américo. 1966. El folklore de los grupos mexicanos en Estados Unidos. *Folklore Americano* 14: 146–163.

———. 1967. Divergencias en el concepto del folklore y el contexto cultural. *Folklore Americas* 27 (June): 29–37.

———, ed. 1970. *Folktales of Mexico*. Chicago: University of Chicago Press.

———. 1978. Ethnographic Work among Minority Groups: A Folklorist's Perspective. In *New Directions in Chicano Scholarship*, edited by Ricardo Paredes Romo and Raymundo Paredes Romo. San Diego: Chicano Studies Center, University of California.

Paz, Octavio. 1984 (1959). *El laberinto de la soledad*. México: Fondo de Cultura Económica.

Romero, Jesús C. 1943. Observaciones acerca del término folklore. *Anuario de la Sociedad Folklórica de México, 1942* 3: 17–40.

———. 1947. El folklore en México. *Boletín de la Sociedad Mexicana de Geografía y Estadística* 63 (May–June): 700–701.

Toor, Frances, ed. 1947. *A Treasury of Mexican Folkways*. New York: Crown.

Vogt, Evon Z., and Suzanne Abel. 1977. On Political Rituals in Contemporary Mexico. In *Secular Ritual*, edited by Sally F. Moore and Barbara Myerhoff. Amsterdam: Van Gorcum. 173–188.

West, J. O. 1988. *Weeping Women: La Llorona, and Other Stories*. Tempe, AZ: Bilingual Press.

Guillermo De Los Reyes

NAHUA

GEOGRAPHY AND HISTORY

Speakers of Nahua languages number about 1 million and live in the Mexican states of Guerrero, Puebla, Tlaxcala, and Veracruz and in the Pipil and Nicarao regions of Central America. The several dialects of Nahua fall into two groups: Nahuat and

Náhuatl. The only difference between the two is the *tl* sound that dropped out of Nahuat. The Nahuas live in rural communities where they grow corn, beans, chiles, and squash on small plots or *milpas*. They became farmers after the end of the Ice Age, and their skill at farming enabled them to build the great ancient civilizations of Teotihuacán, Tula, Cholula, and Tenochtitlán before the arrival of the Spanish in 1519.

ROOTS OF NAHUA FOLKLORE

The earliest record of Nahua folklore appears in the *Codices*, picture books and narratives telling about the creation of the universe. The most important for understanding the ancient origins of Nahua folklore are the *Cantares mexicanos*, *Codex Telleriano Remensis*, and *La leyenda de los soles*. The *Cantares mexicanos* are Náhuatl songs of ancient Aztec kings who descend from the sky world with the aid of the singer and his god. Drummers accompanied the singers and performed on horizontal log drums and upright skin drums. The *Codex Telleriano Remensis* is a picture book with images of gods and goddesses involved in acts of creation. One of the most important is of the goddess Xochiquetzal, or Quetzal Flower, cutting a flower from the branch of a tree growing in the primordial heaven of Tamoanchán. The gods expel Xochiquetzal, who falls to earth and gives birth to the god of corn, Cinteotl. *La leyenda de los soles* contains many ancient myths that include the four suns or eras, the discovery of corn, the creation of the fifth sun, and the story of the *mixcoah* or cloud serpents who mate with deer women and whose descendant became the priest-king of Tollan during the golden age of Nahua culture.

The Spanish conquest of **Mexico** in 1521 ended the empire of Tenochititlán and ushered in centuries of change under colonial rule. Some Spanish friars learned Nahua languages and introduced biblical stories into Nahua oral tradition. Spanish colonialists developed ties of blood kinship, marriage, and godparenthood with the Nahua through which they introduced Spanish folksongs and folktales. The folklore of the 1 million speakers of Nahua languages today consequently comes from two traditions: the ancient Nahua and Spain.

Contemporary Nahua drum in rhythmical patterns similar to those of the ancients, but words to songs like those in the *Cantares mexicanos* have largely disappeared. The drummers, often accompanied by a flute, play for dance groups, some dating back to the sixteenth century. They include the flying pole dancers, or *cuahpatanini*, representing birds descending from the sky to fertilize the earth. Also of ancient origin are the Quetzal dancers who wear beautiful headdresses of feathers designed to resemble the prized quetzal bird.

Survivals of ancient folklore in oral narratives resemble the creation stories found in the *Codex Telleriano Remensis* and *La leyenda de los soles*. While few contemporary narrators tell of Xochiquetzal picking a flower from the tree in Tamoanchán, a number tell tales of divine women who produce food by having sex. Some contemporary stories describe sexual encounters between men and female deer resulting in the creation of a corn plant. A man plants chiles in the forest and discovers female deer frolicking with his chile plants. He decides to join them, the deer women persuade him to exchange hats, and he puts on antlers that are *chachantic*, or soft and furry like a young stalk of corn. Erotic encounters between humans and deer appear on ancient pottery and in *La leyenda de los soles*.

The Franciscan friar Bernardino de Sahagún believed that the ancient Nahua told a version of the Orpheus tale in which Piltzintecuhtli searched for his beloved Xochiquetzal in the land of the dead. Sahagún did not collect a version of this story, but Danish scholar Akë Hultzkrantz believes that there is a strong native North American Orpheus tradition. Contemporary Nahuas tell stories of a husband who, in deep despair over the loss of his wife, makes a difficult and dangerous journey to find her in the underworld. In some cases, the dead wife has run off with another man, and in others she is the grieving husband's sister.

Nahuas continue to tell stories of "The Origin of the Fifth Sun" and the discovery of corn trapped in Sustenance Mountain, both of which appeared in the ancient *La leyenda de los soles*. In the ancient stories, the god Nanahuatl became the fifth sun by jumping into a pyre in the ancient city of Teotihuacán. Contemporary storytellers still recount how a man and a woman jump into a fire and become the sun and the moon. "The Origin of Corn" describes how an ant removes a kernel of corn trapped inside a mountain. Nanahuatl, this time as an old lightning bolt, breaks open the mountain and releases the corn for starving humans. Nahuas also tell stories about the origin of corn-planting knowledge that may derive from an ancient source but does not exist in any known Codex. Usually Nanahuatl awakens after cracking open Sustenance Mountain and plants his *milpa*. Little lightning bolts ask him how he planted his corn, and he tells them to grind the corn into dough for making tortillas and throw the dough into a big hole. The little lightning bolts do as told, and, of course, their corn does not sprout. So they take their revenge by blowing down Nanahuatl's *milpa*. The old lightning bolt tells them to restore his *milpa* as a condition for giving them corn-planting knowledge, and so the little lightning bolts glue the stalks back together with their mucus.

TALES AND SONGS OF EUROPEAN ORIGIN

Meanwhile, the Nahua have translated and adapted Spanish folk music and tales to fit their own culture. Musicians playing the guitar and violin frequently perform songs in Nahua languages at weddings. One of the most popular is *"Xochipitzahuac"* or "Slender Flower," a ribald tune about a widow left to satisfy her erotic desires by moving her hands much as one does to husk corn and about her dead husband, who threatens to return to her in the form of an armadillo. Dance groups dedicated to St. James, the patron saint of Spain, and representing battles between the Moors and the Christians perform in many villages. Nahua dancers reinterpret themes from Spanish folk dances to represent the conquest and the struggle between God and the devil. Ironically, the devil is also a symbol of Spanish-speaking Mexicans, particularly wealthy landowners.

Contemporary Nahua narrators tell many folktales of Spanish origin. Some are biblical stories, and others are reworked versions of European fairy tales. The biblical stories include "Adam and Eve" in the Garden of Eden, which appears to have replaced the story of Xochiquetzal in Tamoanchán. The early friars noticed the similarity between Xochiquetzal cutting the flower from the tree in Tamoanchán and

Eve eating the forbidden fruit from the tree of knowledge. In both cases, the story is about sexual fault or *tlahtlacolli* in Náhuatl and *pecado* (sin) in Spanish. The Nahuat of the sierra norte de Puebla use *tahtacol* (*tlahtlacolli*) and *pecado* interchangeably, leading some scholars to conclude that the Nahua have adopted Christian sexual morality. However, many Nahua maintain the sixteenth-century meaning of the term *tahtacol*, which applies to any fault that leads to a state of brokenness.

Many popular stories collected in Europe in the nineteenth century by the Brothers Grimm have entered Nahua oral tradition. They include "The Bear's Son," "Hansel and Gretel," "Cap o' Rushes," "Two Travelers," "Blood Brothers," "The Magic Ring," "Blancaflor," "The Rich and the Poor Peasant," and various animal **trickster** tales. Narrators perform these stories at wakes, while drinking in bars, and when working in groups such as those who process sugarcane. As in the case of much folklore that travels from one group to another, the Nahua translated and adapted the European stories to fit their own culture. "The Bear's Son," a very popular dragon-slayer story, is historically related to *Beowulf*, the eighth-century English epic. The Nahuat of the sierra norte de Puebla translated "The Bear's Son" into their own language and turned the hero into Nanahuatl, the ancient god who became the fourth sun, removed corn from Sustenance Mountain, and taught the little lightning bolts how to plant corn. In the Spanish versions of this story, the hero is the son of a bear father and a human mother. He helps his mother escape from his father and return to her village, where he goes to school and has trouble with his teacher. He leaves town and joins two or three companions who live in a haunted house. The bear's son vanquishes the house-haunting demon, who escapes into the underworld, and follows a trail of the demon's blood to find an enchanted princess. At this point, the Nahuat hero turns into the Nanahuatl, who now is the captain of the rain gods. He makes his home on a mountain high above the community until rain gods take him toward the sea so that he will not destroy humans with a flood.

"The Bear's Son" is a good example of a story that meant one thing in Spain and something quite different for the Nahuat. In Spain the story may be an allegory of a boy's maturation into a man, and the key moment is the hero's redemption when he vanquishes the house-haunting demon. By turning the hero into Nanahuatl, the Nahuat remove the meaning of redemption and make the central character a god who personifies a powerful force of nature. Rather than maturing so he can fit into the human community, Nanahuatl acts with *ilihuiz*, an adverb that means "with excessive strength" or "without consideration." One who acts with *ilihuiz* is a danger to others and unfit to live in the human community. Removing the meaning of redemption from the story exemplifies oikotypification, altering a tale that came out of European Christianity so that it fits another cultural tradition.

A second example of translating and changing a European story to fit Nahua culture is "Hansel and Gretel," which becomes a sad tale about the complete disintegration of a family. In many parts of Europe, this folktale begins with a father and stepmother who abandon their children in the forest for want of food. The children end up in the house of a witch who intends to eat them, but they cleverly escape and return to their parents, often bringing the witch's wealth to end the famine. The story is about the disintegration and the reconstitution of the family. Nahuas sometimes change the tale into a sad story of the complete and final destruction of a family brought about by some fault or excess. The ancient Nahuas told many such stories such as the tale of Topiltzin Quetzalcoatl, who got drunk on *pulque* and approached his sister sexually, bringing down the golden age civilization of Tollan. Nahuat stories of "Hansel and Gretel" that have a plot resembling the tale of Topiltzin Quetzalcoatl begin when a boy and a girl, abandoned by their parents, end up in the home of an old woman who wants to use them to make children she can eat. The boy and girl escape but must separate when the girl is seduced by a Spanish-speaking Mexican man. The boy must leave his sexually awakened sister to avoid incest and ends up becoming a wealthy man through his skill as a gambler. His father finds him and asks for some money but is dismayed by the boy's lack of generosity and pays a priest to kill his own son.

Nahuas have altered the plots of other European stories to fit their family and kinship system. They transformed "Cap o' Rushes," for example, by shifting the focus from the European prince's search for a beautiful heroine, with whom he fell in love at a ball, to a Nahua boy's search for his father. The shift to the father-son relationship fits Nahua kinship that emphasizes ties among fathers, sons, and brothers. Some Nahua narrators have changed "The Two Travelers" from a tale of two envious brothers, one who is good and the other who is bad, into a story about brothers who quarrel and then settle their differences because they have compassion (*teicneliliz*) for each other. Compassion is the foundation of the respect (*icnoyot*) among brothers that Nahua parents take great pains to instill in their children. Nahua narrators are fond of telling "Blood Brothers" and give the story a special twist to express their view of the fraternal bond. In Spain, the story usually features identical twin or triplet boys who ask for their inheritance and head out into the world. They reach a fork in the road, and each goes his separate way. The first ends up a prisoner in The Castle Where One Goes and Never Returns, and the other brothers try to rescue him. The youngest successfully removes his brother from the Castle and then confesses that he spent the night with his twin or triplet brother's wife. At this point, many Spanish narrators introduce the motif of "The Jealous Brother." The twin who is married kills his brother who rescued him from the Castle but then uses a magic ointment to resuscitate him. Nahuat narrators add a mystical connection among the brothers enabling them to know each other's experiences and eliminate the motif of the "Jealous Brother."

The plots of other European fairy tales remain intact, but the Nahua interpret them to fit their culture. "The Magic Ring" is a very popular story of European origin that Antti Aarne and Stith Thompson describe as a tale about a hero who receives a magic ring that can make all his wishes come true. A thief steals the ring and takes it across an ocean, and helpful animals bring it back to the owner. The Nahuat identify the wounded animal as a snake, whom they consider the animal companion spirit of a human lightning bolt. The ring has magical qualities because lightning bolts are divine beings with power to produce vast quantities of wealth. Some Nahuat interpret the story as an allegory demonstrating the power of *teicneliliz* or compassionate understanding, which is the basis of *icnoyot* or respect the hero shows toward the wounded serpent.

"Blancaflor" is a recasting of the ancient Greek story of Medea, who fell in love with Jason and uses her magic to help him obtain the Golden Fleece and then escape from her cruel father. Jason abandons Medea when they arrive at another kingdom and marries the king's daughter. Medea uses her magic one final time to punish the daughter and then kills her own children. The story probably changed when adopted by Spaniards who brought it to Mexico and introduced it to the Nahuas. The Spanish and many Nahua Blancaflors use their magic to gain back their husbands. Nahua narrators, particularly in the sierra norte, regard Blancaflor as *nahueh*, an affectionate term applied to a mother or any woman in the family. *Nahueh* is in the center of the household, and she uses her magic to produce children, feed her family, and show love (*tazohtaliz*) by teaching respect (*icnoyot*).

EUROPEAN TRICKSTER TALES

European trickster tales enter Nahua oral tradition without much change in meaning. One is "The Rich and the Poor Peasant," featuring two brothers—one of whom is poor but manages to become rich by selling something worthless to someone else. The rich brother perishes when he tries to repeat the transaction so he might become even richer. Nahuas as well as Spaniards tell this story to depict the evils of greed and envy, particularly between brothers.

Stories of a smaller and weaker animal who tricks a larger and more powerful one are very popular among Nahua narrators. They tell versions of the "Rabbit and Coyote" stories found all over the Americas and that Franz Boas traced to Spain and Portugal. The Nahua stories, particularly from the sierra norte de Puebla, begin when the rabbit is caught eating flowers in a woman's garden. The woman places the rabbit in a basket to boil him for dinner, and a coyote appears, setting up a series of trickster episodes in which the rabbit outwits the coyote. The Nahua include many episodes found elsewhere, but they apply them to their own lives. For example, one well-known Nahuat narrator in the sierra norte de Puebla used the Rabbit and Coyote story to interpret the political conflict in his community. For him, Coyote represents armed men who took over his village and acted big when carrying their large and powerful rifles. Rabbit represents the unarmed Nahuat, who must use their wits to get rid of their well-armed oppressors. *See also* **Maya; Otomí**.

BIBLIOGRAPHY

Aarae, Antti, and Stith Thompson. 1964. *The Types of the Folktale: A Classification and Bibliography*. 2nd edition. Folklore Fellows Communications, No. 184. Helsinki: Suomalaimen Tiedeakatema.

Bierhorst, John. 1985. *Cantares Mexicanos: Songs of the Aztecs*. Stanford: Stanford University Press.

———. 1992. *History and Mythology of the Aztecs: The Codex Chimalpopoca*. Tucson: University of Arizona Press.

Boas, Franz. 1912. Notes on Mexican Folk-lore. *Journal of American Folklore* 25: 204–260.

Pruess, Konrad T. 1982. *Mitos y cuentos nahuas de la sierra madre occidental*. México: Instituto Nacional Indigenisa.

Quiñones Kever, Eliose. 1995. *Codex Telleriano-Remensis: Ritual, Divination, and History in a Pictorial Aztec Manuscript*. Austin: University of Texas Press.

Sandstrom, Alan. 1991. *Corn Is Our Blood: Culture and Ethnic Identity in a Contemporary Aztec Indian Village.* Norman: University of Oklahoma Press.

Taggart, James M. 1983. *Nahuat Myth and Social Structure.* Austin: University of Texas.

———. 1997. *The Bear and His Sons: Masculinity in Spanish and Mexican Folktales.* Austin: University of Texas Press.

James M. Taggart

OTOMÍ

GEOGRAPHY AND HISTORY

A member of the Otopamean language family, Otomí includes Pame-Chichimeco, Otomí-Mazahua, and Matlatzinca-Ocuilteco. It is spoken in the central highlands mainly north and northeast of Mexico City. Otomí was the name the Nahuatl-speaking Aztecs gave speakers of the language and possibly means "carrier of bows and arrows." However, speakers call themselves *ñhañhu* or similar variants, which means "a speaker of the language." There are 17,083 speakers of Otomí in Mexico City, 114,043 in Hidalgo, 1,019 in Guanajuato, 104,357 in the state of Mexico, 732 in Michoacán, 8,225 in Puebla, 22,077 in Querétaro, 834 in Tlaxcala, and 17,584 in Veracruz—almost 300,000 in all. Primarily marginal subsistence farmers and small-scale merchants, they are gradually being incorporated into wage labor in industries and service sectors in urban areas as well as into the flow of international migration.

Otomí man holding a sculpture. (© Danny Lehman/CORBIS)

The Otomí were present in the central valley of **Mexico** for several thousand years before the Spanish arrived in 1519. In the fourteenth century, the Aztecs, who consolidated their power and extended their domination throughout central Mexico, defeated the Otomí kingdom at Xaltocan. Forced to flee, many became integrated into other kingdoms independent of Aztec rule, such as Tlaxcala and Michoacán, usually as defenders of their borders. Otomí warriors who remained under Aztec rule frequently defended the empire's northern borders against invading nomadic groups or the eastern border against the Tarascans in Michoacán. Two Otomí kingdoms, Meztitlán and Xilotepec to the northeast of the central valley, remained independent until a few decades before the arrival of the Spanish. This area in Hidalgo, called the Mezquital Valley, was considered the main center of the Otomí, though a large percentage of Otomí are also located in the neighboring Valley of Toluca.

The extent of Otomí territory in pre-Hispanic times denotes their importance. Most likely they transmitted many Mesoamerican cultural traits to the Aztecs, who never acknowledged this cultural legacy. Generally, they characterized Otomí as lazy or stupid. This ethnocentrism has persisted until today, possibly having a negative impact on language use. Furthermore, Náhuatl spoken by the Aztecs was the *lingua franca* before the Conquest, and many words were incorporated into Spanish. Also Otomí is a much more difficult language to write or speak than Náhuatl.

When the Spanish arrived in Tlaxcala, they formed an alliance with its rulers and their Otomí vassals against the Aztecs. Later, Otomí nobles from Jilotepec were instrumental in the conquest and colonization of the areas north of the Mesoamerican frontier occupied by nomadic groups called Chichimecs. The Otomí had prolonged contact with these groups, with whom they shared cultural characteristics and spoke similar languages. These factors facilitated the colonization process. Gradually, they expanded the territory they occupied as they moved north into Querétaro and Guanajuato. "Chichimec" referred to a variety of ethnic and linguistic groups who shared a nomadic lifestyle. Today only Pame and Chichimec-Jonáz still survive. In fact, both Otomí and Aztecs were considered to be Chichimecs because of their northern origin.

Overall, the Otomí cultural configuration is similar to the general Mesoamerican pattern. However, because the Otomí have occupied a diversity of regions and have been dispersed among other ethnic groups, local populations have developed distinctive characteristics, making it difficult to delineate a single Otomí cultural pattern. The northern groups retain more Chichimec elements, for example. Because the Spanish chroniclers used Aztec informants, the ethnohistorical information on the Otomí for the pre-Hispanic period remains unclear. In pre-Hispanic times, cultural borrowing was common, and deities and traditions were assimilated by different ethnic groups. Since the Conquest, an ongoing process of syncretism with Catholicism has led to some homogenization of religious practices throughout the country based on the worship of crosses, saints, and virgins. Despite strong acculturative pressures during the past five centuries and language loss in main areas, however, the Otomí have retained many characteristic beliefs and traditions.

The move north by the Spanish and their allies began a few years after the defeat of the Aztecs in 1521. Otomí nobles and warriors were instrumental in the conquest and colonization of the northern frontier occupied by Chichimecs who resisted the invasion throughout the sixteenth century. Their purpose was to obtain privileges, concessions, and land grants. When gold and silver were discovered in Guanajuato, San Miguel el Grande (now San Miguel de Allende) was founded as a commercial and supply center for the mines and as a point of defense from the Chichimec attacks along the Silver Road. Otomí were utilized both as warriors and as colonists sent to civilize the nomads by their example. By the end of the colonial period, however, they had lost their position, and most were dispersed as workers and sharecroppers on the estates and ranches of the elites. Otomí from Hidalgo, Querétaro, and

Guanajuato participated in the independence movement that originated in the cities of Querétaro, San Miguel, and Dolores Hidalgo, but their role in this and other movements of the post-independence period has not yet been fully researched.

The Otomí who settled along the Laja River valley of Guanajuato and in the traditional neighborhoods (*barrios*) of the city of San Miguel de Allende provide the focus here. The chapels and crosses of *barrios* and rural communities form part of a network of religious participation integrating the entire region, including Mexico City. Most participants are of Otomí origin, but other groups, such as the Chichimeca-Jonáz settled in San Luis de la Paz, also form part of the network.

CELEBRATIONS FOR THE CROSSES

The different histories of migration, settlement, adaptation to diverse physical settings, dialects, and cultural contacts with other ethnic groups, including the Spanish, make it difficult to speak of the Otomí as a highly integrated ethnic group with uniform beliefs and traditions. Therefore, the traditions and beliefs found in this area are not necessarily found in all Otomí groups. Characteristics that seem to permeate throughout are the devotion to a variety of crosses and the presence of small family chapels. Participants in religious celebrations are incorporated as ritual kin by calling each other *compadres* (co-godparents), a term normally used by Spanish speakers to indicate the relationship between the parents and godparents of a baptized child.

In the area studied, celebrations for a number of crosses take place throughout the year, but the Sacred Cross of Calderón Pass has been the main one that agglutinated communities and *barrios* throughout the region. Despite its being stolen in 2000, the cross remains the focus of worship. Other important elements include the worship of Saint Michael the Archangel and Saint James, divine warriors and protectors adopted from Spanish traditions, and dance groups known as *concheros*, who perform material from a genre called dances of the Conquest. They are called *concheros* because they accompany their dances with mandolin-like instruments made from armadillo shells (*conchas*). The groups are organized in a military hierarchy, and "true" groups have a leader or captain with direct genealogical linkage to the founder who participated in the Conquest. Prior to all important religious celebrations, night-long vigils (*velaciones*) are held.

OTOMÍ ORIGIN MYTH

The origin myth for Otomí groups of the Laja River valley is closely associated with the Sacred Cross of Calderón Pass. It describes the animosities between opposing native groups during the conquest of this highly dynamic multicultural and multilinguistic region, but it also provides a model for future interaction by incorporating them into a single system. According to the account transmitted from generation to generation, on 14 September 1531, christianized Otomí and Chichimec warriors confronted non-Christianized Chichimecs in a battle near Calderón Pass. After fifteen days and nights of fighting, it suddenly grew dark, and a shining cross appeared in the sky. Upon seeing this supernatural sign, non-Christianized natives cried out, "*Él es Dios*" (He is God)—a phrase that *conchero* dancers still call out as they perform.

The appearance of the cross was a sign to surrender and accept the Catholic faith. A replica of the vision was carved out of stone from a nearby streambed and taken to the pass where a chapel was built.

The stone cross is about four feet tall and rests on a small pedestal. It is covered with a thin layer of tin painted dark brown and covered with figures representing the passion and death of Christ. Also represented are two native dancers, the sun and moon at each point of the horizontal axis, a bloodied dagger at the base, the sacred heart of Christ, and a pair of severed feet and hands with the palms showing. While the three images are related to Christian beliefs, in pre-Hispanic times the feet and hands of sacrificial victims were consumed ritually by the principal lords. The heart was eaten only by the high priests or emperor. On a short crosspiece at the top of the cross, a mirror is encrusted in the stone painted with the letters *INRI*. It is topped with a small metal crown. A head of Christ is placed in a hollow at the intersection of the axes making it appear as though the figure is completely enveloped by the cross. This type of cross is common in areas inhabited by Otomí, and usually the hands, feet, and heart are also exposed. Wooden crosses of this style are covered with mirrors painted with the figures of the passion of Christ.

The two principal celebrations in the zone related to the Sacred Cross coincide with the beginning and end of the annual agricultural cycle. In May festivities for crosses throughout Mexico take place on 3 May. In September, the festivities run from the fourteenth on the day known as the Exaltation of the Sacred Cross until the celebrations for Saint Michael the Archangel at the end of the month. Before the celebrations, *velaciones* are held in the chapel at Calderón Pass. People arrive from different communities carrying images and crosses with offerings of flowers and candles. They enter the chapel accompanied by the clanging of a bell to be ritually cleansed by their spiritual leaders and to leave offerings. People usually spend the night sleeping on blankets and reed mats. Coffee, bread, and liquor are offered. Throughout the night, *copal*, a pine resin incense, is burned while hymns are sung to the four winds, the four cardinal points, and the *ánimas* (souls of the ancestors) and to commemorate important cultural heroes and events such as the Conquest by people playing *conchas*.

During the vigil, a *custodia* (guardian) that always accompanies the cross during celebrations is decorated with *cempaxúchitl* (large orange-colored marigolds) and *cucharillas*. *Cucharillas* are the shiny white spoon-shaped "leaves" broken off the base of the *xotol* cactus. The *custodia* is about three feet high and made of wood. Eight spikes radiate from a round mirror with the head of Christ painted on it. Seven spikes have rhomboid-shaped mirrors with painted figures on them. The one at the top is in the shape of a cross.

The cycle of celebrations in September in which the Sacred Cross plays a central part always begins with a vigil at Calderón Pass on the night of the thirteenth in preparation for the Catholic feast day called the Triumph of the Sacred Cross the next day. This date coincides with the beginning of the battle in 1531. Traditionally, people from La Cieneguita took the cross on a pilgrimage to its community, making several stops along the way. On the day of the celebrations for Saint Michael, which always falls on the weekend following the twenty-ninth, they carried it in a procession of traditional dances and flower offerings called *xúchiles* to the main church in the city of San Miguel. This mutual cooperation has been broken, however, since the cross was stolen.

For the main celebration, dance groups from many parts of Mexico and communities with their respective images and large flower offerings called *xúchiles* congregate on the outskirts of town. Before the procession, a ceremony called the *Encuentro* (Encounter) is held. The spiritual leaders accompanying the Sacred Cross burn incense and ritually cleanse participants who ask forgiveness for the offenses they committed against each other during the year. This ceremony commemorates the reconciliation between Christianized and non-Christianized natives after the battle in 1531. After the *Encuentro*, they proceed to the main church at the center of town in an impressive display of color and sound.

The *xúchiles* are prepared by different communities and *barrios* to be placed in front of the main church in honor of their ancestors who died in the battle of conquest. *Xúchil* means "flower" in Náhuatl. The *xúchiles* are formed by two tree trunks from twelve to twenty feet long and two crosspieces about five feet wide. Upon this rectangular frame, different designs are formed with small reeds tied with string. *Cempaxúchitl* and *cucharillas* are woven into this bed of reeds. Amaranth, a long purplish-colored wild plant, and fennel, a green plant used for medicinal purposes, are also used, as well as tortillas, bread, fruit, and other offerings.

According to tradition, the *xúchiles* represent the stretchers used to carry the dead from the battlefield. White *cucharillas* represent the skulls of the dead, and *cempaxúchitl*, a symbol of the sun, was the flower offered to dead warriors and leaders. The *xúchiles*—or *chimales* as they are called in some places—are symbols found throughout the region colonized by Otomí during the Spanish Conquest. *Cucharillas* cut like fringe are also used to decorate short reed staffs or long ones that represent lances. Some believe that the short staffs represent candles carried during a funeral procession, but they look like war clubs represented in images found in native drawings called *codices*. These items are left as offerings to certain crosses. Two of the long staffs are crossed and tied to each point of the crosspiece. A short one is leaned against the cross.

Participants also carry wooden crosses of different sizes representing the souls of their important ancestors, as well as banners with images, emblems, and slogans. The slogans of the *concheros* dance groups usually say "Union, Conformity, and Conquest." Leaders of the groups carry staffs of command that have been passed down from colonial times. These are short wooden poles with a red flag attached and a small metal cross at the point. Ribbons are tied to the shaft at the base of the cross. Some leaders are chosen from the same family and hold the position for life. Other positions, called *cargos*, are rotated each year.

The battle and appearance of the cross as related in the origin myth continue to integrate numerous groups throughout the region. The reconciliation, re-enacted every year, forms the basis for a common identity. Veneration of the fallen ancestors links them directly to the past. Like myths and legends elsewhere, the account tells how supernatural forces and the ancestors created a new social and cultural reality and established norms of conduct to regulate social interaction.

The myth contains many Mesoamerican components. For example, for a new life to be formed, the gods must die or be sacrificed. In the myth, the ancestors who died were buried in the atrium of the church where the *xúchiles* are placed every year in their honor. Popular belief holds that these ancestors transmit special power to those who venerate them, indicating that they have become sacralized. The divinization of leaders and warriors by their mixing personal attributes with those of their deities to create new targets for devotion was a pre-Hispanic tradition.

Fertility symbols are also present. Water runs in the streambed, and the cross was formed from its stones. The armadillo, whose shell is used for *conchas*, is closely associated with the earth. Another element present is a *nahual*, an animal or other being that is the alter ego of a person or god. Saint Michael the Archangel plays such a role to the Sacred Cross. He is the messenger of God and guardian of the faith. This is reflected in the practice of beginning celebrations in September on the day of the Triumph of the Sacred Cross and ending with observances honoring Saint Michael.

Dualistic elements are also present. In Mesoamerican cosmovision, though, these are not opposing but complementary and form a cycle of life emerging from death. The battle initiated a cycle of lasting peace resulting from violent confrontation. It is re-enacted symbolically every year. The ritual number four referring to the cardinal points of the universe is also present. Also, four captains led the armies.

The myth is a reflection of syncretic processes combining elements from Mesoamerican beliefs and European traditions related to the miraculous appearances of saints and crosses during crucial moments of battle such as the appearance of Saint James in Spain during the reconquest of the Iberian Peninsula from the Moors. Rather than adopt the position that the persistence of these customs demonstrates that members of ethnic groups in Mexico resist change or have traditional mentalities, their continuation indicates their relevance for reinforcing social cohesion and providing meaning for life in a continually changing and uncertain world.

The myth also commemorates the historical role played by Otomí in the formation of the Spanish colonial order. The exclusion of the Spanish from the myth, however, provides a noteworthy means of reinforcing a unified identity as native brethren despite their violent confrontation in opposition to the unnamed foreign invaders who received the real benefits of the conquest.

STUDIES OF OTOMÍ FOLKLORE

Most literature on the Otomí has been published in Spanish. Some exceptions include an entry in the *Handbook of Middle American Indians* (Manrique 1969); a description of the *concheros* dance groups in the 1940s (Stone 1975); three works by Dow: a doctoral dissertation describing religious practices and the cargo system (1973), a seventy-two-page monograph on the Otomí of the northern mountain zone of Puebla (1974a), and a lengthier work on shamanism (1986); Sandstrom on curing and fertility rituals (1981) and the making and use of paper figures (1986) among the mountain Otomí of Puebla; a native **ethnography** by Salinas in collaboration with Bernard (1989); an ethnoarchaeological study of maguey exploitation in the Mezquital Valley (Parsons and Parsons 1990); chapters on Otomí verbal art and language preservation (Lastra 2000a, 2000b); and an article on religious traditions in Guanajuato (Correa 2000a).

Literature in Spanish covering Otomí in general includes a volume compiling ethnohistorical information on the Otomí from the Spanish chronicles (Carrasco 1979 [1950]); Soustelle's linguistic, historical, and ethnographic text on the Otopame language family (1993 [1937]); and a volume on language and narrative from various regions by Lastra (2001). *Estudios de cultura otopame* is published annually.

Other texts are regionally or locally focused. For the mountainous area of northern Puebla, Dow's dissertation was published in Spanish (1974b), and two lengthy ethnographies by Galinier, originally in French, are available in Spanish (1987, 1990). For the Mezquital Valley in Hidalgo, several works are relevant: a detailed although somewhat ethnocentric overview of Otomí culture (Basauri 1990 [1940]); Tranfo's monograph on Otomí village life and magic (1974); Medina and Quezada's survey of Otomí crafts (1975); a study of the economies of two Otomí communities by Finkler (1974); Franco's monograph on households, economy, and ideology (1992); a study of bilingualism in Otomí markets by Flores Farfán (1984); and Sierra's study of power relations and discursive practices (1992). The mountainous area of Hidalgo is represented with a study of religion and identity by Vélez (1993).

For the valley of Toluca, works include Lagarriga on mortuary practices (1978) and linguistic studies by Lastra de Suárez (1989, 1992). Texts on Querétaro and Guanajuato include ethnographic descriptions of celebrations and religious traditions in San Miguel de Allende (Fernández 1941; Correa 1998, 2000b) and the *Bajío* in general (Moedano 1972); an analysis of Spanish words used in the context of Otomí religious practice (Correa 2000b); a description of family oratories in Tolimán (Chemín 1993); an ethnography of the annual pilgrimage of Otomí from Tolimán to the Zamorano mountain (Piña 2002); and a study of the Otomí of Amealco (Van de Fliert 1988). For Michoacán, see Fabila's monograph of Zitácuaro (1954), and for Tlaxcala, Lastra's book on language and narrative in Ixtenco (1997).

Several works contain important historical information: Powell's classic on the resistance by Chichimecs during the sixteenth century (1952); Jiménez Moreno on colonization and evangelization in Guanajuato (1984); several volumes of paleographed documents and commentary focusing on the conquest and colonization of Querétaro and Guanajuato (Wright 1988, 1989, 1998); and a study on the effects of the introduction of livestock grazing in the Mezquital Valley (Melville 1997). *See also* **Maya**; **Nahua**.

BIBLIOGRAPHY

Basauri, Carlos. 1990 [1940]. La familia otomiana: Los otomíes. In *La población indígena de México*. México: Instituto Nacional Indigenista/CONACULTA. 3: 233–314.

Bernard, H. Russell, and Jesús Salinas Pedraza. 1989. *Native Ethnography: A Mexico Indian Describes His Culture*. Newbury Park: Sage Publications.

Carrasco Pizana, Pedro. 1979 [1950]. *Los otomíes: Cultura e historia prehispánicas de los pueblos mesoamericanos de habla otomiana*. México: Bibliotaca Enciclopédica dal Estado de México.

Chemin de Bässler, Heidi. 1993. *Las capillas oratorios otomíes de San Miguel Tolimán*. Querétaro, México: Fondo Editorial de Querétaro.

Correa, Phyllis M. 1998. La religión popular en el Estado de Guanajuato: El culto a la Santa Cruz del Puerto de Calderón. *Revista Mexicana de Estudios Antropológicos* 43: 69–90.

———. 2000a. Otomí Rituals and Celebrations: Crosses, Ancestors, and Resurrection. *Journal of American Folklore* 113: 436–450.

———. 2000b. Lenguaje, cultura e identidad entre los grupos otomianos del estado de Guanajuato. *Estudios de cultura otopame* 2: 147–162.

Dow, James W. 1973. Saints and Survival: The Function of Religion in a Central Mexican Indian Society. Diss., Brandeis University.

———. 1974a. *The Otomí of the Northern Sierra de Puebla, Mexico: An Ethnographic Outline.* Monograph Series, No. 12. Latin American Studies Center, Michigan State University.

———. 1974b. *Santos y supervivencias: Funciones de la religión en una comunidad otomí, México.* México: Instituto Nacional Indigenista/Secretaría de Educación Pública.

———. 1986. *The Shaman's Touch: Otomí Indian Symbolic Healing.* Salt Lake City: University of Utah Press.

Fabila, Alfonso.1954. *Los otomianos de Zitácuaro.* México: Instituto Nacional Indigenista.

Farfán, Flores, and José Antonio. 1984. *La interacción verbal de compra-venta en mercados otomíes.* México: SEP.

Fernández, Justino. 1941. *Danzas de los concheros en San Miguel de Allende.* México: Gráfica Panamericana.

Finkler, Kaja. 1974. *Estudio comparativo de la economía de dos comunidades de México.* México: Instituto Nacional Indigenista.

Franco Pellotier, Victor Manuel. 1992. *Grupo doméstico y reproducción social: Parentesco, economía e ideología en una comunidad otomí del Valle del Mezquital.* México: CIESAS.

Galinier, Jacques. 1987. *Pueblos de la Sierra Madre: Etnografía de la comunidad otomí.* México: Instituto Nacional Indigenista/Centro de Estudios Mexicanos y Centroamericanos.

———. 1990. *La mitad del mundo: Cuerpo y cosmos en los rituales otomíes.* México: Universidad Nacional Autónoma de México, Centro de Estudios Mexicanos y Centroamericanos, Instituto Nacional Indigenista.

Jiménez Moreno, Wigberto. 1984. *Colonización y evangelización de Guanajuato en el siglo XVI.* León, México: Pliant.

Lagarriga Attias, Isabel. 1978. *Ceremonias mortuorias entre los otomíes del norte del Estado de México.* Toluca, México: Gobierno del Estado de México.

Lastra, Yolanda. 1997. *El otomí de Ixtenco.* México: UNAM.

———. 2000a. An Otomí Story of a Nahual. In *Translating Native Latin American Verbal Art*, edited by Kay Simmons and Joel Sherzer. Washington, DC: Smithsonian Institution Press. 13–21.

———. 2000b. Otomí Language Shift and Some Recent Attempts to Reverse It. In *Can Threatened Languages Be Saved?* edited by Joshua A. Fishman. Multilingual Matters, Series No. 116: 142–165.

———. 2001. *Unidad y diversidad de la lengua: Relatos otomíes.* México: Instituto de Investigaciones Antropológicas, Universidad Nacional Autónoma de México.

Lastra de Suárez, Yolanda. 1989. *Otomí de San Andrés Cuexcontitlán, Estado de México.* México: El Colegio de México.

———. 1992. *El otomí de Toluca.* México: UNAM.

Manrique C., Leonardo. 1969. The Otomi. In *Handbook of Middle American Indians*, edited by Robert Wauchope. Austin: University of Texas Press. 8:682–722.

Medina, Andrés, and Noemí Quezada. 1975. *Panorama de las artesanías otomíes del Valle del Mezquital.* México: Universidad Nacional Autónoma de México.

Melville, Elinor G. K. 1997. *A Plague of Sheep: Environmental Consequences of the Conquest of Mexico.* Cambridge: Cambridge University Press.

Moedano, Gabriel. 1972. Los hermanos de la Santa Cuenta: Un culto de crisis de origen chichimeca. *Memorias de la XII Mesa Redonda de Antropología.* Sociedad Mexicana de Antropología. 599–609.

Parsons, Jeffry R., and Mary H. Parsons. 1990. *Maguey Utilization in Highland Central Mexico: An Archaeological Ethnography*. Ann Arbor: Museum of Anthropology, University of Michigan.

Piña Perusquía, Abel. 2002. *La paregrinación otomí al Zamorana*. Querétaro: Universidad Autónoma de Querétaro.

Powell, Philip W. 1952. *Soldiers, Indians, and Silver: The Northward Advance of New Spain, 1550–1600*. Berkeley: University of California Press.

Sandstrom, Alan. 1981. *Traditional Curing and Crop Fertility Rituals among Otomi Indians of the Sierra de Puebla, Mexico: The Lopez Manuscripts*. Bloomington: Indiana University Museum.

Sandstrom, Alan, and Pamela Effrein Sandstrom. 1986. *Traditional Papermaking and Paper Cult Figures of Mexico*. Norman: University of Oklahoma Press.

Sierra, María Teresa. 1992. *Discurso, cultura y poder: El ejercicio de la autoridad en los pueblos hñähñús del Valle del Mezquital*. Pachuca, México: Gobierno del Estado de Hidalgo and CIESAS.

Soustelle, Jacques. 1993 [1937]. *La familia otomí-pame del México central*. México: Fondo de Cultura Económica.

Stone, Martha. 1975. *At the Sign of Midnight: The Concheros Dance Cult of Mexico*. Tucson: University of Arizona Press.

Tranfo, Luigi. 1974. *Vida y magia en un pueblo otomí del Mezquital*. México: Instituto Nacional Indigenista/Secretaría de Educación Pública.

Van de Fliert, Lydia. 1988. *El otomí en busca de la vida*. Querétaro, México: Universidad Autónoma de Querétaro.

Vélez Arétia, Elena. 1993. *La fuerza de la costumbre en un pueblo otomí: Un estudio sobre los ritos de Tenango de Doria*. Pachuca, México: Gobierno del Estado de Hidalgo/Instituto Hidalgüense de Cultura.

Wright, David. 1988. *Conquistadores otomíes en la guerra chichimeca. Documentos de Querétaro*. Querétaro, México: Talleres Gráficos del Gobierno del Estado de Querétaro.

———. 1989. *Querétaro en el Siglo XVI: Fuentes documentales primarias. Documentos de Querétaro, No. 13*. Querétaro, México: Talleres Gráficos del Gobierno del Estado de Querétaro.

———. 1998. *La conquista del Bajío y los orígenes de San Miguel de Allende*. México: Fondo de Cultural Económica. 1998.

Phyllis M. Correa

RARÁMURI

GEOGRAPHY AND HISTORY

Also known as the Tarahumara, the Rarámuri are an indigenous people of northwestern Mexico, whose contemporary homeland covers approximately 35,000 square kilometers of semi-arid but forested mountains and subtropical canyons. This rugged region, a component of Mexico's Sierra Madre Occidental range referred to as the Sierra Tarahumara, is located in the southwestern corner of the state of Chihuahua. The Mexican national census for 2000 recorded over 86,000 speakers of the Rarámuri language in Chihuahua and an additional 6,000 speakers elsewhere in Mexico, the majority in the adjacent states of Durango, Sinaloa, and Sonora. There were more speakers of Rarámuri than any other indigenous language in northern Mexico and, except for Diné (Navajo), in all of North America north of central Mexico.

"Rarámuri," sometimes written "Ralámuli," is the Rarámuri's name for themselves. Because the Rarámuri are renowned long-distance runners and the Rarámuri word *rará* means "sole(s) of the foot," many writers have concluded that *Rarámuri* should be translated as "foot runners." This analysis is suspect, however, and although no conclusive etymology exists, the Rarámuri use the term with increasing degrees of specificity to designate all human beings in contrast to plants and animals, all indigenous people in contrast to non-indigenous people, Rarámuri people in contrast to other indigenous people, and Rarámuri men in contrast to Rarámuri women. The semantic scope and pronunciation of the term varies among the Rarámuri themselves, reflecting regional variations. Linguists classify the language as belonging to the Taracahitan subgroup of the southern branch of the Uto-Aztecan language family and have proposed that it includes as many as seven distinct dialects.

Exactly when the Rarámuri arrived in western Chihuahua is unknown: only a handful of archeological sites in the Sierra Tarahumara have been excavated, and the relationship between the inhabitants of these sites and the contemporary Rarámuri has never been properly evaluated. At the time of European contact in the late sixteenth and early seventeenth centuries, the Rarámuri's ancestors lived in the basin-and-range country of central Chihuahua and the mountains and canyons of western Chihuahua. Spanish colonial expansion into the region was driven by the discovery of silver and gold, with miners and the farmers and ranchers who supported them soon being joined by Franciscan and Jesuit missionaries. The Rarámuri were proselytized primarily by Jesuits, who founded their first mission among the Rarámuri around 1608 and, during the next century and a half, developed a network of missions that extended throughout Rarámuri territory.

The Rarámuri response to the mission program and to Spanish **colonialism** as a whole was ambivalent. Some Rarámuri embraced Christianity and rapidly integrated into the Spanish colonial system. Many others resisted by withdrawing from the missions and Spanish settlements or by organizing a series of military campaigns against the intruders that involved large numbers of people from many different Rarámuri communities. Usually characterized by the Spanish as "rebellions," these campaigns were motivated by a number of factors, including the Spaniards' forced labor programs and the displacement of Rarámuri people from their lands by Spanish settlers.

Most of these campaigns took place in the second half of the seventeenth century. By the early eighteenth century the devastating impact of introduced Old World diseases and an increasingly effective Spanish military strategy overwhelmed the Rarámuri's ability to organize and coordinate large-scale resistance. Some Rarámuri shifted to small-scale raiding of Spanish settlements as an alternative form of violent resistance, either on their own or in alliance with the members of other indigenous societies, especially the Apache. At times, they also joined multiethnic raiding bands whose members included not only indigenous people but Europeans, Africans, and individuals of mixed descent. Such raiding did not prevent the Spanish from expanding and consolidating their colonial system across Rarámuri territory, but it did undermine their efforts to establish full control over the region.

In 1767, the Spanish Crown expelled the Jesuits from its empire, assigning most of the Rarámuri missions in the Sierra Tarahumara to Franciscan missionaries and the remainder to diocesan priests. This arrangement remained unchanged following Mexican Independence in 1821, but in 1859 the Mexican government prohibited the Franciscans and other religious orders from operating within its borders. The Rarámuri missions in the Sierra Tarahumara were then transferred to the diocesan clergy, which lacked the human and economic resources to administer them. The Catholic presence in the area was negligible until 1900, when the Jesuits resumed responsibility for the religious administration of the Rarámuri in the Sierra.

Between the late eighteenth and late nineteenth centuries, expansion and consolidation of non-indigenous settlements and economic endeavors within traditional Rarámuri territory outside the Sierra Tarahumara was accompanied by the gradual integration of Rarámuri people there into the Spanish colonial and Mexican national systems. In contrast, in the Sierra, where the impact of outsiders was less and resistance to integration greater, the Rarámuri continued to flourish as a distinct cultural group. Their autonomy began to diminish, though, near the end of the nineteenth century with the onset of commercial exploitation of the Sierra's natural resources.

Much of the twentieth century was characterized by an influx of non-indigenous, or *mestizo*, settlers into the Sierra. Initially they were attracted by economic opportunities offered by large-scale mining and lumbering and later, during the second half of the twentieth century, by **tourism** and, in certain areas, illegal drug production. These settlers displaced the Rarámuri from many of the best agricultural lands and subjected them to various forms of social and economic discrimination. Such abuses dramatically increased interethnic tensions and conflicts in the Sierra that were exacerbated by the growing *mestizo* presence. By the end of the century, the non-indigenous population in the Sierra was more than four times greater than the indigenous population.

Throughout the twentieth century the Catholic Church re-established its influence across the Sierra Tarahumara, combining religious activities with programs in education, health, and social welfare. Similar programs developed by the Mexican government and to a limited extent by Protestant organizations paralleled and at times competed with the Catholic efforts. As part of the agrarian reform instituted by the Mexican Revolution of 1910–1920, the Mexican government organized most Sierra communities into communal landholding and economic units known as *ejidos*. Intended to improve economic conditions for the region's residents and to enhance their control over natural resources, this approach legitimized *mestizo* claims to Rarámuri lands and provided Sierra communities with the means to join private companies in exploiting and destroying the Sierra's forests.

By the end of the twentieth century, local ecosystems had been thoroughly disrupted and thousands of Sierra residents, both Rarámuri and *mestizos*, had been forced to abandon the Sierra to seek a livelihood in economic centers elsewhere in Mexico and, to a lesser degree, the United States. This out-migration fragmented many Rarámuri communities and increased the integration of Rarámuri people into the Mexican national culture, a process reinforced by participation of Rarámuri children in the national primary education system. The members of a number of Rarámuri communities began to express concern about the potential loss of their culture and language and to develop strategies to ensure their survival.

ADOPTION OF FOREIGN CULTURAL PRACTICES

During more than four centuries of interaction with non-indigenous people, those Rarámuri who have sustained a separate cultural identity have responded to outside cultural influences by recontextualizing certain foreign cultural elements within their own evolving cultural system. This process, better characterized as appropriation than as acculturation or assimilation, is well illustrated by several examples from the Spanish colonial period.

The ancestors of the contemporary Rarámuri eagerly adopted Old World livestock and agricultural technology, but they incorporated these innovations to enhance rather than replace their indigenous agricultural practices. They accepted the designation by colonial Catholic missionaries of specific locations as civil-religious centers and the construction of churches there,

The woman waving a white banner accepts responsibility for organizing a ritual from the woman kneeling before an altar constructed on a dance patio adjacent to a Rarámuri homestead. The ritual, performed annually to promote the productivity of crops and livestock, is a Rarámuri adaptation of the Catholic blessing of the fields and animals. A *matachine* dancer performs to one side to the music of violins and a guitar. Rejogochi, June 1981. (Photograph by William Merrill)

but they rejected missionary attempts to congregate them into these centers, known in Spanish as "*pueblos*." Instead they maintained the dispersed settlement pattern that was a more suitable adaptation to the local landscape and an effective mechanism for limiting intervention by outsiders into their daily lives. They made the Spanish colonial form of town government, with its hierarchically organized complement of officials, the central component of their political organization, but they limited the power of these officials by retaining consensus as the principal mechanism for community decision making. Similarly, they continued to regard wisdom, moral rectitude, oratorical ability, and commitment to serve others as the qualities most desired in their leaders. Finally, they "converted" to Catholicism by radically reinterpreting Catholic beliefs and rituals and integrating them into the framework of their indigenous religion. They also adapted the Catholic ritual calendar to their own ceremonial cycle, which was structured around the maize-growing season, and they directed the Catholic ceremonies that they had appropriated toward the achievement of indigenous goals such as ensuring the survival of the universe, enhancing individual health, and promoting agricultural productivity.

CULTURAL VARIATION

Contemporary Rarámuri society is one of the most vibrant indigenous societies in North America, with active and evolving traditions in music, dance, sports, the plastic arts, folklore, and oratory. The dynamism of these traditions is evidenced in the significant variation associated with them, which is found both within single communities and between different communities across the region. Broad generalizations about the Rarámuri usually are possible only if such variation is ignored, and even characterizing the Rarámuri as a single cultural group is problematic. Rarámuri people across the Sierra Tarahumara share an identity as "Rarámuri," but they distinguish two major subdivisions within this general category. Most Rarámuri refer to themselves as "baptized ones" (*pagótame* or *pagótuame*), acknowledging their affiliation with the Catholic Church although not necessarily their acceptance of orthodox Catholicism. The members of a small number of Rarámuri communities, however—known as *simaróni*, from Spanish *cimarrón*, "renegade" or "runaway," and *hentíli*, from Spanish *gentil*, "heathen" or "pagan"—reject a formal relationship with the Church.

This variation comes from the interaction of many factors, ranging from differences in the history of interaction with outsiders to the ecological diversity of the Sierra Tarahumara. In some cultural domains, like **worldview** and cosmology, it also reflects the high value that the Rarámuri place on individual autonomy and the absence of mechanisms, such as a formal education system, that would promote the standardization of knowledge. In fact, the only indigenous practice through which basic cultural values and perspectives are consistently presented to the members of different households is the public speech or "sermon" (*nawésari*), delivered by traditional authorities and other community and ritual leaders when people assemble for ceremonies and other social events.

ORATORY

Rarámuri orators deliver their speeches rapidly, averaging about 500 syllables per minute compared to the 300 syllables per minute or less of ordinary conversation. Although each sermon is unique, they all tend to include special vocabulary and constructions seldom encountered in daily speech and to be structured by the presentation of a set of common themes related especially to how people should conduct their lives to maintain proper relations with one another and with their deities. These deities include Our Father (*Onorúame*, also referred to as *Ripá Bitéame*, "One Who Resides Above," and as *Riosi*, from Spanish *Dios*, "God") and his wife, known as Our Mother (*Eyerúame*), often equated with the Virgin Mary and specifically the Virgin of Guadalupe. In most Rarámuri communities Our Father is associated with the sun and Our Mother with the moon, but in others these associations are reversed. In general, however, the Rarámuri identify Our Father and Our Mother as their creators and benefactors in contrast to the devil (*Riré Bitéame*, "One Who Resides Below," or *Riáblo*, from Spanish *diablo*, "devil"), who created and protects nonindigenous people, known as *Chabóchi*, "Whiskered One(s)."

Through explicit references to these beings and standardized admonitions on how to promote the beneficence of Our Father and Our Mother while deflecting the malevolence of the devil, orators implicitly convey many concepts basic to Rarámuri cosmology. The Rarámuri conceive the universe as a series of three to seven levels, with the earth situated in the middle. Levels above the earth are regarded as the abode of Our Father, Our Mother, and their allies, who usually are envisioned as having human form, as well as the ultimate destination of the souls of Rarámuri dead. Levels below the earth, where the souls of non-indigenous people travel after death, are the domain of the devil and his allies, who often are given animal form and include malevolent beings associated with bodies of water, especially deep pools and springs.

The specific details of cosmological knowledge are transmitted across generations in more informal settings, often from grandparents to grandchildren and typically in the privacy of individual households. Accounts of the ancient past often provide the medium through which this information is conveyed, and such accounts allow for considerable individual creativity. The result is that more variation is associated with this knowledge than with the basic cosmological concepts communicated through public oratory.

FOLKTALES

Rarámuri oral literature incorporates a wide variety of themes and protagonists. Some examples recount origins, usually not of the world per se, but of specific features of the world—unusual geological formations, notable characteristics of plants and animals, or specific cultural practices, for example. Many others fit readily into the genre of "**trickster** tales," in which certain animals, often deer, rabbits, foxes, or coyotes, attempt to outwit one another or assume human form to seduce, deceive, or occasionally help human beings. Related stories describe transformations of one kind of animal into another. Human encounters with powerful beings also are a common theme. Accounts of such encounters sometimes are inspired or enriched by dream experiences.

The Rarámuri consider many of these stories to be equivalent to reports, handed down from one generation to the next, of actual events that took in the ancient past. They regard others as simply entertaining and others to be fictions that nonetheless convey important information or perspectives. They also occasionally attribute cosmological significance to accounts that appear on the surface to be insignificant. One example explains that the burro originally had a long tail, but it was burned to its present length when Our Father, displeased by the cannibalism and other misdeeds of the original human inhabitants of the world, dispatched the sun to destroy them. The burro's short tail provides the subject for an engaging explanatory tale while providing concrete evidence of this major cosmological event.

Like oral traditions around the world, these stories are replete with moral lessons, but Rarámuri moral principles tend to be less absolute in concept and more flexible in application than the stark opposition between good and evil of orthodox Christianity. The beings of the Rarámuri pantheon, for example, tend to be either benevolently or malevolently inclined toward humans, helping or harming them in response to how humans behave toward them. Rarámuri religion also places little emphasis on the afterlife or individual salvation. Instead it promotes health and happiness in this life and ensures the continued existence of the universe by maintaining equilibrium among its diverse inhabitants.

RELIGIOUS BELIEFS

Historical evidence from the Spanish colonial period suggests that many Rarámuri accepted Christian baptism because they believed this sacrament could cure European diseases, a view that the missionaries promoted. Meanwhile, others appear to have rejected baptism because they interpreted Christian doctrine regarding the Second Coming of Christ to mean that if all Rarámuri converted, the world would end, something that they wanted to avoid. This perspective is echoed in contemporary Rarámuri ideology, which proposes that by refusing to be baptized, "gentile" Rarámuri ensure that their souls will remain on earth after death to fulfill their role in protecting the pillars that support the sky.

The Rarámuri sustain the universe and fulfill their obligations to their deities primarily through performance of religious ceremonies. Most of these ceremonies include offerings of food and maize beer, feasting, and diverse rituals, all of which reflect indigenous and European influences. Among the most important indigenous rituals are the *yúmari* and *tutubúri*, directed by ritual chanters (*wikaráame*) whose songs typically are melodic intonations rather than songs with words that are intelligible to non-specialists. They accompany themselves with rattles as they move back and forth across a dance patio in front of an altar composed of wooden crosses, usually draped with cloths and adorned with bead necklaces, and a plank or platform for food and beer offerings. Similar patios are constructed for performances of the matachine dance, adapted from Spanish dances dramatizing the conflict between Christians and Moors. The flamboyantly costumed *matachine* dancers also shake rattles but in a rhythmic pattern distinct from that of the chanters, and they dance to tunes played by musicians on violin and sometimes guitar. Such European-inspired music also is performed without dancing as entertainment during social gatherings, but *yúmari* and *tutubúri* songs are restricted to ritual contexts. Other songs with no ritual significance are sung by individuals in their homes.

Statues representing Christ and the Virgin Mary, dressed as a Rarámuri woman, are carried in a procession led by Easter ceremonial officials and local political authorities. Norogachi, April 2003. (Photograph by Lars Krutak)

FESTIVALS AND CELEBRATIONS

The Rarámuri stage their major ceremonies at pueblo centers, usually in conjunction with the principal dates of the Catholic liturgical year. The Easter ceremony is the most elaborate, attended by hundreds of Rarámuri people from the widely dispersed homesteads affiliated with each pueblo. It also is the ceremony that varies most extensively in content and interpretation from one Rarámuri community to another.

Most Rarámuri communities hold their Easter ceremonies between Maundy Thursday and Holy Saturday. This ceremony differs from those of the remainder of the year in that neither the *yúmari* and *tutubúri* nor the matachine rituals are performed. Instead groups of men and boys dance to the music of drums and reed whistles, played only during the Easter season, which begins for many Rarámuri communities on Candlemas (2 February) rather than Ash Wednesday. These groups, along with the pueblo political officials, women and girls, and other community members complete a series of processions around the church and pueblo center along a route marked by crosses and arches corresponding to Stations of the Cross. These processions' prominence is reflected by many Rarámuri communities referring to the Easter ceremony as *Norírawachi,* meaning "When We Walk in Circles." The ceremony culminates on Holy Saturday with the destruction of an effigy identified as Judas. This effigy is the focus of ritual humor and is interpreted in distinct ways in different communities, ranging from a rather straightforward icon of a non-Indian to a complex symbolic representation of disorder in the universe; however, in no Rarámuri communities is this effigy seen as simply a representation of the apostle who betrayed Christ. The remainder of Holy Saturday is devoted to drinking maize beer, which continues for one or more days, usually in the hamlets where the majority of Rarámuri live rather than in the pueblo centers.

The Easter celebrations of some Rarámuri communities also have become major attractions for tourists, whose presence many Rarámuri resent but others value as a ready market for their arts and crafts. Easter ritual

Spotted with white clay paint and carrying elaborately decorated swords, Easter participants known as "pintos" dance to the accompaniment of a drum and reed whistle. Norogachi, April 2003. (Photograph by Lars Krutak)

A woman spins wool with a wooden spindle-and-whorl in front of her home; two bundles of cleaned but unspun wool lie on the ground to her right. Rejogochi, July 1981. (Photograph by William Merrill)

paraphernalia such as drums, reed whistles, and the feathered headgear worn by some participants are favorite tourist purchases, and the Rarámuri produce other items primarily for sale to them: woven belts, headbands, bracelets, necklaces, bows and arrows, and carved wooden figurines and masks. Violins, rattles, woolen blankets, baskets, and pottery are made for both local use and export. The Rarámuri gain access to the external market through arts and crafts stores in tourist centers of the Sierra or through traders who export Rarámuri goods to other areas of Mexico, the United States, Canada, and Europe. Rarámuri craftspeople usually receive poor compensation for their work, but some efforts have been made to reduce exploitation. These efforts, usually initiated by outsiders, include attempts to increase prices (and thus returns to artisans) by portraying Rarámuri arts and crafts as "authentic" expressions of indigenous culture or by organizing artisan cooperatives and then promoting the sale of arts and crafts as a way of benefiting the communities where they are produced.

MAIZE BEER

Of all Rarámuri productions, the large, low-fired clay pots used for fermenting maize beer are perhaps the most prized by private collectors of indigenous art. These pots also are highly valued by the Rarámuri themselves, in part because they are difficult to make but, more important, because of their relationship, both practical and symbolic, to maize beer. This beer, called *sugí, suwí,* or *batári,* is central to Rarámuri social life. Regarded as a gift from Our Father, it is referred to metaphorically as "Our Father's Water" (*Onorúame Ba'wíra*) and is valued as an intoxicating but nourishing beverage and as a medicine.

Maize beer is prepared most frequently by the members of a single household to compensate people who assist them in the completion of some task, like planting or weeding their fields, during communal work parties. It is also obligatory for all ritual events, including those sponsored by households or groups of neighboring households to provide food and other necessities for their dead relatives, to protect their crops and livestock, and to prevent or cure illness. Some of these rituals can include *yúmari, tutubúri,* and matachine performances and thus—on a smaller scale—resemble ceremonies held at the pueblo centers. Curing rituals especially incorporate many elements not seen in the pueblo ceremonies.

FOLK MEDICINE

Rarámuri etiology and curing practices reflect the concept of the soul, an aspect of Rarámuri worldview about which considerable variation exists despite wide sharing of fundamental concepts. Each individual is believed to have multiple souls, and except for accidents and minor ailments, all sickness is associated with soul loss or other threats to the souls. Death occurs when all of a person's souls abandon the body. Most preventative and alleviative curing is directed toward strengthening the souls, and Rarámuri doctors (*owirúame*) typically rely on their ability to control their dreams, which are interpreted as the activities of their principal souls, to locate and recover souls captured by sorcerers (*sukurúame*) and other malevolent beings. The doctors restore the souls to the affected person during curing rituals.

The most elaborate curing rituals aim to placate two categories of powerful beings: *híkuri*, which is associated with the peyote cactus (*Lophophora williamsii*) and other plants, and *bakánowa* or *bakánawi*, usually identified with the tubers of a bulrush (*Scirpus* sp.). The *híkuri* and *bakánowa* beings are believed to be each other's mortal enemies, and they also steal the souls of people who fail to provide them with offerings or to observe certain prohibitions.

The Rarámuri organize their ideas about these beings into sets of binary oppositions (*híkuri*, for example, is linked to fire and the east, *bakánowa* to water and the west), but the rituals oriented toward them share formal similarities: both take place on special patios, access to which is restricted to a limited group of participants and dangerous to all others, and both are directed by the most highly regarded ritual specialists. These specialists are known as raspers (*sipáame*) because they communicate with these beings through special songs accompanied by rasping a smooth stick against a notched one resting on an overturned half bottle gourd.

Despite their dangers people acquire both *híkuri* and *bakánowa* to protect themselves from sorcerers and other enemies and to improve their performance in sports and games, which usually are associated with wagering. The Rarámuri rely on these and other ritual elements and activities to influence the outcome of competitive events, but unlike the members of many other Native American societies, they tend not to regard games as preeminently religious in nature.

SPORTS AND GAMES

Today the Rarámuri play several games of chance, including card games adopted from their *mestizo* neighbors and native games—especially *romayá*, similar to pachisi and more widely known as *patole*, which uses stick dice. Games of skill include *rihibári* and *hubára*, which are based on the same principle as quoits or horseshoes. In *rihibári*, the goals are depressions in the ground, and players use disks made of stone, metal, or pottery. In *hubára*, fresh tree branches, preferably of oak and about the thickness of a finger, are cut with a section of the adjacent trunk to provide stability. One of these sticks is tossed ahead to serve as the goal, and players toss their other sticks toward it, with points going to the one who comes closest. Men and boys play all three games, whereas women and girls usually play only *romayá*.

A sport called *ra'chuéla*, similar to lacrosse or field hockey, is found in some Rarámuri communities, but more widely distributed and by far the most famous of Rarámuri sports is long-distance running. Teams of children or young to middle-aged adults compete in two

A girl runs the stick-and-hoop race, urged along by her supporters who run with her. Rejogochi, August 1981. (Photograph by William Merrill)

different kinds of races: one, for men and boys, is called *rarahípuami* or *rarahípari*, in which a wooden ball is propelled along the course by flipping it with the foot; the other, known in different areas as *ariwéta*, *nakíwari*, *rowéari*, and *rowécuami*, is for women and girls, who use curved sticks to toss a single hoop, two interlinked hoops, or two small sticks bound together ahead of them as they run.

Despite their prominence in contemporary Rarámuri culture, these races may have been developed or adopted by the Rarámuri during the Spanish colonial period. The women's race is not described until the twentieth century, an omission that could be explained by the general neglect of most female activities in the historical and ethnographic literature. Male sports, in contrast, are well documented as far back as the seventeenth century, and the ball race is not mentioned until the second half of the eighteenth century. That the repertoire of Rarámuri sports has changed is unquestionable: the rubber-ball game, widely distributed in various forms in the Americas prior to European contact, is recorded for the Rarámuri in the seventeenth and eighteenth centuries but not thereafter.

STUDIES OF RARÁMURI FOLKLORE

No comprehensive, systematic study of Rarámuri folklore exists, but considerable information is available in books and essays published primarily in English, German, Spanish, and, beginning in the 1970s, Rarámuri. Of particular significance is the work of Rarámuri authors, which usually combines compilations of Rarámuri oral literature or descriptions of contemporary cultural practices with Rarámuri commentary on them, presented in both Rarámuri and Spanish. Such studies include Mares Trías (1975, 1982), Mares Trías and Burgess (1996), López Batista (1980), López Batista and others (1981), Palma Batista (1994), Gardea García and Chávez Ramírez (1998), Cruz Huahuichi (2000), and Palma Aguirre (2002).

The linguist Don Burgess participated in many of these studies and has drawn upon them in his own work, which includes collections of Rarámuri stories and songs in Rarámuri and Spanish (Burgess 1970, 1973), English translations of diverse examples of Rarámuri oral literature (Burgess 1985), and the only review in English of the state of research on Rarámuri folklore (Burgess 1981). A brief compilation of Rarámuri "legends" in Spanish is found in Muñoz (1965).

Other non-Rarámuri writers have explored specific aspects of Rarámuri folklore and culture in focused studies of oratory (Deimel 2001), philosophy and religious practices (Kennedy and López 1981; Velasco Rivero 1983; Merrill 1988, 1998; Bonfiglioli 1995; Deimel 1996, 1997), arts and crafts (Fontana and others 1977; Fontana and Teiwes 1979; Levi 1992; Salmón and Adams 1996; Adams and Salmón 1997), and sports (Kennedy 1969; Kummels 2001). These topics also are discussed in the ethnographic monographs of Lumholtz (1987 [1902]), Bennett and Zingg (1935), Pennington (1996 [1963]), Kennedy (1990, 1996 [1978]), and González Rodríguez (1993b [1982]). Spicer (1962) provides an overview of the history of the Rarámuri and other indigenous societies of northwestern Mexico between the early seventeenth century and the 1960s. His comparative study is complemented for the Spanish colonial period by that of Deeds (2003). Rarámuri history in the Spanish colonial period also is presented in essays (González Rodríguez 1993a; Merrill 1993, 1994) and in annotated collections of Spanish colonial period documents (Sheridan and Naylor 1979; González Rodríguez 1987). Sariego Rodríguez (2002) presents more contemporary historical information in his study of indigenous policies and programs in the Sierra.

BIBLIOGRAPHY

Adams, Karen R., and Enrique Salmón. 1997. Raramuri Necklaces: A Rapidly Changing Folk-Art Form in the Sierra Madre Occidental of Northern Mexico. *Journal of Ethnobiology* 17.1: 1–16.

Bennett, Wendell C., and Robert M. Zingg. 1976 (1935). *The Tarahumara: An Indian Tribe of Northern Mexico*. Glorieta, NM: Rio Grande Press.

Bonfiglioli, Carlo. 1995. *Fariseos y matachines en la Sierra Tarahumara: Entre la Pasión de Cristo, la transgresión cómico-sexual y las danzas de Conquista*. Mexico City: Instituto Nacional Indigenista/ Secretaría de Desarrollo Social.

Burgess, Don H. [Donaldo Burgess McGuire]. 1970. *Anayábari Ra'icháriara Jipe Nerúgame Ra'íchari (Cuentos de Antes y Hoy)*. Mexico City: Instituto Lingüístico de Verano.

———, comp. 1973. *Ralámuli Huicala (Canciones de los Tarahumaras)*. Mexico City: Instituto Lingüístico de Verano.

———. 1981. Tarahumara Folklore: A Study in Cultural Secrecy. *Southwest Folklore* 5: 11–22.

———, comp. 1985. Leyendas Tarahumaras. In *Tarahumara* by Bob Schalkwijk, Luis González Rodríguez, and Don Burgess. Mexico City: Chrysler de México. 71–176 [English translations appear on pp. 167–176].

Cruz Huahuichi, Clemente. 2000. *Je riká ra'icha ochérame: Así cuentan los mayores*. Chihuahua City, Mexico: Doble Hélice Ediciones.

Deeds, Susan M. 2003. *Defiance and Deference in Mexico's Colonial North: Indians under Spanish Rule in Nueva Vizcaya*. Austin: University of Texas Press.

Deimel, Claus. 1996. *Híkuri ba: Peyoteriten der Tarahumara*. Hanover, Germany: Niedersächsisches Landesmuseum.

———. 1997. *Die rituellen Heilungen der Tarahumara: Mit einer Chronik zur Literatur 1902–1991*. Berlin: Dietrich Reimer Verlag.

———. 2001. *Nawésari: Texte aus der Sierra Tarahumara*. Berlin: Dietrich Reimer Verlag.

Fontana, Bernard, Edmund J. B. Faubert, and Barney T. Burns. 1977. *The Other Southwest: Indian Arts and Crafts of Northwestern Mexico*. Phoenix: Heard Museum.

Fontana, Bernard, and Helga Teiwes. 1979. *The Material World of the Tarahumara*. Tucson: Arizona State Museum/University of Arizona.

Gardea García, Juan, and Martín Chávez Ramírez. 1998. *Kite amachíala kiya nirúami. Nuestros saberes antiguos*. Chihuahua City, Mexico: Gobierno del Estado de Chihuahua.

González Rodríguez, Luis. 1987. *Crónicas de la Sierra Tarahumara*. Mexico City: Secretaría de Educación Pública.

———. 1993a. *El noroeste novohispano en la época colonial*. Mexico City: Universidad Nacional Autónoma de México y Miguel Porrúa.

———. 1993b [1982]. *Tarahumara: La sierra y el hombre*. Chihuahua City, Mexico: Editorial Camino.

Kennedy, John G. 1969. La carrera de bola tarahumara y su significación. *América Indígena* 29.1: 17–42.

———. 1990. *The Tarahumara*. New York and Philadelphia: Chelsea House.

———. 1996. [1978]. *Tarahumara of the Sierra Madre: Survivors on the Canyon's Edge*. Pacific Grove, CA: Asilomar Press.

Kennedy, John G., and Raúl A. López. 1981. *Semana Santa in the Sierra Tarahumara: A Comparative Study in Three Communities*. Occasional Papers of the Museum of Cultural History, University of California, Los Angeles, No. 4. Los Angeles: Regents of the University of California.

Kummels, Ingrid. 2001. Reflecting Diversity: Variants of the Legendary Footraces of the Rarámuri in Northern Mexico. *Ethnos* 66.1: 73–98.

Levi, Jerome M. 1992. Commoditizing the Vessels of Identity: Transnational Trade and the Reconstruction of Rarámuri Ethnicity. *Museum Anthropology* 16.3: 7–24.

López Batista, Ramón. 1980. *Qui'ya Iretaca Nahuisarami (Relatos de los Tarahumaras)*. Mexico City: Instituto Nacional Indigenista.

López Batista, Ramón, Ignacio León Pacheco, Albino Mares Trías, and Luis Castro Jiménez. 1981. *Rarámuri Ri'écuara (Deportes y Juegos de los Tarahumaras)*. Chihuahua City, Mexico: Don Burgess (privately published).

Lumholtz, Carl S. 1987 (1902). *Unknown Mexico: A Record of Five Years' Exploration among the Tribes of the Western Sierra Madre*. 2 vols. Glorieta, NM: Glorieta Press.

Mares Trías, Albino. 1975. *Jena Ra'icha Ralámuli Alué 'Ya Muchígame Chiquime Níliga (Aquí relata la gente de antes lo que pasaba en su tiempo)*. Mexico City: Instituto Lingüístico de Verano.

———. 1982. *Ralámuli Nu'tugala Go'ame (Comida de los Tarahumaras)*. Chihuahua City, Mexico: Don Burgess McGuire (privately published).

Mares Trías, Albino, and Don Burgess McGuire. 1996. *Re'igí Ra'chuela: El Juego del Palillo*. Chihuahua City, Mexico: Escuela Nacional de Antropología e Historia, Unidad Chihuahua.

Merrill, William L. 1988. *Rarámuri Souls: Knowledge and Social Process in Northern Mexico*. Washington, DC: Smithsonian Institution Press.

———. 1993. Conversion and Colonialism in Northern Mexico: The Tarahumara Response to the Jesuit Mission Program, 1601–1767. In *Conversion to Christianity: Historical and Anthropological Perspectives on a Great Transformation*, edited by Robert W. Hefner. Berkeley: University of California Press. 129–163.

———. 1994. Cultural Creativity and Raiding Bands in Eighteenth Century Northern New Spain. In *Violence, Resistance, and Survival in the Americas: Native Americans and the Legacy of Conquest*, edited by William B. Taylor and Franklin Pease G. Y. Washington, DC: Smithsonian Institution Press. 124–152.

———. 1998. Rarámuri Easter. In *Performing the Renewal of Community: Indigenous Easter Rituals in North Mexico and Southwest United States*, edited by Rosamond B. Spicer and N. Ross Crumrine. Lanham, MD: University Press of America. 365–421.

Muñóz [sic], Maurilio. 1965. *Leyendas tarahumaras*. Mexico City: Instituto Nacional Indigenista.

Palma Aguirre, Francisco. 2002. *Vida del Pueblo Tarahumara: Mápu Regá Eperé Rarámuri*. Chihuahua City: Doble Hélice Ediciones.

Palma Batista, Jesús Manuel. 1994. Rarajípari: Las vivencias de Jesús Manuel Palma. In *Rarajípari: La carrera de bola tarahumara* by Fructuoso Irigoyen Rascón and Jesús Manuel Palma Batista. Chihuahua City, Mexico: Centro Librero La Prensa. 33–102 (English translation: 127–156).

Pennington, Campbell. 1996 (1963). *The Tarahumar of Mexico: Their Environment and Material Culture*. Guadalajara: Editorial Agata.

Salmón, Enrique, and Karen R. Adams. 1996. For Beauty and For Prayer: Artistic Expressions in Raramuri Necklaces. *American Indian Art* 22.1: 48–55, 91.

Sariego Rodríguez, Juan Luis. 2002. *El indigenismo en la Tarahumara: Identidad, comunidad, relaciones interétnicas y desarrollo en la Sierra de Chihuahua*. Mexico City: Instituto Nacional Indigenista/Instituto Nacional de Antropología e Historia.

Sheridan, Thomas E., and Thomas H. Naylor, eds. 1979. *Rarámuri: A Tarahumara Colonial Chronicle, 1607–1791*. Flagstaff, AZ: Northland Press.

Spicer, Edward. 1962. *Cycles of Conquest: The Impact of Spain, Mexico, and the United States on the Indians of the Southwest, 1533–1960*. Tucson: University of Arizona Press.

Velasco Rivero, Pedro de. 1983. *Danzar o morir: Religión y resistencia a la dominación en la cultura tarahumar*. Mexico City: Centro de Reflexión Teológica.

William L. Merrill and Lars Krutak

TARAHUMARA. *See* Rarámuri

Caribbean

CUBA

GEOGRAPHY AND HISTORY

The folklore of Cuba, the largest island in the Caribbean, is extremely rich in popular music, dance, and oral literature. These are products of a peculiar cultural blend that has been occurring since the European conquest of America. The island was conquered by the Spaniards at the beginning of the sixteenth century. The Native Americans were killed or died of disease imported by Europeans. After a century of colonization, they had almost all disappeared. Their cultural influence is nevertheless evident in Cuban toponymy (the very name Cuba is Indian), in cooking habits (manioc bread, for instance), and of course in the cultivation of tobacco used for making the famous Cuban cigars. After the decimation of Indians, Spaniards imported many slaves from West and Central Africa to work on plantations and in the cities. Cuban folklore is mainly based on the melding of Spanish and African

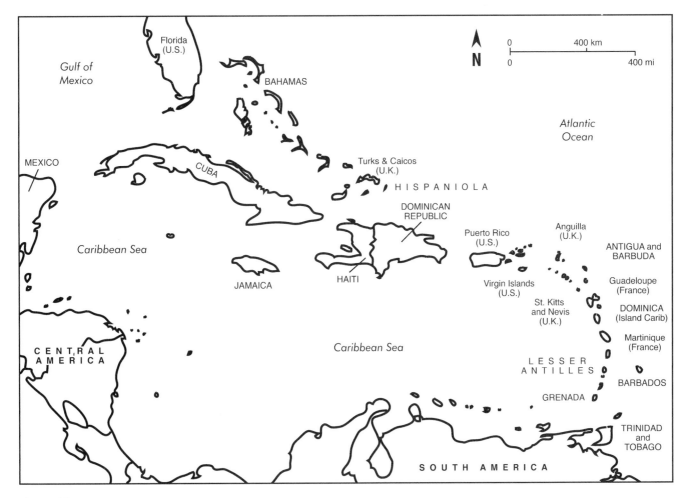

The Caribbean.

A Santería ceremony in the colonial city of Trinidad, Cuba, 23 July 2002. Santería is a blending of Catholicism, brought to Cuba by the Spanish, and traditional African religions, brought to Cuba by slaves imported by the Spanish. (© Jack Kurtz/The Image Works)

cultural influences, which developed during the colonial era and after independence from Spain in 1898.

SACRED MUSIC AND DANCE

Sacred music and dance are an essential part of Afro-Cuban religion and are deeply grounded in drumming and singing. Three drums, called *bata*, are used in Santería, a religion derived from traditional Yoruba polytheism. They are of different sizes, but they all have an hourglass shape, with two membranes each. The rhythms of the *bata* are especially complex, sometimes binary, sometimes ternary or of mixed pattern (6/8). As the drummers use a total of six different membranes to play various tones, they can structure melodies with their instruments. Each of these melodic rhythms is linked to a god of the pantheon and is performed to honor and to invoke him. For instance, there are specific rhythms for Elegua, god of crossings, for Ogun, god of iron, and for Ochosi, god of the hunt. During a drum ceremony called *tambor*, mystical songs in call-and-response form are performed by the believers' choir in accompaniment of these rhythms. The participants also dance for the gods in a standardized manner. Each divinity has its own choreography linked to specific rhythms and songs. The movements of the dancers are usually a representation of some of the characteristics of the spiritual entity. The dancer for Yemaya, goddess of the ocean, moves his skirt as if it were waves. The dancer who honors Chango, god of thunder and sexuality, raises high his hand and simulates the striking of lightning on the earth. This set of esthetic behaviors (dance, songs, rhythms) often leads some individuals to be possessed by one of the invoked spirits. Far from becoming frightened, the community of believers rejoice at this presence of a god among men.

Palo Monte, a religious tradition from Congo, also has a set of rhythms, dances, and songs linked to its creed, which focuses more on the relationship between the dead and the living. Drums are mono-membranophones, and songs are usually sung in a blend of Spanish and Kikongo that comprises the ritual language called *bozal*. Dances usually have a connotation of confrontation or rebellion, which stylistically differentiates Palo Monte from Santería. Rituals are rawer and stronger. But both religions have greatly influenced the secular folklore of the island.

SECULAR MUSIC AND DANCE

Secular Cuban music and dance have reached a high degree of popularity in the world. "Salsa" music, songs, and dances are in fact grounded in various forms of traditional Cuban entertainment, which have been given a new life with modern technology and adapted to the world market.

Carnival (*Carnaval*) was a prominent institution as far as folklore is concerned because it included public music, songs, dancing in the street, and fancy outfits. Specific associations, known as *comparsas*, were devoted to organizing the celebration, which corresponded to dates in the Catholic calendar. Each neighborhood had its *comparsa*, and in large cities such as Havana and Santiago, there was often an informal competition among them. In Santiago de Cuba, *comparsas* danced in the street in June and July in masked celebrations known as *fiestas de mamarrachos* from St. John's Day (24 June) to St. Ann's Day (26 July). In Havana, the celebration took place on the *Día de los Reyes*, or Epiphany (6 January). One of these associations was very peculiar. Members were known as *diablitos* or *ñáñigos*. They were fully hidden by their costumes, which closely resembled traditional African costumes. In fact, this association was more than a *comparsa*; it was a secret society of mutual help, founded on an African myth derived from Nigerian Calabar. This society was called the *abakuá*. Though some of these carnival traditions have weakened since the 1950s, they still exist. Carnival is still a very popular festival, but its date is no longer linked to religious celebrations.

The *tumba francesa* was born when French colonists and their domestic slaves settled in the eastern part of Cuba after Haiti achieved independence in 1804. In Santiago de Cuba, there still are *tumba francesa* societies in which the founders' descendants meet regularly to dress in eighteenth-century costumes and dance in a way very much influenced by French court dances such as the *menuet* or *quadrille*, but with African-derived drumming.

The *rumba* is very different from the "Americanized" Latin dance, which was very popular in the 1950s. The original *rumba* is usually improvised by one or two drummers-singers and dancers on the sidewalk. There are three main types of rumbas, and the public always encourages the performers. The *columbia* is danced by a solitary man who shows his virtuosity by manipulating a handkerchief and sometimes doing fast-paced acrobatic tricks around a glass bottle put on the ground. The *guaguanco* is a form of *rumba*, which involves a man trying to seduce a woman. She tries to avoid getting "caught" by her partner. The last form is known as *yambu*: dancers imitate the slow gestures of old women at work. The rhythmic basis of all kinds of rumbas is the *clave*, a very popular five-beat rhythm.

The *son* is a dance and musical style also based on a *clave* rhythm but performed by a band comprised of a percussion section, a guitar, a bass, horns, or even a full big band. The *son* is danced by couples at a relatively slow pace. The dancers hold each other gently and move slowly following the rhythm in a manner much closer to European social dances such as the waltz. Born more or less at the same moment as jazz in New Orleans, the *son* was created in the eastern part of the Cuba and became extremely popular from the 1920s, dominating ballrooms and lounges for many years.

In the 1940s and 1950s, Cuban popular music evolved quickly under the influence of the entertainment industry, which favored a frequent renewal of popular culture. It was the era of *mambo* and *cha cha cha*, which became widely popular outside Cuba. The former especially, based on a 1–2/1–2–3 rhythm pattern, was a genuine expression of the Cuban spirit. The words of the songs were often rife with social critique and satirical content.

MUSICAL LITERATURE

Popular Cuban literature was originally oral and came from the Hispanic and African traditions. It was transcribed in the twentieth century by folklorists who gave it a literary form similar to what Perrault, Andersen, and the Grimm brothers had done earlier in Europe. Exchanges between the popular and scholarly versions of these stories, as transcribed by clerks, are not uncommon in a country founded in modern times. Some of these myths, tales, and legends are at times variants of narratives from Europe or Africa; others are popular local inventions or are creations of the folklorists themselves.

The term *musical literature* describes sung works in which the literary content is more important than the melody or harmony. It includes texts in verse, improvised or set, with a fixed meter, such as a stanza with ten octosyllables. An example is the form called the *décima*. This form has been known since the the end of the Middle Ages in Spain and was set in the sixteenth century by the poet Vincente Espinel, which is why the term *espinela* is sometimes used to describe the *décima*. The ten verses are organized in the following manner (each capital letter symbolizing the last syllable of the verse): A–B–B–A–A–C–C–D–D–C. *Décimas* occur throughout Latin America. According to Pasmanick (1997), "[D]écima entered Cuba through theater, the church, and immigrant farmers, cowboys, and mule skinners" and became a very popular genre there. The Cuban *décima* is often sung in the form of a *punto*, the characteristics of which (Phrygian and Mixolydian modes in 3/4 rhythm) came from the Canary Islands. The *punto* is accompanied by a six-string guitar or, in the eastern part of the country, by a *tres*, a three-string guitar. There are regional variations in the form both rhythmically and in the number of performers (solo, duet). *Punto* aficionados organize poetic competitions in which the singers attempt to show that they are the most virtuosic in improvisation. (Music for these is simple and repetitive.) One of the most entertaining forms of *punto* is the *controversia*, in which each poet completes the tenth verse of his adversary's song to begin his own *décima*. Since the fifteenth century *décimas* have been written and published, and since the beginning of the twentieth century they have been recorded, played on the radio, and used in advertisements. Today literary competitions are held at a national level and shown on Cuban television.

The *décima*, whose easily traced origins are Hispanic, is combined in Cuba with the *rumba*. Some 40 percent of the rumbas that Philip Pasmanick studied have the form of *décimas*. Here is an example of a *décimas rumberas*:

Hoy se encierra en este ritmo	A	Today this rhythm contains
Un Eden lleno de flores	B2x	An Eden full of flowers,
Para ti miles de honores	B	Thousands of honors to you.
Te quiero más que a mi mismo	A	I love you more than myself.
En mi decir sin egoísmo	A	In my own voice, without egotism,
Claro te voy a cantar	C	I will sing to you clearly
Con mi sincera amistad	C	With my sincere friendship.
Yo soy un hombre correcto	D	I am a righteous man,
Para ti va mi afecto	D	So I offer you my affection
Y mi sincera amistad.	C	With my sincere friendship.

In short, the *décima* is not exclusively a Hispanic or peasant genre. It has been integrated into the *rumba* by the Afro-Cuban population. It is a typical illustration of folkloric transculturation, of which there are many examples in Cuba.

MYTHS, LEGENDS, AND FOLKTALES

Just as the *décima* was imported from Europe and then creolized, so too was a body of tales, legends, and myths whose origins are demonstrably African and that have also been transformed in the Caribbean. The myths of Santería relate primarily to the adventures of the gods. They are tales related to divining by use of shells (cowries) or palm nuts. The followers of Santería consult their gods when they have a decision to make or a problem to solve. The signs they receive from throwing shells on the ground are interpreted as referencing certain myths related to the real-life situation of the petitioner. These stories feature the gods and also the signs for divination themselves, which act as characters in the tales. In other words, the function of these tales is not simply a speculative one but, rather, it is a practical one. The following story of the sign Obbara exists in many variations:

> Olofi [the god of creation] invited all of the *orishas* [the deities] to a feast. Obbara Shango was very poor, he was dirty; that is why he did not heed the invitation. When all of the *orishas* were together at the home of the eldest god, he gave them calabashes. They believed that the gifts were ordinary and insignificant, and they delivered them to Obbara to mock him. Obbara accepted them and, far from despising them, he said, "I know how to cook the calabash." In taking one he thought that there were insects inside. Nevertheless he opened it, and while removing the seeds, he saw that it was full of gold. They were all full of gold. After some time Olofi invited the *orishas* to another feast, and when it had begun and they were playing the drums, they saw a man dressed entirely in white on a white horse.
> "Who is that? He looks like a prince."
> "You are welcome! Enter!" said Olofi.
> It was Obbara, who had the treasure from the calabashes and who came to thank Olofi.

The diviner strives to find the meaning of this story for the petitioner. For example, did he recently give or receive gifts? Does he have calabash in his garden? Is he invited to a feast? Does he have money trouble? All these elements should make it possible to counsel the individual by replacing his specific case in the mythical structure of which his life is a distant echo. Here we see how the folklore is socially alive. In Santería life imitates myth.

These Afro-Cuban myths often stem from transculturation. In other words, if identical African tales have survived in the body of myths, many others have been integrated into Catholicism. First, the African divinities are identified with saints or the Virgin Mary. That is why the divining manuals refer indistinctly to Obatala, the androgynous god of purity and wisdom, as *Virgen de las Mercedes*, or to Oshun, goddess of love, gold, and copper, as *Virgen de la Caridad del Cobre*. This phenomenon is well known. On the other hand, we are less aware of myths of European origin because they have often been perfectly integrated into Afro-Cuban divining procedures. Here as an example is the tale associated with the sign Oragun:

A man already had many children when his wife again gave birth. He wondered how he would feed this new infant and refused to have it baptized. The devil offered to be his godfather, but he refused. Instead he accepted that death be his godmother. Death protected the child until he grew up. He told Death that he wanted to be a doctor. Death took him to an iroco and told him that in giving the sick a leaf of this tree, they would be cured. But if he saw a candle at the foot of the bed, the invalid was supposed to die, and he should not treat the person in any way.

The king was sick and had the doctor called. When he arrived, he saw his godmother at the foot of the bed. But the king's men made so many promises that he ignored her and healed the king. Once outside, he gave a gift to his godmother, and she pardoned him. But, shortly thereafter, the king's daughter fell ill. Death was at her feet; she was condemned. The doctor did not want to treat her, but they promised him the princess's hand in marriage. He treated her, and she was healed. When he was finished, Death took him to a place where there were a large number of candles lit. She said to him, "You see this candle which is about to go out; it is your life ending." Death's godson died in spite of his pleas.

This story, which is completely recontextualized in the Afro-Cuban mythological system, is a well-known tale from European folklore. Called the "Tale of Godmother Death," it illustrates the close relationship between the institution of Catholic godparents and life after death. Here this story has an entirely different meaning. In terms of Afro-Cuban divinity it means that his alliance with Ifa, the god of destiny, is dangerous. We condemn ourselves to death if we save someone who has been condemned by destiny. Here we see how much Afro-Cuban folklore is an open and pragmatic system.

The creolization of African and European sources created much of Cuban culture. Nevertheless, it would be wrong to suggest that it is simply a melting pot. A large part of Cuban folklore is of purely local origin, closely tied to the history of the island. Some tales are particularly interesting because they are intimately linked to the creation of the Cuban nation. The legend of the Light of Yara (*la Luz de Yara*) tells of Hatuey, a sixteenth-century Indian chief who resisted the Spanish and was burned to death by the conquistadors. Here is the literary version of this legend as published by Luis Vicoriano Betancourt in 1875:

Hatuey courageously threw himself into the flames; the Spaniards shouted out with a ferocious joy, and Bartolomé de Las Casas fell to his knees, sending to the sky a funeral oration, while the angel of freedom collected the last sigh of the first martyr for the independence of Cuba.

Since then a subtle and mysterious light, separated from the enormous pyre, roams the night in this great plain, watching the dreams of those who still sleep in servitude, and waiting for the time of eternal light and eternal vengeance. This light was the soul of Hatuey. It was the light of Yara.

It is difficult to know if Betancourt invented this story from scratch or if the legend already existed in eastern Cuba. In either case we can see here the political use of folklore: this story was published in the midst of Cuba's war of independence, thus providing a myth of resistance against European guardianship. The supporters of independence gave their struggle a historic legitimacy through this story by proclaiming their alliance with the Caribbean Indians. Many Cubans in the Yara region still say that they have seen this light when on night walks.

FUSION OF CULTURES

It is obvious from the few genres discussed thus far that Cuban folklore went through a double process of transculturation. The first was a phenomenon of exchange and of the fusion of African and Hispanic culture that Fernando Ortiz (1995) has studied extensively. The second, less studied, can be defined as the series of exchanges between popular and scholarly culture. Writers, poets, and also ethnographers such as Lydia Cabrera have been inspired by popular tales and legends, but in quite a few cases the tales invented by the cultural elite were adopted by the people. In short, we can in no way see Cuban folklore as a stable and closed system. On the contrary, it is the product of interpenetration of European and African civilizations, as well as the cultural exchanges between the people and the dominant classes in the colonial and postcolonial era. After the Cuban revolution of 1959, dramatic social and cultural changes occurred, but the socialist state encouraged the preservation of folklore by creating the National Folklore Dance Company, **museums**, and various academic journals dedicated to Cuban folklore. *See also* **Haiti; Island Carib (Dominica); Jamaica.**

BIBLIOGRAPHY
Cabrera, Lydia. 2004. *Afro-Cuban Tales*. Lincoln: University of Nebraska Press.

Carpentier, Alejo. 2001. *Music in Cuba*. Minneapolis: University of Minnesota Press.

Daniel, Yvonne. 1995. *Rumba—Dance and Social Change in Contemporary Cuba*. Bloomington: Indiana University Press.

Dianteill, Erwan, and Martha Swearingen. 2003. From Hierography to Ethnography and Back: The Relationship between Lydia Cabrera's Texts and the Written Tradition in Afro-Cuban Religions. *Journal of American Folklore* 116: 273–292.

Ortiz, Fernando. 1995. *Cuban Counterpoint, Tobacco, and Sugar*. Durham: Duke University Press.

Pasmanick, Philip. 1997. Décima and Rumba: Iberian Formalism in the Heart of Afro-Cuban Song. *Latin American Music Review* 18.2: 252–277.

Perez Sarduy, Pedro, and Jean Stubbs. 1993. *Afrocuba—an Anthology of Cuban Writing on Race, Politics, and Culture*. Melbourne: Ocean Press.

Erwan Dianteill (Translated from the French by David Wick)

HAITI

GEOGRAPHY AND HISTORY

The nation of Haiti covers approximately a third of western Hispañola, part of the Antillean island chain that arches across the Caribbean Sea. Like its sister islands of **Jamaica, Cuba,** and Puerto Rico (the Greater Antilles), Hispañola is mountainous and sedimentary. Five major mountain systems link Haiti and the Dominican Republic, its neighbor on the island to the east, and the courses of streams and other natural features define the frontier between them. Within Haiti, natural features generally bound the nine administrative departments and their local divisions. Political upheaval resulting in poor conservation policy has thinned Haiti's rich natural woodland cover, provoking erosion of topsoil and a grave agricultural dilemma. Trees tend to be pine, mahogany, other hardwoods, and fruit trees such as avocado, orange, and lime. Some species of trees and plants provide medicinal benefits. Indigenous fauna include various birds (parrots, guinea hens, flamingos), reptiles (iguanas, crocodiles, snakes), and insects (spiders, scorpions, centipedes).

The written history of Haiti generally begins with the first voyage of Christopher Columbus, though the ancestors of the people who greeted the Italian navigator had presumably migrated from northern South America from about 4000 B.C.E. In 1492 they called themselves Taíno, meaning "good" or "noble," to distinguish themselves from other island peoples. The Taíno had developed agriculture, a nature-based religion, crafts, and sports, and they traded with other peoples by sea. Spanish colonization introduced diseases for which the Taíno had no natural defenses as well as a forcibly imposed work regime that killed many and drove others into mountain shelters. As the indigenous population declined, the Spanish monarchy authorized the use of enslaved Africans to mine the land for gold. The population remained sparse as the Spanish discovered greater quantities of gold in Central America; but when France took control of the western third of the island in the late seventeenth century, naming it Saint Domingue, French merchants increased exponentially the trade in enslaved Africans along with the cultivation of sugar. Africans resisted enslavement and in 1791 rose up in the northern part of the colony. The struggle for liberation and then independence from France ended on 18 November 1803. The revolutionaries declared independence on 1 January 1804, renaming their land Haiti (from "*ayiti*," Taíno for "mountainous land"). Haiti was the second American colony to free itself and the only nation on earth born from a slave revolution.

The post-revolutionary story of Haiti unfolded as a struggle over how the new republic would integrate into the larger circle of nations. Initially repulsed for its apparent threat to other slaveholding powers that feared the "Haitian example," Haiti secured a treaty with France in the 1820s that exchanged diplomatic recognition for a substantial indemnity to the former plantocracy. During the 100 years that passed before the indemnity was paid off, Haitian peasants denounced it and sometimes resorted to armed revolt because the deal rewarded the descendants of those who had exploited their ancestors and choked the development of their own economy. Privileged Haitians continued to court political recognition and trade links with other states. In the early twentieth century the United States, seeking control over Central America and the Caribbean, invaded and occupied Haiti, secured the cooperation of Haitian elites, and crushed militant peasant resistance. The occupation ended in 1934, but Haiti has since lived within the North American sphere of influence. The United States backed the infamous Duvalier dictatorship (1957–1986) until a grassroots movement ejected it, reviving hopes for democracy. In the twenty-first century popular organizations struggle with international forces over control of Haiti's economic development.

The culture of Haiti, both pragmatic and expressive, draws on African and European roots and on a unique historical experience in the Americas. Very broadly, the descendants of enslaved people, who were largely from the Guinea coast (modern **Benin**, Togo, and Nigeria) and the Angola coast (the modern Congos and Angola), make up the Creole-speaking peasantry and urban masses. Their classic unit of social organization, the *lakou*, revolves around a family patriarch and inhabits a compound that includes a peristyle for service to the Afro-Haitian divinities. Traditionally, these people farmed the land and traded in marketplaces that followed African models. In the twentieth century many quit the land for the cities, where they either continued in urban marketplaces or took up such occupations as nanny, taxi driver, or artisan. Most of the urban masses are self-employed and poor. The bourgeoisie and the petty bourgeoisie, largely the mixed-blood descendants of French planters and merchants, generally gravitate to the capital (Port-au-Prince) and engage in business, government, and the professions. They identify as Christians, acquire a European-style education, speak French much of the time, and keep tight control over the parliamentary government. The Haitian **diaspora**—scattered through the United States, Canada, France, and other Caribbean states—has given rise to a middle class that makes a substantial contribution to the economy through remittances and to the culture through its migrant experience.

Throughout its tumultuous history, Haiti has scored remarkable achievements in expressive culture. Haitian visual art, spanning the continuum from sacred to secular, has found an international following. Dealers have sought Haitian canvas painting since the 1940s, but other forms such as sequin and metal art have made an impact as well. A major exhibit of Vodou (sacred Afro-Haitian) art traveled across the United States in 1997–1998. The performing arts of Haiti, particularly Afro-Haitian dance and drumming, formed the core of the national theater that opened in 1949. African American dancer Katherine Dunham's widely adopted technique relied primarily on traditional Afro-Haitian dance, and Afro-Haitian music probably influenced North American jazz by way of New Orleans. Finally, Haiti has produced an astonishing volume of literature despite its high illiteracy rate. The expressive culture of Haiti is a gumbo of African and European **motifs** and inspiration, brewing in the Caribbean pot, wafting through the diaspora.

RELIGIOUS BELIEFS

Haiti's multiple heritages, taking on a new life in the Caribbean, manifest in the field of spirituality. Most people today affiliate with Vodou or a Christian denomination and in far smaller numbers with Islam or Judaism. They have constructed

Vodou drums, Haiti (1910). Since the slavery period, Haitians have imported Christian symbols into Vodou, and today Christian churches might use the Vodou drum during services. (General Research & Reference Division, Schomburg Center for Research in Black Culture, The New York Public Library, Astor, Lenox and Tilden Foundations)

Vodou temples in the diaspora and built Christian churches in the homeland on their return from abroad. Haitian spirituality might answer a personal quest and a collective search for cultural identity.

The word *vodou* has recently come into use as the name for Afro-Haitian spirituality. In Fongbe, spoken by the Fon of modern Benin, *vodou* signifies a spiritual entity, often ancestral. Rather than naming the belief system Vodou, it was long customary in Haiti to say, simply, "I serve the spirits," using the word *lwa* from the Yoruba *oluwa*, "spirit." In the twentieth century Haitians and observers began to name the system Vodou and classify it as a religion. Prior to the twentieth century, travelers, missionaries, statespersons, and scholars regarded Vodou as superstition, sorcery, even cannibalism. The Haitian government criminalized it, and Roman Catholic missionaries persecuted its adherents. Scholarship, pressured by nationalist critiques in the wake of the U.S. occupation, shifted to a more sympathetic perspective on Afro-Haitian spirituality, but in truth the brave persistence of believers explains the survival of Vodou. A legacy of racist stereotypes rooted in the fears that the revolution inspired outside of Haiti still dishonors its image, but they live in tension with a heightened respect on the part of many.

The biases that have characterized writing about Vodou warrant a brief clarification of its beliefs and practices. Believers may serve the spirits on a personal level by keeping a small private altar, or *ogatwa*, and some choose initiation into a society (*sosyete*). The activities of Vodou societies do not focus on a supreme entity (Gran Mèt, or Great Master) so much as the spirit intermediaries between that entity and humans. These envoys live *anba dlo*, "beneath the waters," a metaphor for the divide that separates matter and spirit. The spirits called *lwa* dramatize the forces that move nature and humans—from life to love, power to destruction, death to regeneration. Vodou spirits also recall the African ancestors who brought them to Haiti, and they group into corresponding *nasyon* (nations), each with its own music, dance, and images. The spirits respond to these sonic, kinetic, and visual cues through the society, whose members serve as mediums so that the spirits may speak with the community of believers dispensing advice and keeping the community whole.

Haitians have imported Christian symbols into Vodou since the period of slavery, and today Christian churches might use the Vodou drum in services. However, Christianity has not been as ecumenical toward Vodou as vice versa. Since the

1860s when the Haitian government ended a long rift with the Vatican (over the Haitian constitution's separation of church and state), the Roman Catholic Church has implemented several unsuccessful campaigns to abolish Vodou. The centralized and orthodox nature of Roman Catholicism has thwarted its own efforts to uproot the decentralized, heterodox Afro-Haitian faith, and along the way many Catholics have come to an enlightened understanding of it. Protestant denominations, largely a sign of North American influence, have taken up where the Catholic Church has left off. Fundamentalists mandate that converts take oaths of renunciation of the *lwa*, but the convert

A *vèvè* (cosmogram) for Gede, spirit of death and cemetery, traced in coffee and corn flour on the floor of a temple in Port-au-Prince, 1987. (Photograph by Lois Wilcken)

usually retains a belief in the reality of the Vodou spirits as well as a tendency toward possession, albeit in the Christian fashion of "speaking in tongues." Meanwhile, Haitians establish Vodou societies in the diaspora and initiate foreigners of Christian extraction.

Islam and Judaism live in Haiti in far more subtle forms. Many of the enslaved undoubtedly adhered to Islam, but the slave trade followed on the heels of the reconquest of the Iberian Peninsula from the Muslims and the ensuing repression of the latters' faith. Traces of Islam survive in Vodou art and perhaps song. A small number of Jewish planters and then refugees settled in Haiti from the colonial period to the time of the Holocaust, but they tended to assimilate and established no synagogues. Some diagrams on Vodou temple floors, though, may be cabalistic in origin. The diagrams fuse diverse belief systems, including Freemasonry, and typify the synthetic nature of Haitian folklore.

JEAN PRICE-MARS AND HAITIAN ETHNOGRAPHY

Jean Price-Mars, a medical doctor widely regarded as the author of Haiti's first **ethnography**, introduced the word *folklore* into Haitian scholarship and letters. He explained the term in his *Ainsi parla l'oncle*, first published in 1928 during the U.S. occupation. Nationalist sentiment and the use of Afro-Haitian folk forms in its expression were not new, but Price-Mars's call to study Haiti's African heritage and incorporate its forms into a national art found resonance within a larger anti-colonialist movement sweeping Africa and the Americas. His call inspired a generation of intellectuals and artists who created, among other things, a bureau of ethnology, a national theater, and a national folklore troupe. The inventory that follows owes much to the Haitian folklorists and ethnologists who devoted their careers to the valorization of the people's proverbs, tales, performing arts, visual arts, and games.

Proverbs

The proverbs of the Haitian people imaginatively fashion a code of moral behavior on the levels of the individual, the family, and the society. Scholars believe that they reinterpret European and African insights through the Caribbean experience. Many proverbs appeal because they are full of word play and double meaning. The representative Haitian proverbs below give literal and more figurative translations into English from the Haitian Creole: *"Lang pa lanmè, men li antere anpil moun"* (The tongue is not the sea, but it drowns many people—that is, gossip destroys many reputations); *"Ranje kabann ou avan dòmi nan je ou"* (Make your bed before you get sleepy, which means be prepared); *"Sak vid pa kanpe"* (An empty bag doesn't stand up, or a hungry person can't fight for his or her rights); *"Sonje lapli ki lève mayi ou"* (Remember the rain that makes your corn grow—that is, give credit where credit is due); *"Mwen, m se kiyè bwa, m pa pè chalè"* (I am the wooden spoon; I don't fear the heat, meaning I keep my cool, whatever the problem); and *"Yon sèl dwèt pa manje kalalou"* (A single finger does not eat okra, which suggests that one cannot accomplish alone).

Nearly 1,500 proverbs have made their way into print, and more will follow as Haitians invent or resurrect them in response to unfolding experience. During the late 1980s Father Jean Bertrand Aristide, who later became president, popularized *"Men anpil, chay pa lou,"* or "With many hands, the burden is light." This proverb has replaced the French motto *"L'union fait la force"* (Unity makes strength) on a Creole version of the Haitian flag.

Folktales

Like the proverb, the Haitian folktale transmits wisdom, values, and guidelines by which to live. The narrative element, of course, distinguishes the folktale and fuses entertainment with principle. Folktales afford gifted storytellers opportunity to display their talents while inciting audience participation. Haitians blended folktales from Africa and Europe to make a stew of their own. The beloved Bouki and Malis cycle resurrects the rabbit (Malis) and the hyena (Bouki) of many African tales (in the United States, Br'er Rabbit and Br'er Fox). The Haitian experience transforms these characters so that Bouki recalls the newly arrived, unbaptized slave, and Malis the creolized, superior one. In another interpretation, Bouki represents the uncultivated man of the people, subject to the exploitation of the elite Malis. Such ingredients from Europe as kings and princesses surface even in the Bouki and Malis collection, and many tales feature the werewolf, whose Haitian name, *lou gawou*, clearly derives from the French *loup garou*. Specialists, though, remind us of the universality of such characters as this.

Storytelling entails a level of artistry that earns the title *mèt kont* (literally, tale master). Professional storytellers traveled throughout colonial Haiti performing at festivals and wakes, for which they were paid through food and lodging. The story-teller continues to spin his or her magic today, but rarely in the city, where television and radio monopolize entertainment. Collectors have described the performance of the *mèt kont* as one-woman or one-man theater. The storyteller assumes the voices and gestures of each character, embellishes the narrative with song and dance, and provokes the listeners to respond—perhaps even to contribute to the narrative line. Following the classic form of his or her medium, the Haitian storyteller greets the listeners with *"Krik?"* And they respond, *"Krak!"* What are these words literally? The French *cric* means "small sound" or "peep," and *crac* means "bang" or "pop"—just like "creak" and "crack" in English. In Haitian *"pou ti krik ti krak"* means "at the slightest provocation." In the context of storytelling, *"Krik? Krak!"* opens the session. The storyteller might continue with the following interchange:

STORYTELLER: *Tim, tim?* (Those piles?)

LISTENERS: *Bwa chèch.* (Dry wood.)

STORYTELLER: *Konbyen li pòte?* (How many does he or she bring?)

LISTENERS: *Twa.* (Three, meaning, "Tell us three stories." The number varies.)

Such formulas characterize traditional storytelling in the Americas. The formulaic ending for the Haitian tale is, generally, "They gave me a little kick that sent me all the way here to tell you this tale."

MUSIC AND DANCE

Music and dance further enrich Haitian folk theater. The Vodou ceremony (usually called a "dance" in Haiti) is theater, as are the more public *kanaval* (Carnival) and *rara* festivals (pre-Lent and Lent, respectively) because they feature the endless flow of melody, beat, and movement; the dazzling display of costumes, masks, and banners; and the dramatic interplay of traditional characters and spectators.

The indispensable role of song in the lives of ordinary Haitians moved Harold Courlander to name his first ethnography of Haiti *Haiti Singing* (1939)—later revised and renamed *The Drum and the Hoe* (1973). As Courlander observed, songs mark any and every occasion or activity. Haitian workers, notably in the countryside, organize into labor cooperatives called *konbit*, which have their own song repertories. A rich corpus of children's songs accompanies play. Traditional songs have carried news and messages of protest. During the festivities of *kanaval* and *rara*, competition centers on the songs bands compose for their fans and for the season. Not least, a vast repertory of Christian and Vodou songs links ordinary people with divine powers.

More often than not, song structure stresses collective and recollective needs. Although Haitians use various song forms, call-and-response stands out as characteristic. A soloist "sends" (*voye*) a stanza or a phrase, and a chorus "answers" (*reponn*) with either the same melody and text or an abbreviated version of it. The soloist may ornament his or her part. The role of the chorus goes beyond interaction for pleasure.

Traditional song demands the participation of the collective for integrity and efficacy. The participatory nature of singing prescribes economy of song structure: concise phrases within relatively narrow range. Meanwhile, the folk roots of Haitian song poke through in the frequent use of penta- and heptatonic modes in distinction to the major and minor modes of Europe's "art" music. A generous sprinkling of Fongbe, Yoruba, Kikongo, and other words through the texts of Vodou songs recollects Haiti's specifically African heritage.

Much, if not most, traditional music in Haiti accompanies dance, and dancers derive their energy from a pronounced beat, or pulse. A slow pulse guides the dancer and highlights key words in song text. The organization of pulse in Haitian folk music follows principles from West Africa and the Congo. The spice of Afro-Haitian rhythm is the simultaneous or successive subdivision of a pulse by two and three. Try tapping three beats with one hand in the same time you take to tap two beats with the other hand! A simultaneous three-against-two creates interesting relationships that feel offbeat, or syncopated. The division of successive slow pulses can also achieve a syncopated effect. Tap two slow, evenly spaced pulses with your foot: "one, two, one, two . . ." As you continue, use hand claps to divide the "one" into three even mini-pulses and the "two" into two even mini-pulses. After you have mastered that, try omitting the second mini-pulse in the set of three and the first mini-pulse in the set of two. (Continue to tap your foot in slow, even pulses.) Pick up the speed and ask yourself how it feels. African people breathe this pattern, and it permeates jazz.

Instruments, especially drums and percussion, articulate the principles of rhythm. Drums undoubtedly attract the most attention in folk music. Most consist of a hollowed log of slightly conical bore with a cowhide or goatskin stretched across the larger opening. These come most often in sets of three: *maman* (mother, or first), *segon* (second), and *boula* (baby, or third). A few Haitian drums use a cylindrical bore, and the *timbal* (Congolese) sports a skin at each opening. Ensembles sometimes use a tambourine called *bas* (for its bass tone). An assortment of bells, rattles, and scrapers accompany the drums in nearly all kinds of folk music. Most derive from Africa, but the *tcha-tcha*, a gourd filled with seeds or pebbles, recalls the Taíno *maraka*. The small iron gong, called *ogan*, provides a musical mantra for the Vodou ensemble.

Other categories of instruments besides drums and percussion expand the sonic palette. Among wind instruments the simple six-hole end-blown flute carries melody, whereas long metal trumpets (*klewon*) and sets of bamboo trumpets of variable length and pitch (*vaksin*) serve a more percussive or harmonic function in *kanaval* and *rara* processions. We hear string instruments most rarely in Haitian folk music, but rural bands may include the African-derived banjo, and children like to make a one-string arched bow they call the *tanbou marengwen* (mosquito drum, although not actually a drum). In the rural south musicians have incorporated such European instruments as violins and silver side-blown flutes into their ensembles.

Most traditional music in Haiti derives from dance, and the roots are deep. Sixteenth-century woodcuts and the diaries of Spanish colonists document the dancing of the Taíno, primarily for sacred functions. In the revolutionary Maroon

culture of the French colonial period, dances might have absorbed
some degree of Taíno character as
the African dances mutually
shaped one another. Moreau de
Saint-Méry, a white creole from
Martinique, published detailed
descriptions of the dances of enslaved Africans just before the
revolution (1969 [1789]). Because many Africans in St.
Domingue were not creole—that
is, not born in the colony—they
danced exactly as they had in
their native lands. Moreau por-
trays the *chika*, a dance he attributes to the Congo slaves, as
centering on a gentle yet seductive swaying of the hips to the
pulse of the drum. Interestingly,

La Troupe Makandal performs *kanaval*. (Photograph by Lois Wilcken)

the dance that Haitians call *kongo* today follows Moreau's eighteenth-century description. We can identify elements of European dances in the folk repertory, with
kontredans an obvious adaptation of the contradance. Some communities have preserved the minuet, the lancer, and the polka.

The dances of Vodou, which ranks among the world's "danced religions," are
both functional and representational. Maya Deren (1983 [1953]), a Vodou initiate
who was also daughter of a renowned psychologist, explained the moment of possession as the "concentration of this physical-psychic meditation." Dancer Katherine
Dunham (1983) also wrote of the connection between physical movement and the
Vodou spirits. The Vodouist believes that movement to drumming invites the divine literally to possess the dancer. Because divinities, or *lwa*, differ in character, the
nature of the movement determines the *lwa*. A supple wave through the spine mim-
ics the serpentine spirit Danbala and all of his Rada nation, who also share an affinity for undulant water. By contrast, the Petwo nation is fiery and nervous, so they
respond to a tight, shivering movement of the arms and torso.

While Vodou initiates learn sacred dances as part of their instruction and often excel at them, public festivals in Haiti invite the participation of non-
specialists. Crowds dance as they follow their favorite *kanaval* and *rara* bands
through urban streets and countryside roads. But even the bands that conduct
these rites feature dance specialists, like the *kanaval* queens and the *majè jon*
(baton major) of *rara*. These two festivals exhibit their own dances: *rabòday*, *chay
o pye*, *maskawon*. The Port-au-Prince *kanaval* has lost much of its traditional quality in recent years. Large floats play pre-recorded commercial music without featured dance specialists. Other cities and villages consciously preserve the traditional
festivals.

ARTS AND CRAFTS

Haitian festivals and the ceremonies tell their stories in multiples modes, including the visual. Art forms have developed over generations, but they earned international recognition only in the years following World War II. Until that time, canvas painting of the educated class celebrated the Haitian countryside and the heroes of the revolution, but stylistically imitated the fine arts of Europe. By contrast, Haitian fine artists in the twentieth century have embraced the folk arts, and along with folk artists they enjoy the attention of critics, scholars, and collectors all over the world.

Little remains of Taíno material culture, but recent research has assembled artifacts and generated a new excitement among scholars and students. The *zemi*, an image of a deity (also called *zemi*) or an ancestor carved from stone, clay, bone, shell, or wood, survived through integration into the ritual paraphernalia of Vodou temples. Most Taíno art utilizes bold rectilinear and curvilinear motifs, either carved or painted. The current revival of interest in Taíno culture has the potential to influence modern Haitian art. Meanwhile, most forms of Haitian folk art derive from the outstanding art traditions of the West Africa and Congo regions, and they draw likewise from spiritual and esthetic standards.

Metalwork traces back to the ironwork of the blacksmiths of revolutionary Haiti. They fashioned weapons resembling multi-pronged African throwing knives as well as crosses for family burials. The crosses incorporate ideas about the structure of the cosmos and the processes of time. Haitian artists practice ironwork with less frequency today, but they often specialize in two-dimensional sculptures cut from the metal of oil drums. Such artists favor human, animal, and mythological subjects.

Although they function as spiritual magnets, the *vèvè* of Haitian Vodou, cosmograms sketched on the temple floor, belong unequivocally among art forms. Perhaps hundreds of *vèvè*, each capable of individual variation, adorn the notebooks of priests and priestesses, and any person within the priesthood must know how to transfer these line drawings to the earthen temple floor, preferably around the center post of the dance space. The artist pinches the medium (usually fine-ground corn-flour or coffee) from a small plate and sifts it through the fingers to the earth. The figure of the cross structures most *vèvè*, but certain designs for the turbulent Petwo nation lack symmetry. Motifs evoke specific spirits: for example, a heart shape for Ezili (love) or a flag and machete for Ogou (power). The artist seemingly ornaments the work with symbols from Freemasonry, but these "points" reinforce the attraction of the *vèvè*—that is, their power to summon the deities they embody.

Sequin art has grabbed center stage in recent exhibits. Vodou artists traditionally embroider sequins and beads onto banners, altar bottles, and medicinal packets (*pakèt kongo*); and the dancers of the springtime Rara Festival create costumes embellished with sequins. Each Vodou society owns a set of banners or flags (*drapo*) that herald the spirits special to the society by means of *vèvè* and color portraits called *imaj*. Altar bottles contain libations used in Vodou rites. The textile itself is usually satin, velvet, or some other sumptuous material. The artist embroiders designs and images onto the textile with beads, sequins, and portraits. Most flags and bottles leave little of the textile surface unadorned. In the temple peristyle, servants dance with the banners. The finished product dazzles the spectator with glittering color and movement. The sequin arts have made an impressive journey from the humblest of Haitian temples to the world's most famous art museums. They are both sacred objects and collector's items.

Woodcarving flourishes in Haiti despite deforestation. Various types of wood have replaced mahogany, once sculptors' first choice but now rare. Tourists find in abundance sculpted mortar and pestles, bowls, vases, and other functional items turned decorative, but some woodcarving lives on a higher level of artistry. Imaginatively exquisite carvings on the surfaces of drums and walking sticks are not only functional, especially when they represent divinities; and wooden figurines, some standing on Vodou altars, maintain a tradition of wood sculpting from Africa. Haitian artist Deenps Bazile beguiled the custodians of Prospect Park in Brooklyn, New York, when ordinary tree stumps all over the park were magically transformed into three-dimensional portraits of people and spirits. The site of the most compelling of these sculpted stumps is now recognized by park officials as Gran Bwa, named after the spirit of the woods in Haitian Vodou.

SPORTS AND GAMES

The traditional games of Haiti have received little attention among folklorists and anthropologists. Courlander devotes part of a chapter to games, drawing for the most part from the work of Haitian ethnologist Emmanuel Paul (1962). The introduction to Haitian musicologist Claude Dauphin's collection of children's songs (1981), which often make up the texture of games, eschews social context for a classification by acoustic structure. Equating Haitian folklore with "the African presence in Haiti," Paul dismisses games of French origin that children of the privileged play in school. But the games in his inventory, collectively called *gage* after the French for "forfeit," likely derive from both Europe and Africa, as do children's songs and tales. The games in Paul's collection have in common the temporary forfeiture of a personal possession such as a scarf, ring, or pen when a player loses a round. A master (*mèt*) directs most of these games. Players might arrange themselves in circles or semicircles, and the acquisition of cooperative and competitive skills is often the outcome.

In conformity with my observations, Paul notes that most of these games have vanished from the Haitian cityscape, but some Haitians report that they continue to play the games at wakes all over Haiti. The Haitian wake (*vèy*) brings friends and family together at the home of the deceased for one or more evenings of song, games, food and drink, and remembrance. Unlike the solemn Christian wake, which coexists with and perhaps complements the *vèy* in Haiti, this Afro-Haitian practice joyfully celebrates the life of a loved one. If the departed was a Vodou initiate, members of his or her society hold a series of prayer vigils that terminate in an all-night feast called *dènyè priyè*, or last prayer, at which they also play the traditional games. That Haitians hold traditional wakes complete with songs and games in diaspora communities testifies to their value.

CHALLENGES OF THE MODERN WORLD

How does the folklore of Haiti fare as forces of **globalization** and the **modernization** that accompany it progress? Haiti has had long experience with these forces. What we know as Haiti began as the fruit of emerging globalism with most of its indigenous base decimated five hundred years ago. We can argue that the Columbus voyages triggered globalization—the convergence of traders and immigrants from western Europe, enslaved workers from distinct regions of Africa, and interspersed indigenous survivors. For the nation of Haiti, then, globalization is not new. Even when we use the term in today's more narrow sense—that is, the integration of capital and commerce following the dissolution of the Soviet bloc—then Haiti is experiencing a new albeit intense phase of a familiar process. Traditional culture has met such challenges in the past. Can it do the same today?

Vodou drumming and dance invite critical evaluation of how folklore survives in the modern world. In the twentieth century, prodded by foreign invasion and occupation, Haitian intellectuals woke up to Africa as the mother of Haiti's national identity. Since the Haitian masses lived a culture rooted in Africa, ethnologist Jean Price-Mars (1973 [1928]) applied the word *folklore* to Afro-Haitian culture. Writers and ethnologists embarked on the study and valorization of that culture, and by the 1940s performing groups that specialized in folkloric music and dance were representing it on the modern stage. In the ensuing decades, scholars and critics debated whether or not this mode of representation transformed culture into commodity, vacating it of meaning and leading to its demise. In a comprehensive study of the phenomenon, folklorist Alan Goldberg (1981) argues that Haitian folkloric performers construct a mask in order to protect their cultural resources and maintain a strong sense of identity. The co-existence of staged folklore and Vodou temples thriving abroad and at home makes Goldberg's point.

One of Haiti's most inscrutable proverbs says, "*Dèyè mòn, gen mòn*"—that is, "Behind mountains, there are mountains." The adage offers multiple interpretations as well as an astute description of Haitian topography. We might see the folklore of Haiti through the metaphor of mountains, one range layering another and another and another. Essays such as this one represent folklore as do **museum** exhibitions, audio recordings, and stage performances. Behind these mountains of representation one finds the people of Haiti embroidering ever more elegant banners for a Vodou society, dancing down a countryside road in a Carnival band, singing for the spirits in a Brooklyn basement, and coining new proverbs in the marketplace in response to new challenges.

STUDIES OF HAITIAN FOLKLORE

For general reading on Haitian history, society, and culture, the reader may begin with Bercht and others (1997). This beautifully illustrated catalog accompanied the Taíno exhibit at New York City's El Museo del Barrio in spring 1998. Its comprehensive essays make it the first English language publication of its kind. Brown (1991) accounts for five generations of spiritual women, focusing on one who put down roots in Brooklyn, New York. Characterized as experimental ethnography, the book reveals much about Vodou and the people who practice it in the diaspora. Consentino (1995) offers over 400 pages of Vodou art with sixteen interpretive essays from mulitple disciplines. This catalog accompanied a groundbreaking exhibit that traveled across the United States.

Courlander's work (1973 [1960]) remains a classic in the ethnography of Haiti. Courlander approaches Haitian culture through its folk arts, particularly music. Deren (1984 [1953]) is one of the most fascinating explorations of Vodou. The experimental filmmaker melds artistic insight and erudition as she explicates the cosmology of Vodou. Leslie Desmangles (1992), a Haitian scholar and professor of religion, discusses the folk religion of Haiti as the intersection of African, Christian, and Amerindian belief systems. He emphasizes the fluidity of spiritual forms and practices.

In *Tell My Horse* (1990 [1938]) the celebrated African American novelist, folklorist, and anthropologist Zora Neale Hurston writes of her personal experience in Haiti during the period of the first U.S. occupation. Hurston questions the stereotyping of Caribbean culture that was typical of her time. Trinidadian novelist C.L.R. James (1989) weaves his classic account of Haiti's struggle for independence and freedom from slavery. The late thinker and novelist plied his creative talents while leaving no stone of documentation unturned. Métraux (1972) is essential for those interested in the details of Vodou practice, its history, and its turbulent relationship with Roman Catholicism. The author stands out as one of the most skilled ethnologists of his generation.

Wilcken and Augustin (1992) introduces the reader to Vodou drums and drumming. Its central chapter analyzes basic structures of the rhythmic patterns that accompany some sixteen Vodou dances, and it notates them. The authors relate rhythm and instrumental practice to Vodou cosmology. The reader may find descriptions of traditional dances in Yarborough (1959). The author, an African American who danced with Katherine Dunham, gave more than thirty years of her life to the promotion of Haitian dance. In this richly illustrated book, she describes all of Haiti's sacred and secular folk dances.

Drawing from memories of the stories her mother told her, professional storyteller Liliane Nérette Louis brings utmost affection and respect to her medium in *When Night Falls, Kric! Krac! Haitian Folktales* (1999). The volume includes Bouki and Malis, animal stories, tales of kings and princesses, ghost stories, and stories of love and courtship. The author also contributes traditional Haitian recipes and a "*Kreyòl-English*" glossary. Perhaps the best-known collection is Diane Wolkstein (1997). The author has assembled a fine introduction to the folktales of Haiti from her fieldwork in the 1970s. Wolkstein acquaints the reader with the storytellers as well as their stories. Because the tellers typically weave songs into their performances, this book concludes with a short collection of song texts and their melodies.

Recording media, sound and visual, have captured the folklore of Haiti. Smithsonian Folkways has re-released *Caribbean Revels: Haitian Rara and Dominican Gaga* (1992), recordings by Verna Gillis with new notes by Gillis and Gage Averill. Smithsonian also distributes *Music of Haiti, Vols. I–III* (Courlander 1952), with Harold Courlander's recordings and notes, and *Rhythms of Rapture: Sacred Musics of Vodou Ritual* (1995), a compilation of various ritual specialists and popular artists. *The Drums of Vodou* (1992), featuring Frisner Augustin and La Troupe Makandal, accompanies the book of the same name. Other recordings of traditional music directly available from La Troupe Makandal are *Èzili* (2002) and *Prepare* (2004).

Black Dawn (1981), an animated film about the Haitian revolution by Robin Lloyd and Doreen Kraft, features some of Haiti's finest artists. The same filmmakers have given us *Haitian Pilgrimage* (1995), an account of a Haitian family's return to its roots from their new home in Massachusetts. Maya Deren's *Divine Horsemen: The Living Gods of Haiti* (1985) captures Vodou dance in mid-twentieth-century Haiti and closes with a segment on the dances of Rara and Carnival.

The World Wide Web is evolving in its access to Haitian folklore and folk arts, and more construction is needed. Those looking for a Haitian search engine should check fouye.com, but educators would benefit from a direct visit to educavision.com, the site of Educa Vision, Inc., a Haitian-owned company based in Florida that develops, designs, publishes, and distributes materials on Haiti, including its folklore. Haitiglobalvillage.com, a Haitian communications network, provides information and resources on all aspects of Haitian culture and society. A limited selection of Haitian traditional music is interspersed among commercial recordings listed on the musical chronicles page of windowsonhaiti.com. Makandal.org, the Web site of La Troupe Makandal, features a more specialized "boutique" and is planning a series of essays on the Haitian folk arts. Finally, selections from the Sacred Arts of Haitian-Vodou exhibit that toured the United States in 1997–1998 are now on the site of the American Museum of Natural History in New York City at amnh.org/exhibitions/vodou. *See also* **Cuba; Island Carib (Dominica); Jamaica.**

BIBLIOGRAPHY

Augustin, Frisner, and La Troupe Makandal. 1992. *The Drums of Vodou* (sound recording). White Cliffs Media Company CD 9338.

Benson, LeGrace. 2001. How Houngans Use the Light from Distant Stars. *Journal of Haitian Studies* 7.1: 106–135.

Bercht, Fatima, and others, eds. 1997. *Taíno: Pre-Columbian Art and Culture from the Caribbean.* New York: Monacelli Press and El Museo del Barrio.

Brown, Karen McCarthy. 1991. *Mama Lola: A Vodou Priestess in Brooklyn.* Berkeley: University of California Press.

Caribbean Revels: Haitian Rara and Dominican Gaga (sound recording). 1992. Smithsonian Folkways SFW40402.

Consentino, Donald J., ed. 1995. *Sacred Arts of Haitian Vodou.* Los Angeles: UCLA Fowler Museum of Cultural History.

Courlander, Harold. 1939. *Haiti Singing.* Chapel Hill: University of North Carolina Press.

———. 1952. *Music of Haiti. Volumes I–III* (sound recording). Smithsonian Folkways 04403.

———. 1973 (1960). *The Drum and the Hoe: Life and Lore of the Haitian People.* Berkeley: University of California Press.

Dauphin, Claude. 1981. *Brit kolobrit: Introduction méthologique suivie de 30 chansons enfantines haïtiennes recueillies et classées progressivement en vue d'une pédagogie musicale aux Antilles.* Sherbrooke, Québec: Éditions Naaman.

Deren, Maya. 1983 (1953). *Divine Horsemen: The Living Gods of Haiti.* Kingston, NY: McPherson.

———. 1985. *Divine Horsemen: The Living Gods of Haiti* (film). New York: Mystic Fire Video.

Desmangles, Leslie. 1992. *The Faces of the Gods: Vodou and Roman Catholicism in Haiti.* Chapel Hill: University of North Carolina Press.

Dunham, Katherine. 1983. *Dances of Haiti.* Los Angeles: University of California Center of Afro-American Studies.

Gillis, Verna, and Gage Averill. 1991. *Caribbean Revels: Haitian Rara and Dominican Gaga* (sound recording). Smithsonian Folkways CD 40202.

Girouard, Tina. 1994. *Sequin Artists of Haiti*. Port-au-Prince and Cecilia, LA: Haitian Arts and Girouard Art Projects.

———. 1995. The Sequin Arts of Vodou. In *Sacred Arts of Haitian Vodou*, edited by Donald J. Consentino. Los Angeles: UCLA Fowler Museum of Cultural History. 357–377.

Goldberg, Alan. 1981. Commercial Folklore and Voodoo in Haiti: International Tourism and the Sale of Culture. Diss., Indiana University.

Hurston, Zora Neale. 1990 (1938). *Tell My Horse: Voodoo and Life in Haiti and Jamaica*. New York: Harper and Row.

James, C.L.R. 1989. *The Black Jacobins: Toussaint L'Ouverture and the San Domingo Revolution*. 2nd edition. New York: Vintage Books.

La Troupe Makandal. 2002 (1986). *Èzili* (sound recording).

———. 2004. *Prepare* (sound recording).

Lloyd, Robin, and Doreen Kraft. 1981. *Black Dawn* (film). Burlington, VT: Green Valley Media.

———. 1995. *Haitian Pilgrimage* (film). Burlington, VT: Green Valley Media.

Louis, Liliane Nérette. 1999. *When Night Falls, Kric! Krac! Haitian Folktales*, edited by Fred Hay. Englewood, CO: Libraries Unlimited.

McAlister, Elizabeth. 2002. *Rara: Vodou, Power, and Performance in Haiti and Its Diaspora*. Berkeley: University of California Press.

Métraux, Alfred. 1972. *Voodoo in Haiti*. New York: Schocken Books.

Moreau de Saint-Méry. 1969 (1789). De la danse. *Conjonction* 24.3: 46–62.

Paul, Emmanuel. 1962. *Panorama du folklore Haïtien (Présence Africaine en Haïti)*. Port-au-Prince: Imprimerie de l'État.

Price-Mars, Jean. 1973 (1928). *Ainsi parla l'oncle*. Ottawa: Leméac.

Rhythms of Rapture: Sacred Musics of Vodou Ritual (sound recording). 1995. Smithsonian Folkways CD 40464.

Rigaud, Milo. 1974. *Ve-Ve: Diagrammes rituels du voudou*. New York: French and European Publications.

Wilcken, Lois, and Frisner Augustin. 1992. *The Drums of Vodou*. Tempe, AZ: White Cliffs Media.

Wolkstein, Diane. 1997. *The Magic Orange Tree and Other Haitian Folktales*. New York: Random House.

Yarborough, Lavinia Williams. 1959. *Haiti-Dance*. Frankfurt-am-Main: Brönners Druckerei.

Lois Wilcken

ISLAND CARIB (DOMINICA)

GEOGRAPHY AND HISTORY

Dominica, an independent West Indian country still loosely affiliated with Great Britain, is the rainiest and most rugged island in the Caribbean. Because the land is so mountainous, it did not attract early European plantation owners and so provided an effective sanctuary for Caribs forced to abandon other islands. Dominica's economy is based largely on the export of bananas grown primarily on small farms. Unemployment is widespread, tourism lags behind that of the other Lesser Antilles, and the only exportable natural resources are fresh water and lumber from virgin rainforests. The latter is particularly difficult to harvest commercially because of the challenging terrain.

Carib men. (Photograph by Anthony Layng)

Carib elder with grandchild. (Photograph by Anthony Layng)

The majority of Dominicans are Creoles of mostly African ancestry with many exhibiting various amounts of white or Carib admixture. Dominicans are very aware of subtle and numerous racial differences within their population, and most tend to view behavior and character as being more or less determined by one's racial makeup. Individuals of various complexions unself-consciously refer to straight hair as "good" and equate Caucasian features with beauty. When speaking to new acquaintances, it is not unusual for Dominican Creoles to mention their white or Carib relatives.

Carib populations are found in Dominica, St. Vincent, Venezuela, Belize, Guatemala, Honduras, and Nicaragua. These populations are sometimes referred to as "Garifuna" or "Black Caribs." The Caribs of Dominica are the largest indigenous population in the Caribbean Islands. Most of the Caribs of Dominica live within the Carib Territory (established in colonial times as the Carib Reserve) on the eastern side of the island. This minority of some 2,000 persons is by and large culturally assimilated within the general Creole population of Dominica. Although they tend to see themselves as having little in common with the far larger Creole population (approximately 70,000), most Dominicans, Creoles and Caribs alike, speak English, adhere to Christianity, are poor, and depend on cultivating crops for their livelihood.

Tourists visit the Carib Territory in search of a distinct cultural setting and are inevitably disappointed to discover that most Caribs look like other Dominicans and appear to have a lifestyle indistinguishable from that of Creole farmers. A few remaining skilled basketmakers produce distinctive traditional baskets for sale, and these are eagerly purchased as evidence that one has spent time among the Dominican Caribs.

Unlike Creole village councils, the Carib Territory has a council chaired by a "chief." This elected leader has very limited political power and serves mainly to reinforce the idea that Caribs are a culturally distinctive population. It is ironic that traditionally the island Caribs consisted of egalitarian aggregates without any designated authority figures.

Although Carib houses tend to be less clustered than do Creole houses, there are no evident architectural distinctions between Carib houses and those of Creoles who live in nearby villages. Since a number of Creoles reside within the Carib Territory, who is and who is not a Carib is primarily a matter of self-ascription. However, in general, persons born in the Carib Territory are considered Caribs, and individuals born elsewhere are not. According to most Caribs, their values and moral behavior clearly distinguish them from Creoles. In interaction with outsiders, Caribs are usually

Carib children. (Photograph by Anthony Layng)

self-conscious about their ethnic identity and often preoccupied with efforts to illustrate or otherwise confirm assumed racial and cultural traits that make them different from other Dominicans. Their folklore plays an important role in this regard.

FOLKTALES

Individual Carib **worldviews** include elements of European Catholicism, American Protestant fundamentalism, Creole magic and witchcraft, and Carib folk beliefs. The Carib population has been influenced by the Catholic Church since the seventeenth century. Currently, Catholic priests have baptized nearly everyone born in the reserve, but most residents are seldom seen in church. Even though the Jesuits in the eighteenth century complained that the Caribs were very difficult to convert, by the nineteenth century most considered themselves to be Catholics. Protestant missionaries have in recent years "saved" only a small minority of Caribs, and the Catholic priest (a Belgian) who currently holds weekly masses for Caribs admits that very few of his parishioners have any serious commitment to Catholic doctrine. This priest is little admired and frequently criticized. However, a popular folktale idealizes a former priest:

> Was an old French priest from Vieille Case [just outside the reserve]. Was the only one to reach Calvary; he got all the nails and that. He could stop rivers, and did, more than once. He came this way one day during Holy Week where some men was working a sugar mill. He told them to stop. They didn't when he leave, and the mill said to them, "Oh, I is so tired, so tired." They certain scared and went and told the white man [plantation owner], and the syrup boil all over everywhere. This priest never ask for money. When he need money, he have a black marble and place it on the bed, on a white sheet, and money come when his hand over the marble; it just there.

Such tales justify prevalent feelings about the present priest, who is often accused of being mercenary ("He only want money for mass, for wedding, for everything") and ineffectual, since he neither has nor claims to have any magical abilities. Most Caribs express little interest in doctrinal differences between Catholic and Protestant teachings, and although they are disinclined to support any religious organization, they do consider God to be an active agent in their lives. When crops or homes are destroyed by hurricanes, or when a child dies or a family member loses a job, such events are explained as resulting from "God's will." Whenever someone has suffered from some tragedy, friends will offer, "God is good," as a reminder that he knows what is best. This expression is heard in nearly every conversation regarding serious personal misfortune.

Carib house. (Photograph by Anthony Layng)

Caribs also express considerable interest in the supernatural abilities of their Indian ancestors. Children are told about how, "in the old days," Caribs had considerable wisdom and used powerful magic in warfare. For example, one tale describes how two small islands just offshore were converted to giant war canoes whenever Caribs wanted to attack colonial plantations in Martinique and elsewhere in the Lesser Antilles. Another popular folk narrative recounts how the ancestors were able to approach a cave where a sacred serpent lived and ask it for guidance. Since this serpent spoke only the traditional Carib language, this source of intelligence was regrettably lost. According to the

Caribs, this same serpent constructed what is an unusual but natural stepped incline from the top of a cliff into the sea. Caribs are eager to have tourists walk to this site and hear the story associated with it.

Some versions of this "Escalier Tete Chien" tale describe the serpent as having the head of a white man, and other stories of times past also include references to whites, as in the following:

> After a hurricane that destroy all the provisions, a family was out, look for wild yams when they see some white people. As they did in those days, they run into the bush so the whites not see them. They were in such a hurry they leave a small girl who the whites find. They wash her and take her with them to England. There she became a white person. When she live with whites, she became white. I believe the Elizabeths are descended from her.

Some of their tales reflect the belief that the Carib Territory contains special resources. The following are typical.

> About twenty years ago a man went to drink from that river [a small steam], and he saw kerosene running out of the ground. When he went to get a bottle, it stopped. If he took some right away, kerosene would still be running there.

> There is a cliff near here I've seen something shining, probably gold, but where it can't be reached. Early in the morning, this was about thirty years ago, a girl saw something shining like fire. She wanted to touch it but warned not to by her uncle. When she returned it was gone. Perhaps the shining thing was a gift from her father [deceased], but she didn't know how to take it.

These accounts have a parallel in the widely held belief that "if you're offered something in a dream and don't take it straight away, you will never get it."

FOLK MEDICINE

Additional folk beliefs involve the use of traditional remedies to treat maladies such as colds, diarrhea, stomach pains, skin infections, and even emotional problems associated with unremitting fear or unrequited love. A white flower is said to bloom on top of a large rock formation on a ridge near the northern boundary of the Carib Territory, and the finder of this rare blossom may use it to attract the affection of any desired person.

Many adults make and use numerous medicines according to magical formulas that vary from household to household. When one medicine proves to be ineffectual, the recipe is altered or another substituted. In this way, creative experimentation is likely to be continued until a cure is "achieved," or at least until the complaint is resolved. Formulas for these medicines are exchanged freely among friends, usually accompanied by the assurance that "this is certain sure to cure you." Much concern focuses on the proper time to administer these folk medicines. Remedies for illness, swelling, or infection are to be taken while the moon is waning, while potions for increasing one's strength or luck must be administered during the waxing of the moon.

Traditional healer. (Photograph by Anthony Layng)

Similarly, crops are planted at this time to ensure their rapid growth. To the Caribs, it is a matter of simple logic that an effort to reduce inflammation or cure a cold may be associated with the waning moon and that the fertility of a garden is more likely insured by planting while the moon is waxing.

When home remedies prove inadequate, help may be sought from medical doctors in Roseau, the capital of Dominica, or from an elderly Carib healer who uses rituals and plants to cure her patients. Some younger Caribs claim that these old healers use sorcery to make people sick in order to drum up business. In spite of these accusations, these practitioners do have some patients who patronize them, often as a last resort, after both home remedies and modern medicines have been tried. In such cases, the failure of medicine is likely to be attributed to *obeah* (witchcraft). Doctors are considered impotent in dealing with patients afflicted by *obeah*, and even though certain folk remedies are designed to ward off witches, if the witch is powerful, it is believed, only a skilled healer can help.

The few remaining healers say that they are able to cure many ailments caused by witches, but they confess to being unable to divine the identity of an offending witch. Caribs generally agree that only certain gifted Creole diviners are able to do that. However, sometimes a Carib healer may inadvertently expose a witch. One elderly woman healer recounted how, when she removed a hairy caterpillar from an afflicted neighbor's infected foot and "sent it back" to the (unknown) witch, that person's foot became infected, and he came to the healer for treatments. The healer's suspicions were confirmed when, according to her, this man failed to pay for her services, thus proving to the healer at least that "he was an evil man."

Most Caribs are convinced that the most powerful Creole diviners live on other islands. Although these practitioners charge far more than do locals, they are considered capable of not only identifying particular witches but for an additional fee, using sorcery to kill or otherwise punish them. Carib confidence in Creole diviners is illustrated by an incident that occurred at a government construction site in the Territory. Upon discovering that a locked chest containing valuable tools had been stolen, the Creole owners publicly threatened to go to Guadeloupe and hire someone to kill the unknown thief. During the following night, the chest and all its tools were surreptitiously returned to the site.

WITCHCRAFT AND MAGIC

Although most Caribs are convinced that some residents of the Carib Territory use *obeah* to harm neighbors who offend them (usually because of jealousy), it is unlikely that any Carib individuals believe they themselves have such powers. And when very serious maladies or other traumatic misfortunes are attributed to *obeah*, it usually is assumed that the offending witch is a Creole. In this way, Caribs maintain the belief that they are quite different from Creoles.

The many stories concerning the antics of Creole witches told by Caribs are typical of those heard throughout the West Indies. For example, frequent reference is made to the fact that some witches remove their skin at night, the time during which they are most likely to act out their malevolence. One account related by several young men involved a witch whose skinless body was allegedly exhibited some years ago in Roseau, following her death in the hospital. The witch died, they said, because a man who discovered her skin one night poured salt on it, causing it to harden and shrink to such an extent that the returning witch was unable to slip back into it before the sun rose. Presumably, she succumbed to dehydration.

Many accounts describe the activities of Creole witches, nearly all of whom are women, within the Carib Territory. The following narratives illustrate these themes:

A Carib man told his Creole wife is a witch. She hurt him sucking his blood. A friend saw her out one night, so the husband took something that keep him awake. Pretend to sleep, he saw her rub something on herself. He did too and went after her. He found her in Haiti, with other witches. He came back without her knowing. When she came back, he shot her. She died, but you can't tell how a witch dies, how she is killed. When you meet a witch and kill her, she is dead at home. If you cut off a finger or her hair, she will be home when she lose it, not where you cut it.

The ex-chief killed a witch from Castle Bruce [south of the reserve], a woman who came to the reserve about ten years ago. She came every night to cause trouble, take chief's blood and make noise. He soaked a bullet in seawater three days. The witch jumped on the roof and crowed. Others in the house were asleep. He went out, he was naked, and heard it crow. It was too early for real fowl. He shot where he heard it. It didn't wake up people in the house, but others heard. There was blood going to Castle Bruce. Found out the woman died in Castle Bruce. When witches here, it make you sleep through everything.

Caribs express a great deal of fascination concerning the activities of witches, but few indicate any apprehension of *obeah* during the day. At night when some witches are said to travel by assuming the form of fireflies, window shutters are closed even on the hottest nights for fear that a witch might happen to fly inside. Hex signs are painted on some houses to ward off passing witches. Some believe that prayers to Moses are efficacious in this regard. Even when such precautions have been employed, if someone becomes ill during the night or is plagued by wakefulness, members of the household are inclined to assume that a witch is responsible. Any otherwise unexplained phenomenon occurring at night such as unusual noises or sensations is likely to be interpreted as evidence that a witch may be present.

God, magic, and witchcraft represent powerful supernatural forces according to most rural Dominicans, and the Caribs are no exception to this generalization. However, Carib folklore does reflect some distinctive beliefs that are very important to this minority. As their tales and legends indicate, Caribs consider themselves to be more closely related to Caucasians than to Creoles, and they are convinced that their native ancestors possessed magical powers that were far more extraordinary than those known to Creoles. Although they view contemporary Creoles as being peculiarly adept when it comes to divining evil and perpetrating black magic, they claim that Carib folk medicines are far more reliable than those produced elsewhere and certainly more humane than Creole witchcraft. Such beliefs are fully compatible with the prevailing stereotype in the Territory that Creoles, in contrast to Caribs and whites, are immoral and cannot be trusted. In this way, Carib folklore bolsters their ethnic claim that Caribs and Creoles have very little in common. *See also* **Cuba; Haiti; Jamaica.**

BIBLIOGRAPHY

Layng, Anthony. 1979–1980. Ethnic Identity, Population Growth, and Economic Security on a West Indian Reservation. *Revista/Review Interamericana* 9: 577–584.

Taylor, Douglas. 1945. Carib Folk Beliefs and Customs from Dominica, British West Indies. *Southwestern Journal of Anthropology* 1: 507–530.

————. 1952. Tales and Legends of the Dominican Caribs. *Journal of American Folklore* 65: 267–279.

Anthony Layng

JAMAICA

GEOGRAPHY AND HISTORY

An English-speaking island nation in the Caribbean Sea with a population of approximately 2.7 million people, half of whom live in or near its capital of Kingston, Jamaica gained its independence from Britain on 6 August 1963. To appreciate Jamaican traditions one needs to understand the circumstances through which many different peoples contributed to creating the folklore of this mountainous tropical island, situated south of Cuba and west of Haiti. While English was the language of the colonial government, Twi-Asante or Ashanti was the African language of the Akan people brought as slaves. Over time "patois" evolved as the *lingua franca*. These patois-speaking slaves, often forbidden to leave their owner's property, interacted with not only English but also Irish, Scottish, and Welsh, each contributing to the distinctive lilt of today's Jamaican English. Many of the grammatical conventions as well as the rhythmic pattern are attributable to a variety of African tonal languages, primarily Twi-Asante and later Kikongo. Spanish, French, Indian, and Chinese settlers have also added to the vocabulary of Jamaican Creole.

Jamaican Creole began to emerge as a "respectable" language during the period leading up to internal self-government in 1944, when poetry and stories by Jamaicans using the language were first published. By helping to legitimize oral and written Jamaican English through her poetry and storytelling, Louise Bennett Coverley became a Jamaican icon loved and honored by the nation as Jamaica's leading lady of folklore. Similarly, Rex Nettleford, through his leadership of the Jamaican National Dance Theatre, and Olive Lewin, who created the Jamaican Folk Singers, succeeded in bringing folk elements of those arts to national consciousness after independence.

Originally Taíno Indians inhabited Jamaica, but just a few place names remain from their Arawak language, including *Xaymaica*, land of wood and water; a few oral narratives such as the "Legend of Mountain Pride," which recounts the tragic death of a Taíno woman in love with a young chief or *cacique*; and some archeological sites where artifacts including *Zemis*, religious statues seen as intermediaries between man and Taíno deities, have been found. These fragments are what is left of their world, though remnants of Taíno culture are more prevalent on other Caribbean islands. The demise of the Taíno Indians was a result primarily of diseases, including small-pox and influenza, coupled with harsh working conditions imposed by Spanish colonizers after Christopher Columbus and his crew took possession of Jamaica for Queen Isabella and King Ferdinand of Spain in 1494.

The Spanish settled in Jamaica during the following decade. Jamaica was never one of Spain's prize possessions, but its cattle ranches and export crops served as a re-stocking depot for ships traveling between Spain and South America with vast treasures of silver and gold. The search for such treasure, believed to be buried in graves, hidden in rivers—as suggested in "The Legend of the Golden Table" and the Riva Muma stories—or concealed in large ceramic containers known today as Spanish jars, is now part of Jamaica's folklore. Poorly defended Spanish settlements were attacked by Cromwell's English forces in 1655, sending the Spaniards fleeing, leaving a few place names, some linguistic contributions, and distinctive forms of construction, including the Spanish wall of stones held by canes, overcast with mortar of white lime and sand, and sometimes covered with tiles. The English tradition used mortar with cut stone or bricks, while wattle-and-daub construction was the architectural norm for Africans, first brought by the Spanish at the start of the sixteenth century. Elaborate Great Houses—developed from English Georgian architecture with multiple stories, sloping shingle roofs, verandas, and carved fretwork design or wrought ironwork—eventually became the Jamaican Vernacular style that appeared in the latter part of the eighteenth century. Today the risk of hurricanes and earthquakes has put greater emphasis on buildings of cement block reinforced with steel, even in the poorer areas where zinc is often used as an interim measure.

Sephardic Jews, who had hidden their true religious affiliation to escape persecution under the Spanish Inquisition, remained in Jamaica when the Spanish fled. Joined by others in the late seventeenth century, they today form one of the oldest Jewish communities in the Western Hemisphere. The descendants of African slaves established communities in the hilly interior, independent of the British conquerors, and became known as Maroons.

From 1655 to 1963 the British government ruled from afar while those living in Jamaica gradually developed their own ways of dealing with an agrarian life dominated by the need for fieldworkers, which gave rise to the importation of bonded white servants and then forced labor from Africa. According to historian Philip Curtin, the European population in 1700 was approximately 7,000 and the African 40,000. Though historians dispute the exact figures, by 1800 hundreds of thousands of Africans had arrived while the white population remained at little more than 20,000. All things English—race, religion, government, language, and customs—were considered the ultimate standard in contrast to African culture. Through constant migration on both sides, European and African standards were constantly reinforced even as the interaction of those living permanently in Jamaica created a Creole population that synthesized aspects of both worlds.

After England defeated the Spanish, 3,000 of Oliver Cromwell's Protestant soldiers and 1,500 royalists were granted land and settled on the island, governed by military rule. Cromwell's army had just conquered Ireland, so many Irish came as bonded servants, and many Scottish arrivals were prisoners of war who served in menial capacities. Hundreds more Scots were shipped to Jamaica later in 1745–1746 after they supported James the Young Pretender's unsuccessful bid for the British throne. By 1750 a third of the white population of Jamaica was of Scottish origin, and their customs influenced plantation life so much that in the early 1800s, Lady Nugent, the governor general's wife, noted that Scottish reels were one of the most popular forms of dance at after-dinner estate parties or the balls that formed the center of British social life. A French ballroom dance, the quadrille, found its way into Jamaica in the early nineteenth century and was adopted into Afro-Jamaican tradition through house servants and musicians who played at these functions. The source of the quadrille was likely refugees fleeing slave revolts on the French colony of St. Dominique. Some whites and free coloreds stayed and account for the revival of Catholicism and the input of Haitian Voudou. A now famous legend, "The White Witch of Rose Hall," is based on the life of Annee Palmer, who grew up in Haiti, married Jamaican estate owner John Palmer in 1820, and reputedly used her knowledge of Voudou practices to murder four husbands before her terrorized slaves murdered her.

Festivals and Celebrations

The mid-eighteenth and early nineteenth centuries were the height of the plantation era. Many of London's wealthiest people were absentee landowners whose Jamaican sugar estates were run by "attorneys"—so called because they were given the power of attorney over properties in the absence of the owners. At Christmas, masters had to grant slaves three days off and give them clothing and better food. Christmas parties in Jamaica still commence at the beginning of December and last throughout the month, with communities whitewashing curbs and homes and spending Christmas Eve shopping. Growing out of West African secret society masquerades, Jonkunu was one of the most colorful folk traditions. The name possibly derives from the words *dzono* (sorcerer) and *kunu* (deadly) in the Ewe language of eastern Ghana and Togo, and though menacing in nature, Jonkunu surfaced during the relaxed Christmas season when licenses were granted to permit masqueraders freedom of movement on the roads. First appearing around 1720, groups of male slaves roamed, wearing masks depicting cow heads, horse heads, and boars' tusks and various costumes, especially pitchy-patchy covered in tattered cloth; accompanied by musicians playing fife, grater, bass, and rattling drums; frightening children; and expecting money or refreshment. Its popularity peaked in the late 1700s, when owners promoted the festival or Christmas carnival on their properties, allowing European elements such as Set Girls, Morris dancers, and steps from Scottish reels to creep into the festivities. As slaves began to outnumber whites and word of emancipation spread through religious gatherings in the early nineteenth century—culminating in a slave rebellion throughout western Jamaica in 1831—Jonkunu was actively discouraged. Christian missionaries and their followers deplored the licentious dancing and drinking that accompanied Jonkunu, and the 1841 Kingston riots became known as the John Canoe Riots. Though suppressed, Jonkunu survives today in rural variants in the communities of Clarendon and St. Catherine.

Bruckins arose as a joyous African celebration of emancipation from slavery after 1 August 1838 and included songs thanking Queen Victoria and costumes and dances mimicking the Royal Court. One group in red and the other in blue, led by their king and queen, competed in communities to see which queen could " 'bruck" her waist and hips the best. The celebrations included bombastic "speechifying" at a tea meeting within a bamboo-frame shed covered in palm fronds, where bids were taken to see who could unveil the queen and showbread. Revived dancers continued through the night with instruments, including two kinds of drums and calabash shakers.

MAROON CULTURE

Maroons were better able to retain their cultural identity than many other Africans because of their isolation in mountain settlements and their eventual freedom from British interference. Maroons were descended primarily from the Ashanti of Ghana, then called the Gold Coast, and other West Africans with whom they mixed over the years. Creoles born on plantations who successfully fled slavery joined Maroons, as did a few Taíno and Miskito Indians. The dominant belief system of the West African Akan people (and all African religions in Jamaica) recognized a creator deity of infinite goodness as well as ancestral spirits and other gods; and one notable tradition that continued on plantations and among small groups where African retentions exist even today is the sacrifice of a fowl or goat, accompanied by ritual singing, dancing, and drumming to invoke the intercession of an ancestor with the rulers of the world beyond.

Death ceremonies were one area where authorities granted leeway in terms of group assembly, which may account for the persistence of these African-derived retentions. Funerals today remain major social occasions, but in the folk tradition the spirit returns on the ninth night to its earthly home. Relatives and friends sit up each night and by the ninth, if the spirit has been properly entertained and honored with libations, food, song, and dance, the spirit passes on to its spirit home. If unhappy, it returns to cause problems for the living. Dinki Mini in St. Mary—similar to Zella in Portland, Ettu and Gerreh in Westmoreland and Hanover, and Tambo in Trelawny—are all ways in which people follow burial rituals to ensure the smooth transition of the spirit from this

Dinki Mini dancers. (Photograph by Laura Tanna. Copyright 1986)

earthly experience to the spirit world. Dinki Mini is joyous, including ring play and extremely suggestive dancing accompanied by the *benta*, a stringed instrument made with a long length of bamboo at each end of which musicians sit—one rubbing the string with a gourd producing a twanging sound and the other striking it with thin bamboo sticks. Maracas, guitar, grater, and a drum set may be used. Gerreh differs in that it specifically includes a dance in which lengths of bamboo held parallel to the ground are constantly moved while young dancers maintain their balance. Some songs may be critical of the dead. Tambo in Wakefield, Trelawny, was kept alive up until the early 1970s by master-drummer Benjamin Reid, who straddled a large drum, using his heel to change pitch, while another man struck the sides with two sticks. Many songs are laments and may be repeated during ceremonies such as tombing, when one builds a proper tomb forty days or even a year after a burial.

Although a limited amount of traditional knowledge and folklore of Africa survives in Maroon villages today, the symbolism of their successful fight for freedom gives them great significance within Jamaica's cultural heritage. Accompong in the west and Moore Town in the east are the two largest communities, each with its own colonel. The Accompong Maroons fought the British for fifty-seven years and gained their freedom in 1738. The Maroons have legends about the miraculous feats of their leaders, including Kwaku and Cudjoe. Every 6 January the Accompong Maroons celebrate Cudjoe's brave struggle for Maroon freedom with music, song, libations, and ceremonial rites.

The freedom fighter Nanny of the Windward Maroons of Portland and St. Thomas was so highly revered that she has been elevated to the status of National Hero by the Jamaican government for having forced the British to sign a treaty in 1740. Oral history attributes the Maroon "war bush" or caucoon plant to "Grandy Nanny," who originated the idea of camouflaging warriors in this foliage, then surrounding and ambushing British soldiers. Popular lore has Nanny catching British bullets under her skirts and firing them back at the enemy. While myths and legends surrounding Maroon leaders were important psychological tools, the practical ability to use leaves, roots, and saps of specific plants to heal warriors wounded in battle contributed much to their victory. One of the chief symbols of Maroon independence is the *abeng*, a cow horn blown to signal an enemy approach.

Maroons have hundreds of songs for communicating with ancestral spirits. Some Akan Twi-Ashanti language survives in Maroon songs. The *prenting* and the *goombeh* are the two most important Maroon drums, used on both religious and secular occasions. The tall *prenting* is sometimes accompanied by systematically beating a piece of bamboo with two sticks and striking a machete with a piece of metal. Dance style, dictated by the rhythm of the drums, depends upon occasion, whether for the military, healing, funerals, or recreation. The *goombeh* drum is square, covered with goatskin, with a second square frame inside for tuning the instrument. The rhythms or drum language, like much of Maroon language and knowledge, has been protected from outsiders for reasons of survival. In Jamaica at large, various percussion instruments have become the hallmark of Afro-Jamaican music, even during those times when bans on drums were periodically enforced. Even without instruments, music was an integral part of traditional life, with digging or worksongs to accompany every kind of labor. *Mento*, a once-popular folk music genre, carries the same emphasis on the fourth beat as do digging songs.

CHILDREN'S SONGS AND GAMES

Singing and ring games also formed part of children's play activities alongside evening storytelling sessions. Undoubtedly the most popular character in Jamaican folklore today is Anansi, the trickster-hero, originally a sky god of Akan-Ashanti heritage brought to the Caribbean by West African slaves. This spider, sometimes referred to as a little man carrying a sack, may be small in stature and may speak with a slight lisp in the broadest of Jamaican English patois, indicating a low social standing, but his cleverness can outsmart even the biggest foe. A mischievous rather than a malicious **trickster**, he is undone only by greed. His ability to use brains to overcome both inferior social status and dangerous oppressors readily made Anansi a powerful symbol of enduring resistance against overwhelming odds. Because so much Afro-Jamaican religion and culture was suppressed, this individual character has assumed social and political significance in the larger Jamaican context and has long lent his name to all Jamaican folk stories, even when they do not include the trickster himself.

FOLKTALES

Non-trickster tales tend to be longer than their trickster brethren, though no Jamaican narrative has the length or complexity that can be found in African narratives and no single **hero** emerges to dominate this genre as does Anansi in trickster tales. The Jamaican role of hunter most closely resembles the West African culture hero. Similar to his African prototype, this character has knowledge of magical chants and objects such as arrows, whips, and exploding limes, marbles, or eggs. Unlike the trickster, the hunter-hero rarely acts alone but is assisted by his hunting dogs or his mother, who is endowed with supernatural powers. He travels on a journey, usually through a dangerous forest, and overcomes dangerous obstacles such as an evil witch-woman, a dangerous bull, or a monstrous flying bird. Trickster tales may have etiological endings, purporting to explain why an animal today looks or behaves in a certain way as a result of Anansi's actions, which are usually based upon self-interest. In heroic tales, the protagonist does something beneficial for others, demonstrating more consciousness of social responsibility than does Anansi.

Popular imaginative tales incorporating Jamaica's European cultural heritage include cumulative narratives, a kind of word game in which new actions are constantly added to an original action and then the whole sequence repeated in perfect order—the more quickly, the more the audience appreciates the performance. Also popular are lying stories or tall tales that reveal who can exaggerate the most, parson stories in which the hypocritical actions of religious figures are ridiculed, and "big boy" stories—bawdy tales in which a young man either indulges in sexual activity or exposes an authority figure doing so. Duppy stories may be examined in the context of burial rites but are considered a kind of ghost story in which the performer

Storyteller Adina Henry. (Photograph by Laura Tanna. Copyright 1983)

delights an audience when the duppy is revealed by speaking or singing in a nasal voice. Rolling Calf tales deal also with spirits of the dead returning to haunt the living, identified by the sound of a clanging chain. Storytelling sessions were most often associated with night, either prior to bedtime or when keeping company with families after a death before the body was buried.

Storytelling in Jamaica has never traditionally been a paid profession but, rather, a means of entertaining and educating children, though adults seem always to gather as well. Anyone, male or female, may perform stories as long as he or she can hold the audience's interest through the skillful use of words, sounds, and physical movement. Children learn to perform by observing others and then practicing among themselves, usually starting with riddles and rhymes that are shorter and easier to learn. Proverbs are used to teach children, make a rhetorical point in discussion, or summarize the conclusion of a narrative. Rarely these days does one hear the traditional ending formula, "Jack Mandora me no choose none." A number of the oral narratives, especially non-trickster narratives, have a chant or song that a child learns, repeating the tune while changing some of the words to advance the plot. The spread of electricity in the past few decades—and with it radio, television, and musical sound systems—has virtually obliterated storytelling in the home. The Jamaica Library Service, Jamaica Commission for the Development of Culture (JCDC), and a few professional storytellers now strive to keep this performing art alive.

But Maroon leaders and the Akan trickster-hero Anansi were not the only ones to become part of Jamaican folklore. In 1760 rebel leader Tacky led a slave uprising in the Parish of St. Mary that took almost six months to subdue, and although he was eventually captured and beheaded, he became a folk hero known for his daring and courage. He was believed to be an *obeahman*—*obeah* coming from the Ashanti word *obayifo*, for "sorcerer." Because slaves were not allowed to congregate in large numbers outside their own plantations and organizing religious meetings was difficult, it has been argued that African religious leaders lost their positions of authority to *obeahmen*, who functioned as individuals whose knowledge of poisons, use of ground glass, and deadly spells cast fear not only into other Africans but into Europeans as well.

SPELLS AND MAGIC

Laws against *obeah* and *obeahmen* were instituted in 1781. *Obeah* is still considered a form of magic capable of manipulating forces of evil, while the *myalman* or spirit man was thought of as a person who could manipulate forces of good, especially for healing. *Myalism* came to be regarded as the most common form of African-derived religion among slaves. Formal Christian teaching to slaves began in earnest when some 400 Moravian families and the accompanying 4,000 to 5,000 African American slaves left the United States in 1783 and settled on four estates in St. Elizabeth in western Jamaica. Black preachers, especially Native Baptists, arose with leaders practicing their individual interpretations of the faith. As Christianity influenced *Myalism*, the religious forms of Revival, Zion, and Pukumania, stressing spirit possession, developed around individual shepherds or leaders whose followers are often seen dressed completely in white. Mallicah Reynolds, better known as Kapo, one of the most famous modern Revival leaders, was also highly regarded as a folk artist. Today a collection of his painting and sculpture is displayed in the National Gallery of Jamaica, as is the work of Everald Brown, whose large decorated guitars and unique instruments represent the creativity of many members of the Rastafarian faith, another offshoot of Christianity, which has found international acceptance since its inception in the 1930s.

RELIGIOUS BELIEFS

Rastafarianism grew out of the same consciousness of Africa as Marcus Garvey's teachings of the period, and an oral tradition of prophecies and miraculous feats is attributed to Garvey. When Emperor Haile Selassie of Ethiopia was crowned King Ras Tafari in November 1930, the poorest and blackest of Jamaica's dispossessed found hope in the belief that Ras Tafari was God returned in their image. Photographs of East Africans with long locks and biblical admonitions against cutting one's hair inspired dreadlocks, a tangible symbol of Rasta faith that took courage to wear in the early decades of the movement when authorities dealt harshly with followers whose spiritual gatherings or *groundations* included drumming, chanting, and the use of marijuana or *ganja*. Some Rastafarians follow the teachings of the Ethiopian Orthodox Coptic Church, which recognizes Christ; others follow no organized church. Singer Bob Marley is the best-known Rastafarian, and the lyrics of his reggae songs are the religion's greatest proponent.

Kumina, another Afro-Jamaican religion of which spirit possession is an integral part, appears more directly related to the last great influx of Africans, who came from Central Africa as indentured laborers between 1841 through 1865. One of Rastafarianism's tenets of repatriation to Africa may have come down through indentured laborers who were originally

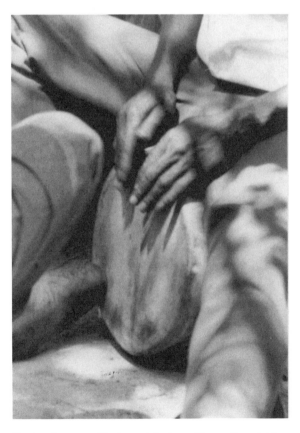

Kumina drummer. (Photograph by Laura Tanna. Copyright 1986)

343

promised passage back to their homes. Britain abolished the slave trade in 1807 before the Portuguese did so. Some Africans, primarily from Angola and the Congo, destined for slavery in Brazil, found their ships intercepted and themselves "liberated" by the British and sent instead to work in Jamaica. The last generation of Jamaican elders who as children had contact with these Africans is almost all dead now, but they influenced people who even twenty or thirty years ago could share their memories. Cyrus Wallace, better known as Baba C, a Kumina king in West Kingston with roots in St. Thomas, learned Kimbundu and Kikongo words and songs from his African grandmother, who taught him the Congolese belief in the supreme god *Ndzambi-amphuungu ngolo*. Communicating with ancestral spirits both to honor them and ask for their intercession and assistance for specific purposes is the main function of Kumina ceremonies. Essential to those ceremonies are the rhythm of drums—the *kbandu* and the smaller *cyas*, which direct the dancers and call forth spirits—and the language of the songs, of which there are two kinds: *bailo*, primarily in Jamaican Creole, and *country*, in what Kumina followers call African *language*, identified by linguists as words and creolized phrases of Kikongo or Kimbundu or even words in sound and structure reminiscent of these languages. The *bailo* songs are for entertainment, while *country* songs are invocations to communicate with ancestral spirits. Another folk tradition of Congolese heritage, almost unknown and isolated in Galloway, Westmoreland, is Beele play, a game in which players face each other and must perform specific arm movements to win.

Tazia, replica of Imam Hosain's tomb, built by Sidney Byjoo of Kemps Hill for Hussay in Clarendon, 21 August 1999. (Photograph by Laura Tanna. Copyright 1999)

EAST INDIAN CULTURE

Following emancipation, East Indians also came as indentured laborers aboard ships with Africans to serve on sugar estates. This and their small numbers are reasons no racial animosity exists between them in Jamaica. *Ganja*, the Hindi word for marijuana, and the concept of its being a holy herb as well as the use of it are not the only contributions East Indians have made to Jamaican traditions. As both Hindus and Muslims arrived in Jamaica, many adopted Christian religions but retained elements of their own traditions, though now diminished somewhat. The most popular of these is Hosay or Hussay, a Muslim festival to mourn the death of the Prophet Mohammed's grandson Hosain. A replica of his tomb—a *tazia* or *tadjah*—constructed out of a bamboo frame on wheels and covered with brightly colored paper, forms the center of a street parade or road march, accompanied by musicians playing *tassas* tied to their waists—small earthenware drums heated over charcoal to tighten their goatskin drumheads and beaten with small sticks. Brass cymbals or *janj* and barrel-drums also keep the dancers moving toward the river or bay into which the *tazia* will be thrown at sunset. Indians of all faiths join in this festival, held in Jamaica on the sighting of the first new moon in August, rather than the Shia Islamic sighting of the moon in January-February, which is the busy harvest time on Caribbean sugar estates. All Jamaicans are welcome in this celebration now, which included stick fighting in the old days and took place near Indian communities in St. Mary, Westmoreland, Clarendon, Kingston, and Spanish Town, but the cost of building the *tazia* and the loss of those with the knowledge of how to create and play the instruments and construct the *tazia* means that as recently as 1999 only one Hosay was held in the entire country.

STUDIES OF JAMAICAN FOLKLORE

Olive Senior's *Encyclopedia of Jamaican Heritage* (2003) is invaluable on all aspects of Jamaican art and culture. For a fascinating account written in 1835 of the realities of daily life for Africans and Europeans on Jamaican properties, read Bernard Martin Senior (1969). For history on early African arrivals in Jamaica and its subsequent impact, read two books by Curtin (1955, 1969) and one by Brathwaite (1971). Jamaican language and folklore expressions are treated in Cassidy (1971) and Cassidy and Le Page (1980). Further knowledge on the concept of a continuum of language and culture, African arrivals, their religion, music, and dance, especially Maroon culture, can be found in Alleyne (1988, 1999). Kenneth M. Bilbey's video on the Maroons (1979) and his work on Kumina with Fu-Kiau kia Bunseki (1983) are extremely interesting. For a sensitive and detailed study of Maroon, Kumina, Rastafarian, and all folk music, song, dance, and spirituality, including many isolated groups with African retentions, see Lewin (2000). On related topics see Tanna and Ramsay on death rituals (1987) and Owens on Rastafarian philosophy and religion (1976). Schuler (1980) did much to open research on Central African and **Yoruba**, as opposed to earlier Ghanaian Akan contributions, and Carter (1996) built on that opening. Warner-Lewis (2003) comprehensively covers Central African influences in the Caribbean, with emphasis on linguistic derivations. For drama see Hill (1992), and for an introduction to Jamaican art, including folk art, see Boxer and Poupeye (1998). Tanna and Baugh (1999) contains rare photographs of traditional pottery techniques. Louise Bennett's groundbreaking poetry appears in *Jamaica Dialect Poems: Jamaica Labrish* (1966), while Jekyll (1966 [1907]) and Beckwith (1924, 1969a [1928], 1969b [1929]) presented the first serious examinations of Jamaican songs and folktales. For a detailed collection of oral narratives, with photographs of performers, analysis of oral narrative performance, and an extensive bibliography on folktales in print, see Tanna (2000a) accompanied by *Jamaican Folk Tales and Oral Histories*, a 104-minute (2000b [1987]) and two 60-minute audio cassettes of storytellers (1987, 1992) recorded in the 1970s and 1980s. For an extensive bibliography of excellent works on all aspects of Jamaican culture, see Senior (2003) or the

University of the West Indies Press catalog. *See also* **Cuba**; **Haiti**; **Island Carib (Dominica)**; **Sephardim**; **Suriname Maroons**.

BIBLIOGRAPHY

Alleyne, Mervyn. 1988. *Roots of Jamaican Culture*. London: Pluto Press.

———. 1999. Linguistics and the Oral Tradition. In *General History of the Caribbean*. Vol. VI, edited by B. W. Higman. London: Unesco Publishing/MacMillan Education. 19–45.

Beckwith, Martha Warren. 1924. *Jamaica Anansi Stories*. Memoirs of the American Folk-Lore Society, No. 17.

———. 1969a (1928). *Jamaica Folk-Lore*. New York: Kraus Reprint.

———. 1969b (1929). *Black Roadways: A Study of Jamaican Folk-Life*. New York: Negro Universities Press.

Bennett, Louise. 1966. *Jamaica Dialect Poems: Jamaica Labrish*. Kingston: Sangster's Book Stores.

Bilbey, Kenneth M. 1979. *Capital of Earth: The Maroons of Moore Town* (film). Penn State University Audio Visual.

Bilbey, Kenneth M., with Fu-Kiau kia Bunseki. 1983. *Kumina: A Kongo-Based Tradition in the New World*. Brussels: Centre D'Etude et de Documentation Africaines. 1–114.

Boxer, David, and Veerle Poupeye. 1998. *Modern Jamaican Art*. Kingston: UWI/Ian Randle.

Brathwaite, Edward Kamau. 1971. *The Development of Creole Society in Jamaica, 1770–1820*. Oxford: Oxford University Press.

Carter, Hazel. 1996. The Language of Kumina and Beele Play. *African Caribbean Institute of Jamaica Research Review* 3: 66–83.

Cassidy, Frederic G. 1971. *Jamaica Talk: Three Hundred Years of the English Language in Jamaica*. London: MacMillan Education.

Cassidy, Frederic G., and R. B. Le Page. 1980. *Dictionary of Jamaican English*. Cambridge: Cambridge University Press.

Curtin, Philip D. 1955. *Two Jamaicas: The Role of Ideas in a Tropical Colony, 1830–1865*. Cambridge, MA: Harvard University Press.

———. 1969. *The Atlantic Slave Trade: A Census*. Madison: University of Wisconsin Press.

Hill, Errol. 1992. *The Jamaican Stage, 1655–1900*. Amherst: University of Massachusetts Press.

Jekyll, Walter. 1966 (1907). *Jamaican Song and Story*. New York: Dover.

Lewin, Olive. 2000. *Rock It Come Over: The Folk Music of Jamaica*. Kingston: University of the West Indies Press.

Owens, Joseph. 1976. *Dread: Rastafarians of Jamaica*. Kingston: Sangster's Book Stores.

Schuler, Monica. 1980. *"Alas Alas Kongo": A Social History of Indentured African Immigration into Jamaica, 1841–65*. Baltimore: Johns Hopkins University Press.

Senior, Bernard Martin. 1969 (1835). *Jamaica, As It Was, As It Is, And As It May Be, Comprising Interesting Topics for Absent Proprietors, Merchants and Valuable Hints to Persons Intending to Emigrate to the Island: Also an Authentic Narrative of The Negro Insurrection In 1831; with A Faithful Detail of the Manners, Customs and Habits of the Colonists and A Description of the Country, Climate, Productions, Including An Abridgment of the Slave Law*. New York: Negro Universities Press.

Senior, Olive. 2003. *Encyclopedia of Jamaican Heritage*. Kingston: Twin Guinep.

Tanna, Laura. 1987. *Jamaican Folk Tales and Oral Histories* (sound recording). Miami: DLT Associates.

———. 1992. *Maroon Storyteller* (sound recording). Miami: DLT Associates.

———. 2000a (1984). *Jamaican Folk Tales and Oral Histories*. 3rd edition. Miami: DLT Associates.

———. 2000b (1987). *Jamaican Folk Tales and Oral Histories* (film). Miami: DLT Associates.

Tanna, Laura, and Cecil Baugh. 1999. *Baugh: Jamaica's Master Potter*. Revised edition. Miami: DLT Associates.

Tanna, Laura, and Hazel Ramsay. 1987. Death Rituals and Responses: Dinki Mini. *Jamaica Journal* 20.2: 27–31.

Warner-Lewis, Maureen. 2003. *Central Africa in the Caribbean*. Kingston: University of the West Indies Press.

Laura Tanna

Geographical Guide to Peoples, Cultures, and Regions

The following guide will help users quickly and easily ascertain the main geographical locations of unfamiliar peoples, cultures, and regions.

Africa

Abanyole: Kenya
Baule: Ivory Coast
Benin: Nigeria
Berber: Algeria, Burkino Faso, Libya, Mali, Morocco, Niger, Tunisia
Bushmen. *See* San, below.
Comoros Islands: in Indian Ocean off northern coast of Mozambique
Ga: Ghana
Igbo: Nigeria
Ijo: Nigeria
Jie: Uganda
Lunda: Democratic Republic of the Congo, Zambia
Mascarene Islands: in Indian Ocean east of Madagascar
Nuer: Sudan
San: Botswana, Namibia
Shona: Mozambique, Zimbabwe
Swahili: Kenya, Mozambique, Somalia, Tanzania
Tuareg: Algeria, Burkina Faso, Libya, Mali, Niger
Wolof: Senegal, Gambia
Xhosa: South Africa
Yoruba: Nigeria, Ghana, Togo
Zande: Central African Republic, Congo, Sudan
Zulu: South Africa

Asia and the Middle East

Ainu: Japan, mainly the northern island of Hokkaido
Assam: state of India
Bali: one of the islands comprising Indonesia
Bihar: state of India
Duna: Papua New Guinea
Gaddi: northern India
Haryana: state of India
Iban: Malaysia
Isaan: northeastern Thailand

Kadazandusan: Malaysia
Kaliai: Papua New Guinea
Karnataka: state of India
Kashmir: state of India
Kewa: Papua New Guinea
Khasi-Jaintia: northeastern India
Kurds: Iran, Iraq, Syria, Turkey
Maluku: Indonesia
Manchu: northern and northeastern China
Molucca. *See* Maluku, above.
Mongol: Mongolia and northern China
Nagaland: northeastern India
Orissa: state of India
Semai: Malaysia
Siberia: China, Russia, and Central Asia
Tairora: Papua New Guinea
Uttar Pradesh: state of India
Uyghur: northwestern China

Australia and Oceania

(For the location of other islands in Oceania, see the "Australia and Oceania" map in Volume 1)
Guam: Mariana Islands
Kiribati: Gilbert Islands
Malaita: Solomon Islands

Europe

Ashkenazim: Eastern and Central Europe
Basque: southwestern France, north-central Spain
Brittany: northwestern France
Catalonia: northeastern Spain
Flanders: northwestern Belgium
Galicia: northwestern Spain
Gypsies. *See* Roma, below.
Lapps. *See* Sámi, below.
Piedmont: northwestern Italy
Roma (Gypsies): worldwide, but especially southeastern Europe
Sámi: Finland, Norway, Sweden
Sephardim: expelled from Spain in fifteenth century
Val d'Aosta: Italy

North America

Apache: Arizona, New Mexico, Oklahoma
Cherokee: southeastern United States, Oklahoma

Cheyenne: Montana, Oklahoma
Choctaw: Mississippi, Oklahoma
Eskimo. *See* Western Inuit and Yupik, below.
Haida: Haida Gwaii (Queen Charlotte Islands) off British Columbia, Canada;
   Alaska
Hopi: Arizona
Iroquois: northeastern United States, mainly New York State; Ontario, Canada
Kiowa: Oklahoma
Lakota: northern Plains states, mainly North and South Dakota, Montana,
   Minnesota
Navajo: Arizona, New Mexico
Nez Perce: Idaho, Oregon, Washington State
Ojibwe: Ontario, Canada; northern Great Lakes region
Seminole: Florida, Oklahoma
Tlingit: British Columbia and Yukon, Canada; Alaska
Western Inuit and Yupik: Arctic Canada; Alaska

South and Central America, Mexico, and the Caribbean

Caipira: Brazil
Candoshi: Peru
Island Carib: island of Dominica in the Caribbean
Kaingang: Brazil
Maroon: Suriname
Maya: Mexico, Guatemala
Nahua: Mexico
Otomí: Mexico
Quechua: Bolivia, Ecuador, Peru
Rarámuri: northern Mexico
Sertão: Brazil
Shuar: Ecuador
Sibundoy: Colombia
Tarahumara. *See* Rarámuri, above.
Xavante: Brazil
Yanomami: Brazil, Venezuela

Glossary

Anecdote. Short, usually single-episode narrative told as believable and often focusing on a person.

Animal tale. A fictional narrative in which the main roles are taken by personified animals. Frequently, the same plots may also be used with human characters. Animal tales become fables when explicit morals are added, and they may often have purportedly etiological significance.

Animism. Belief that not only humans but aspects of nature, both animate and inanimate, have spiritual dimensions.

Ballad. A narrative folksong, relatively brief and composed in stanzas. The form is usually associated with northern European folksong traditions, but similar forms occur in many parts of the world.

Bowdlerization. Expurgation of materials deemed unsuitable, usually because of erotic or scatological content.

Calendar custom. Traditional behavior, usually in the form of a ceremony or festival, that recurs regularly in the annual cycle. Calendar customs often correspond with economic activities such as planting and harvest and are frequently coordinated with astronomical phenomena such as the solstices and equinoxes.

Cante-fable. A story that mixes prose narration with poetry or song.

Caste. A level in a stratified society into which one is assigned for life. Membership is determined by birth and cannot be changed through social mobility.

Clan. A kinship group, usually consisting of several lineages, in which members have a sense, often vague, of descent from a common ancestor, who may in fact be a figure from myth.

Contagious magic. Magic based on the principle that once two objects have been in physical contact with one another, they will continue to exert spiritual influence on each other even after the physical contact ceases.

Cosmology. A society's theory of the nature of its universe. This often represents a codification of the society's worldview.

Cross-cousin. A child of a parent's different-sex sibling—for example, of a father's sister or a mother's brother. Frequently, a preferred marriage partner.

Divination. A custom used to ascertain the future and to disclose the will of spiritual beings or forces. Many Western divination customs focus specifically on the identity of a future spouse, but in other parts of the world divination responds to a range of other issues.

Emic. The perspective of the cultural insider.

Endogamy. Marriage rule that requires that a spouse be found within a particular group.

Epic. A long narrative poem or folksong, often performed to simple musical accompaniment. The oral epic, which has flourished in many parts of the world, frequently narrates events in the career of a culture hero in language that may be highly stylized and formal.

Etic. The perspective of the cultural outsider.

Etiological tale. A story that purportedly accounts for the origin of a specific, usually natural phenomenon. Frequently, etiological tags are added to narratives, whose main purpose is not to explain origins. Very often these tags—and in fact whole stories with etiological emphasis—are not meant to be taken literally.

Exemplum. A story told for the purpose of providing an example, either positively or negatively, of what a society believes constitutes moral conduct.

Exogamy. Marriage rule that requires that a spouse be found outside a particular group.

Fable. A folk narrative that is intended as fiction but that makes a clear moral or ethical point, which may be stated explicitly usually at the conclusion of the story.

Fairy tale. A folk narrative that is intended as fiction and whose setting is a fantastic otherworld and in which an often naive protagonist achieves success. Most folklorists prefer such terms as *märchen* and *wonder tale*, and some may reserve *fairy tale* to refer to a literary production written in imitation of a folk narrative.

Folklife. Sometimes used as a synonym for *folklore*. The term, though, implies not only verbal traditions—to which some authorities would restrict the application of *folklore*—but to the full range of customary behavior, especially including material folk culture.

Folktale. A folk narrative that is intended as fiction. Sometimes, particularly in early literature, the term was used synonymously with the more inclusive *folk narrative*.

Homeopathic magic. Also called imitative magic. Magic based on the principle that "like produces like"—that the magic practitioner must imitate in miniature the results that he or she expects the spiritual powers to produce.

Informant. The person who provides data about folklore to a folklorist. Many contemporary folklorists now prefer less potentially pejorative terms such as *consultant* for such a person.

Legend. A folk narrative set in the recent past and intended to be accepted as true or plausible.

Lineage. A kinship group in which all members can clearly trace their descent to a common ancestor and in which all members have a definite sense of how they are related to each other.

Magic. Ritual behavior that is believed to have compulsive power. This means that the person performing the ritual, which may often be very complex in terms of both what is done and what is said, believes that properly following the procedure will compel spiritual forces or beings to do what is desired.

Märchen. A story told as fiction. Usually set in a magical otherworld, this kind of story typically delineates a quest by a young protagonist to attain fame, fortune, or a good marriage. Also called wonder tale and sometimes used as a replacement for *fairy tale*.

Matrilineal descent. A system for reckoning kinship in which relationships are traced only through female relatives.

Memorate. A first-person folk narrative that relates a single experience, often involving an encounter with the supernatural.

Mnemonic Device. An aid to memory. Particularly important for the recitation of lengthy folklore forms.

Moiety. One-half of a kinship-based society. A society with moieties will always have two and only two of them.

Myth. A folk narrative set in sacred time (before and at the creation of the cosmos or when the cosmos was very young). Myths may be intended as truth literally or symbolically. They often articulate a society's worldview.

Parallel-cousin. A child of a parent's same-sex sibling—for example, of a father's brother or a mother's sister. Occasionally, a preferred marriage partner.

Participant observation. The research methodology in which an ethnographer spends time living with the group of people whose culture he or she is researching in order to determine how the various aspects of the culture interrelate.

Patrilineal descent. A system for reckoning kinship in which relationships are traced only through male relatives.

Polygyny. A marriage pattern in which one man is married to more than one woman.

Proverb. A short, pithy statement, often using figurative language and other poetic devices, that articulates conventional wisdom. Proverbs are often used to comment upon specific situations, and their meaning may depend upon those situations.

Riddle. A question, often stated using metaphor and other figures of speech, that tests verbal agility or cultural knowledge. Riddles may be principal devices of enculturation that teach young people how to use language artistically.

Rite of passage. A ceremony that accompanies a change in identity. Rites of passage frequently occur at birth, at initiation from childhood to adulthood, and at death. Sometimes they may be called life-cycle rituals.

Shaman. A religious specialist who acquires knowledge and power through direct contact with spiritual beings rather than through formal education.

Sib. *See* clan.

Syncretism. Blending of aspects from more than one culture. Though often used in regard to the merging of religious traditions, the process applies to any aspect of culture.

Tall tale. A humorous fictional narrative that employs excessive exaggeration. Often told in a straightforward manner, such a story often catches the audience off-guard through a preposterous conclusion.

Totem. A clan's symbol. Usually an object from nature such as an animal, a plant, or a topographical landmark.

Tradition. The process by which folklore passes from one person to another.

Vocable. A wordless syllable used in singing. Not a nonsense syllable, since it may have important connotative and emotional significance.

Witchcraft. Traditionally, the use of magic in order to harm someone else. Modern reinterpretations of the term have recast it sometimes in a more positive light, and contemporary witches argue that they are following longstanding traditions of nature worship.

Worksong. A song that accompanies labor for the purpose of synchronizing effort, setting a pace that all the laborers can maintain, relieving tedium, and voicing concerns and protests. The subject matter need not be work.

General Bibliography

Bauman, Richard, ed. 1977. *Verbal Art as Performance*. Rowley, MA: Newbury House.

———, ed. 1992. *Folklore, Cultural Performances, and Popular Culture: A Communications-Centered Handbook*. New York: Oxford University Press.

Bausinger, Hermann. 1990. *Folk Culture in a World of Technology*, translated by Elke Dettmer. Bloomington: Indiana University Press.

Ben-Amos, Dan, ed. 1976. *Folklore Genres*. Austin: University of Texas Press.

Bødker, Laurits. 1965. *Folk Literature: Germanic*. Copenhagen: Rosenkilde.

Bohlman, Philip. 1988. *The Study of Folk Music in the Modern World*. Bloomington: Indiana University Press.

Bolte, Johannes, and Georg Polívka. 1913–1932. *Anmerkungen zu de Kinder- und Hausmärchen der Brüder Grimm*. 5 volumes. Leipzig: Dieterich.

Brown, Mary Ellen, and Bruce A. Rosenberg, eds. 1998. *Encyclopedia of Folklore and Literature*. Santa Barbara: ABC-CLIO.

Campbell, Joseph. 1949. *The Hero with a Thousand Faces*. New York: Pantheon.

Chadwick, H. Munro. 1912. *The Heroic Age*. Cambridge: Cambridge University Press.

Claus, Peter J., Margaret Mills, and Sarah Diamond, eds. 2004. *South Asian Folklore: An Encyclopedia*. New York: Routledge.

Cocchiara, Giuseppe. 1981. *The History of Folklore in Europe*, translated by John N. McDaniel. Philadelphia: Institute for the Study of Human Issues.

Davies, Christie. 1990. *Ethnic Humor around the World: A Comparative Analysis*. Bloomington: Indiana University Press.

De Caro, Frank A. 1983. *Women and Folklore: A Bibliographic Survey*. Westport, CT: Greenwood Press.

De Vries, Jan. 1963. *Heroic Song and Heroic Legend*. New York: Oxford University Press.

Dorson, Richard M. 1961. *Folklore Research around the World*. Bloomington: Indiana University Folklore Series.

———, ed. 1972. *Folklore and Folklife: An Introduction*. Chicago: University of Chicago Press.

Dundes, Alan, ed. 1964. *The Study of Folklore*. Englewood Cliffs, NJ: Prentice-Hall.

———. 1975. *Analytic Essays in Folklore*. The Hague: Mouton.

———, ed. 1984. *Sacred Narrative: Readings in the Theory of Myth*. Berkeley: University of California Press.

———, ed. 1991. *The Blood Libel Legend*. Madison: University of Wisconsin Press.

———, ed. 1999. *International Folkloristics: Classic Contributions by the Founders of Folklore*. Lanham, MD: Rowman and Littlefield.

Edmonson, Munro S. 1971. *Lore: An Introduction to the Science of Folklore and Literature*. New York: Holt, Rinehart and Winston.

Falassi, Alessandro, ed. 1987. *Time Out of Time: Essays on the Festival*. Albuquerque: University of New Mexico Press.

Fine, Elizabeth C. 1984. *The Folklore Text from Performance to Print*. Bloomington: Indiana University Press.

Finnegan, Ruth. 1977. *Oral Poetry: Its Nature, Significance, and Social Context*. Cambridge: Cambridge University Press.

Foley, John Miles. 1988. *The Theory of Oral Composition: History and Methodology*. Bloomington: Indiana University Press.

Frazer, James. 1922. *The Golden Bough: A Study in Magic and Religion*. Abridged edition. New York: Macmillan.

Graburn, Nelson H. H., ed. 1976. *Ethnic and Tourist Arts: Cultural Expressions from the Fourth World*. Berkeley: University of California Press.

Green, Thomas A., ed. 1997. *Folklore: An Encyclopedia of Beliefs, Customs, Tales, Music, and Art*. 2 volumes. Santa Barbara: ABC-CLIO.

Hobsbawn, Eric, and Terence Ranger, eds. 1983. *The Invention of Tradition*. Cambridge: Cambridge University Press.

Honko, Lauri, ed. 1990. *Religion, Myth, and Folklore in the World's Epics*. New York: Mouton de Gruyter.

Hultkrantz, Åke. 1960. *General Ethnological Concepts*. Copenhagen: Rosenkilde and Bagger.

Jolles, André. 1930. *Einsache Formen*. 2nd edition. Tübingen: Max Niemeyer.

Kartomi, Margaret J. 1990. *Concepts and Classifications of Musical Instruments*. Chicago: University of Chicago Press.

Krappe, Alexander H. 1930. *The Science of Folklore*. New York: Barnes and Noble.

Leach, Maria, and Jerome Fried, eds. 1972. *Standard Dictionary of Folklore, Mythology, and Legend*. Revised edition. New York: Funk and Wagnalls.

Legman, G. 1964. *The Horn Book: Studies in Erotic Folklore and Bibliography*. New Hyde Park, NY: University Books.

———. 1968–1975. *No Laughing Matter: An Analysis of Sexual Humor*. 2 volumes. Bloomington: Indiana University Press.

Littleton, C. Scott. 1982. *The New Comparative Mythology*. Berkeley: University of California Press.

Lomax, Alan. 1968. *Folk Song Style and Culture*. Washington, DC: American Association for the Advancement of Science.

Lord, Albert B. 2000. *The Singer of Tales*. 2nd edition, edited by Stephen Mitchell and Gregory Nagy. Cambridge, MA: Harvard University Press.

MacDonald, Margaret Read, ed. 1999. *Traditional Storytelling Today: An International Sourcebook*. Chicago: Fitzroy Dearborn.

Middleton, John, ed. 1967. *Myth and Cosmos: Readings in Mythology and Symbolism*. New York: Natural History Press.

Mieder, Wolfgang. 1982–1993. *International Proverb Scholarship: An Annotated Bibliography*. 3 volumes. New York: Garland.

———, ed. 1993. *Wise Words: Essays on the Proverb*. New York: Garland.

Mieder, Wolfgang, and Alan Dundes, eds. 1981. *The Wisdom of Many: Essays on the Proverb*. New York: Garland.

Nettl, Bruno. 1983. *The Study of Ethnomusicology: Twenty-nine Issues and Concepts*. Urbana: University of Illinois Press.

Nettl, Bruno, and others, eds. 1998–2002. *The Garland Encyclopedia of World Music*. 10 volumes. New York: Garland.

Oinas, Felix J., ed. 1978a. *Folklore, Nationalism, and Politics*. Columbus, OH: Slavica Publishers.

———. 1978b. *Heroic Epic and Saga: An Introduction to the World's Great Folk Epics*. Bloomington: Indiana University Press.

Paredes, Américo, and Richard Bauman, eds. 1972. *Toward New Perspectives in Folklore*. Austin: University of Texas Press.

Peek, Philip M., and Kwesi Yankah, eds. 2003. *African Folklore: An Encyclopedia*. New York: Routledge.

Propp, Vladimir. 1984. *Theory and History of Folklore*, translated by Ariadna Y. Martin and Richard P. Martin; edited by Anatoly Lieberman. Minneapolis: University of Minnesota Press.

Rank, Kurt, and others, eds. 1977– . *Enzyklopädie des Märchens*. 11+ volumes. Berlin: Walter de Gruyter.

Roebuck, A. A. 1944. *A Dictionary of International Slurs (Ethnophaulisms)*. Cambridge, MA: Sci-Art.

Sebeok, Thomas, ed. 1972. *Myth: A Symposium*. Bloomington: Indiana University Press.

Sumner, William Graham. 1960. *Folkways*. New York: Mentor Books.

Thompson, Stith. 1955–1958. *Motif-Index of Folk-Literature: A Classification of Narrative Elements in Folktales, Ballads, Myths, Fables, Medieval Romances, Exempla, Fabilaux, Jest-Books and Local Legends*. Revised edition. 6 volumes. Bloomington: Indiana University Press.

———. 1977 (1946). *The Folktale*. Berkeley: University of California Press.

Toelken, Barre. 1996. *The Dynamics of Folklore*. Revised edition. Logan: Utah State University Press.

Uther, Hans-Jörg. 2004. *The Types of International Folktales: A Classification and Bibliography*. Helsinki: Academia Scientarum Fennica.

Van Gennep, Arnold. 1960. *The Rites of Passage*, translated by Monika B. Vizedom. Chicago: University of Chicago Press.

Vansina, Jan. 1985. *Oral Tradition as History*. Madison: University of Wisconsin Press.

Zumthor, Paul. 1990. *Oral Poetry: An Introduction*, translated by Kathryn Murphy-Judy. Minneapolis: University of Minnesota Press.

Editors, Contributors, and Translators

Editors

William M. Clements, General Editor
Arkansas State University
State University, Arkansas

Thomas A. Green, Advisory Editor
Texas A&M University
College Station, Texas

Guy Lancaster, Editorial Associate
Arkansas Encyclopedia of History and Culture
Little Rock, Arkansas

Francesca M. Muccini, Editorial Associate
Arkansas State University
State University, Arkansas

Jennifer Klotz, Editorial Assistant
Arkansas State University
State University, Arkansas

Daniel Turner, Editorial Assistant
Arkansas State University
State University, Arkansas

Contributors

Abu S. Abarry
Temple University
Philadelphia, Pennsylvania

Rustambek Abdullaev
Tashkent Institute of Fine Arts and Design
Tashkent, Uzbekistan

Ezekiel Alembi
Kenyatta University
Nairobi, Kenya

Martha G. Anderson
Alfred University
Alfred, New York

Richard W. Anderson
Oregon State University
Corvallis, Oregon

Galiev Anuar
Kazakh State University
Almaty, Kazakhstan

Temsula Ao
North East Hill University (NEHU)
Shillong, Meghalaya, India

Subhasini Aryan
Home of Folk Art
Gurgaon, Haryana, India

Camilla Asplund-Ingemark
Åbo Akademi University
Lund, Sweden

Chukwuma Azuonye
University of Massachusetts at Boston
Boston, Massachusetts

Robert Baron
New York State Council on the Arts
New York, New York
W.E.B. DuBois Institute of African and American Research
Harvard University
Cambridge, Massachusetts

Cynthia Becker
Boston University
Boston, Massachusetts

Margaret H. Beissinger
University of Wisconsin
Madison, Wisconsin

Mark Bender
Ohio State University
Columbus, Ohio

Gillian Bennett
Folklore Society
London, England, United Kingdom

Niko Besnier
University of California, Los Angeles
Los Angeles, California

S. Elizabeth Bird
University of South Florida
Tampa, Florida

Stephanie Rose Bird
Oak Park, Illinois

Ágnes Birtalan
Eötvös Loránd University
Budapest, Hungary

Anne Leonora Blaakilde
Danish Institute of Gerontology
Copenhagen, Denmark

Marta Botiková
Comenius University
Bratislava, Slovakia

Gian Luigi Bravo
University of Turin
Turin, Italy

Simon J. Bronner
Pennsylvania State University, Harrisburg
Middletown, Pennsylvania

Naomi Brun
McMaster University
Hamilton, Ontario, Canada

Anna Brzozowska-Krajka
Maria Curie-Skłodowska University
Lublin, Poland

Margaret Buckner
Missouri State University
Springfield, Missouri

Raymond A. Bucko, S. J.
Creighton University
Omaha, Nebraska

Mary E. Lawson Burke
Framingham State College
Framingham, Massachusetts

Richard Allen Burns
Arkansas State University
State University, Arkansas

John W. Burton
Connecticut College
New London, Connecticut

Erik Camayd-Freixas
Florida International University
Miami, Florida

Shirley F. Campbell
Australian National University
Canberra, Australia

Robert Cancel
University of California at San Diego
La Jolla, California

Kenneth L. Carriveau Jr.
Baylor University
Waco, Texas

Ray Cashman
University of Alabama at Birmingham
Birmingham, Alabama

Steven C. Caton
Harvard University
Cambridge, Massachusetts

Ileana Citaristi
Art Vision
Bhubaneswar, Orissa, India

Peter J. Claus
California State University, Hayward (Emeritus)
Hayward, California

William M. Clements
Arkansas State University
State University, Arkansas

Chip Colwell-Chanthaphonh
Center for Desert Archaeology
Tucson, Arizona

Phyllis M. Correa
Universidad Autónoma de Querétaro
Querétaro, Mexico

David R. Counts
Oyama, British Columbia, Canada

Dorothy Ayers Counts
Oyama, British Columbia, Canada

Yvonne Creswell
Manx National Heritage
Douglas, Isle of Man, British Isles

Kathy Curnow
Cleveland State University
Cleveland, Ohio

Elguja Dadunashvili
Georgian Academy of Sciences
Tbilisi, Georgia

Gabriella D'Agostino
Università di Palermo
Palermo, Sicily, Italy

Birendranath Datta
Gawuhati University
Tezpur University
Guwahati, Assam, India

Nora Marks Dauenhauer
Juneau, Alaska

Richard Dauenhauer
Juneau, Alaska

Frank De Caro
Louisiana State University
Baton Rouge, Louisiana

Guillermo De Los Reyes
University of Houston
Houston, Texas

Robert Knox Dentan
State University of New York at Buffalo
Buffalo, New York

Thérèse de Vet
University of Arizona
Tucson, Arizona

Erwan Dianteill
EHESS
Paris, France

James R. Dow
Iowa State University
Ames, Iowa

Barbara R. Duncan
Museum of the Cherokee Indian
Cherokee, North Carolina

Arbnora Dushi
Institute of Albanology
Prishtinë, Kosova

Meredith Filihia
La Trobe University
Melbourne, Australia

Elizabeth C. Fine
Virginia Polytechnic Institute and State University
Blacksburg, Virginia

Annette B. Fromm
The Deering Estate at Cutler
Miami, Florida

Nicola Frost
Goldsmith's College, University of London
London, United Kingdom

Ulugbek Ganiev
Tashkent Institute of Fine Arts and Design
Tashkent, Uzbekistan

Andrew L. Giarelli
Portland State University
Portland, Oregon

Christine Goldberg
University of California, Los Angeles
Los Angeles, California

Stefan Goodwin
Morgan State University (Emeritus)
Baltimore, Maryland

Uddipana Goswami
Centre for Northeast India
South and Southeast Asia Studies
Giwahati, Assam, India

Laura R. Graham
University of Iowa
Iowa City, Iowa

Piercarlo Grimaldi
University of Eastern Piedmont
Vercelli, Italy

Mathias Guenther
Wilfrid Laurier University
Waterloo, Ontario, Canada

Terry Gunnell
University of Iceland
Reykjavík, Iceland

Mon'im Haddad
Al-Boqai'a, Israel

Lalita Handoo
Central Institute of Indian Languages
Mysore, Karnataka, India

Gregory Hansen
Arkansas State University
State University, Arkansas

Lee Haring
Brooklyn College (Emeritus)
Brooklyn, New York

Galit Hasan-Rokem
Hebrew University
Jerusalem, Israel

Patricia Haseltine
Providence University
Shalu Taichung, Taiwan, Republic of China

Terence E. Hays
Rhode Island College
Providence, Rhode Island

Elissa R. Henken
University of Georgia
Athens, Georgia

Maria Hnaraki
Cornell University
Ithaca, New York

Mary Hufford
University of Pennsylvania
Philadelphia, Pennsylvania

Charles Illouz
University of La Rochelle
La Rochelle, France

Linda J. Ivanits
The Pennsylvania State University
University Park, Pennsylvania

Jason Baird Jackson
Indiana University
Bloomington, Indiana

Lisette Josephides
Queen's University
Belfast, Northern Ireland, United Kingdom

Francisco Josivan
Faculdades Integradas Claretians
São Paulo, Brazil

Molly Kaushal
Indira Gandhi National Centre for the Arts
New Delhi, India

Daniel A. Kelin II
Honolulu Theatre for Youth
Honolulu, Hawai'i

Doreen Helen Klassen
Sir Wilfred Grenfell College
Corner Brook, Newfoundland, Canada

Barbro Klein
The Swedish Collegium for Advanced Study in the Social Sciences (SCASSS)
Uppsala, Sweden

Natalie Kononenko
University of Alberta
Edmonton, Alberta, Canada

Philip G. Kreyenbroek
Georg-August-Universität Göttingen
Göttingen, Germany

S. A. Krishnaiah
MGM College Campus
Udupi, Karnataka, India

Lars Krutak
Arizona State University
Tempe, Arizona

Belma Kurtişoğlu
İstanbul Technical University
Turkish Music State Conservatory
İstanbul, Turkey

Bülent Kurtişoğlu
İstanbul Technical University
Turkish Music State Conservatory
İstanbul, Turkey

Reimund Kvideland
University of Bergen
Bergen, Norway

Ermis Lafazanovski
Institute of Folklore
Skoje, Macedonia

Guy Lancaster
Arkansas Encyclopedia of History and Culture
Little Rock, Arkansas

Luke Eric Lassiter
Marshall University
Charleston, West Virginia

Kimberly J. Lau
University of Utah
Salt Lake City, Utah

John Laudun
University of Louisiana
Lafayette, Louisiana

Anthony Layng
Wake Forest University
Winston-Salem, North Carolina

Nathan Light
University of Toledo
Toledo, Ohio

Lamont Lindstrom
University of Tulsa
Tulsa, Oklahoma

Ron Loewe
Mississippi State University
Starkville, Mississippi

Ernesto Lombeida
Arkansas State University
State University, Arkansas

Ivan Lozica
Institute of Ethnology and Folklore Research
Zagreb, Croatia

Elke Mader
University of Vienna
Vienna, Austria

Jeannette Marie Mageo
Washington State University
Pullman, Washington

Frances M. Malpezzi
Arkansas State University
State University, Arkansas

Pierre Maranda
Université Laval
Québec, Québec, Canada

Laura R. Marcus
Santa Fe, New Mexico

Peter Jan Margry
Meertens Institute
Amsterdam, The Netherlands

Ntongela Masilela
Pitzer College
Claremont, California

Gregory G. Maskarinec
University of Hawai'i
Honolulu, Hawai'i

Stein R. Mathisen
Finnmark University College
Alta, Norway

Max Matter
Institut für Volkskunde der Albert-Ludwigs-Universität
Freiburg, Germany

Joseph L. Mbele
St. Olaf College
Northfield, Minnesota

John Holmes McDowell
Indiana University
Bloomington, Indiana

Thomas S. McIlwain
University of Stockholm
Stockholm, Sweden

Thomas A. McKean
University of Aberdeen
Aberdeen, Scotland

Lisa McNee
Queen's University
Kingston, Ontario, Canada

William L. Merrill
Smithsonian Institution
Washington, D.C.

Clyde A. Milner II
Arkansas State University
State University, Arkansas

Mustafa Kemal Mirzeler
Western Michigan University
Kalamazoo, Michigan

Tom Mould
Elon University
Elon, North Carolina

Jane Freeman Moulin
University of Hawai'i at Manoa
Honolulu, Hawai'i

Francesca M. Muccini
Arkansas State University
State University, Arkansas

Patrick B. Mullen
The Ohio State University
Columbus, Ohio

William J. Nichols
Georgia State University
Atlanta, Georgia

Johnston Akuma-Kalu Njoku
Western Kentucky University
Bowling Green, Kentucky

Ranjini Obeyesekere
Princeton University
Princeton, New Jersey

Ted Olson
East Tennessee State University
Johnston City, Tennessee

Mahmoud Omidsalar
California State University
Los Angeles, California

Low Kok On
Universiti Malaysia Sabah
Labuan International Campus
Labuan, Malaysia

Carme Oriol
Rovira i Virgili University
Tarragona, Catalonia, Spain

Gus Palmer Jr.
University of Oklahoma
Norman, Oklahoma

Hwan-Young Park
Chung-Ang University
Seoul, Korea

Richard J. Parmentier
Brandeis University
Waltham, Massachusetts

Patricia H. Partnow
Partnow Consulting
Anchorage, Alaska

Dorji Penjore
Centre for Bhutan Studies
Thimphu, Bhutan

Benedito Prezia
Faculdades Integradas Claretianas
São Paulo, Brazil

Richard Price
College of William and Mary
Williamsburg, Virginia

Sally Price
College of William and Mary
Williamsburg, Virginia

Ravshan Rahmonov
Tajik State National University
Dushanbe, Tajikistan

Dilshod Rakhimov
Tajik State Institute of Arts
Dushanbe, Tajikistan

Mojca Ramšak
Center for Biographic Research
Ljubljana, Slovenia

Susan J. Rasmussen
University of Houston
Houston, Texas

Celeste Ray
University of the South
Sewanee, Tennessee

Rebecca Read
Mississippi State University
Starkville, Mississippi

Beatrise Reidzane
Institute of Literature, Folklore, and Art
Rīga, Latvia

Alfons Roeck
Catholic University of Leuven
Leuven, Belgium

Klaus Roth
Universität München
Munich, Germany

Robert A. Rothstein
University of Massachusetts
Amherst, Massachusetts

Steven Rubenstein
Ohio University
Athens, Ohio

John S. Ryan
University of New England
Armidale, New South Wales, Australia

Sarita Sahay
Oakleigh East, Victoria, Australia

Frank Salamone
Iona College
New Rochelle, New York

Glauco Sanga
Università Ca' Foscari
Venice, Italy

Harold Scheub
University of Wisconsin
Madison, Wisconsin

Ropo Sekoni
Lincoln University
Lincoln University, Pennsylvania

Soumen Sen
North-Eastern Hill University
Shillong, Meghalaya, India

Jacqueline Simpson
The Folklore Society
London, England

Thomas Solomon
University of Bergen
Bergen, Norway

Birgitte Sonne
University of Copenhagen
Copenhagen, Denmark

Pamela J. Stewart
University of Pittsburgh
Pittsburgh, Pennsylvania

Kathleen Stokker
Luther College
Decorah, Iowa

Monique R. Carriveau Storie
University of Guam
Mangilao, Guam

Andrew Strathern
University of Pittsburgh
Pittsburgh, Pennsylvania

Pauline Turner Strong
University of Texas
Austin, Texas

Alexandre Surrallés
Centre national de la recherche scientifique
Laboratoire d'anthropologie sociale
Paris, France

Vinson H. Sutlive Jr.
The College of William and Mary
Williamsburg, Virginia

Verjiné Svazlian
Institute of Archaeology and Ethnography
National Academy of Sciences
Yerevan, Armenia

Michael Taft
Archive of Folk Culture
American Folklife Center
Library of Congress
Washington, D.C.

James M. Taggart
Franklin and Marshall College
Lancaster, Pennsylvania

Laura Tanna
African Caribbean Institute of Jamaica (1983–1997)
Jamaica Memory Bank (1982–1997)
Miami, Florida

Jean-Pierre Taoutel
Iowa State University
Ames, Iowa

Noriah Taslim
Universiti Sains Malaysia
11800 Minden
P. Pinang, Malaysia

Jeannie Banks Thomas
Utah State University
Logan, Utah

Lana Thompson
Florida Atlantic University
Boca Raton, Florida

Jeff Todd Titon
Brown University
Providence, Rhode Island

Wajuppa Tossa
Mahasarakham University
Mahasarakham, Thailand

Rainer Tredt
Katholische Universität Eichstätt-Ingolstadt
Eichstätt, Germany

Luqman Turgut
Georg-August-Universität Göttingen
Göttingen, Germany

Natalie Underberg
University of Central Florida
Orlando, Florida

Eugene Valentine
Arizona State University
Tempe, Arizona

Kristin B. Valentine
Arizona State University
Tempe, Arizona

Rand Valentine
University of Wisconsin
Madison, Wisconsin

Kira Van Deusen
Bellingham, Washington

Juracilda Veiga
Center for Indigenous Culture and Education
São Paulo, Brazil

Fabio Viti
Università degli Studi di Modena e Reggio Emilia
Modena and Reggio Emilia, Italy

Vilmos Voigt
ELTE University
Budapest, Hungary

Susan S. Wadley
Syracuse University
Syracuse, New York

Deward E. Walker Jr.
University of Colorado
Boulder, Colorado

Frederick White
Slippery Rock University
Slippery Rock, Pennsylvania

Linda White
University of Nevada
Reno, Nevada

Kahikāhealani Wight
University of Hawai'i
Honolulu, Hawai'i

Lois Wilcken
La Troupe Makandal/City Lore
Brooklyn, New York

Takako Yamada
Kyoto University
Kyoto, Japan

Juwen Zhang
Willamette University
Salem, Oregon

Zora D. Zimmerman
Iowa State University
Ames, Iowa

Translators

Scott Darwin
Arkansas State University
State University, Arkansas

Marta Innocenti
Bologna, Italy

Ernesto Lombeida
Arkansas State University
State University, Arkansas

Don Mader
Amsterdam, The Netherlands

Francesca M. Muccini
Arkansas State University
State University, Arkansas

Robert A. Orr
Ottawa, Canada

Tigran Tsulikian
Yerevan, Armenia

David Wick
Arkansas State University
State University, Arkansas

Cumulative Index

American Folklife Preservation Act, **1**:77

American Folklore Scholarship: A Dialogue of Dissent (Zumwalt), **1**:13

American Folklore Society (AFS), **1**:5, 6, 13, 30, 84

American Indians, **4**:1–142

American Romani weddings, **3**:401

Amirani (Georgia), **3**:356

Amulets: Ashkenazim, **3**:332, 338; Berber, **1**:103–105, 107, 109; Denmark, **3**:83; England, **3**:1; Galicia, **3**:203; Greenland, **3**:109–110; Israel, **2**:380; Kiribati, **1**:343, 347; Kurds, **2**:385; Russia, **3**:412; Sephardim, **3**:213; Tajik, **2**:333; Tlingit, **4**:118; Tuareg, **1**:117, 119; Wolof, **1**:211

"Analog" copies, **1**:4–5

Analytical Survey of Anglo-American Traditional Erotica (Hoffmann), **1**:56

Anansi (Jamaica), **4**:341

Anatsui, El, **1**:201

Ancestors and dead: Ainu, **2**:288, 290, 291–292; Albania, **3**:326, 327; Ashkenazim, **3**:333, 334; Australian Aborigines, **1**:293–294, 297, 298; Austria, **3**:253–255; Bali, **2**:159–160; Baule, **1**:164; Benin, **1**:174–176, 178; Brittany, **3**:171, 172; Caribs of Dominica, **4**:332–333; Catalan, **3**:200; China, **2**:213; Chinese living abroad, **2**:235, 238–239; Duna, **2**:166; Ecuador, **4**:197–198; England, **3**:1, 6, 13, 19; Ga, **1**:181–182; Gaddi, **2**:36; Galicia, **3**:206–207; Germany, **3**:269; Guam, **1**:337–338; Haiti, **4**:318; Hawai'i, **1**:368; Hopi, **4**:45–46; Hungary, **3**:278; Iban, **2**:173, 174–175; Igbo, **1**:199; Ireland, **3**:27, 34; Isaan, **2**:132–134; Israel, **2**:377, 379; Japan, **2**:273, 276; Kadazandusun, **2**:176; Kaingang, **4**:194; Kaliai, **2**:183–184, 186; Kashmir, **2**:61; Khasi-Jaintia, **2**:67, 72–73; Kiribati, **1**:342; Korea, **2**:296–298, 302, 303; Lunda, **1**:235–236, 239; Madagascar, **1**:139; Maluku, **2**:202; Manchu, **2**:250; Maroons of Jamaica, **4**:339–340; Marquesas Islands, **1**:380; Marshall Islands, **1**:351; Mexico, **4**:271–273; Nepal, **2**:117; New Caledonia, **1**:311, 312; Norway, **3**:127, 128, 132; Orissa, **2**:83, 87; Palestine, **2**:407; Persia, **2**:423; Piedmont and Val d'Aosta, **3**:477; Poland, **3**:385–386, 388; Roma, **3**:401, 402, 406; Russia, **3**:412, 413, 416; San, **1**:242–246; Semai, **2**:148; Shona, **1**:251; Sibundoy, **4**:230–231; Sicily, **3**:490; Slovakia, **3**:290; Tairora, **2**:206, 207; Taiwan, **2**:261, 266; Tlingit, **4**:122–123; Ukraine, **3**:440, 445; Vanuatu, **1**:327, 328; Xavante, **4**:247; Yoruba, **1**:224, 225; Zande, **1**:229, 232. *See also* Funerals and burials

Andersen, Hans Christian, **3**:12, 85

Anderson, Benedict, **2**:278

Anderson, Hugh, **1**:285

Anderson, Walter, **3**:196

Andes: Quechua, **4**:208–209; Sibundoy, **4**:229–230

Andrew, Saint, **3**:206, 289, 349, 388

Anecdotes: Albania, **3**:328, 329; Australia (British), **1**:286, 287; Bali, **2**:163; Cheyenne, **4**:29; China, **2**:222; England, **3**:6, 9, 10, 13; Guam, **1**:337, 339; Ireland, **3**:38–39; Kashmir, **2**:61; Latvia, **3**:362; Macedonia, **3**:372; Manchu, **2**:248; Marshall Islands, **1**:351; Maya, **4**:259; Poland, **3**:380, 392; Roma, **3**:406; Russia, **3**:420; Siberia, **2**:322; Sicily, **3**:491; Slovakia, **3**:292; Tajik, **2**:326; Turkey, **2**:432; Uyghur, **2**:339, 340; Wales, **3**:75, 76–77; Western Inuit and Yupik, **4**:133; Xhosa, **1**:259, 260

Anglicanism in Australia, **1**:278

Aniakor, Chike, **1**:201

Animal dances: Cherokee, **4**:15; Cheyenne, **4**:28; Choctaw, **4**:33

"The Animal Languages" (Mascarene Islands), **1**:146

Animism and animal tales, **1**:94; Ainu, **2**:287–288; Australian Aborigines, **1**:293–296; Bali, **2**:152, 160; Bangladesh, **2**:96, 103; Benin, **1**:177; Caribs of Dominica, **4**:332–333; Cherokee, **4**:12–13; Cheyenne, **4**:26–27; China, **2**:213; Ga, **1**:184; Guam, **1**:335–336; Haiti, **4**:320; Hawai'i, **1**:368; Iban, **2**:173; Igbo, **1**:195–196; Iroquois, **4**:55–56; Italy, **3**:472; Lakota, **4**:71–72; Lunda, **1**:237–238; Malaita, **1**:302; Malay, **2**:142; Maya, **4**:259; Mongol, **2**:256–257; Nahua, **4**:283–284; Nez Perce, **4**:100–101; Nuer, **1**:153; Palau, **1**:360–361; Peru, **4**:202; Poland, **3**:381; Quechua, **4**:210; Rarámuri, **4**:301; Russia, **3**:418–419; Samoa, **1**:394; San, **1**:242–247; Shona, **1**:250, 253; Siberia, **2**:316–319; Sibundoy, **4**:232; Suriname Maroons, **4**:238; Tlingit, **4**:121–123; Trobriand Islands, **1**:317; Western Inuit and Yupik, rapport with, **4**:134; Wolof, **1**:216; Xavante, **4**:250; Yanomami, **4**:253–254; Yoruba, **1**:219, 223–224; Zande, **1**:230–231. *See also specific types of animals*

Ankou (death, Brittany), **3**:171–172

Ankrah, Roy, **1**:186

Anne of Austria, **3**:164

"Annual Bibliography," **1**:5

"Annual Folklore Bibliography," **1**:5

Anthony the Abbot, Saint, **3**:470–471

Antiquarianism, **1**:1–3; and museums, **1**:57

Antiquitates Vulgares (Bourne), **1**:1, 2

Antiquities, **1**:1–3

The ANZAC Book (Australia [British]), **1**:285

Apache, **4**:1–8; arts and crafts, **4**:6; geography and history, **4**:1–3; modernization, challenges of, **4**:6–7; rituals and ceremonies, **4**:5–6; stories and tales, **4**:3–4; studies of Apache folklore, **4**:7

Apache Wars, **4**:3

Apartheid: Xhosa, **1**:258, 262; Zulu, **1**:269

ap Nudd, Gwyn, **3**:74

Apollonia, Saint, **3**:229

Appadurai, Arjun, **1**:42

Appalachia, **4**:156–166; architecture, **4**:163–164; arts and crafts, **4**:164; dance and drama, **4**:161–162; festivals and celebrations, **4**:161; food, **4**:164; geography and history, **4**:156–158; and invented tradition, **1**:51; modernization, challenges of, **1**:79, **4**:165; myths, legends, and folktales, **4**:159–160; and race, **1**:79; religious beliefs, **4**:158–159; songs, ballads, and music, **1**:79, **4**:160–161; sports and games, **4**:162–163; studies of Appalachian folklore, **4**:165

"Applied folklore," **1**:77

Aqa Jamal, **2**:425

Arabian Nights, **3**:12

Arabic language (Berber), **1**:101

Arabs: Berber influenced by, **1**:101–103; Spain influenced by, **3**:180, 182. *See also* Palestine

Archaisms in Macedonian legends, **3**:372

Architecture: African Americans, **4**:153–154; American southwest, **1**:39; Appalachia, **4**:163–164; Ashkenazim, **3**:338; Australia (British), **1**:282–283; Austria, **3**:257–259; Bangladesh, **2**:102; Benin, **1**:176; Bhutan, **2**:111–112; Caipira, **4**:180; Cherokee, **4**:18–19; China, **2**:226–228; Chinese living abroad, **2**:242; Flanders (Belgium), **3**:232; Igbo, **1**:200–201; Jamaica, **4**:337; Japan, **2**:278; Kazakh, **2**:313; Maluku, **2**:201–202; Mississippi Delta, **4**:167; Moorish, **3**:218; The Netherlands, **3**:244–245; Shona, **1**:253–254; Slovenia, **3**:303–304; Sri Lanka, **2**:128–130; Ukraine, **3**:446–447; Uyghur, **2**:344; Vanuatu, **1**:330–331. *See also* Housing

Archives, **1**:3–5; Latvia, **3**:364; and modernization, **1**:52; and repertoire, **1**:82

Arctic region: Western Inuit and Yupik, **4**:128–131

Arendt, Hannah, **1**:29–30

Arhuaran (son of Oba Ozolua), **1**:177

Ari fróði (the Learned), **3**:113

Arizona: Apache, **4**:1–3; Hopi, **4**:44–45; Navajo, **4**:82–83

Arjuna, **2**:40

Armenia, **2**:357–372; epics and historical narratives, **2**:359–362; geography and history, **2**:357–359; modernization, challenges of, **2**:369; songs and legends, **2**:362–369

Armes Prydein (poem), **3**:73

Arminius, **3**:268

Armor. *See* Weapons and armor

Arnamagnean Institute, **3**:114, 115

Arngrímur Jónsson the Learned, **3**:116

Arnim, Achim von, **3**:312

3:168–169; Galicia, 3:206–208; Germany, 3:262–265; Hopi, 4:47; Hungary, 3:281–282; Ireland, 3:26–27; Isle of Man, 3:47–51; Kiowa, 4:66; Korea, 2:301; Maya, 4:257; Mexico, 4:272; Navajo, 4:89; Nepal, 2:120; The Netherlands, 3:241–243; Palestine, 2:404; Persia, 2:423; Peru, 4:204–205; Piedmont and Val d'Aosta, 3:474–477; Poland, 3:386–388; Quechua, 4:211–212; Rarámuri, 4:299; Roma, 3:403–404; Russia, 3:415–417; Scotland, 3:64–66; Serbia, 3:429–432; Sicily, 3:487–489; Slovakia, 3:289–290; Slovenia, 3:296–299; Switzerland, 3:314–317

Calendimaggio (May Day feast), 3:475

California: Australia (British) social influence by, 1:278; Proposition 187 to limit public services to non-citizens, 1:66

Call-and-response stories: Ga, 1:185, 191; Guam, 1:338; Igbo, 1:196; Lunda, 1:236; Shona, 1:250, 253; Wolof, 1:216; Yoruba, 1:218, 221; Zande, 1:233

Callaway, Henry, 1:270, 271, 273

Callegari, Adriano, 3:460

Calvin, 3:238

Camayd-Freixas, Erik, 1:74

Camés (Kaingang myth), 4:195–196

Campbell, J.F., 3:114

Campos, Rubén, 4:279

Cana'an, Tawfiq, 2:411

Canada: Haida, 4:38–39; Iroquois, 4:50–51; Ojibwe, 4:103–105; Tlingit, 4:117; Western Inuit and Yupik, 4:128–131

Canales, Antonio, 3:185

Candoshi, 4:181–187; geography and history, 4:181–182; religious beliefs, rituals, and celebrations, 4:182–185; songs and music, 4:185–187; studies of Candoshi folklore, 4:187

Cannibalism: Haiti, 4:318; Yanomami, 4:253, 254

Canoes: Ainu (Japan), 2:291; Benin, 1:174; Hawai'i, 1:373, 375; Ijo, 1:207, 208; Kaliai, 2:183; Kiribati, 1:342, 343, 347; Malaita, 1:306; Maluku, 2:202; Marshall Islands, 1:355; Palau, 1:361, 363; Seminole, 4:115; Tlingit, 4:126; Trobriand Islands, 1:321–322, 324; Tuvalu, 1:409

Cantomble (Brazil), 1:79

Canzuna (folksong, Sicily), 3:485

Capitalism, 1:42

Capmany, Aureli, 3:196

Capping (African American), 4:150

Captain Cook Chased a Chook: Children's Folklore in Australia, 1:284

"The Captain of the Push" (Australia [British]), 1:285

Caracalla, Abdel Halim, 2:397

Card games: China, 2:226, 242; Persia, 2:424; Rarámuri, 4:305; Slovakia, 3:293, 294

Caribs of Dominica, 4:329–336; folk medicine, 4:333–334; folktales, 4:331–333; geography and history, 4:329–331; witchcraft and magic, 4:334–336

Carlos IV, 3:186

Carlyle, Thomas, 1:46

Carnival: Catalan, 3:197; Croatia, 3:348, 349; Cuba, 4:311; Flanders, 3:227; Galicia, 3:206; Georgia, 3:360; Hungary, 3:282; Italy, 3:457, 464; Piedmont and Val d'Aosta, 3:471, 472, 474; Poland, 3:387; Quechua, 4:210–211, 213; Sibundoy, 4:234–235; Sicily, 3:488; Slovakia, 3:289. See also Mardi Gras

Carnival societies (Switzerland), 3:316

Carolina Sea Islanders, 1:20

Caroline Islands, 1:333, 339

Carpenter, Inta Gale, 1:82

Carpitella, Diego, 3:461

Carribean, 4:309–347

Carucci, Laurence, 1:353

Carving and sculpture: Australian Aborigines, 1:297; Baule, 1:164, 167; Cherokee, 4:18; Ecuador, 4:192; Guam, 1:339; Haida, 4:42; Haiti, 4:324, 325; Hawai'i, 1:374; Igbo, 1:201; Ijo, 1:205; Marquesas Islands, 1:378, 383–384; Navajo, 4:91–92; Palau, 1:359–360, 364; Shona, 1:253, 254; Suriname Maroons, 4:241; Tlingit, 4:126; Tonga, 1:402; Trobriand Islands, 1:320, 324; Western Inuit and Yupik, 4:138; Wolof, 1:213; Yoruba, 1:225; Zande, 1:233

Caseponce, Esteve, 3:195

Casimir the Great, 3:381

Cassian, John, 3:160, 439

Castelló i Guasch, Joan, 3:195

Caste system. See Social structure

del Castillo, Bernal Díaz, 4:275

"The Castle of Dimdim" (Kurds), 2:387

Catalan, 3:195–201; calendars, 3:199; festivals and celebrations, 3:197–198; food, 3:199–200; geography and history, 3:195–197; music and dance, 3:198–199

Catherine, Saint, 3:164, 388

Catherine the Great, 3:409

Catholicism: and Afro-Cuban myths, 4:314; anti-Catholic nativism in U.S., 1:65; Australia (British), 1:278, 280–281, 289; Caribs of Dominica, 4:331–332; Chinese living abroad, 2:239; France, 3:161, 166, 167; Haiti, 4:318–319; immigrants to U.S., 1:66; Kewa, 2:189; Kiribati, 1:341, 348; Latvia, 3:365–366; Maluki, 2:198; Marquesas Islands, 1:380; Mauritius and Rodrigues, 1:145; Mexico, 4:269–271; Otomí, 4:290; Peru, 4:200–202, 206; Quechua, 4:209; Rarámuri, 4:297–300, 302; Réunion, 1:148; Sertão, 4:217, 218; The Seychelles, 1:149; Shuar, 4:220–221;

Sibundoy, 4:230, 234–235; Spain, 3:180–182; Sri Lanka, 2:125, 126, 128; Taiwan, 2:261; Tonga, 1:401; Turkey, 2:430; Tuvalu, 1:405. See also Christianity

Cattle: India, sacredness of, 2:13; Jie, importance to, 1:132–135; Nuer, importance to, 1:150, 153

"The Cattle-Killing" (Xhosa), 1:264

Cattleshed as community gathering-place, 3:473

Cauld Blast Orchestra, 3:66

Cautionary tales, Isle of Man, 3:46–47

Cayurucrés (Kaingang myth), 4:195–196

Céilidh (visiting house), 3:26, 57, 117

Celebrations. See Festivals and celebrations

Celtic influence, 3:70; Brittany, 3:171–173; England, 3:4–5; France, 3:158–159; Galicia, 3:203; Iceland, 3:112; Ireland, 3:23, 34; Piedmont and Val d'Aosta, 3:474; Spain, 3:179; Wales, 3:72, 75

Cemetery rites. See Funerals and burials

A Centennial Index (American Folklore Society), 1:6

Central Africa. See Western and Central Africa

Central America, 4:256–308

Cepenkov, Marco, 3:372

Ceramics: Australian Aborigines, 1:297; Baule, 1:163; Berber, 1:109, 111; Caipira, 4:179; Candoshi, 4:186; Cherokee, 4:17–18; Hopi, 4:49–50; Igbo, 1:201; Iroquois, 4:52; Lakota, 4:75; Mexico, 4:272; Navajo, 4:91, 92; Shona, 1:253; Tajik, 2:330–331; Turkey, 2:436–437; Uzbek, 2:354; Vanuatu, 1:330; Yoruba, 1:226

Ceremonies. See Rituals and ceremonies

Cernunnos, 3:171

Cervantes, Miguel de, 3:183

Cetshawayo (Zulu king), 1:269

Cha cha cha (Cuba), 4:312

Ch'a-don Lee, 2:299

Chadwick, Nora, 3:173

Chagnon, Napoleon, 4:251–252

Chain structure, tales (Russia), 3:419

Chameleon as theme (Yoruba), 1:222

Chamisso, Adelbert von, 1:350

Chamorros. See Guam

Chamula and worldview, 1:98

Changeling, fairy, 3:47

Chant of Urdmau (Palau), 1:362

Chants: Assam, 2:29; Benin, 1:178; Bhutan, 2:109; Ga, 1:191; Gaddi, 2:35, 36; Haryana, 2:40; Hawai'i, 1:366, 369–371, 375; Iban, 2:174, 175; Igbo, 1:197; Isaan, 2:134, 136–137; Kadazandusun, 2:178; Kashmir, 2:64; Kiribati, 1:344; Marquesas Islands, 1:381–382; Marshall Islands, 1:352; Palau, 1:360, 361–362; Samoa, 1:394; Shuar, 4:226; Yoruba, 1:222–223

Charioteers' folksongs, Sicily, 3:485–486

Charlemagne, 3:161–162, 167, 250, 261, 269

Charles II (England), 3:3, 15, 19

Charles, Thomas, 3:74

Charms and spells: England, **3:**9; Greenland, **3:**109–110; Jamaica, **4:**343; Poland, **3:**382; Shuar, **4:**226. *See also* Incantations

Chaseworld: Foxhunting and Storytelling in New Jersey's Pine Barrens (Hufford), **1:**30

Chastushki (Russia), **3:**421

Cherokee, **4:**8–21; architecture, **4:**18–19; arts and crafts, **4:**17–18; festivals and ceremonies, **4:**15–16; food, **4:**19; geography, **4:**8; history, **4:**9–10; modernization, challenges of, **4:**20; music and song, **4:**14–15; myths, legends, and folktales, **4:**12–14; religious beliefs, **4:**11–12; social structure, **4:**9–10; studies of Cherokee folklore, **4:**20–21; writing system of, **1:**24, **4:**14

Cherokee Nation of Oklahoma, **4:**8

Cheyenne, **4:**21–30; arts and crafts, **4:**28; geography and history, **4:**21–23; modernization, challenges of, **4:**29; myths, legends, and folktales, **4:**25–26; religious beliefs and rituals, **4:**23–25; songs and dance, **4:**26–28; sports and games, **4:**28; studies of Cheyenne folklore, **4:**29–30

Chiang Kai-shek, **2:**260

Chickee (Seminole), **4:**114

Child, Francis James, **1:**94, **3:**13, 59

Childbirth and birth rituals: Abanyole, **1:**125; Albania, **3:**325; Ashkenazim, **3:**332–333; Bali, **2:**156; Chinese living abroad, **2:**236; Croatia, **3:**348; Gaddi, **2:**36; Igbo, **1:**196; Jie, **1:**134; Kashmir, **2:**61; Korea, **2:**298; Malaita, **1:**305; Malta, **3:**505–506; Nepal, **2:**115–116; Orissa, **2:**83; Palestine, **2:**404, 406; Persia, **2:**418–421; Poland, **3:**384–385; Roma, **3:**397; Samoa, **1:**393; Seminole, **4:**114; Tairora, **2:**204; Taiwan, **2:**263; Tajik, **2:**333; Ukraine, **1:**444; Vanuatu, **1:**329; Yoruba, **1:**223. *See also* Baptism; Circumcision

Child naming: Abanyole, **1:**125; Ashkenazim, **3:**333; Bangladesh, **2:**104; Benin, **1:**177; Berber, **1:**104; and ethnicity, **1:**26; Greece, **3:**495–496; Khasi-Jaintia, **2:**71; Malaita, **1:**306; Nagaland, **2:**78–79; Nepal, **2:**116; Samoa, **1:**387; Sephardim, **3:**220; Shona, **1:**250; Slovakia, **3:**291; Tuareg, **1:**104, 108; Yoruba, **1:**222

Children's Crusade, **3:**268

Children's games: Ashkenazim, **3:**337; Croatia, **3:**348; Denmark, **3:**86, 87; Greece, **3:**499–500; Haiti, **4:**325; Jamaica, **4:**341; Norway, **3:**131; Western Inuit and Yupik, **4:**133, 139–140; Xavante, **4:**244–245. *See also* Games, sports, and recreation

Children's songs, stories, and verses: Albania, **3:**328; Armenia, **2:**366; Australia (British), **1:**284; England, **3:**20; Finnish-Swedish, **3:**100–101; Ga, **1:**187–190; Italy, **3:**462; Jamaica, **4:**341; Malaita, **1:**301; Nagaland, **2:**77; Nez Perce, **4:**101–102; Palestine, **2:**409; Tuvalu, **1:**407; Uzbek, **2:**352; Vanuatu, **1:**330; Western Inuit and Yupik, **4:**133, 139–140

CHIME, **2:**231

China, **2:**211–233; arts, crafts, and architecture, **2:**226–228; clothing styles and food, **2:**228–229; drama, **2:**224–225; folksongs, **2:**218–221; folktales and legends, **2:**216–218; geography and history, **2:**211–213; India, comparison with, **2:**9; modernization, challenges of, **2:**229–231; music, **2:**222–223; myths, **2:**215–216; narrative poems, **2:**216; opera, **2:**224; oral folklore traditions, **2:**214–215; paper cutting, **2:**228; preserving Chinese folklore, **2:**214; religious beliefs, **2:**213–214; sports and games, **2:**225–226; storytelling and musical performance, **2:**221–222; studies of Chinese folklore, **2:**231

Chinese Exclusion Act (U.S. 1882), **1:**65

Chinese living abroad, **2:**233–245; anti-Chinese nativism, **1:**65; arts, crafts, and architecture, **2:**242; food and medicine, **2:**240–241; history, **2:**233–235; Mississippi Delta, **4:**173; modernization, challenges of, **2:**243; myths and folktales, **2:**241–242; religious beliefs, **2:**235–236; rituals, festivals, and celebrations, **2:**236–240; sports and games, **2:**242; studies of overseas Chinese folklore, **2:**243

Chingisizm, **2:**308

Chinoperl Papers, **2:**231

Chinyanta Shadrack Nankula (Mwata Kazembe XIV), **1:**235

CHIPAWO (Children's Performing Arts Workshop), **1:**254

Chippewa. *See* Ojibwe

Chivalrous combat in Georgian folktales, **3:**357

Choctaw, **4:**30–38; arts and crafts, **4:**32, 34–35; dance, **4:**33–34; geography and history, **4:**30–32; modernization, challenges of, **4:**37; myths, legends, and folktales, **4:**35–36; studies of Choctaw folklore, **4:**37–38; supernatural lore, **4:**36–37

Choctaw Fair, **4:**32–33

Choeten Zangmo, **2:**110

Chomsky, Noam, **1:**69

Choris, Louis, **1:**350

Christening ritual. *See* Baptism

Christian V, **3:**83

Christianity: African American, **4:**145; Armenia, **2:**357, 363, 368; Assam, **2:**18; Australia (British), **1:**289, 290; Bangladesh, **2:**95, 96; Baule, **1:**164; Benin, **1:**179; Bihar, **2:**25; Caipira, **4:**180; Candoshi, **4:**182; Caribs of Dominica, **4:**331–332; Cherokee, **4:**11; Cheyenne, **4:**24; China, **2:**213; Chinese living abroad, **2:**236, 239; Choctaw, **4:**37; Duna, **2:**166, 167; Ecuador, **4:**191–192; Guam, **1:**333, 337; Haiti, **4:**317–319, 321; Iroquois, **4:**59; Israel, **2:**372, 374; Jamaica, **4:**343; Kadazandusun, **2:**177, 181; Karnataka, **2:**48; Kazakh, **2:**308; Kewa, **2:**189, 196; Khasi-Jaintia, **2:**66, 73; Kiowa, **4:**62–63; Kurds, **2:**385, 389; Lakota, **4:**69;

Lebanon, **2:**392, 398, 399; Lunda, **1:**236; Malaita, **1:**301–303; Maluku, **2:**197, 198–199; Marquesas Islands, **1:**378, 380, 381; Maya, **4:**261; Mexico, **4:**269–270; Mongol, **2:**253; Navajo, **4:**87, 88; Nepal, **2:**114–115; New Caledonia, **1:**313; Ojibwe, **4:**109; Otomí, **4:**290–292; Palestine, **2:**401, 406; Peru, **4:**200–201, 205–206; Quechua, **4:**209; Rarámuri, **4:**297–298, 301–302; Samoa, **1:**394–396; Seminole, **4:**112; Shona, **1:**249, 252; Shuar, **4:**220, 224; Siberia, **2:**320; Sri Lanka, **2:**125, 126; Tairora, **2:**209; Taiwan, **2:**261; Tlingits, **4:**119; Tonga, **1:**399–401; Trobriand Islands, **1:**319–320; Turkey, **2:**430; Tuvalu, **1:**405; Vanuatu, **1:**325, 326–327; Western Inuit and Yupik, **4:**131–132; Xhosa, **1:**258, 260, 263, 266–267; Zande, **1:**228; Zulu, **1:**272

Christianity, early: Brittany, **3:**174; Denmark, **3:**83; England, **3:**4; Finland, **3:**90; France, **3:**160–161; Georgia, **3:**354; Germany, **3:**261; Hungary, **3:**279; Latvia, **3:**365–366; Macedonia, **3:**371; Malta, **3:**504; Poland, **3:**380; Russia, **3:**411–412, 415–417; Sámi, **3:**136; Scotland, **3:**55; Serbia, **3:**426, 429, 430; Slovakia, **3:**286–287; Ukraine, **3:**438; Wales, **3:**73

Christiansen, Reidar, **3:**137

Christmas customs: England, **1:**2; Jamaica, **4:**338; Russia, **3:**416; Serbia, **3:**431–432

Christmas tree (Austria), **3:**253

Chronological primitivism, **1:**73

Chulkov, M.D., **3:**410

Chunkey game (Cherokee), **4:**16–17

Churchill, Winston, **3:**38

Church of England, **1:**1–2

Ciarmavermi (magician, Sicily), **3:**490

"Cinderella," **1:**22, 95; England, **3:**12; Germany, **3:**266; Ireland, **3:**29; San, **1:**241

Circumcision: Abanyole, **1:**125; Bangladesh, **2:**104; Berber, **1:**108; and ethnicity, **1:**26; Palestine, **2:**406; Roma, **3:**398; Tajik, **2:**329, 333; Vanuatu, **1:**329; Wolof, **1:**211

Civilization and Its Discontents (Freud), **1:**74–75

Civil rights (Tlingits), **4:**126

Civil wars. *See* Wars and conflicts

Clans: Australian Aborigines, **1:**295; Brittany, **3:**174; Hopi, **4:**45–47; Iroquois, **4:**51; Japan, **2:**273, 275, 276; Jie, **1:**136; Kazakh, **2:**309; Kewa, **2:**189, 191; Khasi-Jaintia, **2:**67; Kiribati, **1:**341, 342; Malaita, **1:**301; Manchu, **2:**246; Marshall Islands, **1:**350; New Caledonia, **1:**310; Roma, **3:**397; Serbia, **3:**426; Tlingit, **4:**117; Trobriand Islands, **1:**316, 317; Tuareg, **1:**114; Wolof, **1:**214. *See also* Family relationships

Classes of society. *See* Social structure

The Classic of Mountains and Seas (China), **2:**215

Clavie (Scotland), **3:**65

Clavijero, Francisco, **4:**276

Cleansing ritual (Isle of Man), **3:**48

Cleverness. *See* Trickster
"The Clever Peasant Girl," 1:95; Mascarene Islands, 1:146
"Click Go the Shears" (Australia [British]), 1:286
Clifford, James, 1:48
Clinton, Bill, 2:381
Clothing: Austria, 3:258–259; Berber, 1:106; Cherokee, 4:18; China, 2:227, 228–229; and colonialism, 1:7–8; Gaddi, 2:35; Greece, 3:499; Hawai'i, 1:371–372; Iceland, 3:117–119; Igbo, 1:201–202; Ijo, 1:207; and invented tradition, 1:50; Kazakh, 2:312; Kiribati, 1:347; Lumba, 1:240; Malaita, 1:303, 304; Malta, 3:506; Manchu, 2:246, 250, 251; Marquesas Islands, 1:379, 384; Maya, 4:262–263; Norway, 3:130; Palestine, 2:407, 408; Seminole, 4:112–113; Siberia, 2:316, 323; Sibundoy, 4:234; Slovakia, 3:294; Tairora, 2:205, 208; Tajik, 2:331–332; Trobriand Islands, 1:324; Tuvalu, 1:409; Wales, 3:77; Western Inuit and Yupik, 4:130; Wolof, 1:212; Yoruba, 1:224–225
Clottey, Attuquaye, 1:186
Clovis, 3:161
Club War (Finland), 3:91
Coal miners and mining. *See* Miners and mining
Cockfighting: Bali, 2:161; Ecuador, 4:192; Iban, 2:175; Kadazandusun, 2:180. *See also* Games, sports, and recreation
"Codding" (expressive lying, Ireland), 3:37
Cohen, Erik, 1:86
Coleman, Simon, 1:86
Colenso, J.W. (bishop of Natal), 1:271, 274
Collier, Michael, 3:36
Collins, Samuel, 3:410
Colmcille, Saint, 3:30–31
Colombia: Sibundoy, 4:229–230
Colonialism, 1:7–10; and diaspora, 1:19; and ethnicity, 1:25; and Ga, 1:181; and globalization, 1:42; and Shona, 1:248; and Swahili, 1:154, 159, 160; and Zande, 1:228. *See also* British rule and influence; France; Spanish exploration and conquest
Comedia (Spanish drama), 3:184
Comedy. *See* Humorous stories, skits, etc.
Communication and translation, 1:89
The Comoros, 1:142–143; beliefs and folklore, 1:142–143; geography and history, 1:142
A Comparative Study of Kashmiri and Hindi Folksongs (Handoo), 2:62
Competence and performance, 1:69–70
Competition as theme (Swahili), 1:158, 159

Confucianism: China, 2:212–213; Chinese living abroad, 2:235, 236; Japan, 2:275, 276; Korea, 2:300; Taiwan, 2:261
"Confusion of Tongues" (Nagaland), 2:76
Conjuring. *See* Incantations
Conspiracy rumors (African American), 4:151
Constantine (Emperor), 3:160
Constantine VII Porphyrogenitus, 3:347
Constellation stories. *See* Astrology
Constitution (Mexico), 4:269
Contes du Temps passé, 3:266
Contests. *See* Games, sports, and recreation; Races
Contrary Dance (Cheyenne), 4:28
Cook, James, 1:309, 366, 374, 378
Cooking. *See* Food customs and beliefs
"The Coon in the Box" (African American), 4:144
Corn (Cherokee), 4:19
Coronado, Francisco Vásquez de, 4:1; and Hopi, 4:44
Corridos (Mexico), 4:273
Cortés, Hernán, 4:275–276
Cortés, Martín, 4:275–276
Cortez, Joaquín, 3:185
Corvinus, Matthias, 3:276
Cosmogonic myth (Poland), 3:380
Cosmology. *See* Worldview
Costumes. *See* Clothing; Masks and masquerades
Cotters, Denmark, 3:134
Council of Forty-Four (Cheyenne), 4:22–23, 25
Counter-Reformation (Italy), 3:457
Courtship: Appalachia, 4:161; Choctaw, 4:34; France, 3:163; Italy, 3:454; Kewa, 2:194; Lakota stories, 4:72; Scotland, 3:56; Shona, 1:250; Tlingit, 4:124
Coyote tales (Nez Perce), 4:100–103
"Cracker Night" (Australia [British]), 1:290
Cradleboards (Apache), 4:6
Crafts. *See* Arts and crafts
Crang, Mike, 1:86
Creation stories: Apache, 4:3–4; Armenia, 2:357; Australian Aborigines, 1:293–294, 297, 298; Bangladesh, 2:99; Cherokee, 4:11, 12; Cheyenne, 4:25–26; China, 2:215; Chinese living abroad, 2:235; Duna, 2:166, 168–169; Equador, 4:198–199; Gaddi, 2:32–34; Guam, 1:335; Haida, 4:40–42; Hawai'i, 1:366, 370; India, 2:5; Iroquois, 4:54, 56; Isaan, 2:135; Japan, 2:274; Kadazandusun, 2:177, 178; Kazakh, 2:307–309; Kewa, 2:191; Khasi-Jaintia, 2:67–68; Kiribati, 1:342; Korea, 2:295–296; Lakota and Dakota, 4:72; Malaita, 1:302; Malay, 2:142; Maluku, 2:198–199; Manchu, 2:247–248; Mescalero Apache, 4:4; Mongol, 2:255; Nagaland, 2:75, 77; Navajo, 4:85; Orissa, 2:80–81; Otomí, 4:290–293; Palau, 1:360–361; Palestine, 2:404; Persia, 2:414–416; Roma, 3:406; Samoa, 1:388–389; San, 1:242; Seminole, 4:115;

Siberia, 2:317–318; Tairora, 2:206–207; Tonga, 1:397, 400; Turkey, 2:432; Tuvalu, 1:406; Vanuatu, 1:328; Xavante, 4:249–250; Xhosa, 1:259–260; Yanomami, 4:252, 254; Zulu, 1:269–270
Creoles, 1:10–12; and Dominica, 4:330, 335–336
Creolization, 1:10–12; and Caribbean, 1:10; and globalization, 1:42; and hybridity, 1:47; and Indian Ocean, 1:10; and Latin America, 1:10; and Louisiana, 1:10; and Madagascar, 1:10; and Mascarene Islands, 1:144; and Mauritius and Rodrigues, 1:144, 146; and nativism, 1:65; and race, 1:78
Crick, M., 1:86
Criollos (Mexico), 4:275–276
Croatia, 3:341–352; Central, 3:345–346; history, 3:347–352; Littoral, 3:341–343; Lowland, 3:346–347; Mountainous, 3:343–344
Croatian Peasant Party, 3:351
Cromwell, Oliver, 3:3, 15, 36
Crooked Mick of the Speewah, 1:286
Crops. *See* Agriculture and farming
Crosh cuirns (Isle of Man), 3:47, 48
Cross-dressing. *See* Transvestites, transsexuals, cross-dressing
Crusades, 3:162–164, 365–366, 509
Cruz, San Juan de la, 3:181
Cuba, 4:309–315; and diaspora, 1:20; fusion of cultures, 4:315; geography and history, 4:309–310; music literature, 4:312–313; myths, legends, and folktales, 4:313–315; sacred music and dance, 4:310; secular music and dance, 4:311–312
Culin, Steward, 2:241–242
Cultural absolutism, 1:15
Cultural and Natural Areas of Native North America (Kroeber), 1:16
Cultural continuity of Greece, 3:494, 495
Cultural creolization, 1:10–11
Cultural evolution, 1:12–14; geology as influence, 1:12; and translation, 1:91
Cultural exceptionalism. *See* Nationalism
Cultural imperialism, 1:38
Cultural primitivism. *See* Primitivism
Cultural relativism, 1:14–16; Boas, Franz, 1:14–15; and cultural evolution, 1:14; and Plato, 1:14; and religion, 1:14
Cultural studies tradition, 1:72
Culture area, 1:16–18; and motif, 1:54, 55; and museum, 1:57. *See also* Geography
Cunning. *See* Trickster
Cunningham, Allan, 3:59
Cures. *See* Medicine and cures
Curutons (Kaingang myth), 4:196
Customs and Traditions of Palestine, 2:411
Cycles of life. *See* Life-cycle rituals and beliefs
Cyfarwyddiaid (storytellers, Wales), 3:72
Cyril, Saint, 3:371, 426, 429

Dabke dance (Lebanon), 2:395, 396–397
Dadié, Bernard, 1:168

Dainihonkoku Hokekyokenki (Buddhist tales, Japan), **2:**274

Dakota: "as-told-to" stories, **4:**73–74; geography and history, **4:**67–70; modernization, challenges of, **4:**75–76; music and songs, **4:**74, 77; myths, legends, and folktales, **4:**70; storytelling, **4:**73–74; vision talks, **4:**73; war stories, **4:**73

Dal, V.I., **3:**410

Dalí, Salvador, **3:**186

Damatian Klapa Festival (Croatia), **3:**343

Danaher, Kevin, **3:**23

Dance. *See* Music and dance

Danilov, Kirsha, **3:**410

Da-ño're (Xavante), **4:**246–248

Dansk Folke Museum, **1:**58

Daoism, **2:**217; China, **2:**213, 223; Chinese living abroad, **2:**236, 241; Japan, **2:**276; Taiwan, **2:**261, 268

Darcy, Les, **1:**286

Darkness khan (Mongol), **2:**255

Darwin, Charles, **1:**12

Das, Tulsi, **2:**92

Daun, Áke, **3:**150

Davenport, William Henry, **1:**353

David (Biblical King), **3:**357

David (Dewi), Saint, **3:**73–74

Davidson, Alan, **1:**11

David the Builder, **3:**357

Davies, Owen, **3:**10

Da-wawa (Xavante), **4:**248–249

Day of the Dead (Mexico), **4:**271, 272–273

Dayworkers, Italy, **3:**457

Dead. *See* Ancestors and dead

"Dead" water (Ukraine), **3:**444

Death and mourning rituals: Ashkenazim, **3:**333; Bhutan, **2:**110; Brittany, **3:**172; Croatia, **3:**349; Kiribati, **1:**343, 346; Madagascar, **1:**140; Malta, **3:**505; Marshall Islands, **1:**351; Nepal, **2:**116, 121; Réunion, **1:**148; Roma, **3:**401–402; Vanuatu, **1:**329; Yoruba, **1:**222; Zande, **1:**232. *See also* Funerals and burials

Death wedding (Ukraine), **3:**441

Décima (Cuban song form), **4:**312–313

Decolonization and diaspora, **1:**19

Deep Benin language (Benin), **1:**171

"Defiant girl" story (Mauritius and Rodrigues), **1:**146–147

Dégh, Linda, **1:**68, **3:**280, 283

Deities. *See* Gods and goddesses

DeKeyser, P., **3:**229

Delafosse, Maurice, **1:**165

Delargy, James, **3:**28

Delarue, Paul, **3:**196

Demographics: Assam, **2:**18–19; Bangladesh, **2:**95–96; Israel, **2:**278; Malta, **3:**506–507; Serbia, **3:**426; Swahili, **1:**158; Taiwan, **2:**260. *See also* History

Denmark, **3:**80–89; calendars, **3:**85–88; celebrations, **3:**88; geography and history, **3:**80–82; music and dance, **3:**85; religion

and beliefs, **3:**83; supernatural lore, **3:**83–85

Dennis, C.J., **1:**285

"The Derby Ram" (Australia [British]), **1:**285

Derwêshê Ebdî story (Kurds), **2:**388

A Description of the Isle of Man, **3:**43

Deutsche Gesellschaft für Volkskunde (German Folklore Society), **1:**6

Deutsche Legenden, **3:**267

"The Devil's Riddle," **1:**95

Devotional art, Sicily, **3:**489–490

Dhlomo, H.I.E., **1:**261

Dhola tale (Uttar Pradesh), **2:**91

Dhuwa (Australian Aborigines), **1:**295–296

Dialects: Assam, **2:**21; Bihar, **2:**30; Haryana, **2:**44. *See also* Creolization; Language

Diamondback rattlesnake motif (Choctaw), **4:**35

Días de los Muertos, **1:**7

Diaspora, **1:**18–22; Australia (British), **1:**281; and globalization, **1:**19, 21, 42; and hybridity, **1:**47; Jewish Diaspora, **1:**18–20; and race, **1:**78; Shona, **1:**254; Swahi, **1:**158; Vlach, John Michael, **1:**20

Díaz, Porfirio, **4:**278–279

Dice games: Cherokee, **4:**17; Peru, **4:**207. *See also* Gambling

Dickens, Charles, **3:**13

Diddley bows (Mississippi Delta), **4:**172

Diffusion, **1:**13, 22–24; and modernization, **1:**53; and motif, **1:**54

Digitalization, **1:**5

Dikes and drainage, **3:**234–235

Dilemma stories: Abanyole, **1:**123; Bhutan, **2:**108; Bihar, **2:**26–27

Dimitri-Taikon, Johan, **3:**149

Dinaric cultural zone. *See* Croatia, Mountainous

Dingane (Zulu king), **1:**269

Dinka, **1:**151

Dinnsenchas ("place lore"), **3:**35

Dinuzulu (Zulu king), **1:**273

Diocletian (Emperor), **3:**347

Dipendra (Crown Prince of Nepal), **2:**114

Diple musical instrument, **3:**344

Dirges. *See* Laments; Poetry

Discrimination and racism, **1:**79; African American, **4:**149; Haiti, **4:**318; Mauritius and Rodrigues, **1:**145

Diseases: effects on frontier, **1:**37–38; Hopi, **4:**44–45

"Dismantling Local Culture" (Shuman), **1:**43

Disney, Walt, **3:**267

Disobedience tales: Mauritius and Rodrigues, **1:**146; Nez Perce, **4:**101–102; San, **1:**244

"Disobedient Boy" (Nez Perce), **4:**101

Dispute settlement: Marshall Islands, **1:**350; Nuer, **1:**151; Tairora, **2:**209

Divani Lugat-at-Tiurk (Collection of Turkik Language), **2:**310

Divination. *See* Diviners and divination

Divine Right of Kings, **3:**161, 163

Diviners and divination: Baule, **1:**166, 167; Benin, **1:**171, 174–176, 179; China, **2:**213; Duna, **2:**167; Finnish-Swedish, **3:**99; Ga, **1:**191–192; Iban, **2:**172; Igbo, **1:**197; Isle of Man, **3:**48–49; Japan, **2:**273; Kaliai, **2:**187; Kewa, **2:**189; Kurds, **2:**386; Madagascar, **1:**139; Malaita, **1:**305; Nuer, **1:**152; Persia, **2:**419; Piedmont and Val d'Aosta, **3:**474; Russia, **3:**416; Shona, **1:**252; Siberia, **2:**319, 320; Tairora, **2:**206; Tuareg, **1:**114; Vanuatu, **1:**327; Yoruba, **1:**222; Zande, **1:**229, 230. *See also* Prophets and prophecies

"Doctor Know-All" (African American), **4:**144

Doctors. *See* Healers; Medicine and cures

Dodge, Mary Mapes, **3:**235

Dodola (rain dance, Serbia), **3:**431

Dolls: Hopi, **4:**49; Western Inuit and Yupik, **4:**139, 140

Dolphins as Christian symbol (Malta), **3:**509

Dominica. *See* Caribs of Dominica

Donohoe, Jack (Australian folk hero), **1:**286

Don Ramiro I, **3:**205

Doornbosch, Ate, **3:**244

Dorson, Richard, **1:**13, 36, 67, 83

Dorst, John, **1:**30, 48

Dotson, Louis, **4:**172

Dough-based cuisine, **3:**339

Douglas, Mary, **1:**28

"The Dowie Dens o Yarrow" (song), **3:**58–59

Dowry system: Bangladesh, **2:**104; Greece, **3:**499; Roma, **3:**398; Russia, **3:**414; Sephardim, **3:**219; Slovakia, **3:**288; Tuareg, **1:**119; Uttar Pradesh, **2:**93; Uzbek, **2:**354

The dozens (African Americans), **4:**150

Dragoi (Albania), **3:**324–325

"The Dragon Slayer," **1:**94–95

Drakos, Georg, **3:**153

Drama and theater: Abanyole, **1:**124–130; Appalachia, **4:**162; Ashkenazim, **3:**336–337; Bali, **2:**161–163; Bangladesh, **2:**99; Basque, **3:**190; Bhutan, **2:**110; China, **2:**214–215, 224–225; England, **3:**16–17; Flanders (Belgium), **3:**231–232; Ga, **1:**192; Georgia, **3:**359–360; Haiti, **4:**321; Haryana, **2:**44; Hungary, **3:**281–282; Igbo, **1:**198–199; Iroquois, **4:**58; Japan, **2:**276–277; Kaliai, **2:**187; Karnataka, **2:**53–54; Kashmir, **2:**63–64; Kiribati, **1:**344; Lakota and Dakota, **4:**74; Macedonia, **3:**374–375; Malay, **2:**143; Manchu, **2:**251; Marquesas Islands, **1:**383; Maya, **4:**261; Mongol, **2:**256; Orissa, **2:**83–84; Quechua, **4:**212–213; Sertão, **4:**219; Shona, **1:**252–253; Shuar, **4:**227; Sicily, **3:**488; Slovakia, **3:**293; Spain, **3:**184; Sri Lanka, **2:**128; Taiwan, **2:**264; Tajik, **2:**329–330; Tlingits, **4:**124–125; Turkey, **2:**435–436; Ukraine, **3:**446; Uttar Pradesh, **2:**92–93; Vanuatu, **1:**329–330

Dramitse Nga Cham dance (Bhutan), **2:**110

"Dream Ballad," **3:**128

Dreamcatchers (Ojibwe), **4:**108

Dream of the Red Chamber (China), **2:**222

Dreams: Australian Aborigines, 1:292–299; Denmark, 3:84; Iceland, 3:116; Israel, 2:373, 380; Kewa, 2:196; Lakota, 4:74; Malaita, 1:304–306; Nepal, 2:118; Nez Perce, 4:98; Rarámuri, 4:304; Suriname Maroon, 4:238; Xavante, 4:247–249

Dresses. *See* Clothing

Drinking songs and rituals: China, 2:214, 219; Ga, 1:191–192; Germany, 3:271; Khasi-Jaintia, 2:69; Mongol, 2:258; Russian wedding, 3:414; Shuar, 4:225–226

Drinks: Candoshi, 4:185; Kariri, 4:217. *See also specific types*

Drmeš dances (Croatia), 3:345

"Droll-tellers" (Cornish), 3:13

Drums: Cherokee, 4:14; Cuba, 4:310; Haiti, 4:322; Iroquois, 4:59; Maroons of Jamaica, 4:340; Nahua, 4:283; Navajo, 4:87; Shuar, 4:226; Western Inuit and Yupik, 4:136–137

Dual faith belief system (Russia), 3:411, 412

Dube, Violet, 1:271

Duendes (Guam), 1:338

Duhovi (Souls' Day, Serbia), 3:431

Dukhovnye stiki (Russia), 3:421

Dumy (epic poetry, Ukraine), 3:440

Duna, 2:165–170; folktales, 2:168–169; geography and history, 2:165–167; medicine and ritual, 2:167; songs and ballads, 2:169–170

Duncan Dhu, 3:184

Duneier, Mitchell, 1:80

Dunlop, Weary, 1:286

Duo Dinámico, 3:184

Dušan the Mighty, 3:427

Dwellings. *See* Housing

Dybeck, Rikard, 3:145

Dylan, Bob, 2:220, 3:184

"Eagle Catches the Chicks" game (China), 2:226

Eagle clan (Haida), 4:39

Easter ceremonies (Rarámuri), 4:302–304

Easter eggs: Slovenia, 3:298; Ukraine, 3:445–446

Eastern Africa, 1:123–162

Eastern Band of Cherokee Indians, 4:8, 15–16

East Indian culture (Jamaica), 4:344–345

East Slavs (Russia), 3:411, 412

E bukura e Dheut (Beauty of the Land, Albania), 3:325

Ecuador, 4:187–192; arts and crafts, 4:192; festivals and celebrations, 4:191–192; medicine and magic, 4:191; poetry, 4:188–189; religious beliefs and rituals, 4:197–199; roots of Ecuadorian folklore, 4:187–188; Shuar, 4:219–221; songs and narrative games, 4:189–190; studies of Ecuadorian folklore, 4:188

Eddas, 3:270

Eddic poems (Iceland), 3:113

Edict of Expulsion (1492), 3:212

Edo people. *See* Benin

Edward I (England), 3:71

Edward I (Scotland), 3:55

Edwards, Ron, 1:286, 287

Eemut (Jie), 1:131

Eggs: as cure for illness, 3:439; Slovenia, Easter eggs, 3:298; Ukraine, Easter eggs, 3:445–446

Egudu, 1:197

Ehn, Billy, 3:151

"Eight Immortals" stories (China), 2:217

Einar Ólafur Sveinsson, 3:115

Eira, Mathis Aslaksen. *See* Siri-Matti

Eiríkur Laxdal, 3:113

Eisteddfod (Wales), 3:75

"Elastic ball game" (Lower Piedmont), 3:477

El bosta ("The Bus") song (Lebanon), 2:394–395

El Cordobés, 3:186

"Elder Cuckoo" story (Semai), 2:146

Elders: Shona, 1:249; Western Inuit and Yupik, 4:133; Xavante, 4:249

Elegiac poetry (Igbo), 1:197

El Greco, 3:181, 186

Eliade, Mircea, 1:73

Elias, John, 3:74

Elias, Norbert, 3:151

Elijah (prophet), 3:334, 417

Elijah, Saint, 3:403, 418

Elizabeth I (Queen of England), 3:54

Ellamma (Hindu goddess), 2:50–51

El-Shamy, Hasan, 1:56

Elustafev, Ilia, 3:423

Emancipation from slavery: African American, 4:146; Jamaica, 4:339. *See also* Slavery

Embree, Ella, 2:277

Embroidery: Greece, 3:500; Macedonia, 3:375; Ukraine, 3:444–445. *See also* Textile arts

Emeneau, Murray, 2:3

Emergence mythology. *See* Creation stories

Encyclopedia of a Malay History and Culture (Lumpur), 2:145

Engiro (Jie), 1:135, 136

England, 3:1–21; calendars, 3:17–20; celebrations, 3:20; Celtic influence, 3:4–5; children's folklore, 3:20; drama, 3:16–17; geography and history, 3:1–4; ghost lore, 3:10–11; life-cycle customs, 3:20; music and dance, 3:13–15; myths and legends, 3:11–13; religion and beliefs, 3:4; stories and tales, 3:11–13; storytelling, 3:11–13; superstition and fairy lore, 3:5–8; witchcraft and popular magic, 3:8–10. *See also* British rule and influence

The English and Scottish Popular Ballads (Child), 1:94

English Anglicanism in Australia, 1:289

English Civil War, 3:3

English Folk Dance Society, 3:14

English language: Ga, 1:181; Guam, 1:339; Hawai'i, 1:371; Kiribati, 1:348; Malaita, 1:300; Mascarene Islands, 1:144; The Seychelles, 1:149; Vanuatu, 1:326, 327

Englynion y Beddau (poem), 3:71

Entrada (Quechua), 4:213

Environmental determinism, 1:16–17

Epic of El-Zir Salem (Palestine), 2:404

Epic of Kajoor (Wolof), 1:215

Epic stories, tales, poetry: Ainu, 2:287; Armenia, 2:359–362; Australian Aborigines, 1:293, 297; China, 2:215–216; Croatia, 3:350; Iban, 2:174; India, 2:8–9; Japan, 2:275; Karnataka, 2:49, 50; Kazakh, 2:312; Malaita, 1:302; Manchu, 2:246, 247–248; Mexico, 4:280; Mongol, 2:254–255; Nahua, 4:285; Ojibwe, 4:105; Persia, 2:415; Russia, 3:423–424; Siberia, 2:317–318, 323; Turkey, 2:432; Ukraine, 3:440, 441; Uttar Pradesh, 2:90–91; Uyghur, 2:337; Uzbek, 2:350; Wolof, 1:215; Xhosa, 1:264; Yemen, 2:442. *See also* Hero

An Epoch of Miracles (Burns), 4:260

Epos (heroic songs), 3:327

Erasmus, 1:57, 3:238

Erdélyi, János, 3:283

Erinmwin (Benin), 1:172, 174

Erixon, Sigurd, 3:146–148, 154

Escalade festival (Switzerland), 3:315

Eschenbach, Wolfram von, 3:263

Escuder, Tomàs, 3:196

Esigie, Oba, 1:178

Eskimos. *See* Western Inuit and Yupik

Es Safi, Wadih, 2:396

Ethical concepts: Madagascar, 1:139. *See also* Taboos

Ethiopia's influence in Israel, 2:381

Ethnic cleansing and romantic nationalism, 1:62

Ethnicity, 1:25–27; Caucasia, 3:356; and diaspora, 1:19; and globalization, 1:42; Lumba, importance of assertion, 1:240; Mexico, 4:270; Sri Lanka, 2:124–126; Swahili, 1:158

Ethnocentrism and nativism, 1:64

Ethnography, 1:27–31; and fieldwork, 1:27, 33; and gender, 1:39–41; Haiti, 4:319–320, 326–327; Maya, 4:256–257; and museums, 1:59; and performance theory, 1:69; Peru, 4:200–201; and public folklore, 1:76; and race, 1:81; Sibundoy, 4:229; and text, 1:84; and translation, 1:91; Western Inuit and Yupik, 4:129; and worldview, 1:98, 99; Yanomami, 4:251

Ethnography and Folklore Archive of Catalonia, 3:196

Ethnology (Sweden), 3:146–151

Ethnomusicology (Hungary), 3:280

Ethnopoetics, 1:31–32; and translation, 1:91

Ethnotourism, Macedonia, 3:377

Finnish National Museum, **1**:58

Finnish School, **1**:22–23

Finnish-Swedish, **3**:97–103; calendars, **3**:101–102; children's lore, **3**:100–101; geography and history, **3**:97–98; language, **3**:97, 102–103; medicine and cures, **3**:99; music and dance, **3**:100; storytelling, **3**:99–100; supernatural lore, **3**:98–99

Finsch, Otto, **1**:354

Firdausi (Tajik-Persian poet), **2**:326

Firebird: Armenia, **2**:365; Russia, **3**:419

Fisher, Archie, **3**:66

"Fisher's Ghost" (Australia [British]), **1**:286

Fishing: Ga, **1**:182; Ijo, **1**:204; Kaingang, **4**:194; Lunda, **1**:234; Marquesas Islands, **1**:379; New Caledonia, **1**:309; Seminole, **4**:114; Sicily, **3**:483–484; Western Inuit and Yupik, **4**:129–130; Wolof, **1**:209

Fishponds (Hawaiʻi), **1**:376

Fiske, John, **1**:72

Flags and nationalism, **1**:63

Flamenco, **3**:183, 184–185

Flanders (Belgium), **3**:223–233; architecture, **3**:232; brewing, **3**:232; calendars, **3**:226–229; drama, sports, and games, **3**:231–232; geography and history, **3**:223–225; medicine, **3**:229; myths, legends, songs, and folktales, **3**:229–230; religion and ritual, **3**:225–226; town rivalries, **3**:230–231

Flanders, Helen Hartness, **1**:41

"The Fleeing Pancake," **1**:95

Flood, Bo, **1**:339

Floods: Kaingang, **4**:195–196; Mississippi Delta, **4**:170–171; Yanomami, **4**:252, 254

Flores, Judy S., **1**:339

Flores, Rosario, **3**:183

Flores, Tomasito, **3**:183

Florida: Seminole, **4**:111–112

"Flower of Scotland" (song), **3**:57–58

Flower symbolism: Isle of Man, **3**:47–48; Malta, **3**:509

Flutes (Quechua), **4**:211, 212

Flying Canoe myth (Trobriand Islands), **1**:321–322

Folk Arts Program, **1**:77

Folk high schools (Denmark), **3**:82

Folk idioms. *See* Language

The Folk Literature of a Yucatecan Town (Redfield), **4**:259

Folk Literature of the South American Indians, General Index (Wilbert & Simoneau), **1**:56

Folklore Fellows, **1**:94

Folklore Handbook (Japan), **2**:279

Folklore Institute of Indiana University, **1**:161

Folk-lore Journal (Zulu), **1**:272

Folklore of the Holy Land (Hanauer), **2**:411

Folk-lore of Yucatán (Brinton), **4**:278

Folk-Lore Society (Bangladesh), **2**:95

The Folklore Text from Performance to Print (Fine), **1**:85

Folklorism, **1**:35–37; and modernization, **1**:52

Folklorism Bulletin, **1**:37

Folk medicine. *See* Medicine and cures

Folksong. *See* Music and dance

Folk Songs of Australia (Australia [British]), **1**:285

Folk Songs of Australia and the Men and Women Who Sang Them (Australia [British]), **1**:285

Folk Song Style and Culture (Lomax), **1**:17

Folktales. *See* Stories and tales

Folk Traditions of the Arab World (El-Shamy), **1**:56

Food customs and beliefs: Appalachia, **4**:164; Ashkenazim, **3**:332; Australia (British), **1**:290; Australian Aborigines, **1**:297; Bali, **2**:159; Bangladesh, **2**:101, 104; Caipira, **4**:179–180; Catalan, **3**:199–200; Cherokee, **4**:19; China, **2**:213, 228–229; Chinese living abroad, **2**:239, 240–241; and creolization, **1**:10–11; Denmark, **3**:87; Duna, **2**:167; and ethnicity, **1**:26; Greece, **3**:498–499; Haida, **4**:42–43; Iceland, **3**:118–119; Igbo, **1**:201–202; India, **2**:5, 13–14, 64; Iroquois, **4**:56; Israel, **2**:379; Kaingang, **4**:193–194; Kaliai, **2**:187; Kiribati, **1**:340, 343; Korea, **2**:296, 304; Lebanon, **2**:395; Malta, **3**:509; Marquesas Islands, **1**:379; Marshall Islands, **1**:349, 355; Nepal, **2**:116–118; Nez Perce, **4**:103; Palestine, **2**:410; Persia, **2**:419, 423; Seminole, **4**:113–114; Sephardim, **3**:219–220; Serbia, **3**:430; Sertão, **4**:216–218; Sicily, **3**:487, 491; Taiwan, **2**:261–263, 266; Trobriand Islands, **1**:316; Uyghur, **2**:345; Wales, **3**:77; Western Inuit and Yupik, **4**:129–130; Zande, **1**:228

Footwear (Western Inuit and Yupik), **4**:130

Foragers: Apache, **4**:1; Cherokee, **4**:19; and cultural shift, **1**:16–17; Kaingang, **4**:193

Ford Foundation, **2**:15, 58

Fortis, Alberto, **3**:350

Fortune-telling: Chinese living abroad, **2**:235; Korea, **2**:303. *See also* Diviners and divination

Forty Day Party (Tlingit), **4**:120

Foster, George, **1**:97

Founding myth of Switzerland, **3**:308–309

Four Sacred Mountains (Navajo reservation), **4**:84

"Fox as Nursemaid for Bear" (Mascarene Islands), **1**:144

Fraguas Fraguas, Antonio, **3**:207

France, **3**:157–170; Baule colonization by, **1**:164; calendars, **3**:168–169; Celts and Roman Gauls, **3**:158–161; ecomusées in, **1**:60; Frankish kingdom, **3**:161–162; French Revolution and Napoleon, **3**:165–167; geography, **3**:157–158; globalization, **3**:169; Greek influence, **3**:158–159; Louis XIV, **3**:164–165; Madagascar occupation by,

1:138; Marquesas Islands annexation by, **1**:377, 380; medieval era, **3**:162–164; nationalistic folk beliefs, **3**:166–167; New Caledonia colonization by, **1**:308–309, 314; open-air museums in, **1**:60; Réunion, as overseas department of, **1**:147; Sahara colonization by, **1**:103, 111, 114, 117; The Seychelles occupation by, **1**:149; storytelling, **3**:163–164; Vanuatu colonization by, **1**:325; Wolof colonization by, **1**:209, 211

Franciscans and Rarámuri, **4**:297

Franco, Francisco, **3**:181, 183, 187, 190, 203, 205

Frankish kingdom, **3**:161–162

Franz Joseph (Emperor), **3**:347

Frazer, James George, **1**:96, **3**:17

Freedom celebrations (African American), **4**:146

Freeman, Derek, **2**:176

French Guiana: Maroon, **4**:236–237

French language: The Comoros, **1**:142; Mascarene Islands, **1**:144; Mascarene Islands, creolization of, **1**:144; The Seychelles, **1**:149; Vanuatu, **1**:326, 327

French Revolution, **3**:165–167

Freney, James, **3**:36

Freud, Sigmund, **1**:74–75

Friedmann, Frederik, **3**:453

Friedrich II, Wittekind, **3**:268–269

Friedrich Wilhelm III (King), **3**:265

Friis, J.A., **3**:137, 140

Frontier, **1**:37–39; Australia (British), **1**:288–289; cultural imperialism, **1**:38; and diffusion, **1**:22; and invented tradition, **1**:50; and nationalism, **1**:37, 38, 62; Roman frontier, **1**:38; Zulu Difaqane, **1**:38

Frybread (Seminole), **4**:114

Frykman, Jonas, **3**:151, 153

Fudoki compilations (Japan), **2**:274

Fundamentalism, **1**:65

Funerals and burials: Abanyole, **1**:128–130; Armenia, **2**:368–369; Australian Aborigines, **1**:294; Baule, **1**:164, 168; Benin, **1**:174; China, **2**:228; Chinese living abroad, **2**:235, 237, 238; Duna, **2**:170; Haiti, **4**:325; Igbo, **1**:196; Ijo, **1**:205, 207; Kadazandusun, **2**:179; Kazakh, **2**:311, 313; Kewa, **2**:191–192; Khasi-Jaintia, **2**:71, 72; Korea, **2**:296–298; Kurds, **2**:386, 387, 389; Lebanon, **2**:398–399; Lunda, **1**:238; Madagascar, **1**:139; Malaita, **1**:303–304; Maroons of Jamaica, **4**:339–340; Marshall Islands, **1**:355; Nepal, **2**:116–117; New Caledonia, **1**:311; Palau, **1**:362; Peru, **4**:201–202; Poland, **3**:385–386; Roma, **3**:402; Russia, **3**:413; Samoa, **1**:393; Shona, **1**:250, 252–254; Suriname Maroons, **4**:239–240; Tairora, **2**:206; Taiwan, **2**:263; Tajik, **2**:329; Tlingit, **4**:120; Ukraine, **3**:443–444; Uzbek, **2**:351; Yoruba, **1**:224; Zande, **1**:232. *See also* Death and mourning rituals; Potlatches

Furniture: Appalachia, **4**:164; Zande, **1**:233

Fürst, Walter, **3**:309

Gerald of Wales, **3:**70

Gerholm, Lena, **3:**150, 152

"German Charlie" (Australia [British]), **1:**286

German Folklore Society, **1:**6

Germanic National Museum, **1:**58

Germany, **3:**260–273; Australia influenced by, **1:**278, 279; calendars, **3:**262–265; folklore under Nazi regime, **1:**62, **3:**272; geography and history, **3:**260–262; Marshall Islands colonization by, **1:**350, 356; myths, legends, and folktales, **3:**265–271; Palau colonization by, **1:**360; songs and material culture, **3:**271

Geronimo, **4:**3

Gesamtregister, **1:**6

Gesellschaft für Volkskunde, **1:**6

Geser epic (Mongol), **2:**254–255

Gessler, Governor, **3:**308–309

Gessner, Salomon, **3:**310

Gherip-Sänäm story (Uyghur), **2:**339

Ghiglier, Michael, **4:**251–252

Ghost Dance (Kiowa), **4:**63

Ghost stories: England, **3:**10–11; Ireland, **3:**34; Iroquois, **4:**59; Karnataka, **2:**51; Norway, **3:**127; Seminole, **4:**115. *See also* Supernatural beliefs

Ghul (ghoul) tales and superstitions (Persia), **2:**418

"Gifting money" practice (Greece), **3:**498

Gilbert, Thomas, **1:**349

Gilferding A.F., **3:**410

Ginzburg, Carlo, **3:**457

Girls' Puberty Ceremony, **4:**5, 6–7

Giuliano, Salvatore, **3:**486

Glasgow Missionary Society, **1:**258

Glassie, Henry, **1:**70, **3:**35

Globalization, **1:**42–44; Australia (British), **1:**290; Brittany, **3:**175; Croatia, **3:**352; and culture area, **1:**18; and diaspora, **1:**19, 42; and diffusion, **1:**24; Finnish-Swedish, **3:**102–103; France, **3:**169; Georgia, **3:**362; Guam, **1:**339; Hungary, **3:**283; and hybridity, **1:**42, 47; Madagascar, **1:**141; Malta, **3:**511; Marquesas Islands, **1:**384; and nationalism, **1:**42, 62; The Netherlands, **3:**240–242, 245; Piedmont and Val d'Aosta, **3:**479; Samoa, **1:**390–392; San, **1:**240; Slovakia, **3:**294; Swahilization, **1:**158; and tourism, **1:**86; Ukraine, **3:**448; Wales, **3:**77; Wolof, **1:**216

Glyndŵr, Owain, **3:**71–72

Gods and goddesses: Baule, **1:**164; Caipira, **4:**178; Cuba, **4:**310, 313; Hawai'i, **1:**369; Igbo, **1:**195; Ijo, **1:**204; Japan, **2:**272; Malaita, **1:**301; Rarámuri, **4:**300–301; Russia, **3:**411–412; Sámi (Lapps), **3:**136; Serbia, **3:**429–430; Yoruba, **1:**222. *See also specific religions and deities*

Godunov, Boris, **3:**423

Goetz, Herman, **2:**32

Goldbert, David Theo, **1:**79

The Golden Bough (Frazer), **1:**96, **3:**17

"Goldilocks and the Three Bears," **1:**55

Gold rushes: Australia (British), **1:**289; and Western Inuit and Yupik, **4:**132

Goldstein, Kenneth S., **1:**27, 68, 82

Goldwater, Robert, **1:**74

Golem, **3:**334

Gombrich, Ernst, **1:**74

Gomis, Cels, **3:**195

Gomme, Alice Bertha, **3:**20

González, José Edwardo, **1:**74

González Caturla, Joaquim, **3:**196

González Sanz, Carlos, **3:**196

Good fortune, portents of (Ashkenazim), **3:**333

Goombeh (Maroons of Jamaica), **4:**340

Gordimer, Nadine, **1:**270

Gordon, Adam Lindsay, **1:**284–285, 288

Gorgasali, Vakhtang (King), **3:**357

Gossen, Gary, **1:**98

Gourd dances (Kiowa), **4:**65

Gow, Nathaniel, **3:**63

Gow, Niel, **3:**63

Gowdy, Bob, **3:**34

Gowlett, Derek F., **1:**274

Goya, Francisco, **3:**185, 186

Grabrijan, Dusan, **3:**375

Graburn, Nelson, **1:**87

Gradén, Lizette, **3:**153

Grain-growing culture, **3:**348

Granada, Luis de, Fray, **3:**181

"Grandfather's Clock," **1:**55

"Grandmother Samsin" stories (Korea), **2:**298

Granlund, John, **3:**148

Grant, E.W., **1:**272

Graphic arts. *See* Arts and crafts; Painting

"The Grateful Dead," **1:**95

Graven images: animals as decorative elements, **3:**338; ban on making, **3:**337–338

Great Britain. *See* British rule and influence; England

Great Lakes region: Ojibwe, **4:**103–105

Great Moravian Empire (Slovakia), **3:**286

Great Plains: Lakota, **4:**67–69

Great Siege (Malta), **3:**511

Greco-Roman antiquity, **1:**5

Greece, **3:**493–502; arts, crafts, and architecture, **3:**500; food and celebrations, **3:**498–499; geography and history, **3:**493–494; music and dance, **3:**497–498; myths, legends, and folktales, **3:**496; proverbs and jokes, **3:**497; roots and themes of folklore, **3:**494–496; sports and games, **3:**499–500

Greek mythology, **3:**496, 497, 499

Green Corn Ceremony (Cherokee), **4:**15

Green Corn Dance ceremony (Seminole), **4:**115

Greenland, **3:**103–111; celebrations, **3:**108–109; games, **3:**108–109; geography and history, **3:**103–105; shamanism, **3:**105–107; spells and songs, **3:**109–110; storytelling, **3:**107–108; supernatural lore, **3:**105–107

Greig, Gavin, **3:**58

Greyerz, Otto von, **3:**313

Grigorovich, V.I., **3:**372

Grimm, Jacob, **1:**94, **3:**269

Grimm, Wilhelm, **1:**61, 94

Grimm brothers, influence of, **1:**2, 55, 61, **3:**12, 114, 243, 265–271; and Nahua tales, **4:**285

Grots-Brots (Servandztiants, Armenia), **2:**364

"*Gruagach òg an fhuilt bhàin*" (Fair-haired Young Girl), **3:**60

Grundtvig, N.F.S., **1:**76, **3:**82

Grundtvig, Svend, **3:**82

Gstanzl (verse form), **3:**257

Guam, **1:**333–340; geography and history, **1:**333–334; *Kantan Chamorrita,* **1:**338; magical and adventure tales, **1:**335–336; modernization, challenges of, **1:**339; myths and *pourquoi* tales, **1:**334–335; spirits and the supernatural, **1:**337–338; tales of social instruction, **1:**336–337

Guam Council on the Arts and Humanities Agency (KAHA), **1:**339

Guarani and Caipira, **4:**177–178

Guardiola, Pepa, **3:**196

Guatemala: Maya, **4:**256–268

"The Gucci Kangaroo" (Australia [British]), **1:**287

Gugga Chauhan (Rajput warrior), **2:**41

A Guide for Fieldworkers in Folklore (Goldstein), **1:**27

A Guide to Folktales in the English Language (Ashliman), **1:**94

Guilds (Switzerland), **3:**315

Guilhem, **3:**162

Gunaddhya (early writer, Kashmir), **2:**60–61

Gunner, Elizabeth, **1:**272

Guru Padmasambhava (Indian Buddhist saint), **2:**106, 107, 110

Gusle musical instrument, **3:**344

Gustafsson, Lotten, **3:**153

Gustavus Adolphus II, **3:**102, 144, 149

Guy Fawkes Night (Australia [British]), **1:**290

Gwala, Mafika, **1:**272

Gyanendra (King of Nepal), **2:**114

Gypsy. *See* Roma

Habsburg, Rudolf von, **3:**250

Habsburg monarchy, **3:**309, 350, 351

Hagen, Friedrich Heinrich von der, **3:**312

Hagiographies (Ireland), **3:**30–31

Haida, **4:**38–44; geography and history, **4:**38–39; myths, legends, and folktales, **4:**40–42; potlatches, **4:**42–43; social structure, **4:**39–40; studies of Haida folklore, **4:**43–44

Hainteny (Madagascar), **1:**140

Hairstyles and head coverings: Berber, **1:**104, 107; Igbo, **1:**201; Maya, **4:**262; Tuareg,

Ivandan (John the Baptist Day, Serbia), 3:431

Ivan Kupalo (summer solstice), 3:417

Ivan the Terrible, 3:409

Ivrea, festival (Piedmont and Val d'Aosta), 3:474

Izaga nezimo zikukhuluma (Zulu), 1:274

Izibongo, 1:272–274

Izibongo: Zulu Praise-Poems, 1:272

"The Izibongo of the Zulu Chiefs," 1:272

Izibongo ZamaKhosi, 1:272

Izwi Labantu (newspaper) (Xhosa), 1:262, 264

Jaarsma, Dam, 3:243

Jabavu, John Tengo, 1:263, 264

"Jack and the Beanstalk," 3:12

Jack in Two Worlds (McCarthy), 1:85

"Jack the Giant-Killer," 3:12

Jadwiga, Queen, 3:381

Jae-hyo Shin (early writer, Korea), 2:300

Jaguar stories (Yanomami), 4:253–254

Jainism: Bihar, 2:25; Gaddi, 2:31; Haryana, 2:39; Karnataka, 2:48; Orissa, 2:80

Jakobson, Roman, 1:90, 91

Jamaica, 4:336–347; children's songs and games, 4:341; and diaspora, 1:20; East Indian culture, 4:344–345; festivals and celebrations, 4:338–339; folktales, 4:341–342; geography and history, 4:336–338; Maroon culture, 4:339–341; religious beliefs, 4:343–344; spells and magic, 4:343; studies of Jamaican folklore, 4:345–346

James I (England), 3:54

James II (England and Scotland), 3:54

James IV (Scotland), 3:54

James VI (England and Scotland), 3:54

James VII (England and Scotland), 3:54

James, Saint, 3:204–206, 349

James, Richard, 3:410

Jánošík, Juraj, 3:292

Janša, Anton, 3:304

Japan, 2:271–284; arts, crafts, and architecture, 2:278; folk religion and performing arts, 2:276–277; geography and history, 2:271–273; Marshall Islands influence by, 1:350; medicine, 2:278; modernization, challenges of, 2:278–279; modern studies of Japanese folklore, 2:279–281; and nationalism, 1:63; Palau influence by, 1:360; periods of cultural history, 2:273–275; religious beliefs, 2:275–276; sports and games, 2:277–278; Taiwan, influence in, 2:261, 265. See also Ainu

Jataka tales (birth stories of the Bodhisattva): Bhutan, 2:108; India, 2:7; Isaan, 2:135; Sri Lanka, 2:127

Jean du Doigt, Saint, 3:170, 175

Jelacic, Josip, 3:351

Jenkins, J. Geraint, 3:78

Jenn tales and superstitions (Persia), 2:417–418

Jesuits: Italy, 3:457–458; Rarámuri, 4:297

Jewelry and personal adornments: Baule, 1:167; Benin, 1:176; Berber, 1:106; Hawai'i, 1:372; Igbo, 1:201; Kiribati, 1:347; Marquesas Islands, 1:381, 384; Navajo, 4:91; Tlingit, 4:125–126; Tuareg, 1:107, 119; Wolof, 1:211. See also Amulets; Beadwork

Jews: Diaspora, 1:18–20; folklore of, 1:20, 62; immigrants to Mississippi Delta, 4:174; immigrants to U.S., 1:66; Nazi genocide of, 1:64

Jhangar epics (Mongol), 2:254–255

Jicarilla Relay Race (Apache), 4:5–6

Jie, 1:131–137; geography, 1:131; social structure, beliefs, and historical tradition, 1:133–137; stories, tales and historical tradition, 1:131–133

Jingoism and nativism, 1:64

Jinx as theme (Wolof), 1:213

Jnoun (Berber), 1:103–104, 111

Joan of Arc, 3:164

John, Saint, 3:199, 200, 265, 268

John Frum movement (Vanuatu), 1:327

John III Sobieski (King of Poland), 3:381

Johnson, Robert, 4:170

Johnson, Samuel, 3:38, 63

John Stands in Timber (Cheyenne), 4:22

John the Baptist, Saint, 3:290, 349, 388, 417, 429, 471

Jokes and joking rituals: Albania, 3:328, 329; Ashkenazim, 3:334; Greece, 3:497; Ireland, 3:38–39; Latvia, 3:362; Malaita, 1:302, 304; Roma, 3:406; Shona, 1:249, 250; Slovakia, 3:292; Swahili, 1:158; Wolof, 1:214–215; Yoruba, 1:224–225

Jolobe, J.J.R., 1:262

Jolted work system, 3:456

Jón Árnason, 3:114, 117

Jónas Jónasson frá Hrafnagili, 3:117

Jones, Mary, 3:74

Jones, Michael Owens, 1:77

Jones, Stephen, 2:222

Jón Guðmundsson the Learned, 3:113

Joning (African American), 4:150

Jonkunu (Jamaica), 4:338–339

Jón Ólofsson frá Grunnavík, 3:113

Jonsson, Bengt R., 3:149

Jordan, A.C., 1:261

Joseph II (Emperor), 3:347

Joseph, Saint, 3:199, 200

Journal of American Folklore, 1:5

Journal of Asian American Studies, 2:243

Journal of Folklore Research, 1:95

Journal of Palestine Oriental Society, 2:412

Journal of the Royal Anthropological Institute, 2:178

Journal of the Royal Asiatic Society, 2:30

Judaism: Australia (British), 1:290; Haiti, 4:319; Israel, 2:372; Jamaica, 4:337; Palestine, 2:401; Turkey, 2:430. See also Jews

Juju music (Yoruba), 1:223, 225

Julius Caesar, 3:261

Jung, C.G., 1:92

Junjappa stories (Karnataka), 2:50

Jurjans, Andrejs, 3:368

Júrjenson, Kaarjel, 1:81

Just, Saint, 3:160

"Just-so" stories (Nuer), 1:153

Kabua the Great (Marshall Islands leader), 1:350

Kabyle (Berber), 1:108, 110

Kadazandusun, 2:176–182; arts and crafts, 2:180–181; celebrations and games, 2:179–180; geography and history, 2:176–177; modernization, challenges of, 2:181; music, 2:179; myths, legends, and folktales, 2:178–179; religious beliefs and rituals, 2:177–178; studies of Kadazandusun folklore, 2:181–182

Kadoazi, 4:183

Ka'ililauokekoa (Hawai'i), 1:376

Kaingang, 4:193–199; food, 4:193–194; geography and history, 4:193; symmetry in myths and folktales, 4:194–197

Kairus (Kaingang subgroup), 4:194–195

Kakárma (Shuar), 4:222–223

Kalabari, 1:204, 208

Kalákaua (Hawaiian king), 1:371

Kalevala, 3:92–96

Kaliai, 2:183–188; geography and history, 2:183–184; modernization, challenges of, 2:188; myths, legends, and folktales, 2:184–186; songs and music, 2:186; storytelling, 2:187; themes in folktales, 2:188

Kalila Wa Demna (animal) tales (Palestine), 2:405

Kamahualele (foster son of Hawaiian chief), 1:370

Kambule, Mpondo, 1:270

Kamehameha (Hawaiian king), 1:367, 374

Kamês (Kaingang subgroup), 4:194–195

A Kammu Story-Listener's Tales (Lindell, Swahn & Tayanin), 1:81

Kammu traditions, 1:81

Kanak people. See New Caledonia

Kanaval festival (Haiti), 4:323

Ka Niam Khasi, 2:66–67

Kantan Chamorrita (Guam), 1:338

Kanyembo Lutaba, Paul (Mwata Kazembe XVII), 1:238, 239

Kapchan, Deborah A., 1:47, 48

Karadžić, Vuk Stefanovik, 3:372, 373, 431, 432, 434

Karagiozis (shadow theater, Greece), 3:500

Karimov, Islam, 2:349

Kariri culture (Sertão), 4:217

Karl-Emanuel, count of Savoy, 3:315

Karl of Savoy, Duke, 3:310

Midwives: Abanyole, **1:**125; African Americans, **4:**147; Norway, **3:**126; Persia, **2:**417, 420; Poland, **3:**384; Ukraine, **3:**444. *See also* Childbirth and birth rituals

Migration: Albania, **3:**322, 323; Armenia, **2:**367–368; Australia (British), **1:**286; Austria, **3:**250; Basque, **3:**189; Baule, **1:**165; Benin, **1:**170–171; Brittany, **3:**173–174; Croatia, **3:**347, 350–352; Denmark, **3:**81; Finland, **3:**90; France, **3:**158–159; Galicia, **3:**202–203; Georgia, **3:**362; Germany, **3:**261; Greenland, **3:**103–105; Hopi, **4:**45–46; Hungary, **3:**275–276; Iceland, **3:**111–112, 118; Ireland, **3:**23–24; Island of Man, **3:**42, 43; Jie, **1:**131–132; Kadazandusun, **2:**179; Lunda, **1:**235; Macedonia, **3:**376; Malta, **3:**504; Nagaland, **2:**74, 75, 77; The Netherlands, **3:**235–236; Norway, **3:**126; Palau, **1:**359–360; Palestine, **2:**404–405; Persia, **2:**417, 420; Piedmont and Val d'Aosta, **3:**470; Poland, **3:**381, 384; Roma, **3:**395; Sardinia, **3:**465; Scotland, **3:**54; Sephardim, **3:**212–213; Serbia, **3:**426; Sicily, **3:**480–482; Slovakia, **3:**285–287; Slovenia, **3:**296; Spain, **3:**179–180; Ukraine, **3:**444; Wales, **3:**70

Milad, myth of (Palau), **1:**359, 364

Miladinov, Dimitri, **3:**372, 373

Miladinov, Konstantin, **3:**372, 373

Milligan, Jean, **3:**63

Milošević, Slobodan, **3:**427

Mime: Ga, **1:**192; Lunda, **1:**237; Malaita, **1:**303; Samoa, **1:**394

Miners and mining: Ainu (Japan), **2:**286, 293; Appalachia, **4:**165; Australia (British), **1:**279; Duna, **2:**168; Finland, **3:**91; Isle of Man, **3:**42; Italy, **3:**454, 465; Ojibwe, **4:**105; Rarámuri, **4:**290; Scotland, **3:**53; Shona, **1:**252, 255; Sicily, **3:**481; Slovakia, **3:**285, 287; Spain, **3:**179; Suriname Maroon, **4:**238

"Min Min Lights" (Australia [British]), **1:**286

Minnesota: Lakota, **4:**67–69

Minstrels (Ukraine), **3:**440–442

Miošić, Andrija Kačić, **3:**350

Miracle plays (Piedmont and Val d'Aosta), **3:**475

Mishnah (Israel), **2:**373

Missionaries: Benin, **1:**171; Candoshi, **4:**181–182; Hawai'i, **1:**374; Kiribati, **1:**341; Madagascar, **1:**138, 140, 141; Malaita, **1:**303, 306; Marquesas Islands, **1:**378, 380, 385; Marshall Islands, **1:**354; Mascarene Islands, **1:**146; Navajo, **4:**87; New Caledonia, **1:**314; Quechua, **4:**212; Rarámuri, **4:**297; Samoa, **1:**391–393, 395, 396; Shona, **1:**252; Tonga, **1:**400, 401; Trobriand Islands, **1:**316, 319–320; Tuvalu, **1:**405, 408; Vanuatu, **1:**327, 329; Xhosa, **1:**258; Zande, **1:**228, 233; Zulu, **1:**266, 271

Mississippi: Choctaw Indians, **4:**30–38. *See also* Mississippi Delta

Mississippi Delta, **4:**166–175; field hollers and worksongs, **4:**168–169; folk medicine,

4:171; folktales, **4:**171–172; geography and history, **4:**166–167; musical instruments, **4:**172–173; non-African American folklore, **4:**173–174; spirituals and blues, **4:**169–171; studies of Mississippi Delta folklore, **4:**174

"Mixed breed," **1:**48

Moccasin Game (Navajo), **4:**89–90

Moddey Dhoo (Black Dog), **3:**43

Modernization, challenges of, **1:**52–54; Ainu, **2:**290–293; Apache, **4:**6–7; Appalachia, **4:**165; Armenia, **2:**369; Assam, **2:**23–24; Australia (British), **1:**290; Bali, **2:**163–164; Baule, **1:**168; Benin, **1:**179; Berber, **1:**111–112; Bhutan, **2:**112; Brittany, **3:**175; Cherokee, **4:**20; Cheyenne, **4:**29; China, **2:**229–231; Chinese living abroad, **2:**243; Choctaw, **4:**37; and cultural area, **1:**18; Dakota, **4:**75–76; and diaspora, **1:**19; Guam, **1:**339; Haiti, **4:**325–326; Haryana, **2:**45–46; Hawai'i, **1:**374–375; Ijo, **1:**208; India, **2:**14–15; Ireland, **3:**39; Isaan, **2:**139; Japan, **2:**278–279; Kadazandusun, **2:**181; Kaliai, **2:**188; Karnataka, **2:**57; Kazakh, **2:**314; Kewa, **2:**195–196; Khasi-Jaintia, **2:**73; Kiribati, **1:**347–348; Kurds, **2:**391; Lakota, **4:**75–76; Lebanon, **2:**400; Madagascar, **1:**138; Malay, **2:**144; Maluku, **2:**202–203; Marquesas Islands, **1:**384; Marshall Islands, **1:**356; Maya, **4:**264; and nationalism, **1:**61; Navajo, **4:**86–87, 92–93; The Netherlands, **3:**240, 245; New Caledonia, **1:**313–314; Nuer, **1:**153; Palestine, **2:**409–410; Peru, **4:**207; Quechua, **4:**214–215; and race, **1:**79; Sámi (Lapps), **3:**141–142; Semai, **2:**149–150; Shona, **1:**254; Siberia, **2:**324; Sibundoy, **4:**235; Slovakia, **3:**286; Slovenia, **3:**294; Suriname Maroons, **4:**238, 241–242; Tairora, **2:**208–209; Tajik, **2:**334; Tlingits, **4:**126–127; and tourism, **1:**86; Tuareg, **1:**111–112, 120; Uttar Pradesh, **2:**94; Uyghur, **2:**345–346; Vanuatu, **1:**331; Western Inuit and Yupik, **4:**139–140; Wolof, **1:**216; Xavante, **4:**250; Xhosa, **1:**258, 261–267; Zande, **1:**233

Modern Language Association International Bibliography (MLAIB), **1:**5–6

Modlitewki (prayers), **3:**382–383

Moe, Moltke, **3:**138

Mohammed, Prophet, **1:**115, 212

Mohammedan Saints and Sanctuaries in Palestine (Cana'an), **2:**411

Moieties: Apache, **4:**5–6; Haida, **4:**39; Iroquois, **4:**51; Tlingit, **4:**117–119, 124, 125; Xavante, **4:**243–245

Molina, Tirso de, **3:**183

Moluccas. *See* Maluku

Monasteries (France), **3:**160–161

Moneo, Rafael, **3:**187

Money transaction stories (Palau), **1:**360

Mongol, **2:**252–259; dance, crafts, and festivals, **2:**258–259; geography and history,

2:252–254; heroic epics and folktales, **2:**254–255; proverbs and riddles, **2:**258; religious beliefs, **2:**256–258; songs and poetry, **2:**255–256

Monsters and creatures: Abanyole, **1:**124; Bali, **2:**160; Cherokee, **4:**13; Croatia, **3:**348; Georgia, **3:**354; Iceland, **3:**115; Mauritius and Rodrigues, **1:**147; Navajo, **4:**85; Nez Perce, **4:**103; Piedmont and Val d'Aosta, **3:**471–472

Montaldi, Danilo, **3:**456

Montana: Cheyenne, **4:**21–22; Lakota, **4:**67–69

Montanini song, Italy, **3:**461

Montefiore, Judith, **2:**375

Mooinjer Veggey (Isle of Man), **3:**44

Moonlight rituals: Benin, **1:**177; Igbo, **1:**196; Shona, **1:**253; Zande, **1:**230

Moorish architecture, **3:**218

Morality lessons: Haiti, **4:**320; Ijo, **1:**206; Nez Perce, **4:**100–101; Rarámuri, **4:**301; Shona, **1:**250; Shuar, **4:**225; Wolof, **1:**216; Yoruba, **1:**222

Morant, Harry, **1:**285

Morelos, José María, **4:**277

Morgan, Louis Henry, **1:**15

Morganwg, Iolo, **3:**75

Morgon Kara legends (Siberia), **2:**321

Mori, Yoshiro, **1:**63

Morphology of the Folktale, **3:**419

Morris dance, **3:**15

Morrison, Toni, **1:**79

Morrisseau, Norval, **4:**108–109

Moser, Hans, **1:**36, 37

Mother Damp Earth (Russia), **3:**413, 422

Mother Friday (Russia), **3:**417

Mother Goddess (Russia), **3:**412

"Mother" image of Greek nation, **3:**494

Motif, **1:**11, 54–57; and type, **1:**54, 94, 95

Motif-Index of Folk-Literature (Thompson), **1:**55, 56, 286

Mounds (Cherokee), **4:**19

Mt. Graham (Apache sacred site), **4:**7

Mountain dwellers (Italy), **3:**453–455

Mountain pasture system (Italy), **3:**454–455

Mountain Spirits (Apache), **4:**5

Mourides, **1:**212

Mourning. *See* Death and mourning rituals

"Mouse oracle" (Baule), **1:**167

Mpande (Zulu king), **1:**269

Mqhayi, Samuel Edward Krune, **1:**261–264, 267

Mugabe, Robert, **1:**249

Mules and Men (Hurston), **4:**143

"Mulga Bill's Bicycle" (Australia [British]), **1:**285

Mullen, Patrick B., **1:**80

Mummers' Play: England, **3:**16–18, 20; Isle of Man, **3:**50

Murad I (Sultan), **3:**434

Murals. *See* Painting

Rouget de Lisle, Claude-Joseph, 3:157
Round dance: Georgia, 3:359, 360; Hungary, 3:282; Kiowa, 4:64; Siberia, 2:319; Slovenia, 3:302
Roure Torent, Josep, 3:195
Rousseau, Jean Jacques, 1:74, 3:310
Royal House of Orange, 3:242
Royal Institute of Amazingh (Berber) Culture, 1:111
Royal Scottish Country Dance Society, 3:63
Royalty: Georgian folktales, 3:356–357; Igbo, 1:8; Lunda, 1:235, 236; Nagaland, 2:77; Wolof, 1:210; Zande, 1:228. *See also specific names of kings, queens, etc.*
Royaume, Catherine, 3:315
Rózsa, Sándor, 3:277
Rubin, William, 1:74
Rudd, Steele, 1:286
Rugs. *See* Textile arts
Rumba (Cuba), 4:311
Rumor stories (African American), 4:151, 169
Runeberg, Johan Ludvig, 3:101
Runge, Philipp Otto, 3:267
Rupayan Sansthan (Rajasthan), 2:15
Rushnyky (ritual towels, Ukraine), 3:444–445
Russia, 3:408–425; calendars, 3:415–417; epics, 3:421–424; history, 3:411–412; Israel, influence on, 2:376–377; legends, folktales, and other oral genres, 3:417–420; life-cycle celebrations, 3:413–415; preservation of folklore, 3:408–411; Siberia, influence on, 2:316; songs, 3:420–421; Tajik, influence on, 2:325–326; Uzbek, influence on, 2:349, 350; witchcraft and magic, 3:412–413
Ryan, John S., 1:291
Rybnikov, P.N., 3:410

"Sabour" (Mascarene Islands), 1:146
Sacred Arrows (Cheyenne), 4:23–24
Sacred Buffalo Hat (Cheyenne), 4:23–24
Sacred Cross of Calderón Pass (Otomí), 4:290–293
The Sacred Remains: Myth, History, and Polity in Belau, 1:365
Sacred story archives (Vanuatu), 1:328
Sacrifices: Albania, 3:324; Baule, 1:166; Benin, 1:172, 173; Bihar, 2:27; Chinese living abroad, 2:237, 238; Duna, 2:166–167; Gaddi, 2:35–36; Iban, 2:175; Jie, 1:135–137; Kadazandusun, 2:178; Karnataka, 2:51; Kazakh, 2:307; Khasi-Jaintia, 2:69; Korea, 2:297; Malaita, 1:304; Manchu, 2:250, 251; Marquesas Islands, 1:381; Maya, 4:265; Mongol, 2:258; Nepal, 2:121; Nuer, 1:152; Palestine, 2:408; Sámi (Lapps), 3:136; Semai, 2:146, 148; Siberia, 2:321; Taiwan,

2:261–262; Tajik, 2:334; Tonga, 1:399; Yoruba, 1:224
Sagyrbayev, Kurmangazy, 2:312
Sahagún, Fray Bernardino de, 4:275
"Said Hanrahan" (Australia [British]), 1:285
Saint cults: Brittany, 3:174; France, 3:160; Sicily, 3:487
Saint's day holidays: Greece, 3:497; Malta, 3:504–505, 508–509; Roma, 3:403–404; Sicily, 3:488
Saivism, 2:20
Saktism, 2:20
Salam,sina (Samoan chief), 1:388
Salesians (Shuar), 4:220–221
Sálote (queen of Tonga), 1:401
"Salsa" music (Cuba), 4:311
Salt making: Lunda, 1:234; Sicily, 3:484–485
Salvà, Adolf, 3:195
Sámi (Lapps), 3:90, 112, 134–144; geography and history, 3:134–135; modernization, challenges of, 3:141–142; narratives, 3:139–140; preservation of folklore, 3:136–139; religion and beliefs, 3:136; Russian influence, 3:140; stories and tales, 3:140–141; witchcraft, 3:135
Samoa, 1:386–397; ceremonies and rituals, 1:393–394; genealogical stories, 1:386–387; history, 1:387–388; origin tales, 1:388–389; spirit lore, 1:392–393; stories of humans and spirits, 1:389–390; theater and dance, 1:394–396; Tonga in Samoan folklore, 1:388; Western-influenced folklore, 1:390–392
Samuelson, R.C.A., 1:272
San, 1:240–248; animals and hunting lore, 1:246–247; geography and society, 1:240–242; the mythological Early Times, 1:242–244; stories, myths, and legends, 1:242; studies of San folklore, 1:247; transformation of the Early Times, 1:245–246; trickster tales, 1:244–245
San Carolos Apache, 4:6
Sand drawings: Navajo, 4:86, 92; Vanuatu, 1:330
Sandile (Xhosa chief), 1:260, 266
Sankaradeva (spiritual leader of Assam), 2:19–20
Sanskrit: Assam, 2:17; Bali, 2:152, 154; Bihar, 2:26; forerunner of other languages, 1:22; India, 2:3; Isaan, 2:135; Karnataka, 2:51, 53; Kashmir, 2:60; Manchu, 2:247; Nepal, 2:115
Santéria myths (Cuba), 4:313
San Vitores, Luis Diego de, 1:333
Sardana (dance), 3:198–199
Sardinia, 3:464–465; circle dances, 3:465; funeral lament, 3:465; poetic contests, 3:465; shepherd's code of honor, 3:465
Saressalo, Lassi, 3:140
Sargadelos ceramic factory (Galicia), 3:208–209
Sassoontsi Davit (Davit of Sassoon, Armenia), 2:364

Sastre, Alonso, 3:184
Sather, Clifford, 2:176
Satire: Bangladesh, 2:99; Igbo, 1:196, 197; Nepal, 2:119; Russia, 3:418; Sri Lanka, 2:128; Wolof, 1:214; Yemen, 2:444; Yoruba, 1:223
Sava, Saint, 3:427
The Savage Mind (Lévi-Strauss), 1:47
Saveen (Gaddi), 2:35–36
Sayrami, Mulla Musa, 2:341
Scarves. *See* Hairstyles and head coverings
Scéalaíocht (Ireland), 3:27–28, 30, 31, 37
Schapkarev, Kuzman, 3:372
Scheub, Harold, 1:272
Schiller, Friedrich, 3:309
Schilling, Diebold, 3:310
Schnitzelbängler (poems), 3:316
Schoolcraft, Heny Rowe, 4:105
School of Oriental and African Studies of London University, 1:161
Schools: Navajo children, 4:92; Western Inuit and Yupik, 4:131–132, 140–141
Schreiner, Olive, 1:270
Schrijnen, Jos, 3:237
Schwizerdütsch language, 3:307
Scotland, 3:52–69; Australia (British) influence by, 1:278, 279, 281; ballads, 3:57–62; calendars, 3:64–67; geography and history, 3:52–55; music and dance, 3:57–64; political autonomy, 3:55; regional divisions, 3:53–54; sports and games, 3:64; storytelling, 3:57; supernatural lore, 3:55–57
The Scots in Australia (Australia [British]), 1:281
Scott, Bill, 1:278, 287
Scott, Walter, 3:3, 59
Sculpture. *See* Carving and sculpture
Seal, Graham, 1:291
Seanchas (Ireland), 3:27–28, 30, 31, 34–35, 37
Sea stories: Croatia, 3:347; Marshall Islands, 1:352; Swahili, 1:156
Sechseläuten festival (Switzerland), 3:315
Secola, Keith, 4:108
Second sight (Ireland), 3:55
The Secret History of the Mongols (Mongol), 2:253–254
Secret societies (Japan), 2:272
Seers. *See* Diviners and divination
Sega (Mascarene Islands), 1:148, 150
Self-mutilation (Karnataka), 2:49
Sellmann, James, 1:334
Semai, 2:145–151; geography and history, 2:145–146; modernization, challenges of, 2:149–150; religious and folk beliefs and Semai peaceability, 2:146–149; social structure and Semai democracy, 2:149
Seminole, 4:111–116; arts and crafts, 4:114; clothing, 4:112–113; food, 4:113–114; geography and history, 4:111–112; housing, 4:114; social structure, 4:116; Studies of Seminole folklore, 4:116

and rituals, **4:**238–240; roots of Maroon culture and folklore, **4:**237–238; studies of Maroon folklore, **4:**242

Surrallés, Alexandre, **4:**185–186

Survivalist narratives (Igbo), **1:**195–196

"Survivals," study of, **1:**2–3, 50

Suryamati (Kashmir Queen), **2:**60

Svensson, Birgitta, **3:**152

Svensson, Sigfrid, **3:**148, 150

Swahili, **1:**154–162; class and competition, **1:**159; dance, **1:**157–158; elements of Swahili folklore, **1:**156–157; geography and history, **1:**154–155; myths, legends, and folktales, **1:**155; outside influences, **1:**158; proverbs, **1:**159; race and demographics, **1:**158; sources of Swahili folklore, **1:**160; studies of Swahili folklore, **1:**161; urban and rural, **1:**160–161

Swahn, Jan-Öjvind, **1:**81, **3:**148

Swamp cabbage (Seminole), **4:**114

Swan maiden motif, **1:**56; Manchu, **2:**247; Tairora, **2:**208

Sweat lodges (Choctaw), **4:**37

Sweden, **3:**144–156; cultural anthropology studies, **3:**146–148; cultural theory studies, **3:**151; early twentieth-century folklore studies, **3:**146–148; ethnology studies, **3:**146–150; folklore scholarship, **3:**152–154; late twentieth-century folklore studies, **3:**148–151; Lund University folklife archives, **3:**148, 150; multiethnic studies, **3:**151–152; music and dance, **3:**146; nineteenth-century folklore studies, **3:**144–146; peasant culture, **3:**144–146; Stockholm, Institute for Folklife Research, **3:**146, 148; storytelling, **3:**147; Uppsala University studies, **3:**149

Sweet Medicine (Cheyenne), **4:**23, 25

Switzerland, **3:**306–319; calendars, **3:**314–317; festivals, **3:**311–312; founding myth, **3:**308–309; geography, **3:**306–307; history and folklore, **3:**308–312; language, **3:**307–308; religion, **3:**308; songs, yodeling, and music, **3:**312–314

Sword-Dance Play (England), **3:**16

Sword dances: Basque, **3:**194; Croatia, **3:**343; England, **3:**15; Piedmont and Val d'Aosta, **3:**476

Swordfish fishing traditions (Sicily), **3:**483

Sy, Cheikh Ahmadou, **1:**212

Sylvester (high priest), **3:**374

Symbolism. *See* Simile and metaphor; *specific types of symbols*

Symmetry, concept of (Kaingang), **4:**194–197

Synagogues, **3:**338

Syncretism, **1:**47. *See also* Hybridity

Syv, Peder, **3:**85

Taarab (Swahili), **1:**155, 157–159

"The Table, Ass, and the Stick," **1:**95

Taboos: Australian Aborigines, **1:**297; Bali, **2:**158; Bangladesh, **2:**103–104; Chinese living abroad, **2:**239; Greenland, **3:**107–108; Hawai'i, **1:**374; Kadazandusun, **2:**178–179; Khasi-Jaintia, **2:**70; Kiribati, **1:**343; Madagascar, **1:**139; Malaita, **1:**302, 303; Nagaland, **2:**79; Nez Perce, **4:**98; Roma, **3:**396; Samoa, **1:**393–394; Siberia, **2:**318; Tlingit, **4:**118; Tonga, **1:**399

Tacitus, **3:**261

Tagore, Rabindranath, **2:**95

Táin Bó Cualigne (The Cattle Raid of Cooley), **3:**28

Taíno: Haiti, **4:**316; Jamaica, **4:**337

Tairora, **2:**203–210; arts and crafts, **2:**208; geography and history, **2:**203–205; modernization, challenges of, **2:**208–209; myths and folktales, **2:**206–208; religious beliefs and rituals, **2:**206; studies of Tairora folklore, **2:**209–210

Taiwan, **2:**260–270; arts and crafts, **2:**264–265; festivals, **2:**266–269; food, **2:**266; geography and history, **2:**260–261; medicine and folk arts, **2:**265–266; opera, **2:**263–264; puppet performances, **2:**264; religious beliefs and rituals, **2:**261–263; songs, **2:**263; studies of Taiwanese folklore, **2:**269

Tajik, **2:**325–335; arts and crafts, **2:**330–331; clothing styles, **2:**331–332; drama, **2:**329–330; drama and theater, **2:**329–330; festivals and celebrations, **2:**332–334; folksongs and dance, **2:**329; geography and history, **2:**325–326; medicine and rituals, **2:**327–328; modernization, challenges of, **2:**334; music, **2:**328–329; proverbs and riddles, **2:**326–327; sports and games, **2:**330

Taj Mahal, **2:**11

The Tale of Genji (Japan), **2:**274, 275

The Tale of the Heike (Japan), **2:**275

Tales. *See* Epic stories, tales, poetry; Stories and tales

Tales of Gods and Spirits (China), **2:**218

Tales of the Bewitched Corpse (Mongol), **2:**255

Talismen: Madagascar, destruction of, **1:**138; Siberia, **2:**318; Ukraine, **3:**446

"Talking Turtle" (African American story), **4:**147–148

Tall tales (Ireland), **3:**37–38

Tamajaq language (Tuareg), **1:**112

Tamar (Queen), **3:**357

Tamazgha (Berber), **1:**101

Tambor (Cuba), **4:**310

Tamil people. *See* Sri Lanka

Tanac dances (Croatia), **3:**343, 345

Tanahill, Reay, **1:**11

Tangherlini, Timothy R., **1:**82

Tangun mythology (Korea), **2:**295–296, 304

Tannahill, Robert, **3:**59

Tantrism, **2:**80

Taoism. *See* Daoism

Taotaomo'na (Guam), **1:**337–339

Tarahumara. *See* Rarámuri

Tarankanje singing style (Croatia), **3:**341

Tarantella (dance, southern Italy), **3:**463

Tarantism (Italy), **3:**463

"Tar Baby" (African American), **4:**148

"The Tar Baby and the Rabbit," **1:**94; Mascarene Islands, **1:**144, 146; Réunion, **1:**148; The Seychelles, **1:**149

Target language (TL), **1:**89, 90

Tartit, **1:**112, 120

Tatars, **3:**422, 423

Tattoos and body markings: Australian Aborigines, **1:**297; Bangladesh, **2:**101; Benin, **1:**173; Berber, **1:**104–105; Bihar, **2:**28; Igbo, **1:**201; Ijo, **1:**207; Kiribati, **1:**347; Lumba, **1:**240; Malaita, **1:**300, 303, 306; Maluku, **2:**202; Marquesas Islands, **1:**380–381; Marshall Islands, **1:**354; Nagaland, **2:**77–78; Siberia, **2:**317; Tairora, **2:**202, 203; Trobriand Islands, **1:**324; Wolof, **1:**215; Yoruba, **1:**226

Taufa'ahau (King George Tupou, Tongan chief), **1:**399

Tautasdziesma (Latvia), **3:**368

Tayanin, D., **1:**81

Taylor, Archer, **1:**27, **3:**148

Teaching spirits (Nez Perce), **4:**98

Tea drinking: Appalachia, **4:**164; Candoshi, **4:**185; China, **2:**221, 227; Finnish-Swedish, **3:**101; Gaddi, **2:**36; Korea, **2:**296; Taiwan, **2:**262; Wales, **3:**77

Teatro de virtudes políticas (Sigüenza y Góngora), **4:**276

Tebutalin (Manchu), **2:**247

Technicians of the Sacred (Rothenberg), **1:**31

Tedlock, Dennis, **1:**31, 32, 85

Television: Baule, **1:**168; Marquesas Islands, **1:**384; Swahi, **1:**161; Wolof, **1:**216

Tell, William, **3:**308–309

Tendlau, Abraham, **3:**335

Tenzone dei Mesi (folk drama, Sicily), **3:**488

Teresa de Ávila, **3:**181

Terms of address (Shona), **1:**250

Ternhag, Gunnar, **3:**153

Terton Pema Lingpa, **2:**110

Teuta (Queen), **3:**322

Teutonic Mythology, **3:**269

Text, **1:**11, 83–85; and diffusion, **1:**23; and ethnography, **1:**27, 84; and ethnopoetics, **1:**31; and translation, **1:**83, 91

Textile arts: African Americans, **4:**154; Australia (British), **1:**283; Baule, **1:**167–168; Benin, **1:**176; Berber, **1:**110; Cherokee, **4:**18; Croatia, **3:**345; Ecuador, **4:**192; Guam, **1:**339; Hawai'i, **1:**374; Hopi, **4:**49; Igbo, **1:**201; Italy, **3:**457; Kiribati, **1:**346–347; Marquesas Islands, **1:**378; Marshall Islands, **1:**354; Navajo, **4:**90; Quechua, **4:**214; Samoa, **1:**387; Shona, **1:**253; Suriname Maroons, **4:**241; Tlingit, **4:**126; Tonga, **1:**402; Tuareg, **1:**119; Tuvalu, **1:**409;

Tumba francesa (Cuba), **4:**311

Tuna fishing traditions (Sicily), **3:**484

Tupi-Guarani culture and Caipira, **4:**177–178

Tupilaks (amulets), **3:**110

Tupinikim and Caipira, **4:**177

Turkey, **2:**429–439; arts and crafts, **1:**26, **2:**436–437; dance, **2:**434–435; geography and history, **2:**429–432; music, **2:**433–434; sports, games, and puppet theater, **2:**435–436; studies of Turkish folklore, **2:**437; verbal arts, **2:**432–433

Turkish influence or occupation: Croatia, **3:**350; Greece, **3:**494–495; Macedonia, **3:**373; Malta, **3:**511

Turner, Frederick Jackson, **1:**38, 39

Turner, George, **1:**393

Turner, Louis, **1:**87

Turner, Othar, **4:**172–173

Turner, Patricia, **4:**151

Turriff, Jane, **3:**58

Tursunzoda, M., **2:**326

Tuvalu, **1:**404–411; arts and crafts, **1:**409–410; games and sports, **1:**409; geography and history, **1:**404–405; magic and ritual, **1:**406–407; music and dance, **1:**407–408; oratory, myths, and legends, **1:**406; religion, **1:**405–406; studies of Tuvaluan folklore, **1:**410

Tu Wei-ming, **2:**234

"The Two Brothers," **1:**55

Two-part singing (Croatia), **3:**341–346

Tyabashe, Mdukiswa, **1:**267

Tylor, Edward Burnett, **1:**2, 12, 71

Type, **1:**11, 94–96; and cultural area, **1:**18; and diffusion, **1:**23; and motif, **1:**54, 94, 95; and translation, **1:**91

Type and Motif Index of the Folktales of England and North America (Baughman), **1:**94

The Types of Folktale (Aarne), **1:**23, 94

uBaxoxele (Zulu), **1:**272

Udechukwu, Ada, **1:**201

Udechukwu, Obiora, **1:**201

Udo dress, **1:**7–8

Uhland, Ludwig, **3:**312, 314

uHlangakula (Zulu), **1:**272

Újváry, Zoltán, **3:**283

Ukraine, **3:**437–449; architecture, **3:**446–447; arts and crafts, **3:**444–445; calendars, **3:**445–446; epics and minstrals, **3:**440–442; geography and history, **3:**437–439; legends, **3:**440; life-cycle celebrations, **3:**442–444; witchcraft and folk medicine, **3:**439–440

uKulumetule (Zulu), **1:**272

Ulster Cycle, **3:**28–30

Ulster Folklife (folklore journal), **3:**40

umkaSethemba, Lydia, **1:**270, 271

Unamuno, Miguel de, **3:**179

Unani system (Uttar Pradesh), **2:**90

Uncle Remus (African-American), **4:**143

UNESCO: Committee of Government Experts on the Safeguarding of Folklore, **1:**291; Memory of the World Register, **3:**363; recommending founding of open-air museums, **1:**58; Register of Intangible World Culture Treasures, **3:**364

Union song (Italy), **3:**461

Unison singing (Croatia), **3:**346

United Keetoowah Band, **4:**8

United States: Australia (British) influenced by, **1:**290; and globalization, **1:**43; Guam influenced by, **1:**334; Hawai'i influenced by, **1:**374–375; Marshall Islands influenced by, **1:**350, 356; Palau influenced by, **1:**360

Unity of opposites as theme (Yoruba), **1:**224

"Universal Declaration of Human Rights" (1948), **1:**15

University of Dar es Salaam, **1:**161

Unspunnen Festival (Switzerland), **3:**311–313

"Untombi-yaphansi" (Zulu), **1:**271–272

Urban II (Pope), **3:**162

Urban legends (African American), **4:**151

Urban life: Armenia, **2:**369; Australia (British), **1:**287, 290; Australian Aborigines, **1:**293; China, **2:**119; Denmark, **3:**82; Haryana, **2:**45; Kiribati, **1:**348; Korea, **2:**296; Marshall Islands, **1:**349, 356; Nepal, **2:**119; New Caledonia, **1:**313; Piedmont and Val d'Aosta, **3:**478; Shona, **1:**254–255; Swahili, **1:**154, 157, 160–161; Sweden, **3:**145; Switzerland, **3:**309; Uttar Pradesh, **2:**89; Vanuatu, **1:**325–326, 329, 331; Wolof, **1:**216; Xhosa, **1:**261; Yoruba, **1:**220, 221

Urry, John, **1:**86, 87

Ursula, Saint, **3:**506

Ursus, Saint, **3:**471, 478

U.S. Food and Drug Administration, **2:**440

Uttar Pradesh, **2:**88–94; arts and crafts, **2:**94; cultural tradition, **2:**4; folk beliefs and medical practices, **2:**90; folk theater, **2:**92–93; geography and history, **2:**88–90; modernization, challenges of, **2:**94; songs and music, **2:**91–92; sports and recreation, **2:**93; stories and epics, **2:**90–91

uTulasizwe (Zulu), **1:**272

uVusezakiti (Zulu), **1:**272

Uyghur, **2:**335–348; arts, crafts, and architecture, **2:**344; dance, **2:**343–344; folktales and folksongs, **2:**339–341; food, **2:**345; geography and history, **2:**335–337; modernization, challenges of, **2:**345–346; music, **2:**341–343; myths and legends, **2:**338–339; religious beliefs, **2:**337–338; shamanism, **2:**338

Uzbek, **2:**348–355; arts and crafts, **2:**353–354; epics, **2:**350; geography and history, **2:**348–350; music, **2:**352–353; performance arts, **2:**353; songs, **2:**351–352; studies of Uzbek folklore, **2:**354

Vaishnavite sects: Karnataka, **2:**48; Orissa, **2:**80

Valdemar the Victorious, **3:**81

Valkeapää, Nils-Aslak, **3:**142

Valle-Inclán, Ramón del, **3:**184

Vallejo, Antonio Buero, **3:**184

Valor, Enric, **3:**195

Van Gennep, Arnold, **2:**296

Vanuatu, **1:**325–332; architecture, **1:**330–331; games, sports, arts, and crafts, **1:**330; geography and history, **1:**325–326; language and religion, **1:**326–327; modernization, challenges of, **1:**331; music and plays, **1:**329–330; oral tradition: stories and myths, **1:**327–328; song and dance, **1:**328–329; studies of Vanuatu folklore, **1:**331

Vargyas, Lajos, **3:**279

Vasa, Gustav (King), **3:**90

Vave (Swahili), **1:**155, 156

Velázquez, Diego, **3:**186

Ven, Dirk Jan van der, **3:**237

Venezuela: Yanomami, **4:**251–252

Verbal folklore. *See* Oral tradition

Verdaguer, Jacint, **3:**195

Verga, Giovanni, **3:**453

Verkovich, Stefan, **3:**372, 373

Verse. *See* Children's songs, stories, and verses; Poetry

Vetalapanchavingshati (Bangladesh), **2:**99

Vèvè (Haiti), **4:**324

Vico, Giambattista, **1:**73

Victoria (Queen), **3:**65

Victorian Anthropology (Stocking), **1:**12

Victorian period (England), **3:**3

Vidyapiti (Indian poet), **2:**30

Viennese Expo (1873), **1:**57

Vierbergerwallfahrt (Austria), **3:**251

Viking period (Denmark), **3:**81

Vila (fairy, Serbia), **3:**432–433

Vilakazi, Benedict Wallet, **1:**261, 271, 272–273

Vinokurova, Natal'ia, **3:**419

Violant, Ramon, **3:**196

Violins: Apache, **4:**6; Croatia, **3:**346; Mongol, **2:**258; Norway, **3:**130, 131; Sicily, **3:**486; Slovenia, **3:**301

Virgil, **1:**44

Virginity: Berber, **1:**105, 110; Kiribati, **1:**348; Roma, **3:**401; Russia, **3:**415; Samoa, **1:**390, 393, 396; Shona, **1:**252; Ukraine, **3:**442

Virgin of Guadalupe, **4:**273–275

Visionary poets, **1:**31–32

Vision quests: Cheyenne, **4:**22, 26; Iroquois, **4:**55; Nez Perce, **4:**98; Shuar, **4:**222–223, 226

Vision talks (Lakota and Dakota), **4:**73

Višnjic, Filip, **3:**434

Vitolinš, Jekabs, **3:**368

Vitus, Saint, **3:**268

Vizenor, Gerald, **1:**93

Vlach, John Michael, **1**:10, 20

Vladimir (Prince), **3**:411, 422

Vlas, Saint, **3**:417

Vodou in Haiti, **4**:317–319, 321, 323, 324, 327

Vodoun, **1**:47

Volkhvi (priest-magicians, Russia), **3**:411, 412

Volkskultur in der technischen Welt (Bausinger), **1**:52

Volkskundliche Zeitschriftenschau, **1**:5

Volodymyr of Kyiv (Prince), **3**:438–439

von Sydow, Carl Wilhelm, **1**:23, 67, **3**:147, 148, 154

Voskuil, J.J., **3**:237

Voudouri, Lilian, **3**:501

Vraz, Stanco, **3**:373

Vrbitsa (Day of Willows, Serbia), **3**:431

Vries, Jan de, **3**:237

Waan Ailin Kein (Canoes of These Islands), **1**:355

Wackernagel, Hans Georg, **3**:309

Wagner, Richard, **3**:271

Wagner, Sigmund von, **3**:313

Waikhuu chant (Isaan), **2**:136–137

Wailing: Russia, **3**:411, 414; Xavante, **4**:248–249. *See also* Funerals and burials

Wakwatshange, Ngqeto, **1**:270

Waldron, George, **3**:43, 46

Wales, **3**:69–79; Celtic influence, **3**:72; *eisteddfod,* **3**:75; English influence, **3**:71–72, 76–78; geography and history, **3**:69–72; poetry, **3**:75; religion and beliefs, **3**:72–75; songs, **3**:76; storytelling, **3**:75–76

Walking sticks (Mississippi Delta), **4**:173

Wallace, William, **1**:50

"Waltzing Matilda" (Australia [British]), **1**:285

Wandjina (Australian Aborigines), **1**:298–299

Wangchuck, Jigme Dorji, **2**:106

Wangchuck, Jigme Singye, **2**:106

Wan language (Baule), **1**:165

Wannan, Bill, **1**:281, 287

Ward, Russel, **1**:281

Warren, William, **4**:107

Wars and conflicts: Australia (British), **1**:289; Benin, **1**:172; Candoshi, **4**:181–182; Cheyenne, **4**:23, 26; Comanches, **4**:61–62; Hawai'i, **1**:366, 374–375; Hopi, **4**:45; Kiowa, **4**:61–64; Kiribati, **1**:341; Lakota, **4**:69, 73; Marquesas Islands, **1**:377, 380; Marshall Islands, **1**:350; Mexico, **4**:278–279; Ojibwe, **4**:107–108; Otomí, **4**:288–289; Palau, **1**:360; Rarámuri, **4**:297; Seminole, **4**:111–112; Shuar, **4**:223; Vanuatu colonization by, **1**:325; Western Inuit and Yupik, **4**:132–133; Wolof, **1**:209; Xhosa, **1**:257, 262; Yanomami, **4**:251; Zande, **1**:231; Zulu, **1**:269

War songs and dances: Baule, **1**:166; Hawai'i, **1**:366; Igbo, **1**:196; Ijo, **1**:207; Kiowa, **4**:65; Kiribati, **1**:344–345; Lunda, **1**:239; Malaita, **1**:303; Marshall Islands, **1**:352; New Caledonia, **1**:313; Palau, **1**:360

Washington (state) Nez Perce, **4**:97

Water drumming: Malaita, **1**:304; Zande, **1**:232

Waters, Edgar, **1**:285, 286

Water shrines: Brittany, **3**:170; France, **3**:159, 160

Water spirits: Ijo, **1**:204, 207; Wolof, **1**:209, 210

Waulking songs (Gaelic Scotland), **3**:59, 61–62

Wealth: Bangladesh, **2**:100; Benin, **1**:170, 172, 176, 177; Berber, **1**:106; Chinese living abroad, **2**:239; England, **3**:20; Finnish-Swedish, **3**:99; Haryana, **2**:43; Ijo, **1**:205, 206; Ireland, **3**:28; Jie, **1**:135; Kazakh, **2**:312; Khasi-Jaintia, **2**:66; Nahua, **4**:285, 286; Navajo, **4**:83, 91; Nepal, **2**:121; Netherlands, **3**:238, 244; New Caledonia, **1**:310–311; Orissa, **2**:86; Quechua, **4**:208–216; Spain, **3**:179, 180; Tonga, **1**:402; Trobriand Islands, **1**:317, 318, 321, 322; Uttar Pradesh, **2**:89, 92; Uyghur, **2**:344; Wales, **3**:71; Wolof, **1**:209

Weapons and armor: Cherokee, **4**:18; China, **2**:227; Haiti, **4**:324; Hawai'i, **1**:374; Ijo, **1**:205; Karnataka, **2**:55–56; Kiribati, **1**:347; Lunda, **1**:239; Maluku, **2**:200–201; Seminole, **4**:114; Switzerland, **3**:315; Tairora, **2**:205, 208; Tuareg, **1**:113; Western Inuit and Yupik, **4**:130

Weaving. *See* Textile arts

Weddings: Abanyole, **1**:127–128; Albania, **3**:325–326; Armenia, **2**:367; Ashkenazim, **3**:333; Bali, **2**:156–157; Berber, **1**:105, 108; China, **2**:228; Chinese living abroad, **2**:236–237; The Comoros, **1**:143; Croatia, **3**:348–349; Greece, **3**:499; Haryana, **2**:43–44; Israel, **2**:378–379; Kadazandusun, **2**:180; Kazakh, **2**:311, 314; Kiribati, **1**:345; Kurds, **2**:386; Lebanon, **2**:396–398; Malaita, **1**:304; Malta, **3**:505–507; Marshall Islands, **1**:355; Palestine, **2**:403; Poland, **3**:383–384; Roma, **3**:398–401; Russia, **3**:413–415; Shona, **1**:252; Tairora, **2**:206; Taiwan, **2**:262; Tajik, **2**:328, 329, 332; Tuareg, **1**:105, 120; Ukraine, **3**:442–443; Uzbek, **2**:351; Vanuatu, **1**:329

Weepers (Malta), **3**:505

Weeping Woman legend (Mexico), **4**:271

Weiers, Michael, **2**:247

Weinreich, Beatrice Silverman, **3**:339

Weinreich, Uriel, **3**:339

Weiss, Richard, **3**:309

Welcoming ceremonies: Candoshi, **4**:184–185; China, **2**:218

Welters, Henri, **3**:243

Western and Central Africa, **1**:163–233

Western Inuit and Yupik, **4**:128–142; arts and crafts, **4**:138–139; dance, songs, and music, **4**:136–138; festivals and games, **4**:138, 139–140; geography and history, **4**:128–132; religious beliefs and rituals, **4**:134–135; social structure, **4**:132–133; studies of Yupik and Inuit folklore, **4**:140–141

Whaling and Western Inuit and Yupik, **4**:131

Wheel Game (Cheyenne), **4**:28

White, Richard, **1**:39

White Boys (Isle of Man), **3**:50

White Buffalo Calf Woman (Lakota story), **4**:70

Whiteman tales: Apache, **4**:4; Western Inuit and Yupik, **4**:135–136

White Painted Woman (Apache), **4**:5

Whiting, Robert, **2**:277–278

Wicca, **1**:50

Wilbert, Johannes, **1**:56

"The Wild Dog" (Nagaland), **2**:76

Wild Hunt (England), **3**:8

"Wild Huntsman" (Germany), **3**:269

Wild man imagery: Austria, **3**:255; Italy, **3**:472

Wilhelmina (The Netherlands), **3**:242

Willem II (Netherlands), **3**:242

William of Newburgh, **3**:10

William of Orange, **3**:54

Williams, John (missionary to Samoa), **1**:391

Williamson, John, **1**:288

Williamson, Roy, **3**:57

"Willy Reilly" (Australia), **1**:285

Wilson, William A., **1**:78

Windmills (Sicily), **3**:484

Wine feasts (Greece), **3**:499

Winifried (Germany), **3**:261

Winter activities: Haida, **4**:39; Iroquois, **4**:58; Lakota, **4**:68; Russia, **3**:413; Slovenia, **3**:302–303

Winter houses (Cherokee), **4**:18–19

Wintu Indians (northern California), **1**:97

Wisdom question (Greece), **3**:496

Witchcraft: Bali, **2**:155–157, 160–161; Baule, **1**:164; Benin, **1**:171, 174; Caribs of Dominica, **4**:334–335; Choctaw, **4**:36–37; Denmark, **3**:83–84; Duna, **2**:166, 167; England, **3**:8–10; Flanders (Belgium), **3**:230; Ga, **1**:184; Hungary, **3**:278; and invented tradition, **1**:50; Italy, **3**:457–458; Kewa, **2**:189; Malaita, **1**:306; Norway, **3**:126; Palestine, **2**:408; Piedmont and Val d'Aosta, **3**:473; Russia, **3**:412–413; Sámi, **3**:135–136; Slovenia, **3**:299–300; Tairora, **2**:205, 209; Tlingits, **4**:118–119; Trobriand Islands, **1**:315, 324; Tuvalu, **1**:406–407; Ukraine, **3**:439–440, 444; Wolof, **1**:211; Zande, **1**:228–230

Witchcraft Act (England), **3**:8

The Witch-Cult in Western Europe (Murray), **1**:50

Witches' Sabbath (Italy), **3**:457

Witch trials: Denmark, **3**:83; England, **3**:8–9; Norway, **3**:125; Sámi, **3**:135–136

Wolof, **1**:208–217; caste system, **1**:213–214; change and tradition, **1**:216; economy and society, **1**:209; folktales, **1**:216; geography and history, **1**:208–209; oral traditions: poems, epthets, and epics, **1**:214–215; religious history, beliefs, and performances, **1**:210–213; songs, games, and performances, **1**:215